ÉTIENNE MORIN:
FROM THE FRENCH RITE
TO THE SCOTTISH RITE

Seal of the Order of the Royal Secret (1767)

ÉTIENNE MORIN: FROM THE FRENCH RITE TO THE SCOTTISH RITE

ARTURO DE HOYOS, 33°, Grand Cross, KYCH

Past Master, McAllen Lodge No. 1110, AF&AM of Texas

Grand Archivist and Grand Historian

and

JOSEF WÄGES, 32°

Plano Lodge No. 768, AF&AM of Texas

Valley of Dallas, Orient of Texas

Westphalia Press
An Imprint of the Policy Studies Organization
Washington, DC

ÉTIENNE MORIN: FROM THE FRENCH RITE TO THE SCOTTISH RITE

All Rights Reserved © 2024 by Policy Studies Organization

Westphalia Press
An imprint of Policy Studies Organization
1367 Connecticut Avenue NW
Washington, D.C. 20036
info@ipsonet.org

ISBN: 978-1-63723-680-2

Daniel Gutierrez-Sandoval, Executive Director

PSO and Westphalia Press

Updated material and comments on this edition
can be found at the Westphalia Press website:
www.westphaliapress.org

In memoriam

Ill. Rex Richard Hutchens, PhD, 33°, Grand Cross, KYGCH
(November 29, 1942 – December 17, 2022)

Past Grand Master of Arizona
Deputy of the Supreme Council, 33°, S.J.

whose friendship, wit and scholarship continue to inspire

CONTENTS

PART 1 — History

Masonic Mystery	1
The First Lodges (1740–49)	1
Morin's First System: The Élus Parfaits (1745–60)	2
Morin, Grand Inspector of the Grand Lodge of France (1761–65)	8
Continuity of Masonic iconography	12
Conflict with Brother Martin (1766)	20
The Order of the Sublime Princes of the Royal Secret (1767–75)	23
The Provincial Grand Lodge, a force of stability (1766–89)	28
Revolutionary Chaos (1789–99)	30
Grand Lodge of Pennsylvania Lodges (1801–04)	31
Progression of the rituals (1740–1804)	32
Grand Lodge of France ritual (1774–87)	32
Grand Orient de France ritual (1788–1804)	33
Rit Écossais ritual (1788–1804)	35
Pennsylvania "Ancient Masonic Rite of York" ritual (1789–1804)	39
Scottish Mason's Guide (1804)	41
Conclusion	45

PART 2 — Ritual Ancestry and the Scottish Rite Blue Degrees

[1] Complete Corpus of Masonry, Adopted by the Respectable Grand Lodge of France (1774)

Apprentice

Disposition of the Candidate	53
Apartment of Brother Terrible	54
Arrangement of the Lodge	54
Procedure for Opening the Lodge	55
Discourse of the Orator	57
Obligation	58
Instruction	59
Procedure for Closing the Lodge	65

Fellow Craft

Arrangement of the Lodge	68
Procedure for Opening the Lodge	68
Obligation	70
Instruction	71
Procedure for Closing the Lodge	78

Master

Arrangement of the Lodge	80
Reception	80
Opening of the Lodge	80
Discourse	84
Instruction	85
Procedure for Closing the Lodge	88

[2] The Regulator of the Mason (1801)

Foreword	91

Apprentice

First Section: Preliminaries	93
Second Section: Reception	97
Obligation	109
Instruction	113
Closing	116
Work of the Banquet	116

Fellow Craft

First Section: Preliminaries	127
Second Section: First Preliminary	128
Second Preliminary	128
Opening of the Work of the Lodge	129
Obligation	134
Instruction	135
Closing of the Work	141

Master

First Section: Preliminaries	145
Second Section: Reception. First Preliminary	146
Second Preliminary	146
Opening of the Work	146
The Actual Reception	148
Obligation	158
Closing	162
Instruction	162

[3] The Regulator of the Knight Masons (1801)

1st Order. Degree of Elect. Most Wise.

Opening	169
Obligation	171
Instruction	173
Closing	176

2d Order. Degree of Scots. Most Grand.

Opening	179
Reception	180
Obligation	182
Proclamation	185
Instruction	186
Closing	188

3d Order. Degree of Knight of the East. Sovereign Master.

Opening	193
Reception	195
Obligation	200
Instruction	203
Closing	206

4th Order. Degree of Rose-Croix. Most Wise and Perfect Master.

Opening	211

Reception 212
Obligation 215
Instruction 220
Closing 223
Banquet 223

[4] Rit Écossais Rituals (1788)

First Degree. Apprentice.

Opening 229
Questions and Answers of the Wardens 229
Questions for the Visitors 231
Reception 232
Invocation 232
Explanation of the Tracing-Board 238
Honors to be Rendered to the Current Worshipfuls 239
To Wardens 239
To Knights of the East 240
To the Princes of Jerusalem 240
To Rose Croix 240
To Sublime Prince Masons 240
Closing 241

Second Degree. Fellow Craft.

Opening 245
Reception 245
Brother Orator's Speech 248

Third Degree. Master.

Opening 255
Reception 256
Discourse 265
Closing 266

[5] Scottish Masons Guide (1804/1820)

Apprentice

Introduction	270
Opening	271
Reception	274
Prayer	276
Questions	277
Obligation	282
Prayer	286
Closing	287
Instruction	287
Table Lodge or Banquet	294

Fellow Craft

Opening	306
Reception	307
Obligation	310
Closing	312
Instruction	313

Master

Essential Introduction	319
Clothing	320
Titles in a Lodge of Masters	320
Arrangement of the Middle Chamber	320
Opening	321
Reception	323
Preparation of the Candidate	323
Obligation	326
Historical Discourse	327
Oath	331
Proclamation	331
Instruction	333

Appendix A
Saint Domingue Lodges 341

Appendix B
Correspondence and documents 359

1763

February 6 / No. 603 M — La Parfaite Union to de Joinville, ... 359

June 21 / No. 991 M — Morin to de Joinville 363

June 24 / No. 607 M — La Corde to de Joinville 366

June 24 / No. 608 M — La Corde to de Joinville 370

July 25 / No. 912 M — Morin to de Joinville 374

October 6 / No. 628 M — de Villers Deschamps to de la Chaussee 375

December 7 / No. 629 M — de Villers Deschamps to Pingré 376

1764

May 3 / No. 913 M — Morin to Brest de la Chaussee 377

May 3 / No. 604 M — La Parfaite Union and Morin to the Grand Lodge of France 378

May 3 / No. 609 M — La Concorde to de la Chaussee 380

May 3 / No. 611 M — La Concorde to de la Chaussee 381

May 3 / No. 613 M — La Concorde to de la Chaussee 383

May 3 / No. 612 M — La Concorde to de la Chaussee 385

May 3 / No. 614 M — La Concorde to de la Chaussee 386

May 3 / No. 615 M — La Concorde to de la Chaussee 387

August 28 / No. 914 M — Morin to du Mourier 388

1765

March 7 / No. 915 M — Morin to Lantoine and Daubertin 390

March 10 / No. 605 M — Grand Lodge of France to Morin 391

June 23 / No. 606 M — La Parfaite Union to the Grand Lodge of France 392

July 19 / No. 181 M — Poncet to Lamarque 393

July 30 / No. 610 M — Bérindoague to Bassett 393

November 22 / No. 182 M — Lamarque and Perrot to Puisieux 395

November 23 / No. 183 M — Puisieux to de la Chaussee 395

1766

May 7 / No. 184 M — L'Amitié Indissoluble to the Grand Lodge of France 396

July 3 / No. 185 M — L'Amitié Indissoluble to the Grand Lodge of France 397

July 18 / No. 186 M — L'Amitié Indissoluble to the Grand Lodge of France 398

1767

July 19 / No. 187 M — L'Amitié Indissoluble to the Grand Lodge of France 400

June 1 / FM2 544 — Sov. Coun. Princes of Jerusalem, St. Marc Reconstitutes L'Étoile Union.. 401

June / No. 188 M — L'Amitié Indissoluble to the Grand Lodge of France 406

June / No. 189 M — L'Amitié Indissoluble to the Grand Lodge of France 407

June 29 / No. 190 M — Perrot to La Chaussee 409

1768

February 28 / No. 191 M — Perrot to la Chaussee 411

1770

February 1 / FM2 543 — La Verite report on Parfaite Harmonie 412

June 1 / FM2 543 — La Verite correspondence with La Concorde 417

Illustrations

Frontispiece ii

Ritual of "Perfection" or "Ecossais ou Elu Parfait de la L[oge]" (ca. 1750) 4

Knight of the Sun Coco shell snuff box (1757) 6

Distinctive jewel of the Maître Illustre, said to have been bestowed by Frederick the Great 12

Chevalier d'Aigle, Grand Elu Grand Inspecteur. Chevalier de Beauchaîne, 1760 13

Chevalier d'Aigle, Grand Elu Grand Inspecteur. Boucher de Lenoncourt, 1763 13

Seal of the Order of the Sublime Princes of the Royal Secret. Étienne Morin, 1767 14

Francken's seal of the Sublime Princes of the Royal Secret […] Same, used in Charleston 14

Patent of Charles Fabien Janare, September 30, 1758, issued by Beauchaîne 15

Patent of Claude de Brie, March 14, 1762, issued de Lenoncourt 16

Patent of Samuel Stringer, December 6, 1768, issued by Francken 17

Martin succeeds Morin as deputy for the Grand Lodge of France, July 17, 1766 20

Francken flees New York. Supplement to the New York Gazette, April 17, 1769 25

Pierre Dupont Delorme's 1797 ritual cahier 40

February 4, 1794 member list for the Lodge La Tendre Amitié Franco-Américain 43

1801 Constitutions for Triple Unité Ecossais 44

Part 1
HISTORY

Introduction

...contacts between traveling freemasons played almost a more important part then for the history of Freemasonry than it does in our time. It might be the reason why, at least up to the middle of the nineteenth century, it does not make much sense to consider separately one subject (a brother, a lodge, a town, a country or a rite) without remembering constantly that, in a way, it was probably in relation with the whole masonic world.

—Alain Bernheim, AQC 100 (1987), 53

Masonic Mystery

The Ancient and Accepted Scottish Rite has long been confronted with an enigma: whence came its Craft ritual, and *why* was it created?[1] Although the first part of this question was recently (but only partially) answered, the second part remained elusive. A more complete answer, however, lay concealed within an intimate knowledge of the early rituals, but only when considered in their historical context. This investigation was complicated by an obstacle: sources suggest a late 18th century origin in Saint Domingue but, due to the extremely violent nature of the Haitian revolution, little to nothing remains there from Freemasonry before 1804. Although a majority of the colonial records of Saint Domingue are lost, some documents and records survived, scattered about in foreign archives. Fortunately, enough of the surviving data exists to reassemble much of the puzzle, to gain a better sense of the macro-Masonic history, through the creation of meta-data for every lodge which has existing materials available. In reassembling this data we will see not only the arrival of Freemasonry on the island, with its rise and fall, but also the life cycle and Masonic networks of Étienne (Stephen) Morin's *Élus Parfaits* and his *Order of the Sublime Princes of the Royal Secret*. This provides additional evidence as to how Morin's work was the driving force which ultimately led to the creation of the Scottish Rite. Viewing his Orders as living and evolving organisms not only provides a genealogical context for the future Scottish Rite, but it helps us understand the dynamic relationships upon which the early membership depended.

Not only was Morin a founding Masonic figure there but the systems he gave birth to created a national identity so strongly entrenched that the Grand Lodge of France could not gain a firm foothold. It was only after his death that the *Grand Orient de France* succeeded in bringing the island under its control. The sovereign aspirations of Morin's systems were a foreshadowing of things to come.

The arrival of the Grand Orient's "French Rite" ushered in a period of stability, peace, and prosperity, that was a calm before the storm of the Haitian revolution, which upended the colony and severed old associations. Revolutionary struggles gave way to the lodges seeking new recognition from the Antients in the Grand Lodge of Pennsylvania as well as the *Rit Écossais* in Paris, which became the Philosophical Scottish Rite in 1805. These Masonic lodges continued to labor in earnest right up until the final moments, despite the chaos outside their doors. It's in this meta-data that we can discover the Masonic history of Saint Domingue, by placing the evolution of Masonic ritual in context within these different periods, leading up to the creation of the Scottish Rite craft ritual and answering why, with a great degree of satisfaction.

The First Lodges (1740–49)

Freemasonry arrived in Saint Domingue between 1738 and 1740 in Les Cayes with the founding of the lodge *La Concorde*.[2] This story was recorded about thirty years after the fact and is likely a second-hand

---

[1] Although the first Scottish Rite Craft ritual was created in 1804, it wasn't until 1868 that the Southern Jurisdiction created its version, which was printed in 1872. For the complete text, see Arturo de Hoyos, *Albert Pike's Porch and the Middle Chamber: The Book of the Lodge. A Ritual of the Scottish Rite Blue Degrees* (Washington, D.C.: Scottish Rite Research Society, 2022).

[2] FM2 543, in the Bibliothèque nationale de France (hereinafter *BnF*). François Lamarque remarked in his 1776 report concerning the Cap Français lodge *Saint Jean de Jerusalem Ecossais* that the Lodge *Frères Réunis* of Les Cayes was "established in 1738–40 by the English." In 1779 the Provincial Grand Lodge of St. Domingue wrote to the Grand Orient of France that the Lodge *Frères Réunis* "obtained in 5765 constitutions from the gr[an]d∴ L[odge]∴ of France, but it worked constantly before 1747 which it has always done since,

account. Said to have been established by English Masons from Jamaica, English records revealed that the only lodge active at that time was St. Johns Lodge, later called '*The Mother Lodge*' in Kingston, founded April 14, 1739, by the Premier Grand Lodge of England.[3] Some twenty months later a state of war existed between England and France, with the war of Austrian Succession beginning in earnest on December 16, 1740, and ending October 18, 1748. It is within a twenty month window that *La Concorde* came into existence. The state of war brought direct English and French Masonic collaboration to an end, or so it seemed.

Mercantilism practiced in England and France dictated that their colonial possessions were strictly obliged to engage in commerce only within the spheres of their respective nations. Although this principle existed as a policy, in reality the lines were blurred as the protocols of necessity dictated a different practice. We see evidence of this first hand in the founding of *La Concorde*. Its location was key to its relationship with Kingston. Both cities were major producers and exporters of sugar for their respective colonies. Les Cayes lay at the southwestern tip of Saint Domingue and was far from the heavily trafficked shipping lanes on the northern coast of the island. Strategically it lay due East of Kingston, providing an ideal location for direct unsanctioned commerce. Masonic membership was the means of facilitating such relationships.

Utilizing the seas—the highways of the 18th century—Freemasonry spread across the globe, bringing together merchants, landowners, ships captains, local government and the military, under a common association which, occasionally, transcended nationalism. Nearly every major port city in both English and French colonial possessions had a lodge. Saint Domingue was exceptional by comparison, counting at least thirty-nine known lodges and many more "high degree" bodies attached to them throughout the life of the colony. One would expect nothing less from the *Pearl of the Antilles*, whose output counted for half of French GDP during its existence. Understanding the Masonic social networks of the 18th century is key to understanding the trade networks.

Morin's First System: The Élus Parfaits (1745–60)

Masonic membership was vital to commercial success, and offered the additional prospect of substantially better treatment, if one were taken prisoner. There are several contemporary accounts of Masonic courtesy superseding foreign policy out of fraternal respect. The most germane was that of Étienne Morin who was taken prisoner twice by the English: first in 1745 and again in 1762.[4] These two events changed the course of Freemasonry on the island.

In 1744 Morin travelled from Bordeaux to Martinique during his initial voyage. He was initiated as a Scots Master or *Maître Ecossais* by Governor William Mathew at *The Great Lodge* in St. John, Antigua, when the merchant vessel *La Pallas* was being reloaded. Variations of this account have been preserved in two separate versions of the same ritual. The earlier version, called *Le Quarre ou le parfait Elu Ecossais* (dated 1763) provides details concerning the result of Morin's first encounter, and about what transpired in 1762.

---

without almost any suspension; its first register, wherein no doubt were its constitutions, were from Milord Penn, has been lost; it only dates from the second, which was inspected, as you will see, by your Experts and by two Wor[ship]ful∴ Deputies for these purposes from the L[odge]∴, each a member. She desires that her work be regularized from the time of 1747, which she merits by her zeal and amity…" (*BnF FM2 544*, fo. 2). Morin regularized this lodge in 1747. Compare to document No. 607 M in the Appendix. "It was he who raised our August and S[ublime]∴ edifice, which still exists today under the gracious title of *La Concorde*." The surgeon Jean Castaing was the oldest member of the Lodge in 1774, and was initiated on May 10, 1745.

3 John Lane, intro by William James Hughan, *Masonic Records, 1717–1894: Being Lists of All the Lodges at Home and Abroad Warranted by the Four Grand Lodges and the "United Grand Lodge" of England, with Their Dates of Constitution, Places of Meeting, Alterations in Numbers &c., &c. Also Particulars of All Lodges Having Special Privileges, Centenary Warrants, &c., &c.* 2d ed. (London: Freemason's Hall, Great Queen Street, 1895), 82.

4 Josef Wäges, "Étienne Morin and the Santo-Domingo Manuscript," in *Heredom: The Transactions of the Scottish Rite Research Society*, vol. 26 (Washington, D.C.: Scottish Rite Research Society, 2018).

This eminent Degree was established in France by the Most Respectable Brother Morin who received it from William [Mathew] governor-general of the English islands, who had taken up residence in Antigua in 1744. The Grand Lodge of England, having recognized him as such, had granted him authority to establish his Lodge of Perfection in 1745 when he was made a prisoner of war, and the said Respectable Brother Morin, having spent some time in Les Cayes, left and deposited the powers there in the Respectable Scottish Lodge which he had established in 1762 through the Grand Lodge of London, through the Most Respectable Brother Comte, [Earl Ferrers, Viscount Tamworth] whence the Respectable Brother Étienne Morin went on a voyage and established his permanent residence in Saint Domingue in 1763.[5]

In the later Les Cayes version (dated 1767), called *Le Grand Elu Parfait Maître et Sublime Ecossais*[6], we're given a general sense of what transpired.

The Brother Estienne Morin was the first to have the happiness to be admitted and initiated into this eminent Degree by the Respectable Brother Admiral [William] Mathew, Governor General of the English Windward Islands, in Antigua, when he was captured. This zealous brother, having made since that time multiple trips to England, improved himself and formed several Lodges in America and in France, in accordance with the powers he had received from him.[7]

Scots/Scotts/Scottish Masonry, which was practiced in London in the early 1730s, was closely connected to the Master Masons Degree, and it added to the story of Hiram Abif, architect of Solomon's temple. "The Worshipfull and Most Respectable Scottish Union Lodge" was founded in Berlin on November 30, 1742, and worked in French, before the rituals were translated to German in 1746. The "Scots" tradition would become the foundation of the most important high French degrees, and would have a great impact on Morin.

His misfortune at sea and his Masonic affiliation led to his being granted authority to establish a new type of Masonic lodge in Bordeaux: a Parfaite Loge d'Ecosse or Perfect Scottish Lodge. This name would later evolve, and is the origin of the "Lodge of Perfection." A copy of the original degree, in the Bordeaux Municipal Library, sheds light on its earliest form. Titled the Grade de vrais maître Ecossois, exactement trâduits[8] (Degree of the True Scots Master, exactly translated), it is a primitive form of ritual which evolved to become the Elu Parfait (Perfect Elect) by 1749, and by the following year it was last in a ten-degree system bearing the same name[9] and containing the following:[10]

1. Apprentice.
2. Fellow Craft.

---

5   *Le Quarre ou le parfait Elu Ecossais*, Grand Collège des Rites Ecossais, 29–30.

6   Grand Elect Perfect Master and Sublime Scots was rendered initially by Francken as Grand Elect Perfect Master & Sublime Mason in 1769. By 1783 it had become Grand Elect, Perfect & Sublime Mason. Their assemblies are called Lodges of Perfection (14°).

7   *Le Grand Elu Parfait Maître et Sublime Ecossais*, Ms. 5328. B.11.828/3, Grand Collège des Rites Écossais. 7–8.

8   *Grade des Vrais maitres Ecossois exactement traduit*. Ref. 6 E 9. Bibliothèque Municipale de Bordeaux. This is a 1740s translated copy of the English original brought to Bordeaux by Morin from London in 1745.

9   Just as the *Elu Parfait* was the last in its system, so was the Royal Secret the last in the 25-degree "Order of the Royal Secret." This also explains why Charleston initially called its system the "Supreme Council of the 33d" until it was rebranded in 1804 by de Grasse-Tilly as the Ancient and Accepted Scottish Rite.

10 In a letter written May 16, 1750 (Sharp document 15.3), an attorney name Boulard noted that in 1744 Morin initiated him "into the mysteries of *Scottish Perfection*." He also added that "to be a Perfect Elect, that is to say Scots, one must have obtained the nine degrees of Masonry." The nine degrees are presented, in full, in a manuscript of the "Ecossais ou Elu Parfait de la L[oge]" (ca. 1750), in the *Bibliothèque Universitaire de Toulouse*.

3. Master.
4. Secret Master.
5. Perfect Master.
6. Secretary or Master by Curiosity.
7. Provost and Judge or Irish Master.
8. (Super)intendant of the Buildings or English Master.
9. Elect Master.
10. Perfect Elect, Grand Scots.

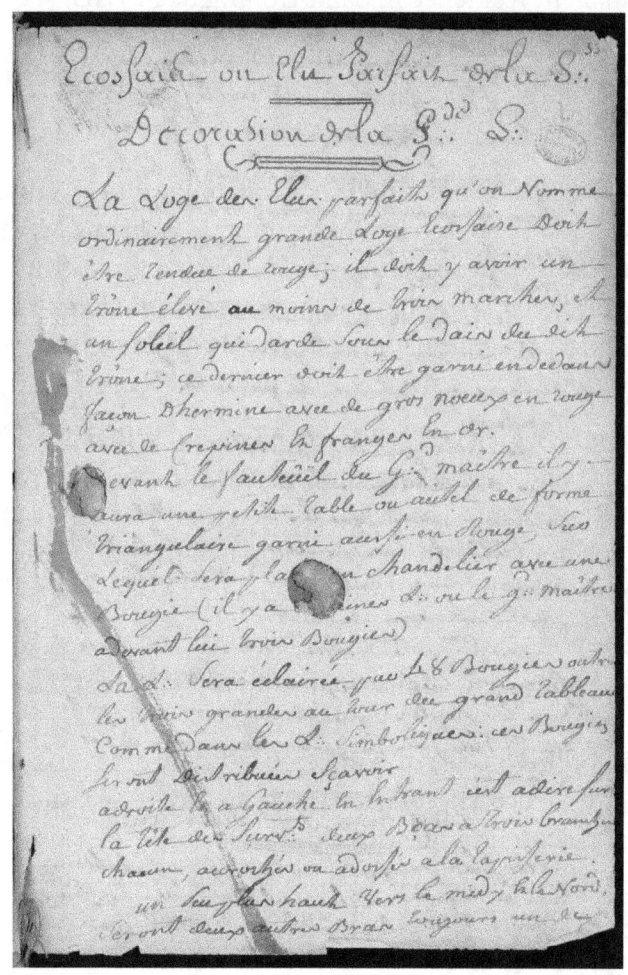

Ritual of "Perfection" or "Ecossais ou Elu Parfait de la L[oge]" (ca. 1750)
The ritual also included a summary of the preceding nine degrees.
—*Bibliothèque Universitaire de Toulouse*

The early date and inclusion of a single Élus degree,[11] suggests that the degree system transitioned from being a single degree, into a system of ten degrees in the mid 1740's, as a means of arresting control of the spread of Scottish degrees, under a local central authority. Local Scottish degrees were organized into a system, with the original degree becoming the terminal degree. This was about the same time that the Élus degrees were being created, given the inclusion of only a single Élus degree and simple title.

The Élus Parfaits met at the *Parfaitie Loge d'Ecosse* of Bordeaux founded in 1745 and was the Scottish

---
11   "Ecossais ou Elu Parfait de la Loge" (1750), MS 209, Fonds du Service commun de documentation de l'Université des sciences sociales (Toulouse), bibliothèque de l'Arsenal.

Lodge attached to the symbolic Lodge *L'Anglaise*, which was founded by English and Irish Masons in 1732.¹²

Morin founded the Perfect Scottish Lodge using the constitution he received from London and became their inspector in Saint Domingue in 1747. In a 1757 letter to the Élus Parfaits, he shed light upon the nature of their mutual association. He informed them that he conferred the degree of *Parfait Elu Grand Ecossais* on ten brothers at the Les Cayes lodge *La Concorde*, and had established a Scottish Lodge there.

> In order to enable them to work for the Perfection of the Royal Art, I handed them the certificate which your Respectable Lodge gave me, dated July 25th, 1747, at the bottom of which are the constitutions I was given by the Respectable Mother Lodge of London on the 25th of June 1745 and which you certified so that they may have recourse to them if needs be.¹³

We see that on Saint John's day 1745 Morin was given authority to establish a *Parfaite Loge d'Ecosse* in Bordeaux, itself becoming a Mother Lodge in her own right, and making Morin her deputy in Saint Domingue in 1747. The Élus Parfaits constituted Perfect Scottish Lodges in Paris, Toulouse, Marseilles, Montpellier, and in the colonies in Saint Pierre, Martinique, New Orleans, Louisiana, and in Saint Domingue at Cap-Français, Port-de-Paix, Saint-Marc, and Les Cayes before expiring sometime around 1760.

Curiously, Morin established the Perfect Scottish Lodge, and granted the degrees of Knight of the East and Knight of the Eagle or Sun to *La Concorde*, after he had been stripped of his deputy powers on December 24, 1752. He had been replaced by Lamolere de Feuillas, the first Master of the Bordeaux *Parfaite Loge d'Ecosse*, who resided far away in Fort Dauphin. He in turn passed his authority over to Bertrand Berthomieux of Saint-Marc, deputizing him on March 28, 1754.¹⁴ Although Morin's authority as Deputy over Saint Domingue only lasted from 1747 through 1752, his influence continued thereafter.

La Concorde had become a daughter of Morin's Bordeaux lodge *La Française* on December 28, 1747, just a few months after he became the Deputy of the Élus Parfaits. The timing suggests something more than coincidence. Its Scottish Lodge, Knight of the East Chapter, and Knights of the Sun bodies were established on June 26, 1757, as indicated by the separate member lists.¹⁵ This early graduated high degree structure, with separate bodies for each degree, became a draft framework for his future system.

The island, as Deputy Morin found it in 1747, only had three lodges: *La Concorde* in Les Cayes, *Saint Esprit* in Léogane, and its daughter lodge *l'Union* in Petit-Goave. *Saint Esprit* was organized sometime before 1746 and only appears once in name, in the founding records, when Dominique-Laurent Radoux, Commandant of the Petit-Goave militia, sought a constitution from the *Grande Loge Provincial* of the *Grand Orient de France* in October 1784. Radoux had come into possession of the original papers of *l'Union* from Armand-Robert Caignet de Lester, its first Worshipful Master. The lodge did not exist after 1752 as Caignet de Lester appears as a founding member of the *Parfaite Loge d'Ecosse* in Saint-Marc on December 2, 1752. Authorized by Feuillas, and under the local authority of Berthomieux, it was attached to the St. John's lodge *La Concorde* which too had been reconstituted by Morin at some point in 1749. Caignet de Lester later succeeded his cousin Martines de Pasqually in Port-au-Prince as the head of what little remained of the *Élus Coëns* in 1774.¹⁶

---

12 G.W. Speth, "The English Lodge at Bordeaux," *AQC* 12 (1899), 6–22.

13 Jean-Pierre Gonet et al., *Les Élus Parfaits, Une Aventure Transatlantique. Les Documents Sharp*, vol. 1 (Paris: Grand Collège des Rites Écossais Suprême Conseil du 33ᵉ degré en France, 2022), 172–73.

14 Gonet et al., *Les Élus Parfaits* (2022), vol. 1, 153–55.

15 Gonet et al., *Les Élus Parfaits* (2022), vol. 1, 175.

16 The Élus Coëns, who were decidedly esoteric, reinterpreted and modified Masonic ritual to include occult practices. See Stewart Clelland, Josef Wäges and Steve Adams, *The Green Book of the Élus Coens* (London: Lewis Masonic, 2021); Clelland, Wäges and Adams,

This coco shell snuff box was a 1757 Masonic Gift given to Sauveur Balanque, Commander of the King's frigate "Le Duc," celebrating the re-constitution of *La Concorde* by the Bordeaux Lodge *La Française*. Note that in addition to a symbolic tracing board, it also contains on the obverse, 3 letters S and a sun inside of a delta, alluding to the Knights of the Sun body created by Morin.

—*Musée de la franc-maçonnerie (Paris), GODF collection; photo by Ronan Loaëc.*

Morin founded a *Parfaite Loge d'Ecosse* in Cap-Français, on March 1, 1749, called *Saint Jean de Jérusalem Ecossaise*.[17] In this early period Cap-Français was the largest city and center of commerce in the French colony, serving as the capital until 1770, and being described as the *Paris of the Antilles*. Its proximity to the shipping lanes on the Northern coastline and deep harbor made it the ideal location for trade and commerce. This lodge became one of the main hubs of activity of Morin's second system. Its founding, however, was not without controversy and ultimately contributed to Morin losing his deputy powers as he had conferred degrees and established the lodge in advance of notifying the Élus Parfaits in Bordeaux. Technically, Morin's deputy powers came from the Élus Parfaits. However their existence was due to his actions, which complicated the picture. This theme of conflicting authority would surface again later. Morin appears to have resided in Cap-Français through 1753, serving as Grand Orator for the lodge in 1752.[18]

At that time a Scottish lodge was typically attached to a Symbolic lodge, given that it is membership was derived from the body of local Masons. On March 13, 1752, Brother Rivière, the Secretary of *Saint Jean de Jérusalem Ecossaise*, wrote to Bordeaux informing them that they had given the local Symbolic Lodge *La Bonne Intelligence* constitutions after changing its name to *La Parfaitie Harmonie*.[19] The lodge was formed sometime before this, perhaps by the Languedoc-infanterie lodge *La Bonne Intelligence*, and formed locally after the regiment moved. This story has been repeated countless times in the British and French armies and informs us of the particular group of Masons, composing *Saint Jean de Jérusalem Ecossaise*.

The Master's Voice. The Letters & Rituals of Martines de Pasqually, 1767–1774 (London: Lewis Masonic, 2022)

17 Gonet et al., *Les Élus Parfaits* (2022), vol. 1, 135–38.
18 Gonet et al., *Les Élus Parfaits* (2022), vol. 1, 141.
19 Gonet et al., *Les Élus Parfaits* (2022), vol. 1, 142.

Morin's unauthorized founding of the *Parfaite Loge d'Ecosse* in Saint-Marc in 1752 resulted in his being stripped of deputy powers. This Perfect Scottish Lodge was the daughter of Cap-Français, which had yet to be officially recognized by Bordeaux. The circumstances of their founding are clearly defined in their letter seeking to be recognized by the Mother Lodge in Bordeaux.

> Our Respectable Mother Lodge of Le Cap, from which we received our powers and constitutions through Brother Morin whom it had deputized to receive and install us in a regular manner, will also notify you of this, in order to enable us to start corresponding with you.[20]

This was the event that caused Bordeaux to sever relations with Morin. Not only had he founded a lodge in Cap-Français without their consent, but they also learned that this new lodge had itself founded a daughter lodge in a neighboring town, *under their own authority and before they themselves had been recognized, and after having deputized their own Deputy Morin, to act on their behalf*. A marginal note on their letter, informing Bordeaux about what had transpired, records that they had "written on January 6th, 1753, to Brother Morin that we would recognize this lodge after it has been constituted by Respectable Brother Feuillas, our deputy."[21]

Morin had lost his powers only 13 days before this note was added and points to the founding of Saint-Marc as the inciting incident. This lodge was never recognized by Bordeaux and disappeared before the end of the 1750s. It simply vanished from the Bordeaux records after a single piece of correspondence from them.

Although Lamolere de Feuillas had delegated his powers and deputized Bertrand Berthomieux to provide provisional constitutions to St. Marc and Port-de-Paix, no surviving evidence suggests that this occurred. *Saint Jean de Jérusalem Ecossaise's* constitution was not healed until May 22, 1759, which act was performed by Lamolere de Feuillas himself.[22] This regularization was the last significant act that remained of the Élus Parfaits. Correspondence from Saint Domingue and Martinique continued in 1760, and Louisiana corresponded until 1764, but in France the situation had become quite different. The final document from Bordeaux was a speech that hinted that the lodge was on the verge of ruin, and aimed to inspire the brethren to come together.[23] We do not know the impact of this speech, as all records cease in 1760, but in spite of this the lodges they constituted in the colonies continued. Their demise may have motivated Morin to return to France, when he became the deputy of the Grand Lodge of France.

What had begun in 1754 as a conflict over colonial territory between England and France in North America, had exploded in 1756 becoming the Seven Years War, lasting through 1763. Battles erupted on the continent as well as the seas across the globe, becoming an effective world war. The effects of this conflict were also felt in the colonies, with no new lodges being established in Saint Domingue from 1752 through 1762. Sea-going vessels were frequently captured, the English seizing some 1,875 ships between 1752–63.[24] The disruption of the flow of goods back and forth between the colonies and mother country had disastrous effects.

By the close of 1760 at least seven lodges had been founded in Saint Domingue. Three lodges, *Saint Esprit* in Léogane, *l'Union* in Petit-Goave, and the *Parfaite Loge d'Ecosse* of Port-de-Paix had demised. The remaining four lodges, *La Concorde* in Les Cayes with its high degree bodies, the Perfect Scottish lodge *Saint Jean de Jérusalem Ecossaise* and its symbolic lodge *La Parfaitie Harmonie* in Cap-Français, along with *La Concorde* in Saint-Marc, were all united as members of the system of the Élus Parfaits

---

20 Gonet et al., *Les Élus Parfaits* (2022), vol. 1, 144–45.
21 Gonet et al., *Les Élus Parfaits* (2022), vol. 1, 144.
22 *BnF FM2 543*.
23 Gonet et al., *Les Élus Parfaits,* (2022), vol. 1, 67–69.
24 File *HCA 32 180-252*, National Archives, Kew, England.

and all under the direct influence of Morin. This is why he was the obvious choice of deputies for Saint Domingue.

MORIN, GRAND INSPECTOR OF THE GRAND LODGE OF FRANCE (1761–65)

By 1761 Morin was in Paris and became the Deputy of the Grand Lodge on August 27, 1761. A close examination of the powers ascribed to him are instructive in determining precisely what were the limitations on these powers and privileges, in comparison to what occurred.

> We have by general Consent, Constituted and Instituted and by these present Constitutions, we institute and give Full and Entire Power to Brother Stephen Morin, whose signature is in the margins hereof, to Form and Establish a Lodge, to receive and multiply the Royal Order of Free Masons in all Perfect and Sublime Degrees, to take care that the statutes and regulations of the Grand and Sovereign Lodge, General or Particular, be kept and observed and never to admit therein except true and Legitimate brethren of Sublime Masonry.
>
> To regulate and govern all the members who will compose the said Lodge that he can establish in the 4 parts of the world, where he will arrive or will be able to remain, under the title of Lodge of St. John and called *La Parfaite Harmonie*, giving him power to Choose such officers to help him to govern his lodge as he sees fit, whom we command and enjoin to obey and respect him. Ordain and Command all masters of regular Lodges of whatever dignity they May be, cast upon the surface of the earth and the seas, Pray, and enjoin them in the name of the Royal order and in the Presence of our most Illustrious Grand Master to recognize as such and as we acknowledge our Dearest Brother Stephen Morin as Respectable Master of the Lodge of *La Parfaite Harmonie* and Deputize Him as our Grand Inspector in all parts of the New World to enforce the observance of our Laws in General &c. And by these present Constitutions our Very Dear Brother Stephen Morin our Grand Master Inspector, authorizes and empowers him to establish in all parts of the world, perfect and Sublime Masonry &c. &c. &c.[25]

Morin had "Full and Entire Power… to receive and multiply the Royal Order of Free Masons in all Perfect and Sublime Degrees" and was given authority to establish a Lodge called *La Parfaite Harmonie*. Moreover, the Grand Lodge "authorize[d] and empower[ed] him to establish in all parts of the world, Perfect and Sublime Masonry." He was charged to keep and observe all statutes and regulations of the Grand Lodge, both general and particular, and holds the rank of Grand Master Inspector. The intention of the Grand Lodge appeared to be that he would establish his new lodge "where he will arrive or will be able to remain"—meaning that this would become a fixed lodge once Morin established his permanent residence. Deviation from these boundaries would become problematic.

La Parfaite Harmonie appeared on the list of Regular Lodges in both 1765 and 1769, and it was recorded as having been founded in Port-au-Prince in 1762, though its date is in error.[26] Based on Morin's correspondence, we learn that he landed in Saint-Marc on January 20, 1763.[27] After departing Bordeaux abord *Le Succès* for Cap-Français, his ship was captured at sea[28] and brought into Plymouth on April 9, 1762. Morin spent two months in London and later claimed he had been appointed an Inspector of

---

25 Extracted from *BnF FM1 285*, which is the "Golden Book" of de Grasse-Tilley. It was printed *in toto* in facsimile, with a transcription, as in *Livre d'Or du Grasse-Tilly. Premier Souverain Grand Commandeur du Suprême Conseil de France* (Paris: 8 rue Puteaux, 2003); see esp. 86–87.

26 *Tableau General de tous les Vénérables Maîtres des Loges tant de Paris que la Province, Régulièrement Constituées, par la Grand Loge de France. 1769.* Archives, Grand Orient de France.

27 Jean-Pierre Gonet et al., *Les Élus Parfaits, Une Aventure Transatlantique. Les Documents Sharp*, vol. 2 (Paris: Grand Collège des Rites Écossais Suprême Conseil du 33ᵉ degré en France, 2022), 165

28 *HCA 32 245*, National Archives, Kew, England, 115

English lodges for the Sublime degrees by Washington Shirley, 5th Earl Ferrers, who was Grand Master of Freemasons of the Premier Grand Lodge from 1762-64.

> As I pointed out to you in my previous letter, when I embarked at Bordeaux to travel to America I was captured by the enemy of the French State and taken to England. I spent two months in London, where Earl Ferrers [Viscount Tamworth], Grand Master of all the Lodges under English jurisdiction, has appointed me Inspector of its jurisdiction for the part of the New World and has bestowed on me the sublime degrees by giving me a certificate stating that I alone am able to establish lodges of Grand Elect Scots, Knight, and Prince Mason.[29] I will share with you some of these rarities, which I admire and of which I am overcome with joy at being the depositary.[30]

Given the alignment of the supporting evidence of his capture at sea it is clear that *something* happened—but was it simply an endorsement of his French patent as he indicates in his letter on May 3, 1764, or was it something more?[31] Morin's new claims to the high degrees are, in effect, an expansion of his original powers from 1745, reaffirming his right to confer them along with Knight of the East and Prince Mason. This narrative was repeated in his June 21, 1763, letter to Chaillon du Jonville, the Grand Substitute of the Grand Master of the Grand Lodge of France, with more detail and candor.

> At the beginning of 1762 I was captured at sea and conducted by the enemy of the French State to London, where I received all the consolations and enjoyed all the pleasures and benefits that a Freemason can expect in such circumstances, especially as I had been so highly recommended by your good self. I often had the pleasure of working with the Most Respectable Brother Earl Ferrers, Viscount Tamworth, the Grand Master and Protector of all the Lodges under English jurisdiction.
> I told him in open lodge about the patent you were kind enough to grant me, to which he added his approval, congratulating me and bestowing on me the title of life member of all the lodges of England and Jamaica, in which places I received in this capacity all the services which I needed until my departure for Saint Domingue.[32]

This clarifies what transpired: the Grand Master of the Premier Grand Lodge endorsed Morin's patent issued by the Grand Lodge of France, and declared him a life member of the lodges of England and Jamaica. This opened the door for Morin to operate anywhere in the Caribbean. His statement "in which places I received in this capacity all the services which I needed until my departure for Saint Domingue" suggests that he attended lodge in London and Jamaica in 1762, given that these capacities and services were contingent upon the recommendation of the Grand Master.

With these new powers in tow, Morin traveled first to Jamaica, and immediately began his mission after arriving in Saint-Marc, and establishing himself at *La Concorde*. He intended to place all of the lodges under the protection of the Grand Lodge of France. We see that just one month later that Morin constituted a new lodge in Port-au-Prince called *La Parfaitie Union* on February 26, 1763.[33] He sent Bertrand Berthomieux as "Deputy Representative of the Respectable Lodge of St. Marc for their

---

29 The first two are Grand Elect, Perfect and Sublime Mason (later 14°) and Knights of the East (later 15°), but it is unclear what is meant by "Prince Mason." It may be the Prince of Jerusalem (later 16°).

30 Gonet et al., *Les Élus Parfaits*, (2022), vol. 2, 173

31 Josef Wäges, "Étienne Morin and the Santo-Domingo Manuscript," in *Heredom: The Transactions of the Scottish Rite Research Society vol. 26* (Washington, D.C.: Scottish Rite Research Society, 2018).

32 Gonet et al., *Les Élus Parfaits* (Paris: 2022), vol. 2, 166–67

33 File *113-1/118 Loge de la Parfaitie Union, Orient Port-au-Prince (Saint Domingue) No.603–606M*, Archives of the Grand Orient de France.

installation," and was Morin's first Deputy in Saint Domingue. Morin's new local administration mirrored the system of Grand Lodge, and deputies were made to govern the island, by maintaining a local presence. *La Parfaitie Union*, which was founded perhaps in 1762, was the daughter of *La Concorde* in Saint-Marc, and became one of the principle lodges of the Order of the Sublime Princes of the Royal Secret. Port-au-Prince became the capital city of Saint Domingue about 1770 and hosted the central and governing body of Morin's system, the *Grand Conseil des Sublimes Princes Maçons*.[34]

Morin also made Brother François Ignace de Villiers Deschamps a deputy. Deschamps wrote to Brest de la Chaussée, keeper of the seals of the Grand Lodge, and informed him that Morin gave him a constitution in Port-au-Prince to establish a Lodge of Perfection in Brest, France.

> Brother∴ Morin, whom I had the pleasure of seeing in Port-au-Prince and with whom I have often worked, has sent me a parcel to send to you to pass on to Monsieur de Joinville, your Worshipful. He has also delivered to me a charter empowering me to establish a Lodge of Grand Scots in this town, but only after it has been approved by your own Respectable∴ Lodge∴, our Mother Lodge. As this charter is pasted onto canvas, I dare not risk sending it by post. I hope, my dear Brother∴, that you will kindly obtain for me an official permission approving what Brother∴ Morin has done and will attach to it the title of Lodge Inspector so that I can shut down an irregular lodge which has been established in this town.[35]

De Villiers Deschamps proceeded cautiously with Morin's constitution, and was referred to Brother Pingré, Grand Secretary of the Grand Lodge. He sent several copies of the same two letters and a final copy on December 7, 1763. It is doubtful that he received a favorable reply as his Lodge *l'Heureuse rencontre* (founded in Brest, France, in 1745), ultimately absorbed the rival Lodge *Constante* (founded in 1762) in 1776.

Les Cayes was informed that their founder Morin became Grand Inspector and sent a glowing reply on May 3, 1764. With these lodges aligned, Morin needed to bring *Saint Jean de Jérusalem Ecossaise* into the fold, to gain a foothold in the North of the Island, and accomplish his objective. This sentiment is reflected in his June 21, 1763, letter from Port-au-Prince to the Grand Substitute:

> As for the Respectable Scottish Lodge of Le Cap-Français, which I founded in 1748, and its daughter the Symbolic Lodge at Fort Dauphin, founded under the title of *La Double Alliance*, I hope to visit this part of the island to fulfil my mission to the ultimate, and will let you have a detailed description of their work and their Masonic conduct.[36]

Saint Jean de Jérusalem Ecossaise had a daughter lodge in Fort Dauphin, *La Double Alliance*, and this likely occurred after Lamolere de Feuillas, then residing in For Dauphin, regularized their constitution in 1759, but before the letter was written in 1763. Morin was now targeting not one, but two lodges. Based on superscripted notes in the Knight of the Sun degree in Morin's cahier of rituals,[37] it appears that

---

34 The Grand Council of the Sublime Princes was the governing body of the Sublime Princes of the Order of the Royal Secret. It was seated in Port au Prince, and used Morin's patent authority to establish a Lodge named *Parfaitie Harmonie*. The *Baylot BnF FM4 15*, source ritual text of the Francken Manuscripts, contains the original version of Sublime Prince of the Royal Secret degree. This 1764 text includes the opening and closing of the 'Sovereign Council of Sublime Princes' which was reserved for Morin's deputies. As the terrain of Saint Domingue was difficult to traverse by land, deputies of the Sovereign Council were appointed to the Lodges in a manner similar to the Provincial Grand Lodge system: Jean Jacques Texier was made deputy for Port au Prince in 1764, Martin Bérindoague was made a deputy for Les Cayes in 1765, and Mennessier de Boissy was made a deputy for Jacmel in 1770.

35 File 113-1/010 Loge L'Heureuse Rencontre, Brest No.628M. Loge Ecossaise de la Véritable Union No.623M. Archives of the Grand Orient de France.

36 Gonet, et al., *Les Élus Parfaits*, (2022), vol. 1, 167

37 *BnF FM4 15 Baylot*.

he travelled North with the Foix Regiment departing Port-au-Prince and arriving in the town of Grand Riviere just 24 kilometers to the South of Cap-Français.

> This degree was granted to me by the Lodge constituted for the Régiment de Foix during our encampment at Grand-Rivière and at our Lodge at the Orient of St. Marc on the 29th of March 1764. By Brother Peyrottes, written at the Camp of Grand-Rivière in the Cap-Français quarter of Saint Domingue, June 1763.[38]

The lodge attached to the Foix Regiment was called *Josué*, and counted Baudry de Balzac, Gaspard-Adrien Boner du Louvat de Champollon, Pierre-André Grainville, and Louis-Claude de Saint Martin as members, who later joined the Élus Coëns. Sometime between June 1763 and March 29, 1764 Morin traveled with them from Port-au-Prince to Grand-Rivière, and then to Saint-Marc in March 1764. His mission must not have been successful, and perhaps there were still hard feelings. Thirty-five days later, on May 3, after returning to Port-au-Prince, he wrote to the Grand Lodge:

> I am sending you three lists which, as you will see, are continuations of those I have already sent, along with the briefs in duplicate for three Lodges, namely those of Saint-Marc, Les Cayes du Fond in the Ile à Vache and Port-au-Prince... There is also a lodge in Le Cap called *Édouard Stuard* which is similarly composed and which we certainly do not want to recognize.[39]

The lodge *Édouard Stuard* had been formed before November 25, 1762, by Nicolas Hector Andraule de Langeron, with dubious authority from Charles-François Radet de Beauchaîne[40] (or Beauchesne), described as "the most fanatical of the irremovable Worshipful Masters of the old Grand Lodge of France."[41] In 1758 Langeron had received the Perfect English Master degree from Beauchaîne under the alleged authority of "the unfortunate Prince Charles Stuart Edward (sic), lawful King of England, Ireland and Scotland, Grand Master and Protector of Legitimate Scottish Lodges."[42] Beauchaîne, who had presided as Worshipful Master of the Frankfurt lodge *Loge Ecossaise et Anglaise la Constance*, was the inventor of the Fendeurs degrees in 1747.[43] He had a disreputable reputation, during the Seven Years' War (1756–63), as a peddler of high degrees, with his French counterpart, Boucher de Lenoncourt.[44]

> During the Seven Years' War, he [Beauchaîne] followed the German army with a trailer equipped as a lodge, filled with rituals, Masonic catechisms, jewels, ribbons and regalia. Thus, he stopped on the main roads to confer degrees. He had forty-five available to amateurs.[45]

---

38 *BnF FM4 15 Baylot*.

39 Gonet, et al., *Les Élus Parfaits*, (2022), vol. 2, 171

40 *BnF FM2 (543)*

41 Jean Marie Ragon, *Francmaçonnerie. Rituel de la Maçonnerie forestière contenant tout ce qui a rapport à la Charbonnerie et à la Fenderie, suivi d'une analyse de 14 associations politiques secrètes provenant de ces deux anciennes institutions, etc.* (Paris: Collignon, 1861), 5.

42 The patent is reprinted in W.H. Rylands, "Two French Documents," *AQC* 15 (1902), 95.

43 Ragon, *Francmaçonnerie. Rituel de la Maçonnerie forestière* (1861), 5.

44 Georg Franz Burkhard Kloss, *Annalen Der Loge Zur Einigkeit (Der Englischen Provincial-Loge, so Wie Der Provincial- Und Directorial- Loge Des Eclectischen Bundes Zu Frankfurt Am Main. 1742–1811. Eine Festgabe, Ausgetheilt Bei D. säcularfeier D. Loge Zur Einigkeit AM 27. Juni 1842.)* (Graz: Akadem. Druck- u. Verlagsanst., 1972), 28

45 Gustave Bord, *La Franc-maçonnerie en France des origines à 1815* vol. 1 (Paris: Nouvelle Libraire Nationale, 1908), 181. Bord, pp. 184–85, further noted: "The lodges of the Chevalier de Beauchaîne seem to have been part of the regime of the Emperors of East and West. They functioned in the same way as the so-called military lodges, which were not in the Orient of any regiment, nor of any city, but in the Orient of the place where they were and which were designated by latitude and longitude. *La Constance*, as well as *Constance et l'Amitié*, was therefore a military lodge like *St-Jean de la Gloire ou St-Alexandre*, the old lodge of the musketeers. The Brethren of these lodges were, in a way, commercial travelers in Freemasonry, and their role was considerable in the spread of the Order."

Beauchaîne's lodge was branded a *Winkelloge* or "irregular lodge," since it lacked recognized authority. Following the war he returned to Paris in 1763 and appeared in the list of Masters of lodges through 1769, but with this note: "Brother Beauchesne. [sic] Not Constituted. The Grand Lodge refused to expedite his letters. He is a degree peddler."[46]

CONTINUITY OF MASONIC ICONOGRAPHY

The enthusiasm of persons like Morin, and to a lesser degree Beauchaîne and de Lenoncourt, was a guarantee that their contributions to Masonry would survive in some manner. We are able to see this when we examine the ancestral lineage of the designs of Masonic patents, as well as the language and symbolism of the degrees. The iconography on Beauchaîne's 1760 seal for the degree of *Chevalier d'Aigle, Grand Inspecteur Grand Elu*, the terminal degree in his 7-degree system and an early Kadosh variant, appears to be the source of the seal of Boucher de Lenoncourt, predating it by three years.[47] It may have been adapted from a ritual first brought to Germany in 1758 by the Marquis Gabriel de Lernay, the French prisoner-of-war who started the chapter of Clermont in Berlin.[48] The ritual described a jewel, with similar features, attributed to Frederick II ("the Great") king of Prussia.[49]

> It was the King of Prussia who gave this jewel to the Illustrious Knights; they wore it from the third buttonhole of the vest, attached to a black moiré ribbon. It is a crowned double [headed] eagle, holding a sword between his talons.[50]

Distinctive jewel of the Maître Illustre, said to have been bestowed by Frederick the Great.

---

46 *Tableau General de tous les Vénérables Maîtres des Loges tant de Paris que la Province, Régulièrement Constituées, par la Grand Loge de France. 1769.* Archives of the Grand Orient de France.

47 *Chevalier de l'Aigle, Grand Elu, Grand Inspecteur,* patent of Charles Fabien Janare (dated September 30, 1758) in the Riga Museum of Freemasonry. The printed patent was created in 1760 by Johann Samuel Mund, and Janare's copy was backdated, authorizing what had already transpired, albeit in an attractive form.

48 *The Marquis Gabriel de Lernay* petitioned the Baron de Printzen, of The Three World Globes, for permission to form a lodge for his compatriots. The *Marquis also conferred the* Chevalier Elu de la St. Jean de Jérusalem on the Baron, and four others, and permission was granted to organize the "chapter of Clermont" *in 1760 in Berlin.*

49 Frederick the Great was himself founder of the Grand Lodge of the Three World Globes in 1740.

50 See the *Maître Illustre* ritual in "Recueil des différents grades de la Franc-Maçonnerie," at < *http://gallica.bnf.fr/ark:/12148/btv1b9061836 n.r=franc-maconnerie.langFR* >.

The crowned double-headed eagle, clutching a sword, and its association to Frederick the Great, would become most identified with the Scottish Rite's tradition. Significantly, Lenoncourt was a signatory on Morin's 1761 patent. Based on the strong similarities between Lenoncourt's and Morin's seals, the attribution of Morin's ritual version of *Chevalier d'Aigle, Grand Inspecteur Grand Elu*,[51] to Frederick the Great, and also the near identical design of all of their patents, it is clear that the iconography of the seals and forms of the patents are evolutionarily linked. The attribution to Frederick the Great was an artifact of Lenoncourt's time in Germany, and Morin built his liturgy on these foundations. Morin's most important deputy, Hendrick Andriessen Francken (aka "Henry Andrew Francken") copied these from him, and had his own patent, which was copied by William Gamble in Albany in 1768, and which became the template for both the English branch of the Order of the Royal Secret as well as the early Scottish Rite.

Chevalier d'Aigle, Grand Elu Grand Inspecteur.
Chevalier de Beauchaîne, 1760.

Chevalier d'Aigle, Grand Elu Grand Inspecteur.
Boucher de Lenoncourt, 1763.

---

51   *BnF FM4 15 Baylot.*

Seal of the Order of the Sublime Princes of the Royal Secret.
Étienne Morin, 1767.

(Left) Henry Andrew Francken's seal of the Order of the Sublime Princes of the Royal Secret, on the patent of Samuel Stringer, December 6, 1768, and (right), seal of the same, used in Charleston.

Patent of Charles Fabien Janare, September 30, 1758, issued by Beauchaîne, creating him a
"Knight of the Eagle, Grand Elu, Grand Inspector, protector of Innocence."
This patent was produced by Johann Samuel Mund in 1760, and appears to be a backdated copy.

Patent of Claude de Brie, March 14, 1762, issued by François le Boucher de Lenoncourt, Worshipful Master of the lodge St. Jean de Metz, and countersigned by Henri-Joseph Brest de la Chaussée, Worshipful Master of lodge de L'Écossaise de l'Exactitude. Both de Lenoncourt and la Chaussée were signatories on Morin's patent. —BnF FM5 (27)

Samuel Stringer's Knights Kadosh patent, December 6, 1768, issued by Henry Andrew Francken and illustrated by William Gamble

Jean Baptiste Marie Delahogue had a similar patent dating from 1766, and later used it to successfully establish the Charleston Lodge *La Candeur* in 1796, which then joined the Grand Lodge of South Carolina Antient York Masons.[52] The thought of including *Édouard Stuard* was unconscionable, not only because

---

52   Josef Wäges, "De Grasse-Tilly and the early Supreme Council," in *Heredom: The Transactions of the Scottish Rite Research Society* vol.

it was of doubtful origins, but also because it owed allegiance, not to the Grand Master of the Grand Lodge of France, but to the pretender Charles Edward Stuart:

> We the Master, Inspectors and Laborers of the Most Respectable English and Scottish Lodge of Saint John. Established in the Army of our Very Dear King in Germany, with the distinct title of *La Constance*, decorated with all honors, and authorized by our most dignified, most dear, and Most Respectable Grand Master Charles Stuard Edouard [sic], regularly assembled by the mysterious numbers.[53]

Édouard Stuard founded a daughter lodge *L'Etroite Union* in Gros-Morne on November 25, 1762. They become aware of their irregular founding and take a constitution from *La Parfaitie Harmonie* in Cap-Français on November 25, 1764, and *Édouard Stuard* itself vanishes, being rechartered as *Le Vérite* in 1767.[54]

At the same time that Morin sought to bring the Island under the control of the Grand Lodge, the cessation of hostilities in the seven years wars led to a rapid expansion of other new lodges. The *Loge du Choix des Hommes* may have been established in Jacmel in 1762 under unknown authority. It is recorded that the first Worshipful Master was named Fourmont,[55] and it may have been a military lodge which transitioned into a local lodge at the end of the war.

In the North another lodge, *L'Amitié Indissoluble* in Léogane joined the Grand Lodge of France on November 26, 1765. It had been formed sometime prior to April 1765, according to their Worshipful Master Poncet, who wrote to the Grand Lodge informing them that "Our Worshipful died three months ago: he alone, through his Letters Patent, had the right to constitute a Lodge, but he did not do this while he was alive, with the result that our labors would become useless if we continued without the approval of the other Lodges."[56] The lodge was received and at that time was the only lodge in the Colony not directly involved with Morin, and was outside his sphere of influence.

Morin gathered the member lists and forwarded them to the Grand Lodge seeking to obtain constitutions for *La Concorde* in Saint-Marc, *Parfaitie Union* in Port-au-Prince and *La Concorde* in Les Cayes. The Grand Lodge complied and Port-au-Prince received all three constitutions on March 10, 1765, writing to the Grand Lodge on March 23, 1765 that,

> As the Respectable Brother Morin has been absent from this colony for some time he is not here to be able to fulfil the intentions which you have laid down for him in a brief which was sent to his address. During his departure for Jamaica, where he is currently to be found, he entrusted our Lodge *La Parfaite Union* with the task of opening indiscriminately any packages that might be addressed to him, and as for those which concerned the establishment of our Lodge he instructed us to comply with everything that he might be ordered to do. This is the course of action which we have followed with exactitude, as you will see from the report on our installation which we are sending you today.[57]

---

29 (Washington, D.C.: Scottish Rite Research Society, 2022).

53 Wäges, "De Grasse-Tilly," *Heredom* (2022).

54 *BnF Fm2 543*.

55 A document transcribed by Jean Doszedardski in 1813 states, "1st∴ Constitution. – In the year 1762 by the M[ost]∴ R[espectable]∴ and W[orshipful]∴ Brother Fourmont. the date is unknown." See facsimile in Kamel Oussayef, trans., Jean Doszedardski, *Book of Wisdom* ([Lexington, Mass.:] Supreme Council, 33°, NMJ), 2013), p. 123. Original document in the Van Gorden-Williams Library and Archives, Lexington, Massachusetts.

56 See Appendix. *113-1/044 Loge de L'Amité Indissoluble, Orient de Léogane : No.183–191 M*. Archives of the Grand Orient de France.

57 See Appendix. *113-1/044 Loge de L'Amité Indissoluble, Orient de Léogane: No.183-191 M*. Archives of the Grand Orient de France.

Morin departed for Jamaica and made Martin Bérindoague his second deputy for Les Cayes, who represented him at their installation for their new constitution on June 9th, 1765. Because of the confusion of having two lodges with the same name, *La Concorde* is renamed *Les Frères Réunis* by the Grand Lodge on their new constitution, dated February 26, 1765.[58] Bérindoague wrote to the Grand Lodge on July 30, 1765, to send them the member lists of the lodge, and to confirm his own powers.

> By Letters Patent sent to me by the Respectable∴ Brother∴ Morin dated the fifth day of the first month of the Masonic∴ Year 5764 and by virtue of the powers that your Sublime∴ Lodge∴, Our Mother, has granted him by bestowing upon him the title of Deputy Inspector of the Grand∴ and Sublime∴ Lodge∴ of France and England for the New World, by the said Letters Patent he has appointed me in his stead Deputy for the southern part of Saint-Domingue. I would be sincerely flattered, my Respectable Brother, if your Grand and Sublime∴ Lodge∴, Our Mother Lodge, would confirm the choice of our Respectable∴ and much-loved Brother∴ Morin who departed a short while ago for Jamaica.[59]

Apparently even his deputy wondered whether or not this course of action was legal. In the member lists of his lodge we see for the first time the new local structure of the Sublime Princes of the Order of the Royal Secret, based on the member lists for each body. The membership was sorted into separate high degree bodies according to their degrees held.

1. Worshipful Lodge of Les Cayes du Fond. (1°-3°)
2. Chapter of Elects of Les Cayes du Fond. (9°-11°)
3. Respectable Lodge of Perfect Elect, Grand and Sublime Scots of Les Cayes du Fond. (14°)
4. Council of the Knights at the Orient of Les Cayes du Fond. (15°)
5. Grand Council of the Knights of the East and West, Princes of Jerusalem, established at the Orient of Les Cayes du Fond. (17°)[60]

This was the local structure of the Sublime Princes of the Order of the Royal Secret in Saint Domingue. Presumably, each city had these five bodies, given that there are mentions of bodies from Port-au-Prince and St. Marc founding lodges. Each local lodge and its appendant bodies were connected to the Grand Council in Port-au-Prince, and each local lodge could confer degrees as high as Princes of Jerusalem, while degrees above it were bestowed by the Grand Council. All local deputies apparently held the Sublime Princes of the Royal Secret degree, while the local leadership underneath them were Knights Kadosh. Based on the lists it isn't possible to say whether all the other degrees Morin possessed were actually worked, but it appears that it was at least a terminal degree system of sorts, and that one had to have certain degrees corresponding to the list above before advancing, though not necessarily all. The French arm of the Order worked a different degree structure initially as it evolved and this tradition prevailed, whereas the English arm had a fully developed, graduated system, when their lodges were formed.

By the end of 1765 Morin was in Jamaica, by which time he had largely completed his original mission and still more lodges were created. The net result was that his influence had diminished with the increase in lodges. There were then eleven lodges on the island; four of which, *Les Frères Réunis*, in Les Cayes, *La Concorde* in Saint-Marc, *La Parfaitie Harmonie* in Port-au-Prince and *Parfait Union* in Port-au-Prince were aligned with him. He had temporarily failed in the North of the island and the lodges there were

---

58 *BnF FM2 543*

59 See Appendix. *113-1/043 Loge La Concorde, Orient Les Cayes, Fond de l'Ile à Vache (St. Domingue) : No. 607-615*. Archives of the Grand Orient de France.

60 See Appendix. *113-1/044 Loge de L'Amité Indissoluble, Orient de Léogane: No.183-191 M*. Archives of the Grand Orient de France.

aligned with the oldest lodge, *St. Jean de Jérusalem Ecossaise*, which still operated under its Élus Parfaits constitution. Subordinate to it were its daughters, *Parfaitie Harmonie* in Cap-Français along with its own daughter *L'Etroite Union* in Gros-Morne and *La Double Alliance* in Fort Dauphin. *L'Amitié Indissoluble* of Léogane had directly contacted the Grand Lodge to alleviate itself from destruction. Unaffiliated with either side were *Loge du Choix des Hommes* in Jacmel and *Édouard Stuard* of Cap-Français, but the latter was considered clandestine and about to vanish. The following year brought even more change and conflict with it.

Conflict with Brother Martin (1766)

From the Grand Lodge's perspective Morin had succeeded in gaining it lodges, but had yet to achieve its conquest of the island. More troubling, however, was direct evidence in his own hand that he also claimed Deputy Powers from the Grand Lodge of England. He also claimed to have sole authority over the degrees "Grand Elect Perfect Master and Sublime Mason, Knight of the East, and Prince Mason."[61] Further, he had made at least two deputies: Bertrand Berthomieux for Saint-Marc, and Martin Bérindoague for Les Cayes, and had given a constitution to François Ignace de Villiers Deschamps in Port-au-Prince to establish a Lodge of Perfection in Brest, France,[62] well outside of his theatre of operation. Most alarming of these was that he was creating entirely new bodies of lodges, as evidenced by the member lists in Les Cayes from 1765. All of these facts considered together, led to his removal as deputy on July 17, 1766.

> Brother∴ Martin member of the Grand∴ Lodge∴ of France, obliged to pass to America gives his demission – To reward his Zeal and Labor the Grand∴ Lodge∴ gives him the patent of Inspector of Lodges∴ in America, and revokes the powers allegedly given in the same capacity to Brother Maurin [sic], given that the latter responds badly to the confirmation of the Grand∴ Lodge∴[63]

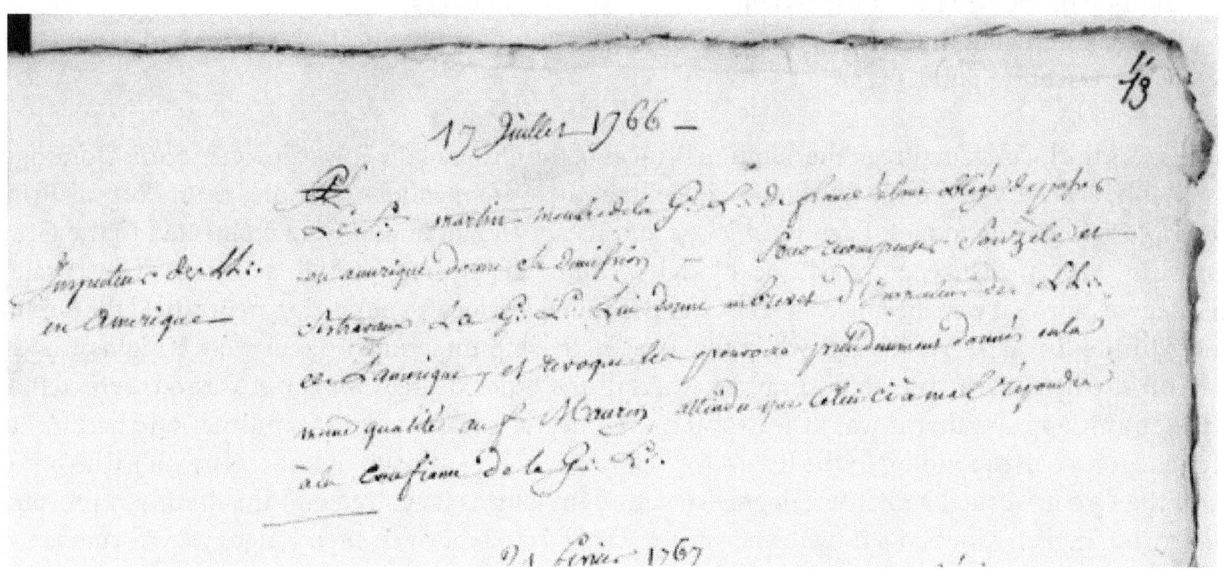

Martin succeeds Morin as deputy for the Grand Lodge of France July 17, 1766. BnF FM1 98.

Martin arrived later that year in Cap-Français and began visiting the local lodges. According to the

---

61 Gonet, et al., *Les Élus Parfaits* (2022), vol. 2, 173

62 See Appendix. File *113-1/010 Loge L'Heureuse Rencontre, Brest No.628M. Loge Ecossaise de la Véritable Union No.623M.* Archives of the Grand Orient de France.

63 *BnF FM1 541. f.13*

reports of *Le Vérité* he visited *St. Jean de Jérusalem Ecossaise, Parfaitie Harmonie,* and *Édouard Stuard*.[64] His brief stay in Cap-Français was primarily driven by business. No advance notice of this was given to the local lodges, creating chaos and confusion. Morin likely never received word of this and learned later, after returning to Saint Domingue, as he never wrote again after 1765. From his perspective this act, which would have looked like betrayal, would further solidify his resolve in forming his emerging rite as a sovereign system, independent of the Grand Lodge of France. According to *Le Vérité*, Martin had determined that none of the lodges in Cap-Français were regularly founded after examining their records, and he reconstituted *Édouard Stuard* as *La Vérité* on March 1, 1767, before returning to France. This formerly clandestine lodge became the beachhead for the Grand Lodge of France's deputy Martin, but none of the other lodges on the island recognized it as regular. In a 1771 report from *Le Vérité* to the Grand Lodge, they complain that

> The Respectable Regular Lodges of the Isle of Saint-Domingue are, due to an unpardonable irregularity, so intimately bound up with the irregular ones that they actually support their error, their paradoxical nature, and their disobedience to the laws of the Sublime Grand Lodge. They even regard them as their 'compass,' a disgrace that the Respectable Lodge *la Vérité*, constituted by the Respectable∴ Brother∴ Martin and whose Constitutions you have confirmed, is suffering from. The refusal of the Respectable∴ Regular Lodges to recognize the Respectable∴ Lodge *la Vérité* as regular is based on two grounds: 1) The fact that the Sublime Grand Lodge did not give them notice of the powers it had bestowed upon Brother∴ Martin, and 2) the fact that they have a Council of the Prince of the Secret [sic], compared with which, the Sovereign Council of this Orient is very little.[65]

Based on the context in the letter it appears that Martin's choice of lodges was not well received and the only possible lodge to convert, given that the influence of the 'Council of the Prince[s] of the [Royal] Secret' was dominant on the island. From Martin's perspective, all lodges were irregular if they did not have a constitution issued by the Grand Lodge of France. Thus, the only "regular" lodges during his stay were *La Concorde, Parfaitie Union, Les Frères Réunis, L'Amitié Indissoluble,* and *La Vérité* which he had personally regularized. Had Martin travelled outside of Cap-Français he would have learned that three out of the five lodges he thought were loyal to the Grand Lodge, were in fact the core of Morin's system. Unfortunately for *Le Vérite*, their pleas fell on deaf ears as the Grand Lodge had slumbered since February 21, 1767, and was powerless to act. This created a power vacuum that was filled by the Order of the Royal Secret, its network having been long since established. This was not the first time *Le Vérité* complained to the Grand Lodge about its unjust treatment.

Earlier in 1770, *Le Vérité* wrote to *La Concorde* informing them of their new foundation. Secretary Mathéus of *Le Vérité* wrote to Secretary Pierre Constant de Castellin of *La Concorde*, sending him a copy of their certificate and immediately a scandal erupted, charging the tone of their letters with bitterness. At dispute was the name of Martin as Grand Inspector, begging the question as to who, in fact, was the legitimate inspector? De Castellin wrote informing Mathéus that he would not address him as Brother since

> These procedures have been recommended to us in many circumstances by the Grand and Sovereign Lodge of France, which, by letters patent of 27th August 1761, appointed the Most Respectable Brother Étienne Morin as its Deputy and Grand Inspector in this Colony, with the power to admit and constitute to the sublime degree of the highest perfection those Brethren whom he might find there to be worthy of such Degrees. This patent was recorded in our Register

---

64 *BnF FM2 (543)*
65 *Bnf FM2 543*

of Deliberations at Brother Morin's request. He travelled here for this express purpose and attended our labors. Since that time we have duly recognized him.

To the prejudice of such powers, we see from the documents enclosed in your letter that an attempt has been made to substitute the so-called 'Brother' Martin, who, during his stay with you, did not deign to make the slightest approach to any Regular Lodge in this Colony, to have himself recognized in that capacity (if such existed), nor to request the registration of the powers he might have. Indeed, on the contrary, we see that he was in a hurry to constitute you provisionally without – in defiance of the law of nations – at least asking the lodges of the Colony for their advice and agreement, and without even taking the trouble to consult them about the Ancient lodge regularly established at the Orient of Le Cap-Français.[66]

Le Vérite received a copy of Morin's powers and made the case for Brother Martin's legitimacy, writing:

We will not argue about the validity of the letters patent borne by your Brother Étienne ~~Martin~~ Morin. I believe him to be your Grand Inspector, although I have as much reason to be suspicious of him as you have to be suspicious of our Respectable Brother Martin, for ultimately the mission of your man has never been confirmed to me any more authentically than the mission of mine. The mission of the latter is not only confirmed at the Lodge *La Vérité* which he constituted, but at all the Legal Lodges of the Colony by means of the collated extracts that the Grand Lodge enjoins the Lodge *La Verité* to pass on, just as I passed it on, in the prescribed form, to your own Lodge in my capacity as Secretary…

If you are in happy correspondence with the Grand Lodge of France then you will find that the General Table says that Brother Martin is Past Master of the Lodge *St. Frederic* in Paris, and an Officer of the Most Respectable and Sublime Grand Lodge of France, and if you have any remaining suspicions left about a Mason of this stature then frankly I have nothing more to say to you.[67]

At issue wasn't just the validity of Grand Inspector Martin, but also his violation of the sovereignty and jurisdiction of *St. Jean de Jérusalem Ecossaise*.

He was aware that this Lodge of Le Cap had a very ancient and very legitimate existence in Masonry, and if he were unaware of it why, when he visited it, did he not ask to see its constitutions, for he would then have seen that they were in good order, and that they emanated from the Most Respectable Scottish Lodge of Bordeaux, recognized as legitimate by the Grand Lodge of France, and all Lodges. He would therefore have been well assured of the genuine existence in Masonry of this Scottish Lodge of Le Cap, its only deficiency being that it was not listed in the General Table in accordance with the new statutes of the Grand Lodge, which only date from 1763. But these new Statutes could not deprive it of its legitimacy, and it would even be on the General Table to confirm the date of its first constitutions if Brother Martin had kept the promise he had given it to have it inserted into the Table on his return from Paris, given the difficulty there was in sending packages to that city.[68]

The lodge correctly noted that Martin was fully aware that the lodge existed since he personally had visited it, but he failed to record its existence on the general table. Its Symbolic Lodge is recorded on the 1769 table, but not as *Parfaitie Harmonie*, but only as *Saint Jean de Jérusalem*. This is because the previous

---

66   *Bnf FM2 543*
67   *Bnf FM2 543*
68   *Bnf FM2 543*

year *Parfaitie Harmonie* merged with *St. Jean de Jérusalem Ecossaise*, which is accounted for by *Le Vérite* as having occurred as, a result of the former realizing that it was founded irregularly.

One of the aforementioned Lodges, called *L'Harmonie*, was aware of the irregular nature of its procedure and decided to remedy it by merging with another Lodge, called *Ecossaise*. Once it had conceived this plan it set about executing it. This merger was achieved in 1768 and please note, Respectable Masters, this Lodge *Ecossaise* (without any Constitutions) was aware of the pretty unbusinesslike behavior of Lodge *L'Harmonie*, regarding which it (Lodge *Ecossaise*) had given Brother Martin a parcel of papers to take to the Sublime Grand Lodge – to what purpose I do not know.[69]

From the perspective of *La Concorde* the powers of Martin were doubtful and his actions irregular:

> [D]uring the suspension of the work of the Grand Lodge, the Council of Knights of the East, with its seat in Paris, certainly has no more right to issue constitutions for a place where another Council of Knights of the East resides than it would have had to issue constitutions for Paris, for a Parliament does not give orders within the jurisdiction of another Parliament. If the Grand Lodge of France, which can be seen as the Council of the Most Serene Grand Master, is no longer in session, then the authority necessary to maintain subordination, and legal guardianship of the laws of Masonry is devolved to the Councils of the Knights of the East, the Princes of Jerusalem, the Sublime Knights of the Royal Secret etc.[70]

Their reasoned position was that they were no longer suffragan to the Grand Lodge of France, not because they deliberately severed ties, but because the Grand Lodge was no longer in session. This became their perspective going forward, since they had been legitimately founded, and the Grand Lodge was in a state of slumber; hence, power devolved to the lower bodies still in existence. The Grand Lodge appeared to have made a grave mistake by replacing Morin, and an even graver acquisition in *Le Vérite*. Moreover, Martin made a diplomatic blunder, and succeeded instead in turning the aligned lodges of Saint Domingue against the Grand Lodge and, by extension, the local lodges loyal to it. Its slumber the following year in 1767, arrested further expansion, and provided the Order of the Royal Secret, an opportunity to thrive. The result of the exchange of letters between *La Concorde* and *Le Vérité* was a refusal to recognize each other as Masons.

> I pray, Sir, the case that I make of most of the members of this so-called Lodge; most of them are linked to me by law and by state, but only civilly. I even advance that the almost immense number of so-called Masons, Grand Scots, Knights of the East, Princes of Jerusalem, of the Royal Secret &c, there are perhaps not four truly good Masons.[71]

Martin, in comparison to Morin, could hardly be considered Grand Deputy. Morin partially resided in Port-au-Prince and had influence everywhere on the island, through his network of deputies. Martin, per contra, resided but briefly in Cap-Français and quickly returned to France initiating a row. He fractured the foundation laid by Morin, isolating *Le Vérite* in the North and *L'Amitié Indissoluble* in the South, who were then surrounded by hostile lodges. This isolation increased their resolve to correct this sorely perceived error.

---

69 *Bnf FM2 543*
70 *Bnf FM2 543*
71 *BnF FM2 543*

THE ORDER OF THE SUBLIME PRINCES OF THE ROYAL SECRET (1767–75)

In the beginning, Morin did not likely intend to build a high degree system outside of the sphere of the Grand Lodge of France, but rather within it and went to great lengths to inform them precisely what he was doing, in order to bring the lodges of Saint Domingue under their control. His decision to pursue a path towards local sovereignty was one borne of necessity; first, because it was the Grand Lodge who abandoned him and not the other way around and, second, since the Grand Lodge's labors had slumbered, their administrative powers devolved to local bodies, to maintain order. From his perspective he had constantly been at labor propagating the high degrees since 1745, and his vision of a Masonically unified Saint Domingue had mostly come to fruition. The historical record shows no clear separation between his work for the Élus Parfaits and his work for the Grand Lodge and it rather appeared to be a continuous string of actions. His actions were a continuity of his original task: to spread the high degrees in general and Scottish Masonry in particular, albeit in slightly augmented forms from the originals. Moreover, he appeared to be creating a unifying system that united both French and English Masons, as well as both Ancients and Moderns.

In March 1765 Morin and Francken were together in Kingston and, by that December, Francken was in New York attending a christening[72] with his newlywed (second) wife.[73] In between these months, a plan had been made to use Morin's English powers and establish an arm of the same system in the English colonial possessions. When Francken departed for New York, he likely had a deputy patent modeled after Morin's, had commissioned a new seal and counter seal for his use in the Order of the Royal Secret, and was travelling with (at least) a copy of the Grand Elect, Perfect and Sublime Master degree.[74] His mission to establish a Lodge of Perfection in New York was achieved on December 20, 1767, and he returned hurriedly to Jamaica by April of 1769. To avoid debtors prison, Francken fled New York with his wife, and his personal effects were auctioned, appearing in the local newspaper as a "Gentleman absconding" from his debts.

> Public Auction. Tomorrow will be sold at Moore & Lynsen's Auction Room, Several rich Cloaths, the Property of a Gentleman absconding. On Wednesday, At the House of Henry Andrew Franckin Esq. near the New Dutch Church, the Household Furniture of that Gentleman, who departs the Province.[75]

Francken had been a party to two very large land grants in New York. In 1767 he petitioned with Cornelius P. Low, for 2,000 acres on the western frontier of Ulster county New York. Low was related to his wife and had been speculating on land in New York as early as the 1730's. The following year Francken was naturalized in the Province of New York and on February 3, and petitioned for 5,500 acres with John Morin Scott and M.G. Van Bergen on April 17, 1769.[76] Francken appears to have been a land speculator[77]

---

72 "Child & Date … Johanna … Dec 8 … Parents … Low Nicholaas / Sara Low … Witnesses … Henry A. Franken / wife Johanna Low." *Dutch Reformed Church Records from Selected States, 1660-1926; New York City*. Vol II, Book 34, p. 89. < *https://www.wikitree.com/photo.php/e/e3/Louw-483-1.jpg* > Accessed March 15, 2023.

73 "After being appointed court interpreter in 1765 and with the permission of Lieutenant Governor Moore, Francken traveled to Albany, New York and New York City, both with Dutch-speaking populations. He married Johanna Low of Newark, New Jersey…"—S. Brent Morris, "Henry Andrew Francken and his Masonic Manuscripts," *Heredom* vol. 23 (Washington, D.C.: Scottish Rite Research Society, 2015), 109.

74 We do not have any evidence that Francken translated and transcribed any rituals into English at this point; he may have simply summarized and "communicated" the contents to the recipients, an occasional practice which continued into the Nineteenth Century.

75 *Supplement to the New York Gazette and the Weekly Mercury*, April 17, 1769.

76 *Calendar of N.Y. Colonial Manuscripts, Indorsed Land Papers: In the Office of the Secretary of State of New York, 1643–1803* (Albany: Weed, Parsons, 1864). 453, 455, 503

77 Francken had owned 600 acres in Jamaica, and partially owned 7,500–8,000 acres in New York. On December 30, 1761, he was granted 300 acres for cultivation in St. Thomas Parrish, Jamaica, adjacent to his son Parker Bennet Francken. In 1767 he petitioned with Cor-

> **PUBLIC AUCTION.**
> To-morrow, will be fold at
> **Moore & Lynfen's**
> AUCTION-ROOM,
> Several rich Cloaths,---the Property of a Gentleman abfconding.
> On *Wednefday*,
> At the Houfe of Henry Andrew Francklin, Efq; near the New Dutch Church, the Houfhold Furniture of that Gentleman, who departs the Province.
> At Moore & Lynfen's *Auction Room*,
> Every Day this Week,
> A large and general Affortment of Irifh Linens, 7-8 and yd. wide Cotton and Linen Checks, yd. and 3-8 do. printed Cottons, Silk and Thread Stockings, Blond Laces, Silk Handkerchiefs, Thickfets, Dowlafs, &c. &c.
> With a Variety of other GOODS.

Francken flees New York. *Supplement to the New York Gazette and the Weekly Mercury*, April 17, 1769.

and borrowed against the land but defaulted on his debts and escaped with his pregnant wife to Kingston, where his daughter Mary Long Francken was born on August 4, 1769.[78] The land in question was later sold on July 11, 1770.

Because Morin was no longer communicating with the Grand Lodge his location became difficult to determine as we only have fragmentary pieces of information. One such example comes from the Léogane lodge *L'Amitié Indissoluble*. Poncet, the Master of the lodge, wrote to the Grand Lodge on June 29, 1767, to find out why the members from his Lodge were rejected at the Scottish Lodges of other Orients.

> It is a question of whether you would be so kind as to inform me as to whether there are several different kinds of Masonry in France. We at the Lodges in Port-au-Prince, Saint-Marc and Le Fond de l'Iîe à Vache, known under the gracious titles of *La Parfaite Union, La Concorde* and *Les Frères Réunis*, dispute the right of what they call Scottish Masonry, whose adherents do not wish to correspond with us in this quality to which they lay claim… I would ask where they got their constitutions of what they call Scottish Masonry from? They tell me from Jamaica. I think that, as Frenchmen, we should all follow uniquely all the constitutions emanating from the Most Respectable Grand Lodge of France, that same France from which, for some 28 years now, I have drawn the 1st principles of the Royal Art, in which I have been deeply immersed as far as the degree of Sublime Elect Grand Master. I have met and frequented some excellent French and English Masons who have never hesitated to receive me in all their Lodges. It is unfortunate, my Most Respectable Brother, that the three Lodges of the New World, where I have lived for some 18 years, flatly refuse to recognize in their Lodges the Masons I initiated with the agreement of

---

nelius P. Low for 2,000 acres in Ulster County New York. On March 2, 1768, he twice petitioned for a sum of 5,500 acres, with John Morin Scott and M. G. Van Bergen and their associates, which was sold July 11, 1770. On May 13, 1773, he petitioned for 300 acres, in St. Thomas Parrish, Jamaica

78 Kingston, Jamaica Church of England Parish Register.

our Mother Lodge, the Grand and Most Respectable Lodge.[79]

Importantly we see that as early as July 1767 the lodges around Morin already considered themselves as sovereign and claim that their form of Scottish Masonry was seated in Jamaica and not France. The Master made it clear in his letter that they did hold regular Masonic communication, but that they "do not wish to correspond with us in this quality to which they lay claim." The meaning is subtle, but significant. They recognized the Grand Lodge's authority over symbolic Masonry, but not over the High Degrees, and instead rely upon Morin's English powers.

After Poncet received a reply form the Grand Lodge, he provided further insight into the personage of Morin.

> From time to time in this colony we see Brother Morin, whom we certainly acknowledge as Master of the Lodge of *L'Harmonie* as listed in the table of Regular Lodges, but who wishes, under titles that he has undoubtedly obtained surreptitiously from the Grand Lodge, to pass himself off as Inspector of Lodges of Saint Domingue. We refused point-blank to recognize him as such, as he does not appear in the General Table, where we find only a Brother Martin who lives in Le Cap, and not Brother Morin who wanders backwards and forwards to Jamaica, for it should be said in passing that there is no Lodge called *L'Harmonie* in all the French territory of Saint Domingue, and therefore could this not be a Brother who is making Masonry into a livelihood and living off the proceeds? He is certainly very enlightened and has all the answers at his fingertips as the saying goes, but he is definitely not my cup of tea. I would be obliged if you could provide me with some clues about this Brother after you have enquired about him at the Grand Lodge from which he must have originally come. He is turning upside down all the Lodges in Port-au-Prince, Les Cayes and Saint-Marc with titles to which he lays claim from both Jamaica and France. All the Brethren of these three Orients look up to him as a tutelary deity, but as for me, speaking as someone who is not so credulous, I would be delighted to know who he really is before bestowing upon him the slightest honors other than those due to the Master of the Lodge *L'Harmonie*, and that is why I am taking this opportunity to repeat my request.[80]

From the context of the letter, Morin's role appeared to be merely the founder of a system which operated autonomously, as he "wanders backwards and forwards to Jamaica." Although he was accused of living off the proceeds of Masonry, this argument doesn't hold up to scrutiny. We know that Morin was a merchant. At one point he loaned Christopher Wood, some £500 (£43,627.65 in today's money), which was recorded as a bad loan in his probate file.[81] This weighty debt was unrecoverable and, given its size, was most likely commercial. The amount suggests that Morin had significant sources of income outside of Masonry. On the other hand, his system was effectively a Saint Domingue Grand Lodge that operated until 1777, some six years after his death. The local lodges, chapters, and councils were self-sustaining, self-funded, and self-governing. Their bylaws addressed powers and initiation fees, how they were to be applied, and further how the lodges were to use these funds. The whole system was well-regulated and operated with what it perceived to be perfect regularity.

On Saint John's Day 1767, *L'Etroite Union* of Gros-Morne was reconstituted by the *Souverain Conseil des Princes de Jérusalem* of Saint-Marc and remained a member of the Order of the Royal Secret until April 23, 1777. As it was the daughter of the Symbolic Lodge *Parfaitie Harmonie*, itself a daughter of *Saint Jean de Jérusalem Ecossaise*, its date of entry suggests that its mother had yet to affiliate at this point, coinciding with the fallout from Martin's visit to Cap-Français.

---

79 *113-1/044 Loge de L'Amité Indissoluble, Orient de Léogane: No.183-191 M.* Archives of the Grand Orient de France.
80 *113-1/044 Loge de L'Amité Indissoluble, Orient de Léogane: No.183-191 M.* Archives of the Grand Orient de France.
81 *1B/11/3/51, f. 131 (Stephen Morin),* Jamaica Archives.

Morin appeared in Les Cayes, and his signature appears on the patent of Guillaume Alexis Delmas (August 22, 1767) for the Degree of Knight of the East. This document was issued by the Council of the Knights Princes from the Orient of Les Cayes, at the top of which is an elaborately designed and stamped copperplate impression bearing the first seal of the Order of the Sublime Princes of the Royal Secret. Morin likely later deposited the plate with *Les Frères Réunis* as it still appeared on their 1774 member list sent to the *Grand Orient de France*, when the lodge went under their jurisdiction, some three years after his death. Curiously, there is a third example of this seal in the papers of Pierre Lambert de Lintot.[82] He appears as "Pierre Lambert" in the 1764 member lists of *La Concorde* in Les Cayes and he was also a member of the Elect Chapter, absent on military duty.[83]

At some point in 1768 *Saint Jean de Jérusalem Ecossaise* joined the Order of the Royal Secret, and in turn, reconstituted *La Double Alliance* its daughter in 1769 and renamed her *Saint Jean de Jérusalem de Nouvelle Alliance*. This lodge was short-lived and disappeared after 1774.

Later in 1769, Morin was back in Kingston. According to the *1771 Francken Manuscript*, Grand Inspector Morin informed the Consistory of the Princes of the Royal Secret that the 24° was no longer to be simply called "Knights of Kadoch" but also "Knights of the White and Black Eagle."

> The Grand Inspector Stephen Morin, Founder of the Lodge of Perfection &c in a Consistory of Princes of the Royal Secret held at Kingston In Jamaica In the year of Masonry 7769, advertized of Princes Masons, that lately a commotion had been at Paris, and that Enquiry had been made, whether those Masons who stiled themselves Knights of Kadoch, were not in reality Knights Templars. It was therefore Resolved, in the grand communication of Berlin & Paris, that said Degree should be stilled, knights of [the] white & black Eagle and the Jewel of the order should be a black Eagle &c as mentioned in the 24th Degree.[84]

Morin's final Masonic act in Jamaica was to "issue a Constitution for a Grand Chapter of Princes of the Royal Secret on April 30, 1770, to Henry Andrew Francken, Deputy Inspector, William Adams Deputy Inspector, William Wynter, Gabriel Jones, John Prendergast, Edward Bowes, and Martin Matthias."[85] William Wynter serves as the first President and Grand Commander of all Grand Chapters, Councils and Consistories and Francken is the local Deputy.

Just a month later he performed his final Masonic act in Jacmel, as his signature appears on the patent of the Worshipful Master of the *Loge du Choix des Hommes*, Mennessier de Boissy (June 1, 1770), creating him a Deputy Inspector.[86] The lodge had been founded in 1762 and was reconstituted by the *Souverain Conseil des Princes de la Maçonnerie* at Port-au-Prince on February 2, 1768 and was installed by Morin's local Deputy, Jean Jacques Texier.[87] Morin's appearance in Jacmel was to officially make de Boissy the local representative and Deputy Inspector for Jacmel. *Loge du Choix des Hommes* was unique in his system, as it survived as the last lodge in Saint Domingue affiliated with the Order of the Royal Secret, since the bulk of their lodges had affiliated with the *Grand Loge Provinciale* of the *Grand Orient*

---

82   David Harrison, *The Rite of Seven Degrees* (Surrey, United Kingdom: Lewis Masonic, 2020).

83   113-1/043 Loge La Concorde, Orient Les Cayes, Fond de l'Ile à Vache (St. Domingue): No. 607-615. Archives of the Grand Orient de France.

84   *1771 Francken Ms.*, Archives of the United Grand Lodge of England.

85   [Jerry A. Roach, unaccredited transcriber] *The 1783 Francken Manuscript. With Essays by Jeffrey Croteau, Alan E. Foulds, Aimee E. Newell* (Lexington, Mass.: The Supreme Council, 33°, NMJ, 2017), 59.

86   Alain Bernheim, "Estienne Morin et l'Ordre du Royal Secret," Acta Macionica vol. 9 (Bruxelles: Grande Loge Régulière de Belgique, 1999), 11–30.

87   Kamel Oussayef and Aimee E. Newell, *Book of Wisdom: Freemasonry through the Veil of an Ancient French Manuscript* (Lexington, MA: Supreme Council, 33° Northern Masonic Jurisdiction, 2013). This book is a translation and facsimile reproduction of SC113H, Doszedardski Collection (Jean Frederic C. Doszedardski 1770-1816) La Maçonnerie Ancien Ecossaise. Van Gorden-Williams Library and Archives, Lexington, Massachusetts.

de France by 1777. In contrast, this lodge resisted joining until March 30, 1785, becoming the last lodge on the island to do so. Morin returned to Jamaica in 1771 and died on November 11, 1771. His legacy in light of this context is not one of a degree merchant but is instead one of a Masonic founder.

In the absence of their founder, the order continued to expand. *Saint Jean de Jérusalem Ecossaise* established the Fond des Nègres lodge *Les Frères Choisis* on May 10, 1773. This lodge worked until November 11, 1783, before affiliating with the *Grand Loge Provinciale*. The high degrees worked by this lodge are retained in the archives of the Grand Lodge of Sweden, and the bound cahier contains two sets of rituals used in the lodge, separated by a decade.[88]

1773	*1783*
4. Expert	4. Expert ou Maître préfet des Ouvrages
5. Elu	5. Élus
6. Ecossisme ou Loge de Perfection	6. Grand Élus ou sublime Ecossais
7. Chevalier d'Orient	7. Chevalier d'Orient
8. Princes de Jérusalem	8. Princes de Jérusalem

The 1773 collection likely contains the rituals of the Order of the Royal Secret as used at the time of the lodge's founding, whereas the 1783 collection appears to be a revision made sometime after the lodge affiliated with the *Grande Loge Provinciale*. Noticeably the revised rituals have the Scottish degree substituted altogether, with substantial revisions to the Knights of the East and Princes of Jerusalem texts. There are no references to a Sovereign Council and, most significantly, the privileges of the Princes of Jerusalem were removed from the revisions. This change was necessary because the Princes of Jerusalem were previously understood to be "the chiefs of Masonry, and they judge sovereignly, all the affairs which relate to it, and have right to annul, revoke or cancel all that is done in lodge, abrasive or contrary to the regulations."[89] These privileges were likely necessary to assert the Order's dominance, in light of competition from lodges aligned only with the Grand Lodge. These powers were codified by Francken in the English arm of the Order, although he limited their jurisdiction from symbolic lodges to Lodges of Perfection and Councils of the Knights of the East (vide *1771 Francken MS.*, Constitutions of 1762, Art. 29).[90]

The *Souverain Conseil des Chevaliers d'Orient* in Port-au-Prince constituted the lodge *L'Unanimité* in 1773 in Petit-Goave, but it was a member for just over a year, before affiliating with the *Grand Orient de France* on May 27, 1774.[91]

Les Frères Choisis constituted a daughter and the last lodge for the Order of the Royal Secret, *Les Frères Zélés* in Cavaillon on March 6, 1775.[92] This lodge was a member for over two years until being reconstituted by the *Grande Loge Provinciale* on November 11, 1777.

The Provincial Grand Lodge, a force of stability (1776–89)

Although the death of Morin eventually had an effect on the Order, as the foundations of their entire

---

88 *Ms. 104 D. LII. Haut Grades de l'Orient de Paris.* Archives of the Grand Lodge of Sweden.

89 "Ils sont les chefs de la Maçonnerie, ils jugent souverainement, toute les affaires qui la concernant, et ont droit de casser et révoquer ou annuler tout ce qui se fait en loge d'abrasif ou contraire au règlemens." *Ms. 104 D. LII. Haut Grades de l'Orient de Paris.* Archives of the Grand Lodge of Sweden. "Ils sont les chefs de la Maçonnerie, ils jugent souverainement, toute les affaires qui la concernant, et ont droit de casser et révoquer ou annuler tout ce qui se fait en loge d'abrasif ou contraire au règlemens."

90 "2ᵈ T[he] Princes of Jerusalem have a Right and Privilege, to annul and repeal, all that might have been done inconsistent to the orders & Laws, in a council of knights of the East, and also in a Royal Lodge of Perfection and in any other Lodges whatsoever, Provided nevertheless, that there is not Present any of the Sublime Princes of a Superior degree." —*1771 Francken Ms.*

91 *BnF FM2 545*

92 *BnF FM2 544*

structure were built upon his powers, they by no means suffered from a lack of administration, and continued growing and expanding in his absence. His death, as well as that of the Grand Master of the Grand Lodge of France, Louis, Comte de Clermont in 1771, made possible a reconciliation in Saint Domingue. Louis Philippe II, Duc de Chartres, succeeded as Grand Master, and at once the Grand Lodge arose from its slumber. The birth of the *Grand Orient de France* in 1773, from the ashes of the former, signified a change in direction. This, coupled with the loss of Morin, led to a softening of hearts and a desire to be affiliated with the reformed Grand Lodge. The principle means of achieving this was the closure of the Council of the Sublime Princes seated at Port-au-Prince.

La Parfait Union was naturally the first acquisition for arresting the chaos in Saint Domingue. It was reconstituted by the *Grand Orient* on May 7, 1774 along with its daughter *L'Unanimité* on May 27 and vanished from the records after 1778.[93] Just ten months later, *La Vérité* was reconstituted on October 9.[94] The alignment of these two lodges made possible the establishment of the *Grand Loge Provinciale* on March 22, 1776 and the remaining lodges were then reconstituted after its founding, with the exception of *Les Frères Choisis* in 1783 and *Loge du Choix des Hommes* in 1785.[95] The birth of the *Grande Loge Provinciale* marked a new era of stability on the island through its regulations and administration, as old conflicts were put to rest.

The *Grande Loge Provinciale* began its work in 1777 to reconstitute the remaining lodges. *La Concorde* was the first and reconstituted on July 27, followed by *L'Etroite Union* on September 14 and *Les Frères Zélés* on November 11.[96] As *La Concorde* was one of the principal lodges in the Order of the Royal Secret, its conversion completed the conquest of the northern part of the island, with resistance only remaining in the South. *Saint Jean de Jérusalem Ecossaise* vanished altogether in 1777. The following year *Les Frères Réunis*, was reconstituted in Les Cayes on July 27, 1778.[97] Only two lodges stubbornly remained attached to the Order of the Royal Secret.

At the same time, the *Grande Loge Provinciale* began chartering new lodges, issuing a constitution for the Petit-Trou lodge *La Raison Perfectionnée* on August 20, 1779. The same year both *L'Amitié Indissoluble* and *Parfait Union* disappeared from the records, leaving the capital city without a lodge until *La Réunion Desirée* was constituted on July 21, 1783.[98] Many of its members had also been members of Parfait Union as its name suggests. Two of its ritual books survive in the Scottish Rite library in Minneapolis. They are preserved in two leather bound cahiers, the first is titled *Maçonnerie du Grand Orient, Chevalier de l'Epée, septième Grade*.[99] The second cahier is titled *Maçonnerie du Grand Orient, Rose Croix. Dernier Grade*.[100] These rituals date to around the founding of the lodge and are beautifully written, providing an insight as to what degrees were being practiced by the Saint Domingue lodges prior to the standardization of the ritual in 1786. These degrees are augmentations of their classical forms, and the structure suggests that it followed the French Rite framework with perhaps the degree of Expert Master being inserted before Elect Master.

On November 11, 1779, *Les Frères Choisis* was at last reconstituted.[101] Its resistance is impressive given that they shared the same city with the *Grande Loge Provinciale* in Fonds-de-Nègres since its creation.

The Petit-Goave lodge *L'Union du Saint Esprit* is constituted October 24, 1784, utilizing the papers

---

93 *BnF FM2 545*
94 *BnF FM2 543*
95 *BnF FM2 545*
96 *BnF FM2 544*
97 *BnF FM2 543*
98 *BnF FM2 546*
99 *Ms. 724*, Minneapolis Scottish Rite Library.
100 *Ms. 720*. Minneapolis Scottish Rite Library.
101 *BnF FM2 544*

from the first lodge *L'Union* founded in 1746.[102] This lodge merged with *Parfait Union*'s daughter, *L'Unanimité* on July 28, 1788, becoming *L'Unanimité et Union de Saint Esprit*.

Several significant events occurred in 1785. The Les Cayes lodge Les *Frères Discrets* was reconstituted on March 1, and the final remaining lodge of the Order of the Royal Secret, *Loge du Choix des Hommes*, submitted and was reconstituted by the *Grande Loge Provinciale* on March 30, 1785.[103] Likely dissatisfied, its membership within the *Grand Orient* was brief, and they petitioned *Saint André d'Ecosse* in Paris to join the *Rit Écossais*, on Saint John's Day 1788.[104] The constitution and rituals for the symbolic degrees for this lodge are preserved in the Jean C. Doszedardski collection at the Van Gorden-Williams Library in Lexington, Massachusetts, and demonstrates the first known example of Scottish Craft or symbolic degrees to include the modes of recognition for the Antients degrees as well.[105] In July a new lodge, *La Réunion des Coeurs* was established in Jérémie and worked under a Kingston, Jamaica warrant from Saint James Lodge, dated June 21, 1785.[106] The following year they were constituted by the *Grande Loge Provinciale* on June 20, 1786.

Two more lodges were founded by the *Grande Loge Provinciale* before the outbreak of the French Revolution. *Les Philadelphes* in Léogane was founded in 1788, as the city had been without a lodge for nearly nine years, and *Les Amis Réunis* in Port-au-Prince was established in 1789.[107]

The French Revolution began on July 14, 1789, with the storming of the Bastille, which destabilized the mother country and her colonies. This same year Antients Masonry arrived on the island with the constitution of *Réunion des Coeurs Franco Americain* in the capital city of Port-au-Prince on December 18 by the Grand Lodge of Pennsylvania at the insistance of Pierre le Barbier Duplessis,[108] who became Grand Secretary of Pennsylvania the following year.

The Grand Orient had successfully brought the entire island of Saint Domingue under its control for only one year in 1787, but its success was short-lived, and the map of her dominion, was ever changing.

Revolutionary Chaos (1789–99)

The revolution, whose motto was liberty, equality, and the rights of man, rang hollow in the ears of the enslaved, whose sweat, blood, and tears fertilized the soil of the island. The first article of the Declaration of the Rights of Man stated that "Men are born free and remain free, equal in rights,"[109] yet the many of the inhabitants in the French dominions remained in bondage: they were not seen as men, but as chattel property. Gathered together in the rain and darkness at Bois Caïman on August 14, 1791, slaves lead by Dutty Boukman performed a voodoo ritual and made a pact with each other to break their chains and burn their plantations to the ground. Within a week the entire Northern Department of the colony was in flames. Some 4,000 whites had been slaughtered and over 1,000 plantations were razed. The survivors organized into militias and proceeded to massacre over 15,000 blacks in reprisal, but they were simply outnumbered ten to one and driven back to Cap Français.

By January 1792 over a third of the colony had been sacked. France sent 6,000 troops and a new governor, Léger-Félicité Sonthonax, to restore order. A genocidal civil war had begun and showed no signs of stopping. We have no way of knowing for certain if lodges met during this period, but if the late

---

102 *BnF FM2 545*

103 *BnF FM2 545*

104 Oussayef and Newell, *Book of Wisdom: Freemasonry through the Veil of an Ancient French Manuscript* (2013)

105 The statutes and regulations are preserved in SC113H, the first and Second degrees are preserved in SC113AF and the third degree in SC113AG, *SC113 Doszedardski Collection (Jean Frederic C. Doszedardski 1770–1816) La Maçonnerie Ancien Ecossaise*. Van Gorden-Williams Library and Archives, Lexington, Massachusetts.

106 *BnF FM2 545*.

107 *BnF FM2 545*.

108 *BnF FM2 545*.

109 Declaration of the Rights of Man. National Assembly, August 24, 1789.

history of the revolution is any indication, they persisted where possible in the large cities, although there are no Masonic records for Saint Domingue from 1789-1796. Thousands of displaced citizens boarded ships, fleeing to America as refugees for their safety, having lost everything. Creoles in the Southern Department invited the British to come and occupy the island, believing that they would preserve the institution of slavery, after it was abolished in Saint Domingue by Sonthonax on August 29, 1793. The landowners felt betrayed by their own government.

Arriving in May of 1794, the British occupation was largely ineffective as they were too few in number and utterly decimated by yellow fever. Spain briefly entered the conflict from their half of the island and met with a similar fate. Forces led by Toussaint Louverture and André Rigaud checked the British advance and kept them largely isolated to Port-au-Prince, leading to their evacuation in May 1798, and a formal agreement to withdraw all British forces from Saint Domingue signed by Colonel Thomas Maitland and Louverture on August 31, the same year. By the end of the year all British forces had withdrawn to Jamaica counting nearly 100,000 casualties. The Revolution began to cool, as the rebel leaders now turned inward and fought amongst themselves for control, with Louverture emerging as the victor.

Slowly lodges began to emerge in this relative peace, returning to normal operation. The first lodge founded after the evacuation of the English was *La Parfaitie Egalité*, constituted by the *Grande Loge Provinciale La Sagesse* of Portsmouth, Virginia on November 6, 1798. Several other lodges were also founded and recorded in the Tableau of *Le Vérité* for 1799. They were likely working under warrant locally from the *Grande Loge Provinciale*, but it is not clear as there are no records for this, having evacuated themselves in 1798 and appearing in New York in 1799 before dissolving the following year. They are *L'Intimité* in Port-de-Paix, *La Céleste Amité* in Dondon, *L'Union des Cœurs sans Fard* and *De Sion des Frères de la Véritable Egalité* in Cap Français.[110] Another lodge *Saint Jean d'Ecosse des Sept Frères Réunis* is established in Le Cap and were originally constituted by *Saint-Jean d'Ecosse de Marseilles* and received a constitution from the *Grand Orient de France* on Saint John's Day 1799. All of these new lodges are founded in the Northern Department around Cap Français, and will remain a stronghold of the French Rite and the *Grand Orient* until the end. By 1800 *Les Frères Réunis* are back at labor in the Southern Department, but we have no evidence except for the petition of some of her members in Paris in 1805 for recognition. There are only a handful of lodges with records after 1800; *Les Sept Frères Réunis* and *Le Vérité* in Cap-Français and *Les Frères Réunis* in Les Cayes who will be reconstituted by the Grand Lodge of Pennsylvania along with *La Concorde* in Saint-Marc, *Loge du Choix des Hommes* in Jacmel, *La Réunion des Coeurs* in Jérémie, *Réunion des Cœurs Franco Americain* in Port-au-Prince, and *Amis Réunis* in Mole St. Nicolas. *Amis Réunis* was formerly a clandestine lodge and sought recognition from the Grand Orient, but there is no indication that it was approved.

The constitution and rituals[111] of *Loge du Choix des Hommes* preserved in the Doszedardski Collection note that 'despite the disasters of the colony of Saint Domingue, which however caused three suspensions and resumptions of labor, finally transferred its meetings to the City of Santo Domingo.'[112] They likely relocated before 1804, as they re-constituted the lodge *Parfaitie Harmonie* in the city of Santo Domingo on Saint John's Day 1805 in advance of their removal from the rolls of the Grand Lodge of Pennsylvania in 1806. Conclusively we can say that no other lodges are founded by the *Grand Orient* from 1800-1802. *Le Vérité* will constitute one final lodge for the *Grand Orient*, constituting a daughter lodge, *Le Enfants du Mars* in Cap Français on June 11, 1803.[113] Her life will be very short perhaps numbering merely months.

---

110 *BnF FM2 543*. Le Vérité 1799.

111 *SC113 AF*, "Premier Grade Apprentif, Ecossais. 2∴ Grade Compagnon, Ecossais"; *SC113 AG*, "Simbolique∴, Troisième Maître Grade Simbolique Ecossais." Doszedardski Collection, Van Gorden-Williams Library and Archives.

112 *SC113 H*, "La Maçonnerie Ancien Ecossaise." Doszedardski Collection, Van Gorden-Williams Library and Archives.

113 *SC113 H*, "La Maçonnerie Ancien Ecossaise."

Grand Lodge of Pennsylvania Lodges (1801–04)

As *Réunion des Cœurs Franco Americain* had survived the revolution, it was in a unique position to spread Antients Masonry across the island in the West and South Jurisdictions, being aligned with *Les Frères Réunis* and *La Concorde*. These lodges were reconstituted *No. 88 Les Frères Réunis* and *No. 89 La Concorde* by the Grand Lodge of Pennsylvania on May 4, 1801. The island began to stabilize through 1801 under the leadership of Louverture and the Grand Lodge founded *No. 95 La Humilité* in Anse-a-Veau on December 6, 1802, before constituting their *Provincial Grand Lodge of Saint Domingue* three days later in Port-au-Prince on December 9.

Louverture expanded his power over the whole island, conquering the Spanish portion and abolishing slavery. Returning to Le Cap, he issued a constitution declaring the island sovereign from France, provoking the wrath of Napoleon, who sent General Leclerc to put down the revolution in 1802. Louverture is tricked into a signing a truce, but is instead imprisoned and sent back to France where he dies in his cell. Initially Jean-Jacques Dessalines succeeds Louverture and fights for the French, but turns on them after learning of the plan to re-institute slavery in Martinique. The French face a final onslaught from the rebel forces and are utterly decimated by disease and fierce fighting, claiming le Clerc himself.

The *Provincial Grand Lodge* founded *No. 97 Parfaitie Harmonie* in Santo Domingo and *No. 98 La Persévérance* in Abricots on September 5, 1803. This short lived Provincial Grand Lodge constituted a final lodge, *No. 99 La Temple du Bonheur* in Archahaye on December 5, 1803, but they likely never met as Dessalines declared the birth of the Republic of Haiti twenty-seven days later on January 1, 1804, sealing the fate of all white people who remained.

Progression of the Rituals (1740–1804)

Regrettably, there are no known examples of the Saint Domingue symbolic degrees from 1740–74. The earliest lodges were aligned with the Élus Parfaits of Bordeaux, which was itself attached to the symbolic lodge *L'Anglaise*, chartered by English and Irish Masons in 1732. It used the same ritual as England, given that all minutes for this lodge are in English until the Comte de Clermont became the Grand Substitute for the Grand Master in 1744. In Saint Domingue however, the Perfect Scottish Lodges were attached to Saint John's Lodges that already existed, making it impossible to say with any certainty what ritual was used in their lodges.

As Saint Domingue lodges had received constitutions issued from several Masonic authorities, a variety of symbolic degrees were conferred over the lifetime of the colony. There were four Grand Lodges chartering symbolic lodges from 1774–1804, each with its own unique ritual. All of these ritual influences are evolutionarily linked and when combined with the Antients degrees, contain all the necessary ingredients to compose the *Guide des Maçons Écossais* (1804).

Grand Lodge of France ritual (1774–87)

The earliest datable Saint Domingue symbolic degrees are the "Bonseigneur rituals," part of a collection ascribed to Jean Bonseigneur, who was a coffee plantation owner in Port-de-Paix. They are in a leather-bound cahier collection of rituals in the George Longe Collection in the archives of the Amistad Research Center at Tulane University. The Latomia Foundation, then ran by Gerry Prinsen, published re-touched facsimile images of the entire collection with useful but errant French transcripts and English translations.[114] While the contribution was important, it included some incorrect assumptions. Prinsen correctly noted that the ritual collection is made sometime after 1786, but he wrote that "the craft degrees show an archaic structure and seem to be copies from originals which are mostly earlier than 1760."

On the contrary, the symbolic degrees were near perfect transcriptions of the official Grand Lodge

---

114 The collection was reprinted in a vastly-improved edition as Gerry L. Prinsen, ed., Forward by Michael R. Poll, *The Bonseigneur Rituals: A Collection of 18th Century New Orleans Masonic Rituals* 2 vols. (New Orleans: Cornerstone, 2008)

of France ritual. Created in 1769, the first standardized French Rite ritual was the *Corps Complete de Maçonnerie* (printed in 1774).[115] These degrees were used after the birth of the *Grand Orient de France* in 1773, as the latter did not standardize their own ritual until 1786, and it did not reach Saint Domingue until 1788.[116] Prinsen also noted that the lodge using these rituals was likely the same *Parfaitie Loge d'Ecosse*, which Morin founded in Port-de-Paix, but concedes that he knew of no evidence for the lodge's existence at that time. This opportunity was used to highlight other unrelated contributions by Latomia on the Élus Parfait featuring the Sharp documents. In reality they paint a clear picture that there was only a single piece of correspondence from them. It is certainly possible that the lodge continued, but there is no evidence to account for this. In light of the data generated in this project, there are at least two possible lodges, *La Parfaitie Egalité*, and *L'Intimité*, both appearing only in the member lists for *Le Vérité* in 1799 and 1800.[117] The inclusion of their names on the member lists suggests that they were *Grand Orient Lodges*, but we have no evidence yet to be definitive. Regardless, this standardized ritual was used in at least one City in Saint Domingue and used in most new lodges chartered after 1774, but before 1788.

Grand Orient de France ritual (1788–1804)

Doszedardski's collection includes a copy of the first three degrees of the French Rite. The original was transmitted from the *Grand Orient de France* to *Le Vérité* after its construction in 1786.[118] The Doszedardski copy was used by *Le Vérité* to charter the Cap Français lodge *Le Enfants de Mars* on June 11, 1803.

> This cahier contains / 1°∴ The three Symbolic degrees. / 2°∴ The Labors of a Workshop L[odge]∴ / 3°∴ Constitutions, & Installations of Lodges. / 4°∴ General Masonic Institutes, of the Modern Rite∴ / Taken from the Collection of the Most Illustrious B[rother]∴ M[aster]∴ Huet de Lachelle∴[119]

The language in the ritual offers clues to its approximate age, as it contains the 1785 variation in the toasts of the Entered Apprentice degree, rendered to the King and his family:

> B[rothers]∴ Senior and Junior Wardens, will you kindly announce on your Columns that the first obligatory health is to the King our Monarch, to the Queen his august Consort, and to all the Sovereign-protectors of the Masons; to this health we shall add our best wishes for the prosperity of France. For a health so precious to us I invite you to produce the best possible fusillade. I reserve the right to give the orders to fire.

This particular line was changed after the royal family was executed in 1793. In the 1803 Republican edition of *Le Régulateur du Maçon*, the first toast is made "to the French Republic and its government" and, in the 1805 Napoleonic edition, it is made to "His∴ Imperial Majesty∴ and his august family," returning to an approximation of the original.[120]

Achille Huet de la Chelle, esquire, was an adviser to the king and lieutenant at the royal seat of Petit Goave. He was the founder of the lodge of *l'Union du Saint Esprit*, a member of *Unanimité et Union de Saint Esprit*, and honorary member of the Port-au-Prince Ancients lodge *Réunion des Coeurs Franco-Américain*, in 1790. This honor, from a different masonic rite, was bestowed because he had been made

---

115 Pierre Mollier, *Le Régulateur du Maçon 1785 / « 1801 »* (Paris: A l'Orient, 2018)

116 *SC113 J*, "Cayers Rite Moderne," Doszedardski Collection, Van Gorden-Williams Library & Archives.

117 *BnF FM2 543*

118 Mollier, *Le Régulateur du Maçon* (2018)

119 *SC113 J*, "Cayers Rite Moderne."

120 Mollier, *Le Régulateur du Maçon* (2018)

Administrator of the Illustrious *Grande Loge Provinciale* of Saint Domingue. Succeeding Buttet in 1785, he then became Grand Master of the Provincial Grand lodge of *Heredom de Kilwinning d'Edimbourg*[121] in Saint Domingue in 1788 after Radoux died. His honorary membership in the first Ancients lodge in Saint Domingue was simply a gesture of goodwill.

A transcript of de la Chelle's 1788 rituals for the Royal Order of Heredom are in a cahier in the Archives of the Supreme Council, 33°, S.J. The copy, which is certified by him, was made for the chapter established at Archahaye on June 26, 1796. It also contains a nearly complete suite of Ancients high degrees—the "Ancient York Rite"—consisting of Past Master, Mark Mason and Royal Arch. This same manuscript was translated by Albert Pike in his *Rit Ancien Maçonnerie D'York* (1879).[122] In the final section of de la Chelle's MS. are the General Masonic Institutes of the Modern Rite; but these appear to be a later version than the copy in Doszedardski. In the final paragraph we gain valuable insight concerning Freemasonry during the revolution, and the fate of the *Grande Loge Provinciale*.

> This Masonic instruction book, received by us from Achille Huet de l'Echelle [sic], Administrator of the Illustrious Provincial Lodge of Saint Domingue, delivered to the Respectable *la Réunion des Coeurs*, Orient of Jérémie, to make its archives pious.

To determine the date we note that *Réunion des Coeurs* affiliated with the Provincial Grand Lodge on June 20, 1786, just after Huet de la Chelle became Administrator. In the example letters a few pages before this note, we get more conclusive information relative to the date.

> In the East of Spanish Town, the 11th Day of the 11th Masonic month, t[he Year]∴ o[f]∴ t[he]∴ T[rue]∴ L[ight]∴ 5794 and of the Vulgar Era, the 11th Day of the Month of January 1794.

> Dearest & Respectable Brother, I have had the favor of drawing for you several boards, since my arrival in Jamaica &c &c…

This note indicates that it was copied in Jamaica for the refugees of *Réunion des Couers* residing there from the archives of Huet de la Chelle. Further, the preceding pages provide a calendar calculation date as 1795, which likely represents the year this section of the manuscript was drafted. These same refugees went on to St. Yago de Cuba, before being expelled in 1807 and arriving in New Orleans. This 1795 Spanish Town, Jamaica date fits nicely in de la Chelle's timeline as he founded *l'Union Française* in New York city in 1797 and served as Provincial Grand Master of the Sovereign Chapter of *Heredom de Kilwinning d'Edimbourg*, of Saint Esprit in New York and was an honorary member of the Chapter *Candeur et Amité* in Philadelphia in 1808. This membership was posthumous as he had returned to Mole in 1799, and died in 1805 on the peninsula of Samana on the Spanish half of the island of Santo Domingo. Since 1795 this region had been a refuge for French planters who escaped with their slaves, occupying the land, and continuing their former plantation lifestyles in relative isolation, until they were expelled by English and Spanish forces in 1809.

A valuable "Piece of Architecture" (Masonic lecture), authored by Huet de la Chelle, is in the Doszedardski Collection. Entitled "Plank or rather erected column at Saint Domingue for the *Grand Orient de France* on the High Degrees," it is included in the "Book of Wisdom" containing the constitutions of the *Rit Écossais*. This piece was drafted June 28, 1799, but never delivered, and was placed in de la Chelle's archives. The text discusses the administrative dispute between the *Grand Orient de France* and

---

121 The French version of the Royal Order of Heredom. The 1786 French Rouen version is very similar to English 1796 versions.

122 Included *in toto* in Arturo de Hoyos, ed., Albert Pike, *Reprints of Rituals of Old Degrees.* (Washington, D.C.: Scottish Rite Research Society, 2015)

the Scottish Mother Lodge of the *Rit Écossais*, *le Contrat Social* concerning which high degrees ought to be practiced. He noted that, starting with Morin, the local lodges had been working the high degrees longer than the Grand Orient had existed. A compromise was struck when the Grand Orient was recognized as Symbolic Mother lodge over Craft degrees and *le Contrat Social* as Scottish Mother Lodge over the high degrees.

> The Respectable Lodges of the Colony, did not have any commitment regarding the High degrees, with the *Grand Orient de France*, which had not yet started its labor; it had not been made known here, because it was still unknown there…
>
> The Grand Orient has since then perceived the usefulness of the High Degrees, but only the announcement that it was working at such degrees reached the colony. Never did the real practice of such take place here.[123]

Ultimately the four Orders of Wisdom comprising degrees 4°-7° of the French Rite were never sent to Saint Domingue, which explains why de la Chelle's collection contains only the first three degrees. The lodges simply continued to work the high degrees they had been working. This accounts for the remnants of Morin's system being present in the 1788 symbolic degrees of the Jacmel *Loge du Choix des Hommes*. Tradition had prevailed.

Rit Écossais ritual (1788–1804)

The *Book of Wisdom* includes the 1788 constitutions of *Loge du Choix des Hommes*, from the Most Respectable Scottish Mother Lodge in the Orient of France, *Le Contrat Social*, Metropolitan Chapter. *Loge du Choix des Hommes* was the last remaining lodge from Morin's Order of the Sublime Princes of the Royal Secret, and had affiliated with the Grand Orient on March 30, 1785, completing the Grand Lodge's conquest of Saint Domingue Freemasonry. By November 21, 1787, they sought to join the *Rit Écossais*,[124] receiving a constitution from them. Huet de la Chelle provides context in his aforementioned piece of architecture.

> The Respectable Grand Lodge *Le Contrat Social*, Orient of Paris constituted in this colony several Scottish Lodges, among others *Les Frères Choisis*, Orient of Fond des Nègres, *Loge du Choix des Hommes*, Orient of Jacmel, *L'Unanimité*, Orient of Petit Goave &c &c.

There were at least three lodges working in the *Rit Écossais* in Saint Domingue according to the Administrator of the *Grande Loge Provinciale*. In a document in the same cahier by Gabriel Jastram, titled "Constitutions granted to the *Loge du Choix des Hommes* at the Orient of Jacmel," we gain a sense of the structure.

> Minutes of Installation. On the 29th∴ day, of the 9th∴ month, 5788 (Nov[ember] 29, 1788.) it was installed by M[ost]∴ R[espectable]∴ B[rother]∴ Couppé, Deputy of the Sovereign Metropolitan Chapter of France. The Respectable *Loge du Choix des Hommes*, today the Scottish Mother Lodge

---

123 Oussayef, trans., *Book of Wisdom* (2013).

124 The *Rit Écossais*, also known as the *Rit Écossais d'Avignon*, became the *Rit Écossais Philosophique* by 1805. This later name was used to distinguish itself from the *Rit Écossais Ancien et Accepté* or Ancient and Accepted Scottish Rite. After returning to Paris in 1804 De Grasse-Tilly first used the term on August 28 of that year when he conferred the 32° on Joseph Louis Louvain de Pescheloche (1751–1805), who was one of the founders of the *Rit Écossais Philosophique* and the Worshipful Master of the Lodge *Saint Alexandre d'Écosse*. De Pescheloche was initiated in the Parisian Lodge *Le Contrat Social* on January 8, 1783, which merged with *Saint Alexandre d'Écosse* in 1805, and then became *Saint Alexandre d'Ecosse et le Contrat Social Réunis*. A colonel in the dragoons when he was killed in the Battle of Austerlitz, de Pescheloche had a celebrated Masonic funeral. See John T. Thorp, "A 'Pompe Fùnebre' in Paris in 1806," *AQC* 16 (1903) 181–88.

of the Isle of Saint Domingue; ceaseless to discontinue its labors in spite of the Disasters of the Colony of Saint Domingue, which however caused three suspensions and resumptions of labor, and finally transferred its sessions to the City of Santo Domingo. It is to that Respectable Lodge that I have the honor of belonging to since 1788 by affiliation, that I owe the feeble knowledge that I have acquired in the Royal Art. At the Orient of Santo Domingo this 5th Day of the 5th Month called Ab, of the Year of the T[rue]∴ L[ight]∴ 5809∴ and of the V[ulgar]∴ E[ra]∴ July 5, 1809.

Gabriel Jastram
S[ublime] P[rince of the] R[oyal] S[ecret,] S[overeign] G[rand] I[nspector] G[eneral] 33D∴

Loge du Choix des Hommes was elevated to the status of Mother lodge of the *Rit Écossais* on November 29, 1788, making it a provincial Grand Lodge of sorts. It is difficult to say when the other two lodges changed their affiliations with the Grand Orient, and if there were any others as well. The last piece of correspondence from *L'Unanimité* received in Paris is dated July 25, 1788, for example. The change in status of *Loge du Choix des Hommes*, and the explosion of hostilities in the revolution limit the possible range from late 1788 through 1791.

Gabriel Jastram was initiated in Saint Pierre, Martinique in the lodge *Sincerité des Couers* according to the 1784 member list for *Les Frères Discrets* in Les Cayes.[125] He would become a member of the Sovereign Senate (later, "Supreme Council") at Kingston, which was created by de Grasse-Tilly (probably in January, 1804[126]). Shortly after authoring the previous memoir, Jastram departed the city of Santo Domingo, and received the 33° in Kingston, Jamaica on August 19, 1809.

I, The Undersigned Sover[eign]∴ G[ran]d∴ I[nspector]∴ G[ene]ral∴ of the 33rd∴ degree, Certify the present Secret Constitutions in conformity with those, recorded on the Register of the Sovereign G[ran]d Inspectors General of the 33rd∴ degree, duly and legally constituted as a Sup[reme]∴ Council of the 33rd degree at Kingston, Jamaica.
Kingston, Jamaica August 19, 1809. 19th day of the 6th month 5809

G[abrie]l Jastram
S[overeign]∴ G[ran]d∴ I[nspector]∴ G[eneral]∴

Some of the members of the Jérémie Rose-Croix Chapter would leave for Santiago, Cuba by 1806, working under Antoine Bideaud, who would later return to France to lobby for their regularization. Jean-Pierre Mongruer de Fondeviolle returned to France and established a consistory *la Triple Unité Ecossaise*, claiming authority from a patent from Kingston in 1804, under nearly the same name. Jastram's stay in Kingston was brief and a few months later he conferred the 33° on Louis Jean Lusson, and Modeste Lefebvre on November 10, 1809, in New Orleans. This version of the 33° appears in the Doszedardski collection, with its secret Constitutions, were printed by Pike in 1859, and are nearly identical to the version carried by Antoine Bideaud. Utilizing the unlimited powers granted in his version of the 33°, Jastram went on to establish the local Scottish Rite bodies. These Secret Constitutions ostensibly gave the bearer, power equivalent to a one man Grand Lodge.

Under the date August 13, 1810, Gabriel Jastram, 33°, "Member of the Supreme Council of the 33rd degree at Kingston, Island of Jamaica, organized by the Count de Grasse-Tilly, Grand Inspector General of the 33rd degree, Grand Commander ad vitam, by authority and power of the Sovereign Grand Council sitting at Charleston, in the State of South Carolina," &c., granted

---

125 *BnF FM2 545.*

126 Alan Bernheim, "Introduction," in *James B. Scot, Outline of the Rise and Progress of Freemasonry* in Louisiana (New Orleans, *1873*; reprint ed., Lafayette: Michael Poll Publishing, *1995*), 12

a Patent to Pierre Joseph Duhalquod, P. R. S., Jean Baptiste Desbois, Rose-Croix, and others for a Symbolic Lodge in New Orleans, under the name *La Bienfaisance*, to confer the degrees of Entered Apprentice, Fellow Craft and Master Mason, of the Ancient Rite.

Then, under the date of December 20, 1810, Gabriel Jastram, by the same authority and in addition, "Under the special protection of the said chiefs of Masonry (the Supreme Council at Kingston) representatives of the Grand and Sovereign Chapter Metropolitan d'Herodom of Kilwinning and Edinburgh in Scotland," granted a Patent to Duhalquod, Savary, Desbois, and others for a Lodge of Perfection, Council of Elect, College of Scots, Council of Knights of the East, Princes of Jerusalem, and Chapter of Scottish Rose Croix, under the distinctive title of La Triple Bienfaisance, to be held in New Orleans, Louisiana, with power to confer the degrees from the 4th to the 18th inclusive.

Under date March 28, 1811, Jean Louis Lusson [sic] and J[ean-Baptiste] Modeste Lefebvre, "Sovereign Grand Inspectors General, of the 33rd degree of the Supreme Council of Jamaica," granted a patent to Duhart, Christian Mittenberger, Duhalquod, Jean Baptiste Desbois, Laurent Sigur, Nicholas Roche, Jean Baptiste Labutut, Soulie, Thomas Urquhart, and Jean Francis Dubourg, for a Special Council and Grand Consistory of Princes of the Royal Secret of Louisiana, with power to confer the grades from the 19th to the 32^{d} inclusive. They were required to report in the shortest time to the Sovereign Grand Councils of Charleston, South Carolina, and of Kingston, Jamaica."[127]

Gabriel Jastram and his disciples, Louis-Jean Lusson and Modeste Lefebvre, used their absolute powers to shape the Masonic landscape in a territory that had yet to become the State of Louisiana, and had no Grand Lodge. The founding of the New Orleans symbolic lodge *La Bienfaisance*, "to confer the degrees of Entered Apprentice, Fellow Craft and Master Mason, of the Ancient Rite" raises an interesting question. Which Ancient rite was this precisely? Was it the Ancient Rite as practiced in French by the lodges in Saint Domingue or was it the symbolic degrees of the Ancient and Accepted Scottish Rite, which were created by 1804?

Jastram had a complete set of Scottish Symbolic degrees in his possession, the *Rit Écossais* craft rituals used by *Loge du Choix des Hommes* and its daughters, and were copied by Doszedardski in New Orleans in 1813 along with its constitutions.[128] In the 18th century, the rituals of the self-styled "Scottish Rite" for the symbolic grades were in fact simply a variant of the rituals of the 18th-century French Rite. Its main difference with the *Grand Orient de France* was not in the symbolic degrees, but exclusively in the different rituals of the high degrees.

These 1788 rituals, used by *Loge du Choix des Hommes*, show evidence of evolution. Sometime after the Ancients Rite arrived in Saint Domingue in 1789, the Ancients words and passwords were added to the degrees. This additional information enabled the lodge to receive Ancients Masons, and allowed the members to be received in Ancients lodges. This same advantage is a defining feature of the Scottish Rite Craft ritual today.

In the tracing board lecture of the Apprentice degree, the variation in the names of the columns is accounted for as well.

---

127 Robert Freke Gould, *A Library of Freemasonry: Comprising Its History, Antiquities, Symbols, Constitutions, Customs, Etc., and Concordant Orders of Royal Arch, Knights Templar, A. A. S. Rite, Mystic Shrine, with Other Important Masonic Information of Value to the Fraternity Derived from Official and Standard Sources Throughout the World from the Earliest Period to the Present Time.* (John C. Yorston, 1906), vol. 5, 299

128 The statutes and regulations are preserved in SC113H, the first and Second degrees are preserved in SC113AF and the third degree in SC113AG, *SC113 Doszedardski Collection (Jean Frederic C. Doszedardski 1770–1816) La Maçonnerie Ancien Ecossaise*. Van Gorden-Williams Library and Archives, Lexington, Massachusetts.

> This tracing-board my Brother represents the entrance to the Temple of Solomon: The first three steps were the only three that the Apprentices had to climb to reach column B. Ancient or J. Modern, where they would gather after work, to receive their wages, which they would only receive after having given the sign, grip and password, as well as a sacred word, and the step of the Apprentices.

This same duality is also seen in the Orator's speech in the Fellow Craft degree:

> We are glad to see that you have remembered and have carried out what we have taught you. At the time of your reception you were given an explanation of the tracing-board which is before your eyes. You were told about the column J. (Ancient) where you were to stand and receive your wages, but no mention was made of column B. The time has come to acquaint you with this column…
>
> Note (Ancient). It will be recalled that the letter J. engraved on the Northern column stands for Jakin, the sacred word in Moderns Masonry, and that the letter B., which stands for Booz, the sacred word of the Ancient Masons, must be placed on the Apprentice column.

And, it also appears in the Master Mason degree:

> (The Grip). He then approaches the Recipient, places his right foot against his and his knee to his knee, and with his right hand takes his wrist in such a way as to join the palm of his hand with that of the Recipient. He then passes his left arm under the same shoulder which brings him stomach to stomach, and then, with the help of the two Wardens, raises the Candidate and speaks into his ear, giving him the accolade M∴B∴N∴ in the moderns usage and M∴H∴B∴ in the ancient. All the Brethren then take their seats as well as the M[ost]∴ R[espectable]∴

In an appeal to the 1740's French Scots Master tradition, the Master Masons were allowed to sit covered in lodge, presumably because this was not just a regular Master Mason ritual, but a Scottish Masters ritual.

> On giving him his hat: Henceforth you will be covered in a Master's L[odge]□∴: this very ancient custom is a token of superiority and freedom.
>
> So far you have served, both as Apprentice and Fellow Craft. Now you will command but take care not to abuse it.

This same tradition of the Master's wearing hats is present in the *Guide des Maçons Ecossais*, and is still used to this day. Indeed we observe many parallels between the *Rit Écossais* Symbolic degrees and those of the Ancient and Accepted Scottish Rite.

The strongest evidence linking the two together is the procedure for receiving a visiting Brother. In the *Loge du Choix des Hommes* version, specific honors are to be rendered if a vising brother is a Worshipful Master, Warden, Knight of the East, Prince of Jerusalem, Knight Rose-Croix or Sublime Prince of the Royal Secret. Presuming that they were carrying their certificate and wearing their regalia, a visiting brother could be received by a varying number of members carrying candles, and under an arch of steel, and then being escorted to their seat, depending on their rank. Interestingly we observe once again the exact local lodge structure of Morin's former system of separate high degree bodies. *Loge du Choix des Hommes* was after all the last lodge to affiliate with the Grand Orient. Curiously in the reception of the Princes of Jerusalem, we observe that they also retained their original powers of administering local lodges granted under Morin's system:

He will pass under the arch of steel, and the Master of Ceremonies will place him at the right hand of the Worshipful, who will hand him the gavel if he is not himself a Prince of Jerusalem.

The Princes have the right to inspect the labors of the symbolic lodges and to revoke all the labors if they are contrary to Masonic laws.

Of particular importance is the procedure for receiving Sublime Princes.

To Sublime Prince Masons.

The Sublime Prince Masons visiting a symbolic lodge will be introduced there by five dignitary officers armed with swords preceded by three Brethren bearing stars and by the Master of Ceremonies. The arch of steel will be formed, and he will be placed to the left of the Worshipful, who will offer him the gavel if he himself does not hold this sublime degree. If he wishes to withdraw before the end of the labors then the same formalities will be observed as on entry. They have much more extensive rights than all the Brethren elevated through the degrees and designated above.

A Sublime Prince is to be received by five lodge Officers carrying swords, preceded by three brothers carrying stars or candles and taken under an arch of steel. This same procedure is almost exactly reproduced in the Scottish Rite craft ritual.

If the visiting Brother is an officer of a Mother-Lodge, or a Deputy near it, a Grand Elect of the Sacred Vault, or Subl[ime]∴ Prince of Royal Secret, he is received at the door with five stars, the gavels beating, and he is made to pass under the vault of steel; with three stars if he is a Worshipful.

All of these clues together make clear that these Jacmel symbolic degrees of the *Rit Écossais* preserve a major source for what became the Scottish rite craft ritual. It makes logical sense as well given that De Grasse-Tilly was initiated in *le Contrat Social* on January 8, 1783 and remained a member until he departed for Saint Domingue in 1787. This lodge became the mother lodge of the *Rit Écossais* and was later renamed *Saint Alexandre d'Ecosse*. It would offer support to De Grasse-Tilly when he returned in 1804, and several of their members would be early members of the French Supreme Council, including Thory, making it almost unavoidable that elements of their ritual would be incorporated into the production of a new Scottish Rite craft ritual.

Pennsylvania "Ancient Masonic Rite of York" ritual (1789–1804)

The Antients ritual arrived in Saint Domingue with the chartering of *La Réunion des Coeurs Franco American* in 1789, yet there are no symbolic degrees recorded in any surviving cahiers. There are, however, surviving copies of the high degrees of the "Ancient Masonic Rite of York" as worked in Pennsylvania. These are the rituals which Thomas Smith Webb received and modified (post-1796) and which formed the basis the current York Rite.[129]

---

129 "[I]nnovations were introduced by Thos. S. Webb, who received these degrees in Philadelphia prior to 1802, and is styled the Father of American Masonry. By what authority he changed the work and ritual, we have not the means of knowing, except to build up for himself the reputation of a learned Mason." —Alfred Creigh, *History of the Knights Templar of the State of Pennsylvania from February 14th, A. D. 1794: A. O. 676 to November 13th, A. D. 1866: A. O. 748. A. O. E. P. 69. Prepared and Arranged from Original Papers Together with the Constitution, Decisions, Resolutions and Forms of the R. E. Grand Commandery of Pennsylvania* (Philadelphia: J. B. Lippencott, 1867), 28. Although many of Webb's modifications were adopted throughout most of the country, he was "regarded by … *Pennsylvania* brethren as having been something of a charlatan." —*Proceedings of the Grand Chapter of Royal Arch Masons, of the State of Wisconsin, at its Forty-sixth Annual Convention, held in the city of Milwaukee, February 18 and 19, A.D. 1896* (Milwaukee: Burdick, Armitage & Allen, 1896), 88.

There are minor variations in the order and number of the degrees in various manuscripts of the Ancient York Rite. For example, in Provincial Grand Master Huet de Lachelle's ca. 1795 copy, the degrees were the 4° Past Master, the 5° Mark Mason, and the 7° Royal Arch Mason. The 6° may have been the Royal Master.[130] Another copy lists them as 4° Past Master, 5° Mark Master, 6° Super Excellent Master, 7° Super Excellent Master, 8° Royal Arch.[131] All of the various copies seem to conform to his style of rituals and contain English language artifacts, particularly in the passwords.

Pierre Dupont Delorme's 1797 ritual cahier of the 15°-25° of the Order of the Royal Secret, also includes a Tyler's manual for the Ancients Craft degrees and the Past Master's Degree.[132] It describes the decorations of the lodge, and indicates a placement of the Wardens which differs from that used by the Moderns in the first degree. The opening and closing procedures are described along with the words, passwords, and grips for each degree. Interestingly, the spellings of the words and password differ slightly from the English originals—preserving a synthesis of both French and English traditions.

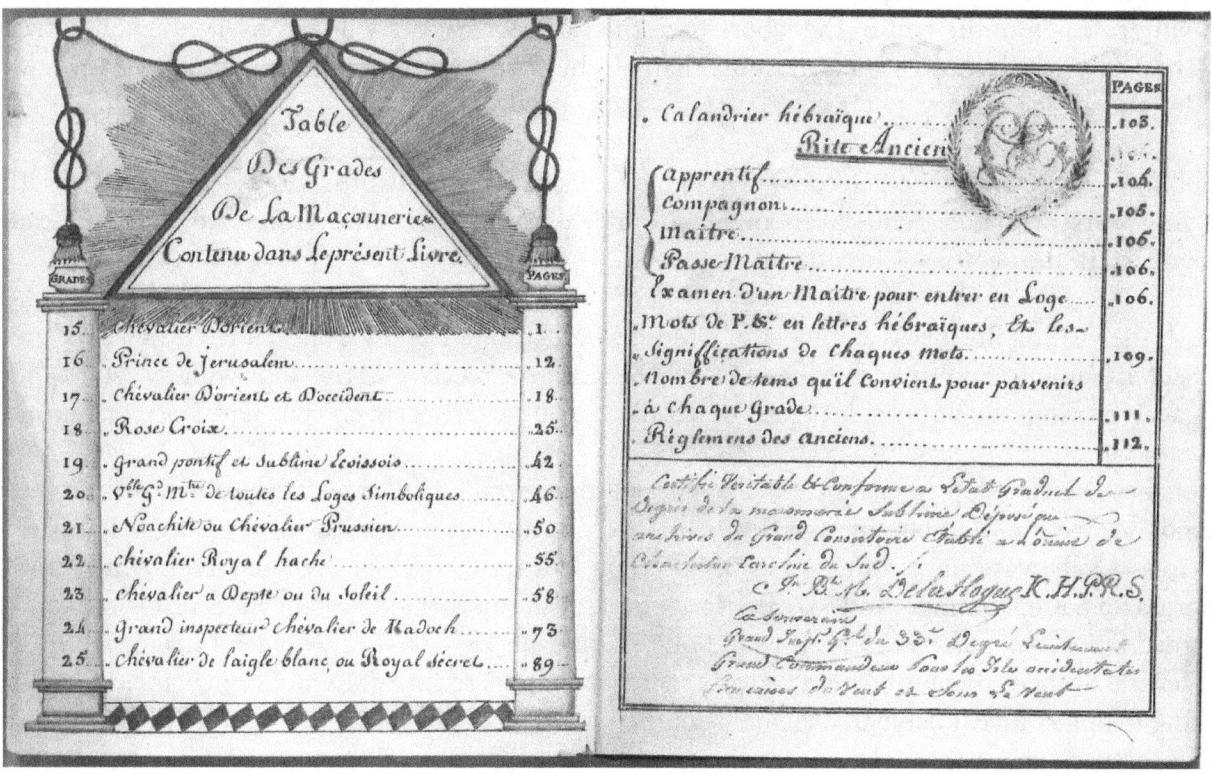

Pierre Dupont Delorme's 1797 ritual cahier was certified in 1804 by J. B. M. De La Hogue, K.H., P.R.S., 33°, as conforming to the rituals in the Grand Consistory in Charleston.

Following the Past Master is the examination procedure used in Ancients lodges for visiting Masters. Penciled in below this section are the position and orientations of the square and compasses, placed on the Bible, during the obligations of the first three degrees.

After the illustration is a French translation of a section from the English exposure *Three Distinct Knocks*, titled in the original as "All the Words explained that belong to Gripes."[133] The inclusion of this

---

130 For the collection, see Arturo de Hoyos, *Reprints of Rituals of Old Degrees* (Washington, D.C.: Scottish Rite Research Society, 2015)

131 Manuscript *167-t-e*, "Collection de rituels du Ancient d'York" Latomia Foundation.

132 *Dupont Delorme D.I.G. P.M. 2me.* [Untitled ritual manuscript, volume 2, dated 1797], Archives of the Supreme Council, S.J., Washington, D.C. The location of the first volume is unknown.

133 *The Three Distinct Knocks: Or the Door of the Most Antient Free-Masonry, Opening to All Men, Neither Naked nor Cloath'd ... Being an Universal Description of All Its Branches ... by W—O—V—N*. Dublin: printed and sold by Thomas Wilkinson, 1785. 51.

passage helps to establish exactly what were the forms and ceremonies of the Ancients degrees in Saint Domingue.

The last entries contain the degree intervals for the Order of the Royal Secret, extracted from the Constitutions of 1762, that first appeared in French in the *Livre d'Or* of De Grasse-Tilly, as well as a French translation of the "Regulations of the Ancients." This translation is the only extant example of the constitution of the Grand Lodge of South Carolina Ancient York Masons, issued March 24, 1787.

This Grand Lodge had been chartered by The Grand Lodge of Pennsylvania, as four local Charleston lodges wanted to operate separately from the existing Grand Lodge that was chartered by the English. This was in the immediate aftermath of the Revolutionary War, when the United States began to assert its own distinct national identity, as expressed by the creation of its own separate institutions from its mother. A sample report is included at the end and identifies the lodge whose archives this account was recorded from as number 12, which was the Charleston lodge *La Candeur*, chartered by French refugees from Saint Domingue in 1796.

Delorme received these rituals from Jean-Baptiste Aveihlé when he was made Deputy Inspector General for Port-au-Prince and Prince Mason on December 10, 1797. Aveihlé was a member of *La Candeur* and had received some of the Order of the Royal Secret degrees initially from de Grasse-Tilly but was made a Deputy Inspector General by Hyman Isaac Long, just before his passing.[134]

The 1797 symbolic rituals of *La Candeur* possessed by de Grasse-Tilly were rediscovered in the Strasburg archives of the *Bibliothèque nationale de France* in 2019, containing in the second section, the only known 18th century example of a French translations of the Ancients rituals.[135] Our study of these rituals reveals that they were themselves a translation of *Three Distinct Knocks*, with the only exception being that the deacons roles and duties were rendered to the Wardens, as there are no deacons in Moderns ritual.

It is unknown if the ritual used by the Grand Lodge of South Carolina Ancient York Masons was similar to *Three Distinct Knocks*, or to that of the Grand Lodge of Pennsylvania, which was the Provincial Grand Lodge for the Ancients in the United States, founded in 1761. The latter Grand Lodge chartered all of the Ancients lodges in Saint Domingue as well, but a Grand Lodge's charter and ritual often came from different sources. However this may be, the rituals of Pennsylvania's "Ancient York Masonry" remain distinctly unique from all other forms of American Craft ritual.[136]

Scottish Mason's Guide (1804)

The following section outlines our synthesis of the events which lead to the creation of the Scottish Rite's Craft ritual. The authorship of the Scottish Rite Craft ritual contained in the *Guide des Maçons Ecossais* may not be the product of a single individual as it is a composite of all of the forms of Freemasonry practiced in Saint Domingue.

Research by Pierre Noël demonstrated that the foundation of the Scottish Rite's Craft ritual is Ancients in form, and is based directly on a translation of *Three Distinct Knocks*.[137] Its influence was so great that

---

134 Jean Baptiste Aveihlé register. [Manuscript, dated December 12, 1797; copied and translated by Albert Pike], Archives of the Supreme Council, 33°, S.J., Washington, D.C. The location of the original is unknown.

135 Josef Wäges, "De Grasse-Tilly and the Early Supreme Council," in *Heredom: The Transactions of the Scottish Rite Research Society*, vol. 29 (Washington, D.C.: Scottish Rite Research Society, 2020).

136 The rituals of *Three Distinct Knocks*, of the Grand Lodge of Pennsylvania, and the Grand Lodge of South Carolina all differ substantially from each other. The *Grand Lodge of Pennsylvania Ritual Manual* (Philadelphia, 2012) reads nearly identical to the cipher text in J.A. Gavitt, ed., *31 King Solomon and His Followers (Keystone). A Valuable Aid to the Memory* (1909). A variant, which may preserve some older practices, is M. Wolcott Redding, ed., *Ecce Orienti or the Rites and Ceremonies of the Essenes. National Series 9 PA* (1880). The latter may have been used in some parts of the Commonwealth, as it includes some features in common with T.S. Webb's revisions. The Craft rituals of the Grand Lodge of South Carolina include some archaic features, but show evidence of revision since at least the mid-1800s. In general, it can be classified as Webb-form.

137 See Pierre Noël, *Guide des Maçons Écossais. A Édinbourg. 58∴ Les grades bleu du REAA: genése et développement* (Paris: A l'Orient, 2006)

it is easier to identify variances with the source-text than to search for them individually. For example, there are no carpets, and the Junior Warden is in the South (a distinguishing feature of Ancients ritual). Notably, unlike the Charleston translation of 1797, which was taken by de Grasse Tilly to Paris in 1804, the *Guide des Maçons Ecossais* version retained the Deacons.

We know that De Grasse-Tilly submitted his ritual cahiers on December 29, 1804[138] to the *Grand Orient de France* which was around the same time that Pierre Mongruer de Fondeviolle established the consistory *la Triple Unité Ecossaise* in Paris. This near-simultaneous occurrence may suggest a cooperative effort in which the Scottish Rite's Craft ritual was the product of men who shared a common Masonic background.

A comparison of ritual texts reveals the *Guide des Maçons Ecossais*, is much more than a mere translation of *Three Distinct Knocks*, with occasional alterations. The ritual is a purposeful composite which blends the forms used in Saint Domingue: an intentional unification of traditions with the Antients' work as the foundation. As we saw earlier, the *Rit Écossais* (aka *Rit Ecossais Philosophique*) contributed prominent features, while the French Rite, as printed in *Le Régulateur du Maçon* contributed other aspects (e.g., the chambers of reflection, the use of a coffin and the procedure of making toasts).

Understanding the manner in which the rituals were combined recalls the contributions of those central figures within the context of our history, while the Scottish Rite's Craft ritual itself preserves some of the Masonry of Saint Domingue. The actors likely responsible for the creation of the Scottish Rite Craft ritual were Alexandre François Auguste de Grasse-Tilly, Pierre Mongruer de Fondeviolle, and Germain Hacquet. By creating this ritual they ensured that some of the practices of those lodges would be perpetuated in the memory of ritual language and procedure.

De Fondeviolle was made a Mason in *La Vérite* in Cap Français in 1777 and fled Le Cap after it was burned during the revolt in 1793. He appeared in 1794 in the New York City lodge *Le Tendre Amité Franco-Américain*,[139] and returned to France in 1796 appearing as a member of the Parisian lodge *Le Centre des Amis*.[140]

Hacquet, Lusson, and two others received an English-language patent on April 8, 1801 for a Lodge of Perfection called *Triple Unity* from the Grand Council of the Sublime Princes of the Order of the Royal Secret of at Kingston, Jamaica, for the members of the Port au Prince lodge, *Réunion des Coeurs Franco-Américain*. The Ancients connection is key as it is signed by Isaac Morales, Provincial Grand Master of the Athol (Ancients) Grand Lodge of Jamaica from 1801–09. The founding members of *Triplé Unité*, a Lodge of Perfection, had already received the 25°, Sublime Prince of the Royal Secret from Dominique St. Paul, who was later censured by Kingston in 1803 for these initiations, and the members he made in Saint Domingue were instructed to be healed by Phillipe Toutain, the Deputy Inspector General appointed by Kingston for the island.[141]

> If the S[ublime]∴ P[rince]∴ St Paul or any other Sublime∴ Prince∴ wishes to constitute a Grand Consistory in a town at a distance of less than twenty leagues, then he shall request prior permission to do so from the S[ublime]∴ P[rince]∴ P[hilipe] N. Toutain, whom we appoint for this purpose as D[eputy]∴ G[rand]∴ I[nspector]∴ of the French island of Saint-Domingue & its dependencies.

---

138 *BnF FM1 285*. Suprême Conseil du 33è degré de Grasse-Tilly. Livre d'Or. Bibliothèque nationale de France. 75

139 Archives of the *Lodge L'Union Française*, New York City, New York. On December 12, 1793, a warrant was granted to *La Tendre Amitié Franco-Américain* which became *L'Unité Américaine* on May 26, 1795. *L'Union Française* was instituted in New York City on December 26, 1797, and received its charter on June 6, 1798.

140 "Folmont-Fortin," Gallica, accessed April 29, 2023, <https://gallica.bnf.fr/ark:/12148/btv1b10000110f/f36.item.>

141 "Décisions du Supreme Conseil des Inspecteurs généraux du 33ᵉ. et dernier degré du Rite ancien et accepté, pour la France, depuis l'année 1804. Jusqu'à et Compris l'année 1815." Unpublished manuscript collection, archives of the Supreme Council 33° S.J.

February 4, 1794 member list for the Lodge La Tendre Amitié Franco-Américain, New York City, New York bearing the name of brother Orator Pierre Joseph de Fondeviolle, 54, Master of all degrees, initiated in 1776 in Cap Français at the Lodge Le Verité. L'Union Française Archives.

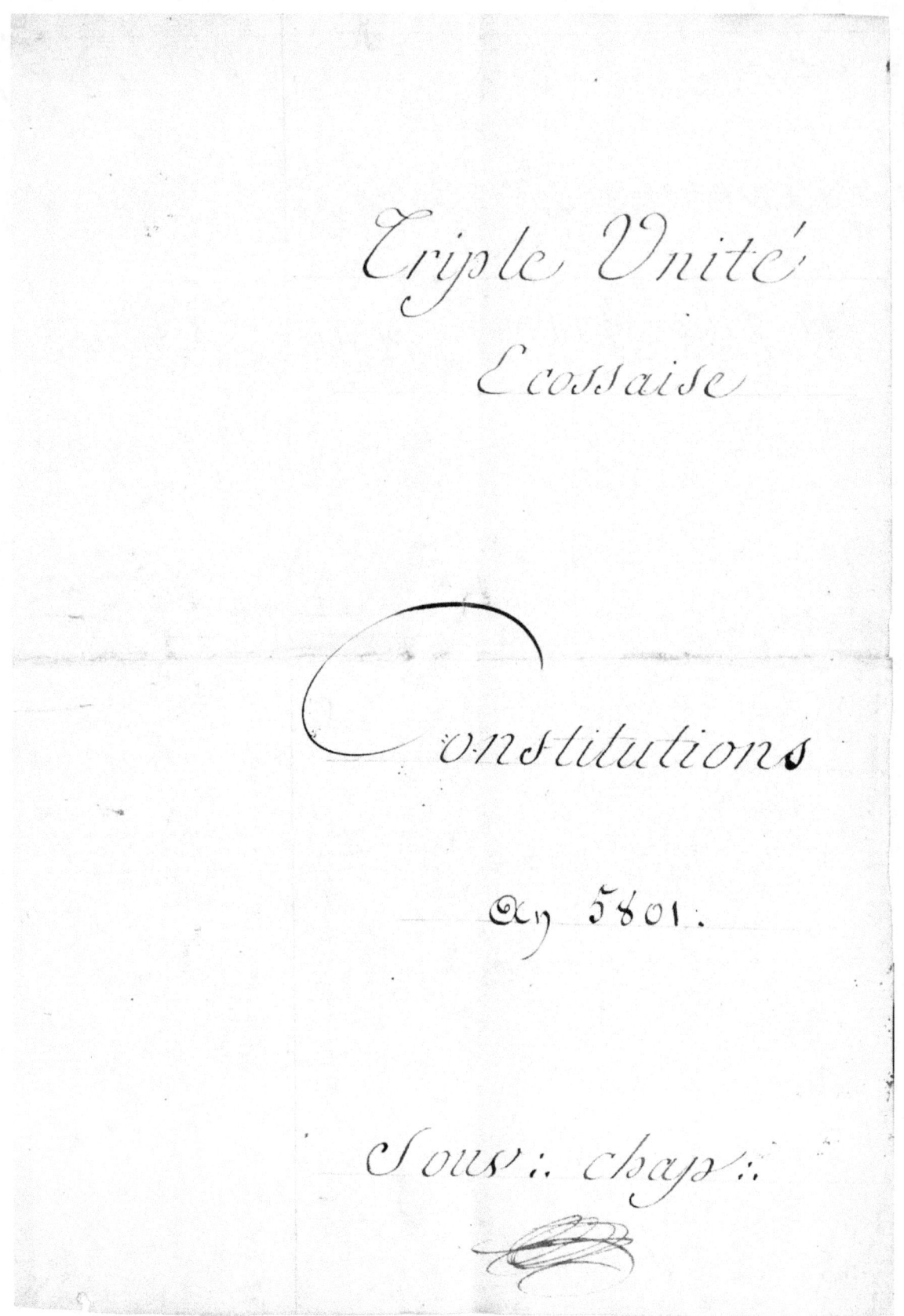

1801 Constitutions for Triple Unité Ecossais. Décisions du Supreme Conseil des Inspecteurs généraux du 33e. et dernier degré du Rite ancien et accepté, pour la France, depuis l'année 1804. Jusqu'à et Compris l'année 1815." Unpublished manuscript collection, archives of the Supreme Council 33° S.J.

Their instruction to submit to Phillipe Toutain explains how Hacquet received a blank patent for a consistory. As the Haitian Revolution drew to its violent conclusion, it is doubtful that they were ever formed and Hacquet returned to France in 1804, patent in hand.

De Grasse-Tilly arrived in Cap Français in July 1802, established his Supreme Council, and made five 33° masons. He was also a member of the lodge *Sept Frères Réunis* which, in May 1803, was in correspondence with the *Rit Ecossais* (which later became the *Rit Ecossais Philosophique*).[142] De Grasse evacuated on December 1, 1803, was captured by the British and was released on February 12, 1804. He then went to Charleston and left in May 1804, based on the sale of one of his servants.[143] He arrived in France in July 1804, and connected with *St. Alexandre d'Ecosse*, the new name of his former lodge *Le Social Contrat* and the mother lodge of the *Rit Ecossais*.

We know that in 1804 De Grasse renamed the 33° system the *Rit Ecossais Ancien et Accepté*, when he made an agreement with the Grand Orient of France.[144] This was most likely to distinguish it from the *Rit Ecossais*, which was similarly renamed *Rit Ecossais Philosophique* to distinguish between them. Hacquet may have supplied the consistory patent for *Triple Unité* from Kingston to de Fondeviolle who opened the first Consistory in France, *la Triple Unité Ecossaise*. De Grasse may have supplied de Fondeviolle with the 1797 translation of *Three Distinct Knocks* used in his Charleston lodge *L'Union Française*, as well as the Saint Domingue variant of the *Rit Ecossais* ritual worked by *Sept Frères Réunis* in Cap Français. The latter was developed by *Choix des Hommes* in Jacmel and included the references to the Sublime Princes of the Royal Secret, as well as the Ancients variations in the craft ritual. We suggest that De Fondeviolle and/or Hacquet merged the three rituals together to create the Scottish Rite's craft ritual.

Conclusion

Symbolic Freemasonry in Saint Domingue was a significant social and cultural force in the region, as it evolved over the course of some 64 years. As the organization grew and changed, it came to exert an increasing influence on the people of Saint Domingue, particularly among the wealthy and educated members of society. The rituals and symbols of Freemasonry became a powerful way for people to express their beliefs and values, and at the same time to connect with others who shared similar ideals within a trade network. It was an integral component of the mercantilist trade system. Over time, the organization adapted to the changing political and social climate in Saint Domingue, importing and developing new traditions and practices that reflected the changing times, before being erased from history altogether as it had been.

The 1804 Scottish Rite craft ritual was a skillful synthesis of the traditions of symbolic Masonry in Saint Domingue. Although created by a small group of men, its influence has been far-reaching. The ancestral traditions, emanating from the French Rite, the Antients Rite, and the *Rit Ecossais*, carried a broad appeal which readily gained enthusiasts. It continues to do so today, for the Scottish Rite craft ritual is the most popular type craft ritual in the Masonic world; it is worked in more countries than any other form of Symbolic Masonry. Thus, even if we ignore the high degrees which became Order of the Royal Secret—and later the Scottish Rite—this ritual of the Blue Degrees, which was created by those influenced by the work of Stephen Morin, remains a legacy to his unbounded energy and unyielding passion in the pursuit of Masonic excellence.

---

142 *BnF FM2 543*

143 *"Degrasse, Alexander Francis Augustus and Sophie Degrasse of St. Domingo to Elias Pohl, Bill of Sale for a female save named Themire. Date: 5/21/1804."* South Carolina Department of Archives and History. Series: S213003 Volume: 003T Page: 00376 Item: 000.

144 *Acta Latomorum, ou Chronologie de L'Histoire de la Franche-Maçonnerie Française et Étrangere* (Paris: Grand Orient du France, 1815), vol. 1, 225

Part 2
*RITUAL ANCESTRY AND THE
SCOTTISH RITE BLUE DEGREES*

COMPLETE
CORPUS
OF
MASONRY,
ADOPTED
BY THE R[ESPECTABLE] G[RAND] L[ODGE] OF FRANCE.

DEGREE
OF APPRENTICE.

NOTICE.

Should a few copies of this very limited Edition of a Complete Corpus of Masonry *the printing of which, in response to the solicitation of certain regularly-constituted lodges we could not refuse, ever fall into profane hands, then good & true Masons will not be able to attribute the cause solely to the carelessness of the Brethren to whom they might be entrusted, partly because the precaution was taken of having it done under the eyes of a Brother whose discretion is well known; that it was composed & printed by other Brethren, also very discreet & who, besides the Obligation they offered at their Reception, have also undertook to deliver beforehand the proofs & even the slightest evidence of the printing of this collection, copies of which will be distributed only on receipts in due form, or from a duly-constituted lodge, or from Masons with whom the Brother charged with this work will have associated in a regular lodge, or in response to Certificates of Reception which will be presented to him. The Profane will not be more enlightened if a few copies do fall into their hands, & the Brethren, by their means, will avoid the trouble of writing down what they need for their instruction. It is up to the lodges which will deliver & distribute them at the Candidates" Receptions, to recommend that they take the greatest care of these notebooks, in which we have limited ourselves to giving each of the Degrees for which they are written, the decoration of the lodge, the manner of opening & closing it, as well as the Receptions, because these explanations are necessary for those who know the practice. Others may search as much as they like, but we can assure them in advance that they will find nothing. Moreover, the precaution that is being taken to henceforth recognize as Brethren only those who are bearers of a Certificate in due form will spare the inquisitive Profane the research they are certain to make & the interpretations they will impute to what they have seen & read. They are advised to give their care & efforts to a small book that is to be found everywhere, & which has been published under the title of* Les Francs-Maçons écrasés, ou leur secret découvert, & mis au jour, imprimée à Jérusalem [*The Freemasons Crushed, or their Secret Discovered & Unearthed, Printed at Jerusalem*].[1]

---

1 By Gabriel-Louis Pérau, 1742.

DISPOSITION
OF THE
CANDIDATE.

To succeed in being received as a Mason, the sincere desire to acquire a superior degree of virtue must guide us, and the spirit of curiosity must not be the motive of our actions.

After being proposed by a Brother, the latter will have made a precise investigation of the motives which persuaded the Postulant to be received as a Mason; he will become fully satisfied that the desire alone to be initiated into the mysteries of Masonry is the only motive which made him act, he will propose it in regularly assembled lodge; the Worshipful will proceed to collect the votes in the usual manner. If they are favorable, the day & hour for the reception will be set for the Proposing Brother, who will report it to the Profane, enjoining him not to miss the appointment, which he will give him for this purpose.

The day of the reception having arrived, the Proposer will go to the place indicated; after joining him, he will take him for a walk, if the time permits, but will not speak to him about his Reception; though he will answer him as briefly as he can to any questions he puts to him on this subject. He will then lead him subtly outside the door of the temple, where he will ask him to wait a moment, while he goes to announce his arrival.

When he has informed the lodge that the Recipient is waiting outside the temple, the Worshipful will depute the Brother of the Porch, with one or two Serving Brethren, or in their absence, two Brethren of the lodge. The first, after having caused him open the door, will approach him with great decency & politeness, but, at the same time, with the coldest air and the most imposing tone that he can. He will ask him to deliver his hat, sword, cane or cloak, will cover his eyes with a handkerchief, and lead him to the Dark Chamber, called the *Chamber of Reflection*. This apartment does not need any decoration or hangings, it is only necessary that the Recipient can sit there. It will be guarded by a Serving Brother or another Brother, who will observe the Candidate, without speaking to him, or allowing him to question him.

The Brother Tyler, or of the Porch, having introduced the Candidate into the Chamber of Reflection, will return to the lodge, & will report to the Worshipful, who will leave him at least one hour, during which time the lodge will be opened, & all the necessary arrangements made for the reception, after he will have requested the consent of the assembled Brethren, & that they will have given it by the Sign of Approbation. All the Brethren will pay the greatest attention to accomplish the charges for which they are each responsible. All the Brethren knowing what they have to do, the Worshipful will ask the Brother Terrible to go to his apartment.

APARTMENT OF BROTHER TERRIBLE.

Although this apartment has nothing designated & is very arbitrary, it should nevertheless be gloomy, & more or less impose horror, according to what one judges appropriate to impose on the Recipient; it may be draped in black, with a dimly lit lamp; it may also have a dungeon door, fitted with locks & chains. Brother Terrible must wear a large black cloak, seated next to a table where a kneeler, upon which will be placed a white handkerchief & a sword.

ARRANGEMENT OF THE LODGE.

The lodge will be hung with blue, covered with a celestial canopy, and sprinkled with golden stars. A Mosaic pavement will be parquetted. In the east will be a throne elevated by three steps, at the lower part of which will be a Blazing Star. At the foot of the throne will be a triangular altar, adorned with a carpet on which the attributes of the Order will be embroidered. On this altar, there must be a square, a Compass, a Bible; a gavel, & three candlesticks, each bearing a candle, & arranged in a triangle; to the left of the altar there must be a table in front of the Secretary's place, on which will be the registers, the seals, an inkstand & a candlestick.

To the right of the altar there will be another table in front of the Orator, on which there will also be a candlestick.

The Wardens will be stationed in the West of the lodge.

The Senior will wear a square at the end of a blue ribbon, arranged in saltire.[2]

The Junior will wear a plumb, also placed at the end of a blue ribbon.

The door of the temple can be drawn in perspective at the West of the lodge.

There must be three windows; namely, one in the East, one in the West & one in the South: they are represented by painting.

The Sun will be depicted in the South of the lodge, with the Moon placed in the North opposite the Sun, with some stars.

The Apprentice Column, called *J*, will be in the North of the lodge: it must be isolated behind the Junior Warden.

The Column *B* will also be in the North of the lodge, behind the Senior Warden.

The lodge tracing-board will be laid out on the pavement; it will be illuminated by three lights placed in three large candlesticks, on which will be carved some of the attributes of the Order. They will be placed at three of the cardinal points of the tracing-board, that is to say, one in the East, one in the West opposite the Senior Warden, & the other opposite the Junior.

The Officers of the lodge will be stationed to the right & left of the Worshipful; it is to be observed that that the Secretary occupies the first position to the left of the Worshipful & the Orator the first on his right.

All the Brethren will wear a white apron with the bib raised, the gloves white. Those of higher degrees may be decorated with their aprons, regalia & jewels.

---

[2] With the riBonribbon folded over in the shape of a St. Andrew's Cross.

PROCEDURE FOR OPENING THE LODGE.

Q. *Brother Senior Warden, what is the hour?*

A. M[ost] W[orshipful], it is high noon.

Q. *What is the duty of a Mason?*

A. To see that the lodge is well tyled, that it is safe from the indiscretions of the Profane, & that all the Brethren here present are worthy to attend our mysteries.

Q. *Order the Brother Tyler to see to it; & you, my Brother, assure yourself of the qualities of the Brethren here present.*

The Brother Tyler goes out &, after examining he enters the lodge & reports to the Junior Warden that he has examined tile by tile, gutter by gutter, & that the lodge is safe from Profane indiscretion. The Junior Warden reports, in the same words, to the Senior Warden, & the latter to the Worshipful, adding that all the Brethren present here are worthy to attend our mysteries.

Q. *Since it is high noon, and that we are entirely safe from the indiscretion of the Profane, & that the Brethren here present are worthy to attend our mysteries, inform the Brethren on the columns of the South & North to assist me in opening the Apprentice's lodge.*

The Wardens inform the Brethren on their column & request them to assist the Worshipful in opening the Apprentice Mason's lodge.

Then the Worshipful raps three blows of the gavel on the altar, & says: *Since it is high noon, my Brethren, come to order & do our duty.* All the Brethren make the sign of the Apprentice & after clapping their hands three times three they make the usual acclamations.

The Master then makes a short speech on the subject of the convocation of the lodge & then exhorts the Brethren to silence, after which the Brother Orator compliments the visiting Brethren, if there are any.

All things necessary for the reception being arranged, the Brother will remove the Recipient from the Chamber of Reflection; he must seize him, & tell him, with a firm tone, to follow him. He leads him to the door of Brother Terrible's apartment, where he knocks as a Mason; after the three knocks, the Brother Terrible must answer, and ask, *Who is knocking?* he answers, *It is a blind man who asks to see the light, & a Profane gentleman who asks to be received as a Mason.* After an interval the Brother Terrible asks the Recipient if he has the inclination & and if the spirit of curiosity does not attract him to it. He answers no. After several questions intended to impress the Recipient he must be handed over to the Brother Terrible very abruptly, saying, *It is done, I deliver him to you & I answer no more.* After a brief silence the Brother Terrible removes his blindfold & asks him several questions: he affirms the danger in which he is & that he cannot endure the trials, & inspires him with both optimism & terror; after which he has him properly clothed, that is to say, stripped of all metals, without buckles, without a coat, his right arm out of the shirt sleeve so that his shoulder shows; the right knee uncovered, & his left foot in a slipper; & after covering his eyes he points his sword at him & says: *Follow me with confidence.* He then leads him to the door of the lodge, where he gives three distinct knocks.

The Brother Tyler (or of the Porch) informs the Junior Warden, & he the Senior, that someone knocks as a Mason at the door of the lodge. The Senior Warden says to the Worshipful: *Worshipful Master, someone knocks as a Mason at the door of the lodge.* The Worshipful tells him to find out who is knocking.

The Senior Warden passes this order to the Junior, & the Junior to Brother Tyler, who inquires & to whom he responds, *It is a Gentleman who asks to be received as a Mason.* The word passes as before from the Brother Tyler to the Worshipful, who orders the Junior Warden to see who is knocking. He asks Brother Terrible, who replies: *It is a blind man who is asks for the light, a corpse who asks for resurrection, & a Profane who asks to be received as a Mason.*

The Senior Warden returns these answers to the Worshipful, who orders him to ask him his age, occupation, name, place of birth & religion.

The information given, the Senior Warden answers: *Worshipful Master, his age is . . . he is . . . his name is . . . he is from . . . & his religion is . . .*

The Worshipful asks him if he thinks he has sufficient strength to withstand the trials to which he is to be subjected. The Senior Warden inquires, & after the Recipient has satisfied him the Warden says: *Worshipful Master, he says that he has sufficient strength to withstand the trials he has to undergo.*

The Worshipful says to him: *Ask him whether he has ever erred in the path of virtue, if he has ever spoken against the Royal Art.* After the Warden put these questions to the Recipient, he says to the Worshipful: *Worshipful Master, the Profane assures that he has never erred in the path of virtue, that he never spoke against the Royal Art, & that he ardently desires to perfect himself in Masonry.*

While all these questions are being asked the Brother Terrible makes the Recipient turn his back towards the door of the lodge. The Worshipful Master orders the Recipient to be brought in, the Warden opens the door again, & says: *Let him be delivered to me.* Then Brother Terrible says to the Senior Warden, who now has his charge, *It is done, I will no longer answer for him.*

He is led to the West of the lodge where, having arrived, a profound silence is observed; the Worshipful then says to the Senior Warden: *Brother Senior Warden, what do you present to me here? Has he made his final reflections upon the trials to which he is about to be subjected? Yes, Worshipful Master,* replies to the Senior Warden, *he agrees to everything that is to be required of him in order to be received as a Mason.* The Worshipful Master says to the Recipient: *Sir, I must not leave you in ignorance of all the risks that you will run if curiosity urges you to penetrate our mysteries; all your trouble would be useless to acquire the knowledge...*

He then continues with a speech designed to prove the Recipient & to try to ascertain his purpose by his answers.

After he has demanded of him complete resolve & he is convinced, by his answers, of his serious desire, he addresses the Brethren of the lodge, and says: *My Brethren, you have heard. Do you think this Profane is worthy of undertaking & finishing with resolve all that he has to do to become a member of our Society?* The Brethren make the sign of approbation. Then the Worshipful says to the Recipient: *Sir, be careful of what you are about to do; you are in great danger; I fear for you. I have seen many who have not been able to withstand the trials; it would be very unfortunate for you & for us if you succumb...* After the Recipient's response, the Worshipful asks him who will vouch for him. The Recipient then names his Patron, who replies to the Worshipful by the sign of approbation. The Worshipful then says to the Senior Warden: *Brother Senior Warden, make this gentleman begin to travel, & take care of him; do not abandon him completely to his own courage; you yourself should tremble, since you answer for his actions.*

Then the Senior Warden places his sword against his heart & makes him walk around the lodge (various obstacles may be encountered by him as the Worshipful may think fit), & as he passes before the Worshipful he is made to bow.

Having arrived at the West end of the lodge, the Brother Senior Warden reports to the Worshipful on the journey the Recipient has just made. The Master questions him again & assures him that he is to be delivered up to even greater trials. After he has answered, the Worshipful again asks for the consent of the Brethren of the lodge, who make the usual sign. Then the Worshipful admits him to his second journey, & the Brethren briefly shake their aprons. (The second journey is observed to be more arduous than the first.) Having reached the West of the lodge the Senior Warden informs the Worshipful that the Recipient has courageously completed his second journey.

The Master addresses him again, & makes him observe that there is infinitely more left for him to do than he has done so far, & that he fears for him. He asks him again if by any chance he feels ill at ease. After he has answered, the Worshipful asks the Brethren for the third time to approve the Recipient's journey, & they confirm this by making the sign of approval. The Worshipful then orders the Recipient to be admitted to his third journey, which is made slightly more rigorous than the preceding ones, with the same ceremonies being observed.

The Recipient having arrived at the West of the lodge the Worshipful Master asks the Senior Warden whether the Candidate has succeeded in his task. He confirms that he has. The Worshipful then says to the Recipient: *Sir, you are about to undergo your final test, & it is by thereby that you will be recognized as a Mason. Will you show the same resolve that you have shown thus far? Many lack it at this moment, & I would not be surprised at any weakness you might display to me. You are the master of your own removal & to tell of everything you have seen & heard, & of what you were told to do. Take care that your courage does not hurry you into dangers that you cannot avoid. I will give you a moment to reflect.*

(He should be observed asking a nearby Brother if the iron is hot, in a low voice so that the Recipient can only just hear him). After he has answered that he consents to everything, the Worshipful Master says: *Brother Senior Warden, do your duty.* The seal of the lodge is then applied to his shoulder. After which the Worshipful Master orders him to make the three steps of the temple & to advance to the altar as an Apprentice; having arrived there, the Orator rises to his feet & makes the following speech:

DISCOURSE OF THE ORATOR.

Sir, the fearlessness you have shown apparently overcome & defeat the obstacles you encountered in the mysterious journeys you were caused to make in this august lodge; & the eagerness you have shown for such a long time to be admitted into a Society as ancient as it is respectable prove to us that you have trampled underfoot the prejudices of the vulgar Profane.

You are about to contract with us a solemn commitment which will unite you, by the ties of tender & sincere friendship, to an Order into which even which the greatest Kings have not disdained to be initiated.

It is at the foot of the tribunal of discretion that you will promise, before the Great Architect of the Universe, to inviolably keep the secret of Masonry. Consummate this great work by repeating, with attention, what our Worshipful Master will ask you to say.

The discourse is finished, he is caused to place his right knee on the ground, his right hand on the Gospel, & with the other he holds a compass, the point to his left breast. The Worshipful says to him: *Sir, do you consent, although blindfolded & in this attitude, to contract a solemn engagement which contains nothing against God, any earthly King, or your neighbor? Remember henceforth that it is an obligation contracted before the Great Architect of the Universe & before this most respectable Assembly.* The Recipient having answered, the Master says to him: *Repeat after me…*

OBLIGATION.

"I promise & engage on my word of honor before the Great Architect of the Universe & before this Assembly never to reveal to any person who has not done what I have done, the secrets that are to be revealed to me, nor to be the direct or indirect cause of said secret being written, engraved, chiseled, or carved in any language, & I consent, if I should ever become perjured, to have my throat cut, my heart torn out, & to be detested by my Brethren & all posterity. *So help me God.*"

After the obligation has been completed, the Worshipful Master says to him: *By the power invested in me by this respectable lodge under the authority of & at the pleasure of our Respectable Grand Master… I make you an Apprentice Mason,* & gives him three small blows of the gavel on the head of the compass which he is still holding to his left breast. This done, he is led to the West of the lodge. All the Brethren grasp their swords & direct the points toward the Recipient. The Worshipful then orders Brother Senior Warden to cause him to see the light. He is briefly allowed to enjoy the surprise, after which the Worshipful said to him: *You see all these swords. There is not one among us who would not be prepared to use them to avenge you, but there is also not one of us who would not bathe in your blood should you break your word.* After this the Recipient is allowed to dress.

Note: At no time during the reception ceremonies should any Brother speak, nor leave his place on any pretext whatsoever; silence being the soul of the ceremony, the Master must strictly ensure this.

The Brother Recipient being dressed, the Master decorates him with the apron & says to him: *Receive the apron of the Order, the most ancient that there is.* He gives him the gloves & says to him: *The whiteness of these gloves symbolizes the purity of our morals. We have signs, grips, & words to recognize ourselves.*

The word is…

It is spelt out, one letter after another, so when you examine a Brother he must always give you the first letter & then you give the second, & then so on to the end of the word.

The grip is made by shaking hands & placing the thumb on the first joint of the [first] finger.

This grip identifies us to our Brethren of any nation.

The sign reminds you of one of the points of your obligation: that of preferring to have your throat cut than reveal the secrets of Masonry.

He then gives him the kiss of association, which is given at the two corners & the middle of the mouth. Then he says to him: *Go, my Brother, & make yourself known to all your Brethren.* The Recipient gives the sign, the grip, the word, & the kiss to all the Brethren, beginning with the two Wardens, Brother Secretary, Brother Orator, Brother Terrible, Brother Tyler, Brother Treasurer & Brother Steward, & then all the Brethren of the lodge according to their position within it, beginning with the visiting Brethren if there are any. He then takes his place beside the Worshipful. Brother Orator then delivers a discourse on the excellence of the Order, on the happiness enjoyed by Masons, on the virtues required of a Profane to be received, & those virtues that must follow the reception.

The discourse finished, the Worshipful gives the usual Instruction & explanation of the tracing-board; then the Constitutions & Statutes are read, after which the following Instruction is given.

INSTRUCTION.

Q. *Are you an Apprentice Mason?*

A. My Brethren recognize me as such.

Q. *How may I know that you are?*

A. By my signs, tokens, words, password, & the circumstances of my reception faithfully rendered.

Q. *Who obtained for you the advantage of being an Apprentice Mason?*

A. A virtuous friend, whom I later recognized as a Brother.

Q. *Where were you prepared to be received an Apprentice Mason?*

A. In the dark.

Q. *What was done with you when you were prepared?*

A. I was handed over to a stranger, whom I later recognized as a Brother.

Q. *What did he do with you?*

A. He introduced me to the lodge.

Q. *How were you introduced to the lodge?*

A. With three distinct knocks.

Q. *What do they symbolize?*

A. These three maxims of Holy Scripture: "Seek & you shall find; knock & it shall be opened to you; ask & you shall receive."

Q. *How were you dressed when you entered the lodge?*

A. I was neither naked nor clothed, but in a manner decent enough to appear before others & deprived of all metals.

Q. *Why neither naked nor clothed?*

A. Because virtue has no need of splendor to appear in broad daylight.

Q. *Why deprived of all metals?*

A. Because they are the symbol of the vices.

Q. *What did you see when you entered the lodge?*

A. Nothing that the human mind can comprehend.

Q. *Who received you at the door of the lodge?*

A. Another stranger, whom I later recognized as the Brother Senior Warden.

Q. *What are the signs of a Mason?*

A. Any square, level & plumb.

Q. *What are his tokens?*

A. Certain regular grips that the Brethren give to identify each other.

Q. *Where were you received?*

A. In a just & perfect lodge.

Q. *Who compose this lodge?*

A. Three, namely one Worshipful Master & two Wardens.

Q. *Who form it?*

A. Five, namely one Worshipful Master, two Wardens, one Apprentice & one Fellow Craft.

Q. *Who make it perfect?*

A. Seven, namely one Worshipful Master, two Wardens, two Apprentices, & two Fellow Crafts.

Q. *What induced you to become a Mason?*

A. Because I was in darkness, & I wanted to see the light.

Q. *Where were you first prepared before being received as a Mason?*

A. In my heart.

Q. *Where were you placed before you were received as a Mason?*

A. In the Dark Chamber.

Q. *Through what did you pass before joining the lodge?*

A. Through the arch of steel.[3]

Q. *After passing through the arch of steel, where were you placed?*

A. In the Chamber of Preparation.

Q. *Who prepared you & presented you to the lodge before you were received as a Mason?*

A. A man armed with a sword, whom I afterwards recognized as a Brother.

Q. *Why was he armed with a sword?*

A. To keep away the Profane.

---

3   Arch of steel and vault of steel are used interchangeably, and appear in all rituals in this text in French as *voûte d'acier*. These terms though identical in French have been rendered differently in this text, in homage to their traditional historical first uses in the English language.

Q. *Could you see clearly when you entered the lodge?*

A. No, because I had my eyes covered.

Q. *Why did you have your eyes covered?*

A. To show that I was in darkness, that the veil of prejudice had not yet fallen, & that I was not yet worthy to see the light.

Q. *What did you see when you entered the lodge?*

A. Nothing that the human mind can comprehend.

Q. *After you entered the lodge what were you made to do?*

A. Travel from West to East by the North.

Q. *Why?*

A. To seek the light.

Q. *After your Journey what did you do?*

A. I was introduced to the Worshipful.

Q. *What did he do with you?*

A. With the desire I had & the agreement of the lodge, he received me as a Mason.

Q. *How did he receive you as a Mason?*

A. With all the necessary formalities: I had my right knee bared, my left foot slipshod & my right hand on the Bible, holding in my left hand a compass open at right angles placed against my heart, forming a square with my body.

Q. *What did you do in this posture?*

A. I took an obligation to keep the secrets of Masons & Masonry.

Q. *Why was your left foot slipshod?*

A. In imitation of Moses, when the Lord appeared to him in the wilderness in the form of a burning bush, & commanded him to remove his shoes, as unworthy to tread the holy ground on which he walked.

Q. *What did you see upon being received as a Mason?*

A. Three great lights.

Q. *What are they?*

A. The Sun, the Moon & the Worshipful.

Q. *What do they signify?*

A. That the Sun rules or enlightens the day & the Moon the night, & so the Worshipful governs the lodge.

Q. *What are the duties of a Mason?*

A. To shun vice & practice virtue.

Q. *What are the secrets of the Masons?*

A. Words, grips, & signs without number.

Q. *What was the principal point of your Reception?*

A. To be stripped of all metals.

Q. *Why?*

A. Because when Solomon's temple was built, no sound of axe or metal tool was heard.

Q. *How could such a vast edifice be built without the aid of any metal instrument?*

A. Because Hiram, King of Tyre, had sent the cedars from Lebanon, all cut & ready to be put in place, & because Solomon had the stones he needed for his temple cut in the quarries.

Q. *Where is your lodge located?*

A. In the valley of Jehoshaphat, or some hidden place.

Q. *Where can one hold a lodge?*

A. In the valleys, on the mountains, & in any hidden place where women do not prattle, dogs do not bark, & cocks do not crow.

Q. *What form is your lodge?*

A. An oblong square.

Q. *How long?*

A. From East to West.

Q. *How deep?*

A. From the surface to the center of the Earth.

Q. *How wide?*

A. From the South to the North.

Q. *How high?*

A. Feet, yards & cubits without number.

Q. *What covers it?*

A. A celestial canopy ornamented with stars.

Q. *What do you understand by its length, width, height & depth?*

A. That all the Earth forms but one lodge, & that all the Masons of the universe compose it.

Q. *What supports it?*

A. Three great columns.

Q. *What do you call them?*

A. Wisdom, strength & beauty.

Q. *Why are they so called?*

A. Wisdom to govern, strength to support, & beauty to adorn.

Q. *Do you have any jewels?*

A. Yes, Worshipful, three movable & three immovable.

Q. *Which are the movable?*

A. The Bible, the square & the compass.

Q. *Which are the immovable?*

A. The tracing-board, the perfect ashlar, & the rough ashlar.

Q. *What is the use of the movable?*

A. The Bible belongs to God & serves to keep us in fear of him & instruct us in our religion; the square to the Master, & serves to correct our works, which are to train us in virtue; & the compass is to the Grand Master, to perfect our works, by giving precision to our morals.

Q. *To whom is your lodge dedicated?*

A. To St. John.

Q. *Why?*

A. Because St. John, as the forerunner of the light of the Faith through the baptism of the Lord, was chosen as our Patron.

Q. *Where was the temple built?*

A. On Mount Moriah in Jerusalem.

Q. *How many kinds of Masons are there?*

A. There are two kinds: Speculative & Operative.

Q. *What are Speculative Masons?*

A. They are those who learn a firm morality, purify their morals, & make themselves agreeable to everyone.

Q. *What are Operative Masons?*

A. Those who cut stones & raise perpendiculars on their bases.

Q. *Where have you worked?*

A. Outside the temple, filling the gaps made by the Fellow Crafts with the rough ashlar.

Q. *Did you have any fixed lights?*

A. Yes, Worshipful, three: one in the East, one in the West, & the third in the South.

Q. *Why was there no fixed light in the North?*

A. Because the Sun's rays penetrate feebly in this part.

Q. *What is the purpose of these lights?*

A. To enlighten the Craftsmen who work in the temple.

Q. *Where did the Masters stand?*

A. In the East, where the Sun rises to open the gates [of day], & where the Master still stands to govern & enlighten his lodge, to open it, & to set the Craftsmen to labor.

Q. *Where did the Fellow Crafts stand?*

A. They were scattered throughout the temple.

Q. *Where did the Apprentices stand?*

A. Outside the temple, to contemplate & imitate the work of the Masons.

Q. *Where did the Wardens stand?*

A. In the West, where the Sun sets, to close the gates of day & also to pay the Craftsmen, dismiss them, & close the lodge.

Q. *How long did you work?*

A. From Monday morning until Saturday evening.

Q. *Have you been paid?*

A. I am satisfied.

Q. *Where were you paid?*

A. At the column *I*.

Q. *How old are you?*

A. Three years old.

Q. *What time is it?*

A. Worshipful, it is high midnight.

After the Instruction the Worshipful Master passes around the charity box, after which he asks the Senior & Junior Wardens to find out whether any Brother has anything to propose for the good of the lodge & the propagation of the Order. The Wardens make the announcement & then make report to the Worshipful, who says: *My Brethren, no Brother has anything to propose. Brother Senior & Junior Wardens, inform the Brethren on your Columns that I am about to close the Apprentice's lodge.* The Wardens announce this & the lodge is closed in the following manner.

PROCEDURE FOR CLOSING THE LODGE.

Q. *Brother Senior Warden, what hour is it?*

A. *It is high midnight.*

Q. *It is therefore time to conclude our work & to cease our labors. Brother Senior & Junior Wardens, inform the Brethren on your Columns that the Apprentice's lodge is closed.*

The Wardens repeat to the Brethren what the Worshipful has said, one after the other, following which he says: *Come to order, my Brethren, & let us do our duty.* All the Brethren come to order, & then, along with the Worshipful, strike their palms with their fists[4] & engage in the usual acclamations. Then the Worshipful says: *Brethren, the Apprentice's lodge is closed.*

End of the Apprentice Degree.

Errata:

Page 7, last line, for notified to the Postulant *read* notified to the Sponsoring Brother.

Page 21, line 18, for three small of the gavel, *read,* three small raps of the gavel. [5]

---

4 This seems to be a striking of the palm with the fist rather than clapping.

5 Already corrected by the printer!

I, the undersigned, acknowledge that I have been given the above printed Copy & other parts of the Degree of Apprentice Mason, regarding which I have given & hereby give my word of honor not to entrust & communicate them to any Profane of either sex. I agree to be dishonored if by my fault or negligence the said Copy should ever fall into any other hands than those of a Brother. In witness whereof I have signed the present for my justification, or for my confusion.

Given at   the

DEGREE
OF
FELLOW CRAFT.

ARRANGEMENT
OF
THE LODGE.

The Lodge should be hung, decorated & illuminated like that of the Apprentice, except for the mysterious lights, which shall be five in number, & placed as follows:

One in front of the Senior Warden, above the Tracing-Board of the Lodge; the second, on the same line, in the middle of the Tracing-Board; the third, below the Tracing-Board, again in the same line as the preceding ones; the fourth in front of the Junior Warden, & finally the fifth below the Tracing-Board, in front of the Worshipful, at least three feet from the Throne.

The Dignitary Officers & other Brethren of the Lodge will occupy the same places as that of the Apprentice, & decorated with their aprons, cordons & jewels, each according to their Degree. The Officers & Dignitaries shall also wear in saltire the ornaments of their offices & their dignities.

All of the Brethren being seated & the candles lit, the Worshipful will open the Lodge in the following manner.

PROCEDURE FOR OPENING THE LODGE.

The Worshipful will give five raps of his gavel on his table; namely three short & two long, which will be repeated by the Senior & Junior Wardens in turn. After which he will ask:

Q. *Brother Senior Warden, what hour is it?*

A. *Most Worshipful, it is high noon.*

Q. *What is the duty of a Mason?*

A. *To see that the Lodge is well-tyled, that it is safe from the indiscretions of the Profane, & that all the Brethren here present are worthy to attend our mysteries.*

The Worshipful says to the Senior Warden: *Would you be so kind, my Brother to order the most scrupulous inspection & assure yourself of the qualities of the Brethren.*

The Senior Warden passes this order to the Junior, & the latter to Brother Tyler, who leaves the Lodge & goes to see that it is well-tyled.

During the tour of inspection by the Brother Tyler all the Brethren come to order but remain seated.

The inspection made, the Brother of the Porch returns & says to the Junior Warden: *My Brother, I have inspected the Lodge tile by tile, gutter by gutter, & the Lodge is absolutely safe from the indiscretions of the Profane.* He passes this account on to the Senior & this one to the Worshipful, adding that *all the Brethren are worthy to attend our mysteries.*

The Worshipful says: *Since it is high noon, since we are sheltered from the indiscretions of the Profane, & since the Brethren here present are worthy to attend our mysteries, would you please, Brother Senior & Junior Wardens, inform the Brethren who are placed on your Columns that I am going to open the Fellow Craft's Lodge & that I ask them for this purpose to lend me their lights & assistance.*

The two Wardens in turn inform each Brother on their respective Columns one by one, after which the Worshipful says, rising to his feet: *To order, my Brethren, & let us do our duty.* All the Brethren rise & come to order as Fellow Crafts. After which they clap their hands five times, as does the Worshipful, & make the usual acclamations. Then he sits down, as do all the Brethren, & strikes a rap with his gavel, which is repeated by the Senior & then by the Junior Warden. The Worshipful then delivers a short speech on the subject of the convocation of the Lodge & exhorts the Brethren to maintain good order & silence. Then the Orator rises & compliments the visiting Brethren, if any be present, on behalf of the Lodge.

If there is a Reception, the Brother Tyler leaves the Lodge and takes the Recipient (who must, during this whole time, remain in the apartment furthest from the Lodge) & take him to the Chamber of Preparation , where he leaves him, saying: *Prepare for your Reception, & dwell carefully upon all the matters set for your reflection. I shall leave you now, but I will soon join you.* He leaves him & then reports to the Worshipful addressing himself, according to custom to the Junior Warden.

After all things are arranged for the reception, the Worshipful orders one of the Brethren of the Lodge, whom he thinks proper to choose for this purpose, with the exception of the two Wardens, who must never leave their places, to fetch the Recipient, who must have been left in the Chamber of Preparation for at least half an hour; where having arrived, he asks him these questions: *Have you, my Brother, made all your reflections, & do you feel you have sufficient strength, courage & fortitude to withstand the trials through which you are about to pass, & which are quite different from those you were made to undergo in order to attain the Degree of Apprentice?* After the Recipient has answered, he takes him by the hand & leads him as honestly, calmly, & gently as possible to the door of the Lodge, where, having arrived, he knocks 5 times, which are repeated by the Brother Tyler, & which must be repeated a second time by the Brother Conductor of the Recipient. After these five knocks have been thus repeated the Brother Tyler says: *Brother Junior Warden, someone is knocking as a Fellow Craft at the door of the Lodge.* The Junior Warden repeats these words to the Senior & the latter to the Worshipful, who orders him to find out who it is. The Senior Warden passes the order to the Junior & the latter to Brother Tyler, who must ask in a firm tone of voice: *Who is knocking as a Fellow Craft at the door of the Lodge?*

The Brother Conductor replies: *It is an Apprentice who desires & requests to be received as a Fellow Craft.*

The Brother Tyler gives the answer to the Junior Warden, the Junior to the Senior, & the Senior to the Worshipful, who replies: *My Brother, kindly assure yourself of the quality of the Recipient, & ask him for the sign, word, & grip of an Apprentice.*

The Senior Warden leaves the Lodge & asks the Recipient for the sign, word & grip of an Apprentice.

After he is satisfied, the Senior Warden returns to the Lodge & reports to the Worshipful.

The report given, followed by a short pause, the Worshipful orders that the Recipient be asked *if he has served his time & if his Masters are satisfied with him.* This order is passed from the Senior to the Junior Warden & from the latter to Brother Tyler, who half-opens the door & asks him these questions, one after the other, which he returns the same way to the Junior Warden, from the latter to the Senior, & from the Senior to the Worshipful, who orders him to be introduced into the Lodge, which the Brother Conductor does. All the Brethren then come to order. The Brother Conductor places the Recipient between the Senior & Junior Wardens, after which the Worshipful asks him the following questions:

Q. *Whence came you?*

A. From the Lodge of St. John.

Q. *What do you bring from there?*

A. A warm welcome & prosperity to all the Brethren.

Q. *Have you not brought anything more?*

A. The Worshipful Master of St. John's Lodge greets you, Most Worshipful, with all the honors due to you, as well as the Dignitaries, Officers & Brethren of this respectable Lodge.

Q. *What are you seeking, Brother?*

A. Worshipful, I request & ardently desire to be received as a Fellow Craft.

Q. *How long have you worked?*

A. From Monday morning until Saturday evening.

Q. *How do you serve your Master?*

A. With zeal, fervor & constancy.

Q. *Is he happy with you?*

A. Yes, Most Worshipful.

Q. *What proof do you bring?*

(The Recipient makes the sign of the Apprentice).

After these questions and answers are given, the Worshipful says to Brother Conductor, *Advance the Brother to the foot of the Throne by way of the North passing that of the South, by the five steps of the Fellow Craft,* so that at the fifth step he is in square at the foot of the Throne, where having arrived the Worshipful causes him to kneel, & says to him, *Repeat after me.*)

OBLIGATION.

I swear & promise on my word of honor & by the same obligations I have already contracted to keep the secret of the Fellow Craft concealed from the Apprentices, as I shall keep that of the Apprentices concealed from the Profane. *May God help me & all my Brethren.*

When the Obligation is over the Brother Conductor raises the Recipient & resumes his place.

The Worshipful descends from his Throne & raises the bib of the Brother's apron & attaches it to a button of his coat, saying to him while giving him five light taps on his left shoulder with his gavel: *By the power I have received from the Order & this respectable Lodge, I hereby receive & admit you to the number of Fellow Crafts.*

He then gives him the Sign, the Word & the Grip of this Degree.

The Sign is to place the hand square on the chest at the place of the heart, drawing it across horizontally, then dropping it as in the Apprentice Sign.

The Grip involves pressing with the thumb of the right hand five times on the knuckle of the second finger of the Brother to whom it is presented.

The Word is *B*

The Word is given like that of the Apprentice, one letter after the other, that is to say, the questioner gives the first, the questioned the second, & so on until the last.

The password is *S*

Then the Worshipful says to him: *Go, my Brother, make yourself known to all the Brethren of the Lodge, beginning, as in your reception as an Apprentice, with the Brother Senior Warden.*

When the recognition is finished, the Brother takes his place beside the last Fellow Craft received; then the Brother Orator rises & delivers a discourse.

When the discourse is finished, the Worshipful gives one rap with his gavel, which is repeated by the Senior & Junior Wardens, & announces to the Brethren that they may be at ease, but he also begs them to pay close attention to the following Instruction.

INSTRUCTION.

Q. *Are you a Fellow Craft?*

A. Yes, I am.

Q. *How do I know that you are?*

A. By my signs, grips, step & words.

Q. *Give me the sign?*

A. (He does so.)

Q. *What does this sign mean?*

A. It is derived from the obligation whereby I consented to have my heart torn out rather than reveal the secrets of Masonry.

Q. *Give me the grip.*

A. (He does so.)

Q. *Give me the Word of the Fellow Craft?*

A. (It is given, spelt out.)

Q. *What does this word mean?*

A. That strength is in God.

Q. *What did you see when you entered the Lodge?*

A. A great light, in the middle of which was placed the letter G.

Q. *From where did this great light come?*

A. From the Blazing Star.

Q. *What do you keep hidden?*

A. The secret of the Masons & of Masonry.

Q. *Where do you conceal it?*

A. In my heart.

Q. *Why did you have yourself received as a Fellow Craft?*

A. For the letter G.

Q. *What does this letter G stand for?*

A. Geometry, or the fifth of the sciences most necessary to a Mason.

Q. *Does it mean anything else?*

A. It is also the initial letter of the word *Good* [sic], which is the name of the Almighty.

Q. *How were you received as a Fellow Craft?*

A. By passing from Column J to Column B.

Q. *In which Lodge were you received?*

A. In a just & perfect Lodge.

Q. *Where is it located?*

A. In a secret or hidden place, where peace & tranquility, union & harmony reign and finally, in the valley of Josaphat[6.]

Q. *What shape is your Lodge?*

A. An oblong square.

Q. *How is it oriented?*

---

6   Book of Joel, 3:2 & 3:12.

A. Like all holy places, from East to West.

Q. *Its length?*

A. From East to West.

Q. *Its width?*

A. From South to North.

Q. *Its height?*

A. Cubits without number.

Q. *Its depth?*

A. From the surface of the Earth to the center.

Q. *What is your Lodge founded upon?*

A. On three Columns.

Q. *What are they?*

A. Wisdom, strength & beauty.

Q. *What do you mean by these three words?*

A. Wisdom to lead, strength to execute, & beauty to adorn.

Q. *With what is your Lodge covered?*

A. With an azure canopy, spangled with stars without number.

Q. *Is there a door to your Lodge?*

A. Yes, but it is so high that the Profane cannot see over it.

Q. *Who has the key to this door?*

A. All good Brother Masons.

Q. *Where do they keep it?*

A. In a coral box, enriched with ivory.

Q. *How many windows does it have?*

A. Three, one in the East, one in the South & one in the West.

Q. *Why is there no window in the North?*

A. Because the Sun shines feebly in this part of the world.

Q. *What adorns the Portico of the Temple?*

A. Two great columns.

Q. *Of what material were they made?*

A. Brass.

Q. *Their height?*

A. Eighteen cubits.

Q. *Their circumference?*

A. Twelve cubits.

Q. *Their thickness?*

A. Three cubits.

Q. *With what were they decorated?*

A. Bases & capitals.

Q. *With what were the capitals surmounted?*

A. Two globes, one shining like the Sun at meridian, & the other shining like the Moon at full.

Q. *What was the purpose of the inside of the two Columns?*

A. To contain the tools of the Apprentices & Fellow Crafts, & the money to pay their wages.

Q. *How are these two Columns reached?*

A. By three great steps.

Q. *How do the Craftsmen receive their wages?*

A. By giving the password of their Degree.

Q. *Do you have ornaments in your Lodge?*

A. Yes, most Worshipful, we have three; namely, the Mosaic Pavement, the Indented Tassel, & the Blazing Star.

Q. *What do they represent?*

A. The Pavement represents the threshold of the Great Portico; the Indented Tassel the external decoration of the Temple; & the Blazing Star the center emanating the light which illuminates the four parts of the world.

Q. *Give me the moral significance of these three ornaments.*

A. The Mosaic Pavement, formed from different stones joined together, & united by stucco & cement, marks the close union that prevails among the Brethren; the Indented Tassel is the emblem of the external adornment of a Lodge by the Brethren who compose it; & the Blazing Star, whose shining rays can hardly be seen, is the emblem of the Great Architect of the Universe, who is the great light.

Q. *How many jewels do you have?*

A. Six, three movable & three immovable.

Q. *What are the three movable ones?*

A. The square worn by the Worshipful, the level worn by the Senior Warden, & the perpendicular worn by the Junior Warden.

Q. *Why do you call them movable?*

A. Because they pass from one Brother to another.

Q. *What can they be used for?*

A. The square is used to reduce all shapes to a perfect square; the level to draw lines parallel to the horizon; & the perpendicular to raise straight buildings on their foundations.

Q. *Do the three movable jewels not contain some morality?*

A. The square tells us that all our actions must be regulated by justice & equity; the level that there must be perfect equality between the Brethren; & the perpendicular shows us that all grace comes from Heaven.

Q. *What are the three immovable jewels?*

A. The rough ashlar, the perfect ashlar & the tracing-board.

Q. *What is the use of these three jewels?*

A. The rough ashlar is used by Apprentices to learn how to work; the perfect ashlar is used by Fellow Crafts to sharpen the tools of the Masters; & the tracing-board is used by the Masters to draw their designs.

Q. *What is their moral significance?*

A. The rough ashlar, on which the Apprentices work, is the emblem of our soul, susceptible to both good & bad impressions; the perfect ashlar which serves the Fellow Crafts, tells us that it is only by watching our actions that we can protect ourselves from iniquity; the tracing-board, on which the Masters work, is the good example that facilitates the practice of the most eminent virtues.

Q. *Why do the first three officers of the Lodge use only gavels & not hammers?*

A. Because during the construction of the Temple no sound was heard of tools made of metal as the stones & timber had already been worked & prepared in the quarries & in the forests, so that it was only a question of putting them in place.

Q. *Why are the Sun & Moon represented in your Lodge?*

A. The Sun is to enlighten our work, the Moon to help us find our homes when the work is finished.

Q. *What do the two globes mean?*

A. To show us that Masonry is spread over the whole surface of the Earth.

Q. *What is the trowel for?*

A. To conceal the faults of our Brethren.

Q. *Where do you conceal them?*

A. In the heart.

Q. *What is the key to this?*

A. A wise & discreet tongue accustomed to eloquence which, in the absence as well as in the presence of the Brethren, never speaks ill.

Q. *How many kinds of Masons are there?*

A. Two: Speculative & Operative.

Q. *What are Speculative Masons?*

A. They are those of our Order who erect Temples to virtue & dig dungeons for vices.

Q. *What is the purpose of Speculative Masonry?*

A. Its precepts are those of a morality, which tends to purify our morals & render us agreeable to everyone.

Q. *What are the Operative Masons?*

A. The Craftsmen who physically raise perpendiculars on their bases.

Q. *How many points are there in Masonry?*

A. They are without number, but they are reduced to four principal ones, namely guttural, pectoral, manual & pedal.

Q. *Have you seen your Master?*

A. Yes, Most Worshipful.

Q. *How was he dressed?*

A. In blue & gold.

Q. *What do the blue & gold mean?*

A. That a Mason preserves wisdom in the midst of honors, of which he is not dazzled.

Q. *How many pieces of furniture does the Worshipful have?*

A. There are three in number.

Q. *What are they?*

A. The Gospel, the compass & the gavel.

Q. *What is their use?*

A. The Gospel is used to swear obligations, the compass for Receptions, & the gavel to repel the Profane.

Q. *How long do you usually work?*

A. From Monday morning until Saturday evening.

Q. *How do you serve your Master?*

A. With zeal, fervor & constancy.

Q. *What should a good Mason observe?*

A. Silence, discretion, prudence & charity towards his Brethren, avoiding gossip, calumny & intemperance.

Q. *Where are the Fellow Crafts placed in the Lodge?*

A. In the Eastern part of the North.

Q. *Why?*

A. To see more closely the great light they must reach.

Q. *Where do the Fellow Crafts receive their wages?*

A. At Column B.

Q. *How do they receive it?*

A. By giving the password.

Q. *Give it to me?*

A. (He does so.)

Q. *How old are you?*

A. Five years old.

Q. *What hour is it?*

A. Noon to open the Lodge, & midnight to close it.

After the Instruction the Worshipful Master passes around the charity box, after which he asks the Senior & Junior Wardens to find out whether any Brother has anything to propose for the good of the Lodge & the propagation of the Order. The Wardens make the announcement & report to the Worshipful, who says: *My Brethren, since no Brother has anything to offer, Brethren Senior & Junior Wardens, inform the Brethren on your Columns that I am about to close the Fellow Craft's Lodge.* The Wardens announce this & the Lodge is thus closed in the following manner.

PROCEDURE FOR CLOSING THE LODGE.

Q. *Brother Senior Warden; what hour is it?*

A. *It is midnight full.*

Q. *It is therefore time to conclude our work & to cease our labors. Brother Senior & Junior Wardens, inform the Brethren on your Columns that the Fellow Craft's Lodge is closed.*

The Wardens repeat this to the Brethren, one after the other, following which the Worshipful says: *To order, my Brethren, & let us do our duty.* All the Brethren come to order along with the Worshipful, followed by the clapping of hands and the usual acclimations. Then the Worshipful says: *My Brethren, the Fellow Craft's Lodge is closed.*

End of the Fellow Craft's Degree.

I, the undersigned, acknowledge that I have been given the above printed Copy & other parts of the degree of Fellow Craft, regarding which I have given & hereby give my word of honor not to entrust & communicate them to any Profane of either sex. I agree to be dishonored if by my fault or negligence the said Copy should ever fall into any other hands than those of a Brother. In witness whereof I have signed the present for my justification, or for my confusion.

Given at   the

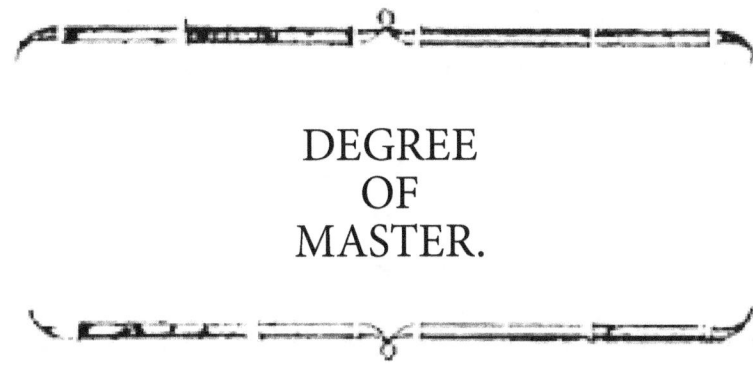

DEGREE OF MASTER.

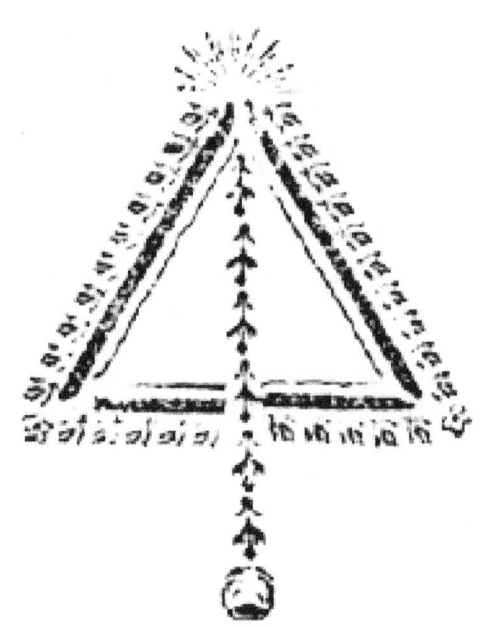

ARRANGEMENT
OF
THE LODGE.

The Lodge must be hung in black, adorned with skulls & bones, as well as an altar, on which there will also be a Bible, a gavel, a square & a candle.

In the square of the Lodge there will be a coffin-shaped object, covered with a burial shroud under which will lie the most recently received Master. There will be three candelabra, each with three candles, which will be placed at three of the corners of the coffin, namely one in front of the Junior Warden, one in front of the Senior, & the third at the corner opposite the latter. At each end of the coffin there will be, respectively, a square & a compass. The Brethren should, as far as possible, be dressed in mourning clothes, with the exception of military personnel, who will wear a piece of black crêpe on their left arm. They will all be decorated with their aprons & cordons & will take their places according to their rank of seniority, with the Lodge Officers being placed as in the two preceding Lodges.

All the Brethren who compose the Lodge will be called WORSHIPFUL MASTERS, & the Worshipful Master shall have the title of MOST RESPECTABLE MASTER.

RECEPTION.

The Recipient will spend one hour in the Chamber of Reflection before his Reception, during which period the Worshipful Masters will prepare to receive him in the following manner.

Opening of the Lodge.

The Respectable will ask: *Worshipful Master Senior Warden, what hour is it?*

The Senior Warden will reply: *Most Respectable, it is high noon.*

Q. *What is the principal duty of a Master Mason?*

A. To see that the Lodge is well-tyled & that the Brethren here assembled are worthy to attend our mysteries.

Q. *Will you therefore see that the Lodge is well-tyled & that all the Brethren here assembled can participate in our mysteries?*

Note: At this, all the Brethren make the sign of the Master.

The Senior Warden passes this order to the Junior & the latter to Brother Tyler, who goes out to make his inspection, after which he returns to the Lodge & says: *Worshipful Brother Junior Warden, I have examined the Lodge tile by tile, gutter by gutter, & the Lodge is absolutely safe from the indiscretions of the Profane.* The Junior Warden passes this report to the Senior, & the latter to the Respectable, adding that *all the Brethren are worthy to attend our mysteries.*

The Respectable says: *Since it is high noon, that the Lodge is well-tyled, since we are safe from the indiscretions of the Profane & since the Brethren here assembled may participate in our mysteries, inform the Brethren on your Columns, Worshipful Brother Senior & Junior Wardens, that I am going to open the Master's Lodge & that to achieve this I ask them to lend me their assistance & support.*

The Senior & Junior Wardens inform each Brother on their Column.

The Respectable then says: *To order, my Brethren, & let us do our duty.*

All the Brethren rise, come to order, & clap their hands nine times while making the usual acclamations. The Respectable then says:

Worshipful Brethren, we are assembled here to proceed regularly to the reception of Master, of Brother * * *. Do you agree that we should show him the tomb?

All the Brethren make the Sign of Approval. The Respectable then says to the Master of Ceremonies: *Will you please go and fetch the Recipient from the Chamber of Reflection, Worshipful Brother, & then bring him to the door of the Lodge.*

The Master of Ceremonies goes to him, & dresses him as a Fellow Craft. He then leads him to the door of the Lodge, where having arrived, he knocks nine times, which is repeated by the Brother Tyler, & which must be repeated a second time by the Master of Ceremonies; after these nine knocks have been thus repeated, Brother Tyler says: *Worshipful Brother Junior Warden, is someone knocking as a Master at the door of the Lodge?* The Junior Warden passes this question to the Senior & the latter to the Respectable, who orders him to find out who it is, the Senior Warden passes the order to the Junior & the latter to the Brother Tyler, who must ask, in a firm tone, *Who knocks as a Master at the door of the Lodge?*

The Brother Conductor replies: *It is a Fellow Craft who desires & requests to be received as Master.*

Brother Tyler passes the answer to the Junior Warden, the Junior to the Senior, & the Senior to the Respectable, who answers him as follows:

Be so good, my Brother, as to assure yourself of the quality of the Recipient, & ask him for the Sign, Word & Grip of the Apprentice & the Fellow Craft.

The Senior Warden leaves the Lodge & asks the Recipient for the Sign, Word & Grip of the Apprentice & Fellow Craft.

After he is satisfied, the Senior Warden returns to the Lodge & reports to the Respectable, who asks the Recipient by way of the Senior Warden: if he has served his time; if his Masters are satisfied with him; he has not erred in the paths of virtue; if he perseveres in making further progress; if a spirit of curiosity has induced to seek this Degree; & if he has seen the tomb, & wishes to see it.

After the Recipient has answered all these questions, he introduces him at the West of the Lodge, holding the point of his sword against the Recipient's heart & ensuring that the Recipient's back is turned so that he cannot see the coffin; he places him between the two Wardens, & then resumes his place. The Respectable then asks the Recipient the following questions.

Q. *Fellow Craft, what are you seeking?*

(He is prompted to give the answer).

A. To be received as Master.

Q. *Have you served your time?*

A. Yes, Most Respectable.

Q. *Are your Masters happy with you?*

A. Yes, Most Respectable.

Q. *What proof do you bring?*

A. (He makes the sign of Apprentice & that of Fellow Craft).

Q. *Are you not one of those traitors whom we suspect of being accomplices in the death of our Respectable Master?*

A. No, Most Respectable! On the contrary, I have come, full of confidence, to seek due reward for my labors.

Q. *Take care! Do not try to deceive us, and be assured, we punish treachery.*

A. Most Respectable, I am a zealous & innocent Fellow Craft.

The Respectable Master then says: *Worshipful Masters, you have heard what he said, do you agree that I should admit this Fellow Craft to his first journey?*

All the Brethren give the Sign of Approval.

The Respectable then says: *Worshipful Master Senior Warden, have the Fellow Craft travel from the West to the East by way of the South. Stay close to his heels & try to discover if he is not moved by the sight of everything he sees. Look at him, my Brethren, to see whether horror does not show in his features, & whether you cannot determine his guilt.*

(The Senior Warden makes the Recipient undertake his journey with his face turned to the wall, while the Brethren affect an air of sadness).

At the end of his first journey three Brethren, each holding a roll, tap him on the shoulder with it.

When the first journey has been completed the Senior Warden informs the Most Respectable Master that the Brother Fellow Craft has finished his first journey, who orders him to ask for the Sign, Word & Grip of the Apprentice.

After he is satisfied the Respectable admits him to his second journey in the same way as the first, & the ceremony of the roll is repeated.

When the second journey is completed the Senior Warden reports this to the Most Respectable, who orders him to ask the Recipient for the Sign, Word & Grip of a Fellow Craft. After he has done this satisfactorily the Senior Warden says: *Most Respectable, the Fellow Craft seemed to me to be anxious & unsteady.* Then he[7] asks the Worshipful Masters of the Lodge whether his conduct during his journey was not suggestive of his guilt & served to confirm suspicions of the murder of the Respectable Father HIRAM.

The Brethren continue with their assumed air of sadness, & the Respectable asks them if the Fellow Craft should be admitted to his third journey.

They make the Sign of Approval.

Then the Respectable tells the Senior Warden to make the Recipient travel for the third time & to inspire him with great confidence and terror.

The third journey complete & the recipient having arrived at the West of the Lodge between the two Wardens, with his back still turned to the coffin, the Senior announces that the Fellow Craft has made his third journey with intrepidity.

The Respectable Master then says to the Recipient: *You have done nothing yet. Prepare yourself for the severest trials to reach the Degree of Master, which is the key of Masonry. I fear that you will succumb. The sadness of this place & their doleful decorations should announce to you how serious your Reception is. Do you persist?*

After he answers, the Respectable Master says to him: *Aren't you afraid to see the tomb? Do you really want to be a witness to our tears?* He answers: *Yes, Most Respectable.* After his response, he tells the Senior Warden to give him the light. He turns the Recipient to face the coffin, & after a short interval the Respectable Master says to him: *Now you see the subject of our grief. This coffin contains the most perfect Mason & the most Respectable Master. Will you join us in making a thorough search for his assassins?*

The Fellow Craft answers, *yes*.

Then the Respectable tells the Senior Warden to bring him forward to the foot of the Throne by three steps of the Master, asking him to cross over the coffin & warning him not to tread on the corpse but to show respect to the Brethren even after their death.

The Senior & Junior Wardens make him step across the coffin. Arriving at the foot of the Throne he is made to stand as a Mason, his feet in square.

The Wardens take care to place their feet behind his in the form of a fulcrum, in order to easily fell him, & for this purpose they each place an arm on his shoulder.

Note. All the Brethren have the point of their swords turned towards the coffin.

In this attitude, the Master makes him renew his obligation & to promise not to reveal to the Apprentices & Fellow Crafts anything that will be entrusted to him concerning the Mastership, following which the Respectable addresses him as follows.

---

7   The Most Respectable Master?

DISCOURSE.

"You know, my Brother, that the Apprentices assembled at Column *J.*, there to receive their wages, & that the Fellow Crafts were paid at the foot of Column *B.*, the price of their emulation. The order that prevailed in the construction of the Temple was established by HIRAM, from the Tribe of *Naphtali,* whom Solomon had chosen to ensure the good order & execution of his plans, & who was a famous craftsman in all kinds of metals. This ingenious Administrator wished to reward each craftsman according to his merit, he divided them into three classes: the first consisting of Apprentices, the second of Fellow Crafts, & the third of Masters. To be able to identify them, & and not to confuse them, the Apprentices had *J.* as their watch- word & the Fellow Crafts *B.*, while the Masters, who were indifferently in the extent of the Temple, had the word *JEHOVA.* Jealousy overwhelmed the three perfidious Fellow Crafts, who hatched a plan to learn the Master's word from HIRAM willingly or by force & carried out this plan as I will you."

(Here the Respectable descends from his Throne & says to remove the corpse).

"One day, after the craftsmen had left, these three villains went, one went to the West gate, another to the North, & the third to the East. When HIRAM presented himself at the West gate to leave the Temple, the first of these scoundrels asked him for the Master's word, but HIRAM refused to give him what he did not deserve & begged him to desist from seeking the degree of Master by violence. The Fellow Craft, dissatisfied with this answer, threatened him, but the threats could not shake the Respectable Master's resolve. The scoundrel therefore struck him on the head with his roll." (Here the Respectable strikes the Recipient on the head with his roll.) "HIRAM ran to the North gate to save himself, but how surprised he was when, having reached it, he found there the second villain who, asking him for the Master's word, but in vain, struck him on the shoulder with a gavel, which caused HIRAM to stagger." (Here the Respectable strikes the Recipient on the shoulder with his gavel.) "Our Respectable Master mustered what little strength he had left to escape from the obvious danger that threatened him, but he was assured of his doom when he saw, at the East gate, the third of those scoundrels, who asked him in a terrifying manner for the Master's word, which Hiram stubbornly refused to give him. The scoundrel therefore struck him on the chest with a crowbar, which felled him." (Here the Respectable Master strikes the Recipient with a kind of small lever. The Wardens then tumble him onto the coffin, & four Brethren cover him with the burial shroud they are holding, so that his face is covered.) The Respectable Master then continues: "This the most respectable of the Masters preferred death to perjury."

"These villains then carried HIRAM's body to a neighboring mountain, where they buried it, marking the place with a branch of *acacia* so as to be able the more easily to remove it, at their leisure, ahead of the pursuits of Solomon..."

(Here there is silence for a moment, after which the Respectable says: *"Let us go to the grave"*. All the Brethren surround the coffin, with the point of their swords turned towards it, & the Respectable passes around, ear to ear, the Master's word *M. B.*, which is then returned to him, after which he continues the story in the following words).

"Solomon chose nine experienced Masters to search for HIRAM: three left by the West gate, three by the North gate, and three by the East gate. Six days passed without their having discovered any trace of their Master & without any hope of learning his fate. But on the seventh day one of them, worn out with fatigue, wanted to sit down; & to do so more comfortably he took hold of the branch of *acacia* which the murderers had planted to mark HIRAM's burial-place. This branch gave no resistance. What is more, the disturbed soil aroused his suspicions. He called over his Fellow Crafts, who decided to dig, but just imagine their astonishment when they saw the body of the respectable Master HIRAM!" (Here the Recipient is uncovered.) "One of them seized his index finger, but the flesh came away, & he uttered the word *J*... The second grasped him by the middle finger, & once again the flesh cleaved from the bones, & he pronounced the word *B*... A third took him by the hand, in the form of a claw, foot to foot, knee to knee, breast to breast, raised him up, & uttered *M... B...*, which means the flesh is rotten.»

(*Note*. The two Wardens & the Respectable take the Recipient by the index finger in turn, but it is the Respectable who raises him).

When the Recipient has been raised the Master says to him: *That is the word & grip of the Master, which has been handed down to us since the murder of HIRAM. Go, my Brother, & identify yourself to the Brethren of the Lodge.*

The Recipient then gives all the Brethren the grip & word of a Master. The Sign is made by abruptly bringing the right hand to the left breast with fingers extended & the thumb & forefinger forming a square & then withdrawing the hand horizontally. Then the Recipient takes his place beside the Respectable & the Orator delivers a discourse on the Reception. When the discourse is over the Respectable begins the following instruction.

INSTRUCTION.

Q. *Are you a Mason?*

A. Prove me or disprove me, the *acacia* is known to me.

Q. *How were you received?*

A. With three great blows.

Q. *What do these three great blows mean?*

A. They are the three blows that our Father HIRAM received.

Q. *How many Orders are there in Masonry?*

A. Five: the Tuscan, Doric, Ionic, Corinthian & Composite.

Q. *What do the three letters* M. B. N. *stand for?*

A. They signify stability, perseverance, & assemblies of Regular Brethren.

Q. *What is the perfect point of your admission?*

A. I guard it, & keep it hidden.

Q. *Of what does it consist?*

A. The secret of the Masons.

Q. *Where do you keep it?*

A. In my heart.

Q. *Where were you received as a Master?*

A. In the Middle Chamber.

Q. *Where do the Masters stand in the Lodge?*

A. Everywhere.

Q. *Why?*

A. To watch over the works & perfect them.

Q. *What came you here to do?*

A. To overcome my passions & make further progress in Masonry.

Q. *Have you seen your Master?*

A. Yes, I have seen him.

Q. *How was he dressed?*

A. In blue & gold.

Q. *How long do you serve him?*

A. From Monday to Saturday.

Q. *With what do you serve him?*

A. With chalk, clay & charcoal.

Q. *What do these materials mean?*

A. Fervor, constancy & the impenetrability of the secret.

Q. *How many kinds of Masons are there?*

A. Of two kinds: the Operative Mason & the Speculative Mason.

Q. *What is a Speculative Mason?*

A. A man who learns good morals, humility & to never speak of Religion except with respect.

Q. *Is there nothing more than that?*

A. He is equal to the Greatest Prince.

Q. *What is a Mason called?*

A. GABAON, that is to say, perfect Mason.

Q. *If a Mason was lost, where would you find him?*

A. Between the square & the compass, which must guide our passions & encompass our steps.

Q. *What secrets have you promised to keep?*

A. All the secrets of Masonry.

Q. *Where do you keep them hidden?*

A. In my heart.

Q. *Do you have the key?*

A. Yes, I have.

Q. *Where do you keep it?*

A. In a box made in the form of an arch.

Q. *Of what metal is it made?*

A. It is not made of any metal. It is a tongue accustomed to praising the Brethren.

Q. *Where is it hanging?*

A. It is neither hanging nor lying down but attached.

Q. *Do you have any signs?*

A. Yes, we have guttural, pectoral, pedal & manual.

Q. *What do you understand by the guttural?*

A. It is the memory of my commitment to have my throat cut rather than to reveal the secrets of Masonry.

Q. *What do you understand by the pectoral?*

A. I understand the pain that the Masters feel at the loss of HIRAM.

Q. *What do you understand by pedal & manual?*

A. The manner of walking, one's postures as a Mason, & the touching of hands.

Q. *How do the Masters travel?*

A. From East to West, to spread the light.

Q. *Where were you paid?*

A. In the Inner Chamber.

Q. *How is this reached?*

A. By a spiral staircase, which ascends in threes, fives & sevens.

Q. *What is the Mason's Sign of Help?*

A. Placing one's arms & hands interlaced on one's head while calling out, *Help me, Sons of the Widow*.

Q. *How old are you?*

A. Seven years & more.

Q. *What is the Master's word?*

A. M. B. N.

After the Instruction the Respectable passes around the charity box, after which he asks the Senior & Junior Wardens to find out whether any Brother has anything to propose for the good of the Lodge & the propagation of the Order. The Wardens announce & then report to the Respectable, who says: *My Brethren, since no Brother has anything to propose, Brother Senior & Junior Wardens, inform the Brethren on your Columns that I am about to close the Master's Lodge.* The Wardens announce this & the Lodge is closed in the following manner.

PROCEDURE FOR CLOSING THE LODGE.

Q. *Worshipful Brother Senior Warden, what hour is it?*

A. It is midnight full.

Q. *It is therefore time to conclude our work & to cease our labors. Worshipful Senior & Junior Wardens, inform the Brethren on your Columns that the Master's Lodge is closed.*

The Wardens repeat this to the Brethren, one after the other, following which the Respectable says: *To order, my Brethren, & let us do our duty.* All the Brethren come to order & then, along with the Respectable, clap their hands & engage in the usual acclamations. Then the Respectable says: *Brethren, the Master's Lodge is closed.*

End of the Degree of Master.

I, the undersigned, acknowledge that I have been given the above printed Copy & other parts of the Degree of MASTER, regarding which I have given & hereby give my word of honor not to entrust & communicate them to any Profane of either sex. I agree to be dishonored if by my fault or negligence the said Copy should ever fall into any other hands than those of a Brother. In witness whereof I have signed the present for my justification, or for my confusion.

Given at   the

THE

REGULATOR

OF THE MASON.

~~~~~~~~~~~~~~~~~~~

HEREDOM,

The year of the G[reat]∴ L[ight]∴ 5801.

FOREWORD.

The ORDER of Freemasons is an association of wise and virtuous men whose objects are to live in perfect equality; to be closely allied by bonds of respect, trust, and friendship under the name of BRETHREN; and to encourage each other in the practice of virtue.

According to this definition, the wisdom and self-interest of all lodges require that they grant the right of participation in our Mysteries only to those who are worthy of sharing in all these advantages, who are capable of achieving the envisaged goal, and who would not cause them any embarrassment in the eyes of Masons throughout the Universe.

Thus, when it comes to the admission of a Profane, the lodge to which he is presented must consider that it will be offering a new member to the general association and a Brother to each member; that, once he is received, Masons throughout the Universe, of whatever status, quality, and social condition, will be obliged to recognize him as such; that, therefore, the honor of the lodge is as much at stake as the glory and prosperity of the Order in assuring that this aspirant is worthy of introduction to all Masons; finally, that on the testimony of his lodge, he should deserve to be received by all Brethren as a virtuous man and Brother who, in that capacity, merits their most intimate friendship, with the lodge acting, by his admission, as a moral guarantor towards all Masons of the qualities that his Reception implies he must be assumed to possess.

Lodges cannot, therefore, be too scrupulous, punctilious, and severe in their scrutiny of the information relating to the aspirants presented to them. Another point, no less important, is the long-desired uniformity in the manner of initiation.

Animated by these principles, the Grand Orient of France has finally taken up the task of drafting a protocol of initiation to the first three degrees, *or symbolic degrees*. They deemed it a duty to return Masonry to those ancient customs which some innovators have tried to alter, and to restore those primary and important initiations to their ancient and respectable purity.

The lodges of its Obedience must therefore conform thereto in every point to cease offering travelling Masons a diversity which is as repulsive as it is contrary to the true principles of Masonry.

THE REGULATOR
OF THE MASON.

FIRST DEGREE,
OR
DEGREE OF APPRENTICE.

FIRST SECTION.
Preliminaries.

No Profane may be admitted until he has reached the age of twenty-one; he must be of a free and non-servile condition, and master of his own person.

A servant of any kind will only be admitted as a Serving Brother.

No one pursuing any vile and abject occupation can be admitted. Only rarely will a craftsman be admitted, even if he is a master craftsman, especially in locations where there are no guilds and corporations.

Those workers in the arts and crafts known as *journeymen* will never be admitted.

The admission of a Profane may only be decided upon at the third meeting, including the one at which he was proposed.

The interval between proposal and initiation shall be three months, but this interval may be reduced to forty-five days provided that, within that time, three general meetings have taken place.

Any eligible Profane will be announced, to the installed Worshipful, by a member of the lodge.

The same applies to any Mason who desires to be affiliated.

The Worshipful Master shall propose, by the following form, the Profane to the assembled lodge during its labor, without naming or identifying, in any way, the Sponsoring Brother:

"My Brethren, the Profane N∴ (first name(s), surname, age, social status or occupation, place of birth, place of domicile) has been proposed and requests to be initiated into our mysteries as a member of this lodge. B[rothers]∴ Senior and Junior Wardens, announce it to your Columns, and ask the B[rethren]∴ to obtain, by the next meeting, information regarding the proposed Profane for the purpose of establishing whether there is a need to appoint Commissioners."

The Senior Warden says: "B[rother]∴ Junior Warden, and Brethren who adorn the column of the South, the W[orshipful]∴ proposes the Profane N∴ (he repeats the Profane's names, age, social status or occupation, place of domicile, etc.) to be initiated into our mysteries as a member of this lodge, and invites us to obtain, by the next meeting, information regarding the proposed Profane for the purpose of establishing whether there is a need to appoint Commissioners."

The B[rother]∴ Junior Warden says: "B[rethren]∴ who adorn the column of the North, the W[orshipful]∴ and the B[rother]∴ Senior Warden invite us, etc." (he repeats his statement in exactly the same words).

At the next meeting, the proposal of the Profane will be dealt with, with the W[orshipful]∴ saying: "Brethren Senior and Junior Wardens, ask the Brethren∴ to disclose any information they may have been able to obtain about the Profane N∴ who was proposed at the last meeting."

The Wardens repeat this announcement, each at the head of his own Column.

If any of the Brethren have any observations to make, then they successively ask to speak by raising and extending their hands.

The Warden at whose Column they stand strikes one rap of the gavel, which the other Warden repeats, then the W[orshipful]∴ with a similar rap. The Warden then says:

"W[orshipful]∴, a B[rother]∴ on my Column requests permission to speak."

The W[orshipful]∴ replies:

"My B[rother]∴, you may speak."

The B[rethren]∴ in the East who have any comments to make will ask the W[orshipful]∴ for permission to speak.

Note: This formula of circulating by threes, all the announcements made in the lodge is required in all circumstances and determines the essential character of regular labor.

Should several B[rethren]∴ concurrently request the floor, it is for the Warden to see who requests it first, and to announce his name to the W[orshipful]∴

If no one rises then the B[rother]∴ Junior Warden says to the Senior Warden in a low voice: "There are no comments on my Column."

The Senior Warden in turn says, audibly: "M[ost]∴ W[orshipful]∴, there are no comments on either of the two Columns."

The W[orshipful]∴ says:

"Brother Orator, present your conclusions."

The B[rother]∴ Orator rises and makes such comments as he thinks fit, after which he waits for a moment to see whether his comments have not given rise to others. If so, these comments should be heard and discussed.

If there are no new comments, or if there are and they have been adequately discussed, he may then conclude that Commissioners be appointed to acquire further information about the proposed Profane. If, however, the nature and importance of the comments lead the Orator to conclude that the appointment of Commissioners is unnecessary then he shall state that fact, but in either case the W[orshipful]∴ shall order the Ballot to be performed by means of the following formula:

"B[rother]∴ Senior Warden, ask the B[rother]∴ Master of Ceremonies to confirm to you the number of voters, and have the ballots distributed accordingly."

The Junior Warden passes this order to the Master of Ceremonies, who distributes to each B[rother]∴ one white and one black ball, and reports to the Senior Warden the number of votes to be cast.

The Senior Warden passes this information to the W[orshipful]∴

Note: visiting Brethren are entitled to vote, since what is being decided is the gift of a new B[rother]∴ to the whole Order.

Then the W[orshipful]∴ says:

"Brethren Senior and Junior Wardens, announce on your columns that the Ballot is to be circulated on the basis of the conclusions of the B[rother]∴ Orator, which argue that Commissioners should (or should not) be appointed (depending on the conclusions presented) expressly to acquire information about the proposed Profane; the white balls being to accept the conclusions of the B[rother]∴ Orator and black balls the opposite."

The B[rother]∴ Senior Warden strikes a rap of the gavel and says:

"B[rother]∴ Junior Warden, Brethren who adorn the column of the South, the Ballot will now passed, etc."

The Junior Warden gives a rap of the gavel and makes the same announcement.

An Expert or, in his absence, a B[rother]∴ appointed for the purpose, circulates the Ballot in the following order: he first offers the ballot-box to the W[orshipful]∴, then to the Wardens, then the Orator, then the B[rethren]∴ in the East, then the B[rethren]∴ of the column of the South, then to those of the column of the North, and then, after casting his own ballot, takes the ballot-box to the W[orshipful]∴, who, before opening it, calls a second Expert to be present with the first at the opening of the ballot-box. He then opens the box and compares the number of ballots with the number of votes of which he was previously advised (they must always be the same).

If there are more or fewer ballots than votes then the ballot is voided and must be repeated.

If the Ballot is equal and correct then the W[orshipful]∴ strikes a rap of the gavel, which the Wardens repeat, and announces the result.

If the votes are unanimous, the W[orshipful]∴ says:

"B[rothers]∴ Senior and Junior Wardens, announce on your Columns that the conclusions of B[rother]∴ Orator have been unanimously adopted, and that Commissioners are to be appointed, more specifically to acquire information about the proposed Profane. At the same time, invite all the B[rethren]∴ to join me in applauding the decision."

If the ballot concluded that no Commissioners should be appointed, then the W[orshipful]∴ would announce so, and there would be no applause.

The B[rother]∴ Senior Warden then says: "B[rother]∴ Junior Warden and Brethren of the column of the South, the Ballot has unanimously adopted the conclusions of the B[rother]∴ Orator. Accordingly, Commissioners, etc., will be appointed. The W[orshipful]∴ invites us to join him with applause."

The Junior Warden makes the same announcement.

Then the W[orshipful]∴ says:

"With me, my Brethren."

All now applaud simultaneously with the battery of two quick raps and one slow o o, o, repeated three times, and end with a triple *vivat*.

The W[orshipful]∴ then secretly appoints three Commissioners from among the Brethren, both present and absent.

At the next assembly, the B[rother]∴ Master of Ceremonies shall, by order of the W[orshipful]∴, pass to the East, and along the two columns, a bag called the *Proposal Bag*: it will be presented to all the Brethren successively, each being required to put his hand into it as if he wished to put something into it without being seen. By this means the Brethren who were appointed Commissioners at the previous meeting will be able to place their written report into the bag without anyone being able to notice it. This report should be written on a fairly small piece of paper, folded in such a way that nothing is seen when held; and thus, the Commissioners remain unknown. These reports need not be signed, and it will be sufficient to refer to the proposed Profane by the initial letter of his surname.

The B[rother]∴ Secretary will only make, in the day's minutes, and in that, when the proposal was made and the Commissioners appointed, a general mention of a proposed Profane, without any indication of his forenames, surnames, social status and occupation, age, place of birth, or place of residence of the Profane; but he shall transcribe on a separate sheet, stamped, sealed and signed with at least three signatures, the forename, surnames, etc., of the Profane, as well as everything that relates to him, such as the appointment of Commissioners, the report of those Commissioners, the ballot, etc. Until the moment of admission, if it takes place and, in that case, he will transcribe into the Book of Architecture[8] everything written on the loose sheets.

The information that each member of the lodge, and more particularly the Commissioners, is invited to contribute must have as its object not only the lifestyle and morals of the proposed, but also knowledge regarding his temperament and character, his habits, his imperfections and, above all, whether he has any vices that might be sufficient reason for not admitting him.

If the report of the three Commissioners is favorable, or if any two out of the three are, then the W[orshipful]∴ says:

"My Brethren, at the meeting of *** the Profane N∴ was proposed for initiation into our mysteries. I have, in consequence of the ballot, appointed three Commissioners to acquire the necessary information. These three Brethren have made their report, and their conclusion is that, by admitting the Profane, the lodge will have made a good acquisition. The Profane persists in his desire to be received. B[rothers]∴ Senior and Junior Wardens, propose the Profane N∴ to the B[rethren]∴ of your columns, and ask them if they have any comments to make."

The B[rothers]∴ Senior and Junior Wardens make this announcement. If anyone has any comments to make then these are heard; at last, the B[rother]∴ Orator concludes.

The B[rother]∴ Master of Ceremonies distributes the ballot, following the same procedure as before.

---

8   The Minuet book or Protocols of the lodge.

A B[rother]∴ Expert rises and carries it to the W[orshipful]∴, who counts the votes in the presence of a second Expert. If the ballot is unanimous he reports it audibly to the lodge, and they applaud.

Then the B[rother]∴ Secretary transcribes into the minutes everything written on the loose sheets.

If the Ballot has three or more black balls the Profane is rejected without appeal, and the loose sheets are burned.

If the Ballot has only one or two black balls it will be so noted on the loose sheets and the proposal postponed until the next (ordinary) meeting.

If, at this fifth meeting, the ballot contains only one black ball then the W[orshipful]∴ shall invite, and cause the Wardens to invite out loud, the Brother who cast the black ball to inform him, outside the lodge and under the seal of Masonic secrecy, of the reasons for his opposition.

At this secret conference the W[orshipful]∴ will judge the importance of the grounds for opposition and, if he finds them to be slight, he will try to persuade the opposing B[rother]∴ to withdraw them, without being allowed to compel him to do so on any pretext.

Finally if, at a final meeting, the ballot still contains a black ball then the Profane will be rejected.

If the grounds for opposition were due only to some specific statutes or general regulations of the lodge, the objector may rise, request the floor, and explain them, so that the lodge may then deliberate and, whatever is then decided, following the conclusion of the B[rother]∴ Orator, by a plurality of votes in an ordinary ballot, shall be implemented.

If the B[rother]∴ who opposes admission is reluctant to explain the reasons to the W[orshipful]∴, either because he fears making an enemy or because he loathes to associate with the proposed Profane, then he may refrain from making himself known to the W[orshipful]∴ and will wait for the final Ballot where, as has been said, one black ball rejects the Profane.

In this case it is better if the lodge retains a member whose character, mind and qualities are known than to acquire a stranger who is unknown to it.

~~~~~~

SECOND SECTION.
Reception.

First Preliminary.

All members of the lodge must be summoned on the day of the meeting indicated by the W[orshipful]∴, and the summons must indicate a reception in the First Degree.

No one shall be absent from the meeting without a legitimate reason, such as civil affairs, duties of state, etc. If anyone fails to attend then he must apologize to the lodge by means of a letter addressed to B[rother]∴ Secretary or, alternatively, pay a fine to benefit the poor.

Second Preliminary.

The Profane aspirant will be brought to the door of the lodge by the Sponsoring B[rother]∴ at least half an hour before the opening of the lodge. This door should not, if possible, be the usual entrance. The B[rother]∴ will there take leave of the Aspirant as if he abandoning him.

The Preparing B[rother]∴ will, if the time has not yet arrived to open lodge, take charge of the Profane and lead him to some secluded place where he cannot converse with anyone, nor see or recognize anyone.

The Preparing B[rother]∴ will maintain a stern expression without brusqueness, avoid making conversation, and respond curtly and vaguely to questions that might be put to him, so as to deprive him of the desire to ask any others.

About half an hour before the opening of the lodge the Preparing B[rother]∴ will take the Profane to the Chamber of Reflection.

This room must be sealed off from daylight and be lit by a single lamp. The walls must be blackened and decorated with funerary emblems to inspire self-reflection, sorrow, and fear. Statements of moral purity and maxims of austere philosophy are legibly written on the walls or framed and hung in various parts of the room; a skull, or even a skeleton, if one can be procured, will recall the emptiness of human concerns.

In this room there should only be a chair, a table, a loaf of bread, a vase filled with clear water, some salt and sulfur in two small vases, paper, pens, and ink.

Above the table is depicted a rooster and an hourglass; below these emblems, are the words *vigilance* and *perseverance*.

Inscriptions.

If mere curiosity has brought you here, depart.

If you fear being enlightened about your faults, you will be troubled among us.

If you are capable of concealment, tremble, for we shall see right through you.

If social distinctions matter to you, depart, for we know none here.

If your soul feels dread, go no further.

If you persevere then you will be purified by the elements; you will emerge from the abyss of darkness and will see the light.

The Profane will be left alone for some time in the Chamber of Reflection, after which the Preparing B[rother]∴ will give him the following or similar questions in writing, to be answered also in writing:

What does an honest man owe to himself?

What does he owe to his fellow man?

What does he owe to his country?

These questions should be written in such a way as to leave enough room for the Profane's answers.

When the B[rethren]∴ are assembled in the room, properly clothed[9] and decorated, the W[orshipful]∴ strikes a rap of the gavel to call the lodge to work. Everyone takes his place and stands.

The W[orshipful]∴ says:

Q. B[rother]∴ Senior Warden, are you a Mason?

A. My B[rethren]∴ recognize me as such.

Q. What is the first care of the Wardens in the lodge?

A. To see that the lodge is tyled without and within.

Note: That is to say, the door of the temple must be closed, and there must be no Profanes inside the hall of lost steps[10] who might eavesdrop.

The W[orshipful]∴ says:

"satisfy yourself, my B[rother]∴."

The Senior Warden says to the Junior Warden: "B[rother]∴ Junior Warden, satisfy yourself that the lodge is tyled."

The B[rother]∴ Junior Warden says: "B[rother]∴ Expert (or B[rother]∴ Tyler), perform your duty."

Then the B[rother]∴ Expert, sword in hand, opens the door of the lodge, takes the key, and places it on the table between the two Wardens, orders B[rother]∴ Tyler to stand guard outside the porch for which he is responsible, closes the door, and stands at the inner entrance to the porch, sword in hand. When this has been done, the B[rother]∴ Tyler tells the Junior Warden in a low voice that the works are tyled. The Junior Warden tells the Senior who says, audibly, "M[ost]∴ W[orshipful]∴, the works are tyled without and within."

The M[ost]∴ W[orshipful]∴ says:

"To order, my Brethren" (he adds):

Q. B[rother]∴ Senior Warden, what is the second duty of a Warden in lodge?

A. It is to ensure that all the B[rethren]∴ are in order.

Q. And are they?

The Junior Warden says to the Senior: "All the B[rethren]∴ are in order on the column of the North."

The Senior Warden says, audibly: "M[ost]∴ W[orshipful]∴, all the B[rethren]∴ are in order on both Columns."

Q. At what hour do the Masons open their works?

A. At noon.

---
9   Wearing his apron.
10 I.e., the vestibule.

Q. What is the hour?

A. It is noon.

The W[orshipful]∴ then says:

"Brethren Senior and Junior Wardens, since it is the hour at which we must open our works, invite the B[rethren]∴ of each Column to join me in opening the works of the lodge of… at the Orient of… in the Degree of Apprentice."

The Senior Warden says: "B[rother]∴ Junior Warden and Brethren of the column of the South, the W[orshipful]∴ invites us to join him in opening the works of the R[espectable]∴ lodge of… at the Orient of… in the Degree of Apprentice."

The Junior Warden makes the same announcement.

The W[orshipful]∴ strikes the three mysterious blows upon the altar…

The B[rother]∴ Wardens repeat, after which he says:

"With me, my B[rethren]∴."

All, with their eyes upon the W[orshipful]∴, make the Sign of the Apprentice, and applaud with the ordinary battery[11].

Finally the W[orshipful]∴ says:

"My B[rethren]∴, the work is open, take your seats."

The Wardens repeat what the W[orshipful]∴ just said, and everyone sits down.

The W[orshipful]∴ then says:

"B[rother]∴ Secretary, will you please read out the Minutes of our previous work."

"B[rothers]∴ Senior and Junior Wardens, ask the Brethren to pay attention to the reading of the Minutes."

The Wardens repeat this invitation.

The B[rother]∴ Secretary reads out the Minutes.

Note: The minutes must necessarily contain all the deliberations taken and proposals made during the course of the work.

However experienced the Brother Secretary may be, however attentive he may be, it is difficult for the minutes to be written while at labor to a standard that will bear a thorough subsequent reading. What is more, something may have occurred that may initially have been recorded which, subsequently, the lodge may decide should not be included in the Minutes, thus necessitating erasures, marginal annotations, etc. For this reason B[rother]∴ Secretary should produce, during the labor, only a rough draft, which he can then correct and delete according to circumstances, provided that he writes up the fair copy of it in a register dedicated to that purpose. He will therefore write the rough draft on loose sheets bearing the stamps of the lodge. At the end of the work, the B[rother]∴ Secretary will read out this rough draft so that each Brother may make such corrections as he thinks fit. These corrections should serve only to render more clearly and accurately what has happened during the work. In order to legally affirm what has been agreed in the rough draft, B[rother]∴ Secretary will have it signed by the W[orshipful]∴ and the B[rother]∴ Orator.

---

11 Two quick raps and one slow rap repeated three times, thus o o, o, and ending with a triple vivat" mentioned above.

While the B[rother]∴ Secretary reads out the redaction from the register the B[rother]∴ Orator compares with the rough draft he has before him to ensure that the B[rother]∴ Secretary has not changed or omitted anything from the proceedings of the previous meeting.

When the reading is finished, the B[rother]∴ Orator must audibly report any changes or omissions he has noticed. If there are none, he says:

"M[ost]∴ W[orshipful]∴, the Minutes conform to the rough draft."

Since other B[rethren]∴ might have noticed something needing correction, the W[orshipful]∴ will say:

"B[rothers]∴ Senior and Junior Wardens, I request you to ask the Brethren of each Column to comment upon the draft of the Minutes recorded at the last assembly, which they have just heard read out."

The Wardens make this announcement.

Note: Comments can only relate to the manner in which the minutes are edited; no substantial changes can be made, they being irrevocably settled at the previous meeting.

If any B[rother]∴ has any comments to make then he rises, requests the floor, and having obtained it, makes his observations, which are then discussed to the extent that they are reasonable.

If there are no comments the Wardens will announce it audibly,

The W[orshipful]∴ says:

"B[rothers]∴ Senior and Junior Wardens, invite the Brethren of each Column to join me in adopting the Minutes of our previous work."

The Wardens make this announcement.

The W[orshipful]∴ says:

"With me, my Brethren."

All applaud in the customary manner.

If any visiting B[rethren]∴ are present they must not be introduced until after the Minutes have been read out, so that if the Minutes contain some fraternal sanctions imposed on B[rethren]∴, or the last work of the lodge involved some dispute, or some matter has been dealt with which must be confined to the Brethren of the lodge, then no Visitor shall have knowledge of it.

If there are visiting Brethren in the hall of lost steps then B[rother]∴ Master of Ceremonies quietly alerts the B[rother]∴ Junior Warden, who gives a rap for attention; he quietly alerts the B[rother]∴ Senior Warden, who gives a rap, to which the W[orshipful]∴ responds and the Senior Warden says: "M[ost]∴ W[orshipful]∴, there are some B[rethren]∴ in the hall of lost steps who ask to be admitted to our labors."

The W[orshipful]∴ replies:

"B[rother]∴ Junior Warden, ask the B[rother]∴ Senior Expert to find out who these B[rethren]∴ are; demand their names, that of their lodges, their certificates, and to tyle them to the work of the degree."

The B[rother]∴ Junior Warden charges the B[rother]∴ Expert with this commission. He exits, questions all the Brethren, each in turn, in particular writes down their names, that of their lodges, and takes charge of their certificates.

He then knocks on the door with the battery of the degree. The B[rother]∴ Tyler answers him in kind, and the Expert also replies in kind. The B[rother]∴ Tyler alerts the Senior Warden, who says it aloud to the W[orshipful]∴ after striking a rap of the gavel.

The W[orshipful]∴ says:

"My B[rother]∴, go see who knocks. If it is a member of the lodge, let him enter after he has given the password and order-word."

The Senior Warden repeats this order to the B[rother]∴ Tyler, who then opens the door, introduces the B[rother]∴ Expert, if it was he who knocked, and closes the door. If it is a member of the lodge, the B[rother]∴ Tyler notifies the Junior Warden, who says loudly, "It is B[rother]∴ N∴, M[ost]∴ W[orshipful]∴,"

Whoever enters must do so by the three Apprentice steps, place himself to order between the two Wardens, and wait for the W[orshipful]∴ to tell him to take his place.

If it is the B[rother]∴ Expert, he places himself between the two Wardens, asks to speak and, after obtaining it, he reports on his mission and delivers the certificates to the B[rother]∴ Master of Ceremonies, who will then take them to the W[orshipful]∴

It is appropriate to have the B[rethren]∴ visitors sign their names on a separate sheet of paper, so that these signatures can be compared against those on the certificates.

If there are no problems the W[orshipful]∴ orders that they be granted entry. The moment they enter the temple the B[rother]∴ Expert asks them for the annual word, which they give in a low voice. To welcome them, all the Brethren stand up and come to order. When they are introduced into the temple the W[orshipful]∴ tells them what a pleasure their visit gives the Brethren. He then invites them to take their places on the columns, whither they are led by the B[rother]∴ Master of Ceremonies.

If the visiting Brethren include any Worshipful Masters of lodges or a deputation from a lodge, any of the three Grand Officers of the Order, or any Serving Officer of the G[rand]∴ O[rient]∴, then they shall be introduced as follows:

For a W[orshipful]∴ or a deputation from a lodge, or for an Officer of the G[rand]∴ O[rient]∴, three Brethren shall be assigned to receive them at the door of the temple preceded by the Master of Ceremonies. They shall be received sword in hand. For the Grand M[aster]∴ of the G[rand]∴ O[rient]∴ of France, the deputation shall consist of nine Brethren, preceded by the Master of Ceremonies.

For a Grand Master from a foreign Orient, seven Brethren.

When these Brethren have arrived between the Wardens (and at the moment of thir introduction the W[orshipful]∴ and the Wardens strike three times nine raps of the gavel, after which the W[orshipful]∴ will give a louder rap to demand silence), the W[orshipful]∴ will congratulate them on behalf of the lodge on the favor they have bestowed upon it and will invite them to take their places in the East, to which the Master of Ceremonies will conduct them. The B[rethren]∴ who accompany them form the arch of steel, while the other B[rethren]∴ stand to order, sword in hand.

The W[orshipful]∴ will offer his gavel only to the three Grand Officers of the Order. When the visiting Brethren have taken their places, the W[orshipful]∴ will invite the B[rother]∴ Wardens to ask the B[rethren]∴ of the lodge and others to join him in applauding the presence of these Brethren.

The Wardens will announce this, after which the customary battery will be given.

If they express thanks the W[orshipful]∴ orders to drown out their applause.

The last are introduced Brethren distinguished by their Masonic qualities or by their dignities in the Order, in such a way that the most qualified of them is introduced last.

When this ceremonial has been completed the W[orshipful]∴ says:

"Let us be seated, my B[rethren]∴"

This is repeated by the Wardens; he then adds:

"My Brethren, by two unanimous votes you have admitted the Profane N∴ to present himself for initiation into our mysteries. If there is no further opposition then I beg you to demonstrate your contentment in the customary manner."

The Wardens repeat this announcement.

All the Brethren, as a sign of their consent, extend their hands and let them fall on their aprons.

If there is any new opposition then this must be discussed.

If there is none, the W[orshipful]∴ says:

"Brother Master of Ceremonies, have the B[rother]∴ Tyler notify the Preparing B[rother]∴ that the lodge awaits the account he is charged with rendering."

The Preparing B[rother]∴ being informed, knocks on the door in the manner described and which is observed in every circumstance.

He reports on the Candidate's disposition, and hands the B[rother]∴ Master of Ceremonies the piece of paper on which are written the three questions proposed to him and the answers he has given to the W[orshipful]∴

The W[orshipful]∴ says:

"The Preparing B[rother]∴ will prepare the Recipient in the required state; send me his sword (if he has one) and his metals."

During the preparation, the W[orshipful]∴ reads aloud the answers the Recipient has given to the questions put to him. If the Recipient arrives late then the W[orshipful]∴ reads out the lodge regulations, which would be interrupted at the first stroke of the gavel.

The Preparing B[rother]∴, returning to the Candidate, comments on the importance of his approach, and then, when he is satisfied of his resolve he stops speaking to him and even affects the most imposing silence and no longer answers any of his questions.

He is then taken out of the Chamber of Reflection and put in the state in which he is to enter the lodge, that is to say he must be bareheaded and carefully blindfolded, wear his shirt[12], with his left arm and breast uncovered, without garters, his right knee bare, and his left foot slipshod. He must not have upon him any gold, silver, watches, buckles, or any other jewelry or metals.

The Preparing B[rother]∴ collects the Recipient's metals, jewels, sword, etc. and brings them to the lodge. He knocks at the door of the lodge and hands them over to the B[rother]∴ Master of Ceremonies, who takes them to the W[orshipful]∴

Returning to the Recipient, the Preparing B[rother]∴ brings him to the door of the lodge, at which he strikes three distinct irregular knocks.

The Junior Warden strikes one rap and says to the Senior Warden:

"Someone knocks on the door as a Profane."

The Senior Warden raps the same, and makes the announcement to the W[orshipful]∴, who also strikes one rap and says:

"See who knocks in this manner."

The Senior Warden relates it the Junior, and the latter to the B[rother]∴ Tyler, who opens the door and asks somewhat brusquely, "Who knocks in this manner?"

The Preparing B[rother]∴ or Expert, without leaving the Recipient, says: "He is a Profane who asks to be received as a Mason."

The B[rother]∴ Tyler closes the door rather abruptly, makes the announcement to the Junior Warden, who relates it to the Senior Warden, who conveys it to the W[orshipful]∴

Note: All these formalities must be observed in order to increase the Recipient's embarrassment.

The W[orshipful]∴ says:

"Ask him his forename, surname, age, nationality, occupation, and his present residence. Ask him what he desires of us, and what is his will."

The B[rother]∴ Tyler half-opens the door and asks all these questions.

The Preparing B[rother]∴ answers them, and the B[rother]∴ Tyler relates them to the Junior Warden, and the latter to the Senior who says them aloud to the W[orshipful]∴

The W[orshipful]∴ says:

"Let him enter."

As the doors are thrown open noisily, with the sound of opening locks, the Preparing B[rother]∴ holds the Recipient by both hands and pulls him between the two Wardens; the doors are close noisily, the locks are again secured, and at that moment the Preparing Brother says: "I deliver him to you. I will no longer answer for him."

---

12   If the weather is cold then he can wear a coat over his shoulders.

The Brethren Wardens, without putting down their gavels, leave their places and approach the Profane, each seizing one of his hands; and after a few moments of silence the Senior Warden says:

"M[ost]∴ W[orshipful]∴, here is the Profane."

The W[orshipful]∴ says:

"Sir, the first qualities we require for admission to our midst, and without which one cannot be initiated into our mysteries, are the greatest sincerity, absolute obedience, and unfailing constancy. Your answers to the questions I am going to put to you will make it possible for us to form an accurate opinion about you."

Q. What is your intent in coming here?

Who encouraged you to do it?

Isn't curiosity the bigger part of it?

The W[orshipful]∴ awaits the Recipient's answers and makes objections in a manner analogous to his type of mind and character.

Q. What is your idea of Masonry?

Answer frankly, and above all be truthful.

(He awaits his answers).

Q. Are you ready for the trials through which you must pass?

(He awaits his answers).

Q. Do you know that obligations are contacted among us?

Q. Who introduced you here?

Q. Are you sure he is a Freemason?

Q. Did he warn you about anything that the Freemasons do?

Q. How can you desire to know something about which you tell me you have no idea?

Q. What thoughts did the objects, presented to your eyes in the room where you were confined on your arrival, cause you to have?

Q. How do you feel about your current condition? What idea do you have of a society in which the Recipient is required to be dressed in a way that must seem strange to you? Again, be truthful in your answers, for we read your heart.

Q. Isn't your confidence and demeanor a bit frivolous?

Q. Don't you fear that we will abuse the state of weakness and blindness in which you let yourself to be reduced? Unarmed, defenseless, and almost naked, you surrender to the power of people you do not know.

At each question, the W[orshipful]∴ waits for an answer, to ensure and increase his embarrassment, depending on how the Profane answers.

After these questions the W[orshipful]∴ says:

"We are going to undergo indispensibleengage ourselves in indispensable trials; I warn you, Sir, that if in the course of these trials the courage and strength that you need to endure them should happen to fail you then you will always be at liberty to withdraw; these trials are mysterious and emblematic; give them all the attention of which you are capable."

After a few minutes of the deepest silence, the W[orshipful]∴ says:

"B[rother]∴ Expert, cause the gentleman take the first journey."

The Wardens resume their places.

The B[rother]∴ Expert takes the Candidate by both hands, makes him travel from the West, where he is, passing through the column of the North, from North to East, from East to South, and thence to the West, between the two Wardens, where the journeys end.

The B[rother]∴ Expert walks backwards, during this journey,.

This first journey must be the most difficult, and must be made in small steps, very slowly, and with a very irregular step.

The room should be laid out in such a way as to make the journey difficult by means of skillfully arranged obstacles and challenges without, however, using anything that could injure inconvenience the Recipient. He will be made to walk sometimes at a slow pace and sometimes a bit faster. He should be made to stoop, from time to time, as if passing through an underground passage, or be required to step over something, as if crossing a ditch; finally, he is made to step in a zigzag, so that he cannot judge the nature of the ground he is traversing.

During this journey the sound of hail and thunder will be made to instill some degree of fear. When the Recipient is back in the West, the Junior Warden strikes one rap and says:

"W[orshipful]∴, the first journey is complete."

The W[orshipful]∴ says to him:

"Sir, what did you notice on the first journey you've just made?"

After his answer, the W[orshipful]∴ says:

"This first journey is emblematic of human life: the tumult of passions, the clash of competing interests, the difficulties of undertakings, the obstacles that proliferate in your path, laid by competitors eager to see you fail, all this is represented by the noise and the clamor that assailed your ears and by the unevenness of the road you travelled."

Then the W[orshipful]∴ says:

"Make the second journey."

This Second journey must be made with slower and longer steps; it should be marked only by brief light sword rattling, carefully directed to the ears of the Candidate. Back in the West the Preparing B[rother]∴ will plunge the Recipient's naked arm into a basin full of water which has been carefully set in this place; he then says: "M[ost]∴ W[orshipful]∴, the second journey is complete."

The W[orshipful]∴ says:

"What thoughts did this journey bring to your mind?"

After any response, the W[orshipful]∴ says:

"You must have encountered, in this journey, fewer difficulties and obstacles than in the first. We wanted to impress upon your mind the effect of constancy in following the path of virtue, for the more one advances, the more pleasant it is."

"The rattling of swords that you heard on the course represents the battles that the virtuous man is constantly obliged to endure in order to triumph over the assaults of vice."

"You have been purified by water. You have yet other trials to undergo; arm yourself with courage in order to endure them to the end."

"B[rother]∴ Expert, have him make the third journey."

This third journey is to be made free-footed, but without haste, rather like a stroll. The Recipient will be followed by someone, at some distance from him, waving a torch which produces a great flame. Care should be taken that this flame does not injure him.

With the Recipient having returned in the West, the Junior Warden gives one rap and says, "W[orshipful]∴, the third journey is complete."

The W[orshipful]∴ says:

"Sir, you must have noticed that this journey was even less strenuous than the previous one. The flames through which you passed are the complement of your purification. May the material fire, with which you have been surrounded, forever ignite in your heart a love of your fellow men; let charity preside over all your words and actions; and never forget this precept of a sublime morality, common to all nations: *Do not do to others what you would not wish to be done to you.*"

"The constancy you have just shown in your three journeys inspires in us the hope that you will withstand in the same way the trials that you still have to undergo. Do you wish to persist in this, Sir?"

After he has replied, the W[orshipful]∴ says:

"Sir, one of the virtues whose practice is dearest to us and the one which brings us closest to the Author of our being is charity. The metals of which you have been deprived symbolize vices: can you, without embarrassment, sacrifice for the benefit of the poor whom we assist daily, the money and the proceeds of the jewels belonging to you, and which have been handed over to me?"

"Take care, Sir. You can well imagine that a small group of people is at this very moment watching your every step and paying attention to the answer you are going to give me. I am asking you for an act of charity but take care not to make it an *ostentatious* one."

Note: If the Recipient is slow to respond or seems uncertain then the W[orshipful]∴ can try to encourage him with words somewhat like those noted here:

The charity which recommend to you ceases to be a virtue when it is done to the detriment of more sacred and pressing duties: civil commitments to fulfill, a family to maintain, children to raise, unfortunate relatives to assist – these are the first duties that nature imposes upon us, and they are the creditors of any man who governs his conduct by the principles of equity. What would you think of someone who made an effort to appear charitable before he had fulfilled these duties? I wanted to enlighten you on the obligations that are common to all men. I now return to the first proposal I made to you: can you, without offending against any of these responsibilities, sacrifice all or part of the money and the proceeds of the jewels that belong to you, and which have been handed over to me, for the benefit of the poor whom we assist daily?

"Answer me."

If the Candidate does not want to donate anything, then it will be up to the lodge to determine whether, in the light of other considerations, he still deserves to be received.

The W[orshipful]∴ continues:

"Sir, in a moment we shall require you to offer us an obligation which assures us of your discretion; this obligation must be written by you and signed in your own blood."

"B[rother]∴ Surgeon, do your duty."

Everything is prepared for a bloodletting, but when the tourniquet is put on and the B[rother]∴ Surgeon is about to stick him, the B[rother]∴ Conductor cries for mercy.

Then the W[orshipful]∴ says:

"Sir, your determination is enough for us at this moment; learn from this trial that, in all times and circumstances, you must help your Brethren and, if necessary, shed your blood for them."

After this ordeal, the W[orshipful]∴ says:

"B[rother]∴ Master of Ceremonies, present the cup of bitterness to the profane."

Then, addressing the Profane, he says:

"Sir, swallow this beverage to the dregs."

When he has drunk it (of which the B[rother]∴ Master of Ceremonies informs the W[orshipful]∴) the W[orshipful]∴ says:

"Sir, this beverage, through its bitterness, symbolizes the sorrows that are inseparable from human existence – resignation to the decrees of Providence can only lessen them."

Then, addressing the B[rother]∴ Expert, he says:

"Advance the Neophyte to the foot of the altar, to there offer his obligation. Be upstanding, to order, and sword in hand, all of you, my Brethren."

The B[rother]∴ Master of Ceremonies leads the Recipient to the altar and causes him to place his right knee on a cushion upon which is drawn a square, his left knee raised; he is caused to hold an open compass in his left hand, he presses one of its points (which must be blunted to avoid accident) against his uncovered left breast; his right hand is placed on a sword which is laid flat across the altar. The

W[orshipful]∴, having his left hand over that of the Candidate says to him:

"Sir, the obligation you are about to enter into contains nothing that could injure the respect we all owe to the law and morality, nor to our attachment and loyalty to the government."

"I warn you that it is terrible, but it is essential that you give it of your full and free will. Do you consent to that?"

The Candidate must answer "yes" with sincerity. If he refuses, attempts must be made to persuade him to do so, but if he persists obstinately he must be released.

If he consents then the W[orshipful]∴ says to him:

"Repeat after me:"

Obligation.

I swear and promise upon the general statutes of the Order, and upon this sword, the symbol of honor, before the G[reat]∴ A[rchitect]∴ of the universe,[13] to keep inviolably all the secrets entrusted to me by this R[espectable]∴ lodge, as well as all that I shall have seen done therein or heard spoken; never to write, trace, engrave, or carve them without express permission, and in such a manner as might be indicated to me. I promise to love my Brethren and to assist them according to my abilities. I furthermore promise to conform to the statutes and regulations of this R[espectable]∴ lodge. Should I commit perjurer I consent to have my throat cut, my heart and entrails torn out, and my body burned and reduced to ashes, my ashes scattered to the wind so that my memory may be held in execration by all Masons. So help me the G[reat]∴ A[rchitect]∴ of the U[niverse]∴.

After this Obligation has been said, the Candidate is led back between the two Wardens.

Then the W[orshipful]∴ says to him:

"Sir, doesn't the Obligation you have just made cause you concern? Do you have the courage to observe it? Do you agree to repeat it when you have received the light?"

After the Candidate answers in the affirmative the W[orshipful]∴ says:

Q. What do you desire?

The B[rother]∴ Junior Warden dictates to him quietly the answer he should make.

A. The light.

The W[orshipful]∴ says:

"It shall be granted to you: all of you, my Brethren, do your duty."

(That is the warning to stand up, sword in hand.)

Note: It is necessary at this event to be provided with torches with wicks, in spirit of wine, in the body of which is an inflammable powder that chemists call *lycopodium* or powdered *black colophony,* although it should be noted that the latter produces a thick, acrid smoke. These torches are made in such a way that, when they are shaken, the powder comes out

---

13 In the original manuscript dating from the late XVIIIth century the text of the Obligation includes the phrase, "in the presence of the Great Architect of the Universe, who is God," whereas in the printed edition of 1803 the words "who is God" are omitted.

and is ignited by the spirit of wine, which burns, and produces a very great flame, but it is essential to remain at a sufficient distance from the Candidate so that it is impossible for him to come to any harm.

At the first rap of the gavel all the Brethren turn towards the Recipient, at the second they direct the point of their swords towards him…[14] and at the third the blindfold is removed by a B[rother]∴ untying it from behind. It is at this moment that the torches are shaken (two or three times at the most).

The Recipient is allowed a moment of silence to contemplate the objects around him.

The W[orshipful]∴ says:

"The swords which are turned towards you inform you that all Masons will fly to your assistance, in all circumstances, if you respect the Masonic bond and if you scrupulously obey our laws, but they also inform you that you will find among us only avengers of Masonry and virtue, and that we shall always be ready to punish perjury if you are guilty of it."

The W[orshipful]∴ adds:

"B[rother]∴ Expert, bring the Neophyte closer."

The Neophyte, with the B[rother]∴ Expert on his right and the B[rother]∴ Master of Ceremonies on his left, is led by them to the foot of the altar, where he kneels as on the first occasion, and there repeats his Obligation, during which he holds one of the points of the open compass against his bare left breast.

After this Obligation, the W[orshipful]∴ strikes three raps of the gavel on the head of the compass, saying:

"Learn by the rightness of the compass to direct all the movements of your heart to good."

The W[orshipful]∴ removes the sword from under the Recipient's hand, places the blade upon the Recipient's head, and pronounces the formula of Reception in these words:

To the glory of the G[reat]∴ A[rchitect]∴ of the U[niverse]∴, in the name of the G[rand]∴ O[rient]∴ of France, with the assistance of all my Brethren both absent and present, and by virtue of the powers invested in me by this R[espectable]∴ lodge, I receive you and constitute you an Apprentice Freemason.

At the same time he strikes the blade of the sword three times with his gavel with the usual battery.

The Neophyte stands up, and the W[orshipful]∴ says to him:

"My B[rother]∴ (for that is what we shall call you from now on), receive from me the first fraternal kiss by the mysterious number of three."

If the weather is very cold then it would be proper to urge the Neophyte to go and dress by a warm fire while the W[orshipful]∴ poses some questions from the Catechism. If the weather is clement, or the Recipient has put his clothes back on, he is placed between the two B[rother]∴ Wardens, and the W[orshipful]∴ says:

"B[rother]∴ Master of Ceremonies, advance the Neophyte to the East by the three steps of an Apprentice."

He is led to the altar, to the right of the W[orshipful]∴, by the three steps of an Apprentice, which the

---

14 [Ellipsis in manuscript, presumably indicating a long pause.]

B[rother]∴ Senior Warden will show him how, by making him climb the first three steps of the temple. The steps of an Apprentice are made by bringing the right foot forward as if one wanted to take a large step, then place [the instep of] the left foot in the middle and behind the right heel, so that their approach forms a double-square.

The W[orshipful]∴ says to him, handing him the apron and gloves:

"My B[rother]∴, this apron, which you will always wear in lodge, will serve as a constant reminder that man is condemned to work and that a Mason must lead an active and laborious life."

"The gloves, by their whiteness, alert you to the candor that must always reign in the soul of an honest man and the purity of our actions."

The W[orshipful]∴ says, while handing him the ladies' gloves: "We do not admit ladies into our mysteries, but in paying homage to their virtues, we like to call them to mind during our works: here, my dear Brother, are the gloves that you will give to the woman for whom you have the most esteem."

Then the W[orshipful]∴ continues:

"In order to be admitted to our assemblies and to share that which unites us throughout the world, you must be able to make yourself recognized. I will give you the Signs, Words and Grip by which we recognize each other, and by the aid of which you will be welcomed by all Masons, wherever you may be in the world."

(He gives him the word of the Degree).

"We also have a *password* which is used among us so that we can be even more certain that the person who is presenting himself to us is a Mason."

"We also have an *order word* or *annual word*, which the G[rand]∴ O[rient]∴ of France replaces every year. All these things will become familiar to you as you practice them among us. You will learn that we make everything square, and that the number three is a mysterious number for us."

"The Sign of the Apprentice is made by bringing the extended right hand to the throat in such a way extending the index-finger from the thumb; the elbow is raised as high as the hand, which forms a horizontal line; the hand is then drawn horizontally and dropped perpendicularly. From these two movements, one horizontal and the other perpendicular, a square is formed."

"This sign reminds us of the pledge we have all made, namely that we would rather have our throats cut than reveal our mysteries. The Grip is made by taking each other's hands so that the four fingers of each are in the palm of the other's hand and the thumb is placed on the first phalanx or joint of the index finger of the other; one taps (or rather causes him to feels by unseen movements) three beats with the thumb on the knuckle, two quick and one slow, which can be indicated in this way: o o, o."

"The Sacred Word is ...[15] You see the first letter of it on this column, which is that of the North; when you are asked for it you will answer, "I can only spell it. Give me the first letter and I will give you the second."

"This word means *my strength is in God*."

---

15   Jakin / Jachin.

"The password is…[16] It is the name of the first metal worker."

"The order word or annual word is…."

Note: Serving B[rethren]∴ should never be told the Order Word or Annual Word.

The W[orshipful]∴ then gives the Neophyte the threefold fraternal kiss.

Then he says to the B[rother]∴ Master of Ceremonies:

"Conduct the B[rother]∴ to the West that he may learn to work on the rough ashlar and make himself known to the B[rothers]∴ Senior and Junior Wardens by giving to them the Words, Sign and Grip I have just communicated to him."

The B[rother]∴ Master of Ceremonies leads him to the B[rothers]∴ Senior and Junior Wardens, to whom he repeats the Words, Sign and Grip. The B[rother]∴ Junior Warden then makes him strike three raps of the gavel on the rough ashlar.

The B[rother]∴ Wardens announce that the Neophyte has repeated the Words, Sign and Grip. The Recipient stands upright and at order between the two Wardens.

The W[orshipful]∴ says:

"B[rothers]∴ Senior and Junior Wardens, invite the B[rethren]∴ who adorn your Columns to recognize in the future B[rother]∴ N∴ as an Apprentice Mason of this R[espectable]∴ lodge and to join me in applauding his initiation."

The B[rethren]∴ make the announcement.

The W[orshipful]∴ says:

"Let us applaud, my B[rethren]∴."

The customary applause is given.

The B[rother]∴ Master of Ceremonies requests the floor on the Recipient's behalf. He teaches him how to give thanks, and they join together for this purpose.

The W[orshipful]∴ calls for the Brethren to drown out the applause.

Thus the work of the initiation is completed, and everyone puts his sword back into its scabbard and sits down.

The B[rother]∴ Orator, after asking the W[orshipful]∴ for permission to speak, addresses to the newly initiated Brother some "piece of architecture"[17,] the subject of which must be some point of morality on fraternal union, on equality, on the duties of man, on turning the other cheek, or such other subjects of morality as he might prefer.

When the discourse is finished, the W[orshipful]∴ administers the Instruction, during which the B[rother]∴ Junior Warden will accompany the newly initiated B[rother]∴ to a position near the tracing-

---

16   Tubalkain / Tubal Cain.
17   *Morceau d'architectured'architecture*, i.e. a discourse.

board which, as stated, must be drawn on the floor, and with the sword to point he indicates to him the images whose symbolic meaning the W[orshipful]∴ will explain.

When the Instruction is complete, the B[rother]∴ Master of Ceremonies leads the newly initiated B[rother]∴ to the head of the column of the North, where he takes up this position for this occasion only.

The B[rethren]∴ must position themselves in lodge according to no other rank than that bestowed by the Degrees; finally, if there is no further work, the W[orshipful]∴ closes the lodge, according to the formula indicated below for the closing of the work.

Instruction.

Q. B[rother]∴ Senior Warden, are you a Mason?

A. My B[rethren]∴ recognize me as such.

Q. What is the first care of the Wardens in the lodge?

A. To see that the lodge is well tyled.

"Make sure that it is, Brother."

When the prescribed and detailed formalities for the opening of the lodge have been completed, the W[orshipful]∴ says:

Q. What is a Mason?

A. He is a free man, equally friendly of the rich and poor, if they are virtuous.

Q. What do we come to the lodge to do?

A. To conquer our passions, subdue our desires, and make further progress in Masonry.

Q. Where were you received?

A. In a just and perfect lodge.

Q. What is required for a lodge to be just and perfect?

A. Three to govern it, five to compose it, and seven to make it just and perfect.

Q. How long have you been a Mason?

A. Since I received the light.

Q. How shall I know that you are a Mason?

A. By my Signs, Words and Grip.

Q. How are the Masonic Signs made?

A. By the square, the level, and the plumb.

Q. Give me the Apprentice Sign.

A. (The Sign is given).

Q. What does this Sign mean?

A. That I would rather have my throat cut than reveal the secrets of the Masons.

Q. B[rother]∴ Junior [Warden], give the Grip to the B[rother]∴ Senior Warden.

A. The B[rother]∴ Senior Warden says: "He is just, M[ost]∴ W[orshipful]∴"

Q. Give me the Word.

A. I cannot read or write it. I can only spell it: give me the first letter and I will give you the second.

Q. What does this word mean?

A. *My strength is in God* was the name of a column of brass placed in the North of Solomon's temple, at which the Apprentices received their wages.

Q. Give me the Apprentice password.

A. (It is given).

Q. What does it mean?

A. It is the name of the son of Lamech, who invented the art of metalworking.

Q. Why did you become a Mason?

A. Because I was in a state of darkness and desired to see the light.

Q. Who introduced you to the lodge?

A. A virtuous friend, whom I later recognized as a Brother.

Q. In what state were you when you were introduced to the lodge?

A. Neither naked nor clothed, to represent the state of innocence and to remind us that virtue needs no ornament, and devoid of all metals because they are the emblem and often the occasion of vice, which the Mason must avoid.

Q. How were you introduced to the lodge?

A. By three distinct knocks.

Q. What do these three knocks mean?

A. *Ask* and you shall receive; *seek* and you shall find; *knock* and it shall be opened to you.

Q. What did these three knocks procure for you?

A. An Expert, who asked me my forename, my surname, my age, my nationality, and if it was my will to be received as a Mason.

Q. What did the B[rother]∴ Expert do with you?

A. He led me into the lodge between the two Wardens, and made me travel, as an Apprentice mason must do, in order to familiarize me with the difficulties one encounters in becoming a Mason.

Q. What happened to you then?

A. The Master of the lodge, with the unanimous consent of all the Brethren, received me as a Mason.

Q. How did he receive you?

A. With all the required formalities.

Q. What are these formalities?

A. I had my right knee bare on the square, my right hand on the sword; with the left I held a compassed opened in a square, the point resting on the left breast which was bared.

Q. What did you do in this posture?

A. I assumed the obligation to keep the secrets of the Order.

Q. What did you see when you entered the lodge?

A. Nothing, M[ost]∴ W[orshipful]∴

Q. What did you see when you were given the light?

A. I saw the Sun, the Moon, and the Master of the lodge.

Q. What relationship can there be between these stars and the Master of the lodge?

A. As the Sun rules the day and the Moon governs the night, so the Master presides over the lodge to enlighten it.

Q. Where does the Master of the lodge stand?

A. In the East.

Q. Why?

A. As the Sun rises in the East to open the day's work, so the Master stands in the East to open the lodge, illuminate the work, and to set the craftsmen to labor.

Q. Where do the Wardens stand?

A. In the West.

Q. Why?

A. To assist the W[orshipful]∴ in his work, to pay the craftsmen, and send them away satisfied.

Q. Where are the Apprentices located?

A. In the North because they can only bear a feeble light.

Q. What is the name of your lodge?

A. The lodge of St. John.

Closing.

Q. How old are you?

A. Three years old, W[orshipful]∴

Q. At what hour do the Masons usually close their works?

A. At midnight.

Q. What hour is it?

A. It is midnight, W[orshipful]∴

"Since it is midnight, Brother Senior, and Junior Wardens, and this is the hour at which Masons are accustomed to close their work, invite the B[rethren]∴ of each Column to close the Apprentice work in the R[espectable]∴ lodge of... at the O[rient]∴ of..."

The Wardens make the announcement.

After the announcement, the W[orshipful]∴ strikes three raps with his gavel with the usual battery. Each Warden strikes the same number, and at this moment all the B[rethren]∴ rise and come to order.

The W[orshipful]∴ says:

"With me, B[rethren]∴"

All make the sign of the apprentice, and the work is completed with the triple battery and the triple *vivat*.

Work of the Banquet.

The room where the banquet is held should be situated so that nothing can be seen or heard from outside. The table, as far as possible, will, be horseshoe shaped: the seat of the W[orshipful]∴ is at the head, and those of the Wardens at the ends.

The B[rother]∴ Orator seats himself at the head of the column of the South, and the B[rother]∴ Secretary at the head of the column of the North, while the West is occupied by the B[rother]∴ Visitors or, if there are none, by the lodge Officers.

Except for the five Officers just named, no one has an assigned seat, except in the case there are visitors decorated with higher degrees, and the E[ast]∴, is occupied by them; the other visitors would be seated at the head of the columns.

Bread is called	*Rough ashlar.*
Wine,	*Strong powder, white or red.*
Bottles,	*Barrels.*

Decanters,	*The same.*
Water,	*Weak powder.*
Plates,	*Tiles.*
Courses of the meal/dishes,	*Boards.*
Burning candles,	*Stars.*
Spoons,	*Trowels.*
Forks,	*Pickaxes.*
Napkins,	*Flags.*
Knives,	*Swords.*
Glasses,	*Cannons.*
Liqueurs,	*Fulminating powder.*

When each has taken his place, it is at the desire of the W[orshipful]∴ to lead the first health before eating or to wait until the soup has been eaten, or at such other moment as he sees fit. When he is ready to propose the first health he gives one rap of the gavel. The Serving B[rethren]∴ immediately come out from within the horseshoe and retire to the West (the same procedure is followed in all the healths). Everyone stops eating. The B[rother]∴ Master of Ceremonies usually stands alone within the horseshoe opposite the W[orshipful]∴ in order to be in a better position both to receive orders and to carry them out, although sometimes he is placed at a small table between the two Wardens. The B[rother]∴ Master of Ceremonies then rises and the W[orshipful]∴ says:

"Brother Senior and Junior Wardens, ascertain that our work is well tyled."

Each of the Wardens satisfies himself of the Masonic quality of all the individuals who are at his Column by casting his eye over them and recognizing them as Masons.

The Junior Warden says to the B[rother]∴ Senior Warden: "I answer for my Column."

The Senior Warden says: "M[ost]∴ W[orshipful]∴, the B[rother]∴ Junior Warden and I are satisfied of the B[rethren]∴ that are on the two Columns."

The W[orshipful]∴ says:

"I answer for those in the East."

"B[rother]∴ Tyler, do your duty."

During this time the B[rethren]∴ adorn themselves with their cordons; an apron is not necessary.

The B[rother]∴ Tyler goes to remove the key from the door which he closes, and hence no one enters or exits anymore.

The Junior Warden informs the Senior that the work is tyled, the latter announces it aloud to the W[orshipful]∴, who raps a blow of the gavel and says:

"My B[rethren]∴, the labor, which was suspended, is resumed."

Note: If, before going to the banquet, they had been closed, they would have to be opened again.

The B[rothers]∴ Senior and Junior Wardens repeat the announcement, after which the W[orshipful]∴ says:

"To order, my B[rethren]∴"

First Health.

Then the W[orshipful]∴ says:

"B[rothers]∴ Senior and Junior Wardens, invite the B[rethren]∴ of each Column to prepare to charge and line up, for the first obligatory health."

The B[rother]∴ Wardens repeat the announcement.

The W[orshipful]∴ says:

"Let us charge and align, my Brethren."

(Note. It is only at this moment should the barrels must be touched, otherwise confusion will arise in the work). Each pours himself a drink as he pleases. If any Brother prefers to drink water out of dietary preference or personal taste then no one must be allowed to pressurize him to change his habits. As each Brother pours himself a drink he places his *cannon* (glass) slightly to the right of his *tile* (plate), at a distance from the edge of the table corresponding roughly to the diameter of the *tile*: this enables the *cannons t*o be immediately aligned.

They also align the *barrels* and *stars* on a second line.

When everything is aligned on the North column, the Junior Warden notifies the Senior who says to the W[orshipful]∴, "All is aligned on both columns."

The W[orshipful]∴ says:

"So in the east; rise to order, with sword in hand."

All rise, the *flag* is over their forearms; the B[rethren]∴ decorated with high degrees put it over the shoulder; They hold the *sword* (if they have any) or a knife with the left hand, and are in order on their right. (If the table is made in a horseshoe the B[rethren]∴ who are on the inside remain seated.)

The W[orshipful]∴ says:

"B[rothers]∴ Senior and Junior Wardens, will you please announce on your Columns that the first obligatory health is to the French Republic and its Government; to this health we shall add our best wishes for their military success. For a health so precious to us I invite you to produce the best possible fire."[18]

---

18   1785 VARIATION.
"B[rothers]∴ Senior and Junior Wardens, will you kindly announce on your Columns that the first obligatory health is to the King our Monarch, to the Queen his august Consort, and to all the Sovereign-protectors of the Masons; to this health we shall add our best wishes for the prosperity of France. For a health so precious to us I invite you to produce the best possible fusillade. I reserve the right to give the orders to fire."
1805 VARIATION.
"B[rothers]∴ Senior and Junior Wardens, will you kindly announce on your Columns that the first obligatory health is to H[is]∴ Imperial M[ajesty]∴ and his august family; to this health we shall add our best wishes for their military success. For a health so precious to us I invite you to produce the best possible fusillade."

The B[rothers]∴ Senior and Junior Wardens repeat this announcement.

When the announcement has been made, the W[orshipful]∴ says:

"Attention my B[rethren]∴ hand to arms! Take aim! Fire! (they drink, and repeat the cannon forward) good fire! (they drink, etc.) the sharpest of fires! (they drink, and one holds one's cannon at about chin height, and against the shoulder) arms forward: one, two, three, (for these three beats, one carries the *cannon* to the left breast, then to the right, then forward); one, two, three! (they repeat the same movements) one, two, three: (they repeat again), and at the stroke of time, forward, they pause there while waiting for the order of the W[orshipful]∴ who informs them to lay down their *cannons,* by three beats, saying "One, two, and three". (At this last beat, all the *cannons* must strike the table once and in unison.) The then applaud by the triple battery and the triple *vivat*.

After which, the W[orshipful]∴ says:

"Let us be seated, Brethren."

The Wardens repeat this.

As long as the work remains in force it is permissible to continue eating, but this must be done in silence.

Second Health.

Sometimes, and this and this is even most suitable for the convenience of everyone, and so as not to interrupt the service, the W[orshipful]∴ orders the second health, as soon as the first is done.

If he does not think fit to have it fired immediately, it is proper to suspend the labor.

If the W[orshipful]∴ has suspended the labor before proposing the Second Health, he must resume; if they paused, he commands it away, and says:

"B[rothers]∴ Senior and Junior Wardens, please invite the B[rethren]∴ of both columns, to prepare to charge and align, for the second obligatory health."

The B[rother]∴ Wardens repeat the announcement.

The W[orshipful]∴ says:

"Let us charge and align, my Brethren."

When everybody has loaded and aimed as above, the Wardens announce this and the W[orshipful]∴ says:

"B[rothers]∴ Senior and Junior Wardens, the second obligatory health which I have the favor of proposing is to the G[rand]∴ O[rient]∴ of France, and all the Officers who compose it; we will join to it a health to all the W[orshipful]∴ M[aster]∴ of the regular lodges, and of their deputies to the G[rand]∴ O[rient]∴ of France; all the Correspondence lodges, and the foreign Orients; finally, we will add our wishes for the prosperity of the Order in general. Invite, I pray you, the B[rethren]∴ of both Columns to join me in making the most Masonic and fraternal fire."

The Wardens repeat; the health is taken, and they applaud as at the first.

If a health has been drunk to any of the Brethren, such as an Officer of the G[rand]∴ O[rient]∴ of France, the W[orshipful]∴ of a regular lodge, or the deputy of a lodge, then such Brethren do not have to drink the health, and can either sit or stand as they please, and when the applause is over they should ask as a body to thank the Brother proposing the health. During these gestures of thanks the Brethren remain standing.

When, after the health has been drunk, they start applauding then the lodge should drown out that applause on the orders of the W[orshipful]∴

When it is all over, the W[orshipful]∴ gives one rap of the gavel and says:

"My Brethren, let us return to our seats."

Then the Master may suspend the labors or leave it in force.

Third Health.

At the time when the Wardens think it appropriate, and especially when he is not on duty, the Senior Warden gives one rap of the gavel, which is repeated by the Junior and then by the W[orshipful]∴ The W[orshipful]∴ then says immediately:

"What do you desire, my B[rother]∴?"

If the labors are suspended then the Senior Warden asks the W[orshipful]∴ to resume them, which he does in these words:

"My B[rethren]∴, at the request of the B[rother]∴ Senior Warden, the labors which were suspended resume activity."

The Wardens repeat the announcement.

After that the Senior Warden raps a stroke of the gavel, which is repeated by the Junior, then by the W[orshipful]∴, and says: "M[ost]∴ W[orshipful]∴, be pleased to charge and align for a health which the B[rother]∴ Junior Warden, the B[rother]∴ Orator and I will have the honor of to propose."

The W[orshipful]∴ charges and aligns, as in the previous Healths. When he is informed that everything is in order, he says:

"B[rother]∴ Senior Warden, announce the health you desire to offer"

The B[rother]∴ Senior Warden says: "It is a health to the W[orshipful]∴, M[ost]∴ W[orshipful]∴ Rise and to order, sword in hand, my Brethren. The health that the Junior Warden, the B[rother]∴ Orator and I have the pleasure of proposing to you is to the M[ost]∴ W[orshipful]∴, who directs the work of this R[espectable]∴ lodge, and that of all who belong to it. Please join us in producing the best fire possible."

The Junior Warden repeats and says: "The health which the Senior Warden, the B[rother]∴ Orator and I, etc.

The Orator repeats the same.

The B[rother]∴ Senior Warden says: "With me, Brethren," and commands the drill or defers the command to the Junior Warden to do so, as he sees fit. He then asks for applause and the *vivat*.

During this health, the W[orshipful]∴ is seated, whereas all the B[rethren]∴ remain standing and to order. When the W[orshipful]∴ has given thanks, the B[rother]∴ Senior Warden says: "With me, B[rethren]∴" and orders the Brethren to drown out the applause. Everyone takes their seats.

The W[orshipful]∴ suspends the labors as he sees fit, or leaves them active.

Fourth Health.

Sometime later, the W[orshipful]∴ resumes the labors, if not already, and causes them to charge for a health.

When all are charges and aligned, he proposes the health of the B[rothers]∴ Senior and Junior Wardens. The B[rother]∴ Orator and the B[rother]∴ Secretary will repeat his announcement.

The W[orshipful]∴ orders the health to be drunk. All the B[rethren]∴ remain seated and the Wardens alone rise. The B[rother]∴ Wardens express their thanks standing, with the B[rother]∴ Senior Warden acting as spokesman.

The W[orshipful]∴ orders the applause to be drowned out.

Fifth Health.

The W[orshipful]∴ then commands, at the moment that seems to him most suitable, the healths of the visiting Brethren. During this health the Visitors stand. They then returns thanks, one of them acting as spokesman. The W[orshipful]∴ covers their applause.

To this fifth health will be added that of the affiliated or corresponding lodges; but if there are no visitors or corresponding lodges, then one will detach from the sixth health that of officers of the lodge. The Orator speaks to return thanks.

Note: After the health to the Visitors, if any B[rother]∴ has songs to sing or a piece of architecture to be read, he can do so by asking to speak.

It is even appropriate at this point to sing some hymns which were made for the purposes of Masonry, and which, sung in chorus, carry in the soul a sweet emotion, by celebrating the advantages of the Masonic union.

Sixth Health.

The health of the B[rethren]∴ Officers and Members of the lodge: to this is added that of the newly initiated Brethren, if there are any. This health is celebrated only by the W[orshipful]∴, the Wardens, and the visiting Brethren if any. The Officers and Members of the R[espectable]∴ lodge stand and return thanks. The B[rother]∴ Orator returns thanks for the Officers, the most senior member for the Members, and one of the Initiates, if there are any, for the others.

Their applause should be drowned out.

Seventh and Final Health.

Finally, the W[orshipful]∴ asks the B[rother]∴ Master of Ceremonies to introduce the Serving Brethren, who bring with them their *flags* and *cannons*.

When they have entered and been placed in the West between the two Wardens, the W[orshipful]∴ gives one rap of the gavel and invites the Brethren to load and aim for the final obligatory health.

The Brother Wardens each strike one rap with their gavel and repeat his announcement.

The W[orshipful]∴ says:

"Let us charge and align, my Brethren."

Everyone loads and aims. When the W[orshipful]∴ is notified that everything is loaded and aimed, he says:

"Rise and to order, Brethren, sword in hand."

All rise, each gives and end of their flag to their neighbors, on his right and left, taking an end of theirs in the same way with their left hand, which does not prevent them from holding the sword with the same hand. The Serving Brethren form, with the Wardens, the same chain, the B[rother]∴ Master of Ceremonies in their midst.

Then the W[orshipful]∴ says:

"Brothers Senior and Junior Wardens, the last obligatory health is that to all Masons spread over the face of the earth, whether in prosperity and in adversity. Let us address our desires to the G[rand]∴ A[rchitect]∴ of the U[niverse]∴ that He may help the unfortunate and lead travelers to safe haven. Invite, I pray you, the B[rethren]∴ of both columns to unite with us, to carry this health with the best of all fires."

The Wardens repeat.

Then the W[orshipful]∴ sings the closing hymn, of which only these last two verses are usually sung:

Brethren and Fellows

of Masonry, }*In chorus, after the W[orshipful]∴ has sung it.*

Without sorrow, let us enjoy,

the pleasures of life,

Furnished with a red border

Thrice the signal of our glasses }*In chorus, after the W[orshipful]∴ has sung it.*

Is a proof of accord

We drink to our Brethren.

Let us join hand-in-hand;

Let us stand together: }*In chorus, id.*

Give thanks to fate;

For the bond which joins us;

And let us be sure

That it is drunk on both hemispheres,   } *In chorus, id.*

There is no more illustrious health

Than those of our Brethren.

 The W[orshipful]∴ says:

"Attention, my Brethren. Hand to arms. Raise arms. Take aim! Fire! Good fire! Triple fire! Advance arms! (they repeat the last two verses three times). One! Two! Three! One! Two! Three! One! Two! Three! Advance arms! One, Two and Three!"

They applause, and sing the last reprise three times.

The W[orshipful]∴ gives one rap of the gavel, which the Wardens repeat, and he says:

Q. B[rother]∴ Senior Warden, how old are you?

A. Three years old, W[orshipful]∴

Q. At what hour do we usually close our labors?

A. At midnight.

Q. What is the hour, B[rother]∴ Junior Warden?

A. It is midnight.

Since it is midnight, etc., (the formula is the same as that used to close the Apprentice lodge. It is a praiseworthy custom to give each other the fraternal kiss before taking leave of each other. The W[orshipful]∴ bestows it upon his neighbor on his right, and it returns to him from the left.

The W[orshipful]∴ orders the Minutes of the Banquet to be read out. He asks for comments, and applause is given. Then he asks if there are any interesting suggestions for the good of the Order in general and for that of the lodge in particular.

If there are any, they are listened to and voted upon if they are brief. If they require more extended discussion they are deferred to the next meeting of the lodge.

The W[orshipful]∴ strikes three raps with his gavel, and says:

"Brethren, the labors are closed; let us retire in peace."

The Wardens repeat this.

Everyone removes his regalia and retires.

THE

REGULATOR

OF THE MASON.

~~~~~~~~~~~~~~~~~~~

HEREDOM,

The year of the G[reat]∴ L[ight]∴ 5801.

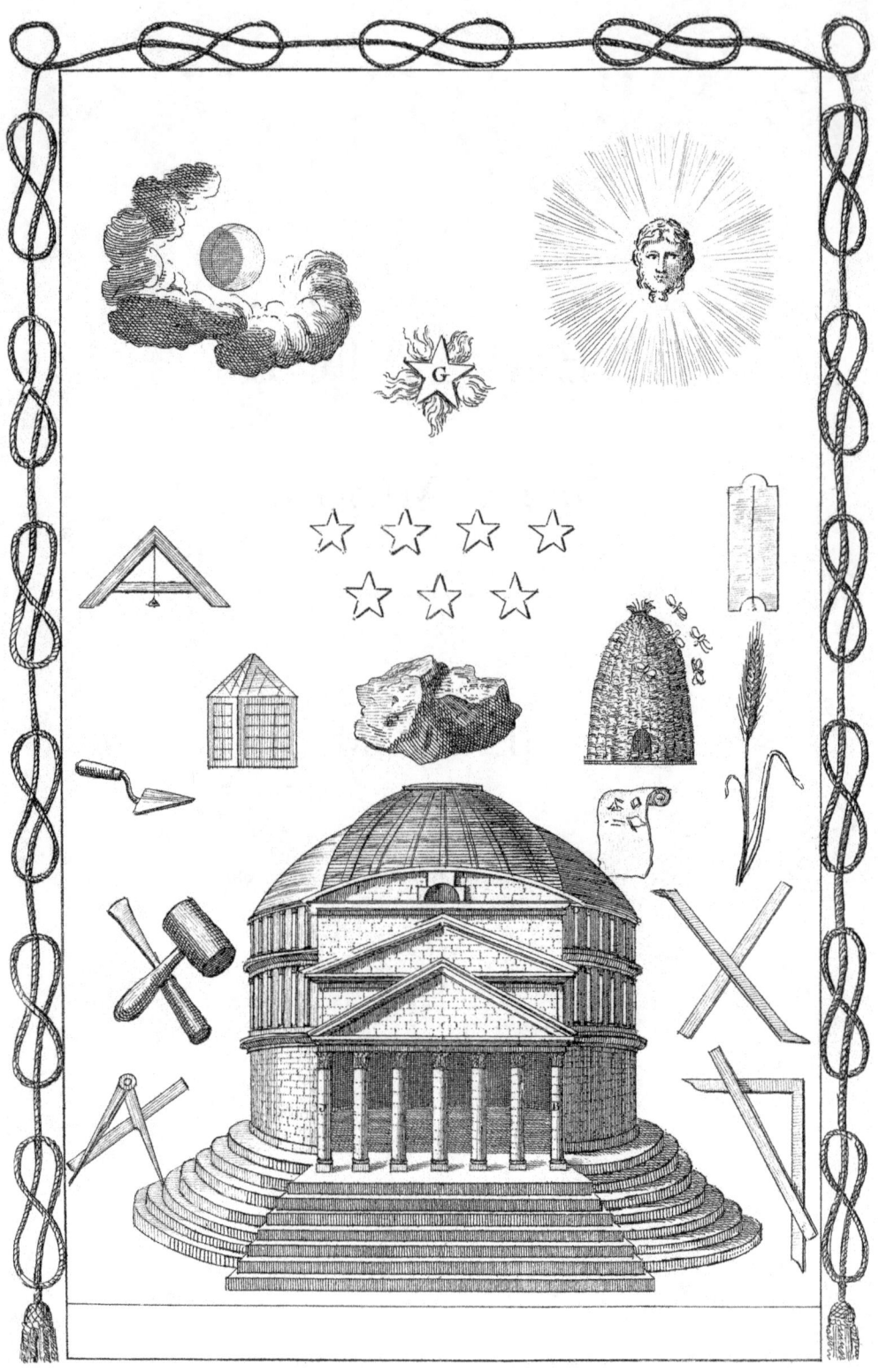

Part 2—Ritual Ancestry and the Scottish Rite Blue Degrees

THE REGULATOR
OF THE MASON.

DEGREE OF FELLOW CRAFT.

FIRST SECTION.
Preliminaries.

An Apprentice may not be admitted to the degree of Fellow Craft until he has served his time, which shall be five ▫. of Instruction in the workshop where he received the Light. He must also be of the age stipulated by the regulations, which is 23 years or more.

Any Apprentice who believes that he possesses the necessary qualities to be promoted to the Degree of Fellow Craft shall apply in confidence to the B[rother]∴ Junior Ward[en]∴ on whose Column and under whose supervision he has had to work since his Reception.

At a suitable pause in the labor the Junior Warden will say:

"M[ost]∴ W[orshipful]∴, B[rother]∴ N∴, an Apprentice of this R[espectable]∴ ▫∴ has asked me to seek on his behalf the favor of being admitted to the degree of Fellow Craft."

The W[orshipful]∴ will ask the Apprentice to stand between the two Ward[ens]∴ where he will be examined on the instruction of the First Degree, after which the W[orshipful]∴ will order him to tyle the temple.

After the Recipient has exited, the W[orshipful]∴ will add: "Brother Senior and Junior Ward[en]∴, please invite the Brethren of each column to comment on B[rother]∴ N∴'s application."

NOTE: When all the comments have been heard (and all Brethren, including Apprentices, are invited to submit them) the W[orshipful]∴ shall order the Apprentices to tyle the temple. When the Apprentices have withdrawn the W[orshipful]∴ will open the labor in the manner to be detailed hereafter.

After the work has been opened the W[orshipful]∴ will say: "Brother Senior and Junior Ward[en]∴, announce on each column that the Apprentice B[rother]∴ N∴ is being proposed for admission to the Degree of Fellow Craft: invite the Brethren to make their comments."

The B[rother]∴ Senior Ward[en]∴ says: "B[rother]∴ Junior Ward[en]∴, Brethren who adorn the column of the South," etc.

The B[rother]∴ Junior Ward[en]∴ repeats the following:

"The lodge, which is presently composed only of Masters and Fellow Crafts, will consider any comments that may have been made by the Apprentices as well as any new comments, and it shall be free to postpone the proposal to another day if shortage of time or the nature and urgency of the subsequent labor does not allow it to be discussed thoroughly or if further clarification is necessary."

If a decision is made to deliberate upon the matter immediately after all the comments have been heard, then B[rother]∴ Orator will argue either for the admission of the Recipient or for a delay. B[rother]∴ Master of Ceremonies will distribute the ballots and a B[rother]∴ Expert will perform the Balloting and carry the ballot-box to the W[orshipful]∴ who, in the presence of another Expert, will count the ballots and announce the result in the usual manner, which announcement will be repeated by the Wardens.

A two-thirds vote is required for admission. If the vote is favorable then the W[orshipful]∴ will invite the Brother Ward[en]∴ to ask the Brethren of the two Columns to applaud it.

The Ward[en]∴ will repeat the announcement.

After this the W[orshipful]∴ says:

"With me, Brethren!"

The Brethren then applaud in the manner to be explained below.

The W[orshipful]∴ then announces that the labor of the Fellow Crafts is closed, after which the Apprentices shall be brought in.

The W[orshipful]∴ announces either that B[rother]∴ N∴ has been approved for admission to the Degree of Fellow Craft, that the ▫∴ has postponed a decision on the matter to another day, or that the B[rother]∴ has been asked to re-apply at another time.

~~~~~~~~~~~~~~~~~~~

SECOND SECTION.

~~~~~~~~~~~~~~~~~~~

FIRST PRELIMINARY.

All members of the lodge must have been summoned in the usual manner for the day of the meeting as indicated by the W[orshipful]∴, the letters of invitation announcing a "Reception in the Second Degree," so that those whose business prevented them from attending the previous meeting may attend this one and cast their vote at it. The invitation that the Secretary will send to the Apprentices must not mention the labor, which they cannot attend.

~~~~~~~~~~~~~~~~~~~

SECOND PRELIMINARY.

~~~~~~~~~~~~~~~~~~~

On the day stipulated for the Reception, all the B[rethren]∴ shall be allowed to attend the lodge. The W[orshipful]∴ will open the Apprentice lodge and, after the Minutes of the last meeting have been read out and have received the customary approval, the W[orshipful]∴ will order all the Apprentices to withdraw.

If there is no other work to be done than that of a Fellow Craft or if there is no Banquet on that day then the Apprentices will not be invited. The only Apprentices admitted will have to wait in the Vestibule.

The Preparing B[rother]∴ will, on being ordered to do so by the W[orshipful]∴, fetch the Aspirant and conduct him to the Chamber of Reflection, and remain with him there until he is summoned for his Reception.

At this moment, the Blazing Star will be drawn with a G∴ in the middle of it, and the column of the South will be illuminated to reveal a transparent B[rother]∴ as well as the Blazing Star, which must, if practicable, be fixed to the ceiling of the lodge in the midst of a sky spangled with stars or, if that is not possible, above the W[orshipful]∴, either above or below the canopy.

Once all this has done the W[orshipful]∴ opens the lodge in the following manner.

~~~~~~~~~~~~~~~~~~~~

OPENING OF THE WORK OF THE LODGE.

~~~~~~~~~~~~~~~~~~~~

The W[orshipful]∴ gives one rap of the gavel which the Ward[ens]∴ repeat, and says:

"My Brethren, be upstanding, sword in hand."

(Which everyone does). Then he adds: "Brother Senior and Junior Ward[en]∴, make sure that all the Brethren on your Column are Fellow Crafts."

Although it is very easy for the Ward[en]∴ to ascertain by simple inspection whether all the Brethren are Fellow Crafts, especially if there are no unknown Visitors, since they must know the Degrees that each of them has achieved, it is nonetheless appropriate for each Warden∴ to go through his Column and ask each B[rother]∴ for the Words, Sign and Grip of the Degree. This formality also helps the Brethren to remember something that they quite commonly forget for want of practice.

When the Ward[ens]∴ have made their rounds they return to their places, each reporting to the W[orshipful]∴ on the outcome of the task he has set them.

When the W[orshipful]∴ has been assured by the report of the Ward[ens]∴ that all the B[rethren]∴ are Fellow Crafts, he says:

"Come to order, Brethren!" (this command will be explained later).

The W[orshipful]∴ will pose the following five questions to the Ward[ens]∴ alternately:

Q. B[rother]∴ Senior Ward[en]∴ are you a Fellow Craft?

A. I am.

Q. Why did you become a Fellow Craft?

A. To know the letter G∴

Q. How old are you?

A. Five years old.

Q. At what hour do the Fellow Crafts start work?

A. At noon.

Q. What hour is it?

A. It is noon.

The W[orshipful]∴ says:

"Since it is noon and this is the hour at which Masons are accustomed to open the work of the Fellow Crafts, Brother Senior, and Junior Ward[ens]∴, invite the Brethren on each of your Columns to join with me in opening that work."

The B[rother]∴ Ward[ens]∴ repeat the announcement.

After the announcement, the W[orshipful]∴ strikes the altar five times with the gavel, giving three fast raps followed by two slow ones, which can be represented as follows: o o o, o o.

These five raps will be repeated in like manner by the Ward[ens]∴, after which the W[orshipful]∴ says:

"With me, Brethren!"

All together make the Sign, then perform the battery by five repeated three times, after which the W[orshipful]∴ says:

"The work of the Fellow Crafts is open."

The Ward[ens]∴ repeat this, and all the Brethren then take their places.

The work of the Fellow Crafts now being in force, the W[orshipful]∴ again states the object of the meeting and, after proposing the B[rother]∴ to be admitted to the Degree of Fellow Craft, he invites the Brother Ward[ens]∴ to ask for comments. If no comments are made then he asks for the sign of approval (raising of the hand).

If the votes are in favor of the Asp[irant]∴ then the W[orshipful]∴ tells the M[aster]∴ of Ceremonies to send word to the Preparing B[rother]∴ that the Asp[irant]∴ must be fetched and introduced.

The Aspirant, now prepared, i.e. clothed as an Apprentice, and unarmed, will be brought to the door of the temple where he will knock as an Apprentice.

B[rother]∴ Tyler then informs the Junior Warden∴ of this in a low voice. The Junior Ward[en]∴ informs the Senior in the same manner, and he informs the W[orshipful]∴ of this audibly.

The W[orshipful]∴ says:

"Go and see who is knocking like this."

This order reaches the B[rother]∴ Tyler via the Senior Warden∴ who passes it on to the Junior. The latter then passes it to the B[rother]∴ Ty[ler]∴.

The B[rother]∴ Tyler opens the door and asks who is knocking.

The B[rother]∴ Expert (or the Preparing Brother) answers:

"It is an Apprentice who is seeking admission to the Degree of Fellow Craft."

The B[rother]∴ Tyler closes the door and passes this reply to the W[orshipful]∴ just like the first time.

The W[orshipful]∴ says:

"Ask him if he has served his time, if he believes that his Master is pleased with him, and if this is his ultimate wish."

When the W[orshipful]∴ has received the Recipient's response, once again by the same route, he will say:

"Have the Apprentice brought in."

As the Recipient is brought in all the Brethren stand up, take their swords in their right hands, and stand in that attitude without actually being at order until otherwise instructed.

The Aspirant will be led between the two Ward[ens]∴ by the three steps of the Apprentice. He will stand there, having come to order as an Apprentice, with his feet in square.

The W[orshipful]∴ will ask him several questions taken from the Apprentice Degree.

NOTE: Care must be taken to ensure that the Recipient has some knowledge of the Degree of Apprentice, otherwise the question asked of him as to whether "his Master is pleased with him" would be meaningless.

The W[orshipful]∴ will then introduce the Recipient to the 5∴ journeys:

"My B[rother]∴, the knowledge you have acquired since you were first admitted to our Mysteries should have enabled you to acquire an understanding of the emblems that accompany the Reception of an Apprentice. We have given you the first inklings, that is to say we have opened up to you the path of knowledge which the common man cannot attain. The further you go, the more satisfying will be the discoveries you will make by dint of sheer hard work. Reflect carefully upon all the emblems that will accompany your Reception."

"B[rother]∴ Expert, have him make the first journey."

The B[rother]∴ Expert will present the Recipient with a mallet and chisel to hold in his left hand while he leads him by the right hand on a journey starting at the South.

When the Recipient arrives back in the West, the W[orshipful]∴ will say to him:

"My B[rother]∴, this first journey illustrates for you the year that every Fellow Craft must devote to instructing himself in the quality and the use of his materials, and to perfecting himself in the practice of cutting and carving the stones that he has had to learn to fashion with the gavel and chisel during his apprenticeship."

The meaning of this Emblem is that an Apprentice, whatever knowledge he may think he has acquired, is still far from being able to finish his work; that the roughness and superfluities of the materials dedicated to the construction of the temple that he is raising to the G[reat]∴ A[rchitect]∴ of the U[niverse]∴ and of which he is both the material and the craftsman, have not yet been removed; that he cannot dispense with the hard and painful work of the gavel and the careful and precise manipulation of the chisel; and that he must never deviate from the line that a skillful M[aster]∴ has drawn for him.

"Br[other]∴ Expert, have him make the second journey."

During this journey, the Recipient will hold a compass and a rule in his left hand. On his return to the West the W[orshipful]∴ will say to him:

"My B[rother]∴, this journey teaches you that, during his second year, a Fellow Craft must master the elements of practical masonry, that is to say how to trace lines on fashioned and dressed materials. That is why you have been equipped with a compass and a rule. This Emblem presents to your mind a very evident truth in the course of human life, as well as among us, namely that ignorance is our first state. Learned men then take care of our childhood and teach us the first elements of the various branches of learning. Our first attempts with our hands are compromised by the weakness of the condition in which we are born. Soon, education opens the way to the various branches of knowledge, and it is to acquire a mastery of them that our youth is particularly devoted until more thoughtful investigation leads us to the discovery of the truth."

"B[rother]∴ Expert, have him make the third journey."

The Recipient hands back the compass which he has been holding, but retains the rule which he shall hold in his left hand while supporting with the same hand a crowbar or lever (*pince*) which rests upon his left shoulder.[19]

Upon his return to the West the W[orshipful]∴ will say:

"My B[rother]∴, this journey symbolizes to you the kind of work a Fellow Craft did during his third year. He was entrusted with the handling of cut stones and other materials. This job presupposed enough knowledge to judge from their shape the place for which they were most suitable, which is why you need a rule. Moving the stones to their destination requires both intelligence and strength. The knowledge that the Fellow Craft has acquired is sufficient to provide the former, while the crowbar makes up for what he lacks in natural vigor. As he was assisted in this work by Apprentices, so it is to the Fellow Crafts that we entrust the care of directing and supervising the Apprentices, under the watchful eye, however, of the M[aster]∴ whom they serve."

"B[rother]∴ Expert, have him make the fourth journey."

The Apprentice will hold a square and a rule in his left hand while holding on to his Conductor with his right.

Upon returning to the West the W[orshipful]∴ will say:

"My B[rother]∴, by this journey we wish to symbolize to you the fourth year of a Fellow Craft, during which he is occupied in the construction and erection of buildings, directing the whole project, and checking the correctness of the laying of the stones and the use of the materials."

This symbolizes the superiority that men acquire over their fellows by zeal, diligence, and the eminence of their knowledge even when they seek it least. Instruct your Brethren therefore by giving them useful lessons, guiding their steps into the paths of virtue, and edifying them by your example."

---

19 In the building-trade a *pince* is an iron lever some 2, 3 or 4 feet in length with a chisel-point at each end, but bent at one end to enable stones to be laid or loads raised by turning it into a lever of the first order [fulcrum in the middle, and load and effort at opposite ends] or second order [load in the middle, and fulcrum and effort at opposite ends] according to need. This *pince* can be made of oak painted black.

"B[rother]∴ Expert, have him make the fifth journey."

During this journey, the Recipient will not carry any tools and will be led by the right hand. On his return to the West the W[orshipful]∴ will say to him:

"B[rother]∴, this journey symbolizes to you the fifth year of the Fellow Craft's time. Now that he is sufficiently instructed in the practice of his art the Fellow Craft must devote this year to the study of theory – that is why your hands are free. It is to the work of the mind that you must now devote yourself. Learn from this emblem that it is not enough for an assiduous education to set us on the path of virtue, for if we are left to our own devices we are soon diverted from it unless continuous effort and constant study keep us on our guard against the seductions of vice and the ardor of the passions. Learn also that all your steps must be directed towards a knowledge of the truth, which is the sole aim we propose. Follow, then, the road that has been marked out for you, and make yourself worthy of being subsequently admitted to new knowledge."

"B[rother]∴ Expert, let the Recipient be shown the five mysterious steps of the temple, so that from there he may discover the Blazing Star and the letter G∴ that adorns its center."

(When the Apprentice has reached the fifth step, the W[orshipful]∴ will say to him:)

"My B[rother]∴, look upon this mysterious Star. Never lose sight of it, for it is the emblem of the genius that raises us to great things, and with still more reason it is also the symbol of that sacred fire and that portion of the divine light with which the G[reat]∴ A[rchitect]∴ of the U[niverse]∴ has formed our souls, and by the rays of which we can distinguish, know, and practice truth and justice."

"The letter G∴ which you see in the center presents to us two great and sublime ideas. First, it is the monogram of one of the names of the Most High, the source of all light, of all knowledge. The second idea that this letter presents to us is derived from that which is commonly explained by the word geometry: this science has as its essential basis the application of the property of numbers to the dimensions of bodies, and above all to the triangle, to which almost all their figures relate, and which provides us with such sublime emblems."

"B[rother]∴ Expert, send the Recipient to the East by the steps of the Fellow Craft preceded by those of the Apprentice."

The Aspirant will take the three steps of Apprentice, which will lead him to the foot of the steps of the temple, that is to say to the lower edge of the tracing-board. He is then asked to ascend five of the seven steps of the temple, after which he is asked to take the three steps of the Fellow Craft. The first∴ to the South, the second to the North, and the third to the East.

At the first∴ step, one drags the right foot diagonally and places the left foot behind it in a double square, at the second step one carries the left foot diagonally and places the right foot behind it, again in a double square, and at the third, which is that of repose, one drags the right foot diagonally and then forms the single square with the left foot.

This irregular step symbolizes a Fellow Craft's right to move from one Master to another and to change his work as the need arises.

He is then led to the East, where, with his right knee on the kneeler and his left knee in square, he pronounces the following Obligation.

OBLIGATION.

"I swear and promise to the G[reat]∴ A[rchitect]∴ of the U[niverse]∴ between your hands most W[orshipful]∴, and to all my B[rethren]∴ under the oath of my first obligation, to keep and preserve faithfully the secrets that are to be entrusted to me and not to communicate them to Apprentices in any manner whatsoever. In the event of a breach of this obligation I submit myself to the penalties stated in my first Obligation."

During the swearing of this Obligation the Bro. Expert will stand on the right of the Recipient and the M[aster]∴ of Ceremonies on his left, with all the B[rethren]∴ standing in order, sword in hand. After the Obligation the W[orshipful]∴ will place the blade of his sword on the Recipient's head and give five light raps of the gavel upon it according to the battery indicated, saying: "To the glory of the G[reat]∴ A[rchitect]∴ of the U[niverse]∴, in the name of the G[rand]∴ O[rient]∴ of France, and by virtue of the powers invested in me by this R[espectable]∴ L[odge]∴, I receive you and constitute you a Fellow Craft Mason;"

The Recipient stands up and the W[orshipful]∴ says to him:

"My B[rother]∴, in this Degree as well as in the previous one, we have a Sacred Word, a Password, a Sign and a Grip, as well as a way of coming to order."

"Coming to order involves placing the right hand on the heart with the four fingers close together and the thumb raised, thus forming a square."

"The Sign is made by coming to order, withdrawing the hand and forearm from left to right horizontally to below the shoulder and then dropping the hand perpendicularly, thus forming a square."

"This Sign reminds us of one of the points of our first pledge, to have our hearts torn out rather than reveal our secrets."

"The Grip is made by tapping three times with the thumb of the right hand on the first∴ joint of the index finger of the one whose hand is taken in the same manner as in the Apprentice Grip, but with two more taps on the same joint of the middle finger."

"The Sacred Word is… it means "perseverance in goodness".

"The Password is… and means "as abundant as the ears of corn".

"Go now my B[rother]∴ and have yourself recognized by the B[rother]∴ Sen[ior]∴ and Jun[ior]∴ Ward[ens]∴"

The Ward[ens]∴ then confirm the correctness of the Words, Sign and Grip∴ given to them by the Fellow Craft.

After this the W[orshipful]∴ says:

"B[rother]∴ Sen[ior]∴ and Jun[ior]∴ Ward[ens]∴, please invite the Brethren of each Column to recognize B[rother]∴ N∴ in future as a Fellow Craft of this R[espectable]∴ ☐ ∴ and to applaud his Reception."

The Ward[ens]∴ repeat this announcement.

After the announcement, the W[orshipful]∴ says:

"With me, Brethren!"

All applaud with the battery of the Degree.

The new Fellow Craft who, all this time, has had to stand to order between the Ward[ens]∴, asks the Sen[ior]∴ Ward[en]∴ for the floor, and having obtained it, gives thanks.

The W[orshipful]∴ orders the applause to be drowned out and says:

"Brethren, be seated again."

All sheathe their swords and sit down.

The new Fellow Craft sits opposite the tracing-board during the instruction that is to be given. B[rother]∴ J[unio]r∴ Ward[en]∴ uses his sword to point out to him the images whose symbolic meaning the W[orshipful]∴ will be explaining.

After the instruction the B[rother]∴ M[aster]∴ of Ceremonies leads the Fellow Craft to the head of the column of the South (on this occasion only; in other assemblies he may station himself at the head of either Column as he chooses).

Finally the W[orshipful]∴ closes the labor using the procedure for the opening as described above. If there are any matters to be dealt with then the Apprentice work shall remain open and the Apprentices, if there are any, shall be brought into the Vestibule. Finally the Apprentice lodge will be closed in the usual way.

~~~~~~~~~~~~~~~~~~~

INSTRUCTION.

~~~~~~~~~~~~~~~~~~~

Q. Are you a Fellow Craft?

A. Yes, I am.

Q. Why did you wish to be received as a Fellow Craft∴?

A. To know the letter G∴

Q. What does this letter stand for?

A. Geometry.

Q. Does it not mean anything else?

A. It is the initial of one of the names of the G[reat]∴ A[rchitect]∴ of the U[niverse]∴

Q. How were you received?

A. Moving from the column J∴ to the column B∴ and up the five steps of the temple.

Q. Through which door did you climb them?

A. Through the West Door.

Q. What are you going to do in the temple?

A. Build dungeons for vices and erect temples to virtue.

Q. Who challenged your entry?

A. Brother Tyler.

Q. What did he demand of you?

A. A Sign, a Grip, and a Word.

Q. What did you see when you ascended the steps of the temple?

A. Two large columns.

Q. Of what were they made.

A. Of bronze.

Q. How high were they?

A. Eighteen cubits.

Q. And their circumference?

A. Twelve cubits.

Q. How thick are they?

A. Four cubits.

Q. So they were hollow?

A. Yes, Worshipful

Q. Why?

A. To conceal the tools of the Fellow Crafts and Apprentices, as well as the money to pay their wages.

Q. How did the craftsmen receive their wages?

A. By a Sign, a Grip and a Word, Apprentices by those of the Apprentice and Fellow Crafts by those of their Degree.

Q. How were the columns decorated?

A. Acanthus leaves adorned the capitals, and these were surmounted by innumerable pomegranates.

Q. Where were you received as a Fellow Craft?

A. In a just and perfect lodge.

Q. What shape was it?

A. An oblong square.

Q. How long was it?

A. From East to West.

Q. How wide?

A. From the South to the North.

Q. How high was it?

A. Feet and cubits without number.

Q. What was it covered with?

A. A canopy of blue spangled with stars.

Q. What supported it?

A. Three large triangular columns.

Q. What do you call them?

A. Wisdom, Strength, Beauty.

Q. Why do you call them that?

A. Wisdom to invent, strength to execute, and beauty to adorn.

Q. How deep was it?

A. From the surface of the earth to the center.

Q. Why do you answer like that?

A. To make it clear that all Masons all over the Earth are but one people of Brethren, governed by the same laws and customs.

Q. Do you have ornaments in your lodge?

A. Yes M[ost]∴ W[orshipful]∴

Q. How many?

A. Three in number.

Q. What are they?

A. The Mosaic Pavement, the Blazing Star, and the Indented Tassel.

Q. What was their use?

A. The Mosaic Pavement adorned the threshold of the great portico of the temple, the Blazing Star was in the middle illuminating the center from which the true light that illuminates the four parts of the world emanates, and the Indented Tassel bordered and decorated the extremities.

Q. Explain to me the moral significance of these three ornaments.

A. The Mosaic Pavement is the emblem of the intimate union that prevails among Masons; the Blazing Star is the emblem of the G[reat]∴ A[rchitect]∴ of the U[niverse]∴ who shines with a light that He borrows only from Himself; and the Indented Tassel signifies the bond that unites all Masons and makes them one family throughout the Earth.

Q. Do you have any jewels in your lodge?

A. Yes, M[ost]∴ W[orshipful]∴

Q. How many?

A. Six in number, namely three movable and three immovable.

Q. Which are the movable jewels?

A. The square that the W[orshipful]∴ carries, the level that the Sen[ior]∴ Ward[en]∴ carries and the perpendicular or plumb that the Junior Ward[en]∴ carries.

Q. What are the immovable jewels?

A. The tracing-board, the perfect ashlar, and the rough ashlar.

Q. What is the use of the movable jewels?

A. The square is used to square the materials and set their surfaces at right angles to each other, the level to place the stones horizontally next to each other, and the plumb to raise the buildings perfectly perpendicular on their foundations.

Q. Can you explain this in a moral sense?

A. The square warns us that all our actions must be regulated by righteousness and justice, the level that there must be perfect equality between all Masons, and the plumb that all good things come to us from above.

Q. What is the use of the immovable jewels?

A. The trestle board is used by the M[aster]∴ to draw their plans and designs, the perfect ashlar is used by the Fellow Crafts to sharpen their tools, and the rough ashlar is used by the Apprentices to learn their trade.

Q. What is their moral significance?

A. The trestle board is the emblem of the good example we owe to our Brethren and to all men; the perfect ashlar is the symbol of the care that the virtuous man takes to erase the marks that vice has made on him and to correct the passions against which we all have to struggle; finally, the rough ashlar is the image of the coarse and savage man that only a profound study of oneself can polish and make perfect.

Q. How many kinds of Masons are there?

A. Two, some speculative and some operative.

Q. What do the Speculative Masons learn?

A. A good morality that serves to purify our morals and make us agreeable to all men.

Q. What is an Operative Mason?

A. Someone who constructs buildings.

Q. How shall I know you are a Mason?

A. From my Signs, Words and Grip.

Q. How many Signs are there in Masonry?

A. They are without number M[ost]∴ W[orshipful]∴, but they are reduced to five main ones.

Q. What are they?

A. The Vocal, Guttural, Pectoral, Manual and Pedal.

Q. What are they for?

A. The Vocal to give the Word, the Guttural to give the Sign of the Apprentice, the Pectoral to give the sign of the Fellow Craft, the Manual to give the Grip of both, and the Pedal to perform the step of both.

Q. How many windows are there in a lodge?

A. Three.

Q. Where are they placed?

A. In the East, the West, and the South.

Q. Why are there no windows in the North?

A. Because the Sun shines only weakly upon this part.

Q. What are the windows for?

A. To provide light for the craftsmen when they come to work, while they are there, and when they depart.

Q. Have you seen your Master today?

A. Yes, M[ost]∴ W[orshipful]∴

Q. How was he dressed?

A. In blue and gold.

Q. What do these two colors mean?

A. Gold signifies wealth, and blue signifies Wisdom, both gifts that the G[reat]∴ A[rchitect]∴ of the U[niverse]∴ granted to Solomon.

Q. Where do the Fellow Crafts stand?

A. In the South.

Q. Why?

A. Because they are more enlightened than the Apprentices, and so they can serve the Masters there.

Q. How do you serve your Master?

A. With joy, fervor, and freedom.

Q. How long do you serve him?

A. From Monday morning until Saturday evening.

Q. Did you receive any wages?

A. M[ost]∴ W[orshipful]∴, I am content

Q. Where did you receive them?

A. At the column B∴

Q. What does this letter indicate?

A. It is the initial of a word that serves to identify us.

Q. Tell me that word.

A. You tell me the first∴ letter, then I will tell you the second.

Q. What does this word mean?

A. It means perseverance in goodness.

Q. Tell me the password.

A. (He does so.)

Q. What does it mean?

A. Abundant, like the ears of corn.

CLOSING OF THE WORK.

Q. How old are you?

A. Five years old.

Q. At what hour does the work close?

A. At midnight.

Q. What hour is it?

A. It is midnight.

Since it is midnight and this is the hour at which Masons are accustomed to close their Fellow Crafts Work, B[rother]∴ Sen[ior]∴ and J[unio]r∴ Ward[ens]∴, kindly invite the Brethren, each on your Column, to join with me in closing the Fellow Crafts Work of the R[espectable]∴ ▢∴ of N∴ in the O[rient]∴ of…

The Ward[ens]∴ repeat the announcement. After the announcement, the W[orshipful]∴ strikes 5∴ raps of the Gavel, which the Ward[ens]∴ repeat, after which the W[orshipful]∴ says:

"With me, Brethren!"

All make the sign and engage in the Masonic applause∴

The W[orshipful]∴ says:

"The Fellow Crafts work is closed."

The Ward[ens]∴ repeat this.

THE

REGULATOR

OF THE MASON.

~~~~~~~~~~~~~~~~~~~~

HEREDOM,

THE YEAR OF THE G[REAT]∴ L[IGHT]∴ 5801.

THE REGULATOR
OF THE MASON.

~~~~~~

THIRD DEGREE,
OR
DEGREE OF MASTER.

~~~~~~

FIRST SECTION.
PRELIMINARIES.

A Fellow Craft may not be admitted to the Third Degree until he has served his time, i.e. until at least three and a half months have elapsed since his Reception into the Degree of Fellow Craft.

This is understood to mean that the Fel[low Craft]∴ has attended seven meetings, which are assumed to have been held every fortnight, assuming that he is of the age required by the regulations, which is 25 years completed.

Any Fellow Craft who, having fulfilled the foregoing conditions, desires to be admitted to the Degree of Master shall apply in confidence to the B[rother]∴ Senior Warden.

If the later deems that the burden of labor will allow the application to receive due attention then he shall say in lodge: "Most Wor[shipful]∴, B[rother]∴ N∴, a Fellow Craft of this R[espectable]∴ lodge, requests the favor of being admitted to the Degree of Master."

The Wor[shipful]∴ says:

"Brother Senior and Junior Wardens, announce on your Columns that B[rother]∴ N∴ is proposed for admission to the Degree of Master. Ask the Brethren for their comments."

The Wardens make the announcement in the usual manner. At this moment, if the proposed B[rother]∴ is present, he asks permission to tyle the temple.

Whether comments of any kind are made or not, the Apprentices and Fellow Crafts are obliged to tyle the temple.

After the Apprentices and Fellow Crafts have exited, the Wor[shipful]∴ opens the Master's work as will be described below. He then again calls for comments on the Candidate. If there are any they are discussed, and the lodge, now composed of the Masters only, deliberates upon the conclusions of Brother Orator and proceeds to a Ballot if anyone requests it. If the Ballot is favorable, the W[orshipful]∴ will ask for the result to be applauded by the battery of the Degree, as will be explained in a moment, and the day for the Reception shall be decided upon, with B[rother]∴ Secretary noting it down in the draft Minutes for the present day.

If the Reception is cancelled or postponed then the Master's work is closed and the Fellow Crafts are brought back if the work of this Degree remains in force, otherwise it is closed to continue the Apprentice work, in which case all the Brethren are brought back.

SECOND SECTION.
RECEPTION.
FIRST PRELIMINARY.

All the Masters shall be invited in the usual manner to attend on the day agreed at the last meeting. The letters of invitation must mention that a "Reception in the Third Degree" is to take place, and that the Brethren should dress in black. A letter of invitation shall also be sent to the proposed Fellow Craft.

SECOND PRELIMINARY.

On the day appointed for the Reception, all Masters will be admitted. The Wor[shipful]∴ will open the Apprentice work and then ask for the Minutes of the previous meeting to be read out. He will then open the work of the Fellow Crafts and ask the B[rothers]∴ Senior and Junior Wardens to go through each Column to ensure that all the B[rethren]∴ are Masters by asking them individually in a low voice for the Words, Sign and Grip. It is a good idea to observe this formality, as much to avoid abuse of the lodge as to help the B[rethren]∴ to remember something that they quite commonly forget for want of practice.

When the Wardens have returned to their stations they provide details of those B[rethren]∴ whom they have found to be poorly instructed. If they are B[rethren]∴ of the lodge then the W[orshipful]∴ invites them to become better instructed and gives them the words they have forgotten. If the poorly instructed are Visitors then it is imperative that they tyle the work.

When it has been ascertained that all the B[rethren]∴ are Masters the Wor[shipful]∴ will open the work in the manner described below.

From that moment on, all the B[rethren]∴ have the title of *Worshipful*, and the Worshipful that of *Respectable*.

OPENING OF THE WORK.

When everything has been arranged as just mentioned, the Most Respectable gives one rap of the gavel, and says:

"Come to order, Brethren, sword in hand."

He then draws his own sword, which he holds in his left hand. All the Masters do the same, holding their swords also in their left hand, pointing them at the floor, and coming to order.

Coming to order involves moving the hand horizontally, with the thumb against the chest and the four fingers close together.

This order is the attitude of repose.

The Most Respectable then asks the following seven questions:

Q.   W[orshipful]∴ B[rother]∴ Senior Warden, what is the first duty of the Wardens in a Master's lodge?

A. M[ost]∴ R[espectable]∴, it is to ensure that all the B[rethren]∴ are Masters.

Q. Are you sure of that?

A. M[ost]∴ R[espectable]∴, we are.

Q. W[orshipful]∴ B[rother]∴ Senior Warden, are you a Master?

A. M[ost]∴ R[espectable]∴, try me. The acacia is known to me.

Q. Give me the sign of the Master.

(He does so).

Q. W[orshipful]∴ B[rother]∴ Junior Warden, how old are you?

A. Seven years and more.

Q. What hour do we open our work?

A. At noon, M[ost]∴ R[espectable]∴.

Q. W[orshipful]∴ B[rother]∴ Senior Warden, what hour is it?

A. It is noon.

The M[ost]∴ R[espectable]∴ says:

"Since it is noon, Wor[shipful]∴ B[rothers]∴ Senior and Junior Wardens, ask the B[rethren]∴ on each of your Columns to join with me in opening the work in the Degree of Master."

The B[rother]∴ Wardens repeat the announcement.

After this announcement the M[ost]∴ R[espectable]∴ strikes with his gavel nine raps (consisting of the Apprentice Battery repeated three times). The Wardens do the same, after which the M[ost]∴ R[espectable]∴ says:

"With me, Brethren!"

All the Brethren with their eyes upon the M[ost]∴ R[espectable]∴, make the sign of the Master, and perform the battery by nine, which is the Apprentice battery repeated three times.

Finally the M[ost]∴ R[espectable]∴ says:

"The work of the Masters is open."

The Wardens announce this on their respective Columns.

The Sign is made standing and to order, with the hand at the level of the forehead, palm outwards, the head tilted slightly to the right, and with a backward swaying of the body.

The M[ost]∴ R[espectable]∴ places his unsheathed sword on the altar and then instructs the Wardens to invite the B[rethren]∴ to sit down.

They do so.

The work now being open, the M[ost]∴ R[espectable]∴ says:

"My Brethren, you have agreed to the Reception of B[rother]∴ N∴ to the Degree of Master. If any of you now have legitimate cause for opposing this then now is the time to do so. Your silence will prove that you are persisting in your agreement."

If there is any opposition then it must be heard, discussed, and then judged in the light of the conclusions of B[rother]∴ Orator. If the opposition is judged to be valid then the assembly has to be broken up and dispersed, and the Reception deferred.

If there is silence on the columns then the M[ost]∴ R[espectable]∴ says:

"B[rother]∴ Master of Ceremonies, warn the Preparing B[rother]∴ to fetch the Aspirant."

The Recipient must have been previously conducted to and enclosed in the Chamber of Reflection, on the walls of which maxims relevant to the Reception will have been placed. There, the Preparing B[rother]∴ will have suitably prepared the Recipient's mind and imagination through sensible, serious, and moral speeches appropriate to the importance of the Degree.

If for some reason the Recipient's arrival has been delayed, then the M[ost]∴ R[espectable]∴ will select a few questions from the Instruction.

The Preparing B[rother]∴ will be responsible for handing the M[ost]∴ R[espectable]∴ the Aspirant's hat and sword.

One B[rother]∴ from each column will take charge of the rolls, to be used as described below.

THE ACTUAL RECEPTION.

When the Fellow Craft's entrance is announced the candles will be extinguished. A lamp made of metal or some other opaque material and of antique design, suspended in the middle of the lodge, will be sufficient to light the proceedings until the time of the Reception. Care should be taken to ensure that the light placed within the lamp does not extend beyond its edges so that the objects within the lodge cannot be distinguished.

Another lamp will be placed on the altar, the dim light of which shall reflect only on the M[ost]∴ R[espectable]∴, rather as the dark lanterns are. All the Brethren will be dressed in black, wearing their hats with the brims pulled down, sword in hand, and wearing an apron with a white background and edged in blue.

The Brethren will be arranged in two rows in the middle of the lodge on benches placed along the length of the tracing-board, but at a sufficient distance to allow passage between them and the tracing-board, and in such a way also that the journeys may be made behind them.

When the Recipient arrives at the door of the temple he knocks as a Fellow Craft. He must be clothed, in other words wearing his apron, in such a way that it can be removed without resistance.

The B[rother]∴ Tyler announces to the Junior Warden that someone is knocking as a Fellow Craft, who passes this on to the Senior who audibly informs the M[ost]∴ R[espectable]∴ of this fact.

The M[ost]∴ R[espectable]∴ says:

"Who is this Fellow Craft who is impertinent enough to come and disturb our work?

"B[rother]∴ Senior Warden, see who is knocking."

The Senior Warden passes this order to the Junior, who says to B[rother]∴ Tyler, "My B[rother]∴, see who is knocking."

B[rother]∴ Tyler half-opens the door and asks who is knocking.

The Preparing B[rother]∴ replies: "A Fellow Craft who has served his time and asks to be received as a Master."

When this answer has reached the M[ost]∴ R[espectable]∴, once again via the Wardens, says:

"Ask for his first name, surname, age, and civil status."

This request is passed on to the Aspirant just like the first one.

The Preparing B[rother]∴ responds.

The B[rother]∴ Tyler closes the door, which he only has to half-open each time, and when the answer has reached the M[ost]∴ R[espectable]∴ he says:

"Ask him his Masonic age, where he has worked, and what he has practiced on."

When the request has reached the Preparing B[rother]∴ he replies:

"The Aspirant is five years old, he worked on the outside of the temple on the polished stone, and he has prepared the tools."

When this answer has reached the M[ost]∴ R[espectable]∴ he says:

"Ask him if he is sincerely disposed to fulfil the duties of a Master Mason and if he has nothing with which to reproach himself regarding the oaths he has previously sworn."

When the request has reached the Aspirant he gives his reply, which is passed to the M[ost]∴ R[espectable]∴

The M[ost]∴ R[espectable]∴ gives one rap of the gavel, and says:

"Bring the Fellow Craft in."

The doors open. The Preparing B[rother]∴ introduces the Aspirant, walking him backwards to a position between the two Wardens, where he holds him with his back to the E[ast]∴

The doors are closed noisily.

The M[ost]∴ R[espectable]∴ says in a firm tone of voice:

"Take hold of the Fellow Craft and make sure he can see nothing of what is going on here until we are assured that he is worthy of admission to our mysteries."

The Wardens seize him. The Senior Warden places the point of his sword against his heart.

The M[ost]∴ R[espectable]∴ says:

"Fellow Craft, swear and promise, under the penalties to which you made yourself liable at your first undertaking, not to reveal anything of what you may see here, and not to communicate anything of it to any Fellow Craft or Apprentice even if you are not admitted to the Degree, which you seem to desire."

The Aspirant replies: "I swear."

"Do you promise to answer frankly and honestly the questions that will be put to you?"

The Aspirant must answer: "I promise."

After this answer, the M[ost]∴ R[espectable]∴ says:

"Fellow Craft, what do you seek?"

    (He answers.)

"Is your motivation a desire to learn?"

    (He answers.)

"Do you have any knowledge of the Degree you are seeking?"

    (He answers.)

The M[ost]∴ R[espectable]∴ says:

"B[rother]∴ Expert, have him make the first of the nine mysterious journeys."

The Wardens take up their positions.

The B[rother]∴ Expert, placed on the right of the Recipient, brings the point of a sword to the Recipient's heart, and causes him to grasp the blade with his right hand about a third of the way along its length, while B[rother]∴ Expert holds the hilt of the sword in his right hand and with his left firmly grasps the Recipient's left hand and in this attitude leads him round the lodge, pushing him in front of him, beginning in the South and not stopping in the East. During this journey he will make sure that the Recipient always has his back to the interior.

After the M[ost]∴ R[espectable]∴ has ordered the journey to take place he adds:

"All of you Masters, members of my council, you know this Fellow Craft. Come therefore and give me an account of what you have learnt about him, so that we may regulate our conduct towards him on the basis of the manner in which he has behaved since he was admitted to join us."

"Fellow Craft, whatever you do, do not turn your head."

The Wardens remain in position.

Nine of the masters gather around the Representation, where the past Master has to lie[20]. Between them

---

20 As this Reception is quite long, it is a good idea to have a very narrow mattress on which the most past Master can lie to avoid him feeling cold while lying on the floor.

they form the Chain of Union. The M[ost]∴ R[espectable]∴ passes to his right in a very quiet voice the old master's word J[ehova]∴, which should return to him from the left. This must be done in the greatest silence, with pomp, so as to inspire the Recipient with some concern about the conduct in which he has engaged and the frivolities he may have allowed himself.

Note: If the lodge is too small to allow the Recipient to make the journeys behind the Brethren then the latter should take their places in the center of the lodge on two rows of benches, as stated, but this must be done without noise.

When the Recipient has arrived back in the West the B[rother]∴ Senior Warden gives one rap and says, audibly:

"M[ost]∴ R[espectable]∴, the first journey is complete."

The nine Masters who had risen to their feet to hold council with the Respectable remaining standing around the Representation. The M[ost]∴ R[espectable]∴ alone returns to his place, gives one rap of the gavel, and says:

"Fellow Craft, you are suspected of having committed a serious crime. B[rother]∴ Conductor, tear off his apron, he is not worthy to wear it."

The Preparing B[rother]∴ snatches it from him.

The M[ost]∴ R[espectable]∴ continues:

"Did your conscience not reproach you at all? Speak frankly. Remember the promise you made only a moment ago. Answer!"

After the Recipient's response, the M[ost]∴ R[espectable]∴ tells him:

"Man's life here on Earth is but a passage."

Then he adds:

"Have him make the second journey."

He says:

"Fellow Craft, on this journey, search the recesses of your soul."

The R[espectable]∴ leaves his seat and joins the nine Masters around the representation.

When the Candidate has arrived back in the West, the Senior Warden gives one rap of the gavel and says:

"The second journey is complete."

The M[ost]∴ R[espectable]∴ returns to his seat and says:

"Crime and innocence, lies and truth, have distinctive characters that do not allow confusion. Tell me, Fellow Craft, does not your conscience reproach you?"

He answers: "No" (and that is ordinary). The R[espectable]∴ says:

"B[rother]∴ Expert (or Conductor), turn the Fellow Craft around; let him see to what excesses the neglect of our duties can lead us."

"Consider what caused the grief we find ourselves in."

B[rother]∴ Expert makes him take three steps backward, turning him round towards the Representation. The nine Masters who had remained standing around it take one step backwards, bringing their right hand up over their hearts at the Master's command while using their left hands to direct the points of their swords towards the representation while turning to face the Recipient.

After a moment of silence, the M[ost]∴ R[espectable]∴ says:

"B[rother]∴ Expert, does the Fellow Craft appear moved at all? Is he not showing any signs of guilt?"

The B[rother]∴ Expert replies, "No, M[ost]∴ R[espectable]∴."

The M[ost]∴ R[espectable]∴ Master says, in an imposing tone: "Every moment leads us to our ultimate end; the true Mason neither fears it nor desires it."

Then he adds:

"B[rother]∴ Expert, have him make the third journey."

When the Recipient has returned to the West the Senior Warden gives one rap of the gavel, and says:

"The third journey is complete."

The M[ost]∴ R[espectable]∴ gives one rap with the gavel.

The nine Masters who were standing up return to their places.

If all the Masters were obliged to move towards the center because of the smallness of the room then this is the moment at which they return to their places.

The M[ost]∴ R[espectable]∴ says:

"Fellow Craft, everything here confronts you with mourning and sadness. You are suspected of having participated with other villainous Fellow Crafts in an act of treachery. Do you know anything of their detestable conspiracy?"

He replies: "No."

The M[ost]∴ R[espectable]∴ says:

"Who will be your guarantor?"

"My word of honor, and my promise as a Mason."

The M[ost]∴ R[espectable]∴ says:

"I accept them. Both are sacred among us, so confirm them by a sign that leaves nothing to be desired."

"The Recipient comes to order as a Fellow Craft by placing his hand over his heart.

The M[ost]∴ R[espectable]∴ continues:

"Do not be surprised, Fellow Craft, at the precautions we are taking with regard to you. Since the death of our Respectable Master all Fellow Crafts are suspect, as you must have noticed by the way you have just been treated. However, the confidence and ingenuousness of your answers have completely removed any suspicions we had about you and have earned you our trust."

"Try to make yourself worthy of the favor you are seeking. The common man allows himself to be taken in by appearances, but the true Mason knows how to put them aside in order to rise to the truth."

"B[rother]∴ Fellow Craft, are you persisting in the desire to which you have testified, namely, to attain the rank of Master?"

He replies: "I am persisting."

The M[ost]∴ R[espectable]∴ says to him:

"My Brother, all the trials you have undergone up to now and the precepts you have been given have had no other purpose than to bring you to the inner sanctum, where you will acquire specific and satisfying knowledge. One can only enter there with a pure soul. We cannot penetrate the recesses of your heart, so you must be your own judge and fear the stings of conscience. It has pleased the Masters to train you – now you will be responsible for teaching the Fellow Crafts and the Apprentices. Let virtue be the motive and object of your precepts. Never lose sight of the fact that a good example produces far more reliable effects than even the wisest lessons."

"Yes, my Brother, all that you have seen so far in Masonry and all that you will see thereafter is covered by the mysterious veil of symbolism, a veil that the intelligent, zealous, and hard-working Mason knows how to penetrate. Pay close attention to what has happened to you and what will happen to you. Do not forget the three mysterious journeys you have made: the Degree actually requires nine, but the lodge is willing to reduce them to three."

"B[rother]∴ Expert, lead the B[rother]∴ up the seven steps of the temple. Let him enter it by the Western door and you will present him to me when it is time, by the three mysterious steps. You, Brethren of each Column, do not forget your duty."

(This warning is for the two Brethren who have provided themselves with two paper-rolls).

The B[rother]∴ Expert takes the Candidate up the first three steps, starting with the right foot.

Arriving at the first landing the Candidate gives the Sign of the Apprentice; he climbs two more steps, and on the second landing he gives the Sign of the Fellow Craft; he climbs the last two steps, and stops there on the Mosaic Pavement, still at the sign of Fellow Craft, with both feet in square. Now that he has reached this point, the Recipient finds that his feet are quite close to the head of the B[rother]∴, who, as we have said, is lying on the ground, but he cannot actually see him as his whole body is covered with a black veil. The B[rother]∴ who is lying down must have his left leg extended, the right bent at right angles with the knee raised, the left arm extended, and his right arm to order as a Fellow Craft.

When the Recipient has reached this place the M[ost]∴ R[espectable]∴ says to him:

"The first two Degrees taught you the use of instruments and materials. In this Degree you no doubt expected to find the further development of the emblems under which the truth has so far been hidden from your eyes, but everything in the universe is subject to strange revolutions, and everything perishes!"

"The temple that Solomon was pleased to build for the King of Kings suffered this sad fate. The unexpected death of the head of this magnificent enterprise can retrace for you, by anticipation, the ruin of this famous temple, which history represents to us as being constantly destroyed and constantly rising from its own ruins."

"Solomon, the son of David, famous for his wisdom and the immensity of his knowledge, resolved to raise to the Lord a temple that his father had planned but which the wars that he had to support against his neighbors had prevented him from building. He sent an emissary to ask Hiram, King of Tyre, to provide him with the materials necessary for this undertaking. Hiram accepted this proposal with joy, and sent one of those rare men whose genius, intelligence, taste, superior talents in architecture and vast knowledge of the character of metals had earned him such a degree of consideration and respect from the King of Tyre that he called him his father, because he was named Hiram like himself, although he was the son of a man from Tyre and a woman of the tribe of Naphtali."

"Solomon entrusted Hiram with the stewardship and direction of the work. The enumeration that was made of all the craftsmen totaled 183,300. History calls them *proselytes,* which in our language means *admitted strangers*, that is, *initiated strangers.* They were composed of 30,000 men to cut the cedars on Mount Lebanon, who served for a month, a third at a time; 70,000 apprentices; 80,000 Fellow Crafts; and 3,300 masters. The inhabitants of Mount Gibel shaped the cedars and cut the stones."

"The workers, divided into three classes, had words, signs, and grips by which they recognized each other and received the pay that was proportionate to the kind of work to which they were suited.

"The Apprentices received their wages at the column J∴, the Fellow Crafts at the column B∴, and the Masters in the middle chamber. The name of the apprentice's column means *preparation,* and that of the Fellow Crafts *strength.* From the historical monuments that have come down to us we learn that the column J∴ was in the North and the column B∴ in the South, near the West door."

"The temple was accessed through three doors: the one intended for Apprentices and subsequently for the temple itself was in the West; the one intended for the Fellow Crafts and, after the completion of the temple, for the Levites, was in the South; and the one intended for the Masters and subsequently for the high priests was in the East."

"As soon as the doors had been put in place, Solomon promulgated a decree whereby all Apprentices and Fellow Crafts were enjoined to leave the temple on the eve of the Sabbath and not to return until the morning of the following Sabbath when the doors were opened again, on pain of being punished by death."

"The arrangement that had been established among the craftsmen should have, of necessity, ensured tranquility. Solomon's most recent decree was intended to prevent the observance of the Sabbath from being evaded on any pretext. Thanks to Hiram's care and vigilance, everything was proceeding in accordance with Solomon's wishes and every day the temple was taking on a new aspect when, suddenly, a dreadful crime was committed that caused the work to be suspended and which cast everyone into universal mourning. Three Fellow Crafts, dissatisfied with their pay, hatched a plan to obtain the wages of a Master by using the Master's sign, word and grip, which they hoped to obtain by brute force."

"They had noticed that Hiram visited the work every evening after the craftsmen had gone home. They therefore set up an ambush at the three doors of the temple: one armed himself with a rule, another with a lever or crowbar, and the third with a heavy mallet."

"Hiram, having accessed the temple by a secret entrance, directed his steps towards the West door, where he found one of the Fellow Crafts, who asked him for the Master's word, sign, and grip, and threatened to kill him if he did not give them to him. Hiram said to him: "Malcontent, what are you doing? You know that I cannot and must not give them to you. I myself did not acquire them in this way. Work hard to earn them, and you can be sure of obtaining them." Just a moment later the traitor tried to strike Hiram a violent blow on the head with the ruler he was holding, but Hiram's movement to parry the blow caused it to hit only his shoulder."

At this point the B[rother]∴ Expert makes the Candidate take one of the three mysterious steps. It consists of passing the right foot over the representation, diagonally, from the West, where he is placed, to the South, holding the left leg in square at the level of the calf of the leg, and remaining for a few moments balanced on the right leg. The B[rother]∴ Expert supports the Candidate in this posture by giving him his hand.

The moment the Recipient takes the first step, the B[rother]∴ of the column of the South gives him a light but perceptible tap on the right shoulder with his roll.

The M[ost]∴ R[espectable]∴ continues:

"Hiram wanted to seek safety by fleeing the temple, and tried to leave by the South door where, however, he encountered another Fellow Craft, who made the same request with the same threat. The moment Hiram tried to flee the Fellow Craft pursued him and struck a heavy blow with his crowbar which, however, hit him only on the nape of the neck."

At this point the Recipient is made to take the second mysterious step, which involves passing the left leg over the representation diagonally from South to North while holding the right leg in square against the calf of the left leg.

During this passage, a B[rother]∴ of the column of the North strikes the neck of the Recipient with a light blow of the roll with which he had armed himself.

The Recipient is now made to take the third step, which involves bringing his right leg to the bottom of the representation, where he joins the two feet at right angles.

Immediately, two of the Brethren seize the Recipient, each taking one arm while placing their other hand on his breast and placing one foot behind the Recipient's heels. Meanwhile the B[rother]∴ who was lying down withdraws so quietly that the Recipient does not notice anything, leaving on the ground the veil with which he was covered.

The M[ost]∴ R[espectable]∴ then leaves his seat, comes close to the Candidate, and continues:

"This misdirected blow only stunned our Respectable Master, who nevertheless had enough strength to run to the East door, where he found the third Fellow Craft, who again made the same request and threats and, in response to Hiram's refusal, struck him a severe blow with his mallet on his forehead and laid him out dead."

The M[ost]∴ R[espectable]∴ produces a mallet, which he had kept hidden, and strikes the Recipient's forehead with it. Immediately the two Brethren who were holding the Aspirant push him and carefully turn him over onto his back.

It is for the B[rother]∴ Expert or Master of Ceremonies to perform this duty, but it is in order to entrust it to two Brethren who are strong enough to knock the Recipient down while supporting the weight of his body to prevent injury.

The Recipient has to lie down in the attitude adopted by the B[rother]∴ who previously occupied his place, i.e. with his head slightly raised and resting on a cushion; his left leg extended and his right bent at right angles with his knee raised; his left arm extended, and his right arm also bent at right angles; his hand over his heart, to order as a Fellow Craft; covered with his apron; and, finally, with the black veil spread over him, so that his face is left uncovered.

Everyone takes up their position. The nine candles are lit, and the lamps extinguished.

If there are any other B[rethren]∴ to be admitted to the Degree of Master then the candles would not be lit and their Receptions would proceed although, of course, before anything else a vote would have been taken on the admission of each Brother following the same procedure as we have described for a single Candidate. The B[rother]∴ who has just been laid down would remain in place, just like the last master before him, and as the next one was thrown down so the previous one would take up position on one of the columns.

If there is only one Reception, or if the last Reception has been reached, then the candles are lit as described and the M[ost]∴ R[espectable]∴ continues:

"Brethren, disorder has crept into our work, and the eyes of all our craftsmen are filled with sadness. We can have no doubt that our Respectable Master Hiram is dead. Let us search for his body therefore and seek by our zeal and carefulness to discover him."

"B[rother]∴ Junior Warden, take two Masters with you, and start the search by the North."

The B[rother]∴ Junior Warden takes with him two Brethren. They go round the lodge starting at the North, probing the soil with the points of their swords.

When they have arrived back in the West, the Junior Warden gives one rap and says, "M[ost]∴ R[espectable]∴, our searches have been in vain."

The M[ost]∴ R[espectable]∴ gives one rap, and says:

"B[rother]∴ Senior Warden, take with you two Brethren, and start the search by the South."

The Senior Warden appoints two Brethren, with whom he goes round the lodge, starting at the South, probing the soil with the points of their swords. On their return to the West, the Senior Warden gives one rap and says: "M[ost]∴ R[espectable]∴, our searches have been in vain."

The M[ost]∴ R[espectable]∴ gives one rap of the gavel and says:

"Brother Senior and Junior Wardens, invite the Brethren who have already accompanied you to join you once more. I shall bring two Brethren with me, and all of us together will make a more thorough search. May we be fortunate enough to make this important discovery!"

These B[rethren]∴, nine in number, go round the lodge in the following order:

The Junior Warden, followed by two Masters from his Column, leaves first by the South; the Senior Warden, followed by the other two Masters from his Column, leaves by the North.

In this way they go round, crossing each other's paths. When they have reached the East, the M[ost]∴ R[espectable]∴ joins them, along with two Masters whom he designates, and all of them go round the lodge three times, searching and probing the soil with the points of their swords.

On the second round the Junior Warden stops and says: "M[ost]∴ R[espectable]∴, I see a vapor rising from a small piece of soil. Let us take a closer look."

They make a third lap, after which the M[ost]∴ R[espectable]∴ stops in front of the tracing-board, at the corner where a mound and an acacia branch are depicted.

Note: In the summer it would be much better to have a branch of real acacia, with an artificial one in the winter. In each case it would be given to the Recipient to hold by means of a rent in the veil where his right hand is.

The Senior Warden says, "M[ost]∴ R[espectable]∴, the soil seems to me to be freshly disturbed at this spot. We may well find the object of our searches here."

The M[ost]∴ R[espectable]∴ makes a gesture as if to lean on the acacia branch and says: "W[orshipful]∴ M[aster]∴, this branch did not grow here. This strikes me as suspicious, and I think our search will not be in vain."

"It may be the case that the assassins wrested from our R[espectable]∴ M[aster]∴ by torture the Word and Sign of a M[aster]∴ Do you not agree that the first sign that one of us will make and the first word he will utter if we find the body of Hiram should henceforth be the Master's Word and Sign of Recognition?"

All give the sign of approval, and then drop their right hand against their thigh.

The M[ost]∴ R[espectable]∴, along with the other eight Brethren, uses the point of his sword which he is holding in his left hand to raise a part of the veil that is covering the Recipient. They immediately make the Sign of Horror.

The Junior Warden approaches, takes the Recipient's right index finger, and lets it go, saying J∴ (the Apprentice word) and taking a step backwards while making the sign of horror.

The Senior Warden then approaches, takes the Recipient's second or middle finger, pulls it towards him, and then lets it slip saying B[rother]∴ (the Fellow Craft word) while taking a step back with the sign of horror.

The M[ost]∴ R[espectable]∴ approaches the Recipient and says, making the sign of horror and taking a step back:

"Brother Wardens, who has disturbed the body of our Respectable Master?"

The Junior Warden says: "M[ost]∴ R[espectable]∴, I thought I could raise him by the Apprentice grip, but the flesh cleaves from the bones."

The Senior Warden says: "M[ost]∴ R[espectable]∴, I thought I could raise him by the Fellow Craft grip, but the flesh cleaves from the bones."

The M[ost]∴ R[espectable]∴ says:

"Do you not know that you cannot do anything without me, but that the three of us can do everything together?"

He approaches the Recipient, places his right foot against his, knee against knee; with his right hand he grasps his wrist so that the palms of both hands are against each other, and passes his left arm under his left shoulder, having by this means stomach against stomach; then, with the help of the two Wardens, he raises him up and says in his ear, while giving him the accolade[21] by three, namely the three syllables of the word M∴ B∴ N∴

All the Brethren return to their places.

The M[ost]∴ R[espectable]∴ returns to his own position.

The B[rother]∴ M[aster]∴ of Ceremonies leads the Recipient to the foot of the altar where, with one knee on the ground, he recites the following obligation.

All the B[rethren]∴ are standing, to order, sword in hand.

OBLIGATION.

I swear and promise, in the presence of the G[reat]∴ A[rchitect]∴ of the U[niverse]∴, on my word of honor and upon the faith of a Mason, before this R[espectable]∴ Assembly, not to reveal in any way to any Fellow Craft, Apprentice or Profane any of the secrets of the Mastership which have been and are to be entrusted to me, under the penalties to which I made myself liable by my first obligations. I reiterate at this time all the commitments that I have already contracted in the Order. May the G[reat]∴ A[rchitect]∴ of the U[niverse]∴ help me.

After the Obligation, the M[ost]∴ R[espectable]∴ says:

"To the G[lory]∴ of the G[reat]∴ A[rchitect]∴ of the U[niverse]∴, in the name of the G[rand]∴ O[rient]∴ of France, by virtue of the powers invested in me by this R[espectable]∴ L[odge]∴, I receive you as a Master Mason."

He places his sword upon the head of the recipient and strikes it with his gavel according to the battery of the Degree.

The Recipient stands up.

The M[ost]∴ R[espectable]∴ says to him:

"My Brother, in order to recognize each other in this Degree, as in the previous ones, we have a Sacred Word, a Password, a Sign and a Grip."

"The Sign is made as described above: it portrays the horror with which the Masters were struck at the first sight of the corpse of Hiram."

"The Sacred Word is the one I whispered in your ear when I raised you up: it is given by receiving and giving the accolade in three beats, one syllable to each beat: it means, *the flesh cleaves from the bones.*"

"The password is *Giblin,* which is the name of the inhabitants of Mount Gibel, who drew the stones from the quarry and shaped the cedars for the construction of the temple."

"As a Master you shall be called *Gabaon;* the Grip is that which I gave you when I raised you, with this difference, that you must grasp the wrist in the same way as yours was grasped."

---

21 [An embrace and the threefold kiss of peace.]

"If a Mason finds himself in peril, he must raise his hands clasped together on his head, with the palms of his hands facing heavenwards and say, "Come to my aid, S[ons]∴ O[f]∴ T[he]∴ W[idow]∴"

"Coming to order in this Degree involves extending the hand with the four fingers clasped together, the thumb spread, and placing it on the heart."

"The Sacred Word should only be uttered and the Grip given in a Master's lodge after having ascertained that the person asking for it is a Master."

The M[ost]∴ R[espectable]∴ then puts the apron of his Degree on the new Master, and says to him:

"You shall henceforth wear your apron with the bib turned down. The blue with which it is bordered should serve as a continuous reminder that a Mason must expect everything from Heaven, and that it is in vain that men plan to build if the G[reat]∴ A[rchitect]∴ does not Himself deign to build."

He returns his sword to him and says:

"You know the use you must make of this sword."

He returns his hat to him and says:

"Henceforth you will wear your hat in the Master's lodge; this very ancient custom is redolent of freedom and superiority. Hitherto you have served as an Apprentice and a Fellow Craft: now you shall command but take care not to abuse that privilege."

The M[ost]∴ R[espectable]∴ gives one rap, and says:

"B[rother]∴ Senior Warden, I am sending you the new Master so that you may teach him to work as a Master does, and that you may recognize him in his new capacity."

The Master of Ceremonies leads him between the Wardens. The Senior Warden asks him to strike three raps on each of the three doors represented on the tracing-board – East, West, and South. Then he receives from him the Words, Signs and Grip. Finally he gives one rap after the Junior Warden has likewise received from the Recipient the Words, Signs, and Grip, and says:

"M[ost]∴ R[espectable]∴, the B[rother]∴ is recognized: he has worked as a Master."

The M[ost]∴ R[espectable]∴ orders the Master of Ceremonies to place the Recipient at the head of one of the two Columns, after which he continues the discourse on the Degree, addressing the newly received B[rother]∴ as follows:

"My Brother, the Fellow Crafts had no sooner committed their crime than they were struck by the enormity of it. In order to hide every trace of it, if it were possible, they took Hiram's body some distance from the works and buried it in a hastily made grave, promising themselves to come and remove it at the first favorable opportunity and then carry it far away. So they could recognize the spot easily, they planted an acacia branch."

"The Masters soon noticed Hiram's absence; they told Solomon who, in order to satisfy his impatience, ordered a search to be made for him."

"Three Masters left by the North door, three by the South door, and three by the West door. They agreed not to stray farther from each other than the range of their voices. At sunrise, one of them saw some vapor rising in the countryside at some distance; this phenomenon transfixed his attention; he told the other Masters about it, and they all approached the place from which the vapor was rising. At first sight they saw a small elevation, or mound, and noticed that the soil had been freshly disturbed there which confirmed their suspicions, and the acacia branch that yielded to their first efforts removed any remaining doubts that it served as a marker to identify the place of his burial. They began to search, and soon found the body of our R[espectable]∴ M[aster]∴ already corrupted and concluded that he had been murdered."

"It was feared that the assassins might have extracted from Hiram by torture the Master's Signs and Words. They therefore agreed that the first sign and word that would escape them at the time of the exhumation would be the future sign and word of recognition among the Masters."

"They donned aprons and gloves of white skin as proof that they had not dipped their hands in innocent blood and sent one of their number to Solomon to inform him that Hiram's body had been found."

"When Solomon learned of the terrible crime that had deprived him of a friend and the head of the labors whose perfection he had made into his ultimate ambition, he fell into the most intense grief. He rent his clothes and swore that for such a dastardly crime he would exact a vengeance that all the world would hear about."

"He ordered a general mourning among the temple workers."

"He sent for the body to be exhumed, with pomp, by Masters, and gave it a magnificent funeral, placing it in a tomb three feet wide by five feet deep by seven feet long. He had a triangle of the purest gold inlaid upon it, had the ancient word for "Master," which was one of the Hebrew names of the G[reat]∴ A[rchitect]∴ of the U[niverse]∴, engraved in the middle of the triangle, and ordered that the word, sign, and grip should be changed and replaced with those agreed upon by the nine Masters."

"It should now be easy for you to grasp the analogy between the trials you have just undergone and the historical account of the circumstances of which they are the emblem."

"If you have reflected upon the various circumstances that accompanied your Reception and upon the Degrees to which you were admitted, you may have noticed certain points that seemed to contradict each other or, at least, did not seem to have a perfect interrelationship. Suspend your judgement in this regard. This diversity stems from that of the objects that the first three Degrees presented to you. They are the fundamental points of all Masonic knowledge. You will see afterwards, by dint of study and research, that these apparent contradictions will disappear. The union of all the knowledge given to you will present you with a coherent whole, interconnected, consistent, intellectually satisfying, and destined to lead you to an appreciation of the most sublime subjects. It is enough for now that the Order has pointed out to you the road you have to follow."

"You were treated as a suspicious Fellow Craft: this is an allusion to the profane enemies of our Order, who slander and persecute it without knowing anything about it, and against whom we must use force to repel their attacks, gentleness to bring them back to more moderate feelings, and prudence in the choice of the appropriate means of doing so."

"No sooner had you justified yourself than your Brethren hastened to give you new marks of friendship by admitting you to participate in their most intimate mysteries; at that moment you reached the inner sanctum."

"The journeys and travels are the emblem of the investigation of the crime and denote the endless wandering and the vagabond state of the criminal who seeks in vain to escape remorse and punishment."

"The strange step you were made to do is symbolic of Hiram's efforts to evade the assassin's blows.

"The three blows you received are those that were dealt to him and should make you aware of the danger of three fatal passions with which man is often blinded, namely *pride, envy,* and *avarice.*"

"These same trials are again emblematic of the sublime importance of our mysteries: they must convince us that always, in all places, under all circumstances, we must be ready to suffer everything, like our R[espectable]∴ M[aster]∴ Hiram, rather than reveal our secrets and fail in our commitments."

"Finally, they are also allegorical emblems of an infinity of knowledge with which only deep study can provide you, and which I cannot and must not communicate to you at this moment."

"We helped you to reach the seventh step, which is the third and perfect number of Masonry. You have thereby obtained the age of your Degree; beware of descending again, and falling from the number of perfection with which you have been decorated."

The discourse completed, the M[ost]∴ R[espectable]∴ says:

"Wor[shipful]∴ B[rethren]∴ Senior and Junior, invite the B[rothers]∴ who decorate each Column to, in future, recognize B[rother]∴ N∴ as a Master Mason. Let him be recognized as such by all Masons spread across the face of the Earth."

The Wardens repeat this.

The M[ost]∴ R[espectable]∴ says:

"Let us applaud, Brethren."

The triple Apprentice battery is sounded.

The Recipient gives thanks.

The M[ost]∴ R[espectable]∴ asks for the applause to be drowned out.

All the Brethren sheathe their swords and sit down.

The M[ost]∴ R[espectable]∴ recites the whole Instruction of the Degree.

After the Instruction, the M[ost]∴ R[espectable]∴ says:

"Wor[shipful]∴ B[rothers]∴ Senior and Junior Wardens, ask the B[rethren]∴ of each Column if they have anything to propose."

The Wardens make this announcement.

If there are any matters arising then these are discussed; if the matter is too important then it is deferred to another assembly.

If there is no business to discuss then the M[ost]∴ R[espectable]∴ gives one rap, and says:

"Come to order, Brethren."

All the B[rethren]∴ come to order and draw their swords, which they hold in their right hands pointing downwards.

The M[ost]∴ R[espectable]∴ says:

CLOSING.

Q. Wor[shipful]∴ B[rother]∴ Senior Warden, at what hour should we close our work?

A. At midnight.

Q. What hour is it?

A. Midnight.

Since it is midnight and this is the hour at which we finish our work, B[rothers]∴ Senior and Junior Wardens, invite the Brethren to help me close the work of the M[aster]∴, etc.

The Wardens repeat the announcement.

The work of the Fellow Craft is then closed, and finally that of the Apprentice.

INSTRUCTION.

Q. W[orshipful]∴ B[rother]∴ Senior Warden, are you a Master?

A. Try me; the acacia is known to me.

Q. Where were you received?

A. In the Middle Chamber.

Q. How did you reach this?

A. By a staircase that I climbed by three, five and seven.

Q. What did you see there?

A. Horror, grief, and sadness.

Q. Did you not see anything else?

A. A dark light illuminating the tomb of our R[espectable]∴ M[aster]∴

Q. How big was it?

A. Three feet wide, five feet deep and seven feet long.

Q. What was upon it?

A. A branch of acacia, and in the upper part a triangle of the purest gold, with the name of the Lord engraved in the center.

Q. What happened to you?

A. I was suspected of a horrible crime.

Q. Who reassured you?

A. My innocence.

Q. How were you received?

A. From the square to the compass.

Q. What were you looking for on this road?

A. The word of the Master, which was lost.

Q. How was it lost?

A. By three great blows to which I succumbed.

Q. Who rescued you?

A. The hand that struck me.

Q. How did that come about?

A. I shall never tell except in secret to one of my equals, and then only when I am obliged to do so.

Q. What did you learn?

A. The circumstances of the death of our R[espectable]∴ M[aster]∴ *Hiram,* who was murdered in the temple by three Fellow Crafts who wished to wrest the Master's word from him or to take his life.

Q. What did the Masters do to recognize each other after the death of our R[espectable]∴ M[aster]∴ Hiram?

A. They agreed that the first word spoken and the first sign made at the time of the discovery of *Hiram's* body would be substituted for the former word and sign.

Q. What were the clues to the discovery of the body of our R[espectable]∴ M[aster]∴

A. A vapor from the newly stirred earth, and a branch of acacia.

Q. What was done with the body after it was found?

A. Solomon had him buried with much pomp.

Q. What was the Master *Hiram?*

A. He was a Tyrian, and the son of a widow of the tribe of Naphtali.

Q. What is the name of a Master Mason?

A. *Gabaon.*

Q. How do Masters travel?

A. From the West to the East, and across the entire surface of the Earth.

Q. Why?

A. To spread the light and gather together what is scattered.

Q. What do the Masters work upon?

A. The trestle-board.

Q. Where do they receive their reward?

A. In the Middle Chamber.

Q. What do the nine stars mean?

A. The number of Masters sent to search for Hiram's body.

Q. If a Master was lost, where would you find him?

A. Between the square and the compass.

Q. What are the true marks of a Master?

A. The word, and the five perfect points of Mastership.

Q. If a Master is in danger of his life, what should he do?

A. Make the sign of distress, saying, "Help me, Sons of the Widow!"

Q. How is this sign made?

A. (He makes it.)

Q. Why do we say Sons of the Widow?

A. Because all Masons claim to be the sons of *Hiram*.

Q. How old is a Master?

A. Seven years and more.

Q. Why do you say seven years and more?

A. Solomon spent seven years and more building the temple.

Q. What does the password mean?

A. This is the name of a mountain from which Solomon drew the stones for the building of the temple.

THE REGULATOR
OF THE
KNIGHT MASONS.

THE REGULATOR OF THE KNIGHT MASONS, OR THE FOUR HIGHER ORDERS.

ACCORDING TO THE REGIME OF THE GRAND ORIENT.

PRICE: 15 Fr.

HEREDOM.

SITUATED IN PARIS,

Available from the B∴

CAILLOT, Bookseller, rue Saint André-des-Arcs, N° 57.

BRUN, rue Saint-Honoré, N° 251, where one will also find an assortment of jewels and decorations for all Degrees.

The PRESIDENT is addressed as.......... MOST WISE.

The Sr WARDEN....................... GRAND INSPECTOR.

The J^r WARDEN....................... SEVERE INSPECTOR.

1ˢᵀ ORDER.

DEGREE OF ELECT.

Most Wise.

OPENING.

When the Council assembles, all the Brethren are clothed except for the cordon, which they are to wear over their left arm.

The Most Wise stands at the foot of the altar and passes the black cordon to all the Brethren, one after the other, according to their dignities and offices. Then the Most Wise says:

Q. Brother Grand Inspector, what is the first care of a Grand Elect Inspector?

A. Most Wise, to ensure that all the Brethren are Elect.

M[ost]∴ W[ise]∴ — Make sure of that, Grand Inspector.

(The Grand Inspector assures himself of this and reports it to the Most Wise).

Q. What is the second duty of an Elect?

A. Most Wise, to see that the labors are tyled.

M[ost]∴ W[ise]∴ — Make sure of that, Grand Inspector.

(The Grand Inspector makes sure of this and reports to the Most Wise).

Q. Are you a Secret Elect?

A. A cave is known to me; a lamp has enlightened me; and a spring has quenched my thirst.

Q. What time is it?

A. The Morning Star informs us that the Sun is about to rise, and that it is time to set to work.

M[ost]∴ W[ise]∴ — Since this just purpose animates you, and the Sun is about to rise, Grand and Severe Inspector, Secret Elected Brothers, the Council is about to open. With me, my Brethren!

(All the Brethren, guided by the Most Wise, make the Sign and applaud. The Most Wise gives eight equal raps and one slow one).

M[ost]∴ W[ise]∴ — The Council of the Elect is open.

(He gives one rap, and says:)

M[ost]∴ W[ise]∴ — To your places, my Brethren.

(The Secretary reads out the Minutes[22] of the previous lodge, after which the Visitors, if any, are introduced).

M[ost]∴ W[ise]∴ — Brother Sev[ere]∴ Inspector, take two Elect with you and perform the most scrupulous search outside the Council Chamber. It is important that I be assured that we cannot be heard.

(The Severe Inspector leaves, accompanied by two Elect. A moment there is a knock at the door of a Master.)

M[ost]∴ W[ise]∴ — Who is the Master so reckless, as to come and disturb our labor? Find out who is knocking, Brother Grand Inspector.

(The Grand Inspector, having ascertained this from the Brother Master of Ceremonies, says:)

G[rand]∴-I[nspector]∴ — It is the Elect sent to make their visit, who have seized one of the temple workers and are bringing him.

M[ost]∴ W[ise]∴ — Let them be admitted.

(The doors open; the Brother Inspector takes the Candidate to the West, saying:)

B[rother]∴ I[nspector]∴ — This is one of the temple workers whom we found near here; we do not know his intentions.

(All the Elect cry out *Vengeance* and turn their daggers towards the Recipient. At the same time, the Grand Inspector lays a dagger against his heart, as if ready to stab him.

After a moment of silence:)

M[ost]∴ W[ise]∴ — Who are you?

(The Severe Inspector dictates the answers to him).

A. My name is *Joaben*, a Mason of the Master class.

Q. What do you want?

A. To throw myself at your feet and to beg your grace to be Hiram's avenger.

M[ost]∴ W[ise]∴ — Break his bonds and let him be free, as every Mason should be.

(He is untied).

M[ost]∴ W[ise]∴ — Assure us my Brother, by your answers, of the truth of what you have just stated.

Q. Are you a Master?

---

22 [Planche. Literally the board.]

A. Try me.

(The Most Wise asks him questions from the Instruction of the Master's Degree to ascertain whether he is instructed).

M[ost]∴ W[ise]∴ — Give the Master's Grip, Words and Sign to Brother Grand Inspector.

(He gives them.)

M[ost]∴ W[ise]∴ — Brethren who compose the Council, are you satisfied?

(All the Brethren raise their right hand and then let them fall in unison on their right thigh as a sign of approval).

M[ost]∴ W[ise]∴ — Since the Brother has received a unanimous, vote then ask him, Brother Grand Inspector, to advance nine steps (three as an Apprentice, three as a Fellow Craft and three as a Master), to the Throne, to come to swear his Obligation between our hands.

(The Brother Grand Inspector leads him to the Throne, where having arrived he kneels on his right knee, places his right hand on the Book of Wisdom[23,] and holds, in his left, the compass which embraces a gavel.

The Most Wise places his dagger against the Brother's forehead and the Grand Inspector places his behind the Brother's back. Then the Most Wise says:)

M[ost]∴ W[ise]∴ — My Brother, if your intentions are sincere then repeat after me:

OBLIGATION.

"I promise, upon the faith of a Mason, before the Grand Architect of the Universe and this Assembly, never to reveal the secret of the Elect to any man who has not done what I have done. I promise to scrupulously fulfil my obligations. I shall keep my promises, or may the most horrible death atone my perjury: may my body fall prey to the vultures, and may my memory be an abomination to the Sons of the Widow throughout the world over."

(The Obligation sworn, the Most Wise says:)

M[ost]∴ W[ise]∴ — Brother Grand Inspector, have the Brother return to the West. Make him take those steps backwards to teach him that nothing is ever easy and that he must never take offence at the mortifications ordered by the judgement of the Lodge, since humility is the true path to Masonic perfection; let him take his place among us.

(Arriving at the West, the Grand Inspector makes him sit on the stool between him and the Brother Severe Inspector. Then the Most Wise says:)

M[ost]∴ W[ise]∴ — Elect Brethren, my Brethren! Since a terrible assassination has deprived us of the Architect who, by his virtues and his knowledge, had deserved to have the conduct of the building made to sing the praises of the Great Architect of the Universe, everything is in consternation among the Craftsmen, and in universal mourning; the Morning Star no longer summons the Craftsmen to work. I implored him who makes vain all the works of men, the he does not build himself. He has deigned to answer my prayers. He does not want the crime to go unpunished any longer. A stranger has offered

---

23 Book containing the Statutes and Regulations governing the lodge.

himself to me and has revealed to me the retreat of Hiram's assassins. This discovery deserves the utmost secrecy and prompt deliberation.

(At this moment, all the Brethren shout *Vengeance!*)

M[ost]∴ W[ise]∴ — (*Addressing the Recipient:*) Brother Master, your zeal in fulfilling this important commission undoubtedly equals that of the other members of my Council.

I do not wish to defer the honour upon anyone: fate shall decide who will be chosen.

Brother Master of Ceremonies, do your duty.

(The Brother Master of Ceremonies presents the Ballot to the Candidate, who withdraws a paper on which is written *Joaben,* and then presents it to all the Elect. Then the Most Wise says:)

M[ost]∴ W[ise]∴ — *Joaben,* your wishes are fulfilled. You shall be the head of such a noble enterprise. I need not impress upon you the great importance of the job I am entrusting to you. Go towards Joppa, near a cave by the sea called *Benacar.* There you will find *Abibalc* and his accomplices. Try to capture them. Remember to only take their lives, should yours be in danger. Depart.

(The Voyage is made. The Severe Inspector accompanies the Recipient; after having fulfilled their mission they return, the latter holding the dagger in his right hand, his arm raised ready to strike, and his left extended along his body. He places himself in the West, crying out: *The crime is avenged.*)

M[ost]∴ W[ise]∴ — Let such a just vengeance serve as an example to the perverse, and show them the end that awaits the guilty. Let the heads of the assassins be exposed with their tools within the works for three days; at the end of those three days, their tools shall be broken, their heads burned, and their ashes cast to the winds, that there may no longer remain any remembrance of them amongst men and Masons. Let knowledge of their forfeiture and just punishment forever remain concentrated amongst Masons.

(The curtain is raised, revealing the exposed heads as has been said. The Most Wise continues and says:)

M[ost]∴ W[ise]∴ — Learn, my Brother, that everything that has happened and everything that you have done, was done to remind you, in the strongest way, of the first engagements you contracted on joining the Order and of the punishment that is justly deserved of whomever commits perjury. Everything presented to you has spoken of vengeance, but the Order is far from inspiring you with such a feeling. On the contrary, never forget that anyone armed otherwise than by legitimate power, can only be a criminal.

Come now, my Brother, to receive the reward you have earned. And all of you, my Brethren, help me to make an Elect.

(The Master of Ceremonies conducts the Recipient to the Throne to renew his obligation, during which time all the Elect are face him with their hands outstretched.

The Most Wise places his dagger on his right shoulder and says to him:)

M[ost]∴ W[ise]∴ — I In the name of the Grand Orient of *****, in its Grand Chapter, and by the powers invested in me by the Chapter of ****, I make you an Elect.

(He hands him the black cordon and clothes him in the Elect apron.)

M[ost]∴ W[ise]∴ — We have in this Degree, as in the preceding ones, a Sign, a Word, and a Grip.

Sign... {The Sign is made by the one who asks, drawing his dagger with his right hand, and raising it as if to strike. The respondent clenches his right fist and raises it, then withdraws it.

Grip... {The Grip is made by the questioner clenching his right hand, raising the thumb, and then presenting the thumb to the answerer. The latter must respond by grasping the thumb with his right hand. (*The same procedure is repeated alternately three times*).

Sacred Word... {The Sacred Word is N.....[24], which means *Vengeance*.

Password... {The password is A..... [25]

Go now, my Brother, and make yourself known to all the Brethren by giving them the Sign, the Word, and the Grip, starting with the Brother Grand Inspector.

(Having done this, the Most Wise proclaims it, saying:)

M[ost]∴ W[ise]∴ —Brothers Grand and Severe Inspectors, Secret Elect Brethren, you shall in the future recognize Brother N..... as a Member of the Council of the Secret Elect of the Chapter of *****, in its First Order.

(The Brother Grand and Severe Inspectors repeat this announcement.)

All the Elect, led by the Most Wise, applaud.

The new Recipient gives thanks. His applause is drowned out by an equal battery).

M[ost]∴ W[ise]∴ — (*Addressing the Recipient:*) My Brother, now newly admitted to the Council of the Elect, your desire for new Masonic knowledge has led you to apply for the first Degree above Symbolic Masonry. Perhaps you imagined seeing the various objects uncovered which the emblems have concealed from you in the previous Degrees; do not fear being deceived in your expectations, but, the path you must travel is long and painful; a tireless zeal will lighten your labor; you have pierced the darkness of the night. The light has shone in your eyes from the moment of your initiation: every day it will enlighten you more and if you have the strength to persist, then you will reach the true goal.

Take your place among the Elect, my Brother; lend an attentive ear to the instruction that is about to be given to you. It will enlighten you on what appears before your eyes, of which you have hitherto been unable to comprehend.

(The Master of Ceremonies takes him to his place; then Brother Orator makes a speech, to which he adds the history of the Degree).

INSTRUCTION.

Q. Are you a Secret Elect?

A. A cave is known to me, a lamp has enlightened me, a spring has quenched my thirst.

Q. What did you do in this capacity?

---
24 [Nekum...]
25 [Abibal...]

A. I was entrusted with an important mission, for which I received the award.

(He shows him his cordon.)

Q. What was your design?

A. To avenge the crime.

Q. What revenge was allowed to the Masons?

A. The just punishment of the assassins of their respectable Master, by the express command of the King.

Q. Where did the plan for revenge originate?

A. In a secret Council.

Q. At what hour?

A. In the darkness of the night.

Q. When did you leave?

A. Before daylight.

Q. Who illuminated you?

A. The Morning Star.

Q. Where did you start?

A. With the elimination of two culprits.

Q. Where did you find them?

A. Fleeing through steep rocks.

Q. Have you gone further?

A. I went inside a frightful cavern.

Q. What did you find there?

A. The traitor having just returned preparing to seek rest.

Q. What happened?

A. Frightened by the appearance of a Master, he took justice into his own hands.

Q. What was there left for you to do?

A. Nothing, since the revenge was accomplished.

Q. What hour was it by then?

A. The Sun had just set

Q. How old are you?

A. Nine weeks past seven years, because of the nine weeks that passed before the punishment of the crime.

Q. What does the form of your reception signify?

A. It described the formation and execution of the plan.

Q. Where do the eight lights come from, and a larger one separate from the rest?

A. They represent the nine Elect, with the largest indicating their leader.

Q. What do the other six lights signify?

A. The six Masters who were joined with them as Elect after their return.

Q. What do the colors of the Council Chamber mean?

A. Black signifies the darkness of the deed, the flames express our eagerness to take revenge, and the red denotes that it can only be extinguished by the blood of the guilty.

Q. What do the inscriptions on the pikes upon which the heads are planted mean?

A. That Heaven, which judges the actions of men, is the sure avenger, and never leaves crime unpunished.

Q. What does the dog mean?

A. That the slightest clue is often used to detect the culprit.

Q. What does the cave mean?

A. That there is no place so obscure and hidden that it can protect the perverse from torment or remorse.

Q. What does the arm holding a dagger mean?

A. That our people must always be ready to strike at whatever offends and injures virtue.

Q. What do the Morning Star and the other eight stars mean?

A. The time of departure and the number of the Elect. This means at the same time, that one cannot start too early when it comes to doing a good deed.

Q. What does the difficult staircase cut into the rock mean?

A. That it is necessary to take the most difficult steps to achieve the destruction of vice.

Q. What does the lamp mean?

A. That we receive unexpected light in the steps that are dictated to us by the Great Architect.

Q. What does the unexpectedly discovered spring mean?

A. That Providence never abandons us in pressing needs.

CLOSING.

Q. What is left for you to do?

A. Nothing, since everything is accomplished.

Q. How old are you?

A. Nine weeks past seven years, because of the nine weeks that passed before the punishment of the crime.

Q. What time is it?

A. The hour at which I came out of the cave, and the time when the Sun has just set.

M[ost]∴ W[ise]∴ — Since there is nothing left to do, and the Sun has set, Brother Grand and Severe Inspectors and Secret Elect Brethren, the Council is going to close. — With me, my Brethren!

(All the Brethren, led by the Most Wise, make the sign and applaud.

The Most Wise strikes eight raps and one slow one, and says:)

M[ost]∴ W[ise]∴ — The Council of the Elect is closed. Let us withdraw in peace.

(He gives one rap, then everyone leaves their ornaments and withdraws in peace).

———

2ᴅ ORDER.

DEGREE OF SCOTS.

The PRESIDENT is called the............... MOST GRAND.

The S[ENIO]R WARDEN.................. GRAND S[ENIO]R WARDEN.

The J[UNIO]R WARDEN.................. GRAND J[UNIO]R WARDEN.

All the BRETHREN.... .... GRAND OFF[ICERS]∴ SUBLIME M[ASTE]RS∴

2D ORDER.

DEGREE OF SCOTS.

Most Grand.

OPENING.

Q. Senior Grand Warden, are we tyled?

A. Most Grand, we are tyled.

Q. What led you here, my Brother?

A. The love of my duty, and a desire to attain sublime knowledge.

Q. What do you bring to make yourself worthy?

A. A pure heart, a zealous partisan of virtue and truth.

Q. Where do you work?

A. In an underground vault.

Q. What is the object of your search?

A. The knowledge of the art of perfecting what is imperfect, and arriving at the treasure of true morality.

Q. What was your reward?

A. I was admitted to a place of light and glory, where I completed my work.

Q. How old are you?

A. Nine years old.

Q. What time is it?

A. Noon.

Q. What do you mean by that?

A. That the Sun, at its highest point, illuminates our work.

M[ost]∴ G[rand]∴ — Since the Sun is at its highest point, it is time to set to work. Brothers Senior and Junior Grand Wardens, announce that I am going to open the Sublime Lodge of the Grand Elect at the Chapter of **** by the usual mysteries.

(The Grand Wardens make the announcement.

This done, the Most Grand strikes three raps. The Senior Grand Warden strikes five, the Junior Grand Warden seven and the Most Grand nine, making twenty-four raps and three intervals).

M[ost]∴ G[rand]∴ — Brothers Senior and Junior Grand Wardens, give me the word.

(The Wardens carry out the order, then the Most Grand says:)

M[ost]∴ G[rand]∴ — With me, my Brethren.

(All the Brethren, led by the Most Grand, make the sign of the sash, and applaud by three, five, seven and nine, and say *huzzah three times*).

M[ost]∴ G[rand]∴ — Grand Wardens, Grand Officer, Sublime Masters, the secret vault is opened, as is the work of the Grand Elect in the Chapter of **** in its Second Order.

(The Wardens repeat the announcement.

The Most Grand strikes one rap, and says:)

M[ost]∴ G[rand]∴ — Take your places, my Brethren.

(All the Brethren take their places. The Secretary reads out the Minutes of the previous labor, after which the Visitors, if any, are introduced).

RECEPTION.

(Everything having been prepared, the Most Grand leaves his place and walks forward, followed by the Wardens, then by the Dignitaries, and all the Brethren, two by two. The greatest silence is observed.

Arriving at the Chamber of Reflection, all the Brethren stand in two lines, in the same order as in the previous chamber, standing upright, swords in hand.

The Most Grand, addressing the Recipient, says to him:)

M[ost]∴ G[rand]∴ — My Brother, what do you ask?

(The Recipient makes some kind of response.

All the Brethren, led by the Most Grand, bow to the Recipient in salute, and return in the same order to the Chamber of Reception. The two Sacrificers and the two Purifiers place the Recipient between them and complete the process. The Preparing Brother follows immediately.

All the Officers in their place, the Recipient is placed between the Wardens.

The Most Grand puts questions to the Recipient taken from the previous Degree).

Q. Are you an Elect?

A. A cave is known to me, a spring has quenched my thirst, etc.

(After a few more questions, the Most Grand says to him:

M[ost]∴ G[rand]∴ — My Brother, your previous labor must have led you to make new discoveries. The promises made to you have no doubt animated your zeal. We must assume that your present steps are inspired by a love of knowledge of the good and the true. You are going to be subjected to great trials and we shall be demanding the greatest of sacrifices of you. Do you feel you have the necessary courage and resignation?

(He must answer *yes*).

M[ost]∴ G[rand]∴ — Brother Sacrificer, lead the victim to the Altar.

(The two Sacrificers lead the Recipient to the Altar of Sacrifice, go around it three times, have him kneel on the ground, as one takes the axe and the other the knife that they will find on the Altar; arms raised ready to strike, they remain in this attitude until after the following questions have been answered:[26]

M[ost]∴ G[rand]∴ — (*Addressing the Recipient:*) My Brother, have you scrupulously observed the Masonic obligations that you have contracted?

A. Yes.

Q. If you are pitiable enough to harbor in your heart some feeling of enmity towards your Brethren, do you consent to deposit it here?

A. Yes.

Q. Do you consent to sacrifice any affection unworthy of a virtuous man?

A. Yes.

M[ost]∴ G[rand]∴ — My Brother, your resignation causes you to find favour with us. In this respect we imitate the Great Architect of the Universe at the moment when his most faithful servant was about to consummate a sacrifice greater than if he had been the victim himself... Stand up.

(The two Sacrificers lead the Recipient to the West, where having arrived, the Most Grand says to him:)

M[ost]∴ G[rand]∴ — My Brother, the sacrifice we demand is that of any action, not being directed by the square and compass, which may offend virtue. Brother Purifiers, lead the Recipient to the ablution vase. Let him emerge, purified of everything that might harm innocence.

(The Brother Purifiers lead him to the ablution vase, lead him around it three times, dipping his hands nine times in the water above the wrist, and his feet up to the ankles, nine times also.

The Purifiers wipe the Recipient's feet and hands with a fine cloth; then they lead him between the Wardens, where having arrived, the Most Grand says:)

M[ost]∴ G[rand]∴ — Finish purifying the Recipient and then bring him to me to swear his Obligation.

---

26 The Recipient must be placed facing the South, with his right shoulder tucked in [*le corps effacé vers l"Ouestl'Ouest*], and his head bowed towards the Altar. The Sacrificer who holds the knife aims it at the heart, and the one who holds the axe aims it at the neck.

(The Purifiers lead the Recipient to the Altar, where incense burns slowly; They take him around it three times; passing his hands – flat, fingers extended, nine times over the smoke of the incense that is burning, and from there lead him to the Most Grand, who makes him swear the following obligation:[27]

OBLIGATION.

I swear and promise, in the presence of this Assembly, never to reveal the secrets, directly or indirectly, to the Profane, nor to inferior Masons; never to disregard a good Mason, of whatever status and condition he might be; to assist my Brethren with my advice and services; never to injure their fortune, status, or honour; and in the event of a breach of my engagements, I submit myself to be deprived of the true light, and deliver myself up to the contempt of the disciples of virtue and truth.

(The Recipient being raised, the Sacrificers cause him to step backwards three steps and then withdraw to one side; then the Most Grand says to him:)

M[ost]∴ G[rand]∴ — My Brother, the obligation you have just sworn is a new bond which unites you to us. It is time to reward your zeal: place in our hands the precious deposit you have in yours.

(Upon receiving the reply of the Recipient, who is left alone at this time, the Most Grand says to him:)

M[ost]∴ G[rand]∴ — My Brother, the request I have just made to you is most essential: it is impossible for me to admit you unless you hand over to me the object of my request. I hope that the Brethren will dispense me from this formality, but I cannot take it upon myself to continue without having consulted them. Go to the West.

Brothers Senior and Junior Grand Wardens, go and collect the votes, and come and report to me.

(The Wardens carry out the order, then the Most Grand says:)

M[ost]∴ G[rand]∴ — My Brother, it is impossible for me to go any further with your Reception. There may be concerns about what you have seen and heard, but you seem to us to be a good Mason. Besides, the Obligation you have just sworn reassures us. Withdraw.

(The Preparing Brother accompanies the Recipient out of the labors. He teaches him the Steps and the Password, ties a green cord around his body, the end of which comes back over his left shoulder, and hands him a golden triangle attached to a Master's cordon, on one side of which is engraved the Hebrew name of the Great Architect of the Universe; then he knocks on the door by three, five, seven and nine.

The Most Grand says:)

M[ost]∴ G[rand]∴ — Brother Senior Grand Warden, can you find out who is knocking?

(The Senior Grand Warden, after ascertaining it in the usual manner, says:)

G[rand]∴ S[enio]r∴ W[arden]∴ — The Recipient has taken the necessary steps and has found the object of your request.

M[ost]∴ G[rand]∴ — Let him be admitted.

(The doors open; the Recipient enters with the delta in hand and having reached the West, points to it and cries out: *Elhanam!*

---

[27] The Recipient takes his place as in the previous Degrees, and the Most Grand presents the sword on which the Recipient must place his right hand.

All the Brethren make the Sign of Ecstasy[28] while contemplating the triangle).

M[ost]∴ G[rand]∴ — My Brother, we cannot reward your zeal enough. Approach.

(The Recipient, accompanied by the two Purifiers, reaches the East using the steps of the Degree and hands the Delta to the Most Grand.

The Most Grand addresses all the Brethren as follows:)

M[ost]∴ G[rand]∴ — You know, my Brethren, just how important the ineffable word is. Let us deposit it here in this underground chamber, let us inlay it upon this pedestal, which will forever be the pedestal of knowledge; let us conceal it from the gaze of the Profane.

(The Purifiers raise the cubic stone. The Most Grand places the triangle on the pedestal, and the Purifiers cover it with the cubic stone. This being done, the Most Grand removes the rope which surrounds the Recipient, and says to him:)

M[ost]∴ G[rand]∴ — I release you from the bond of vice; may nothing in the future stand in the way of your career of virtue and truth.

(The Purifiers cause the Recipient to kneel. One of them hands the M[ost]∴ G[rand]∴ the trough, and the other the trowel, which latter the M[ost]∴ G[rand]∴ dips in the mixture and then passes across the forehead of the Recipient, saying:)

M[ost]∴ G[rand]∴ — Let your thoughts be pure.

(On each occasion one of the Purifiers wipes with a thin cloth. The Most Grand then passes the trowel over the lips of the Recipient, saying:)

M[ost]∴ G[rand]∴ — Let your mouth open only to utter words useful to your Brethren.

(He passes the trowel over his exposed heart, saying:):

M[ost]∴ G[rand]∴ — May your conscience be forever blameless and may all your actions be directed to the knowledge of truth.

(The Candidate rises and the Most Grand says:)

M[ost]∴ G[rand]∴ — Conduct the Brother to the Table of Show Bread.

(The Purifiers lead the Recipient there).

M[ost]∴ G[rand]∴ — My Brother, drink with your Brethren from the same cup and break bread together from the same loaf, to teach you that Masons are strengthened by the union and community of mutual assistance.

(The two Purifiers break the same bread with the Recipient, eat it together, and drink from the same cup. Having done so, they lead him to the Most Grand, who places a golden ring on the ring finger of his left hand, saying:)

---

28 ["Raise the open hands, palms foremost, the fingers together, and the thumb forming a square, to the height of the shoulder and lean the head towards the left shoulder, at the same time drawing back the left foot" – E-J Marconis de Nègre, *The Sanctuary of Memphis or Hermes*, translated by W. J. Coombes, p. 138. Original publisher: Bruyer, Paris 1849.]

M[ost]∴ G[rand]∴ — My Brother, this ring is a proof of the covenant you make with us; may your intentions always be pure, and only change when it changes its own nature.

Let us go now, my Brethren, to the Temple, to admire its beauties, and there give thanks to the Great Architect of the Universe.

(The Purifiers lead the Recipient slowly to the West. Meanwhile the pedestal and the smooth ashlar are removed.

The Recipient having reached the West, the Wardens each strike one rap, which is repeated by the Most Grand. At this signal, the lights are made to shine by removing the transparencies. The veil of the East is drawn back to reveal the seven-branched candlestick and all the riches within. At the same signal soft music should be heard).

M[ost]∴ G[rand]∴ — Brother Purifiers, send the Brother to the East, to receive there, the complement of his Reception.

(The Recipient, now walking freely, arrives at the East accompanied by the two Purifiers. The Most Grand enters the interior with the Recipient and hands him whatever is appropriate for lighting the seven-branched candlestick.

The Recipient goes around the candlestick three times, and lights each lamp in turn, NAMELY:

On the first round, the three tallest.

On the second round, the two next tallest.

And on the third round, those of the outer.

When this is done the Most Grand and the Recipient leave the interior, and the Most Grand resumes his place, asking all the Brethren to come to order and standing. The Recipient, kneeling at the foot of the Altar with his hand on the sword, is made to repeat his Obligation. Finally, the Most Grand places a naked sword on the Recipient's head and strikes it three, five, seven and nine times, saying:)

M[ost]∴ G[rand]∴ — In the name of the Grand Orient of *****, acting in its Grand Chapter, and by the powers invested in me by the Chap[ter]∴ of ****, I receive you, my Brother, Grand Elect Scots Master, into the Sovereign Chapter of ****, in its second Order.

(Then the Most Grand raises him up, decorates him with the cordon and sash, and clothes him with the apron. Then he says to him:)

M[ost]∴ G[rand]∴ — My Brother, in this Degree, as in the preceding ones, we have a Sign, a Word and a Grip.

Sign… { The sign is called the Sign of Ecstasy; it is made with the arms extended to the height of the shoulder, the hands open at right angles, the head bent over the left shoulder, and the left foot drawn back. The Sign of the sash is substituted, which is made by raising the right palm upwards to the left shoulder and then drawing it down along the body to the right hip. This sign is used for greeting and for requesting permission to speak.

Countersign…{ The countersign is that of the cutting the belly. It is made by bringing the right hand to the left hip and then withdrawing it horizontally to the right.

Grip… { The Grip is made by taking each other's right hand and turning it from one side to the other three times, saying: B. N. S.[29]

Walk… { The walk is performed by three, five, seven and nine, as you have done.

Steps… { These steps symbolize the descent of the staircase; they are made sideways, because of insufficient space. They are made as follows: three sideways, starting from the left foot; five starting from the right foot; seven from the left, and then three times three, starting first from the right, then from the left, then from the right, and finally forming a square.

Sacred Word… { The sacred word is S∴ H∴ P∴[30] This is the inexplicable name used to express the name of the four letters, or *tetra grammaton*.

Password… { The password is E∴, which means *thanks be to God*.

You come to order by making the Sign of the Sash.

You do not come to order during ceremonies.

Go now, Brother, and make yourself known to all the Brethren, starting with the Grand Wardens, and give them what you have just received.

(The Purifiers lead the Recipient to the Senior and Junior Grand Wardens, and then to all the Brethren.

When this is done, the Most Grand gives one rap and the music stops).

PROCLAMATION.

M[ost]∴ G[rand]∴ — Brother Grand Wardens, Grand Officer Sublime Masters, you will in future recognize Brother ***** as a Grand Elect and member of the College of Scots in the Chap[ter]∴ of ****, in its Second Order.

(The Wardens repeat the announcement.

All the Brethren, led by the Most Grand, applaud by three, five, seven and nine, followed by the triple *huzzah*.

The newly received thanks them, and his applause is drowned out by three, five, seven, nine, and the *huzzah*.

The Most Grand addresses the following speech to the Recipient:

M[ost]∴ G[rand]∴ — Everything is changed in your eyes, my Brother. New emblems are presented to you on all sides, but their meanings become more perceptible to you. Do not allow yourself to fall behind – make a greater effort every day, and you will inevitably discover the true goal.

Now take your place among us and listen carefully to the Instruction you are about to receive.

(One of the Purifiers has the newly-received placed at the South, in the first position after the Officers.

The Orator gives a speech to which he appends the history of the Degree).

---

29 [Berith, Neder, Schelemoth – Covenant, Promise, Perfection.]
30 [Schem, Hamm, Phorasch].

INSTRUCTION.

Q. What led you here, my Brother?

A. The love of my duty, and a desire to attain sublime knowledge.

Q. What do you bring to make yourself worthy?

A. A pure heart, a zealous partisan of virtue and truth.

Q. Where do you work?

A. In an underground vault.

Q. Where was the underground vault located?

A. It was constructed in secret beneath the most mysterious part of the Temple.

Q. What was this secret vault used for?

A. To contain a precious deposit.

Q. In what place was it?

A. The precious delta, on which were engraved the true characters of the ineffable word, was inlaid on a marble pedestal placed in the middle of the vault and covered again with the cubic stone.

Q. What was the cubic stone?

A. A stone of agate cut into a quadrangular shape, containing the secret words of the Royal Art.

Q. How do you decipher the letters inlayed on it?

A. By reading them according to the Art.

Q. How were you introduced?

A. By three, five, seven, nine.

Q. What happened to you?

A. I was subjected to rigorous trials.

Q. What trial did you undergo?

A. The point on my heart and the iron on my neck, I voluntarily sacrificed my passions.

Q. Was that enough to be admitted?

A. After purifying myself, I was sent on a search to earn my full admission.

Q. Were you successful in your search?

A. By a special favour and an unforeseen light, I made the discovery of the precious deposit: I returned holding it in my hand and in the same state I was in when I made the discovery.

Q. What is the object of your search?

A. The knowledge of the art of perfecting what is imperfect, and of arriving at the treasure of true morality.

Q. What has been your reward?

A. The bond of vices has been broken on me; the trowel imprinted with a prepared mixture has been passed over my forehead, lips and heart; I have taken part in the banquet of the Great Elect; I have received the pledge of a new covenant, and finally, I have been admitted to a place of light and glory, where I have finished my work..

Q. What was the mixture composed of?

A. Of milk, oil, wine and flour.

Q. What do these things signify?

A. Gentleness, wisdom, strength, and beauty – qualities essential of the Grand Elect.

Q. What are the Lodges of the Grand Elect Scots Masters called?

A. Lodges of high science, and their labors sublime.

Q. How do you get there?

A. With firmness of heart and on one's countenance the brow; characters of irreproachable men.

Q. What is their first duty?

A. To observe with respect the laws of Masonry, to practise the soundest morals, and to assist their Brethren.

Q. How many lights do you have?

A. Three times nine.

Q. What do they represent?

A. The inextinguishable lamps deposited in the secret vault.

Q. Why is the name *secret vault* at the opening changed to the name *sacred vault* at the closing?

A. Once the deposit was placed there, it was only known by this latter title.

Q. Where do the Grand Elect travel?

A. In all parts of the world, to spread true knowledge.

Q. How old are you?

A. Nine years old.

Q. Why is the number eighty-one honored among us?

A. Because it is the one that contains the most Masonic combinations and, and in terms of the art, it is three times the cube, or the largest square.

CLOSING.

Q. Whence came you?

A. I come from a search.

Q. What do you bring?

A. The precious deposit.

Q. Where did you deposit it?

A. In a secret and impenetrable place.

Q. How did you get there?

A. By three, five, seven and nine.

Q. Why this deposit?

A. To recover, in the event of alteration, the true characters of the ineffable word, and all the secret words of Masonry.

Q. What do you take from here?

A. The price of my zeal and a greater desire to exercise it.

Q. What is its purpose?

A. The glory of the Great Architect of the Universe.

Q. How old are you?

A. Nine years.

Q. What time is it?

A. Midnight, the time to close our labor.

M[ost]∴ G[rand]∴ — Since it is midnight and the time to close our work, Brothers Senior and Junior Grand Wardens, announce that I am going to close the Lodge of the Sublime Grand Elect at the Chapter of ****, by the usual numbers, and that the sacred vault will be closed.

(The Wardens make the announcement).

M[ost]∴ G[rand]∴ — With me, my Brethren!

(All the Brethren, led by the Most Grand, make the sign of the sash, and applaud by three, five, seven and nine, followed by the triple *huzzah*).

M[ost]∴ G[rand]∴ — Brethren Senior and Junior Grand Wardens, the sacred vault is closed, as also is the work of the Grand Elect at the Chapter of ****, in its Second Order.

(The Wardens repeat this.

The Most Grand gives one rap.

Everyone takes off their jewels and ornaments and retires in peace).

———————

3D ORDER.

DEGREE OF KNIGHT OF THE EAST.

East Hall.

The PRESIDENT is called the	SOVEREIGN MASTER.
The SENIOR WARDEN	SENIOR GENERAL.
The JUNIOR WARDEN	JUNIOR GENERAL.
The ORATOR	GRAND ORATOR.
The SECRETARY	GRAND MASTER OF DISPATCHES.
The MASTER OF CEREMONIES	GRAND MASTER OF THE PALACE.
All the BRETHREN	BROTHER KNIGHTS.
The RECIPIENT	ZOROBABEL.

West Hall.

The PRESIDENT is called the	MOST ILLUSTRIOUS MASTER.
The SENIOR WARDEN	ILLUSTRIOUS SENIOR WARD[EN]∴
The JUNIOR WARDEN	ILLUSTRIOUS JUNIOR WARD[EN]∴

III^D ORDER.

KNIGHT OF THE EAST.

Sov[ereign]∴ Master.

OPENING.

EAST HALL.

All the Knights are in their places except for the one presiding, who enters only after being announced by one stomp of the floor next to the door.

The Senior General says:

S[enio]r∴ G[eneral]∴ — Knights, the Sovereign Master assembles us to hold Council. Let us be attentive to what he is going to say and propose. Here he comes.

(The Sovereign Master enters and goes to his place accompanied by the two Guards of the Tower, who return to their places as soon as the Sovereign Master is in place.

The Sovereign Master gives one rap with the pommel of his sword and then salutes all the Knights.

The Knights, led by the Generals, respond by placing their right hand over their heart and bowing. Then the Sovereign Master says:)

Q. Senior General, what is the first duty of a true Knight?

A. It is to provide for the safety of the Council and to ensure that only Knights can enter it.

Sov[ereign]∴ M[aster]∴ — Senior and Junior Generals, perform the inspection.

The two Generals go to examine the doors of the Tower and see if the guards are on duty. Back in their places, they say:)

Gen[eral]∴ — The guards are surrounding the Palace, the Council is safe.

Q. Is that sufficient?

A. We still need to make sure that all those who are here are worthy of attending the Council.

Sov[ereign]∴ M[aster]∴ — Senior and Junior Generals, make sure of that.

(They make sure of this, and report it to the Sov[ereign]∴ Master, saying:)

Gen[eral]∴ — All the Members here present are good Knights.

Q. What time is it?

A. The revolution of the ten weeks of years of the Captivity.

(The Sovereign Master says:)

Sov[ereign]∴ M[aster]∴ — Senior and Junior Generals, since it is so, announce that the Council is about to open.

(The two Generals make the announcement.

The Sovereign Master strikes seven raps with the pommel of his sword, with an interval between the fifth and the last two.

The two Generals repeat the same battery.

The Sovereign Master says:)

Sov[ereign]∴ M[aster]∴ — With me, Knights.

(All the Knights, led by the Sovereign Master, applaud by five and two, and say together in unison: *Honor to the Knights!*)

Sov[ereign]∴ M[aster]∴ — The Council is open as also is the work of the Chapter of **** in its Third Order.

(The Generals repeat the announcement.

The Sovereign Master gives one rap, and says:)

Sov[ereign]∴ M[aster]∴ To your places, Knights.

(The Secretary reads out the Minutes of the previous labor, after which the Visitors, if any, are introduced).

Sov[ereign]∴ M[aster]∴ — All Knights, Members of my Council, the reason I have assembled you today is to give me your opinion on a marvellous dream that I had last night. You, Grand Master of the Palace, who is gifted with the sublime gift of interpreting them, I will tell you what I saw in my sleep.

(The Grand Master of the Palace responds:)

G[rand]∴ M[aster]∴ — Sovereign Master, this gift is not the result of a natural wisdom of which I can avail myself, and which is not found in other men, but it sometimes please the Great Architect of the Universe to pour out upon us weak humans this supernatural knowledge when, through visions, he deigns to manifest his decrees.

G[rand]∴ M[aster]∴ — Grand Master of the Palace, I recognize the spirit which fills you; here is what

I saw: A roaring lion was ready to pounce upon me to devour me; I fled in terror; a brilliant light from a shining glory dazzled my eyes; my predecessors Nebuchadnezzar and Balthazar, seemed to be laden with chains; a formidable voice was heard, saying, " to me: Free the captives, or your crown will pass into foreign hands!" Since that moment I have lost my peace of mind. It is up to you to help me with your opinion, to make careful deliberation.

(The Grand Master of the Palace replies:)

G[rand]∴ M[aster]∴ — This, Sovereign Master, is what this apparition signifies. The voice you heard is that of the Great Architect, who long ago announced you to the world, who has caused victory to march before you, and made you dominate the East. The captives whom you are commanded to set free are those who have been groaning for ten weeks of years, in slavery; the Great Architect orders you to return them to the same condition as they were in; let their possessions be restored to them, their city rebuilt, and their Temple restored to all its splendor.

The chains on your predecessors show you that, if they were used by the hands of the Great Architect as the instrument for punishing his people, that they will be punished for the excesses they indulged in; finally, the lion ready to devour you presages the end that awaits you, if you turn a deaf ear to the voice of the Great Architect.

Sov[ereign]∴ M[aster]∴ — He has spoken, and he must be obeyed.

(He stands up, as does the whole Council, and says:)

Sov[ereign]∴ M[aster]∴ — Let the Captivity end.

(He lowers the point of his sword and then raises it quickly, to signify freedom.)

The two Generals and the Knights present the points of their swords in unison, and lower them to the ground, as a sign of acquiescence to the Sovereign Master's will of the Sovereign Master, and then raise them quickly.

The Knights, led by the Sovereign Master, take their places.

RECEPTION.

(The Recipient, guided by the Master of Ceremonies, sighs at the door of the Temple to make himself heard. The guards half-open the door and seeing a man in mourning, close it again. One of them reports the matter to the Junior General, who tells the Senior, who informs the Sovereign Master, saying:)

S[enio]r∴ G[eneral]∴ — Sovereign Master, a man in mourning wishes to enter the Council.

Sov[ereign]∴ M[aster]∴ — Find out who he is; take the greatest precautions and give me an exact account.

(The Senior General tells the Junior, and the latter the Guards of the Tower. One of them opens the door, and says to the Recipient:)

Q. What do you ask?

A. To speak to your Sovereign Master if I may.

Q. Who are you?

A. The leader of my equals, a Freemason by status, and a captive by disgrace.

Q. What is your name?

A. Zorobabel.

Q. What has brought you here?

A. The tears and misery of my Brothers.

Q. What come you here to do?

A. I come in the name of the Great Architect to beg the Sovereign to display his goodness and justice.

Q. On what?

A. I come to ask for mercy for my compatriots who have been in servitude for ten weeks of years.

Q. What favour do you seek?

A. May the Sovereign's clemency grant us freedom, and allow us to go and rebuild the Temple of the Great Architect.

(The guard says to him:)

I will forward your complaints and requests to the Sovereign.

(He tells the Junior General, and the latter makes the announcement to the Senior General, who says:)

S[enio]r∴ G[eneral]∴ — Sovereign Master, Zorobabel, a captive and the first of his equals, seeks to appear at the foot of the Throne. He comes to solicit the clemency of the Sovereign Master, freedom for his countrymen, and that of rebuilding the Temple of the Grand Architect.

Sov[ereign]∴ M[aster]∴ — Since he was led here by just motives, let him be granted the favour of appearing before me with his face uncovered.

(The Senior General says to the Junior General:)

S[enio]r∴ G[eneral]∴ — Junior General, the Sovereign will permit the captive to appear with his face uncovered.

(The Junior General informs the guards.

The door of the Tower opens, and the Master of Ceremonies enters with the Recipient. He removes the veil from over his head and conducts him between the two Generals in front of the Throne, where he makes him prostrate himself).

Sov[ereign]∴ M[aster]∴ — Zorobabel, I have felt as you have, the weight of your captivity. I am ready to release you from it, granting you your freedom at once, if you will communicate the secrets of Masonry to me, for which I have always had the greatest respect.

(Zorobabel replies:)

Zorob[abel]∴ — One of the principles of our Order is equality, which cannot reign here: your rank, your titles and your grandeur are not compatible with our Brotherhood. The commitments I have made, and which I cannot violate, prevent me from revealing our secrets to you. If my freedom comes at this price, then I prefer captivity.

Sov[ereign]∴ M[aster]∴ — Are you thinking about refusing me? Upon you alone depends the freedom of your nation and the freedom also to raise the walls of your Temple. My intention is to decorate you like the nobles of my court, and to hand over to you all the riches taken from your homeland by my predecessors. Grand Master of Ceremonies, walk with Zorobabel through the halls of the Palace; point out to him all the riches which are up to him to recover.

(The Master of Ceremonies leads him around a full circle, then says:)

M[aster of]∴ C[eremonies]∴ — Sovereign Master, his soul appears to be tested.

Sov[ereign]∴ M[aster]∴ — Can you really look upon this spectacle without being moved? Do you persist in refusing your possessions and freedom?

Zorob[abel]∴ Yes, Sovereign Master.

(The Sovereign Master says, in a firm tone:)

Sov[ereign]∴ M[aster]∴ — I'm going to see your body tested as your soul. Guards, put him through the fire!

(Two guards bring a lighted brazier and place it in front of the Recipient.

The Master of Ceremonies has him stretch out both hands above the brazier, high enough to avoid burning himself).

Sov[ereign]∴ M[aster]∴ — See the severity of the penalties which threaten you if you persist in your refusal. I shall only give you this moment to decide. Answer.

Zorob[abel]∴ — I cannot betray my obligations.

(The Sovereign Master, addressing the Council, says:)

Sov[ereign]∴ M[aster]∴ — Generals and Knights, so much fortitude surprises me, and my respect for his Order only increases. It is not within me to implement the threats which I have used only as tests. Do you think he should be released?

(The Senior General, and all the Knights, nod in agreement with their swords.

The Sovereign Master makes the same sign, and says:)

Sov[ereign]∴ M[aster]∴ — Let Zerubbabel and all his nation be free.

(The Master of Ceremonies removes the chains from the Recipient. The Sovereign Master:)

Sov[ereign]∴ M[aster]∴ — Go now to your own country. I permit you to restore the Temple destroyed by my ancestors. Your treasures shall be returned to you; be recognized as the leader of your equals. I order that all help and assistance be provided to you as if to myself, in all the places of your passage, and that it be delivered to you out of my treasures of what to offer, in sacrifice upon your Altar, oxen, sheep, lambs, and all that shall be necessary to pay homage to the Great Architect of the Universe and to implore his protection over me and my people. Approach and receive the particular marks of friendship and esteem that you have earned.

(The Master of Ceremonies leads him to the foot of the Throne, where he makes him kneel.

The Sovereign Master says:)

Sov[ereign]∴ M[aster]∴ — I arm you with this sword, a distinctive mark among your equals and make you a Knight.

(He strikes him with his sword on each shoulder and kisses him. He then gives him the apron and the green cordon, which he passes from his left shoulder to his right hip, saying:)

Sov[ereign]∴ M[aster]∴ — I have adopted these decorations in imitation of the Craftsmen of your Temple. Although these marks are not accompanied by any mystery, I nevertheless grant them as an honour only to the nobles of my court. From now on you shall enjoy the same advantages. I place you in the hands of my Generals, who will take care of your departure and that of your people, and will provide you with supplies to take you to the place to where you are to re-establish the Temple. I so order it.

(The Master of Ceremonies leads the Recipient between the Generals. The Senior General takes the Recipient by the hand and leads him to the Tower, where he leaves him while the Knights pass in silence into the West Hall and change their decorations).

WEST HALL.

(As soon as all the Brethren are in place, the Master of Ceremonies looks for the Recipient from the Tower and leads him to the entrance of the Bridge, where he takes leave of him and bids him continue on his way.

Several Knights accompany the Recipient to make up the numbers.

The Knights who have acted as Guards lay down their pikes and, armed with swords, go to the Bridge to dispute the Recipient's passage, and represent a fight. The Recipient defends himself but, during the struggle, loses his cordon and apron; but, keeping his sword, he reaches, after having crossed the bridge, as far as the door of the western where he raps by three, five, seven and nine.

The Junior Warden raps seven times with the pommel of his sword, which is repeated by the Senior Warden and then by the Most Illustrious Master, to whom the Senior Warden announces that someone knocks as a Grand Elect Scots Master.

The Most Illustrious Master says:)

I[llustrious]∴ M[aster]∴ — Illustrious Senior Warden, find out who is knocking.

(The Senior Warden tells the Junior Warden, who goes out.

The Brother Expert on the porch half-opens the door and asks who is knocking.

The Recipient replies:)

Recip[ient]∴ — I ask to see my Brethren, the unfortunate remnants who escaped from captivity, to give them the news of my deliverance.

(The Brother Expert passes this on to the Junior Warden, who informs the Senior and the latter to the Most Illustrious Master in these terms:)

I[llustrious]∴ S[enior]∴ — It is one of our captive Brethren, who brings news of his deliverance.

(The Most Illustrious Master says:)

I[llustrious]∴ M[aster]∴ — My Brethren, the news the captive brings appears to be well founded. The ten weeks of years are over, and the day of the rebuilding has arrived. Let us not neglect such a precious omen.

Illustrious Senior Warden, ask him his name, what country he is from, his age, and what news he brings.

(The Senior Ward[en]∴ passes this on to the Junior, and the latter to the Brother Expert, who asks the Recip[ient]∴ as he opens the door:)

Q. What is your name?

A. Zorobabel.

Q. What country are you from?

A. From the land beyond the river, to the west of Assyria.

Q. How old are you?

A. Ten weeks of years.

Q. What news do you bring?

A. Freedom, and permission to rebuild the Temple.

(The Brother Expert reports this to the Junior Warden, who says it to the Senior, and the latter to the Most Illustrious Master, in these terms:)

I[llustrious]∴ S[enior]∴ — Zorobabel, from the land beyond the river, to the west of Assyria, aged ten weeks of years, brings news of freedom and permission to rebuild the Temple.

(The Most Illustrious Master says:)

I[llustrious]∴ M[aster]∴ — Yes, my Brethren, the captivity ceases, and our sleep has ended. The captive is the prince of the tribe who is to raise our Temple. Let him be admitted among us and recognized as the guide and mainstay of our labors.

(The doors open; the Recipient is led in by the Master of Ceremonies and placed between the Wardens. The Brethren who have accompanied the Recipient resume their places.)

(The Senior Warden says:)

S[enio]r∴ W[arden]∴ — This is Zorobabel who desires to be admitted into the brotherhood.

(The Most Illustrious Master says:)

I[llustrious]∴ M[aster]∴ — Zorobabel, tell us the interesting story of your deliverance.

(The Recipient replies:)

Recip[ient]∴ — Cyrus, having allowed me to appear at the foot of the throne, was moved by our miseries. He granted us freedom and permission to rebuild the Temple. He ordered all its riches to be handed over to me and armed me with this sword for the relief and defence of my Brethren, honouring me with his order of chivalry. I departed, escorted according to the order he had given, but I was attacked by enemies who came to meet me when crossing the River. I triumphed over them, but despite the victory, I lost the distinctive marks our liberator had given me.

(The Most Illustrious Master says:)

I[llustrious]∴ M[aster]∴ — The loss you suffered, my Brother, symbolizes the stripping from you of worldly pomp and grandeur. Our principles, founded on equality, could not be known to the prince, your liberator, therefore you have only lost the profane marks of this prince. But before I communicate to you the secrets that have been preserved among the rest of our Brethren, we require assurances from you.

(The Most Illustrious Master asks him the following questions, to which he may add such others as he deems fit:)

Q. What degree do you have?

A. That of the Grand Elect.

Q. Give me the sign of this Degree.

A. (He does so.)

Q. Give the Word and Grip to the Brother Senior Ward[en]∴

A. (He does so.)

(After the questions, the Most Illustrious Master says:)

I[llustrious]∴ M[aster]∴ — I think Zorobabel is worthy of being admitted among us. Do you agree?

(The Brethren show their agreement with the raised hand sign, with the arm held at shoulder height.

The Most Illustrious Master says:)

I[llustrious]∴ M[aster]∴ — Brother Master of Ceremonies, advance the Recipient by the three steps of the Master, that he may come to take the commitment we require.

(The Master of Ceremonies brings him to the foot of the Throne).

OBLIGATION.

That which a man provided with the five senses promises without being provoked by any human force or power, fear or violence, must be an eternal obligation. He cannot depart from it without being a dishonest man. Thus I oblige myself never to reveal to any Profane the secrets of the Knights, nor to any Brother of an inferior degree without having the authority to do so. I wish to be regarded as a false Brother and despicable being, should I violate this commitment, that I make of my own free will. May the Great Architect help me.

(The Most Illustrious Master lifts him up and says:

I[llustrious]∴ M[aster]∴ — My Brother, the destruction of the Temple has subjected the Masons to such severe disgraces that we feared that their captivity and misfortunes must have contributed to their corruption and released them from their duties. This is why, while awaiting the promised moment of the rebuilding, we have withdrawn to secret and private places, where we faithfully preserve some of the remains of the ancient Temple. We only admit those who make themselves known, both by their signs and by their morals, as true and legitimate Masons, to whom we then communicate the mysteries of our union. The freedom you have obtained for us, and the efforts you have made to join us, testify too greatly in your favour for us to conceal anything from you. See then the state to which we are reduced, and the work we must do to regain our lost splendor. Brother Master of Ceremonies, make the Recipient take three Master steps backwards, to signify to him the decline of our labors.

(The three steps lead the Recipient between the Wardens, where he should see a pile of ruins.

With the Recipient positioned between the Wardens, the Most Illustrious Master says:)

I[llustrious]∴ M[aster]∴ — Y Such is the desolation into which the work of even the greatest of Masons can fall: the walls collapsed, the Altar turned over, the ornaments devastated, while among the Craftsmen fear and distrust reign. But at last, the time has come, our hopes are reborn, our fetters are shattered, our losses will be repaired, our mourning is over, and we shall resume our labor.

Brother Master of Ceremonies, take the Recipient on a tour of the interior and exterior works.

(While the Recipient walks around the exterior works, the groups of lights are lit, the red hangings are rare changed to green, leaving the crimson festoons; the curtain is drawn to reveal the Altar ar the rear and the Glory in all its magnificence. All the Knights stand, sword in one hand and trowel in the other.

The Most Illustrious Master stands behind the Altar at the rear.)

SECOND ENTRY.

(The Master of Ceremonies stomps the floor seven times, by five and two.

The Wardens each give one rap, which is repeated by the Most Illustrious Master. The Junior Warden reports this to the SW, and the latter to the Most Illustrious Master:)

S[enio]r∴ W[arden]∴ — Someone knocks at the door as a Knight of the East.

(The Most Illustrious Master says:)

I[llustrious]∴ M[aster]∴ — See who is knocking.

(The Senior Warden, after ascertaining this according to custom, says:)

S[enio]r∴ W[arden]∴ It is Zorobabel who asks to return.

(The Most Illustrious Master says:)

I[llustrious]∴ M[aster]∴ — Let him be admitted.

(The doors open, and the Recipient is introduced between the Wardens.

The Most Illustrious Master says:

I[llustrious]∴ M[aster]∴ — My Brethren, the rebuilding of the Temple is now our principal object. Zorobabel, such a great work was reserved for you, the commitments you have just made with us, ensure its execution. We need a leader to guide us in our work, and at the same time be our defender: the sword with which you are armed, and which you have been able to preserve, guarantees the success of our work. Come now and receive the attributes of your new status and the knowledge of our mysteries.

(The Master of Ceremonies leads the Recipient to the foot of the Altar by the steps of the Degree.

The Most Illustrious Master descends from his place and, standing in front of the Recipient, who must be kneeling, he hands him a trowel, saying:)

I[llustrious]∴ M[aster]∴ — You have been decorated with the title of Knight of the East, and I will decorate you with the title of Knight Mason. This trowel is its symbol; henceforth work with the sword in one hand and the trowel in the other.

(The Most Illustrious Master puts the sash on him, saying:)

I[llustrious]∴ M[aster]∴ — This sash must accompany you in all Lodges, for it is the mark of the [order of] chivalry to which you have just been admitted.

(The Most Illustrious Master puts the apron on him, saying:)

I[llustrious]∴ M[aster]∴ — This apron symbolizes for you our deliverance, and that our former labors are revived.

(The Most Illustrious Master gives him the green rosette, saying:)

I[llustrious]∴ M[aster]∴ — To preserve the memory of our liberator, we have adopted this rosette, which you will place at the bottom of the cordon of your previous Degree.

(The Most Illustrious Master gives him the jewel, saying:)

I[llustrious]∴ M[aster]∴ This jewel, with its addition of saltire swords, announces to you the triumph of Masonry.

(The Most Illustrious Master then gives him the Sign, Word, and Grip, saying:)

Sign… { The Sign is made by bringing the right hand to the left shoulder, from where it is lowered along the body, sliding across to the right hip, to which one responds by bringing the right hand to the left hip, and withdrawing, also sliding it across to the right hip.

Grip… { The Grip is made by bringing the right hand to the sword to draw it from the scabbard as if one wanted to fight; then throwing the body forward and passing the right foot behind the left, and then raising the left arm with the hand outstretched as if one was trying to push someone away, so that in this position, their left hands meet, interlocking their fingers and immediately embracing.

Word… { The Word is *Judas,* and the response is *Benjamin.*

Password… { The password is *Hia vaurum hammem,* which means *They shall pass the waters.*

Order… { The order is, after having drawn his sword, running it flat and perpendicularly along the right side of the body, with the fist at the height of the hip.

The Walk is by seven, as you performed it.

Go now, Brother, and identify yourself to the Brother Wardens.

(The Master of Ceremonies guides him and, after he has been recognized, he places him on a seat between the Wardens to listen to the Discourse and the Instruction.

After the Discourse, the Most Illustrious Master speaks to the Recipient as follows:)

I[llustrious]∴ M[aster]∴ — My Brother, we shall now proceed to your Proclamation, and place you in the Degree you are to have among your equals.

Illustrious Brother Wardens, announce to all our Brethren that they must in the future recognise Brother **** as a Member of the Council of the Knights of the Orient of the Chap[ter]∴ of *****, in its Third Order.

(The proclamation made by the Wardens, the Most Illustrious Master says:)

I[llustrious]∴ M[aster]∴ — Illustrious Brother Wardens, and all Knights, do you consent to Zorobabel presiding over our work?

(All the Knights make a sign of acquiescence with their swords.

The Most Illustrious Master makes the same sign, and says:)

I[llustrious]∴ M[aster]∴ — Pass on then, Brother Knight, to the seat of Master of our Labors.

(The Master of Ceremonies leads the recipient through the Steps of the Knight.

The Most Illustrious Master then takes him by the hand and places him on the Throne. Then, withdrawing from the left side, he says:)

I[llustrious]∴ M[aster]∴ — Brother Knights, this is the Master who will preside over our labor.

(All the Brethren salute with their swords, saying once: *Honor to the Knight!*

The Recipient salutes with his sword and says once: *Honor to the Knights!*

When the work is finished, the Most Illustrious Master stays alongside the new Master and closes the work).

INSTRUCTION.

Q. Are you a Knight?

A. I received the character.

Q. Make yourself better known.

A. Begin and I will finish.

Q. Judas.

A. Benjamin.

Q. How did you reach this Degree?

A. Through humility and patience.

Q. Whom did you speak to?

A. To him upon whom our deliverance depended.

Q. Did he grant you your request?

A. After testing me, he free me and all my Brethren and honored me with the title of Knight of the East.

Q. What did you do after you obtained your freedom?

A. I went to my homeland to find the rest of my Brethren there.

Q. Where did they receive you?

A. In a Council assembled on the ruins of the Temple.

Q. How was the Council illuminated?

A. By ten groups of seven lights.

Q. What does this number of lights mean?

A. The duration of the Captivity.

Q. What was your work?

A. Rebuilding the Temple of the Great Architect.

Q. How did you work upon it?

A. With the sword in one hand and the trowel in the other.

Q. On what plan was the Temple rebuilt?

A. On the plan of the destroyed Temple.

Q. Where were the materials taken?

A. The stones were taken from the quarries of Tyre and the wood from the forests of Lebanon because it should in all respects be like the first.

Q. How should this be applied?

A. That Masonry must be one and cannot suffer change without alteration.

Q. What shapes did the captives' chains have?

A. They were triangular.

Q. Why?

A. The victors, knowing the respect they had for the Delta, gave this shape to the chains, to mortify them further.

Q. What do the words of recognition mean?

A. The name of the class of those who work on the rebuilding.

Q. Why did we adopt the colour sea-green?

A. In memory of the event, out of gratitude and in the hope of recovery.

Q. In what state did you find the Masons when you arrived at the ruins of the Temple?

A. In mourning and dejection; the Elect of all Lodges given over to

confusion and disorder.

Q. What do the overturned columns, displaced instruments and furniture mean?

A. That any Lodge composed of Brothers who are indiscreet and vicious, loses the harmony which is its principal ornament and cannot delay destroying itself.

Q. What do the obstacles encountered when crossing the Bridge mean?

A. The ardent desire which every good Mason must have to learn, and the difficulties which he must strive to overcome in order to discover the truth.

Q. What is the meaning of the resistance that the new builders mounted against their enemies during the rebuilding?

A. The care with which every Mason should oppose, the introduction of vices and abuses.

Q. What art do you profess?

A. Masonry.

Q. What buildings do you build?

A. Temples and tabernacles.

Q. Where do you build them?

A. For want of land, we build them in our heart.

Q. How old are you?

A. Ten weeks of years.

CLOSING.

Q. Brother Senior Warden, what are you?

A. A Freemason and Knight.

Q. How do you work?

A. With the sword in one hand and the trowel in the other.

Q. Whence came you?

A. From the East.

Q. What do you bring?

A. The freedom to work.

Q. What is your work?

A. Restoring the Temple of the Great Architect.

Q. How old are you?

A. Ten weeks of years.

Q. What time are we in?

A. At the time of rebuilding.

(The Most Illustrious Master says:)

I[llustrious]∴ M[aster]∴ — Since the time has arrived, since we are assured of freedom to work, and since all that remains is for us to carry out what we have deliberated, announce, Illustrious Brother Senior and Junior Wardens, that the Council of Knights is about to close, as well as the labor of the Chapter of **** in its Third Order.

(The Wardens make this announcement, then the Most Illustrious Master says:)

I[llustrious]∴ M[aster]∴ — On me, my Brethren!.

(All the Knights, led by the Most Illustrious Master, make the Sign, and applaud by five and two, saying once: *Honor to the Knights*.

T The Most Illustrious Master gives seven raps with the pommel of his sword, by five and two. The Wardens repeat the battery.

The Most Illustrious Master says:)

I[llustrious]∴ M[aster]∴ — The Council is closed, as well as the labor of the Chapter of **** in its Third

Order, is closed.

(The Wardens repeat the announcement.

The Most Illustrious Master gives one rap with the pommel of his sword, and everyone retires in peace).

4TH ORDER.

DEGREE OF ROSE-CROIX.

The PRESIDENT is called.............	MOST WISE AND PERFECT MASTER.
The Sʳ WARDEN....................	MOST EX[CELLENT]∴ AND PERFECT B[ROTHER]∴ S[ENIO]R∴ WARD[EN]∴
The J[UNIO]R WARDEN...............	MOST EX[CELLENT]∴ AND PERFECT B[ROTHER]∴ J[UNIO]R∴ WARD[EN]∴
The OFFICERS.....................	MOST PUISSANT AND PERFECT.
The KNIGHTS......................	MOST RESP[ECTABLE]∴ AND PERFECT B[ROTHER]∴ KN[IGHTS]∴

IVᵀᴴ ORDER.

ROSE-CROIX.

Most Wise and Perf[ect]∴ Master

OPENING.

The Most Wise gives one rap, which is repeated by the Wardens, and says:

M[ost]∴ W[ise]∴ — Most Excellent and Perfect Brethren Knights, assist me in opening the Chapter of R[ose]∴✝

(The Wardens repeat and say:)

Ward[en]∴ — Most Respectable and Perfect Knights, let us assist the Most Wise in opening the Chapter of R[ose]∴✝.

Then the Most Wise says:)

Q. Most Excellent and Perfect Brother Senior Warden, what is your chief care?

A. Most Wise, it is to see that the Chapter is well tyled, and if all the Brethren present are Knights R[ose]∴✝.

M[ost]∴ W[ise]∴ — Most Excellent and Perfect Brother Senior and Junior Wardens, please make sure of that.

(The Junior Warden receives the Signs, Word, and Grip and the Password from the Master of Ceremonies, then says:)

J[unio]r∴ W[arden]∴ — See, Most Puissant Brother, that the Chapter is well tyled.

(The Master of Ceremonies goes out to perform this task, and when he has returned, he reports to the Junior Ward[en]∴

At the same time the Wardens, each on his Column, receives from each Brother the Signs, Words and Grips of the Degree, reports back to the Most Wise.

After returning to their places, the Master of Ceremonies having reported to the Junior Warden, the latter gives one rap on the Senior Warden's gavel and says to him:)

J[unio]r∴ W[arden]∴ — Most Excellent and Perfect Brother Senior Warden, the Chapter is well tyled.

(The Senior Warden gives one rap on the Junior Warden's gavel, which is repeated by the Most Wise, and says:)

S[enio]r∴ W[arden]∴ — Most Wise and Perfect Master, the Chapter of R[ose]∴✝ is well tyled.

Q. Most Excellent and Perfect Brother Senior Ward[en]∴, what time is it?

A. The moment when the veil of the Temple was rent, when darkness spread across the Earth, when the light was obscured, when the columns and tools of Masonry were broken, when the Blazing Star disappeared, when the cubic stone sweated blood and water, and the Word was lost.

(The Most Wise says:)

M[ost]∴ W[ise]∴ — Since Masonry is experiencing such tribulation, let us employ all our strength in new labors to recover the Lost Word, and in order to achieve this let us open the Chapter of R[ose]∴✝.

(The Wardens, each on his Column, says:)

Ward[en]∴ — Most Excellent and Perfect Brethren Knights, the Most Wise will open the Chapter of R[ose]∴✝. Let us join him.

(The Most Wise raps by six and one.

The Wardens repeat the battery.

The Most Wise says:)

M[ost]∴ W[ise]∴ — Let us do our duty.

(The Most Wise makes the Sign of Demand and all the Brethren the Sign of Response. They then take their swords in their right hand and stand at the sign of the Good Shepherd, in such a way that the sword, point upwards, is embraced by the left arm. The Brethren, led by the Most Wise, turn towards the East, genuflect, and return to their places.

The Most Wise says:)

M[ost]∴ W[ise]∴ — The Chapter of R[ose]∴✝ is opened, as is the work of the Sovereign Chapter of **** in its Fourth Order.

(The Wardens repeat this.

One applauds by six and one, saying *huzzah*[31] six times.

The Most Wise gives one rap, which is repeated by the Wardens, and all the Brethren then sit down on benches the height of a step).

RECEPTION.

(The Most Wise says:)

Q. Most Excellent and Perfect Brother Senior Warden, what subject brings us together?

---

31 No clapping takes place in the first apartment, and no one should ever enter or leave it without genuflecting.

A. Most Wise, the propagation of the Order, and the perfection of a Knight of the East who asks to be admitted among us.

(The Most Wise reads out the Candidate's request. The day of his admission is deliberated. During this time the Master of Ceremonies goes to fetch him; he must wait for his request to be decreed.

When the door is opened, the Candidate must kneel to receive his request. The Most Wise will give it to a Knight, who will throw it on the ground to him: the door is closed, he will learn the day and hour of his Reception.

The Master of Ceremonies returned, if there are any Candidates whose day has been fixed or indicated for the forthcoming assembly, then the Most Wise tells him to go and prepare the Recipient.

The Master of Ceremonies goes to find the Recipient in the Chamber of Reflection, greets him, has him decorated as a Kn[ight]∴ of the East, and says to him:)

M[aster of]∴ C[eremonies]∴ — All our Temples are demolished, our tools and columns broken, the Sacred Word is lost, and, despite all our searches, we do not know the means of recovering it. Will you help us search for it?

(The Recipient having consented, he says to him:)

M[aster of]∴ C[eremonies]∴ — Follow me.

(He leads him to the door of the Chapter, his head uncovered, and knocks as a Knight of the East.

The Wardens make the announcement.

The Most Wise says:)

M[ost]∴ W[ise]∴ — See who is knocking.

(The Wardens do so.

The Master of Ceremonies answers the interior Brother Expert on the inside, who says:)

Q. What do you ask?

A. It is a Brother Knight of the East, wandering among the woods and mountains, who lost the Word at the second destruction of the Temple, and who would like, with your help, to find it again.

(The Wardens make the announcement according to custom.

The Most Wise says:)

M[ost]∴ W[ise]∴ — Let him be admitted.

(All Knights seated as it has been said, have their left hand on their neck, their right hand on their face, and their legs crossed.

The Recipient is placed between the Wardens and the Master of Ceremonies beside him. The Senior Warden gives one rap, which is repeated by the Junior Warden and the Most Wise, saying:)

S[enio]r∴ W[arden]∴ — Most Wise, I present to you a Knight of the East who is seeking the Word.

(The Most Wise says:)

M[ost]∴ W[ise]∴ — My Brother, confusion has crept into our labors, and it no longer within our power to work. You must realize this from the consternation that reigns here. At this time there is a disturbance on the face of the Earth. The veil of the Temple is rent (*at these words a black curtain is drawn to hide the Altar*), darkness is spread across the Earth, the light is obscured, the tools and columns are broken, the Blazing Star has disappeared, the cubic stone sweats blood and water, and the Word is lost. As you can see, it is not possible for us to give you the Word. However, it is not our intention to remain idle; we seek to recover it by a new Law. Are you minded to follow us?

(The Recipient answers yes.

The Master of Ceremonies has him travel for thirty-three years, through the North, the East, the South, and the West, to learn the beauties of the new Law.

The voyages are reduced to seven rounds.

Each time the Recipient passes the Altar he genuflects. In the final rounds, the Master of Ceremonies points to each Column as he passes in front of it and makes him repeat the name of it.

Once the voyages have been completed the Recipient is placed between the Wardens. The Senior Warden gives one rap and says:)

S[enio]r∴ W[arden]∴ — Most Wise and Perfect Master, the Recipient has completed his voyages.

(The Most Wise addresses the Recipient as follows:)

Q. My Brother, what have you learned along the way?

(The Master of Ceremonies dictates the answer to the Recipient).

A. Most Wise and Perfect Master, that there are three virtues to guide me henceforth: Faith, Hope, Charity. Teach me if there are others to follow.

(The Most Wise says:)

M[ost]∴ W[ise]∴ — No my Brother, it is positively these columns and their inscriptions that are the principles of our Order and our new mysteries. Come closer and take with us, the pledge to never depart from this Law.

(The Master of Ceremonies leads the Recipient to the Altar, where he kneels. He has him remove his gloves and place his hands on the Book of Wisdom, on which a sword is placed; he then makes him bow his head.

The Most Wise places the gavel on the Recipient's hands and, in this state, makes him swear the Obligation.

All the Brethren Knights are standing at the Sign of the Good Shepherd.

OBLIGATION.

"I promise, on my word of honour, and upon the same obligations that I have sworn in my previous Degrees, never to reveal the secrets of the Knights of the Eagle under the name of R[ose]∴✝ to any Brother of an inferior Degree nor to any Profane, on pain of being forever deprived of the Word, of being left in perpetual darkness, that a stream of blood will flow unceasingly from my body, that I suffer the most severe anguish of the soul, that the most stinging thorn serve as my bedside, that gall and vinegar serve as my refreshment, that the torment of the cross will finally end my fate, should I ever contravene the laws that are about to be prescribed for me. I also promise never to reveal where or by whom I have been received. May the Great Architect of the Universe help me."

(After the Obligation the Most Wise says:)

M[ost]∴ W[ise]∴ — All is consumed.

(All the Brethren cover their faces with their hands and sit down.

The Master of Ceremonies removes his Knight of the East habit.

The Most Wise then passes him a tunic, saying:)

M[ost]∴ W[ise]∴ — This habit for you denotes our belief. It should remind you by its ornaments of what constitutes the main point of our mysteries.

(The Most Wise puts the apron on him, saying:)

M[ost]∴ W[ise]∴ This black apron is the mark of sincere repentance for the evils that have caused all our misfortunes. It should help you to recognize those of us who seek to recover the true Word.

(The Most Wise passes him the cordon, saying:)

M[ost]∴ W[ise]∴ — This cordon must serve as a sign of mourning until the Word is recovered. Go to the West, and you will help us find it.

(The Most Wise strikes seven raps, which are repeated by the Wardens. All the Knights rise and stand at the Sign of the Good Shepherd, holding their swords in their right hand.

The Most Wise then puts the following questions to the Wardens:)

Q. What motive brings us together?

A. Most Wise and Perfect Master, the cubic stone is sweating blood and water due to the laxity of the Masons in their work, and for the success of Masonry being exposed on a high mountain top.

Q. What does this mystery signify?

A. The loss of the Word, which with your help we hope to recover.

Q. What needs to be done to achieve this?

A. We must embrace the new Law; being fully convinced of the three virtues that are its columns, foundation and principles.

Q. What are they?

A. Faith, Hope, Charity.

Q. How will we find these three columns?

A. By travelling and wandering in the most profound darkness.

(The Most Wise says:)

M[ost]∴ W[ise]∴ — Let us travel, my Brethren, from the West to the North, from the East to the South and above all let us not lose sight of the sentiments which guide us.

(All the Brethren travel in silence, according to their Degree, and circle the Chapter seven times, with the Most Wise at the head, followed by the Wardens, the Dignitary Officers, the Members of the Chapter, the Recipient and the Master of Ceremonies.

On the third tour the Most Wise passes into the Red Chamber.

On the fourth the Wardens do so.

On the fifth the Dignitaries do so.

On the sixth all the Knights, except the Recipient and the Master of Ceremonies, who make the seventh round alone, after which they go to the door of the Chapter, where the Master of Ceremonies knocks as a Knight R[ose]∴✝

The Brother Expert in the inner porch opens the door and, seeing that the Recipient who is about to enter, he says to him:)

B[rother]∴ Ex∴ — You cannot enter unless you give me the Word.

(The Recipient replies:)

Recip[ient]∴ — I am a Brother who seeks the Word with the help of the new Law and the three Columns of Mason[ry]∴

At these words, Brother Expert closes the door.

The Master of Ceremonies strips him of his cordon and apron and says:)

M[aster of]∴ C[eremonies]∴ — These tokens are not humiliating enough for you to find the Word. You must undergo even more humiliating trials.

(He covers the Recipient with a black sheet sprinkled with ashes, so that he cannot see anything, and says to him:)

M[aster of]∴ C[eremonies]∴ — I will lead you into the darkest place, from which the Word must emerge triumphant to the glory and advantage of Masonry. Put your trust in me.

(He leads him in this condition into an apartment where changes in elevation have been prepared going up and down, repeated as much as possible. He then leads him to the open door of the apartment, which represents the horrors of a place of pain and suffering. At the threshold of the door he raises the front of the sheet covering him and makes him go around the room three times in silence, and brings him back to the threshold of the door, where he lowers the sheet again, saying:)

M[aster of]∴ C[eremonies]∴ — The horrors you have just seen are nothing compared with what you will suffer if, unfortunately, you do not observe our Law.

(He then leads him to the door of the Chapter and says:)

M[aster of]∴ C[eremonies]∴ — Remember to answer the questions that will be put to you, otherwise you cannot achieve the Degree you desire. Here they are:

Q. Whence came you?

A. From Judea.

Q. Through which town did you pass?

A. Through Nazareth.

Q. Who led you there?

A. Raphael.

Q. Of which tribe are you?

A. Of Judas.

(The Master of Ceremonies makes the Recipient strike seven raps as a Knight R[ose]∴†

After the customary ceremonies of announcing and opening, and ascertaining who is asking for entry, the Master of Ceremonies replies to Brother Expert, who opens the door:)

M[aster of]∴ C[eremonies]∴ — He is a Knight who, having traversed the most profound spaces, hopes to procure the Word for you as the fruit of his searches.

(The Brother Expert announces this to the Junior Warden. After the Wardens have each given one rap and the Junior Warden has repeated the announcement to the Senior Warden, the latter says:)

S[enio]r∴ W[arden]∴ — Most Wise and Perfect Master, it is a Knight who, having traversed the deepest spaces, hopes to procure the Word for you as the fruit of his searches.

M[ost]∴ W[ise]∴ — Let him be introduced to the West, and we will question him.

(This order is passed back to the Brother Expert, the doors are opened, and the Recipient is introduced to the West.

The Wardens each give one rap, after which the Junior Warden says to the Senior Warden, who repeats it to the Most Wise:)

J[unio]r∴ W[arden]∴ — Most Wise and Perfect Master, here is a Brother Knight Mason who comes to help us recover the Word and who wishes to become a perfect Mason.

(The Most Wise then asks the following questions:)

Q. Whence came you?

A. From Judea.

Q. Through which town did you pass?

A. Through Nazareth.

Q. Who led you there?

A. Raphael.

Q. Of which tribe are you?

A. Of Judas.

Q. Give me the initials of these four words.

A. J∴ N∴ R∴ J∴

D: What do these four letters mean together?

A. Jes[us]∴ of Naz[areth]∴ etc.

M[ost]∴ W[ise]∴ — My Brethren, the Word is recovered. May the light be granted to him.

(The Wardens promptly remove the black sheet.)

M[ost]∴ W[ise]∴ — With me, my Brethren!.

(They applaud by seven, saying *huzzah* as many times.)

M[ost]∴ W[ise]∴ — My Brother, I congratulate you upon the recovery of the Word, which has earned you the degree of Perfect Mason. It is not enough to have earned and deserved it, you must always be worthy of retaining it, and of reaping its fruits in the future. May you long enjoy among us, my dear Brother, and derive from it, through a life worthy of a Knight R[ose]∴✝, the reward of those who have walked in the paths of truth. Come closer, my Brother, so that I may communicate to you the mysteries of perfect Masonry.

(The Master of Ceremonies leads him to the East, where having arrived, the Most Wise removes his chasuble and gives him the Signs, the Grip, and the Word, saying:)

M[ost]∴ W[ise]∴ — In this Degree, my Brother, as in the others, Signs, Words, and a Grips, to recognize each other.

There are two Signs, one of Demand and one of Response.

First Sign… { The first Sign involves raising the eyes to the sky, and at the same time raising the two reversed hands to the height of the forehead, with the fingers intertwined, one in the other, and thus letting them fall onto the stomach.

Second Sign… { The second Sign involves raising the right hand to the height of the forehead, on the side, with the thumb and fingers closed, with the exception of the index which points to the sky, while also raising the eyes.

The first Sign is called the Sign of Admiration.

The second teaches us that everything comes from above, and that there is only one Being, the pure source of truth.

Sign of Distress… { We have a third Sign, which is used only according to the circumstances; it might be called the Sign of Distress. It is made by crossing the right leg behind the left and is answered by crossing the left leg behind the right.

Grip… { The Grip is made by crossing the hands on each other's breast; this is called the Grip of Good Faith or of the Good Shepherd. He who asks places his right hand on the right breast of the other. This one does the same thing. Then: the one who asks, places his left hand on the left breast of the other, who does the same. If the approach is from the right, he responds from the left; if it is from the left, he responds from the right.

Word… { The Word is J∴ N∴ R∴ J∴, which is given by questioning each other, as has been said.

Password… { The password is *Emmanuel*, to which we reply P∴ P∴

Order… { The order is crossing the arms, the hands resting on the opposite breasts.

Go now, my Brother, and make yourself known to the Brother Wardens, and then return to me.

(This done, the Master of Ceremonies takes him back to the East and all the Brethren surround him.

The Recipient kneels, and the Most Wise passes him the cordon with the jewel suspended, saying:)

M[ost]∴ W[ise]∴ — In the name of the Grand Orient of **** in its Grand Chapter, and by the powers which I have received from the Sovereign Chapter of ****, I create and constitute you a Knight of the Eagle, Perfect Free Mason, under the title of R[ose]∴✝, to enjoy, now and forever, the privileges attached to this sublime Degree.

Never dishonour this cordon, which a Perfect Mason must wear everywhere. The rosette at the bottom will remind you of the loss of the Word, and the jewel will inform you by its symbol that allegorical Masonry contains truths that are the sole province of the Perfect Mason. The form of the jewel will tell you more than my explanation; I hope that you will never lose the memory of it.

(He places the blade of his sword on the Recipient's right shoulder, then on his left, raises him up and kisses him. Then he says to him:)

M[ost]∴ W[ise]∴ — We also have hieroglyphs in this degree which are known only to us; they will be communicated to you, but beware of abusing them.

Fear no more the vicissitudes of time; may the Columns never fail you my brother, and may the Great Architect be your aid.

Brother Master of Ceremonies, lead the Brother Knight between the Wardens.

(This done, the Most Wise says:)

M[ost]∴ W[ise]∴ Most Excellent and Perfect Brother Wardens, announce to all the Respectable and Perfect Brethren Knights that henceforth they must recognize Brother **** as a Knight of the Eagle,

Perfect Free Mason, under the title of R[ose]∴☦, and Member of the Sovereign Chapter of *** in its Fourth Order.

(The Wardens make this announcement.

The Most Wise then says:)

M[ost]∴ W[ise]∴ — Let us applaud, my Brethren.

(All the Knights applaud by seven, saying *huzzah* as many times.)

The Recipient asks to give thanks, and his thanks are drowned out. Then the Most Wise says:)

M[ost]∴ W[ise]∴ — My Brother, take your place among us.

(The Master of Ceremonies takes him to his place.

The Brother Orator makes a speech, after which the Most Wise gives the Instruction.

INSTRUCTION.

Q. Are you a R[ose]∴☦?

A. Most Wise and Perfect Master, I have this happiness.

Q. Where were you received?

A. In a Chapter where decency and humility reigned.

Q. Who received you?

A. The most humble of all.

Q. What do you mean by these words?

A. That in our assemblies we distinguish ourselves only by humility and obedience.

Q. How were you received?

A. With all the formalities required for such an important matter.

Q. How were you presented in the Chapter?

A. Free of all my senses and my will.

Q. What did you see upon entering?

A. My soul was delighted at what I saw: the silence, the placement of the Knights, everything gave me a great sense of what I was going to learn.

Q. What happened to you after your introduction?

A. I was taken on a voyage.

Q. What did you learn in your voyages?

A. I saw the three supports of our building. I was taught their names, which I repeated, and which I have engraved forever in my heart.

Q. What are these names?

A. Faith, Hope, Charity.

Q. After the voyages were finished, was your work perfect?

A. No. The Most Wise ordered that I be brought to the foot of that object,[32] before which everyone bows, to swear my obligation there.

Q. How did you swear it?

A. In the most reverent state, with my heart penetrated by what I was saying, and with a firm resolution to regularly observe everything I have promised.

Q. What happened to you next?

A. I was clothed with the marks of sorrow and repentance. I was taught what everything meant, and the memory of what I was doing. Then all the Knights made a commemorative voyage, which led us from sadness to joy after travelling dark and murky paths filled with horror, but the firmness with which each one of us endured our toils, earned us the reward we desired.

Q. What were you looking for on this voyage?

A. The true Word lost by the laxity of the Masons.

Q. Have you found it?

A. Our perseverance helped us recover it.

Q. Who gave it to you?

A. I am not allowed to give it to anyone; but having reflected on what I had seen and heard, I found it on my own, with the help of the author.

Q. Give it to me?

A. I cannot. Ask me about my travels, my name, my country, and try to do as I do.

Q. Whence came you?

A. From Judea.

Q. Through which town did you pass?

A. Through Nazareth.

Q. Who led you there?

---
32 [The altar.]

A. Raphael.

Q. Of which tribe are you?

A. Of Judas.

Q. I am no better informed, my Brother.

A. Do as I do: put the initial letters of each word together, and you will find the subject of our journeys and mysteries.

Q. J.

A. N.

Q. R.

A. J.

Q. Were you given nothing more?

A. The password, which is E[mmanuel]∴, Signs and a Grip, to help me be recognized.

Q. Give me the first sign.

A. (He does so.)

Q. Give me the answer.

A. (He does so.)

Q. Give me the Grip.

A. (He who has received it says: It is just, Most Wise).

Q. What is the order of the Degree?

A. The Good Shepherd.

Q. What was done with afterwards, having given the means to be recognized?

A. The Most Wise and all the Knights constituted me a Knight∴ of the Eagle, a Perfect Freemason, under the title of R[ose]∴✝, and decorated me with the cordon and jewel. After making myself known to all the Knights, I took my seat in the Chapter.

Q. What was done next?

A. The Most Wise gave us an exhortation, conducted Chapter business in the usual manner, and then all Kn[ights]∴ retired in peace.

✝

✝ ✝

CLOSING.

(The Most Wise gives seven raps, which is repeated by the Wardens.

All the Kn[ights]∴ are standing and at order, sword in hand).

Q. Most Excellent and Perfect Brother Senior Warden, what hour is it?

A. Most Wise, the hour of the Perfect Mason.

Q. What is the hour of the Perfect Mason?

A. The moment when the Word is recovered, the perfect ashlar has been changed into a mystic rose; the Blazing Star has reappeared in all its splendor; our instruments have regained their shape; the light is restored to our eyes in all its brilliance; the darkness is dispelled; and the new Masonic law must henceforth reign in our work.

(The Most Wise says:)

M[ost]∴ W[ise]∴ — Let us then follow this Law, since it is the consequence of all the wonders that have dazzled our eyes.

Most Excellent and Perfect Brother Wardens, announce that the Chapter is to be closed.

(The Wardens make the announcement.

All the Knights sheathe their swords.

The Most Wise leaves his place retaining his gavel, genuflects, and goes to embrace all the Knights who are lined up in the column of the South. He starts with the Senior Warden, saying: *Profound peace*.

The head of the column does the same to the person after him, giving the kiss and so on, until all have been kissed. When this has been done, they all genuflect.

The Most Wise says:)

M[ost]∴ W[ise]∴ — Excellent and Perfect Brother Knights, the Sovereign Chapter of R[ose]∴✠ and the work of the Chapter of ****, in its Fourth Order, is closed. Let us do our duty.

(All the Brethren make the Sign, then genuflect, and applaud, led by the Most Wise, by seven, shouting *huzzah*.)

NOTE: The Knights wait in silence for the banqueting ceremony to be announced if one is to be held.

BANQUET.

(All the Knights line up around the banqueting table and the Most Wise says:)

M[ost]∴ W[ise]∴ — Great Architect of the Universe, you who provide for the needs of all beings, bless the food we are about to take. May it be for your greater glory and for our satisfaction.

(The Most Wise takes the bread, breaks it, and gives it to the Knight on his right to make the round with it. He makes the Sign of the Index Finger, and eats; then he takes the cup full of wine, makes the

Sign of the Index Finger, and drinks; then he presents the cup to the Knight on his immediate right, who makes the countersign, and takes the cup. The latter does the same as the Most Wise. After the cup and the bread have passed right round the table in this manner and have eventually returned to the Most Wise, the latter throws the remainder of the bread and the wine into the fire, saying:)

M[ost]∴ W[ise]∴ — Everything is consumed.

(All the Knights come to Order and, led by the Most Wise, make the sign.

The Most Wise gives the kiss of peace, and says:)

M[ost]∴ W[ise]∴ — Peace be with you.

(They withdraw in silence).

†

† †

END OF THE BOOKLET OF THE PRESIDENT.

RIT ÉCOSSAIS SYMBOLIC DEGREES

First Degree.
Apprentice, Scottish.

2ⁿᵈ∴ Degree.
Fellow Craft, Scottish
Symbolic ∴

FIRST DEGREE∴
FIRST CLASS∴
APPRENTICE.
FIRST SCOTTISH DEGREE∴

J[ean]∴ Doszedardski

FIRST DEGREE∴
APPRENTICE∴ FIRST CLASS∴

OPENING OF THE LODGE∴

Q. The Worshipful strikes one rap with his gavel and says: Silence, my Brethren.

A. The Wardens repeat this, saying: Silence, my Brethren.

QUESTIONS AND ANSWERS OF THE WARDENS.

Q. B[rethren]∴ Senior and Junior Wardens, ask all the Brethren composing your columns to help assist us in opening the lodge of an Apprentice Mason.

A. The Wardens repeat this.

Q. Brother Senior Warden, are you a Mason?

A. My Brethren and Fellow Crafts recognize me as such.

Q. What is the first duty of a Mason?

A. To ensure that the lodge is tyled.

Q. Make sure that it is, my Brother

The Wardens check with the Brother Tyler to ensure that the lodge is tyled and, depending upon his answer, they reply:

A. It is, Most Worshipful.

Q. What is the second duty of the Wardens?

A. To see that all the Brethren present here are true Masons.

Q. B[rothers]∴ Senior and Junior Wardens, make sure that they are true Masons by asking them for the semester word. (If there is no semester word then the password is requested).

A. All the Brethren present are true Masons.

Q. What is the third duty of the Wardens in lodge?

A. It is to make sure that all the Brethren are to order. [1]

Q. Are you sure, B[rethren]∴ S[enio]r and J[unio]r∴ Wardens?

A. Yes, they are Worshipful.

Q. Where does the Worshipful stand in the Lodge, Senior Warden?

A. In the East.

229

Q. Why?

A. Following the example of the Sun, which begins its progress in that part of the world or of the Globe, so the Worshipful is placed there to open and illuminate the lodge.

Q. Where do the Masters stand in the lodge, Senior Warden?

A. Throughout the lodge, to strengthen and govern its labors.

Q. Where do the Fellow Crafts stand?

A. In the South, being more enlightened than the Apprentices and more able to withstand the fierce heat of the sun.

Q. Where do the Apprentices stand, B[rother]∴ J[unio]r∴ Warden?

A. In the North, being less able to withstand and endure the heat of the sun, which rarely visits this part.

Q. What is the moral of this distribution?

A. It teaches that places are distributed according to talents and the greatest advancements on the path of virtue.

Q. Why do we assemble here, B[rother]∴ Senior Warden?

A. To erect temples to virtue and to dig dungeons for vice.

Q. How long do we have to work?

A. From midday until midnight.

Q. How long does it take to form an Apprentice, J[unior] Ward[e]n?

A. Three years or more.

Q. How old are you?

A. Three years.

Q. What time is it?

A. Noon. [2]

Q. In consideration of the hour and your age, Brethren Senior, and Junior Wardens, inform the Brethren who compose your columns that I intend to open the Apprentice lodge by the customary signs and batteries of Masonry.

A. The Wardens repeat this.

The Worshipful strikes one rap with his gavel, stands, comes to order, and says piously:

Prayer.   Great Architect of the Universe, cast an auspicious gaze upon this lodge and upon the Brethren who compose it, and fill us with your heavenly light. May your wisdom always be with us. Receive the sacrifice of our hearts, and impress upon them your holy fury towards vice. Cause us to sacrifice our resentments to your goodness, wisdom and justice, let our enemies blush with shame at the insults they utter against us. Let our actions serve as an example to the earth. Do not withdraw your light from us, that it may illuminate us in the darkest night. May your divine breath inspire us in our choice of subjects, may the desire for greater virtue procure for them, the sweetness that it helps us to savor within this holy sanctuary, so that one day the same happiness may bring us all together in your heavenly, adorable and eternal lodge. Amen, &c.

In response the Brethren say Amen &c. three times.

Q. The Worshipful strikes three raps · · ·

A. The Wardens repeat: · · ·

The Worshipful accompanied by all the B[rethre]n∴ perform all the customary signs and batteries. He then strikes one rap with his gavel, which is [3] repeated by the Wardens. All the Brethren then take their places.

The Worshipful says: Brethren Senior and J[unio]r∴ Ward[e]ns, inform your respective columns that the lodge of an Apprentice Mason is now open.

The Wardens make this announcement.

The Master of Ceremonies then calls the roll of all the Brethren.

The Secretary reads out the minutes of the previous meeting. After this the Worshipful says: Brethren Senior and J[unio]r∴ Wardens, announce to your columns that if there are Brethren who wish to comment on the minutes[33] which have just been read, to ask for the word,[34] which will be granted, or if not to show their approval by raising their arms.

The Wardens repeat this.

Comments on the minutes are made or not, and when the minutes are approved, the Worshipful raps once with his gavel and stands to the usual applause.

The Master of Ceremonies goes into the Hall of the Lost Steps[35] to make sure there are no visitors there. If there are, he announces them to the lodge through the Brother Wardens. Brother Expert will then go to tyle them and receive their diplomas. After the usual formalities they will be introduced in the ordinary manner.

QUESTIONS FOR VISITORS.

Q. Whence came you, my Brother?

A. From the Lodge of St. John.

Q. Where is it situated?

A. In a holy place, among the highest mountains, where no cock has ever crowed, no dog ever

---

33 *Planche tracée*. The drawing board, or minutes.

34 Permission to speak.

35 *La Salle des Pas perdus*. The Hall of Lost Steps, or vestibule.

barked, and no woman ever scolded. [4]

Q. What do they do there?

A. They erect temples to virtue and dig dungeons for vices.

Q. What do you bring?

A. Health, prosperity, and a warm welcome to all the Brethren.

Q. What come you here to do?

A. To subdue my passions, subjugate my will, and make further progress in Masonry.

Q. What do you mean by Masonry?

A. I mean the study of the sciences and the practice of the virtues.

Q. Tell me what a Mason is.

A. A free man, obedient to the laws, a brother and friend to the virtuous.

Q. What are you seeking?

A. A place among you.

RECEPTION.

Q. What is the reason that brings us together, Brother Junior Warden?

A. The propagation of the Order: There is a Profane who asks to be initiated into our mysteries.

The Worshipful reads out the decree admitting him and asks again if there is any opposition to his reception, making three separate requests to be interrupted in his reflections, &c. &c. &c.

The Recipient is announced with three great knocks.

Q. Who dares to knock thus at the door of the temple?

A. It is a Profane who asks to be received as a Mason. [5]

Q. Ask him his first name and surname, his age, his place of birth, his marital status, and his current residence, as well as what he desires and finally his will.

After receiving answers to these questions the Worshipful says: Let him enter and place him in the hands of the Wardens. The J[unio]r∴ Ward[e]n∴ says: Here is the Profane.

The Profane is made to lie on his stomach between the two columns: then the Orator says:

INVOCATION.

Sovereign Architect of the Universe, who is God, we adore you, we invoke you, and we bless you. Increase in us that spirit of fraternity and gentleness that characterizes the Masons, kindle our hearts with the sacred fire, with this love, of this tender and boundless charity, which springs forth from your radiant throne. May your eye always watch unceasingly, and may your almighty hand direct our steps, in the quarry that we are traveling. Protect and defend this society of free men, whose works are the study of the sciences in contemplation of your infinite works, and the reform of morals. O thou who are the only regulator, the source of all strength and justice, on behalf of this profane, now prostrate between the columns of this temple, erected to thy glory, at the doors of which he has knocked. Guide his faltering steps, sustain his efforts in the midst of the perilous trials that surround him, but do so after carefully considering the importance of his request and the terrible consequences, attached to weakness or presumption. That only after having travelled along the darkest paths [6] and after trials by iron, blood and fire, he can through his courage and constancy obtain the priceless benefit of the light, for that is the recompense which thou bestows oh G[reat]∴ A[rchitect]∴ O[f]∴ T[he]∴ U[niverse]∴, to all those who have not succumbed.

The Worshipful says:

Q. Sir, is it still your intention to be received as a Mason?

A. Yes. (He is raised.)

The Worshipful says: The primary qualities we require for admission, without which one cannot be initiated into our mysteries, are greatest ~~necessity~~ sincerity, absolute docility, and unfailing constancy. Your answers to the questions I will ask you, will make us decide what we should think of you.

Q. What is your purpose in coming here? Who inspired you with desire? Is not mere curiosity the greatest part? What is your idea of Masonry? ~~You~~ Answer frankly and, above all, be true. Do you know what obligation we contract between us? Who introduced you here? Do you know him to be a Mason? Did he not warn you of what we do? Do you have any idea of Masonry? How can you desire to know something, about which you say you have no knowledge? What reflections have the objects caused you, which were offered to your eyes, in the room where you were confined before presenting you here? What do you think about the indecent state you now are in? What do you think of a society in which the recipient [7] is presented in a way that must no doubt seem unique to you? Again be truthful in your answers. We can read your heart. Your confidence, and your steps, are they not too light? Are you not afraid that we will abuse the state of weakness and blindness to which you have allowed yourself to be reduced; unarmed, defenseless and almost naked? How could you, sir, hand yourself over to the power of people you do not know?

We are going to subject you to indispensable trials. I warn you, Sir, that if in the course of these trials, that if the courage and strength which are necessary to endure should fail you, you are entirely at liberty to withdraw.

These trials are mysterious and emblematic, so give them all the attention that you are capable of.

(First voyage: a difficult one, to the sound of thunder and hailstones.)

Brother Expert have the gentleman perform the first voyage, by passing through the North, the East, and the South and from there to the West.

Note. This voyage must be the most difficult one, accompanied by the rumble of thunder and the sound of hailstones falling.

When the voyage is over the W[orship]ful∴ says, What did you notice, Sir, in the first voyage you have just made? This voyage is emblematic of human life: the tumult of the passions, the clash of various interests, difficulties of enterprise, the obstacles which multiply beneath your feet to discourage you, all this is represented by the [8] noise and clatter that assailed your ears and by the unevenness of the road you have just travelled. Are you willing to persist, Sir?

(2nd voyage: the clatter of arms.) Brother Expert have the gentleman make the second voyage.

Note: There must be a slight clatter of a small number of arms, carefully directed at the Candidate's ears.

(Purification by water.) Returning to the West the Expert will plunge the bare arm of the Recipient into a basin of water to purify him.[36]

Q. What reflection has this voyage made in your mind? You must have found this voyage less difficult and embarrassing than the first. By this we wanted to make sensitive to your spirit, the effect of constancy, to follow the path of virtue, for the more we advance there, the more agreeable it becomes. That clatter of arms you heard in course, represents the combat that the virtuous man is constantly obliged to sustain, when attacked by vice. You have been purified by water, but you still have other trials to undergo. Arm yourself with courage to endure them to the end.

(3rd voyage.) Do you still persist, Sir, in your plan? In that case, Brother Expert, have the gentleman make the third voyage.

Note. This should be done at a stroll and be very easy.

(Purification by fire.) In the course of this voyage the Candidate will be passed through the flames.[37] [9]

Q. Sir, you must have noticed that this voyage was even less painful than the previous one. The flames through which you passed are the complement of your purification. May this material fire with which you have been surrounded kindle forever in your soul the love for your fellow men, that charity governs your words and your actions; and never forget this precept of a sublime morality known to all nations: <u>Do not do unto others, what you do not want done unto you.</u>

The constancy you have just shown in your three voyages make us hopeful that you will also be able to withstand the trials you have yet to undergo. Do you persist, sir? There is still time to withdraw.

Sir, one of the virtues whose practice is most familiar to us and which brings you closer to the author of our being is <u>Benevolence.</u> The metals of which you have been deprived are emblematic of the vices.

(Charity.) Can you, without embarrassment, sacrifice for the benefit of the poor, whom we daily assist, <u>the money or jewelry</u> or the proceeds of these objects, which were given to me? Think about it Sir, and beware, a numerous society has its eyes fixed upon you at this moment: it is attentive to the response you are about to make. [10] I am asking you to perform an act of charity: be careful not to make it one of ostentation.

This charity which I ask of you, ceases to be a virtue when it is done to the detriment of the most sacred and pressing duties, civil commitments to be filled, a family to support, children to bring up, relief of parents who are less fortunate. Here Sir, are the primary duties that nature imposes on us, here are the creditors of every man who regulates his conduct according the principles of equity. What would you

---

36 The purification by water in addition to being an elemental trial, is also on homage to the same tradition in early Scottish Masonry.
37 Reference to the custom of blowing Lycopodium powder through a tube or pipe through the flame of a candle.

think of someone who wanted to appear charitable before having satisfied them? I wanted to enlighten you about the obligations that are common to all men. I now return to the first proposal I made to you. Can you, without injuring any of these duties, sacrifice for the benefit of the poor, whom we assist daily, all or part of the money or proceeds of the jewelry, which belongs to you and was given to me?

Sir, in a moment we are going to demand that you to enter into an obligation, which assures us of your discretion. This obligation must be written by you and must be signed with your blood.

Do you consent to it being drawn?

Brother Hospitaller, do your duty.

Sir, your resignation is your praise, but learn that in all times and circumstances you must always help your Brethren and, if necessary, shed your blood for them. [11]

(The cup of bitterness) Brother Master of Ceremonies, present to the gentleman the cup of bitterness. Drink Sir, this potion down to the dregs. This potion of bitterness, Sir, is emblematic of the sorrows that are inseparable from human life, resignation to the decrees of providence can alleviate them.

Brother Expert, bring the Neophyte to the foot of the altar, there to swear the obligation.

Do you consent, Sir, to swear the obligation we shall require of you? Think about it well.

(When he has knelt in the ordinary manner, the Worshipful says to him:) Sir, the engagement you are about to contract contains nothing harmful to the respect which we owe to our religion, or our attachment and loyalty to our sovereign, nor good morals. I warn you that this obligation is terrible, but indispensable. Is it of your own full and free will? Do you consent to it?

(Repeat with me.) The Worshipful strikes a rap with his gavel and all the Brethren stand and come to order.

(Oath.) I, N∴, do swear and do promise on the Holy Bible, on the General Statutes of the Order, and upon this sword, the symbol of honor, before the G[reat]∴ A[rchitect]∴ O[f]∴ T[he]∴ U[niverse]∴ who is God, to inviolably keep all the secrets of Masonry that will be entrusted to me, by this R[especta]ble∴ Lodge, to reveal nothing of what I will have seen or heard therein, [12] never to write, trace, paint, engrave, or print them, on any material which may be visible to man. To be faithful to my religion, as well as to His Imperial and Royal Majesty,[38] against whom I shall never take up arms, and against the laws, of which I will not murmur; nor will I ever conjure. I promise to be faithful to all my Brethren whom I recognize as such, to help them with my strength, my purse and my advice, both in sickness and in health. Never to attend the labors of an irregular lodge but only those which I shall know to be legitimately and regularly constituted. Never to speak in lodge about religion, politics, or any other matter which may interfere with discussion, and to only occupy myself with our labors. I also promise to conform to the regulations of this Respectable Lodge, and I consent, if against my expectation, I should become a perjurer, to have my throat cut (all the Brethren make the sign), my heart and entrails torn out, my body burned and reduced to ashes, these ashes cast to the wind, and may my memory be forever held in abhorrence by all Masons. May the G[reat]∴ A[rchitect]∴ O[f]∴ T[he]∴ U[niverse]∴ help me. Amen, &c. &c. &c.

(The Recipient is returned to the West).

---

38 Napoleon Bonaparte was emperor of France from May 18, 1804 to April 6, 1814 and again from March 20, 1815 through June 22, 1815.

Sir, does the oath you have just taken, does it give you no anxiety?

Do you feel you have sufficient courage not to violate it?

Do you agree to repeat it, freely?

Q.   What do you desire?

A.   The light. [13]

The Worshipful says: It shall be granted to you.

(All the Brethren stand to order.)

All of you, my Brethren, do your duty.

(With the rap of a gavel all the Brethren stand up, sword in hand).

(At the second rap of the gavel all the Brethren turn towards the Neophyte and point their swords at him).

(The Light.)

(At the third rap of the gavel the J[unio]r∴ Ward[e]n drops his blindfold).

The Worshipful says: The swords <which> directed towards you signify that all Masons will come to your aid in all circumstances, if you respect and practice the virtues, the Masonic union, and scrupulously observe our wise laws, but if you ever become perjured, it would be equally vengeful to punish you for it. This august procedure, this vivid and pure clarity, is emblematic of the pleasure that your initiation causes. These swords, which have been almost ready to pierce your breast, if you ever betrayed us, will be ready to defend you when you have need of your B[rethren]∴ Remain faithful therefore to the commitment you have just contracted, and which you will repeat, between my hands.

(The Oath is renewed.)

(The Expert and Master of Ceremonies lead him to the throne, where he renews his obligation on his knees). The Worshipful gently taps on the head of the compass [14] three times with his gavel, saying unto him, <u>Learn by this emblem and from the righteousness of the compass to direct all the movements of your heart towards goodness.</u>

(The Recipient is received and constituted an App[rentice] Mason.)

He places the blade of the sword against the Recipient's head and in this attitude pronounces the following formula of reception:

To the glory of the G[reat]∴ A[rchitect]∴ O[f]∴ T[he]∴ U[niverse]∴ in the name of the G[rand]∴ O[rient]∴ of France and the R[especta]ble∴ Scottish M[o]ther∴ L[odge]∴ of S[ain]t∴ Alexander of Scotland as well as that of the R[especta]ble∴ Scottish M[o]ther∴ L[odge]∴ of N, by virtue of the powers which have been entrusted to me by this R[especta]ble∴ L[odge]∴ I receive and constitute you an Apprentice Mason.

(He gives three raps on the flat of the sword.)

The Recipient stands up and the Worshipful comes over to him and says, my Brother, for that is how we shall henceforth call you, receive from me the first fraternal kiss by the mysterious number three.

(The first 3 steps[39] of the temple.) The new Apprentice is made to ascend the first three steps of the temple:

(Apron.)

Presenting him with the apron, the Worshipful says: My Brother, this apron, which you will always wear in lodge, will be a constant reminder to you that man is condemned to toil, and that a Mason must always lead an active and industrious life.

(Men's gloves) Presenting him with a pair of men's gloves, he says: These gloves, by virtue of their whiteness, symbolize the candor that must always reign in the soul of an honest man as well as the purity of his actions: the Resp[ecta]ble Lodge deems you worthy of it.

(Ladies' gloves) He then presents him with a pair of [15] ladies" gloves, saying: We do not admit ladies among us, but we pay homage to their virtue and we like to remember them in our labors. Here then, my Brother, are some gloves which you should give to the lady whom you love the most.

To be admitted to our assemblies and participate in the bond that unites us all over the world, it is necessary that you can make yourself known. I will therefore give you the sign, words and grips by which we recognize each other and by whose aid you will be welcomed by all Masons wherever you are in the world.

(Sacred word.)

(He gives him the sacred word in the customary manner).

Ancient. Constitution of York. / Modern.

Zoob. - <u>Booz - Boaz.</u>   Nikai. / <u>Jakin.</u>

(Password.)

We also have a password, which is used among us to make especially sure that the one presenting himself is indeed a Mason: You cannot enter the lodge without giving it at the door.

(He gives him the password).

(Sign.)

The sign of the Apprentice is made by bringing the *right*[40] hand in square, &c. &c. &c.

(Grip)

The grip is made by taking each other's hands &c. &c. &c. (he gives it to him).

You will see the first letter of the sacred word on the column placed in the North: When you are asked to give it, remember to do so only while observing the precautions that I indicated, when I taught it to

---

39 The original uses degrees here, but the meaning is the first three Steps of the Apprentice tracing board. *The first three steps were the only three that the Apprentices had to climb to reach Column B.*

40 *Rechte.* Doszedardski used his native German to conceal passwords and secret work throughout his collection. Words in italics appear in German in original manuscript.

you, saying: Give me the first letter and I will give you the second.

(This word means: My strength is in God.) [16]

The password is the name of the first craftsman who worked with metals.

(Semester word.)

We also have a semester word that the G[rand]∴ Orient of France renews every six months. Its purpose is to identify those Masons who frequent the lodges assiduously. (It is given to him.) Serving Brethren must never have it, nor can it be communicated to visitors.

The Master of Ceremonies leads him to the West on the orders of the Worshipful who says to him: (<u>Let him learn to work the rough ashlar and let him be recognized by Brethren Senior and Junior Wardens, to whom he will return the words, signs and grips.</u>)

The Brother J[unio]r∴ Warden makes him rap 3 times with the gavel on the rough ashlar. The J[unio]r∴ Warden, after receiving from him the signs, words and grips, then brings him before the Worshipful.

The Worshipful strikes one rap with his gavel, which is repeated by the two Wardens, all the Brethren stand and come to order. The newly initiated Brother is then placed between the two columns and [the Worshipful] says: Brethren Senior and J[unio]r∴ Wardens, invite the Brethren who decorate your columns to recognize Brother N∴ in the future as an Apprentice Mason and member of this R[especta]ble∴ Lodge and to applaud his initiation.

(This is repeated and done in the ordinary way)

The Orator then delivers a discourse on fraternal union, equality, the duties of man, and on any other a point of morality he might wish.

EXPLANATION OF THE TRACING-BOARD.

Brother Senior Warden explains the tracing-board to him in the following way:

This tracing-board my Brother represents the entrance to the Temple of Solomon: [17] The first three steps were the only three that the Apprentices had to climb to reach column B. Ancient or J. Modern, where they would gather after work, to receive their wages, which they would only receive after having given the sign, grip and password, as well as a sacred word, and the step of the Apprentices. These three steps symbolize and designate the qualities of: <u>silence</u>, <u>zeal</u>, and <u>submission.</u> After these three steps you see the mosaic pavement: by its arrangement, you understand that order and regularity must always be the privilege of those who wish to enter the temple.

The level, the square, the compass, and the plumb are instruments with which one can polish the works of architecture: in the moral sense, they represent the qualities necessary to acquire wisdom and virtue.

The rough ashlar is emblematic of our soul, susceptible to good or bad impressions. It is upon that, which you must work. It cannot be used in this state: It is the same with man, who has not dedicated himself to his cultivation. It is the image of the profane: which are formless, not yet having been worked upon: the germ of the virtues is disfigured and is like a precious stone buried beneath a misshapen exterior, because Masonry has not given it that brilliance that constitutes its true value.

The sun represents to you, the Worshipful, just like this beneficent star, he constantly illuminates [18] the lodge and proves that no matter how learned one may be, man always needs the torch of reason to guide him.

The moon designates that it is not only to the day that the Mason's duties are limited, but that the star of the night must illuminate his benevolence and his humanity, and that there is no time that exempts him from doing good.

The blazing star, which shines continuously in the lodges and whose brilliance has so suddenly struck your eyes, is the emblem of the light, of that sacred fire, that moves and governs this universe. On seeing it, you must always revere the power of the G[reat]∴ A[rchitect]∴ O[f]∴ the Universe and humble yourself before Him. Finally, my Brother, you see on this tracing-board an indented tassel covering the temple: it designates the silence that reigns among us and the secrecy of our actions: Thus the Masonic labors must be shrouded and our temples rendered impenetrable to the eyes of the profane.

That my Brother, is everything that the first steps you have taken in the Order allow me to teach you. You will see by frequenting this workshop diligently, how much we practice what I have just explained to you, and your conduct and diligence will make you reach new lights and new favors. Try to make yourself worthy of them and be sure that the R[especta]ble∴ Lodge will be filled with joy as it helps you climb even more steps when time and your Masonic conduct require it. [19]

Brother J[unio]r∴ Warden is going to ask you to give raps with the gavel on the rough ashlar: that is the start of your work. May God help you.

The Worshipful strikes one rap with his gavel which is repeated by the Wardens: All the Brethren stand and come to order, while the newly initiated Brother is placed between the two columns.

<u>Prayer.</u> The Worshipful says: G[reat]∴ A[rchitect]∴ of the Universe, divine author and eternal regulator of this universe, your creation: cast a favorable regard upon the Brother who has just been initiated into our mysteries. He is a man, and he is fragile, but as a received Mason he has acquired the rights to your supreme goodness.

Make us virtuous, humane, and beneficent, and banish from our hearts any dreadful selfishness. Finally, oh Supreme Being, identify us with yourself through the practice of all the virtues. Amen, amen, &c.

The Brother Master of Ceremonies leads the received Brother to the East and the Worshipful asks the former to take his place.

HONORS TO BE RENDERED.
TO CURRENT WORSHIPFULS.

When the Worshipful presents himself and the labor has been opened, whoever presents him will send out two Masters <armed> with their swords to receive him, preceded by two other Brethren, each bearing a star, and the Master of Ceremonies. They will pass under the arch of steel which will be formed by all the Brethren; The gavels are exchanged. [20]

TO WARDENS.

When the Wardens present themselves and the labor has been opened, they will be led to their places by the Master of Ceremonies. All the Brethren will remain standing until the gavel has been handed to them.

TO THE KNIGHTS OF THE EAST.

Knights of the East presenting themselves with a certificate of their degree and dressed in the vestments and jewels of the Order will be introduced into the lodge by two Brethren armed with swords and by the Master of Ceremonies; who will precede them and pass under the arch of steel to place the knight on the right of the Worshipful who will offer him his gavel if he himself does not have this degree.

A Knight of the East is entitled to visit the labors of the symbolic lodges, and to prohibit them or to set them on the right path, according to his wisdom and prudence. They have the right to enter and remain covered in the lodge.

TO THE PRINCES OF JERUSALEM.

Princes of Jerusalem visiting a lodge must be decorated with the jewels and ornaments of their degree, announcing themselves as such. The Worshipful will delegate the Brethren to go to receive them. They will lead him to the door of the lodge, opening both leaves of that door. He will pass under the [21] arch of steel, and the Master of Ceremonies will place him at the right hand of the Worshipful, who will hand him the gavel if he is not himself a Prince of Jerusalem.

The Princes have the right to inspect the labors of the symbolic lodges and to revoke all the labors if they are contrary to Masonic laws.

The deputation sent to introduce to the lodge, the Valiant Prince of Jerusalem must consist of four dignitary officers, who must be joined by the Brother Master of Ceremonies. If the Valiant Prince wishes to retire before the lodge is closed, the Worshipful will thank him for his visit, invite him to do so often, and after a rap with the gavel, will say: To order, my Brethren, which will be repeated by the Wardens. All the Brethren will stand, come to order, and once again form the arch of steel. The Valiant Prince will be led out by the same deputation. The four deputies having returned, the labors of the lodge will be continued.

TO R[OSE]∴†∴

A R[ose]∴†∴ visiting a symbolic lodge, decorated with their cordons and jewels and recognized as such, will be introduced there by five Brethren bearing stars and by the Master of Ceremonies. They will pass under the arch of steel and he will be placed to the left of the Worshipful, who will offer him the gavel, if he himself does not hold that degree. A Rose ✠ with a certificate of this degree and the jewel of the Order cannot be [22] tyled before entering the lodge, being a Chief of Masonry. They have the right to interrupt the labors of symbolic lodges and ban or even end them.

TO SUBLIME PRINCE MASONS.

The Sublime Prince Masons visiting a symbolic lodge will be introduced there by five dignitary officers armed with swords preceded by three Brethren bearing stars and by the Master of Ceremonies. The arch of steel will be formed, and he will be placed to the left of the Worshipful, who will offer him the gavel if he himself does not hold this sublime degree. If he wishes to withdraw before the end of the labors then the same formalities will be observed as on entry. They have much more extensive rights than all the Brethren elevated through the degrees and designated above.

CLOSING OF THE LODGE.

The Worshipful: Brethren Senior and Junior Wardens, inform your respective columns that the proposal bag is about to circulate.

The Brother Master of Ceremonies then passes around the proposal bag. The Worshipful receives and examines it in the presence of Brother Orator and Expert.

The Worshipful: Brethren S[enio]r∴ and J[unio]r∴ Wardens, inform the Brethren on your Columns that the charity box is to travel. The Brother Hospitaller passes the charity box around and hands it over to the Worshipful, who gives him the funds which are there to deposit. [23]

The Worshipful says: Brethren Senior and J[unio]r∴ Wardens, ask the Brethren of your columns if they have anything to propose for the good of the Order in general or the lodge in particular. Permission to speak will be granted to them.

The Worshipful: Brethren Senior and J[unio]r∴ Wardens, invite the Brethren who are decorating your columns to lend an attentive ear to the lecture that our dear Brother Secretary will give us of the day's labor. (The Worshipful says: Silence, and to order, my Brethren)

(After the lecture.) The Worshipful says: Brethren Senior and J[unio]r∴ Wardens, invite the Brethren who compose your columns to ask for permission to speak if they have any observations to make on the draft of the day's labor. Such will be granted to them. If not, then ask them to indicate their approval with the customary sign.

The Worshipful: My Brethren, join with me in applauding the day's labor. (Applause.)

Q. Brother Junior Warden, where do the Wardens stand in lodge?

A. In the West.

Q. Why?

A. As the sun completes its progress in that part of the world, so [24] stand the Wardens there, to close the lodge and pay the craftsmen.

Q. B[rother] Senior Warden, at what time do the Apprentice Lodges in which you have worked close?

A. At midnight.

Q. How old are you as an Apprentice, Brother Junior Warden?

A. Three years or more.

The Worshipful: In consideration of the time and your age Brethren Senior and Junior and Wardens, announce your respective columns that I intend to close this Apprentice Lodge by all the customary signs and batteries.

(The Wardens repeat this).

The Worshipful says: Let us swear, my Brethren, that nothing that has happened here will be disclosed.

(Each raises his hand and says, I do so swear.)

The Worshipful strikes as an Apprentice, makes the sign and the battery, and announces that the lodge is closed.

End∴ [25]

2∴ᴺᴰ DEGREE∴
FELLOW CRAFT∴
SCOTTISH SYMBOLIC DEGREE∴
FIRST CLASS∴

J[ean]∴ Doszedardski

FELLOW CRAFT∴ 2∴ND SCOTTISH DEGREE

An Apprentice cannot advance to this degree if he has not served his time, in other words, he has not worked in five lodges of instruction – Five Months∴

OPENING OF THE LODGE.

Q. To order, Brethren (The Wardens repeat this).

Q. Brother Senior Warden, are you a Fellow Craft?

A. Yes, I am Worshipful.

Q. Why did you receive the degree of Fellow Craft?

A. To know the letter G.

Q. How old are you?

A. Five years.

Q. At what time do the Fellow Crafts start their labors?

A. At high noon.

Q. What time is it, Brother J[unio]r∴ Warden?

A. High noon.

Q. Since it is high noon and since this is the hour at which the Masons customarily open the Fellow Craft labors, Brothers Senior, and J[unio]r∴ Wardens, invite the Brethren of your respective columns, to join with me in opening them.

RECEPTION.

Q. What is the reason for our assembly, B[rother]∴ S[enior]∴ Ward[e]n∴?

A. The propagation of the Order: an Apprentice asks to be passed to the degree of Fellow Craft. [1]

Q. Ask him his first name and surname, his age, the place of his birth, his current residence, and his profession. Ask him if he has served his time and if he thinks his Masters are pleased with him.

Q. Bring him in. (At the moment of his introduction all the Brethren rise, take their swords in their right hand and stand in this attitude without coming to order, until ordered otherwise).

The Aspirant will be placed between the two Wardens, by the 3 steps of the Apprentice; he will stand there to order. The Worshipful will ask him some questions about this degree, and will then say to him: My Brother, the knowledge you have acquired since you were admitted to our mysteries, must have made sensitive to your spirit, the emblems that accompanied your reception as an Apprentice. We have therefore given you the light, that is to say, opened the path of knowledge which ordinary men cannot attain. The further you penetrate there, by means of assiduous work, the more satisfying the discoveries you will make. Reflect carefully upon the emblems that will accompany your reception.

Brother Expert, have the Aspirant make the first voyage.

The Brother Expert immediately presents the Recipient with a mallet and chisel which he will hold with his left hand, and will lead him by the right; he will make him begin his voyage in the South, and back to the West; the Worshipful says to him: This voyage is the emblem of that year, which every Fellow Craft must devote to his instruction on the [2] knowledge of the quality of the cut stone, that he will be able to roughen out, using a mallet and chisel during his Apprenticeship. The meaning of this emblem is that whatever knowledge an Apprentice believes he has acquired, it is still very far from being the perfection of his work. Consequently, that as long as he exists, whether on the superfluous crude or materials devoted for the construction of the temple, which he elevates to the Great Architect of the Universe; he must persist in the hard and painful work with his mallet and chisel, and direct them only on the traced lines of a skillful Master.

Brother Expert, have him make the second voyage.

He presents him with a pair of compasses, which he holds with his left hand, and a rule, which he holds in his right hand. Returning to the West, the Worshipful says to him: This voyage is the emblem of the second year, in the course of which a Fellow Craft must acquire the elements of practical Masonry, that is to say the art of tracing lines on materials, trimming them and setting them up. For this purpose you have been provided with a compass and a rule. This emblem must also present to your spirit the sensible truth, that ignorance is the prerogative of our childhood, but only by being cultivated by educated men, is the path to the sciences opened to us and we are led imperceptibly with the help of constant and painful works, to discovery of the truth. [3]

Brother Expert, have him make the third voyage.

He presents him with the rule, which he holds in his left hand, and a crowbar, which he will place on his left shoulder and which he supports with the rule. Returning to the West, the Worshipful says to him: My Brother, this journey represents for you the kind of work a Fellow Craft undertakes during his third year, when he is entrusted with the fitting of the stones and cut materials, a job that assumes sufficient knowledge, to judge by their shape, of the place where they were intended, and for which purpose a rule is required. Their removal to their destination also requires intelligence, which it is presumed he acquired during his Apprenticeship, as well as the necessary supernatural strength, that he acquired with the help of the crowbar; and he was assisted in this work by Apprentices: in the same way we entrust to the Fellow Crafts the care of directing them, under the supervision of the Master whom they serve.

Brother Expert, have him make the fourth voyage.

He presents him with a square and a rule, which he will hold in his left hand and the Conductor, whom he will hold with his right. Returning to the West the Worshipful says: Brother, this fourth voyage represents for you the fourth year of a Fellow Craft, during which he is occupied with the construction and raising of buildings, the overall direction, as well as with checking the accuracy of the placement of stones and the use of materials.

It is also the emblem of the superiority that men acquire over their fellow-men through zeal, diligence in their works and the eminence of their knowledge, even when they least seek it. Instruct your Brethren [4] with good lessons and useful works. Guide their steps on the path of virtue and edify them with your example.

Brother Expert, have him make the fifth voyage.

During this voyage the Recipient does not carry any tools in his hands. Returning to the West the Worshipful says to him: This voyage has represented for you the fifth year of Fellowship. Sufficiently instructed in the practice of the art, the Fellow Craft must use this year to study theory. It is for this purpose that your hands are empty and free, because it is to the work of the spirit that you must henceforth devote yourself. Learn then by this emblem that it is not enough for an education to set you on the path of virtue, because left to ourselves, we are soon diverted, if we do not persist in our efforts; a constant study which keeps us on our guard against seduction, vice, and the fire of our passions. May all your steps therefore be directed towards knowledge of the truth. Our sole purpose, to which we aim, is following the path that has been traced out for you, making yourself worthy of being subsequently admitted to a new degree and, consequently, to new knowledge.

Brother Expert, have the Recipient climb the 5∴th <mysterious> step of the temple, so that from there he may discover the blazing star and the letter G that adorns its center. (When he has succeeded, the Worshipful says:) [5]

My Brother, consider this mysterious star, and never lose sight of it; it is the emblem of the genius that elevates to great things, and with greater reason it is still a symbol that sacred fire, that portion of the divine light from which the G[reat]∴ A[rchitect]∴ of the Universe formed our souls, by whose rays, we can distinguish, know, and practice virtue, truth, and justice.

The letter G which you see in the center represents two great and sublime ideas: one is the monogram of one of the names of the most high, the sources of all enlightenment, and of all sciences: <u>God</u>, which in French is <u>Dieu</u>.

The second, the result of what is commonly explained by the word Geometry, a science that has as its essential basis, the application of the property of numbers to the divisions of bodies and, above all a triangle, to which almost all figures are related and which offer sublime emblems.

Brother Expert, make the Brother pass to the East by the step of the Fellow Craft preceded by that of the Apprentice.

The Recipient will take the 3 steps of an Apprentice, which will lead him to the lower edge of the Tracing-Board. He will make him climb 5 steps, after which he will [6] make him take the 3 steps of the Fellow Craft: the first at the South, the second at the North and the third at the East, where having arrived, the Worshipful says to him: This irregular step, is emblematic of the right, which the Fellow Craft has, to pass from one Master to the service of another and to vary his works, according to need.

He is then taken to the East, to take the following oath:

<u>Oath</u>. I do swear and promise to the G[reat]∴ A[rchitect]∴ O[f]∴ T[he]∴ U[niverse]∴ between your hands, Worshipful Master, and on the faith of my first obligation to faithfully keep and preserve the secrets which shall be entrusted to me, and not to entrust or communicate them to the Apprentices, in any way whatsoever, and in case of violation, I submit to the penalties imposed by my previous oath. May <u>God</u> help me.[7]

The Worshipful receives him as a Fellow Craft in the usual manner, and gives him the signs, grips, sacred word, and password, has him recognized in his new capacity, and applauds his reception in the usual manner.

<u>Sign.</u> Bring the *right hand* to the *heart,* etc. etc.

<u>Grip.</u> Strike with two short and one long on the *first joint,* followed by one on the *second* and a further one on the *first,* which form five strokes of the Fellow Craft.

<u>Sacred Word.</u>   Ancient <u>York.</u>   <u>Modern.</u>

                   <u>Jakin.</u>   <u>Booz.</u>

This word means: <u>Strength.</u>

<u>Password</u>: Htel∴o∴bi∴hcs. Sch∴ib∴o∴leth∴

or <u>Schiboleth</u>: which means <u>Abundance</u>.

<u>The Step:</u> Bring the *right foot* diagonally across from the right side, bring *the left* back behind the right, do the same from the left side starting with the *left foot*, and then make the 3∴rd in the East to complete the step of the Fellow Craft.

BROTHER ORATOR'S SPEECH.

When you were received as an Apprentice, my dear Brother, you were given a sign, a grip, a password, a sacred word, and a step. [8]

We are glad to see that you have remembered and have carried out what we have taught you. At the time of your reception you were given an explanation of the tracing-board which is before your eyes. You were told about the column J. (Ancient) where you were to stand and receive your wages, but no mention was made of column B. The time has come to acquaint you with this column.

These two columns were, my dear Brother, built and erected on the orders of the director in charge of the inspection of the works, of the construction of the Temple of Solomon; in order to avoid confusion and disorder that would undoubtedly have reigned among the Fellow Crafts, on the distribution of wages.

The one marked B. was placed in the South and the other, marked J., in the North. The Apprentices assembled at the latter every Saturday to receive their wages for the labors, which they had undertaken during the previous week, while the Fellow Crafts also met at column B., for the same purpose and object. They were both obliged to give their password and to spell out their sacred words, the initial letter you see on these two columns. [9]

You will recall that column J. is called JAKIN and is used by the Apprentices. I shall now teach you that column B. is called BOOZ and is used by the Fellow Crafts.

I hope, my dear Brother, that <by> your assiduity to Masonic labors you will rapidly acquire new enlightenment that will enable you to achieve Mastership.

Believe me that it will be infinitely sweet and pleasant for me to contribute to your advancement.

Note (Ancient). It will be recalled that the letter J. engraved on the Northern column stands for <u>Jakin</u>, the sacred word in Moderns Masonry, and that the letter B., which stands for <u>Booz</u>, the sacred word of the Ancient Masons, must be placed on the Apprentice column.

End∴ [10]

∴

THIRD DEGREE MASTER∴ SCOTTISH SYMBOLIC DEGREE

3∴RD DEGREE∴
FIRST CLASS.
MASTER∴
SCOTTISH SYMBOLIC DEGREE.

J∴ Doszedardski

Scots∴ M[as]ter∴

MASTERSHIP: 3∴RD DEGREE∴

OPENING OF THE LODGE.

The lodge arranged as it should be, the M[ost]∴ R[espectable]∴ raps once with his gavel and says, To Order, my B[rethren]∴ He then draws his sword, which he holds in his left hand with the sword-point touching the ground, and comes to order, which all the Masters present also do at his invitation: this involves extending *the right hand* horizontally with the *thumb* against the breast and the four *fingers* pressed together, the so-called attitude of repose.

In this attitude the M[ost]∴ R[espectable]∴ says:

Q. W[orship]ful∴ B[rethren]∴, what is your first duty in the l[odge]∴?

A. M[ost]∴ R[espectable]∴ To ensure that all the B[rethren]∴ here present are Masters.

Q. And are you sure certain?

A. We are.

Q. W[orship]ful∴ B[rother]∴ Senior Ward[e]n∴, are you a Master?

A. M[ost]∴ R[espectable]∴ Prove me: the acacia is known to me.

Q. Give me the Master's sign?

A. He does so.

Q. W[orship]ful∴ B[rother]∴ J[unio]r∴ Ward[e]n∴, how old are you?

A. Seven years.

Q. At what time does the Master's labor begin?

A. At noon.[1]

Q. W[orship]ful∴ B[rother]∴ Ward[e]n∴, what time is it now?

A. High noon, M[ost]∴ R[espectable]∴

The Worshipful. Since it is high noon, W[orship]ful∴ B[rothers]∴ S[enio]r∴ and J[unio]r∴ Ward[e]n∴, kindly invite the W[orship]ful∴ B[rethren]∴ of your respective columns to assemble before me to open the labors of the degree of Master.

The Wardens then repeat this announcement and the M[ost]∴ R[espectable]∴ strikes 9 raps (like the battery of the Apprentice degree repeated three times) which the Ward[e]ns∴ also repeat.

Then the M[ost]∴ R[espectable]∴ says: With me, Wor[ship]ful∴ Masters.

All the Masters look towards him and make the sign of horror and the applause by 9 raps, a triple Vivat.

Then the M[ost]∴ R[espectable]∴ responds by saying, the labors are open. This is repeated by the Wardens.

The M[ost]∴ R[espectable]∴ places his sword on the altar, then each brother is seated at the invitation of the M[ost]∴ R[espectable]∴.

The labors thus opened, the B[rother]∴ Secretary reads the previous labor, after their customary approval, or in the usual manner, without applause.

The M[ost]∴ R[espectable]∴ says: W[orship]ful∴ Masters, you have given your consent for the admission of Fellow Craft N. to the Mastership. If any of you has legitimate reasons to oppose this, now is the time to deduce them. Your silence will confirm to me that you are persisting in your approval.

If there are any objections, it is necessary to hear them, discuss them, and judge them, in light of the conclusions of the B[rother]∴ Orator, it would be necessary to send the proposal to another vote: appoint commissioners, &c∴, but if silence prevails over the two columns, the M[ost]∴ R[espectable]∴ says: [2]

B[rother]∴M[as]ter∴ of Ceremonies, tell the Preparing B[rother]∴ to bring in the Candidate.

The Preparing B[rother]∴, after having disposed the Aspirant for the reception, with wise, serious, and moral discourses about the importance of this degree, will take the Recipient's sword and hat to the M[ost]∴ R[espectable]∴, and one B[rother]∴ in each column will be given a roll.

RECEPTION.

When the Recipient is announced the candles will be extinguished, and a lamp with an opaque shade will suffice to illuminate the labors thereof, until the moment of reception. Care should be taken to ensure that the light of this lamp does not extend beyond the edges of the shade, so that none of the inferior objects can be distinguished. One will likewise place another lamp on the altar, whose weak light only reflects on the M[ost]∴ R[espectable]∴ which produces a similar effect to a dull lantern. All the Masters will be dressed in black, hats on their heads and turned down, and swords in hand. They line up thus in two lines, towards the middle of the lodge on row benches, arranged according to the length of the tracing-board, but at a sufficient distance, leaving room between them and the tracing-board, a passage for the voyages which will take place behind them.

The Recipient having arrived at the door of the temple, will knock on it. His apron must be tied in such a way that it can be taken from him without resistance. [3]

B[rother]∴ Tyler informs the J[unio]r∴ Ward[e]n∴ that someone is knocking as a Fellow Craft. He repeats this to the S[en]ior∴ Ward[e]n∴ who announces it in turn to the M[ost]∴ R[espectable]∴

The M[ost]∴ R[espectable]∴ says: Who is the Fellow Craft bold enough to disturb our labors? W[orship]ful∴ Sen[io]r∴ Ward[e]n∴, see who is knocking.

A. It is a Fel[low]∴ who has served his time and who now asks to be received as a Master.

Q. (Note that the questions and answers are repeated by the Ward[e]ns∴ and the B[rother]∴ Tyler). Ask him his name and surname, his age, his place of birth, his current residence, and his ~~current~~ marital status.

A. He has worked on the tracing-stone outside the temple and has prepared the tools. He is 5 years old and more.

Q. Ask him if he is sincerely disposed to fulfilling the duties of a Master Mason, and if he has no reason to reproach himself regarding those duties that he has previously contracted?

After his reply the M[ost]∴ R[espectable]∴ raps once and says:

Introduce the Fellow Craft.

(The doors open.) The doors open and the Preparing B[rother]∴ introduces the Aspirant into the temple by making him walk backwards until [4] he is between the two Ward[e]ns∴, where he stands upright, his back towards the East. The doors are closed.

The M[ost]∴ R[espectable]∴ says in a firm tone of voice:

Seize the Fellow Craft, and make sure he cannot see anything of what is happening here until we are sure that he is worthy to be admitted to our mysteries.

(The Ward[e]ns∴ seize the Aspirant.) At this the Wardens seize the Aspirant. The Senior Ward[e]n∴ passes the point of his sword over his heart and the M[ost]∴ R[espectable]∴ immediately says:

Fellow Craft, swear and promise under the penalties to which you subscribed in your first obligation not to reveal to anything to anyone that you might see here, nor to reveal anything to any Fellow Craft or Ap[p]rentice, even if you are not admitted to this degree, which you seem to desire.

A. I do so swear.

Q. Do you promise to answer truthfully the questions I am about to ask you?

A. I do so promise and swear.

Q. Fellow Craft, what are you seeking?

Is it really the desire of instruction that guides you? Do you have any knowledge of the degree you desire? [5]

(First Voyage.) Brother Expert have the Candidate make the first mysterious voyage, of the nine that he has to make.

The Wardens resume their places and the B[rother]∴ Expert who is on the candidate's right puts the tip of his sword against his heart and makes him grasp the blade with his right hand about a third of the way down, while grasping the Recipient's left hand with his and makes him go around the lodge in the same attitude, starting at the South and pushing him before him without stopping in the East, taking care in the course of the voyage, to keep his back turned towards the inside.

The M[ost]∴ R[espectable]∴ then resumes: All you Masters, members of this workshop, who know this Fellow Craft, come and tell me what you know of him, so that we may regulate our conduct towards him according to his conduct both towards us and among us. And you, Fellow Craft, fear and dread turning your head.

(First Representation) The Wardens retain their places while nine Masters ~~and~~ gather around the representation, where the youngest Master must lie down. Forming the chain of union, the M[ost]∴ R[espectable]∴ passes to his right the ancient word of the Master, J · · · ·, which must return to him from the left. This must be done in the greatest silence, with an imposing manner and in such a way as to cause the Recipient some concern about his conduct and the levities he allowed himself.

When the Recipient returns to the West the S[en]ior Warden [6] raps the gavel and says: M[ost]∴ R[espectable]∴, the first voyage is completed. Then the 9 Masters who have risen to hold council with the M[ost]∴ R[espectable]∴ will remain in this attitude. At the end of the Representation the M[ost]∴ R[espectable]∴ alone, will return to his place, saying: Fellow Craft, you stand accused of a serious offence. Addressing the B[rother]∴ Conductor he says: Tear off his apron, he is unworthy to wear it. The Preparing B[rother]∴ then tears off the apron.

The M[ost]∴ R[espectable]∴ continues: Fellow Craft, does your conscience not reproach you for something? Be sincere and remember the promise you made to us. You have only a moment to respond. The life of man passes quickly: whether you are born great or small; poor or rich, Fate makes us all equal in the end. Wealth and greatness are loans from destiny. As one enters this world, so must one leave it.

(2∴d Voyage.) Have the Fellow Craft make the 2d voyage.

Fellow Craft, during this voyage, examine the recesses of your heart.

(2∴d Representation.) The M[ost]∴ R[espectable]∴ leaves his place to meet the nine Masters, who are gathered around the representation. When the Candidate has arrived back in the West the Senior Ward[e]n∴ raps once and says: M[ost]∴ R[espectable]∴, the 2∴d voyage is completed.

The M[ost]∴ R[espectable]∴ resumes his place and continues:

Guilt and innocence; a lie and the truth have characteristics so perceptible that one cannot confuse them. Well, Fellow Craft, doesn't your conscience reproach you for anything yet? [7]

Brother Expert, bring this Fellow Craft back to us, that he might see to what excesses we can be led towards a refractory person, forgetful of his duties, and you Fellow Craft, consider the cause of the mourning where we are at.

(The nine Masters take a step backwards and point their swords at the representation). Here the Brother Expert makes the Candidate take 3 steps backwards, and turns him towards the representation: The nine Masters who are gathered around this representation take a step backwards, holding their right hand to their heart, at the order of the Master, using the other to point their sword at the representation, staring at the Recipient.

Q.   Brother Expert, is the Fellow Craft moved?

Anything in him, does he detect guilt in him?

A.   No, M[ost]∴ R[espectable]∴

(In an imposing tone) Every moment leads us to our end: the true Mason does not fear it, any more than he desires it. All things must pass, everything departs, everything is changing. Time harvests all and ultimately itself. The night chases the day, the day chases the night, the years chase the years, and the hour chases the hour.

(3∴rd Voyage) Brother Expert, have the Fel[low Craft]∴ make the 3∴rd voyage.

(a rap of the gavel and the 9 Masters withdraw) When the Recipient returns to the West the Senior

Ward[e]n∴ gives one rap of the gavel and informs the M[ost]∴ R[espectable]∴ of the Fellow Craft's return, who strikes one rap and the 9 Masters resume their places.

The M[ost]∴ R[espectable]∴ continues: Everything here announces our mourning and sadness to you. You are suspected of having participated in the [8] treachery of certain ruffian Fellow Crafts: do you know of their detestable plot?

A. No.

Q. What guarantees it?

A. My word of honor and my faith as a Mason.

Q. Do not be surprised by the precautions we have taken towards you. Since the death of our R[espectable]∴ M[as]ter∴ all Fellow Crafts have become suspicious to us. You must have noticed this from the way we have treated you, but your assurances and the naivety of your answers have destroyed any suspicions we may have had about you, and you deserve our trust. Try therefore to make yourself worthy of the favor you are asking for. The vulgar man allows himself to be seduced with appearances, but the true Mason sets them aside, that he might be elevated to the truth. Brother Fellow Craft, do you persist in the plan to which you have testified, of attaining the Degree of Master?

A. I persist in it.

M[ost]∴ R[espectable]∴: All the trials you have just undergone and the precepts which are going to be given to you have no other purpose than to purify your soul before allowing you to explore its interior. It is there that you will acquire knowledge. We cannot penetrate the depths of your soul. Be therefore your own judge, but fear remorse, for the Masters are no longer there to train you: as you yourself become one, you will be responsible for the same care towards the Fellow Crafts and the Apprentices. Let virtue, my dear Brother, be also the motive and the object of your precepts. Never lose sight of the fact that a good example has a greater [9] e effect than even the wisest lessons. Yes, my dear Brother, all that you have seen and experienced so far in Masonry, and all that you will see and experience henceforth, is covered by the mysterious veil of emblem; the Mason, intelligent, zealous and industrious always penetrates. Remember well, everything that has happened to you, and which will happen to you. Do not forget the emblem of the three mysterious voyages that you have just made. This degree requires nine, but the Order has kindly reduced them to three.

(The 7 steps of the temple by 3, 2, 2) Brother Expert, have the Brother climb the 7 steps of the temple: Let him enter by the West gate and, when it is time, present him to me by the 3 mysterious steps. And you, W[orship]ful∴ Masters of both columns, do not forget your duty!

(This applies to both Brethren∴ with the rolls).

The B[rother]∴ Expert makes the Candidate ascend the first three steps, starting with the right foot. Arriving at the pillar he make the sign of the Apprentice. He ascends two more steps and then makes the sign of the Fellow Craft. Finally he ascends the last two steps and stops on the mosaic pavement, still in the order of the Fellow Craft, both feet at right angles. (The Recipient's foot must be near the head of the B[rother]∴ who, as we have already said, is lying on the ground, but whom he cannot see as he is entirely covered by a black veil. The Brother who is lying down should have his left leg extended and his right leg in square, with the knee raised, the left arm extended, [10] and the right arm in the order of a Fellow Craft).

My Brother, the first two degrees taught you know the use of the instruments and to employ the materials. You doubtless expect to find in this a development of those emblems beneath which the truth has hitherto concealed itself from your eyes: but everything in the universe is subject to strange revolutions. Everything perishes, and even the temple that Solomon raised to the king of kings experienced the same fate. The death of the head of this magnificent enterprise can also retrace for you, by anticipation, the ruin of this famous temple that history shows us, being constantly destroyed and then constantly reborn from its own ashes.

(Historical) Solomon, the son of David, famed for his wisdom and the study of his knowledge, resolved to erect a temple that his father had planned, but involvement in certain wars did not allow him to build it. He therefore asked Hiram, King of Tyre, to provide him with the materials necessary for such an undertaking. Hiram gladly accepted this proposal and sent Solomon one of those rare men whose genius, taste, intelligence, superior talent in matters of architecture and vast knowledge of the essence of metals had earned him such a degree of consideration and respect from the King of Tyre that he called him father because, like him, [11] his name was <u>Hiram</u>, even though he was the son of a Tyrian and of a woman from the tribe of Naphtali. Solomon therefore made Hiram his intendant of the works and increased the number of his ~~Labors~~ craftsmen to <u>one hundred and eighty-three thousand three hundred</u>, whom history calls proselytes which means in our language admitted <u>foreigners</u>, that is to say <u>initiates</u>, namely <u>thirty thousand</u> to cut the cedars on Mount Lebanon, one-third of whom would serve for a month; <u>seventy thousand</u> Apprentices; and <u>three thousand three hundred</u> Masters, inhabitants of Mount Gebel, who fashioned and cut the stones.

These craftsmen were divided into three classes, in order to get along, recognize each other and receive the wages proportionate to their labor: they had words, signs and grips.

The Apprentices received their wages at column J∴, the Fellow Crafts at column B∴ and the Masters in the middle chamber: The name of this first column means <u>Preparation</u>, and that of the second <u>Strength</u>. Column J∴ was placed in the North, and B∴ in the South near the Western gate.

One entered the Temple through three gates: that intended for the Apprentices and thereafter for the people was in the West, that intended for the Fellow Crafts and, after the perfection of the temple, for the Levites was in the South, and that of the Masters, formerly for the Pontiffs was in the East. As soon as the gates had been put in place, Solomon issued an ordinance to be published, [12] by which he enjoined all Apprentices and Fellow Crafts, on pain of death, to leave the temple on the eve of the sabbath and not enter it again until the gates were opened the following day. The Order that had been established among the craftsmen was bound to ensure tranquility.

This last ordinance of Solomon was designed to prevent observance of the sabbath from being broken on any pretext, and everything in this respect corresponded to the labors of Solomon. Because of Hiram's care and vigilance, the temple took on new growth every day, when suddenly a terrible crime caused the labors to be suspended. Three Fellow Crafts, dissatisfied with their wages, had conceived a plan of obtaining those of a Master by using the signs, words and grips of this degree, which they meditated to obtain by brute force.

They had noticed that Hiram visited the labors every evening after the craftsmen had left, so they laid in ambush at the gates of the temple, = one armed with a rule, the other with a crowbar, and the third with a gavel. Hiram had entered the temple through a secret door and had turned his steps towards that of the West, where he found one of the Fellow Crafts, who threatened to kill him if he did not give him the words, signs and grips of a Master, to which Hiram replied: What are you doing you wretch? You know that I cannot and must not give it to you, I have not received it thus. At that same moment the traitor strikes him on his head with a rule, but a movement that Hiram made to parry it, deflected it onto [13] his right shoulder.

(First Mysterious Step) Here the Brother Expert makes the Candidate take one of the three mysterious steps, which consists of passing the right foot diagonally over the representation from the West, where he has been placed, towards the South, while keeping his left leg in square at the level of the right calf, an attitude in which the B[rother]∴ Expert must support him by holding his hand. At the moment the Candidate takes the first step, the B[rother]∴ of the southern column (First blow with the roll) who is equipped with a roll strikes him a lightly on the right shoulder with it.

and the M[ost]∴ R[espectable]∴ then continues:

Hiram wanted to flee by the South gate, but there he found another Fellow Craft who made the same demand and the same threats; he tried to flee, but the traitor pursued him and struck him with a stroke of the crowbar, which fortunately only struck his neck.

(2∴ᵈ Mysterious Step.) At this instant the Recipient is made to take the second mysterious step, by passing his left leg diagonally over the representation from South to North while holding his right leg in square against his left calf: during his passage the B[rother]∴ of the northern column, who is equipped with a roll, gives the Recipient a light blow with it on the nape of the neck (2∴ᵈ blow with the roll.) and at the same moment the Candidate is made to take the three steps by making him pass his right leg over the representation (3ʳᵈ Mysterious Step.) and place his two feet in square at the end of it.

(Two B[rethren]∴ seize the Neophyte). Two B[rethren]∴ each taking one arm, place their hands on his chest and at the same time place one of their feet behind, him touching his heels. (The representation is withdrawn.) Meanwhile the B[rother]∴ who was under the veil during the representation, quietly withdraws in such a way [14] that the Recipient does not see him, and leaves the veil lying on the ground.

The M[ost]∴ R[espectable]∴ leaves his place, approaches the Candidate, and continues his narration: The misdirected blow only stunned our unfortunate Master, who however still had sufficient strength to flee towards the eastern gate where he found the third Fellow Craft, who made the same demand and threats and who, upon his refusal, gave him a great blow with the gavel on the forehead and laid him dead.

(A blow with the gavel on the Neophyte's forehead). The M[ost]∴ R[espectable]∴ strikes the Recipient's forehead with a gavel, and at that moment the two B[rethren]∴ holding the Candidate pull him carefully to the floor and arrange him in the same manner as the B[rother]∴ who was in the representation, covering him with the black veil, etc.

(The candles are lit). When this performance has been completed everyone resumes their place, the nine candles are lit and the lamps extinguished.

The M[ost]∴ R[espectable]∴ then replies: W[orship]ful∴ disorder has crept into our works, and sadness is on the faces of all the craftsmen. We can no longer doubt that our R[especta]ble∴ Master Hiram is dead. Let us go in search of his body and ensure that our zeal is sufficient for us to find it. W[orship]ful∴ B[rother]∴ Junior Warden take two Masters with you for this purpose and search the northern part.

The J[unior]∴ W[arden]∴ executes the order, starting from the northern part: They go around the lodge probing the earth with the point of their swords. On their return to the East the Junior Warden raps the gavel once and says, <u>Our search has proved useless</u>.

The M[ost]∴ R[espectable]∴ in turn strikes one rap and says: [15]

(2[d] search, by the S[en]ior∴ Ward[e]n∴) W[orship]ful∴ M[as]ter∴ Senior Warden, take with you two other Masters and continue the search for our Respectable Master Hiram, travel towards the South.

(2 raps of the gavel, repeat[ed] by the Senior Ward[e]n∴) He executes this order in the same way as the first one. Returning to the West he strikes one rap of the gavel and says, <u>Our search was fruitless M[ost]∴ R[espectable]∴</u>

(3 raps of the gavel.) The M[ost]∴ R[espectable]∴ strikes one rap and says: W[orship]ful∴ B[rethren]∴ S[enior] and J[unior] Ward[e]ns∴, ask the Masters who accompanied you on these two journeys, to join you and make a third search, in which I myself will accompany you, along with two of our Masters. Perhaps through our mutual efforts we will be fortunate enough to arrive at this important discovery.

(3[rd] search.) The nine Brethren go around the L[odge]□∴ in the following order:

(J[unior] Ward[e]n∴ towards the South: S[enior] towards the North.) The J[unio]r∴ Ward[e]n∴ followed by two Masters from his column go towards the South, the Senior Ward[e]n∴ followed by two M[as]ters∴ from his column towards the North.

(Junction.) They thus go around the L[odge]□∴ crossing each other's path, and when the Senior Ward[e]n∴ has reached the West the M[ost]∴ R[espectable]∴ a as well as the two Masters who must accompany him, join him, and all together go around the lodge three times, probing the ground they are walking with their swords.

After the second round the S[enior]∴ W[arden]∴ says: [16]

(The Junior Warden) I see steam rising from a small patch of land. Let's take a closer look my B[rethren]∴

Once the 3∴[rd] voyage has been completed the M[ost]∴ R[espectable]∴ stops in front of a painting in the corner showing a mound which is placed an acacia branch.

(The Senior Ward[e]n∴) At this instant the S[en]ior∴ Ward[e]n∴ says to the M[ost]∴ R[espectable]∴:

The earth seems to me to have been recently disturbed. We may well find what we are looking for here.

Then the M[ost]∴ R[espectable]∴ says:

This branch does not seem to have taken root here. It seems suspicious to me. That makes me think our search will not be in vain. It could well be that the assassins by use of torture, could have torn from our R[espectable]∴ the word and sign of this degree. Would you not agree, my B[rethren]∴ that the first sign and the first word that one of us will utter when we discover the body of our R[espectable]∴ Master should henceforward be the word and sign of recognition of all Masons?

(Sign of Approval.) All the Brethren∴ then make the Sign of approval by dropping *the left hand onto the* thigh.

(Raising the Veil.) The M[ost]∴ R[espectable]∴ together with the other B[rethren]∴ immediately raise the veil covering the Recipient, using their swords, and upon seeing him make (sign of horror) the sign of horror.

(The Junior Ward[e]n∴ takes the Recipient by the index finger). The J[unior]∴ W[arden]∴ approaches the Recipient, takes his index finger, and then lets go of it, saying J∴ (the Apprentice word), then stakes a step back while making the Sign of Horror. [17]

(The Senior Ward[e]n∴ takes the middle finger). The S[en]ior∴ Ward[e]n∴ approaches him in turn, takes his middle finger, pulls the Recipient towards him, and then dropping it says (B∴ the Fel[low Craft]∴ word) while also taking a step backwards and making the sign of horror.

The M[ost]∴ R[espectable]∴ hen approaches the Recipient, makes the sign of horror, takes a step back and says: Worshipful Masters, which of you has disturbed the body of our R[espectable]∴ Master? The J[unio]r∴ Ward[e]n∴ answers: I thought I could raise him by the grip of the Apprentice, but the flesh cleaved from the bone.

The Senior Warden answers in turn:

I thought I could raise him by the grip of the Fellow Craft, but the flesh seemed to me to be rotten.

Then the M[ost]∴ R[espectable]∴ says: Do you not know my Brethren, that you can do nothing without me, and that we Three ····· can do everything ···· if we work at the same time.[41]

(The Grip). He then approaches the Recipient, places his right foot against his and his knee to his knee, and with his right hand takes his wrist in such a way as to join the palm of his hand with that of the Recipient. He then passes his left arm under the same shoulder which brings him stomach to stomach, and then, with the help of the two Wardens, raises the Candidate and speaks into his ear, giving him the accolade M∴B∴N∴ in the moderns usage and M∴H∴B∴ in the ancient. All the Brethren then take their seats as well as the M[ost]∴ R[espectable]∴

The Brother Master of Ceremonies leads the Recipient to the altar, where the latter kneels on one knee and takes the following oath, during which [18] all the Brethren stand to order, sword in hand.

Obligation. "I promise and swear before the G[reat]∴ A[rchitect]∴ O[f]∴ T[he]∴ U[niverse]∴ on my word of honor and on the faith of a Mason not to reveal in any way to any Fel[low Craft]∴, App[rentice]∴ or Profane any of the secrets that have been or will be entrusted to me, under the pains to which I submitted myself in my first obligations, and repeat at this time all the commitments, which I have previously entered into. May the G[reat]∴A[rchitect]∴ help me∴"

(The Fel[low Craft]∴ raised to Master). The M[ost]∴ R[espectable]∴ places his sword on the Recipient's head and says, To the glory of the G[reat]∴ A[rchitect]∴ O[f]∴ T[he]∴ U[niverse]∴ under the auspices of the Most Serene G[rand]∴M[as]ter∴, in the name of the Grand Orient of France, and of the R[espectable]∴M[other]∴ Scottish L[odge]☐∴ of Saint Alexander of Scotland and by virtue of the powers I have received from this R[espectable]∴ L[odge]☐∴ I hereby receive you and constitute you a Master Mason.

The M[ost]∴ R[espectable]∴ gives nine gavel raps on his sword, which he then lays on the head of the Recipient, who then stands up.

The M[ost]∴ R[espectable]∴ continues: My Brother, to recognize ourselves in this degree, we have, as well as in the preceding ones, a sacred word, a password, a sign and a grip. The sign is the one we made when you were discovered in our search for the body of our R[espectable] it is called the sign of horror. It depicts for you the horror with which the Masters were seized at the first sight of the corpse [19] of

---

41 Similar to the Royal Arch motto, "we three now agree – in peace, love, and unity to raise a Royal Arch".

Hiram. The sacred word is the one I whispered into your ear when I raised you.

The M[ost]∴ R[espectable]∴ repeats it to him in the usual way:

Moderns sacred word, M∴B∴

Ancients sacred word, Nobaham. Mahabon.

Moderns password, Giblim

Ancients password, Naiclabut. Tubalcain.

The password is Giblim, which is the name of the inhabitants of Mount Giblet, who drew the stones form the quarries and cut the cedars for the construction of the temple, and as a Master you will henceforth remember the word Gabanon.

The grip is the one I gave you when I raised you, but with this difference: that you must grasp the others wrist in the same way that he grasps yours. Additionally we have a sign of distress if a Master is in danger: He must raise his clasped *hands to his head* with the palms of *the hands* facing heavenward and say, Help me, Sons of the Widow.

The order of this degree is to extend *the hand* to the *heart* with the four fingers pressed together, and with *the thumb* over the heart but separated to form a square with the other *fingers*.

One must not pronounce the sacred word and give it with the grip, only in a Masters lodge, after making sure that the other person is really of that degree.

The M[ost]∴ R[espectable]∴ puts the apron of the degree on him saying, from now on you will wear the bib turned down. The color Blue, the border of this apron, will constantly remind you [20] that a Mason must expect everything from above, and that it is in vain that men pretend to build if the G[reat]∴ A[rchitect]∴ O[f]∴ T[he]∴ U[niverse]∴ does not himself deign to do so.

On giving him his sword: You know what you must do with this. Take care never to draw it against your Brethren.

On giving him his hat: Henceforth you will be covered in a Master's L[odge]□∴: this very ancient custom is a token of superiority and freedom.

So far you have served, both as Apprentice and Fellow Craft. Now you will command but take care not to abuse it.

(Proclamation) The M[ost]∴ R[espectable]∴ gives one rap and says, W[orship]ful∴ Brother Wardens, I am sending to you our new Master, so that you may teach him to work as a Master should, and may recognize him as such.

(The Master's Work) The Master of Ceremonies leads him between the two Ward[e]ns∴ The Senior makes him give 3 raps on each of the <3> Gates shown on the Tracing-Board at the East, West and South. He then receives the sign, word and grip, as does the J[unio]r∴ Ward[e]n∴, following which the Senior Warden raps once and says, M[ost]∴ R[espectable]∴, the Master is recognized, and has worked as a Master.

The M[ost]∴ R[espectable]∴ then says, B[rother]∴ M[as]ter∴ of Ceremonies, please take the Recipient to the East, to the head of one of the columns. (Which he does.)

The M[ost]∴ R[espectable]∴ continues his narration:

My Brother, the Fellow Crafts had no sooner committed their crime than they experienced all the horror of it, and to conceal knowledge of it and if possible destroy the slightest trace of it: they removed [21] the corpse of Hiram, and carried it some distance from the works and buried him there in a hastily-made grave, having planned to come and recover it at the first favorable opportunity and then to transport it far away. To recognize the place they planted an acacia branch there, but the Masters soon noticed Hiram's absence and informed Solomon who, to quell his impatience, ordered a search for him. Three Masters left for this purpose by the North, three by the South, and three by the West, after agreeing to always remain within earshot of each other.

At sunrise, one of them perceived in the distance a vapor rising from a small mound. He focused his attention on this phenomenon and shared it with the other Masters; all together they approached the place, where they first saw a small mound of earth that seemed to them to have been recently disturbed. What confirmed their suspicions was the little resistance they experienced in uprooting the acacia branch that they found planted there. They began to excavate and to dig up the earth, and it did not take long to discover the body of the sad and unfortunate Hiram already rotten: but whose condition <left them in doubt> did not allow them to doubt that he had been assassinated: Their initial fear was that the assassins had used torture to extract from Hiram, the Master's signs and words. They deliberated and decided amongst themselves, that in order to nullify the effects of this discovery, that the first words and signs and their first gesture when they exhumed the corpse, would henceforward be those of recognition among the Masters. They clothed themselves in white leather aprons and gloves [22] as proof that they had not soaked their hands in innocent blood and deputed one of them to go to Solomon and tell him of this fatal discovery.

When Solomon learned of this dreadful blow, that had deprived him forever of a friend, head of immense and superb works, to the perfection of which he had devoted all his ambition, he fell into the most severe anguish, tore at his clothes, and swore to avenge such a dark and horrible crime.

He ordered a general mourning among all the craftsmen of the temple, sent out a party to exhume the body with pomp, gave him a magnificent funeral, and then had him placed in a tomb three feet wide, five feet deep, and seven feet long: upon which was inlaid a triangle of the purest gold, engraved in the middle of it, the ancient word of the Master, which was one of the Hebrew names of God, i.e. of the G[reat]∴ A[rchitect]∴ O[f]∴ T[he]∴ U[niverse]∴, and gave his support to the changes in the words and signs, to substitute those adopted by the nine Masters.

DISCOURSE∴

It should be easy for you now, my dear Brother, to grasp the etymology of the historical features that I have just presented to you, of the circumstances that gave rise to them, of the emblem, and of the tests that you have just passed. But if you have reflected on the different circumstances that accompanied your reception, the degrees or promotions to [23] which you have been admitted, you will no doubt have observed some points of contradiction between them or that did not seem to you to have a perfect connection. Do not be surprised by this and suspend your judgement in this regard. This diversity is simply a continuation of the objects that the three degrees present to you and which are nevertheless the fundamental points of all Masonic knowledge. You will then see, with the help of study and wise research, that these appearances or apparent contradictions offer you a continuous and satisfying chain of knowledge which must lead you to the highest objects, and that it is sufficient that the Order shows you the path.

If you have been treated as a suspicious Fel[low Craft]∴ it is an allusion to the Profane, the enemies of our Order, let them slander and persecute us without knowing, and may we repel the traitors by force, and return to more moderate feelings through gentleness. You also saw only barely justified, of what you were charged with, your B[rethren]∴ hastened to bestow upon you a new mark of friendship by initiating you into their most secret mysteries and introducing you into the interior of the temple. The journeys and voyages that you have made are emblematic of the investigation of the crime and of the errant and wandering state of the criminal, who seeks in vain to escape punishment, while the mysterious step represents [24] the efforts that Hiram made to evade the blows of his assassins. As for the three blows which you received, they refer to those which were inflicted upon him, and to the danger of man's blindness, and to his pride, his envy, and his greed.

The trials are also emblematic of the great importance we must attach to our mysteries, and that, in imitation of Hiram, we must suffer a thousand torments rather than reveal the least of our secrets and default on our obligations. Finally, they are also an allegory of the infinite amount of knowledge you will acquire by study alone, and of which I must remain silent for the moment.

You have now reached the seventh degree or 3∴rd perfect number of Masonry: Perfect number of Masonry: beware of descending from it and falling from the number of perfection, with which you are decorated∴

Then, addressing the Wardens:

Brethren Senior and Junior Wardens, invite the Brethren who decorate both the columns of the temple to recognize Most Dear Brother N∴ as a Master Mason, that he may be recognized as such in the future by all other Masters, which are found scattered across the surface of the Earth.

The Wardens repeat this and the M[ost]∴ R[espectable]∴ responds: Let us applaud, W[orship]ful∴ Masters, by the usual triple battery, the admission of W[orship]ful∴ Brother N∴ to the degree of Master. The Recipient gives his thanks and the M[ost]∴ R[espectable]∴ covers the applause. All the Brethren sheath their swords and sit down. The proposal bag and charity box are passed round, and the deliberation is read out &c. &c. [25]

CLOSING OF THE LABORS.

Q. W[orship]ful∴ B[rother]∴ Senior Warden, at what time should the labors be closed?

A. M[ost]∴ R[espectable]∴ at midnight.

Q. And what time is it now?

A. Midnight, Most Respectable.

Q. How old are you?

A. Seven years.

Q. In view of the time and your age, Worshipful Brethren Senior, and Junior Ward[e]ns∴, invite the Worshipful Masters of your respective columns to help me to close the labors of the Master.

The Most Respectable gives nine raps; makes the sign of horror and performs the battery and announces that the L[odge]□∴ is closed.

End∴ [26]

∴

GUIDE
OF THE SCOTTISH MASONS,
OR
NOTEBOOKS
OF THE THREE SYMBOLIC DEGREES
OF THE ANCIENT AND ACCEPTED RITE.

Venerable.

IN EDINBURGH.

58∴

INTRODUCTION.

WHATEVER the detractors of Scottish Masonry say, it is no less certain that the lodges of this rite are generally widespread in all the states of Europe and America, and that the rite of Heredon obtained a marked preference over the Modern Rite.

It seems still certain that if all the Scottish workshops continue to be distinguished by the zeal of their workers, by the brilliance which they have until now not ceased to bring to their work, this rite will be, in a few years, universally followed.

Several educated Masons have communicated to each other the various dissimilarities which they have noticed in the course of their long journeys; it is to put an end to them henceforth, and to obtain a greater uniformity in the manner of giving the Symbolic Degrees, that they are published well rectified, under the title of *Guide of the Scottish Masons*.

Correspondence is established, in all languages, so that the lodges, in whatever countries they inhabit, can obtain these ritual books; and steps are being taken for the copies entrusted, for sale, only to Masons who have acquired the highest Degree of esteem and consideration, in order to prevent this *Guide of the Scottish Masons* from experiencing such scandalous publicity as that which is daily given to the ritual books of the French Rite, under the title of *Regulator of the Mason*.

GUIDE
OF THE SCOTTISH MASONS.

Apprentice.

OPENING.

The Ven[erable]∴[42] raps a gavel blow, and says:

Q. V[ery]∴ D[ear]∴ B[rother]∴ Senior Warden∴, what is the first duty of a Warden∴ in lodge?

A. To ensure that the temple is tiled.

Q. You will ensure that, my Brother.

The Brother Tiler performs his office, and reports to the Senior Warden∴

A. M[ost]∴ V[enerable]∴, the temple is tiled.

Q. What is the second duty of the Senior Warden∴ in a lodge?

A. To ensure that all the Brethren who compose it are Mas[ons]∴

Q. Are they, Dear Brother?

A. They are on both columns, Ven[erable]∴

The Venerable raps a blow.

Q. V[ery]∴ D[ear]∴ B[rother]∴ Junior Deacon, what is your place in the lodge?

A. To the right of the Senior Warden, if he will permit it.

Q. Why, my Brother?

A. To carry his orders to the Junior Warden and see to it that the Brethren stand decently on the columns.

Q. Where is the Senior Deacon?

---

42 Translated correctly as Worshipful, but left as Venerable in this ritual, out of tradition.

A. Behind or to the right of Ven[erable]∴, if he will permit it.

Q. Why, V[ery]∴ D[ear]∴ B[rother]∴ Senior Deacon?

A. To carry his orders to the Senior Ward[en]∴ and to all the dignitaries, so that the labor may be carried out more promptly.

Q. Where does the Junior Ward[en]∴ stand?

A. In the South.

Q. Why, V[ery]∴ D[ear]∴ B[rother]∴ Junior Ward[en]∴, do you occupy this place?

A. The better to observe the sun at its meridian, to send the Craft to labor, call them from labor to refreshment, so that the Ven[erable]∴ may derive honor and glory thereby.

Q. Where does the Senior Warden stand?

A. In the West.

Q. Why, V[ery]∴ D[ear]∴ B[rother]∴ Senior Warden?

A. As the sun sets in the West to close the day, so stands the Senior Ward[en]∴ there to open and close the lodge, to pay the Craft, and send them away content and satisfied.

Q. Where does the Ven[erable]∴ stand?

A. In the East.

Q. Why, my Brother?

A. As the sun rises in the East to begin its course and open the day, so stands the Ven[erable]∴ there to open the lodge, direct it in its labors and enlighten it with his light.

Q. At what hour are Apprentice Masons in the habit of opening their labors?

A. At noon, Ven[erable]∴

Q. What is the hour, B[rother]∴ Junior Ward[en]∴?

A. High noon.

The Ven[erable]∴ then raps three blows of the gavel at equal distance o o o, then turning to the Senior Deacon, they mutually make the guttural sign. The Ven[erable]∴ gives to the Senior Deacon the sacred word softly in his ear, to open the L[odge]∴ of App[rentice] Mas[ons]∴ of the Scottish Rite.

The Senior Deacon carries it to the Senior Ward[en]∴, who sends it by his Deacon to the Junior Ward[en]∴, who, having received it, raps a blow with the gavel, and says: Ven[erable]∴ all is just and perfect.

The Ven[erable]∴ removes his hat and says:

Ven[erable]∴ — In the name of God and of Saint John of Scotland, this L[odge]∴ of Apprentices is open. It is no longer permitted for any Brother to speak, nor to pass from one column to another without having obtained permission, to discuss political questions or controversy, under the penalties prescribed by the general statutes of the order. — With me, my Brethren.

All make the gutt[eral]∴ sign and applause.

The Ven[erable]∴ says:

Ven[erable]∴ — Be seated, my Brethren. (*He adds:*)

V[ery]∴ D[ear]∴ B[rother]∴ Secretary, please read to us the tracing board of the most recent labors.

He raps and says:

Ven[erable]∴ — Attention, my Brethren.

The reading finished, Ven[erable]∴ raps.

The Wardens repeat.

Ven[erable]∴ — Brethren Senior and Junior Ward[ens]∴, announce on your columns that if some Brethren have observations to make, the word is granted to them.

The two Wardens rap a blow. The Senior says:

Sen[ior] W[arden]∴ — Ven[erable]∴, silence reigns over the two columns.

The usual sanction is given on the conclusions of the B[rother]∴ Orat[or]∴

Ven[erable]∴ — Brother M[aste]r∴ of Ceremonies, please go to the courts of the temple, to ascertain if there are visiting Brethren.

The Master of Ceremonies goes and returns between the two Wardens to give a report, puts the certificates of the visiting Brethren upon the altar, and returns to keep them company.

The Ven[erable]∴ sends the B[rother]∴ Grand Expert to tile the visitors, and another Expert to take their signatures, in order to verify them with those of their certificates.

Ven[erable]∴ — B[rother]∴ Tiler, inform the M[aste]r∴ of Cerem[onies]∴ that he may present the visiting Brethren.

The B[rother]∴ M[aste]r∴ of Ceremonies raps.

The Ward[ens]∴ announce it.

Ven[erable]∴ — Grant them entrance to the temple. On your feet and to order, my Brethren.

The M[aste]r∴ of Ceremonies places them between the Wardens.

Ven[erable]∴ — Rise, and to order.

The Ven[erable]∴ asks the following questions:

Q. Whence came you? (*One of the visitors responds:*)

A. From the lodge of Saint John of Scotland, Ven[erable]∴

Q. What do you bring?

A. Joy, health, and prosperity to all my Brethren.

Q. Do you bring anything more?

A. The M[aste]r∴ of my lodge salutes you by three times three.

Q. What do we do here?

A. We erect temples to virtue and dig dungeons for vice.

Q. What do you do here?

A. Conquer my passions, subdue my will, and make further progress in Masonry.

Q. What do you desire, V[ery]∴ D[ear]∴ B[rother]∴?

A. A place among you.

Ven[erable]∴ — It is yours. — Brother M[aste]r∴ of Ceremonies, conduct this Brother to the place which is intended for him. (*He leads him there.*)

If the visiting Brother is an officer of a Mother-lodge, or a Deputy near it, a Grand Elect of the Sacred Vault, or Subl[ime]∴ Prince of Royal Secret, he is received at the door with five stars, the gavels beating, and he is made to pass under the vault of steel; with three stars if he is a Venerable.

The Ven[erable]∴ compliments the visitors and causes them to deliver a huzza.

RECEPTION.

Ven[erable]∴ — B[rother]∴ Expert, ascertain if the profane is in the Chamber of Reflection.

He goes there and returns to make his report.

The Ven[erable]∴ raps, and Ward[ens]∴ repeat.

Ven[erable]∴ — My Brethren, the three ballots having been favorable to the profane N___ the order of business brings his reception; are you ready to proceed with it?

All the Brethren stretch out their hands.

Ven[erable]∴ — B[rother]∴ Expert, please take a pen, ink, paper, and conduct yourself to the profane. Tell him that the trials he is about to undergo being very dangerous, it is prudent that he make his will.

The Expert goes there, and when he believes the will is finished, he fetches it, brings it to Ven[erable]∴, who has the B[rother]∴ Orator read it aloud.

The Ven[erable]∴ then asks the B[rother]∴ Treasurer if he is satisfied; and if he is not, he says to him: Perform your duty.

The Treasurer goes to the profane, asks him for the expenses of his reception; he then returns to the lodge, and says: I am satisfied.

Ven[erable]∴ — Brother Expert, return to the profane; prepare him, and bring him to the door of the temple, to the Brother M[aste]r∴ of Ceremonies.

The Expert goes to remove him from the Chamber of Reflection, hoodwinks him, removes any metal, puts him in his shirt from head to waist with his left breast bare, his right knee bare and a slipper for his left shoe.

The M[aste]r∴ of Ceremonies having received the candidate, gives a distinct knock at the door of the temple.

The two Wardens repeat it alternately, and the Senior Warden says, in a loud voice:

Sen[ior] W[arden]∴ — Venerable, someone knocks at the door of the temple as a profane.

Ven[erable]∴ — See who it is, my Brother, and who rashly dares to disturb our august labors.

The B[rother]∴ Tiler gently places the point of his sword on the candidate's breast, turning it to the side for fear of hurting him, and tries to cause him to feel the cold of the iron, saying in a loud voice:

B rother]∴ T[iler]∴ — Who is this audacious person who comes forcibly to enter into the temple?

M[aste]r∴ Cer[emonies]∴ — Stop, stay your sword, it is I, the B[rother]∴ Exp[ert]∴, who introduces a profane to this Respectable lodge.

Ven[erable]∴ (*raising his voice*). — My Brethren, arm yourselves with your swords; a profane is at the door of the temple. — Brother M[aste]r∴ of Ceremonies, how indiscrete to present yourself here with a profane! What do you intend? … What do you ask?

M[aste]r∴ of Cer[emonies]∴ —That he be admitted among us.

Ven[erable]∴ — How dare he hope so?

M[aste]r∴ of Cer[emonies]∴ — Because he is born free and of good report.

Ven[erable]∴ — Since he was free born and of good report, ask him his name, the place of his birth, his age, his religion, his civil status, and his current residence.

The door must be ajar on one of its leaves; the M[aste]r∴ of Ceremonies and the candidate are outside; with an Expert or Tiler within, to return the answers to the Junior Ward[en]∴, the latter to the Senior Ward[en]∴, and the latter to the Venerable.

The secretary transcribes them in his minutes.

Ven[erable]∴ — Let him in.

As he enters, the Brother Terrible lays the point of his sword on his breast and makes him feel it.

Ven[erable]∴ — What do you feel? What do you see?

Profane∴ - I see nothing, but I feel the point of a weapon.

Ven[erable]∴ — Know that the weapon, of which you feel the point, is an emblem of the remorse which should rend your heart, if ever you commit perjury towards the society in which you desire to have the happiness to enter; and that the state of blindness in which you find yourself symbolizes that in which every man is plunged who does not know the paths of virtue, in which you are about to begin to walk.

Q. What do you ask, sir?

A. I beg to be received as a Mason.

Q. Is it of your own free will, without any compulsion or suggestion, that you present yourself?

A. Yes, sir. (*He is prompted with this answer, if deemed necessary.*)

Ven[erable]∴ — Think carefully, sir, about the request you are making. You will pass through terrible ordeals, which will require all the firmness of which the strongest character may be susceptible. Are you resolved to endure them? Do you feel the courage to brave all the dangers to which your indiscretion could expose you?

A. Yes, sir.

Ven[erable]∴ — Since it is so, I will no longer answer for you. — Brother Terrible, take this profane without the courts of the temple, and conduct him where all mortals must pass who are bold enough to present themselves in this august enclosure.

They make him do two or three circuits in the porch. They gently open the two door leaves; the framework is placed opposite; the candidate is brought back, who must be in front of and very close to the paper frame, and the Ven[erable's]∴ order is executed:

Ven[erable]∴ — Thrust this profane into the cave.

Two Brethren forcefully push him, and two others hold him in their intertwined arms. They slam the two door leaves with force and observe the greatest silence for a moment.

The B[rother]∴ Terrible conducts the candidate between the Ward[ens]∴ and remains at his side.

The Ven[erable]∴ strike a gavel blow, and says:

Ven[erable]∴ — Conduct the recipient to the Junior Ward[en]∴ and cause him to kneel.

Profane, take part in the prayer that we are about to offer on your behalf to the Author of All Things.

PRAYER.

My Brethren, let us humble ourselves before the Sovereign Arbiter of the World; let us recognize His power and our weakness; let us keep our minds and hearts within the bounds of equity; and, walking in sure ways, let us rise up to Him. He is One; He exists of Himself; it is to Him that all beings owe their existence. He operates in everything and everywhere. Invisible to the eyes of mortals, He Himself beholds all things: it is He whom I invoke; it is to Him that I address my voice and my prayers.

Grant, O Great Architect! Grant, I beseech Thee, to protect the workers of peace whom I see gathered here; warm their zeal; fortify their souls against the tiring struggle of the passions; inflame their hearts with the love of virtue, and determine their success, as well as that of this new aspirant, who desires to participate in our august mysteries. Lend this candidate Thine aid and support Him with Thy Mighty

Arm in the midst of the trials he is about to endure. Amen.

Q. Profane, in whom do you put your trust?

A. In God.

Ven[erable]∴ — Since you put your trust in God, boldly follow the hand that leads you, and fear no danger.

The Expert causes him stand, places him between the columns, and the deepest silence is maintained.

Ven[erable]∴ strikes.

The Wardens respond.

All sit in silence.

QUESTIONS.

Ven[erable]∴ — Sir, before this assembly, of which I am only the organ, agrees to admit you to the trials, it must probe your heart, by questioning your mind on the first principles of morality.

Q. Do you believe in a Supreme Being?

A. (*He answers in the affirmative*)

Ven[erable]∴ — This belief, which does honor to your heart, is not only the share of the philosopher, but also that of the savage man; as soon as he perceives that he exists, he senses that he does not exist by himself; he seeks for his father from the whole of nature, and the silence of this mute nature is what brings him to the feet of the Organizer of Worlds. It is to Him that he pays homage by the most childish and ridiculous ceremonies.

Q. What do you mean by the word virtue?

A. (*Let him make whatever answer he thinks fit.*)

Ven[erable]∴ — It is a disposition of the soul that leads to doing good.

Q. What do you mean by the word vice?

A. (*Let him answer.*)

Ven[erable]∴ — It is the opposite of virtue. It is an unfortunate habit that leads to evil; and it is to throw a salutary brake on the impetuous impulse of cupidity; it is to raise us above the base interests which torment the weak profane; it is to calm the feverish ardor of the passions that we gather in this temple. Here, we work tirelessly, to accustom our minds to deploy themselves only to great affections, and to conceive only firm ideas of glory and virtue; it is only by thus regulating one's values by the eternal principles of sound morality, that one succeeds in giving one's soul that just balance of strength and sensibility which constitutes wisdom, or rather the science of life.

However arduous the labor is, it is still that to which you will be obliged to deliver yourself, if you persist in the desire which you expressed to be received a Mason.

Whatever different ideas you may have brought here, it is not by the crude and false ideas of a vulgar ignoramus that you present yourself here. If working constantly on your moral perfection seems to you a work beyond your strength, you may retire.

Q. Do you persist with the intent of being received a Mas[on]∴?

A. Yes, sir.

Ven[erable]∴ — Sir, every society has its laws, and every member has duties to perform; and, as it would be imprudent to impose obligations before knowing them, it is the wisdom of this assembly to tell you what your duties will be.

The first will be absolute silence about everything you may have heard and discovered among us, as well as on everything you will hear, see, or know afterwards.

The second of your duties makes Masonry the most sacred of bonds, when it is not the most noble, the most imposing and the most respectable of institutions; this duty, which belongs to the essence of our being, is, as I told you, to combat the passions which dishonor man and make him so unhappy; to practice the sweetest and most beneficent virtues; to help your Brother, anticipate his needs, relieve his misfortune, assist him with advice and enlightenment. And what would be in a profane a rare quality, is in a Mason only the performance of his duties.

Every opportunity to be useful which he does not take advantage of is an act of infidelity; every relief he refuses to his Brother is perjury; and if tender and consoling friendship also has its worship in our temples, it is less because it is a sentiment than because, being a duty, it can become a virtue there.

The third of your duties, and of which you will not contract the obligation until after having been received as a Mason, will be to conform in everything to the general statutes of the order, to the particular laws of this lodge, and to submit to all that which will be prescribed to you in the name of this respectable assembly, into which you solicit the favor of being admitted.

Now that you know the principal duties of a Mason, do you feel the strength, and do you have the unshakeable resolution to put them into practice?

A. Yes, sir.

Ven[erable]∴ — Before going further, we require your oath of honor, but this oath must be made on a sacred cup.

If you are sincere, you may drink with confidence; but if falsity and dissimulation accompany your promise, swear not at all. Rather remove this cup and fear the prompt and terrible effect of this potion.

Q. Do you consent to swear?

A. Yes, sir.

Ven[erable]∴ — Cause this aspirant to approach the altar.

The M[aste]r∴ of Ceremonies conducts him to the base of the steps of the altar.

Ven[erable]∴ — Brother Sacrificer, present to this aspirant the sacred cup, so fatal to perjury.

The Brother Sacrificer brings a cup with water in it, and watches when the Ven[erable]∴ gives him a sign to give the drink to the aspirant. He should also have some bitters in a bottle, which he pours in after the recipient has drunk a large portion of the water.

Ven[erable]∴ — Repeat with me your obligation.

I pledge myself to the most absolute silence about all the types[43] of trials to which my courage will be subjected. If I should falsify my oath and fail in my duties; if the spirit of curiosity leads me here, (*the V[enerable]∴ makes a sign to give him the cup*) I consent that the sweetness of this drink (*the bitters are poured in*) changes into bitterness, and that its salutary effect turns against me into subtle poison. (*He is made to drink what is left in the cup.*)

The Ven[erable]∴ raps a loud blow, repeated by the Wardens, and says:

Ven[erable]∴ — What do I see? Sir, I see some change in you. Would your conscience contradict the assurances of your mouth? And would the sweetness of this drink already be changed to bitterness? Remove the profane.

They lead him back between the Wardens and make him sit down.

Ven[erable]∴ — Sir, if you have intended to deceive us, this evil is not without remedy for you, you are still free to withdraw. I reject, however, the distressing idea that you ever made yourself worthless of the opinion we formed of you; but I cannot keep them from you any longer: to enter our society and to assure us of the reality of your inclination, you still have great trials to undergo.

You have no doubt heard of the rigor of these trials in the secular world, but whatever idea you may have formed of them, those which await you still exceed them.

Think of it, sir, the moment approaches, and once engaged in trials, you will no longer be able to avoid them. If you do not feel the strength to bear them, ask to withdraw, there is still time.

He replies that he persists.

The Ven[erable]∴ strikes a gavel blow, repeated by the Wardens, and says in a loud voice:

Ven[erable]∴ — Brother Terrible, seize this profane; make him sit on the stone of reflection.

The Brother Terrible seizes him with violence, spins him around, and makes him sit on the stone of reflection.

Ven[erable]∴ — Leave him to his own conscience; let the darkness which covers his eyes, the awful silent solitude be his only companions.

The greatest silence is observed.

After a moment Ven[erable]∴ continues:

Ven[erable]∴ — Have you reflected well, sir, on the consequences of your steps? I warn you for the last time, that although our trials are wholly mysterious and emblematic, they are dreadful nonetheless, such

---

43 The phrase *sur tous les genres* (about all the types) was misunderstood by Pike. The word *genres* means type, gender, kind, etc., and he understood it in the second sense. Hence, his ritual reads, to all men- or woman-kind in respect to all the tests.

that many have succumbed to them. So pronounce judgment for yourself. Do you want to return to the profane world, or do you persist in having yourself received a Mason?

He replies: Yes, sir, I persist.

The Ven[erable]∴ strikes a gavel blow, which the Wardens repeat, and says:

Ven[erable]∴ — Brother Terrible, seize this profane, and cause him to make his first journey. Do your best to bring him back safely.

The Brother Terrible takes him on his first journey and brings him back between the Wardens.

In this first journey, the conductor taps three times on the shoulder of the Junior Warden, who rises and says Who goes there?

The B[rother]∴ Terrible responds:

B[rother]∴ T[errible]∴ — It is a profane who begs to be received a Mason.

Jun[ior]∴ W[arden]∴ — How dare he hope so?

B[rother]∴ T[errible]∴ — Because he is born free and of good report.

Jun[ior]∴ W[arden]∴ — Since he is thus, he may pass.

He is taken back between the two Ward[ens]∴

The Junior Ward[en]∴ raps and says:

Jun[ior]∴ W[arden]∴ — B[rother]∴ Senior Ward[en]∴, the first journey is finished.

The Senior Ward[en]∴ knocks, and says:

Sen[ior]∴ W[arden]∴ — Ven[erable]∴, the first journey is finished.

Ven[erable]∴ — Well, sir, how do you feel about this first journey?

The recipient responds.

Ven[erable]∴ — Sir, our trials, as I told you, are mysterious and emblematic; what did you notice on this journey? What moral reflections did it cause you to have? Finally, under what emblems presented themselves to your imagination?

He is allowed to answer; then the Ven[erable]∴ gives him the following explanation:

Ven[erable]∴ — This first journey, sir, is emblematic of human life, the tumult of passions, the clash of various interests, the difficulty of undertakings, and the obstacles multiplied under your feet by competitors eager to rebut you. All this is symbolized by the noise and crash that struck your ears, and by the unevenness of the road you travelled.

Q. Do you desire to hazard the second journey?

A. Yes, sir.

Ven[erable]∴ — Brother T[errible]∴, cause him to make the second journey.

The same ceremonies are performed as at the first; they stop at the Senior Ward[en]∴ as they did at the Junior [Warden].

The [Senior] Ward[en]∴ announces that the second journey is finished.

Ven[erable]∴ — You have overcome many difficulties; it is a happy omen for the rest of your trials. The ones you endured are nothing compared to those which await you. You must gather, at this moment, all the forces of your soul, if they are not already exhausted. If, against expectation, you succumb to this terrible and dangerous journey, we will bemoan your fate, pity your misfortune, and bitterly regret that so much zeal, so much constancy, did not have more success. — Make the third journey.

The same ceremonies are done as on the other two journeys. This time they stop at the Ven[erable]∴ and perform the same questions and answers.

Ven[erable]∴ — Who comes here?

B[rother]∴ T[errible]∴ — It is a profane who begs to be received a Mason.

Ven[erable]∴ — How dare he hope so?

B[rother]∴ T[errible]∴ — Because he is born free and of good report.

Ven[erable]∴ — Since he is thus, he may pass through the purifying flames, so that there is nothing left of a prof[ane]∴

He is made to make the third journey in the midst of the flames; is brought back between the two columns and announced as on the other journeys.

Ven[erable]∴ — Your travels are happily ended, and I cannot praise your courage enough; but let it not abandon you: you are not yet at the end of your labors; the ones you have yet to do, although of a different type, are all the more difficult.

The Order in which you solicit entrance may require you to shed the last drop of your blood. If you feel the courage to offer yourself as a sacrifice, you must give assurance of it by more than verbal promises; it is, by your own blood, shed today, that all your promises must be sealed. Do you agree?

A. Yes, sir.

Q. From what part of the body do you consent to having your vein opened?

A. *(He answers as he desires.)*

Ven[erable]∴ — Brother Surgeon, do your duty; proportion, however, the amount of the sacrifice to the state of this aspirant's strength. The lodge, moreover, relies on your wisdom and your prudence.

He takes instruments as if he desires to bleed him. He pricks him with a toothpick and someone, with a coffee pot, the spout of which is very small, pours water in a small trickle over the sting. When this is over:

Ven[erable]∴ — Each step you have taken in the career you have undertaken has been marked by success, and you have thus far triumphed over all obstacles; but you are not yet at the end of your trials.

Any profane who causes himself to be received a Mason ceases to belong to himself; he belongs to an Order which is spread over all parts of the globe. And for Masonry to facilitate a Mas[on]∴ being recognized as such, wherever his steps carry him, and whatever the difference of languages, there exist in all the lodges of the universe a seal charged with hieroglyphic characters, known only to true Masons, which, after having been reddened with fire and applied to the body, imprints an indelible mark there. Consent to receive this glorious imprint and be able to say by showing it: And I too am a Mas[on]∴!

They blow out a candle and apply the hot side to the arm.

Ven[erable]∴ — Here, sir, is the moment to put into practice the second of your duties. We have in this lodge unhappy Mas[ons]∴, widows and orphans whom we assist daily; I am going to depute a Brother to you, to whom you will tell in a low voice what you intend for the relief of these unfortunate people; for you must know that the acts of beneficence of Masons, not being acts of ostentation and vanity calculated to make the giver proud, as well as the recipient humiliate, must always be buried in secrecy. — Brother Almoner, approach the candidate, and let him tell you, in a low voice, of his intentions; you will come to report to me in secret.

(If the offer is generous.)

Ven[erable]∴ — I expected no less, sir, from your good heart. The R[espectable]∴ lodge, through my organ, testifies to you all its gratitude. You can also count on that of the unfortunate whose fate you are going to help ease.

(If the offer is low.)

Sir, a widow's mite, given willingly to the needy, is as agreeable to the Grand Architect of the Universe, as would be a rich man's piece of gold. Your donation is received and accepted with the greatest gratitude.

You will soon, sir, reap the reward of your firmness in your trials, and of the sentiments so agreeable to the Great Architect of the Universe, and those of pity and benevolence which you have just manifested. — Brother M[aste]r∴ of Ceremonies, deliver the candidate to the Brother Senior Ward[en]∴, so that he can teach him to take the first step in the corner of an oblong square; and you will bring him to the altar of oaths, to offer his obligation.

The Ven[erable]∴ raps, and says:

Ven[erable]∴ — Arise and to order, my Brethren; the new initiate will take the formidable oath. — Repeat with me your solemn obligation.

OBLIGATION.

I swear and promise of my own free will, in the presence of the Grand Architect of the Universe, who is God, and of this Respectable assembly of Masons, solemnly and sincerely, never to reveal any of the mysteries of Fr[ee]∴-Mas[onry]∴ which will be entrusted to me, but to a good and legitimate Brother, or within a regularly constituted lodge; never to write, trace, engrave or chisel them, or form any character by which the secrets can be revealed, under the penalty of having my throat cut, my tongue torn out, and of being buried in the sands of the sea, that the ebb and flow may carry me away into eternal oblivion. Amen.

The recipient kisses the Bible three times.

The Brother M[aste]r∴ of Ceremonies leads the candidate back between Ward[ens]∴ or rather to the [chamber of] lost steps.

The lights are quietly turned off; one places at the entry of the East two vessels filled with resin, one on each side.

A disheveled Brother lies down in the middle, face down, as if dead.

All the Brethren arm themselves with naked swords; they stand, their swords pointed at the candidate.

The Ven[erable]∴ descends from the throne and stands aside; he raps three strokes of the gavel.

At the first stroke of the gavel, the Master of Ceremonies unties the first knot of the handkerchief.

On the second stroke, the second knot.

At the third, the third and last knot.

Ven[erable]∴ — These pale and gloomy lights are the dark fires which must illuminate the vengeance that we reserve for cowards who perjure themselves. These swords directed against you are carried by as many irreconcilable enemies ready to plunge them into your bosom, if you are ever unfortunate enough to violate your oaths. In whatever place of the earth you dare to take refuge, none will be able to grant you an asylum; you will carry with you the mark of your crime. The rumor of your reprobation will have preceded you there with lightning speed. You would find Mas[ons]∴ enemies of perjury, and the most terrible punishment would await there. Brother M[aste]r∴ of Ceremonies, give him his hoodwink.

The candidate is taken out, then all the candles are lit, so that the brilliance of the lodge contrasts with the darkness in which it was.

Care is taken to give the hoodwink to the candidate in the courtyard of the temple; and on the order of the Ven[erable]∴, all the Brethren arm themselves with swords which they point at the candidate when he is brought in, but with the point lowered.

Ven[erable]∴ —Brother Senior Ward[en]∴, you, upon whom rests one of the columns of this temple, now that the courage and devotion of this aspirant have made him emerge victorious from this long combat between the profane man and the man as a Mason, do you deem him worthy of being admitted among us?

Sen[ior]∴ W[arden]∴ — Yes, Most Venerable.

Ven[erable]∴ — What do you ask for him?

Sen[ior]∴ W[arden]∴ — The great light.

Ven[erable]∴ — (*He raps and says:*) Let there be light. (*He adds:*) Sic transit gloria mundi.

The hoodwink is then dropped at his feet.

All the Brethren must have the points of their swords pointed towards his feet, and have a calm and friendly face.

Ven[erable]∴ — (*gently*) May the array of these swords cease to frighten you. They are no longer directed against you. We have received your oaths; we believe them to be sincere. The happy day of trust and friendship has finally dawned for you. Do not see anything in us but Brethren, who are ready to fly to your relief, to use their swords in defense of your life and your honor.

The Ven[erable]∴ raps. All the Brethren set aside their swords, and remain standing and in order.

Ven[erable]∴ — Brother M[aste]r∴ of Ceremonies, lead this new friend to the throne.

When he has succeeded, he kneels on the ground; the Ven[erable]∴ places the end of his sword on his head, and says:

Ven[erable]∴ — To the glory of the Grand Arch[itect]∴ of the Univ[erse]∴, and under the auspices of and by the powers entrusted to me by this Resp[ectable]∴ lodge, I receive and constitute you an App[rentice]∴ Mas[on]∴ of the Ancient and Accepted Scottish Rite, and a member of this Resp[ectable]∴ lodge.

The Ven[erable]∴ raps three equal blows on the blade of his sword. The neophyte rises, and the Master of Ceremonies leads him to the right of Ven[erable]∴, who, putting on the apron, says to him:

Ven[erable]∴ — Receive this apron, which we call clothing; it gives you the right to sit among us, and you should never present yourself in the lodge without wearing it.

The Ven[erable]∴ picks up the men's gloves, and says:

Ven[erable]∴ — Never defile the brilliant whiteness of these gloves, by dipping your hands in the muddy waters of vice; they are the symbol of your admission into the temple of virtue.

He then takes the women's gloves, and says:

Ven[erable]∴ — These are meant for the one you love the most, convinced that a Mason could not make an unworthy choice.

My Brother, Masons have to recognize each other: words, signs, and grips.

The sign is made, etc.

This sign reminds you of the oath you have taken, and the punishment which is attached to its criminal infraction.

The grip is made by, etc.

The sacred word is, etc.

There is no password.

You will have to give the sacred word to the B[rother]∴ Guardian of the temple, each time you enter it.

My Brother, Masonry is known throughout the Universe, although it is divided into two rites, which are distinguished by the Ancient Rite and the Modern Rite. Nevertheless, they rest on the same basis, on the same principles. We work under the Ancient or Scottish Rite, because it is the purest essence of Masonry, because it is the same that was transmitted to us by the first founders of the order. — Here, now, are the words, signs, and grips of the Modern Rite, etc.

The Ven[erable]∴ embraces the neophyte three times, and says:

Ven[erable]∴ — B[rother]∴ Grand Expert, will you receive the words, signs, and grips of the neophyte.

The Expert receives them, and tells the B[rother]∴ Junior Ward[en]∴, who tells the B[rother]∴ Senior Ward[en]∴, and this one to the Ven[erable]∴

Sen[ior]∴ W[arden]∴ — Most Ven[erable], the words, signs and grips are just and perfect.

The Ven[erable]∴ urges the recipient to go get dressed, and then return.

Upon returning to the lodge, the B[rother]∴ M[aste]r∴ of Ceremonies teaches him to knock at the door as an Apprentice, and to make the steps, and leads him to the rough stone, where he makes him work as an Apprentice.

Ven[erable]∴ — B[rother]∴ M[aste]r∴ of Ceremonies, lead this B[rother]∴ between the two columns. (*Addressing the neophyte*) Dear Brother, today is a day of favor and grace for you. Take your place at the head of the South column; it is the one you will occupy in this Degree. Merit it, by your diligence in our work, and by the practice of the Masonic virtues which you imposed on yourself with the obligation, and of which your Brethren will give you the first example; merit also to penetrate further into our mysteries, and to receive the favors which the lodge never refuses to those who know how to make themselves worthy of them.

Ven[erable]∴ raps; the Ward[ens]∴ repeat; he says:

Ven[erable]∴ — Rise and to order, my Brethren. — B[rethren]∴ Senior and Junior Ward[ens]∴ inform the B[rethren]∴, who adorn your columns, that I am going to proclaim the neophyte as a member of this R[espectable]∴ workshop.

The Wardens repeat.

Ven[erable]∴ — I proclaim, for the first time, Br[other]∴ N____ as an Apprentice Mas[on]∴, and as a member of the R[espectable]∴ Wo[rkshop]∴ N____. Consequently, I invite my Brethren to recognize him in this capacity in the future, and to lend him aid and assistance in all cases where he may need it.

The Ward[ens]∴ repeat this proclamation, which is made three times. After the third, the Ven[erable]∴ says:

Ven[erable]∴ — Let us rejoice, my Brethren, at the acquisition that the lodge has just made of a new B[rother]∴, and of a new friend.

He makes the usual signs and applause.

The B[rother]∴ Master of Ceremonies, or the recipient himself, responds with the same signs.

He returns the thanks.

The Ven[erable]∴ asks the B[rother]∴ Orator to gratify the lodge with a piece of architecture, if he has prepared any.

The Ven[erable]∴ inquires of the columns, by the Ward[ens]∴, if anyone has any proposals to make for the good of the order in general, or that of that Wo[rkshop]∴ in particular.

The proposal bag circulates.

The charity box circulates.

The Orator must be present at both accountings.

The B[rother]∴ Secretary reads the plans of the labors.

Ven[erable]∴ — Brethren Senior and Junior Wardens, announce on your columns that if any Brethren have observations to make on the plans of the labors of the day, the floor is granted to them.

The Ward[ens]∴ announce and return the report.

Ven[erable]∴ — (*He raps, and says:*) Rise and order, my Brethren. Let us give thanks to G[rand]∴ A[rchitect]∴ of the Universe of the works of this day.

PRAYER.

Great Architect, fruitful and immortal source of light, happiness and virtues, the workers of this temple, yielding to the beating of their hearts, offer Thee a thousand thanksgivings, and return to Thee all that they have done what is good, useful, and glorious on this solemn day, when they saw the number of their Brethren increase. Continue to protect their works and direct them ever more towards perfection. May harmony, peace and concord be forever the triple cement that binds their work together!

Friendship, charity! Passion of noble and sensitive souls! Delicious enjoyments of delicate and honest hearts! Support and adorn forever this temple, in which all our efforts will always be focused only on Thee. And Thou, prudent discretion! modest comfort! be the constant prerogative of the Brethren of this Wo[rkshop]∴; and that, having returned to the civilian world, they may always be recognized by their discourse, their attitude, and their actions, that they are the true children of the Wi[dow]∴ Amen.

The Ven[erable]∴ raps a blow, and continues with the following questions:

CLOSING.

Q. B[rother]∴ Junior Deacon, what is your place in the lodge?

A. To the right of the Senior Warden, if he permits it.

Q. Why, my Brother?

A. To carry his orders to the Junior Warden and see to it that the Brethren stand decently on the columns.

Q. Where is the Senior Deacon?

A. Behind or to the right of Ven[erable]∴, if he permits it.

The Ven[erable]∴ addresses the Senior Deacon.

Q. Why, my B[rother]∴?

A. To carry his orders to the Senior Ward[en]∴ and to all the dignitary off[icers]∴, that the labor may be more promptly and more regularly executed.

Q. Where does the Junior Ward[en]∴ stand?

A. In the South.

Q. (*Addressing the Junior Ward[en]∴*) Why, my B[rother]∴?

A. The better to observe the sun at its meridian, to call the Craft from labor to refreshment, call them from refreshment to labor, that the Ven[erable]∴ may derive honor and glory thereby.

Q. Where does the Senior Warden stand?

A. In the West.

Q. Why, V[ery]∴ D[ear]∴ B[rother]∴ Senior Warden?

A. As the sun sets at this part to close the day, so stands the Senior Ward[en]∴ there to close the lodge, to pay the Craft, and send them away content and satisfied.

Q. Are the Craft content, my Brother?

A. They bear witness to it on both columns, Ven[erable]∴

Q. B[rother]∴ Junior Ward[en]∴, what is your age as an App[rentice]∴?

A. Three years, Ven[erable]∴

Q. What is the hour, Brother?

A. Full midnight, Ven[erable]∴

The Ven[erable]∴ gives the Senior Deacon the sacred word softly in his ear, to close the L[odge]∴ of App[rentice] Mas[ons]∴ of the Scottish Rite.

The Senior Deacon carries it to the Senior Warden; the latter gives it to the Junior Deacon, who goes to the Junior Warden; the latter says:

Jun[ior]∴ W[arden]∴ - All is just and perfect, Ven[erable]∴

The Ven[erable]∴ removes his hat, and says, after rapping three times:

Ven[erable]∴ — In the name of God and of Saint John of Scotland, the L[odge]∴ of Apprentice Masons of the Ancient and Accepted Scottish Rite is closed. With me, my Brethren.

All make the Gutt[eral]∴ sign and the usual battery.

(NOTE. *When the work ends early, Ven[erable]∴ gives the following instruction, before closing the lodge.*)

INSTRUCTION.

Q. Brother Senior Ward[en]∴, is there anything between you and me?

A. A worship.

Q. What is it?

A. It is a secret.

Q. What is this secret?

A. Masonry.

Q. Are you a Mason?

A. My Brethren and Fellow Crafts recognize me as such.

Q. What man ought to be a Mason?

A. One who was born free.

Q. How were you prepared to be received as a Mason?

A. First in my heart.

Q. Where were you taken next?

A. In a room adjoining the lodge.

Q. What was this preparation?

A. I was neither naked nor clothed, and deprived of all metals; a cable-tow around my neck; I was thus led to the door of the temple by the hand of a friend, whom I have since recognized as my Brother.

Q. How did you know you were at the door of the lodge, since you were hoodwinked?

A. Because I was stopped and then admitted.

Q. How were you admitted?

A. By a distinct knock.

Q. What was said to you?

A. Who comes there? To which I replied: One who begs to be admitted into this R[espectable]∴ L[odge]∴ dedicated to Saint John of Scotland.

Q. How did you dare hope so?

A. Because I was born free and of good report.

Q. What were you then told?

A. To declare my name, my nickname, my age, my civil qualities, my religion, and the place of my birth.

Q. After this what was ordered?

A. To enter.

Q. How did you enter?

A. Upon the point of a sword, or another weapon of war pressing on my left breast.

Q. What were you asked?

A. If I felt or saw anything.

Q. What did you answer?

A. That I felt, but saw nothing.

Q. By whom were you received after your entry?

A. By the Junior Warden.

Q. How did he dispose of you?

A. He delivered me to the Brother Expert, who ordered me to kneel down and participate in a prayer that Ven[erable]∴ recited.

Q. What was asked of you after this prayer?

A. In whom I put my trust.

Q. What did you answer?

A. In God.

Q. What happened to you next?

A. He took me by the right hand, caused me to rise, and then told me not to fear anything and to follow my leader without danger.

Q. Where did this guide take you?

A. He took me around the lodge three times.

Q. Where did you encounter an opposition?

A. In the South, behind the column of the Junior Warden, where I softly rapped three knocks.

Q. What answer did he give you?

A. He asked me: Who comes there?

Q. What did you answer?

A. As at the door: One who begs to be received a Mason.

Q. Where did you meet with the second opposition?

A. Behind the Senior Warden, in the West, where I knocked three times and then gave the same answers to his questions.

Q. Where did you find the third opposition?

A. Behind the M[aste]r∴, where I knocked in the same way, and again gave the same answers.

Q. What did the M[aste]r∴ do with you?

A. He had me conducted to the Senior Ward[en]∴, in the West, to receive instructions.

Q. What instructions did he give you?

A. He taught me to take the first step in the corner of an oblong square, so that I might arrive at the altar to swear my obligation there.

Q. Where do you swear it?

A. At the altar of oaths, on my left knee, and my right foot bare, my body erect, forming a square, my right hand upon the Bible, compasses, and square; my left hand supporting the compasses pressed to my left breast, and I swore the solemn obligation of Masons.

Q. After you swore this obligation, what was said to you?

A. I was asked what I most desired.

Q. What did you answer?

A. Light.

Q. Who gave you light?

A. The M[aste]r∴ and all the Brethren.

Q. When you received the light, what struck your sight?

A. A Bible, a square and compasses.

Q. What were you told they signified?

A. Three Great Lights in Masonry.

Q. Explain them to me.

A. The Bible rules and governs our law; the square, our actions; and the compasses keep us within due bounds towards all men, and particularly towards our Brethren.

Q. What were you shown next?

A. Three sublime Lights of Mas[onry]∴, the sun, the moon, and the M[aste]r∴ of the lodge.

Q. What happened to you next?

R. The M[aste]r∴ took me by the right hand, gave me the grip and the word, and said to me: Arise, my Brother.

Q. What forms a lodge?

A. Three, five, and seven.

Q. Why do three form a lodge?

A. Because there were three grand Masons employed in the construction of Solomon's temple.

Q. Why five?

A. Because every man is endowed with five senses.

Q. What are the five senses?

A. Hearing, smelling, seeing, tasting, and feeling.

Q. Of what use are they in Masonry?

A. Three are of great use.

Q. Explain to me their uses.

A. Seeing, to see the signs; feeling, to feel the grip and recognize a Brother in the darkness as in the light; and hearing, to hear the word.

Q. Why do seven form a lodge?

A. Because there are seven liberal sciences.

Q. Will you name them for me?

A. Grammar, rhetoric, logic, arithmetic, geometry, music, and astronomy.

Q. Of what use are they in Mas[onry]∴?

A. Grammar teaches us about writing and speaking.

Q. What does rhetoric teach us?

A. The art of speaking and discoursing on any subject.

Q. What does arithmetic teach us?

A. The power of numbers.

Q. What does geometry teach us?

A. The art of measuring the land, as the Egyptians practiced it to recover their land in the same quantity after the overflow of the Nile, which frequently submerged that country, during which time they fled to the mountains; and to avoid the disputes which would arise between them in that respect, they invented geometry, by the aid of which they recovered their just quantity of land. This same rule has since been preserved and practiced by all nations.

Q. What does music teach us?

A. The virtue of sounds.

Q. What does astronomy teach us?

A. Knowledge of the celestial bodies.

Q. What shape is your lodge?

A. An oblong square.

Q. How wide is it?

A. From East to West.

Q. What length?

A. From South to North.

Q. What height?

A. From earth to heaven.

Q. How deep?

A. From the surface of the earth to the center.

Q. Why?

A. Because Masonry is universal.

Q. Why is your lodge situated East and West?

A. Because all the temples are like that.

Q. Why is that?

A. Because the gospel was first preached in the East, and then spread into the West.

Q. What supports your lodge?

A. Three great pillars.

Q. What are their names?

A. Wisdom, Strength, and Beauty.

Q. What does the pillar of Wisdom represent?

A. The Master in the East.

Q. What does the Pillar of Strength represent?

A. The Senior Warden in the West.

Q. What does that of Beauty represent?

A. The Junior Warden in the South.

Q. Why does the Master represent the pillar of Wisdom?

A. As he directs the Craft and maintains harmony among them.

Q. Why is the Senior Warden the pillar of Strength?

A. Because the sun sets in the West; so the Senior Ward[en]∴ stands there to pay the Craft, whose wages are the strength and the support of their existence.

Q. Why is the Junior Ward[en]∴ that of Beauty?

A. Because he stands in the South, which at meridian is the beauty of the day, to cause the Craft to refresh, and call them back from refreshment to labor, that the Ven[erable]∴ may derive honor and glory thereby.

Q. Why do we say that our lodge is supported by three great pillars?

A. Because Wisdom, Strength and Beauty are the perfections of all things, and nothing can last without them.

Q. Why?

A. Because Wisdom contrives, Strength supports, and Beauty adorns.

Q. Is your lodge covered?

A. Yes, by a celestial canopy of clouds of diverse colors.

Q. How blows a Masons wind?

A. Due East to West.

TABLE LODGE
OR
BANQUET.

~~~~~~~~~~~

LAYOUT OF THE LODGE.

The room where the banquet is held should be situated so that nothing can be seen or heard from the outside. The table, as far as possible, will be horseshoe shaped. The seat of the Venerable is at the head, and those of the Wardens at the ends.

The Brother Grand Orator seats himself at the head of the South column, and the Brother Secretary at the head of the West one; the East is occupied by the visiting B[rethren]∴, or by officers of the lodge, if there are no vis[itors]∴

Except for the five officers just named, no one has an assigned seat, except in case there are visitors decorated with higher degrees, when the East is occupied by them. The other visitors would be seated at the head of the columns.

The bread is called *rough stone*; wine, *strong powder (white or red)*; bottles and decanters, *barrels*; glasses, *cannons*; water, *weak powder*; liqueurs, *strong powder*; burning candles, *stars*; napkins, *flags*; plates, *tiles*; dishes, *trays*; spoons, *trowels*; forks, *pickaxes*; the knives, *swords*; salt, *sand*; pepper, *yellow sand*; food, *materials*; snuffers, *pliers*; chairs, *stalls*.

When each has taken his place, it is at the desire of the Venerable to lead the first health before eating, or to wait until the soup has been eaten, or such other moment as he sees fit.

When he desires to lead the first health, he raps a gavel blow; instantly the Serving Brethren leave the interior of the horseshoe and retire to the West. It is the same at each health. Everyone stops eating. The Brother M[aster]∴ of Ceremonies is usually alone inside the horseshoe, vis-à-vis the Venerable, to be more within reach to receive his orders and carry them out; sometimes he is placed at a small table between the two Wardens; the Brother Master of Ceremonies stands up and the Venerable says:

Ven[erable]∴ — Brethren Senior and Junior Wardens, ascertain that our work is duly tiled.

Each of the Wardens satisfies himself of the Masonic quality of all the individuals who are at the two columns, by looking at them, and recognizing them as Masons.

The Junior Warden says to the Brother Senior Warden:

Jun[ior] W[arden]∴ — I answer for my column.

The Senior Warden says:

Sen[ior] W[arden]∴ —Most Ven[erable]∴, the Brother Junior Ward[en]∴ and I have satisfied ourselves of the Brethren who are on the two columns.

The Venerable says:

Ven[erable]∴ — I also answer for those who are in the East. Brother Tiler, perform your duty.

During this time the Brethren adorn themselves with their cordons; an apron is not necessary.

The Brother Tiler goes to remove the key from the door, which he closes; and hence no one enters or exits anymore. The Junior Warden informs the Senior that the work is tiled; the latter announces it aloud to the Venerable, who raps a blow with the gavel, and says:

Ven[erable]∴ — My Brethren, the labor, which was suspended, is resumed.

(NOTE. If, before going to the banquet, they had been closed, they would have to be opened again.)

The Brother Senior and Junior Wardens repeat the announcement; after which Ven[erable]∴ says: To Order, my Brethren!

FIRST HEALTH.

Ven[erable]∴ — Brethren Senior and Junior Warden, invite the Brethren of one and the other column to prepare to charge and line up, for the first obligatory health.

The Brethren Wardens repeat the announcement.

Ven[erable]∴ — Let us charge and align, my Brethren.

(NOTE. It is only at this moment that the barrels must be touched, otherwise confusion will arise in the work.)

Each pours himself a drink as he pleases. If someone, by diet or taste, drinks water, none should force him to change his use.

As each pours his drink, he places his cannon (the glass) at the distance from the edge of the table, approximately the diameter of the tile; by this means the cannons are aligned in an instant.

They also align the barrels and the stars on a second line.

When everything is aligned on the South column, the Junior Warden notifies the Senior, who says to the Venerable:

Sen[ior] W[arden]∴ — All is aligned on the two columns.

Ven[erable]∴ — So in the East. Rise, and to order.

All rise; the flag [i.e. the napkin] is over the forearm; the Brethren decorated with high Degrees put it over the shoulder, and are in order. (If the table is a horseshoe, the Brethren who are inside remain seated.)

Ven[erable]∴ — Brethren Senior and Junior Wardens, be pleased to announce on your columns that the first obligatory health is to His Majesty and his august family; we will add to this health wishes for the prosperity of his armies. It is to us a health so precious, that I invite you to make the best possible fire. I reserve to myself the command of cannons.[44]

The Brethren Senior and Junior Wardens repeat the announcement.

When the announcement is made, the Venerable says:

Ven[erable]∴ — Attention, my Brethren!

The right hand to the sword!

Carry swords!

Salute with swords!

Swords to the left hand!

Arms in the right hand!

Carry arms!

To the cheek!

Fire!

Good fire!

The sharpest of fires!

Advance arms!

One, two, three!

One, two, three!

One, two, three!

Advance!

One, two, three!

The right hand to the sword!

Carry sword!

Salute with swords!

Rest sword!

They then applaud with a triple battery and triple huzzah. After which the Venerable says:

Ven[erable]∴ — Let us resume our seats, my Brethren.

---

44 This variation appears in the 1805 édition of le Régulateur: "B[rothers]∴ Senior and Junior Wardens, will you kindly announce on your Columns that the first obligatory health is to H[is]∴ Imperial M[ajesty]∴ and his august family; to this health we shall add our best wishes for their military success. For a health so precious to us I invite you to produce the best possible fusillade.

The Wardens repeat the announcement.

So long as the labor remains active, it is permitted to continue eating, but it must be done in silence.

SECOND HEALTH.

Sometimes, and most convenient for all, so as not to interrupt the service, the Ven[erable]∴ orders the second health as soon as the first is done.

If he does not think fit to have it fired immediately, it is proper to suspend the labor.

If the Ven[erable]∴ has suspended the labor before proposing the second health, he must resume; if they paused, he commands it away, and says:

Ven[erable]∴ — Brethren Senior and Junior Warden, invite the Brethren of one and the other column to prepare to charge and line up, for the second obligatory health.

The Brethren Wardens repeat the announcement.

Ven[erable]∴ — Let us charge and align, my Brethren.

The Wardens announce that all is charged and aligned, as above.

Ven[erable]∴ — Brethren Senior and Junior Wardens, the second obligatory health that I have the favor to propose to you is _____.

(*This health is that of the Masonic authority under which one labors.*)

Finally, we will add our wishes for the prosperity of the order in general. Invite, I pray you, the Brethren of one and the other column, to join me in making the most Masonic and fraternal fire.

The Wardens repeat the announcement.

The health is taken; there is a battery as at the first.

If there are any of the Brethren whose health is toasted, e.g., the Venerable of the lodge, deputies of lodges, etc., these Brethren do not drink the health, but stand or sit. When the battery is over, they ask to thank everyone together; one of them speaking. During this response, the Brethren remain standing.

When, after drinking the health, they have given their applause, the lodge covers the applause, which is commanded by Ven[erable]∴

When all is finished, the Venerable raps a blow of the gavel, and says:

Ven[erable]∴ — Let us resume our seats, my Brethren.

Then the Master may suspend the labors, or to leave them active.

THIRD HEALTH.

At the time when the Wardens deem it appropriate, and especially when he is not on duty, the Senior Warden raps a blow with the gavel, which the Junior repeats, then the Venerable. Immediately the Venerable says:

Ven[erable]∴ — What do you desire, Brother Senior Warden?

If the labors are suspended, the Senior Warden asks the Venerable to resume them; which he does in these words:

Ven[erable]∴ — My Brethren, at the request of the Brother Senior Warden, the labors which were suspended resume activity.

The Wardens repeat the announcement.

After that, the Senior Ward[en]∴ raps a stroke of the gavel, which is repeated by the Junior, then by the Ven[erable]∴, and says:

Sen[ior] W[arden]∴ —Very Ven[erable]∴, be pleased to charge and align, for a health which the Brother Junior Warden, the Brother Grand Orator and I, will have the honor to propose.

The Ven[erable]∴ charges and aligns, as in previous healths. When he is informed that everything is in order, he says:

Ven[erable]∴ — Brother Senior Ward[en]∴, announce the health which you desire to offer.

Sen[ior] W[arden]∴ —It is to you, Most Venerable. — Rise, and to order, sword in hand, my Brethren.

The health which the Brother Junior Warden, the Brother Grand Orator and I, have the honor to propose to you, is that of the Most Venerable who directs the labors of this Respectable lodge, and that of all that may belong to him: Please join us in making the best fire possible.

The Junior Warden repeats, and says:

Jun[ior] W[arden]∴ — The health which the Brother Junior Warden, the Brother Grand Orator and I have the honor to propose, etc.

The Orator repeats the same announcement.

The Brother Senior Ward[en]∴ says: With me, my Brethren! *and commands the drill, or defers command to the Junior Warden, as he sees fit; he does the battery and the huzzah.*

During this health, the Ven[erable]∴ is seated: all the Brethren remained standing and in order.

After the Ven[erable]∴ returns thanks, the Senior Ward[en]∴ says:

Sen[ior] W[arden]∴ — Out of respect for the Ven[erable]∴, applause will not be covered.

Everyone takes their place.

The Ven[erable]∴ suspends the labors as he sees fit, or leaves them active.

FOURTH HEALTH.

After a time, the Venerable resumes the labors, if it is not already, and causes them to charge and align, for a health.

When all are charged and aligned, he proposes the health of the Senior and Junior Wardens. The Brother

Grand Orator and the Brother Secretary repeat the announcement.

The Ven[erable]∴ orders this health: all the Brethren remain seated; the Wardens alone rise and give thanks.

The Brother Senior Warden speaks.

The Ven[erable]∴ covers the applause.

FIFTH HEALTH.

The Ven[erable]∴ then commands, at the moment that seems to him the most suitable, the health of the visiting Brethren. During this health, visitors stand: one of them returning thanks. The Ven[erable]∴ covers the applause.

To this fifth health will be added that of the affiliated or corresponding lodges; but if there are neither visitors nor corresponding lodges, then one will detach from the sixth health that of the officers of the lodge.

The Orator speaks to return thanks.

(NOTE. After the health of the visitors, if some Brethren have hymns to sing, or some pieces of architecture to read, they can do so, asking to speak. It is, moreover, appropriate to sing some hymns which were made for the purposes of Masonry, and which, sung in chorus, carry in the soul a sweet emotion, by celebrating the amenities and the advantages of the Masonic union.)

SIXTH HEALTH.

The health of Brethren officers and lodge members. To this is added that of the newly initiated Brethren, if there are any.

This health is carried only by the Venerable, the Wardens and the visiting Brethren, if there are any; the officers and members of the lodge stand. The Brother Grand Orator returns thanks for the officers; the oldest member, for members; and one of the initiates, if any, for the others.

Their applause is covered.

SEVENTH AND LAST HEALTH.

Finally, the Ven[erable]∴ asks the Brother M[aster]∴ of Ceremonies to introduce the Serving Brethren, who must bring with them their flags and cannons.

They enter and are placed in the West, between the two Ward[ens]∴, the Ven[erable]∴ raps a blow of gavel, inviting the charge and align, for the obligatory health.

The Brethren Wardens each strike a blow of the gavel and make the same announcement. Ven[erable]∴ says:

Ven[erable]∴ — Let us charge and align, my Brethren.

After the Venerable has been informed that all are charged, he says:

Ven[erable]∴ — Rise, and to order.

All rise, each gives an end of their flag to their neighbors, on the right and on the left, taking an end of theirs in the same way, and holding them with their left hand, which does not prevent them from holding the sword with the same hand. The Serving Brethren form, with the Ward[ens]∴, the same chain, the Brother Master of Cerem[onies]∴ being in their midst.

Then the Venerable says:

Ven[erable]∴ — Brethren Senior and Junior Wardens, the last obligatory health is that to all Masons spread over the face of the earth, whether in prosperity or adversity. Let us address our desires to the Grand Architect of the Universe, that he may help the unfortunate, and lead travelers to their destination. Invite, I pray you, the Brethren of both columns to unite with us, to carry this health with the best of all fires.

The Wardens repeat.

Then the Venerable sings the closing hymn, of which only these two verses are usually sung, and all the assistants join in.

Brethren and Fellows

of Masonry

Let us enjoy, without sorrow,

the pleasures of life.

Furnished with a red border,

thrice the signal of our glasses

is a proof of accord,

We drink to our Brethren.

Let us join hand in hand;

Let us stand together:

Give thanks to fate

for the bond which joins us;

And let us be sure

that it is drunk on both hemispheres,

There no is more illustrious health

Than those of our Brethren.

The Venerable says:

Ven[erable]∴ — Attention, my Brethren!

Right hand to sword!

Carry swords!

Salute with swords!

Swords to the left hand!

Arms in the right hand!

Carry arms!

To the cheek!

Fire!

Good fire!

The sharpest of fires!

Advance arms!

The last two verses are repeated twice.

One, two, three!

One, two, three!

One, two, three!

Advance!

One, two, three!

The right hand to the sword!

Carry sword!

Salute with swords!

Rest sword! (*They are put back gently on the table.*)

They applaud and sing the last hymn three times.

The Ven[erable]∴ raps a blow with the gavel, which is repeated by the Wardens, and has the tracing board of the proceedings of the banquet read; he asks for observations and causes applauses; then he asks if there are any interesting proposals for the good of the order in general, and for that of the lodge in particular.

If there are any, they listen to them if he determines if they are brief; otherwise, they are sent back to the first assembly.

Then the Ven[erable]∴ gives the Ward[ens]∴ the following three questions:

Ven[erable]∴ — Brother Senior Ward[en]∴, how old are you?

A. Three years, Ven[erable]∴

Q. At what hour do we usually close our labors?

A. At midnight.

Q. What is the hour?

A. It is midnight, Ven[erable]∴

It is a commendable practice to give each other a fraternal kiss before parting. The Ven[erable]∴ gives it to his neighbor on the right, and it comes back to him on the left. Then he raps three times with the gavel, which the Wardens repeat, causing applause and a huzzah.

Finally, he raps a gavel blow, and says:

Ven[erable]∴ — My Brethren, the labors are closed, let us retire in peace.

The Wardens also each strike a gavel and make the same announcement.

Everyone leaves his regalia and retires in peace.

(NOTE. In the various announcements of the healths, the Ven[erable]∴ and the Ward[ens]∴ instructions need not adhere strictly to the protocol indicated. The variations which they can put there, can only be pleasant to all the brethren, and be a reason for increasing the pleasures of table work.)

GUIDE
OF THE SCOTTISH MASONS.

Fellow Craft.

GUIDE
OF THE SCOTTISH MASONS.

Fellow Craft.

OPENING.

The lodge being open on the Degree of Apprentice, the Ven[erable]∴ raps a blow, and says:

Ven[erable]∴ — Brethren Senior and Junior Ward[ens]∴, announce on your respective columns that the labors are suspended, to pass to those of Fellow Craft, and invite the Apprentices to tile the temple.

The Ward[ens]∴ repeat the announcement, and report to the Ven[erable]∴ that the App[rentice]s∴ have tiled the temple.

Ven[erable]∴ — Brother Senior Ward[en]∴, what is the first duty of a Ward[en]∴ in a Fellow [Crafts] lodge?

Sen[ior] W[arden]∴ —Very Ven[erable]∴, is to ensure that all Br[ethren]∴ present here are Fellow [Crafts].

Ven[erable]∴ raps a blow, and says:

Ven[erable]∴ — Rise and to order, my Brethren.

All the Brethren look West.

Ven[erable]∴ — Brethren Senior and Junior Wardens, ensure that all the members present here are Fellow [Crafts].

The Ward[ens]∴ each go through their column, starting with the last, to receive the signs, grips, and passwords of each Brother. When this labor is completed and the Ward[ens]∴ have returned to their places, the Senior Ward[en]∴ says to Ven[erable]∴

Sen[ior] W[arden]∴ — All the Brethren present here are Fellow Crafts.

The Ven[erable]∴ rises, sets himself to order as a Fellow Craft, sends the sacred word of Fell[ow Craft]∴ to the Senior Ward[en]∴, causing him to say that he is opening a lodge of Fell[ow Craft]∴ Mas[ons]∴

The Senior Ward[en]∴ send the Junior Deacon to take it to the Junior Warden, who says:

Jun[ior] W[arden]∴ — All is just and perfect, Ven[erable]∴

The Ven[erable]∴ raps three blows, repeated by the Ward[ens]∴ and says:

Ven[erable]∴ — With me, my Brethren!

He makes the sign, the battery, and the acclamation, and says:

Ven[erable]∴ — In the name of God and of Saint John of Scotland, this lodge of Fell[ow Crafts]∴ is open. It is no longer permitted for any B[rother]∴ to speak, nor to pass from one col[umn]∴ to another without having permission. B[rother]∴ Secretary, please read us the tr[acing board]∴ of our most recent Fell[ow Craft]∴ labor.

The reading finished and the tr[acing board]∴ sanctioned:

Ven[erable]∴ — Brother M[aste]r∴ of Ceremonies, please go to the temple grounds, and make sure there are no visitors.

The B[rother]∴ M[aste]r∴ of Ceremonies executes the o[rder]∴, and when he returns, he makes his report.

RECEPTION.

Ven[erable]∴ — Brother M[aste]r∴ of Cerem[onies]∴ please go and prepare the candidate, and bring him in the required condition.

He goes and brings him with his hair disheveled over his shoulders, and carrying a ruler in his left hand, one end of which rests on his left shoulder, the bib of his apron turned up. He raps as an App[rentice]∴ at the temple gate.

Ven[erable]∴ — See who knocks thus, Brother Senior Ward[en]∴

The Brother Senior Ward[en]∴ repeats it to the Junior, and he to the B[rother]∴ Tiler, who half-opens the door, and asks: Who knocks thus?

The Master of Ceremonies responds:

M[aste]r∴ Cer[emonies]∴ — I conduct an App[rentice]∴ who desires to pass from the perpendicular to the level.

The Junior Ward[en]∴ repeats it to the Senior, who repeats it to the Ven[erable]∴

The questions and answers pass successively from the Tiler to the Junior Ward[en]∴, and from the latter to the Senior Ward[en]∴, who repeats them to the Ven[erable]∴, and the Brother Secretary writes them down.

Ven[erable]∴ — How does he dare hope to receive this Degree?

M[aste]r∴ Cer[emonies]∴ — Because he is born free and of good report.

The Ven[erable]∴ raps, and says:

Ven[erable]∴ — Let the App[rentice]∴ enter, and place him between the col[umns]∴

After the cand[idate]∴ enters:

Ven[erable]∴ — Brother Junior Ward[en]∴, who commands the App[rentices] col[umn]∴, this one who asks to pass from the perpendicular to the level, has he served his time, and are the Brethren of his col[umn]∴ satisfied with him?

Jun[ior] W[arden]∴ — Yes, Ven[erable]∴

Ven[erable]∴ — Do all the Brethren consent to his advancement?

All members extend their right hand.

The Ven[erable]∴ raps, and says to the candidate:

Ven[erable]∴ — Without asserting, my Brother, to you a particular grace that this Resp[ectable]∴ lodge does for you today, by making you to pass so quickly to the Second Degree of its workers, I must not keep silent that in primitive times it was necessary to work during five years, without interruption, at the col[umn]∴ of Apprentices; but we do not abbreviate this term to all subjects indiscriminately, and those who, like you, my Brother, are exempt from it, must regard it as a favor which invites them to make themselves worthy of it, and to merit, thereafter, that this lodge opens the ineffable treasures of its reward.

We flatter ourselves that you will neglect nothing to fulfil our expectation and justify the favor of this L[odge]∴

Q. Who procured for you, my Brother, the advantage of being a Mason?

A. A wise friend, whom I have since recognized as a Brother.

Q. In what condition were you presented in the lodge?

A. Neither naked nor clothed.

Q. Why is that?

A. To prove to me that luxury is a vice, which is only imposed on the vulgar, and that the virtuous man must trample under foot all feelings of vanity and pride.

Q. Why were your eyes covered?

A. To make me understand how much the darkness of ignorance, and the deep darkness of the passions that blind us, are prejudicial to the happiness of man.

Q. Why were you sent on a journey?

A. To let me know that it is never on the first step that one achieves virtue.

Q. What did you see when your eyes were uncovered?

A. All the Brethren armed with swords whose tips they presented to me.

Q. Why?

A. To show me that they would always be ready to shed their blood for me, if I were faithful to the obligation that I was about to contract; as well as to punish me, if I was despicable enough to violate it.

Q. Why were compasses placed to your left breast?

A.   To show me that a Mason's heart must always be just and true.

Ven[erable]∴ — You have, my Brother, five journeys to make. Brother Master of Cerem[onies]∴, take this Apprentice on his first journey.

The Master of Ceremonies places a gavel and a chisel in his left hand, takes him by the right hand, and leads him around the lodge.

Back in the West, he says:

M[aste]r∴ Cer[emonies]∴ - Brother Junior Warden, the first journey is finished.

The Junior Ward[en]∴ repeats to the Senior, and he to the Ven[erable]∴

Ven[erable]∴ — My Brother, this first journey represents the time of a year that a Fellow Craft must use to perfect himself in the practice of cutting and sizing of stones, which he learned to rough as an Apprentice, with the help of gavel and chisel. This emblem shows you that whatever perfection an Apprentice may have, he is still far from finishing his labors; that the raw materials consecrated to the construction of the temple which he raises to the Great Architect, of which he is the material and the workman, have not yet been removed, and that he cannot dispense with the hard and painful work of the gavel, and the precise and attentive driving of the faithful chisel; that he should never stray from the line which was traced for him by the Masters. — Give me the Apprentice sign. (*He gives it.*)

Q.   What is the meaning of this sign?

A.   It reminds me of the oath I made at my reception, in which I pledged to have my throat cut if I should prove unfortunate enough to reveal the secrets entrusted to me. (*If necessary, we prompt him with this answer.*)

The Venerable raps, and says:

Ven[erable]∴ — Brother M[aste]r∴ of Ceremonies, take this Brother on his second journey.

The candidate takes a compass and ruler in his left hand, and the Master of Ceremonies leads him from the right.

The journey over, Ven[erable]∴ says:

Ven[erable]∴ — My Brother, this second journey announces to you that, during the second year, a Mason must acquire the practical elements of Masonry, that is to say, the art of drawing lines on rough and prepared materials, which is done with a ruler and compasses. — My Brother, give the Apprentice's grip to the B[rother]∴ Senior Ward[en]∴. (*He gives it.*)

The Senior Ward[en]∴ raps, and says:

Sen[ior] W[arden]∴ —The gr[ip]∴ is right, Ven[erable]∴

The Ven[erable]∴ raps, and says:

Ven[erable]∴ — Brother M[aste]r∴ of Ceremonies, take this Apprentice on his third journey.

A ruler is placed in his left hand, and he supports, leaning on his left shoulder, a crowbar; they conduct it, and make the announcement as on the first two journeys.

Ven[erable]∴ — My Brother, this journey symbolizes to you the third year of an Apprentice, during which he is entrusted with conducting, transporting, and laying the materials worked, which is done with the ruler and pincers. The crowbar, rather than the compasses, is the emblem of the power which adds to our individual strengths the knowledge in order to do and effect that which, without its help, it would be impossible for us to execute.

Q. What do you mean, my Brother, by Masonry?

A. (*He is prompted.*) I mean the study of science and the practice of virtues.

The Ven[erable]∴ raps, and says:

Ven[erable]∴ — Brother M[aste]r∴ of Ceremonies, take this Apprentice on his fourth journey.

A square and a ruler are placed in his left hand; he is caused to make the journey, and he is announced as before.

Ven[erable]∴ — This journey, my Brother, is the emblem of the fourth year of an Apprentice, during which he must be directly occupied with the raising of the building, to direct the whole, and to verify the installation of square materials brought to complete the Masonic work; it teaches you that the application, the zeal, and the intelligence that you have shown in your work can alone elevate you above Brethren less instructed and less zealous than you. — Brother M[aste]r∴ of Ceremonies, make the fifth and final journey.

The candidate has empty hands. The Master of Ceremonies holds the point of a sword over the candidate's heart; he holds it fixed there with the thumb and index finger of his right hand. He causes him to make the tour, and they announce that it is finished, as with the other journeys.

Ven[erable]∴ — This fifth and final journey signifies that, sufficiently instructed in manual practices, the Apprentice must use this last year to study theory. Learn from it, my Brother, that it is not enough to be on the path of virtue to be able to maintain oneself there; there are mighty efforts to be made to acquire perfection. So follow the road that has been cleared for you, and make yourself worthy of admission to the knowledge of higher Masonic labors. Give the Brother Grand Expert the sacred word of an App[rentice]∴ (*The candidate gives it.*)

The Brother Great Expert says: The word is right, Ven[erable]∴

Ven[erable]∴ — Brother M[aste]r∴ of Ceremonies, cause the candidate to perform his last labor as an Apprentice.

The Master of Ceremonies puts a gavel in his hands, with which he makes him strike as an Apprentice on the rough stone and announces that this labor is finished.

Ven[erable]∴ — Brother M[aste]r∴ of Ceremonies, bring the candidate to the foot of the throne, and cause him to step in the manner of an Apprentice.

The Brother Master of Ceremonies carries out the order of the Venerable.

The candidate having arrived at the altar:

Ven[erable]∴ — Consider this mysterious star, and may it never depart from your mind; it is the emblem of that genius which elevates us to great things; it is also the symbol of that sacred fire, with which the Grand Architect of the Universe has endowed us, by whose rays we should discern, love, and practice the true, the just and the equitable.

The delta that you see, wholly resplendent with light, offers you two great truths, and two sublime ideas.

You see the name of God as the source of all knowledge and all science; it is symbolically explained by geometry. This sublime science has as its essential basis the most profound study of the infinite applications of triangles under its true form. All these mysterious truths develop in your eyes by degree, and as you progress in our sublime art.

The Master of Ceremonies causes the candidate to kneel.

The Ven[erable]∴ raps and says:

Ven[erable]∴ — Rise and to order, my Brethren. Repeat with me your obligation.

OBLIGATION.

I swear and promise, under the obligations to which I submitted myself previously, to keep the secrets of a Fellow Craft, which will be entrusted to me, from the Apprentices, as I pledged myself to the former towards the profane; and I consent, should I perjure my oath, to have my heart torn out (*Here all the Brethren make the sign*), my body burned, and my ashes scattered to the wind, that there should be no more mention of me among the Brethren whom I have betrayed. May God preserve me from such misfortune. Amen.

The Ven[erable]∴ sets the sword upon his head, and says:

Ven[erable]∴ — In the name of God, and under the auspices N… and by the powers entrusted to me by this R[espectable]∴ L[odge]∴, I receive and constitute you a Fellow [Craft]∴ Mas[on]∴.

He raps three equal blows of his gavel upon the sword.

The Master of Ceremonies raises the candidate.

The Ven[erable]∴ lowers the bib of his apron, and tells him that, being a Fellow Craft, he must henceforth wear it like this.

Ven[erable]∴ — From now on, my Brother, you must labor on the pointed cubical stone, and receive your wages with the column J∴

This new labor should remind you that a Fellow Craft, destined to repair the defects of the building, must employ all his care, not only to cover the faults of his Brethren, but even to correct them by his examples and his advice.

I will now confer upon you the signs, words, and grips of a Fellow Craft.

The sign is made, etc.

The grip is given, etc.

The sacred word is J∴ (*it is given only by spelling out the letters.*)

The password is S∴ (*it is not spelled and is given when entering the lodge.*)

Go now, my Brother, give the Brother Grand Expert the signs, words, and grips, accompanied by the Master of Ceremonies, so that he may make you known as a Fellow Craft.

The Brother M[aste]r∴ of Cerem[onies]∴ and the candidate carry out the orders of the Ven[erable]∴ That finished, the Brother Grand Expert announces that they are right.

Ven[erable]∴ — Brother M[aste]r∴ of Ceremonies, cause this B[rother]∴ to labor as a Fellow Craft, and show him the steps of this Degree.

The Brother Master of Ceremonies causes the B[rother]∴ to labor, by making him strike three equal blows on the pointed cubical stone; he causes him to make the sign, and the steps, and makes him sit on the column intended for the Fellow Crafts.

It is then that the Orator, or the B[rother]∴ who occupies his place, delivers the lecture.

Then the B[rother]∴ Master of Ceremonies leads the Candidate between the two columns.

Ven[erable]∴ — Brethren Senior and Junior Wardens, announce on your respective columns that we are going to applaud the satisfaction felt by the R[espectable]∴ L[odge]∴ to henceforward count Brother N……. among its Fellow Crafts.

The Wardens make the same announcement.

The Ven[erable]∴ raps, and says:

Ven[erable]∴ — Rise, and to order, my Brethren.

All the Brethren rise: the Ven[erable]∴ makes the Fellow Craft sign, battery, and acclamation, together with all the Brethren.

The candidate returns thanks or asks the Master of Ceremonies to do so.

They applaud the thanks.

The bag of proposals is presented to all the Brethren by a Brother Expert designated by the Ven[erable]∴

The Brother Hospitaller also circulates the charitable box. The proceeds are noted by the Ven[erable]∴ and the Brother Orator; and the Brother Secretary records it on the sketch of the day's labor.

Ven[erable]∴ — Brethren Senior and Junior Ward[ens]∴, ask the Brethren who adorn your columns, if they have anything to propose for the good of the order in general, or of this Resp[ectable]∴ lodge in particular.

The Wardens repeat the announcement.

Ven[erable]∴ — Brother Secretary, please read to us the sketch of the day's labor. Silence, my Brethren.

The Brother Secretary reads his sketch.

Ven[erable]∴ — Brethren Senior and Junior Wardens, ask the Brethren if they have any observations to make on the writing of the outline of the labor of the day.

The Ward[ens]∴ announce, and they decide on the observations that can be made, in the usual way.

CLOSING.

Ven[erable]∴ — Brother Junior Deacon, where is your place in the lodge?

A. Behind the Senior Warden, if he permits it.

Q. Why, my Brother?

A. To carry orders from the Senior to the Junior Ward[ens]∴ and see to it that the Brethren stand decently on the columns.

Q. Where is the place of the Senior Deacon?

A. To the right of the Ven[erable]∴

Q. Why, Brother Senior Deacon?

A. To carry your orders to the Senior Warden and to all the Brethren of the lodge, that the labor may be more promptly and more regularly executed.

Q. Where is the place of the Junior Warden?

A. In the South, Ven[erable]∴

Q. Why, Brother Junior Warden, do you occupy this place?

A. To better observe the sun at its meridian, to call the Craft from labor to refreshment, and from refreshment to labor, that the Ven[erable]∴ may derive honor and glory thereby.

Q. Where is the place of the B[rother]∴ Senior Warden?

A. In the West.

Q. Why, Brother Senior Warden?

A. As the sun sets in the West to close the day, so stands the Senior Ward[en]∴ there to close the lodge, to pay the Craft, and send them away content and satisfied.

The Ven[erable]∴ then raps three equal blows of his gavel.

The Wardens repeat them.

The Ven[erable]∴ turns towards his Deacon, gives him the word, his head uncovered, and then covers himself.

The Senior Deacon carries the word to the Senior Warden.

The Senior Ward[en]∴ sends it by his Deacon to the Junior Ward[en]∴

The Junior Ward[en]∴ says:

Jun[ior]∴ W[arden]∴ — All is just and perfect, Ven[erable]∴

The Ven[erable]∴ uncovers himself, and says:

Ven[erable]∴ — My Brethren, in the name of God and of Saint John of Scotland, the lodge is closed. — With me, my Brethren.

All follow his movements, make the Sign of a Fell[ow Craft]∴, and retire in peace after the Venerable says:

Ven[erable]∴ — The labors are closed, my Brethren, let us bless the Eternal.

(NOTE. *The Ven[erable]∴ gives the following instruction, before the close of labor, when he deems it appropriate.*)

INSTRUCTION.

This instruction takes place between the Ven[erable]∴ and the two Wardens.

Q. Are you a Fellow Craft?

A. I am. Try me, prove me.

Q. Where were you received a Fellow Craft?

A. In a regular Fellow Craft's lodge.

Q. How were you prepared?

A. I was neither naked nor clothed, barefoot nor shod, deprived of all metals, and was thus led by a Brother to the door of the lodge.

Q. How were you admitted?

A. By three knocks.

Q. What was said to you?

A. Who comes there?

Q. What did you answer?

A. An Apprentice who has served his time, and who begs to be received as a Fellow Craft.

Q. How did you hope to achieve this?

A. By the password.

Q. Then you have the password?

A. Yes, I have it, Ven[erable]∴

Q. Give it to me.

A. (*He gives it.*)

Q. What were you then told?

A. Pass, Sh....

Q. What was done to you then?

A. I made five journeys around the lodge.

Q. Where did you find the first opposition?

A. Behind the Senior Warden, where I gave the same answer as at the door.

Q. Where did you find the second opposition?

A. Behind the Master, where I gave the same answer again.

Q. What did he do with you?

A. He sent me back to the Senior Warden to receive instructions.

Q. What instructions did he give you?

A. He taught me my duty, and to take the steps on the Second Degree of a right angle of an oblong square, my right knee bent, my left foot forming a square, my body erect, my right hand on the Bible, my left arm supporting the point of a compasses forming a square, and I thus offered my obligation.

Q. Have you got that obligation?

A. Yes, Venerable Master.

Q. Repeat it to me.

A. I will do so with your assistance.

Q. Stand up and begin.

A. I swear, of my own free will, etc.

Q. After this obligation, what did he show you?

A. The sign of a Fellow Craft.

Q. What did he do with you next?

A. He ordered me to be reinvested with my clothes, and brought back, to thank the lodge for my admission.

Q. After being admitted as a Fellow Craft, did you work in this capacity?

A. Yes, Ven[erable]∴, I worked in the building of the temple.

Q. Where did you receive your wages?

A. At the column J....

Q. When you came to this column, who did you see?

A. A Warden.

Q. What did he demand of you?

A. The password.

Q. Did you give it to him?

A. Yes, Venerable.

Q. What is it?

A. Sh....

Q. How did you get to the column J....?

A. Through the porch of the temple.

Q. Do you then see anything remarkable?

A. Yes, Venerable Master.

Q. What did you see?

A. Two beautiful brass columns.

Q. What are they called?

A. B.... and J....

Q. How high were these columns?

A. Twenty-five cubits, with a chapiter of five cubits, which is forty cubits high. (*See Second Chro[nicles]∴, Chap[ter]∴ 3, v. 15; according to the Bible, the cubit is one foot six English inches.*)

Q. With what were the chapiters finished and adorned?

A. With networks of lilies and pomegranates.

Q. Were the columns hollow?

A. Yes, Venerable Master.

Q. How thick was the outer casing?

A. Four inches.

Q. Where were they cast?

A. In the plain of the Jordan, in clay ground, between Succoth and Zarthan, where Solomon's holy vessels of were cast.

Q. Who cast them?

A. Hiram Abif.

GUIDE
OF THE SCOTTISH MASONS.

Master.

GUIDE
OF THE SCOTTISH MASONS.

Master.

ESSENTIAL INTRODUCTION.

The chamber of reflection must be gloomy.

There should be on the walls maxims related to the reception, the smallest particulars of which must be imposing.

The Brother Preparer must be well informed of his duties vis-à-vis the recipient; he must prepare his mind and imagination for it by wise and moral discourse, relating to the importance of the Degree he solicits.

The Preparer must take the hat and the sword of the candidate and have them delivered by the B[rother]∴ Master of Ceremonies to the Venerable, who assume the title of Respectable Master in this Degree.

The Brother Architect must take care to locate, at the altar of each Ward[en]∴, a roll of coarse paper 18 inches long by 9 in circumference.

This room should be lit by a single very large yellow candle.

An impressive skeleton is of particular context, if a lodge is rich enough to procure it.

This room must still contain rubble, broken tools, and instruments.

The grave dignity of the Brother Preparer contributes greatly to making the entire ceremony more imposing. It cannot be too highly recommended.

The lodge should be hung in black, with strewn white death's heads and crossbones, and an hourglass.

Silver tears should be grouped by 3, 5 and 7.

Nine stars, threes on each light, illumine the lodge.

CLOTHING.

All the Masters must, so far as possible, be in black, with slouched hats, a badge of mourning, white gloves, apron of the Degree, and blue cordon.

The ideal outfit is a black tunic in the shape of a domino, hat à la Henri IV, with a white feather.

The Ven[erable]∴ must wear mourning clothes and a mantle.

TITLES IN A LODGE OF MASTERS.

The Venerable is called Most Respectable.

The Wardens, Most Venerable.

Master Masons, Venerable.

This nomenclature strictly required.

ARRANGMENT OF THE MIDDLE CHAMBER.

There must be a coffin in the middle of the lodge, covered with a funerary pall strewn with death's heads, crossbones, and tears.

A partition is formed around the coffin with hanging panels, to represent the Middle Chamber.

At one corner of this Chamber, on the East side, in its West, is placed a spring of acacia on a small mound.

At the head of the coffin is laid a square.

At the foot of said coffin, lies a compass.

GUIDE
OF THE SCOTTISH MASONS.

Master.

OPENING.

The M[ost]∴ Respectable raps a blow of the gavel, which is repeated by the Ven[erable]∴ Brethren Wardens.

M[ost]∴ R[espectable]∴ — V[enerable]∴ B[rother]∴ Senior Warden, what is the duty of a Senior Warden. before opening the Master's lodge?

A.   To ensure that the temple is tiled, within and without.

M[ost]∴ R[espectable]∴ — Ensure that, very Ven[erable]∴ Brother.

The Very Ven[erable]∴ Senior Ward[en]∴ sends his Deacon, who, on his return, assures him that the temple is duly tiled; then he says:

Sen[ior] W[arden]∴ —Most Resp[ectable]∴, the Master's lodge is tiled.

M[ost]∴ R[espectable]∴ — What is your second duty, V[enerable]∴ B[rother]∴ Senior Warden∴?

A.   To ensure that all members present are Masters.

M[ost]∴ R[espectable]∴ — Ven[erable]∴ Brethren Senior and Junior Wardens, repair to your columns, and ensure that all the Brethren here present are Masters.

Then the M[ost]∴ Resp[ectable]∴ turns and faces e[ast]∴; all the Brethren do the same on the columns, so that no one can see what is happening in the West.

Then the Wardens approach the last Brother, the first closest to their respective altars; they recognize him, and so on up to the first, so that all the Brethren present are recognized by the words, signs, and grips of the Degree.

Any Dignitary Brethren wearing the cordon of an officer of the lodge are not tiled.

This finished, the Junior Warden reports to the Senior, and the latter to the Most Respectable, saying:

Sen[ior] W[arden]∴ —Most Respectable, all the Brethren here present are Masters.

M[ost]∴ R[espectable]∴ — Ven[erable]∴ Brother Junior Deacon, where is your place in the lodge?

A. Behind or to the right of the Senior Warden, if he permits it.

Q. Why, Ven[erable]∴ Brother?

A. To carry the orders of the Senior Warden to the Junior and see to it that the Brethren stand decently on the columns.

Q. Where is the place of the Senior Deacon?

A. To the right of the M[ost]∴ Resp[ectable]∴

Q. Why, Ven[erable]∴ B[rother]∴ Senior Deacon?

A. To carry the orders of the M[ost]∴ Resp[ectable]∴ to V[enerable]∴ B[rother]∴ Senior Ward[en]∴, and to all the Brethren of the lodge, that the labor may be more promptly executed.

Q. Where is place of the Ven[erable]∴ Brother Junior Warden?

A. In the South, Most Respectable.

Q. Why, Very Ven[erable]∴ Brother Junior Warden?

A. To better observe the sun at its meridian, to call the Craft from labor to refreshment, and from refreshment to labor, that the Most Respectable Master may derive honor and glory thereby.

Q. Where is the place of the Ven[erable]∴ Brother Senior Ward[en]∴?

A. In the West, Most Respectable.

Q. Why, Ven[erable]∴ Brother Senior Ward[en]∴?

A. As the sun sets in the West to close the day, so stands the Senior Ward[en]∴ there to close the lodge, to pay the Craft, and send them away content and satisfied.

Q. Where is the Most Respectable?

A. In the East, Most Respectable.

The Most Respectable raps three equal blows, which are repeated by the Wardens.

The M[ost]∴ R[espectable]∴ turns toward the Senior Deacon, gives him the Master's word, his head uncovered, and recovers afterwards. The Senior Deacon delivers it to the Senior Warde[en]∴, who, after having received it, sends it, through the Junior Deacon, to the Junior Warde[en]∴

The Deacons must always place a lot of dignity into their office.

After the words and signs have reached him, the Junior Ward[en]∴ strikes a gavel blow, and says:

Jun[ior]∴ W[arden]∴ — All is just and perfect, Most Respectable.

Then the M[ost]∴ R[espectable]∴ uncovers himself, and then all the Brethren.

M[ost]∴ R[espectable]∴ — Venerable Masters, my Brethren, in the name of God and of Saint John of Scotland, this lodge of Master Masons is open; it is no longer permitted for any Brother to pass from one column to another without having obtained the permission of his V[enerable]∴ Warden. — With me, my Brethren.

He makes the signs of Apprentice, Fellow Craft and Master, including that of Horror. These signs are repeated by all members.

After which he says:

M[ost]∴ R[espectable]∴ — Ven[erable]∴ Brethren Senior and Junior Ward[ens]∴ announce on your respective columns that the labors of the Middle Chamber are open.

All the formalities used in the first two Degrees are also observed for the reading of the tracing board, for the entry of visitors, and for the ratification of the consent of the Masters in favor of the Fellow Craft.

RECEPTION.

The reception being approved by a unanimous vote of the Brethren, the last Master received is caused to lie down in the coffin, feet to the East, heels at right angles, right hand on the heart, left extended along the body, and a funerary pall (shroud) must be put on to cover him from the feet to the belt of the apron.

The apron is turned up to the bottom lip, the rest of the face is covered by with a white linen stained with blood.

Everything being prepared, all the lights are extinguished; only one is kept in a large lantern.

This lighted candle must be of yellow wax and placed on the altar of the Most Respectable. The M[ost]∴ Respectable says:

M[ost]∴ R[espectable]∴ — Venerable Brother Master of Ceremonies, go and prepare the candidate.

PREPARATION OF THE CANDIDATE.

The candidate must be barefoot, bare arms and left breast, and without metals. He must have a small square on his right arm, a cable-tow at the waist wound three times, a Fellow Craft's apron, and disheveled hair.

The Master of Ceremonies knocks on the door of the temple as a Fellow Craft, still holding the candidate by the hand.

The Ven[erable]∴ Brother Grand Expert goes to it to acknowledge who knocks, as he must do for all those who present themselves after the opening of the labor.

The recognition done; the Senior Warden says:

Sen[ior] W[arden]∴ —M[ost]∴ R[espectable]∴, The Master of Ceremonies presents to this R[espectable]∴ lodge a Fellow Craft who has served his time, and who asks for initiation as a Master. (*The door opens a crack.*)

M[ost]∴ R[espectable]∴ — (*In a loud voice*) Why does the Master of Ceremonies come to disturb our grief? Our lament should have prompted him to dismiss any suspicious person, especially a Fellow Craft. My Brethren, is it perhaps one of those who causes our grief? Let us arm ourselves! Perhaps Divine justice delivers a culprit to our just vengeance!

Ven[erable]∴ Brother Grand Expert, take the Brother Terrible with you and cause four armed Brethren to accompany you. (*Raising his voice*) Go! Seize this Fellow Craft! Examine him from head to toe! Above all, examine his hands! Carefully examine his garment! Remove his apron and bring it to me to testify to his actions! Finally, ascertain if there is not any trace on him that would reveal the dreadful crime which was committed.

The candidate is suddenly seized; they examine him and pull off his apron.

The Ven[erable]∴ Grand Expert enters the temple, provided with the apron of the Fellow Craft; he leaves the candidate outside, between the four armed Brethren, and the door ajar until the admission of the candidate into the temple.

The Ven[erable]∴ Grand Expert says on returning:

G[rand]∴ E[xpert]∴ — Most Resp[ectable]∴, I carried out your intentions and executed your orders, but I have found nothing on the Fellow Craft to suggest that he has committed murder. His garments are white, his hands are clean, and this apron, which I brought to you, is spotless.

M[ost]∴ R[espectable]∴ — (*To all the Brethren*) Ven[erable]∴ Brethren, may the Grand Architect cause me to be wrong, and this Fellow Craft be not one of those whom our vengeance must pursue! But to receive him among us, we must take the most severe precautions and measures, and perform the most exacting investigation; for, my Brethren, if this Fellow Craft is innocent, he is surely not unaware of the cause of our grief! Would he have chosen such a hazardous time to show up here if he was guilty? It would be a crude ploy, since he would fear that our suspicions would turn against him.

Ven[erable]∴ Brethren, upon admitting him into this chamber, we will question him, and doubtless his answers will inform us what we must think of him. Are you of this opinion, my Brethren? Please manifest it in the usual way.

They raise their hands.

M[ost]∴ R[espectable]∴ — Ven[erable]∴ Brother Expert, guard of the gates, since this Respectable assembly is of the opinion to admit the Fellow Craft, ask him how he dared to hope to be introduced among us.

The request arrives as usual, by the guardian of the gate, to the Junior Ward[en]∴; and from him to the Senior [Warden], who gives it to the M[ost]∴ R[espectable]∴

The recipient must respond: By the password.

The door guard turns around in surprise, from the ambiguity of the answer given, and says to the M[ost]∴ R[espectable]∴, He answers, By the password!

M[ost]∴ R[espectable]∴ — (*With astonishment*) By the password! This rash answer confirms my suspicions. How could he know it? It is undoubtedly the result of his crime. — You see, Ven[erable]∴ Masters, a proof of his audacity and his crimes! — Ven[erable]∴ Brother Senior Ward[en]∴ be pleased to go and examine the candidate very scrupulously.

After examining him, he enters and says:

Sen[ior] W[arden]∴ —M[ost]∴ R[espectable]∴, his audacity is extreme; his approach implies the refinement of villainy. He comes, I am sure, to spy on what is happening here, or to deceive our good faith under the mask of hypocrisy.

He thus examines him more closely; he views his right hand; pushing him away, he says: O Heavens! It is he!

He seizes him by the collar, and says to him in a threatening voice:

Sen[ior] W[arden]∴ — Speak, wretch! How will you give the password? Who told you?

The Candidate replies: My conductor will give it for me, because I know it not.

Ven[erable]∴ Senior Warden says:

Sen[ior] W[arden]∴ —Most Respectable, the Fellow Craft admits that he does not know the password, but that his conductor will give it for him.

M[ost]∴ R[espectable]∴ — Cause it to be given to you, Ven[erable]∴ Brother Senior Warden.

The cond[uctor]∴ gives the password to the Senior Ward[en]∴, who replies:

Sen[ior] W[arden]∴ —The password is correct, M[ost]∴ R[espectable]∴

M[ost]∴ R[espectable]∴ — Let the candidate enter. (*The Master of Ceremonies ushers him in backwards*) Let those guarding him not abandon him for a moment. Let them stand with him to the West.

Everyone takes their places.

The Brother Terrible holds the candidate by the cable-tow.

M[ost]∴ R[espectable]∴ — Fellow Craft, you must be very rash and very indiscreet to present yourself here at a time when all your comrades are suspect to us, quite rightly. The marks of grief and consternation that you see on our faces, the mourning that surrounds us, these sad remains enclosed in this coffin, everything must paint for you the image of death; and even had this death been the effect of natural causes, we would doubtless grieve, but we would not have a crime to punish and a friend to avenge.

Tell me, Fellow Craft, were you involved in this horrible assault? Are you one of the infamous Fellow Crafts who committed it? Behold their deed.

He is shown the body which is in the coffin.

He replies: No.

The candidate is returned to the side of the M[ost]∴ R[espectable]∴ After he returns, the Brother who was in the coffin rises slowly, so as not to be heard or seen by the recipient.

M[ost]∴ R[espectable]∴ — It is well; cause this Fellow Craft to travel.

The Master of Ceremonies takes the candidate by the right hand: Brother Terrible holds him from behind by the cable-tow, and the four armed Brethren escort him, two on each side. In this way he is led around the Middle Chamber; then he is brought behind or next to the M[ost]∴ R[espectable]∴ The Brother Master of Ceremonies takes the recipient's hand and has him tap the Most Responsible on the shoulder. The latter turns around and, laying his gavel on the candidate's heart, he says:

M[ost]∴ R[espectable]∴ — Who comes here ?

The Master of Ceremonies responds:

M[aste]r∴ Cer[emonies]∴ — It is a Fellow Craft who has served his time, and who asks to enter the Middle Chamber.

Q. How does he hope to do so?

A. By the password.

Q. How will he give it, if he does not have it?

A. I will give it for him. (*He gives it*)

M[ost]∴ R[espectable]∴ — Pass, T….

They lead him to the West.

M[ost]∴ R[espectable]∴ — Ven[erable]∴ Brother Senior Warden, advance the candidate to the altar of oaths, stepping on the first Degree of the right angle of an oblong square, forming a square on the second Degree by two steps, and on the third by only one.

He is caused to take the steps and make the signs of an Apprentice; the steps of a Fellow Craft, and finally those of a Master.

He is caused to kneel on the ground, his right hand on the Bible, the two points of the compass on his breasts.

In this attitude, the M[ost]∴ R[espectable]∴ descends from the throne and comes to make him offer his obligation.

All the Brethren rise and to order.

The candidate offers his vow.

OBLIGATION.

I, N… of my free will, in the presence of the Grand Architect of the Universe, and of this Respectable lodge dedicated to Saint John of Scotland, swear and solemnly promise never to reveal the secrets of the Masters but only to those recognized as such; to obey the orders of this Respectable lodge of Masters; to keep the secrets of my Brethren as my own, except in case of murder or treason; never to do them wrong, nor to allow it to be done to them; to serve them in all that will be in my power; never to seek to seduce their wives, daughters, or sisters.

I furthermore promise to fulfil my previous obligations, under the penalty (*Here, the M[ost]∴ R[espectable]∴ raps a gavel, seizes the right hand of the recipient, and causes him to make the sign of Master*) of having my body severed in twain, one part carried to the South, and the other to the North; my bowels burned, and the ashes scattered to the wind, so that nothing remains of me. So may the Grand Architect preserve me. Amen.

All the Brethren answer: Amen.

He kisses the Bible three times and remains on his knees. The M[ost]∴ R[espectable]∴ takes him by the right hand, in the gr[ip]∴ of an Apprentice and tiles up to the sacred word of a Fellow Craft. As soon as he says it:

M[ost]∴ R[espectable]∴ — Rise, Brother J.... You are about, my Brother, to represent the greatest man in the Masonic world, our Resp[ectable]∴ Master Hiram, who was slain at the completion of the temple, as I am about to inform you.

All the Brethren of the lodge gather around the coffin. The Ven[erable]∴ Brother Junior Warden∴ is in the South, armed with a 24-inch gauge.

The Senior Ward[en]∴ in the West, armed with a square, and the Most Resp[ectable]∴ is armed with his gavel.

The Candidate is placed at the foot of the coffin.

HISTORICAL DISCOURSE.

M[ost]∴ R[espectable]∴ — David, king of Israel, having formed the project of erecting a temple to the Eternal, amassed, for this purpose, immense treasures. But this king having left the paths of virtue and being rendered unworthy of the protection of the Grand Architect, the glory of erecting a temple to the Master of the Universe, was given to his son Solomon.

Before commencing this great edifice, Solomon informed the king of Tyre, his neighbor, his friend, and his ally, who sent him Hiram, a celebrated architect.

Solomon having recognized the virtues and the great talents of Hiram, soon distinguished him by the most eminent posts, and confided to him the direction of the craftsmen and the care of drawing up the plans.

The labors were immense, and the number of craftsmen necessary being proportionate to them, it was necessary to divide them in several classes, and to allocate to them a salary proportionate to their talents.

These classes were divided into Apprentices, Fellow Crafts and Masters. Each of these ranks had signs and words to make themselves known, and to receive wages for their labor and efforts.

The App[rentice]s∴ assembled at the column B; the Fellow Crafts at column J, and the Masters in the Middle Chamber.

Fifteen Fellow Crafts, seeing the time coming to an end, and that they had not been able to obtain the Master's word, because their time had not yet been fulfilled, conspired to obtain it by force from the R[espectable]∴ Hiram, at the first opportunity, in order to pass as Masters in other countries, and receive their wages.

Twelve of these Fellow Crafts recanted, the three others, named Jubelas, Jubelos and Jubelum, persisted in their design.

These three Fellow Crafts, knowing that Hiram went every day at noon to pray in the temple, while the workers were resting, went to each of the gates.

Jubelas, at the South gate,

Jubelos, at the West one,

Jubelum, at the East one.

They waited for the moment when Hiram would show up to leave. Hiram first directed his steps to the South gate, where Jubelas demanded of him the Master's word, to which he replied that he could not receive it in that way, that he must wait patiently until his time had arrived; that, moreover, he could not give it alone, that he had to be accompanied by the kings of Israel and Tyre, by the terms of his oath, and not to give it except when assembled with them. Jubelas, dissatisfied with this response, struck him a blow with a 24-inch gauge across the throat.

Here the Master of Ceremonies leads the recipient to the Junior Warden; the latter seizes the candidate by the collar and says to him three times in a loud voice: Give me the Master's word. *The recipient responds each time:* No.

The Junior Warden then strikes him with a gauge across the throat, and the Master of Ceremonies leads him to the Senior Warden.

The M[ost]∴ R[espectable]∴ continues:

M[ost]∴ R[espectable]∴ — The Most Respectable Master Hiram fled to the West gate where he found Jubelas, who made the same demand of him, and upon his refusal, he too gave him a violent blow with a square, with which he was armed.

The Senior Ward[en]∴ does the same as before, giving the recipient a square blow on the breast.

The candidate is then led before the Most Respectable.

M[ost]∴ R[espectable]∴ — Hiram, shaken by the blow, summoned his strength, and fled to the East gate: but there he found Jubelum, who made the same demand of him as the two others, and who, upon his refusal, gave him a terrible blow of a gavel upon the forehead, which felled him dead at his feet.

The Most Respectable gives a light tap of the gavel upon the forehead of the recipient and pushes him.

Two Brethren, posted purposely to support him, using their combined strength, contribute by pulling him down backward into the coffin; and after having laid him there, they cover him with a funerary pall.

At the same moment they light the candles. The M[ost]∴ R[espectable]∴ continues.

M[ost]∴ R[espectable]∴ — The three murderers, having gathered, mutually asked each other for the Master's word; but seeing that they had not been able to obtain it, and desperate from having committed a useless crime, they thought no more of stealing the knowledge. Consequently, they took up the body of Hiram and hid it under rubble, and during the night they carried it out of Jerusalem, to a hill, and buried it. The R[espectable]∴ Master Hiram, not appearing to work as usual, Solomon caused the strictest search to be made, but to no avail.

When the twelve Fellow Crafts, who had recanted, suspected the truth they reunited and resolved between themselves to go to Solomon, with white gloves in the testimony of their innocence, and inform him of what happened.

Solomon sent these twelve Fellow Crafts in search of their Master Hiram, ordering them, should they find him, to seek for the Master's word on him, and observing that if they could not find it, that it was lost, because there were only three persons who knew it, and it could only be given by these three persons together, of which Hiram was one. He observed to them, supposing that he was dead, that in the future the first sign and the first word which should be made and spoken, upon finding and exhuming the body of this R[espectable]∴ Master, would be substituted for the ancient Master's sign and word.

These Fellows having the promise of Solomon to be rewarded with Mastership, if they arrived at the goal of their search, left, and divided themselves into four companies.

Three went North, three South, three West, and three East.

One of these four companies descended the river of Joppa: one of them having rested beside a rock, he heard terrible lamentations through the cleft of a rock. Listening, he heard a voice saying: Oh! that I had rather had my throat cut, my tongue torn out by the roots, and that I had been buried in the sands of the sea at low tide, a cable-tow's length from the shore, where the sea ebbs and flows twice a day, rather than having been an accomplice in the death of our late Master Hiram!

Oh! said another, that my heart had been torn from my breast, and cast as a prey to the vultures, rather than having been an accomplice in the death of so good a Master!

But alas! said Jubelum, I struck him harder than you both, since it was I who killed him! That I had had my body severed in twain, one part in the South, the other in the North, and my bowels burned to ashes and scattered to the four winds, rather than having been the murderer of our Respectable Master Hiram!

This Fellow Craft, upon hearing these lamentable wails, hailed the other two Fellow Crafts; they agreed amongst themselves to enter the cleft of the rock, to seize the craftsmen, and to bring them before King Solomon; which they did.

These murderers confessed to Solomon what happened and the crime they had committed, and expressed the desire not to survive their infamy.

Accordingly, Solomon ordered that their own sentences be carried out, since they themselves had assigned the manner of their death, and ordered that it be done as follows:

Jubelas had his throat cut.

Jubelos has his heart torn.

Jubelos had his body severed in twain, one part was thrown to the North, the other to the South.

Solomon having thus avenged the death of the R[espectable]∴ Master Hiram Abif sent the same Fellow Crafts back to fulfil their first mission.

These twelve Fellow Crafts departed a second time and travelled for five days without finding anything.

The Senior Ward[en]∴ then passes to the right with half of the Masters, and the Junior Ward[en]∴ with the other half, making three circuits.

The Senior Ward[en]∴ then addresses the M[ost]∴ R[espectable]∴, saying: Our searches have been in vain. *The M[ost]∴ R[espectable]∴ continues:*

M[ost]∴ R[espectable]∴ — These Fellow Crafts having reported to Solomon the futility of their search, he ordered nine Master Masons to make a second search. They were on Mount Lebanon, and on the second day, one of them, very wearied, wanted to rest on a small hill. There, he saw newly cut tree branches planted in the ground. He pulled them up, and there saw that the earth had been freshly disturbed. After probing the excavation in its three dimensions, width, length, and depth, he hailed his companions and told them of his discovery. They then began to remove the earth with great care, and thus managed to discover the body of our R[espectable]∴ Master Hiram, who had been murdered; but not daring, out of respect, to push their search further, they covered the hole; and to recognize the place, they cut a sprig of acacia, which they planted thereon, and returned to Solomon, to whom they gave their report.

Let us now imitate our Masters, my Brethren. You, Ven[erable]∴ Brother Senior Warden, set out at the head of your column, and spare nothing in your search.

The Senior Ward[en]∴ makes four circuits, with the corpse in the middle to the right; he lifts the pall, grasps the sprig of acacia, makes the recipient take it, and makes him place his right hand on his chest, and returns to report to the M[ost]∴ R[espectable]∴, saying:

Sen[ior] W[arden]∴ —M[ost]∴ R[espectable]∴, I found a newly excavated grave with a corpse, which I presume to be that of our M[ost]∴ R[espectable]∴ Master Hiram, and I planted a sprig of acacia there, to easily recognize the place.

The Most Respectable continues:

M[ost]∴ R[espectable]∴ — Solomon, pierced with the deepest grief, surmised that it could indeed only be his Grand Architect Hiram. He ordered them to go and exhume the body and bring it back to Jerusalem.

These ancient Master Masons put on their aprons and white gloves. They returned to Mount Lebanon on the second day, and they lifted the body. Let us then again imitate our ancient Masters, and try together, Ven[erable]∴ Brethren, to remove the remains of our unfortunate Master Hiram.

The Most Respectable goes round the coffin twice, at the head of all the Brethren. Arriving at the South gate, on the right side of the candidate, he stops, and pulling the sprig of acacia, he says:

M[ost]∴ R[espectable]∴ — We have arrived at the place that holds the body of our Respectable Master. This sprig of acacia is the ominous clue. The earth appears to have been recently disturbed. Let us clear up our dreadful suspicions.

The Most Respectable gradually withdraws the pall which covers the recipient. Having discovered him, and recognizing in him our Respectable Master Hiram, he raises both hands above his head, with an expression of sorrow, and lets them fall to his thighs, stamping his feet, and says three times: Oh Lord, my God! *All the Brethren do the same.*

M[ost]∴ R[espectable]∴ — It is indeed the body of our Respectable Master, my Brethren: let us fulfil the sorrowful duty that Solomon imposed on us, by exhuming his Respectable corpse.

The Junior Warden takes the first finger of the right hand, and says B…, taking a step back.

The Senior Warden takes the second finger of the same hand, and says J...., the flesh leaves the bones.

M[ost]∴ R[espectable]∴ — Ven[erable]∴ Master Masons, you see that you cannot do anything without me. Join your efforts to mine, and we will accomplish all our designs.

Then the M[ost]∴ R[espectable]∴ grasps recipient's right wrist making a claw; the two Wardens, each on their sides, assist him by raising the recipient.

The M[ost]∴ R[espectable]∴ puts his left hand on the candidate's shoulder.

The Ward[ens]∴ each take him by the elbow and a shoulder.

The M[ost]∴ R[espectable]∴, raises the recipient, saying in each ear, Moh… (the Master's word). In doing so he must set foot to foot, knee to knee, stomach to stomach, breast to breast, the right hands clawed, and the left hands on the right shoulder, forming a square.

The body raised, the word given, the M[ost]∴ R[espectable]∴ ascends to the throne.

The recipient is in placed next to the Master of Ceremonies.

Every Brother takes his place.

M[ost]∴ R[espectable]∴ — Brother Master of Ceremonies, lead the recipient to the altar, to renew his oath. — Rise and come to order, my Brethren, the new Master Mason will renew his oath.

The Wardens repeat the announcement.

The Master of Cere[monies]∴ causes the recipient to kneel.

OATH.

I renew the oath I have already taken, to prefer death rather than divulge any of the secrets of the Master Masons, which have just been entrusted to me.

This ceremony of the oath being finished, the Master of Ceremonies and the Grand Expert hold the two points of a compass to both his breasts; and the M[ost]∴ R[espectable]∴ strikes three equal strokes on the head of said compass, and says:

M[ost]∴ R[espectable]∴ — Learn to always rectify the movements of your heart in favor of humanity. (*He constitutes him.*)

PROCLAMATION.

To the glory of the Grand A[rchitect]∴ of the Universe, in the name and under the auspices of the Metropolitan lodge of Scotland, seated in Edinburgh, and by virtue of the powers confided to me and by this R[espectable]∴ lodge, I create, receive, and constitute you a Master Mason, and member of this Middle Chamber, of the Ancient and Accepted Scottish Rite, and I qualify you with the genial name of Ven[erable]∴ Brother, which must be sacred to you.

He raps three blows on the sword, which is placed upon the recipient's head. He then gives him the signs, words, and grips of this Degree, and gives him the following instructions:

M[ost]∴ R[espectable]∴ — (*To the candidate*) My Brother, the Masters must recognize each other by signs, words, and grips. I will communicate them to you.

The grand sign of a Master Mason is to raise both hands above the head, let them fall to the thighs, stamping the feet at the same time, and saying: Oh Lord, my God!

There are two reasons for this sign.

The first is that when the Fellow Crafts saw their deceased Master, they raised their hands in surprise, saying: Oh Lord, my God!

The second is when Solomon dedicated the temple to the Lord, he raised his hands saying: My God! Thou art above all things, I adore Thy Holy Name.

The password is T…, which you say when you let go of the hand, but immediately give the grip, by placing yourself on the Five Points of Masonry.

The sacred word is pronounced in syllables in the ear. This word is M∴ H∴ B∴

The grip is given in the following manner. When you have made yourself known as an Apprentice and a Fellow Craft, you ask: Do you want to go further? If you are answered in the affirmative, you put your right hand on the left breast, the thumb raised and the left hand on the head, forming a square. You then grasp him by the Master's grip, saying:

Q. What is this?

A. The grip of a Master Mason.

Q. Has it a name?

A. Yes, and something more, that follows.

Q. What is it, my Brother?

A. The Five Points of Masonry.

Q. Will you give them to me?

A. *Draw the open hand across the belly, as if to open it; raise both hands to the head, saying:* Oh Lord, my God! *Then, give the grip of a Master Mason, which is done with the right hand reciprocally, the right foot to the right foot of the Brother, the right knee to the right knee, the right breast to the right breast, and the left hand reciprocally behind the back, and pronounce in the ear* M∴ H∴ B∴

The M[ost]∴ R[espectable]∴ embraces the new Master three times, and says:

M[ost]∴ R[espectable]∴ — Ven[erable]∴ B[rother]∴ Master of Ceremonies, introduce this Ven[erable]∴ B[rother]∴ N____, to the Ven[erable]∴ Wardens, to be recognized in his new dignity.

The Master of Ceremonies executes the order. After the recipient is recognized, the Junior Ward[en]∴ says:

Jun[ior]∴ W[arden]∴ — All is fair and perfect, M[ost]∴ R[espectable]∴

M[ost]∴ R[espectable]∴ — Conduct this Ven[erable]∴ Brother between the two columns. — Rise and to order!

Very Ven[erable]∴ Brethren Senior and Junior Wardens, announce to the Ven[erable]∴ Brethren that we are about to congratulate ourselves on the advancement of the Ven[erable]∴ B[rother]∴ N....., and invite the Ven[erable]∴ Brethren on both columns, to recognize him in this quality, to give him aid and assistance, and to applaud his initiation into the Sublime Degree of a Master Mason.

The Wardens repeat this announcement. The M[ost]∴ R[espectable]∴ gives the usual applause, then everyone says Huzzah! Huzzah! Huzzah!

The newly admitted Master responds, and the M[ost]∴ R[espectable]∴ offers an applause.

Then the M[ost]∴ R[espectable]∴ gives the following instruction and closes the lodge.

CLOSING.

(*It is the same as when opened*)

INSTRUCTION.

Q. Where were you received?

A. In the West.

Q. Where are you going?

A. To the East.

Q. Why do you leave the West to go to the East?

A. Because the light of the Gospel appeared first on that side.

Q. What are you going to do in the East?

A. Seek a lodge of Masters.

Q. Are you a Master Mason?

A. The Masters recognize me as such.

Q. Where were you received?

A. In a lodge of Masters.

Q. How were you prepared to be received a Master?

A. My feet were without shoes, both arms and breast naked, deprived of all metals, except for a square attached to my right arm, I was led to the door of the lodge.

Q. How were you admitted?

A. By three distinct knocks.

Q. What were you asked?

A. Who comes here?

Q. What did you answer?

A. A Mason who has served his time as an Apprentice and as a Fellow Craft, who begs to be received as a Master.

Q. How did you get there?

A. By a password.

Q. Give it to me.

A. (*He gives it*) T….

Q. What was said to you then?

A. Enter, T….

Q. How were you disposed of?

A. I was led around the lodge.

Q. Where did you meet with the first opposition?

A. Behind the Junior Warden.

Q. What did he demand of you?

A. He asked me the same questions as at the door.

Q. How did he dispose of you?

A. He had me conducted to the West, to the Ven[erable]∴ Senior Warden.

Q. How did he dispose of you?

A. He had me conducted to the Most Resp[ectable]∴ Master.

Q. How did he dispose of you?

A. He sent me back to the Senior Ward[en]∴ to receive instructions.

Q. What were the instructions that you received?

A. When I was in the West he taught me how to approach the East as a Master, making the sign of an App[rentice]∴, and to step on the right angle of an oblong square; to take two more steps on the second Degree of the same square, my feet forming the square, and making the sign of a Fellow Craft∴; finally, the Master's step on the same oblong square. Arriving at the altar, I was made to kneel, my right hand on the Bible, the points of the compasses on each breast, and in this attitude, I solemnly swore my obligation.

Q. Can you repeat it?

A. Yes, M[ost]∴ R[espectable]∴, with your assistance.

Q. Stand up and begin.

A. I, N____, of my free will, etc.

Q. What were you shown next?

A. The Master's sign.

Q. Give it to me.

A. (*He gives it*)

Q. What was done to you then?

A. The M[ost]∴ R[espectable]∴ took me by the hand and gave me the grip.

Q. What is this grip?

A. That of Fellow Craft.

Q. Has it a name?

A. Yes, Most Respectable.

Q. Give it to me.

A. (*He gives it as he learned it*) B….

Q. Can you go further?

A. Yes, pass, I will follow you. He put his thumbnail between the first and second knuckles, which is the pass-grip, and I replied Sh….

Q. What was done to you then?

A. He gave me the grip of a Fellow Craft, saying to me: What is this? (*The thumbnail on the second knuckle*)

Q. What did you answer?

A. The grip of a Fellow Craft.

Q. Give it to me.

A. J….

Q. What are you told then?

A. He told me that I was going to represent one of the greatest men in the Masonic world, our Resp[ectable]∴ Master Hiram Abif, who was killed during the completion of the temple.

Q. After the usual narration, what did he do with you?

A. I was taken to Ven[erable]∴ Brethren Senior and Junior Ward[ens]∴ and to the Master, who put to me the questions that Jubelas, Jubelos and Jubelum had put to Hiram, striking me in the same manner.

Q. What was done to you then?

A. After receiving the gavel blow on the head by the Most Respectable, I was laid on the ground.

Q. What were you told next?

A. That I represented Hiram Abif after his death.

Q. What are you told next?

A. The M[ost]∴ Resp[ectable]∴ resumed Hiram Abif's history.

Q. How did Solomon's envoys raise the body of Hiram Abif?

A. By the Five Points of Masonry.

Q. What are they?

A. First the Ven[erable]∴ Junior Ward[en]∴ took him by the index finger, by which the App[rentice's]∴ make their grip; but owing to putrefaction, the skin slipped off and remained on his hand. The Ven[erable]∴ Senior Ward[en]∴ then took him by the second finger, by which the Fellow Craft's grip is made, and the skin again remained in his hand. The Most Resp[ectable]∴ took him by the hand, placing the four fingers on the wrist, the right foot against the right foot, the right knee against the right knee, the right breast against the right breast, and the left hand supporting him by the back. In this posture he raised it, saying: M∴ H∴ B∴ word which means: He is almost rotten to the bone. This word became the sacred word of Master Mason.

Q. Since you were raised by the Five Points of Masonry, explain them to me?

A. 1st – Hand to hand means that I am always ready to reach out to my Brother to rescue him. 2d – Foot to foot, that I am always ready to fly to the defense and aid of my Brethren. 3d – Knee to knee, that when kneeling before the Supreme Being, I will not forget them in the prayers which I address to Him. 4th – Breast to breast, that the secrets they confided to me will be invariably kept there. 5th – The left hand behind the back, that as much as it is in my ability, I will support my Brethren in all the perils that will threaten them.

Q. Why were you deprived of all metals?

A. Because in the construction of the temple, no sound was caused by the blows of any instrument made of metal was heard.

Q. Why?

A. So that it would not be defiled.

Q. How was it possible that such a vast an edifice could have been built without the aid of any tool of metal?

A. Because the materials were prepared in the forests of Mount Lebanon, conveyed in floats, raised, and placed with specially made wooden gavels.

Q. Why were you without shoes?

A. Because the place where I was received was holy ground, upon which God said to Moses: Remove thy shoes, for the place whereupon you stand is holy ground.

Q. What supports your lodge?

A. Three great pillars.

Q. What are they?

A. Wisdom, Strength, and Beauty.

Q. What do they represent?

A. Three Grand Masters: Solomon, king of Israel; Hiram, king of Tyre, and Hiram Abif, who was slain.

Q. Were the Three Grand Masters employed in the construction of the temple?

A. Yes, M[ost]∴ R[espectable]∴, Solomon drew up the plan, according to the order of God. He furnished money and provisions for the workers; Hiram provided the materials and had them prepared in the forests of Mount Lebanon, and Hiram Abif led the execution of this great work.

END OF THE VENERABLE's NOTEBOOK.

APPENDIX A

APPENDIX A

Appendix A.
NEW SAINT DOMINGUE MASONIC LODGES
1740-1749

No.	Lodge Name	Date Founded / Changed, Demised, or Last Record	City	Mother Lodge(s)
1	La Concorde	1740 – 12/27/1747	Les Cayes	*St. John's Lodge, Kingston Jamaica.*
	La Concorde	12/28/1747 – 1/23/1757	Les Cayes	*La Française, Bordeaux.*
	La Concorde	1/24/1757 – 6/23/1763	Les Cayes	*Parfaite Loge d'Ecosse de St. Jean de Bordeaux (Élus Parfaits de Bordeaux).*
	La Concorde	6/24/1763 – 2/25/1765	Les Cayes	*Parfaite Loge d'Ecosse de St. Jean de Bordeaux (Élus Parfaits de Bordeaux).*
	Les Frères Réunis	2/26/1765 – 7/26/1778	Les Cayes	*The Grand Lodge of France. / The Order of the Sublime Princes of the Royal Secret.*
	Les Frères Réunis	7/27/1778 – 12/14/1800	Les Cayes	*Grand Orient de France.*
	No. 89 Les Frères Sincèrement Réunis	5/4/1801 – 1/1/1804	Les Cayes	*The Grand Lodge of Pennsylvania.*
2	Saint Esprit	before 1746 – Unknown	Léogane	*Unknown.*
3	L'Union	6/17/1746 – 1752?	Petit-Goave	*Loge Saint Esprit, Léogane.*
	L'Union du St. Esprit	10/24/1784 – 7/27/1788	Petit-Goave	*Grande Loge Provinciale.*
	L'Unanimité et Union de St. Esprit	7/28/1788 – 1/1/1804	Petit-Goave	*Grande Loge Provinciale.*
4	St. Jean de Jérusalem Ecossaise	3/1/1749 – 1768	Cap-Français	*Parfaite Loge d'Ecosse de St. Jean de Bordeaux (Élus Parfaits de Bordeaux).*
	St. Jean de Jérusalem Ecossaise	1768 – 4/10/1776	Cap-Français	*The Grand Lodge of France. / The Order of the Sublime Princes of the Royal Secret.*
	St. Jean de Jérusalem Ecossaise	4/11/1776 – 4/8/1777	Cap-Français	*Grand Orient de France.*

No.	Lodge Name	Date Founded / Changed, Demised, or Last Record	City	Mother Lodge(s)
5	La Concorde	1749 – 7/5/1758	Saint-Marc	*Parfaite Loge d'Ecosse de St. Jean de Bordeaux (Élus Parfaits de Bordeaux).*
	La Concorde	7/6/1758 – 1/19/1763	Saint-Marc	*Parfaite Loge d'Ecosse de St. Jean de Bordeaux (Élus Parfaits de Bordeaux).*
	La Concorde	1/20/1763 – 6/25/1765	Saint-Marc	*Parfaite Loge d'Ecosse de St. Jean de Bordeaux (Élus Parfaits de Bordeaux).*
	La Concorde	6/26/1765 – 7/26/1777	Saint-Marc	*The Grand Lodge of France. / The Order of the Sublime Princes of the Royal Secret.*
	La Concorde	7/27/1777 – 5/3/1801	Saint-Marc	*Grand Orient de France.*
	No. 88 La Concorde	5/4/1801 – 1/1/1804	Saint-Marc	*Grand Lodge of Pennsylvania.*

NEW SAINT DOMINGUE MASONIC LODGES
1750-1759

No.	Lodge Name	Date Founded / Changed, Demised, or Last Record	City	Mother Lodge(s)
6	La Bonne Intelligence	1750 ? – 3/12/1752	Cap-Français	*La Bonne Intelligence, Languedoc infanterie.*
	Parfaite Harmonie	3/13/1752 – 1768	Cap-Français	*St. Jean de Jérusalem Ecossaise - Cap Français. Merged with mother.*
7	Parfaite Loge d'Ecosse.	Before 1752 – 1759?	Port-de-Paix	*St. Jean de Jérusalem Ecossaise - Cap Français.*

NEW SAINT DOMINGUE MASONIC LODGES
1760-1769

No.	Lodge Name	Date Founded / Changed, Demised, or Last Record	City	Mother Lodge(s)
8	La Parfaite Harmonie (Morin)	1762 – 11/11/1771	Port-au-Prince	*Grand Lodge of France. Patent for a traveling Scottish Lodge Parfaite Harmonie. On the list of regular Lodges through 1769.*
9	Parfait Union	1762 – 2/25/1763	Port-au-Prince	*La Concorde Saint-Marc.*

Appendix A

	Lodge	Dates	Location	Authority
	Parfait Union	2/26/1763 – 2/25/1765	Port-au-Prince	*La Concorde Saint-Marc.*
	Parfait Union	2/26/1765 – 5/6/1774	Port-au-Prince	*The Grand Lodge of France. / The Order of the Sublime Princes of the Royal Secret.*
	Parfait Union	5/7/1774 – 9/24/1778	Port-au-Prince	*Grand Orient de France.*
10	Le Choix des Hommes	1762 – 2/9/1769	Jacmel	*Unknown. Founded by Fourmont.*
	Le Choix des Hommes	2/10/1769 – 3/29/1785	Jacmel	*Souverain Conseil des Chevaliers d'Orient séant au Port-au-Prince.*
	Le Choix des Hommes	3/30/1785 – 11/20/1787	Jacmel	*Grande Loge Provinciale, Grand Orient de France.*
	Le Choix des Hommes	11/21/1787 – 1/1/1804	Jacmel	*Rit Ecossais.*
	Le Choix des Hommes	11/29/1787 – 1/1/1804	Jacmel	*Rit Ecossais.*
	Le Choix des Hommes	1/23/1805 – 1809	Santo Domingo, DR	*Rit Ecossais.*
	Le Choix des Hommes	4/28/1818 – 4/18/1818	Jacmel	*Rit Ecossais.*
	Le Choix des Hommes	4/19/1818 – 9/6/1819	Jacmel	*Grand Orient de France - R† Chapter.*
11	Édouard Stuard	Before 11/25/1762 – 1766	Cap Français	*Mère Loge Ecossais Anglais (Beauchaîne, irregular).*
	Édouard Stuard	1766 – 2/28/1767	Cap Français	*Mère Loge Ecossais Anglais (Beauchaîne, irregular).*
	La Vérité	3/1/1767 – 10/8/1774	Cap Français	*The Grand Lodge of France.*
	La Vérité	10/9/1774 – 8/15/1803	Cap Français	*Grand Orient de France.*
	La Vérité - Refugee Lodge	1791 – May 1794	Baltimore, Maryland	*Grand Orient de France.*
	Verite Sancti Johannes No. 16	May 1794 – 6/1/1798	Baltimore, Maryland	*Grand Lodge of Maryland.*
12	L'Etroite Union	11/25/1762 – 11/24/1764	Gros-Morne	*Édouard Stuard - Cap Français.*
	L'Etroite Union	11/25/1764 – 6/23/1767	Gros-Morne	*La Parfaitie Harmonie - Cap Français.*

	Lodge Name	Date Founded / Changed, Demised, or Last Record	City	Mother Lodge(s)
	L'Etroite Union	6/24/1767 – 4/23/1777	Gros-Morne	*The Grand Lodge of France. Souverain Conseil des Princes de Jérusalem séant au Saint-Marc.*
	L'Etroite Union	9/14/1777 – 8/7/1788	Gros-Morne	*Grand Orient de France.*
13	La Double Alliance	Before 6/21/1763 – 1769	Fort-Dauphin	*St. Jean de Jérusalem Ecossaise, Cap Français.*
	St. Jean de Jérusalem de Nouvelle Alliance	1769 – 1774	Fort-Dauphin	*St. Jean de Jérusalem Ecossaise, Cap Français.*
14	L'Amitié Indissoluble	Before 11/26/1765 – 5/2/1776	Léogane	*The Grand Lodge of France.*
	L'Amitié Indissoluble	5/3/1776 – 5/15/1779	Léogane	*Grand Orient de France.*

NEW SAINT DOMINGUE MASONIC LODGES 1770-1779

<u>No.</u>	<u>Lodge Name</u>	<u>Date Founded / Changed, Demised, or Last Record</u>	<u>City</u>	<u>Mother Lodge(s)</u>
15	Les Frères Choisis	5/10/1773 – 11/10/1783	Fonds-des-Nègres	*St. Jean de Jérusalem Ecossaise, Cap Français.*
	Les Frères Choisis	11/11/1783 – 1789	Fonds-des-Nègres	*Grand Orient de France.*
	Les Frères Choisis	1789 – 1/1/1804	Fonds-des-Nègres	*Rit Ecossais.*
16	L'Unanimité	1773 – 5/26/1774	Petit-Goave	*Souverain Conseil des Chevaliers d'Orient séant au Port-au-Prince.*
	L'Unanimité	5/27/1774 – 8/1/1779	Petit-Goave	*Grand Orient de France.*
	L'Unanimité	8/2/1779 – 1789	Petit-Goave	*Grand Orient de France.*
	L'Unanimité	1789 – 1/1/1804	Petit-Goave	*Rit Ecossais.*
17	Les Frères Zélés	3/6/1775 – 11/10/1777	Cavaillon	*Les Frères Choisis, Fonds-des-Negres.*
	Les Frères Zélés	11/11/1777 – 6/24/1789	Cavaillon	*Grand Orient de France.*
18	Grande Loge Provinciale	3/22/1776 – 4/17/1799	Fonds-des-Nègres	*Grand Orient de France.*

Appendix A

	Grande Loge Provinciale	4/18/1799 – 1800	New York, New York	*Grand Orient de France.*
19	La Raison Perfectionnée	8/20/1779 – 8/9/1785	Petit-Trou	*Grande Loge Provinciale, Grand Orient de France.*

NEW SAINT DOMINGUE MASONIC LODGES
1780-1789

No.	Lodge Name	Date Founded / Changed, Demised, or Last Record	City	Mother Lodge(s)
20	La Réunion Désirée	7/21/1783 – 7/31/1800	Port-au-Prince	*Grande Loge Provinciale, Grand Orient de France.*
	La Réunion Désirée	2/17/1807 – 9/14/1808	New Orleans, Louisiana	*Grand Orient de France.*
	La Réunion Désirée - Refugee Lodge.	1/18/1798 – 1799	New York, New York	*Grand Orient de France.*
	La Réunion Désirée - Refugee Lodge and R.C. de Heredom de Killwining Chapter	5/20/1805 – 9/14/1808	New Orleans, Louisiana	*Grande Loge Provinciale, Grand Orient de France.*
	No. 112 La Réunion Désirée	9/15/1808 – 3/23/1812	New Orleans, Louisiana	*Grand Lodge of Pennsylvania.*
21	Les Frères Discrets	3/1/1785 – 6/24/1788	Les Cayes	*Grande Loge Provinciale, Grand Orient de France.*
22	La Réunion des Cœurs	7/21/1785 – 6/19/1786	Jérémie	*St. James Lodge, Jamaica (Warrant).*
	La Réunion des Cœurs	6/20/1786 – 4/26/1806	Jérémie	*Grande Loge Provinciale, Grand Orient de France.*
	La Réunion des Cœurs	4/27/1806 – 10/22/1807	St. Yago, Cuba	*Grand Orient de France.*
23	No. 47 Réunion des Cœurs Franco Americain	12/18/1789 – 12/27/1799	Port-au-Prince	*Grand Lodge of Pennsylvania.*

345

No.	Lodge Name	Date Founded / Changed, Demised, or Last Record	City	Mother Lodge(s)
24	Rose Croix de Heredom de Killwining Chapter La Vérite	1787 – 6/1/1798	Jérémie	*Grand Lodge de l'ordre Royal d' Heredom de Killwining (Rouen, France).*
	Rose Croix de Heredom de Killwining Chapter	7/29/1796 – 6/1/1798	Baltimore, Maryland	*Rose Croix Chapter regularized by Pr. GM Huet Delachelle.*
25	Les Philadelphes	1788 – 1/1/1804	Léogane	*Grande Loge Provinciale, Grand Orient de France.*
26	Les Amis Réunis	1789 – 4/8/1799	Port-au-Prince	*Grande Loge Provinciale, Grand Orient de France.*

NEW SAINT DOMINGUE MASONIC LODGES
1790-1799

No.	Lodge Name	Date Founded / Changed, Demised, or Last Record	City	Mother Lodge(s)
27	La Parfaitie Egalité	11/6/1798 – 1/1/1804	Port-de-Paix	*Grand Loge Provinciale La Sagesse, Portsmouth, Virginia, Grand*
28	L'Intimité	1799 – 1/1/1804	Port-de-Paix	*Grand Orient de France?*
29	La Céleste Amité	1799 – 1/1/1804	Dondon	*Grand Orient de France?*
30	L'Union des Cœurs sans Fard	1799 – 1/1/1804	Cap Français	*Grand Orient de France?*
31	De Sion des Frères de la Véritable Egalité	1799 – 1/1/1804	Cap Français	*Grand Orient de France?*
32	Saint Jean d'Ecosse des Sept Frères Réunis	Unknown – 6/27/1799	Cap Français	*Saint-Jean d'Ecosse de Marseille.*
	Les Sept Frères Réunis	6/28/1799 – 4/4/1804	Cap Français	*Grande Loge Provinciale, Grand Orient de France.*

Appendix A

NEW SAINT DOMINGUE MASONIC LODGES
1790-1799

No.	Lodge Name	Date Founded / Changed, Demised, or Last Record	City	Mother Lodge(s)
33	Sovereign Grand Council of Sovereign Grand Inspectors General established in the French Isles of the Winward and Leeward America	7/8/1802 – 12/1/1803	Cap Français	*Supreme Council 33°. Charleston, South Carolina.*
34	No. 95 La Humilité	12/6/1802 – 1/1/1804	Anse-a-Veau	*Provincial Grand Lodge of Saint Domingue. Grand Lodge of Pennsylvania.*
35	Provincial Grand Lodge of Saint Domingue	12/9/1802 – 1/1/1804	Port-au-Prince	*Grand Lodge of Pennsylvania.*
	Provincial Grand Lodge of Saint Domingue	11/15/1806 – 1807	Baracoa Isle, Cuba	*Grand Lodge of Pennsylvania.*
36	Le Enfants du Mars	6/11/1803 – 1/1/1804	Cap Français	*Le Verité, Grand Orient de France.*
37	No. 97 Parfaite Harmonie	9/5/1803 – 1/1/1804	Santo Domingo, DR	*Provincial Grand Lodge of Saint Domingue. Grand Lodge of Pennsylvania.*
38	No. 98 La Persévérance	9/5/1803 – 1/1/1804	Abricots	*Provincial Grand Lodge of Saint Domingue. Grand Lodge of Pennsylvania.*
	No. 98 La Persévérance	5/31/1807 – 10/6/1810	St. Yago, Cuba	*Provincial Grand Lodge of Saint Domingue. Grand Lodge of Pennsylvania.*
	No. 118 La Persévérance	10/7/1810 – 8/14/1812	New Orleans, Louisiana	*Provincial Grand Lodge of Saint Domingue. Grand Lodge of Pennsylvania.*

No.	Lodge Name	Date Founded / Changed, Demised, or Last Record	City	Mother Lodge(s)
	No. 4 Persévérance	8/15/1812 – Active	New Orleans, Louisiana	*Grand Lodge of Louisiana.*
39	No. 99 La Temple du Bonheur	12/5/1803 – 1/1/1804	Archahaye [**Archihaie**]	*Provincial Grand Lodge of Saint Domingue. Grand Lodge of Pennsylvania.*

ÉLUS PARFAITS MASONIC LODGES
1745-1760

<u>No.</u>	<u>Lodge Name</u>	<u>Date Founded / Changed, Demised, or Last Record</u>	<u>City</u>	<u>Mother Lodge(s)</u>
4	St. Jean de Jérusalem Ecossaise	3/1/1749 – 1768	Cap-Français	*Parfaite Loge d'Ecosse de St. Jean de Bordeaux (Élus Parfaits de Bordeaux).*
5	La Concorde	1749 – 7/5/1758	Saint-Marc	*Parfaite Loge d'Ecosse de St. Jean de Bordeaux (Élus Parfaits de Bordeaux).*
	La Concorde	7/6/1758 – 1/19/1763	Saint-Marc	*Parfaite Loge d'Ecosse de St. Jean de Bordeaux (Élus Parfaits de Bordeaux).*
	La Concorde	1/20/1763 – 6/25/1765	Saint-Marc	*Parfaite Loge d'Ecosse de St. Jean de Bordeaux (Élus Parfaits de Bordeaux).*
7	Parfaite Loge d'Ecosse.	Before 1752 – 1759?	Port-de-Paix	*St. Jean de Jérusalem Ecossaise - Cap Français.*
1	La Concorde	1/24/1757 – 6/23/1763	Les Cayes	*Parfaite Loge d'Ecosse de St. Jean de Bordeaux (Élus Parfaits de Bordeaux).*
	La Concorde	6/24/1763 – 2/25/1765	Les Cayes	*Parfaite Loge d'Ecosse de St. Jean de Bordeaux (Élus Parfaits de Bordeaux).*

Appendix A

SUBLIME PRINCES OF THE ORDER OF THE ROYAL SECRET MASONIC LODGES 1763-1785

No.	Lodge Name	Date Founded / Changed, Demised, or Last Record	City	Mother Lodge(s)
8	La Parfaite Harmonie (Morin)	1762 – 11/11/1771	Port-au-Prince	*Grand Lodge of France. Patent for a traveling Scottish Lodge Parfaite Harmonie. On the list of regular Lodges through 1769.*
5	La Concorde	1/20/1763 – 6/25/1765	Saint-Marc	*Parfaite Loge d'Ecosse de St. Jean de Bordeaux (Élus Parfaits de Bordeaux).*
	La Concorde	6/26/1765 – 7/26/1777	Saint-Marc	*The Grand Lodge of France. / The Order of the Sublime Princes of the Royal Secret.*
9	Parfait Union	2/26/1763 – 2/25/1765	Port-au-Prince	*La Concorde Saint-Marc.*
	Parfait Union	2/26/1765 – 5/6/1774	Port-au-Prince	*The Grand Lodge of France. / The Order of the Sublime Princes of the Royal Secret.*
1	La Concorde	6/24/1763 – 2/25/1765	Les Cayes	*Parfaite Loge d'Ecosse de St. Jean de Bordeaux (Élus Parfaits de Bordeaux).*
	La Concorde	2/26/1765 – 7/26/1778	Les Cayes	*The Grand Lodge of France. / The Order of the Sublime Princes of the Royal Secret.*
12	L'Etroite Union	6/24/1767 – 4/23/1777	Gros-Morne	*The Grand Lodge of France. Souverain Conseil des Princes de Jérusalem séant au Saint-Marc.*
4	St. Jean de Jérusalem Ecossaise	1768 – 4/10/1776	Cap-Français	*The Grand Lodge of France. / The Order of the Sublime Princes of the Royal Secret.*
10	Le Choix des Hommes	2/10/1769 – 3/29/1785	Jacmel	*Souverain Conseil des Chevaliers d'Orient séant au Port-au-Prince.*

No.	Lodge Name	Date Founded / Changed, Demised, or Last Record	City	Mother Lodge(s)
13	St. Jean de Jérusalem de Nouvelle Alliance	1769 – 1774	Fort-Dauphin	St. Jean de Jérusalem Ecossaise, Cap Français.
15	Les Frères Choisis	5/10/1773 – 11/10/1783	Fonds-des-Nègres	St. Jean de Jérusalem Ecossaise, Cap Français.
16	L'Unanimité	1773 – 5/26/1774	Petit-Goave	Souverain Conseil des Chevaliers d'Orient séant au Port-au-Prince.
17	Les Frères Zélés	3/6/1775 – 11/10/1777	Cavaillon	Les Frères Choisis, Fonds-des-Negres.

RESPECTABLE AND SUBLIME GRAND LODGE OF FRANCE MASONIC LODGES 1762-1773

No.	Lodge Name	Date Founded / Changed, Demised, or Last Record	City	Mother Lodge(s)
8	La Parfaite Harmonie (Morin)	1762 – 11/11/1771	Port-au-Prince	Grand Lodge of France. Patent for a traveling Scottish Lodge Parfaite Harmonie. On the list of regular Lodges through 1769.
5	La Concorde	1/20/1763 – 6/25/1765	Saint-Marc	Parfaite Loge d'Ecosse de St. Jean de Bordeaux (Élus Parfaits de Bordeaux).
	La Concorde	6/26/1765 – 7/26/1777	Saint-Marc	The Grand Lodge of France. / The Order of the Sublime Princes of the Royal Secret.
9	Parfait Union	2/26/1763 – 2/25/1765	Port-au-Prince	La Concorde Saint-Marc.
	Parfait Union	2/26/1765 – 5/6/1774	Port-au-Prince	The Grand Lodge of France. / The Order of the Sublime Princes of the Royal Secret.
1	La Concorde	6/24/1763 – 2/25/1765	Les Cayes	Parfaite Loge d'Ecosse de St. Jean de Bordeaux (Élus Parfaits de Bordeaux).

Appendix A

	Lodge Name	Date Founded / Changed, Demised, or Last Record	City	Mother Lodge(s)
	Les Frères Réunis	2/26/1765 – 7/26/1778	Les Cayes	*The Grand Lodge of France. / The Order of the Sublime Princes of the Royal Secret.*
14	L'Amitié Indissoluble	Before 11/26/1765 – 5/2/1776	Léogane	*The Grand Lodge of France.*
11	La Vérité	3/1/1767 – 10/8/1774	Cap Français	*The Grand Lodge of France.*
4	St. Jean de Jérusalem Ecossaise	1768 – 4/10/1776	Cap-Français	*The Grand Lodge of France. / The Order of the Sublime Princes of the Royal Secret.*
13	St. Jean de Jérusalem de Nouvelle Alliance	1769 – 1774	Fort-Dauphin	*St. Jean de Jérusalem Ecossaise, Cap Français.*

GRAND ORIENT DE FRANCE MASONIC LODGES 1773-1804

<u>No.</u>	<u>Lodge Name</u>	<u>Date Founded / Changed, Demised, or Last Record</u>	<u>City</u>	<u>Mother Lodge(s)</u>
9	Parfait Union	5/7/1774 – 9/24/1778	Port-au-Prince	*Grand Orient de France.*
16	L'Unanimité	5/27/1774 – 8/1/1779	Petit-Goave	*Grand Orient de France.*
	L'Unanimité	8/2/1779 – 1789	Petit-Goave	*Grand Orient de France.*
11	La Vérité	10/9/1774 – 8/15/1803	Cap Français	*Grand Orient de France.*
	La Vérité - Refugee Lodge	1791 – May 1794	Baltimore, Maryland	*Grand Orient de France.*
18	Grande Loge Provinciale	3/22/1776 – 4/17/1799	Fonds-des-Nègres	*Grand Orient de France.*
	Grande Loge Provinciale	4/18/1799 – 1800	New York, New York	*Grand Orient de France.*
4	St. Jean de Jérusalem Ecossaise	4/11/1776 – 4/8/1777	Cap-Français	*Grand Orient de France.*
14	L'Amitié Indissoluble	5/3/1776 – 5/15/1779	Léogane	*Grand Orient de France.*

5	La Concorde	7/27/1777 – 5/3/1801	Saint-Marc	*Grand Orient de France.*
12	L'Etroite Union	9/14/1777 – 8/7/1788	Gros-Morne	*Grand Orient de France.*
17	Les Frères Zélés	11/11/1777 – 6/24/1789	Cavaillon	*Grand Orient de France.*
1	Les Frères Réunis	7/27/1778 – 12/14/1800	Les Cayes	*Grand Orient de France.*
19	La Raison Perfectionnée	8/20/1779 – 8/9/1785	Petit-Trou	*Grande Loge Provinciale, Grand Orient de France.*
20	La Réunion Désirée	7/21/1783 – 7/31/1800	Port-au-Prince	*Grande Loge Provinciale, Grand Orient de France.*
	La Réunion Désirée	2/17/1807 – 9/14/1808	New Orleans, Louisiana	*Grand Orient de France.*
	La Réunion Désirée - Refugee Lodge.	1/18/1798 – 1799	New York, New York	*Grand Orient de France.*
	La Réunion Désirée - Refugee Lodge and R.C. de Heredom de Killwining Chapter	5/20/1805 – 9/14/1808	New Orleans, Louisiana	*Grande Loge Provinciale, Grand Orient de France.*
15	Les Frères Choisis	11/11/1783 – 1789	Fonds-des-Nègres	*Grand Orient de France.*
3	L'Union du St. Esprit	10/24/1784 – 7/27/1788	Petit-Goave	*Grande Loge Provinciale.*
	L'Unanimité et Union de St. Esprit	7/28/1788 – 1/1/1804	Petit-Goave	*Grande Loge Provinciale.*
21	Les Frères Discrets	3/1/1785 – 6/24/1788	Les Cayes	*Grande Loge Provinciale, Grand Orient de France.*
10	Le Choix des Hommes	3/30/1785 – 11/20/1787	Jacmel	*Grande Loge Provinciale, Grand Orient de France.*
22	La Réunion des Cœurs	6/20/1786 – 4/26/1806	Jérémie	*Grande Loge Provinciale, Grand Orient de France.*

Appendix A

	La Réunion des Cœurs	4/27/1806 – 10/22/1807	St. Yago, Cuba	*Grand Orient de France.*
3	L'Union du St. Esprit	10/24/1784 – 7/27/1788	Petit-Goave	*Grande Loge Provinciale.*
	L'Unanimité et Union de St. Esprit	7/28/1788 – 1/1/1804	Petit-Goave	*Grande Loge Provinciale.*
25	Les Philadelphes	1788 – 1/1/1804	Léogane	*Grande Loge Provinciale, Grand Orient de France.*
26	Les Amis Réunis	1789 – 4/8/1799	Port-au-Prince	*Grande Loge Provinciale, Grand Orient de France.*
27	La Parfaitie Egalité	11/6/1798 – 1/1/1804	Port-de-Paix	*Grand Loge Provinciale La Sagesse, Portsmouth, Virginia, Grand*
28	L'Intimité	1799 – 1/1/1804	Port-de-Paix	*Grand Orient de France?*
29	La Céleste Amité	1799 – 1/1/1804	Dondon	*Grand Orient de France?*
30	L'Union des Cœurs sans Fard	1799 – 1/1/1804	Cap Français	*Grand Orient de France?*
31	De Sion des Frères de la Véritable Egalité	1799 – 1/1/1804	Cap Français	*Grand Orient de France?*
32	Les Sept Frères Réunis	6/28/1799 – 4/4/1804	Cap Français	*Grande Loge Provinciale, Grand Orient de France.*
36	Le Enfants du Mars	6/11/1803 – 1/1/1804	Cap Français	*Le Verité, Grand Orient de France.*

GRAND LODGE OF PENNSYLVANIA MASONIC LODGES 1789-1804

<u>No.</u>	<u>Lodge Name</u>	<u>Date Founded / Changed, Demised, or Last Record</u>	<u>City</u>	<u>Mother Lodge(s)</u>
23	No. 47 Réunion des Cœurs Franco Americain	12/18/1789 – 12/27/1799	Port-au-Prince	*Grand Lodge of Pennsylvania.*

353

5	No. 88 La Concorde	5/4/1801 – 1/1/1804	Saint-Marc	*Grand Lodge of Pennsylvania.*
1	No. 89 Les Frères Sincèrement Réunis	5/4/1801 – 1/1/1804	Les Cayes	*The Grand Lodge of Pennsylvania.*
34	No. 95 La Humilité	12/6/1802 – 1/1/1804	Anse-a-Veau	*Provincial Grand Lodge of Saint Domingue. Grand Lodge of Pennsylvania.*
35	Provincial Grand Lodge of Saint Domingue	12/9/1802 – 1/1/1804	Port-au-Prince	*Grand Lodge of Pennsylvania.*
	Provincial Grand Lodge of Saint Domingue	11/15/1806 – 1807	Baracoa Isle, Cuba	*Grand Lodge of Pennsylvania.*
37	No. 97 Parfaite Harmonie	9/5/1803 – 1/1/1804	Santo Domingo, DR	*Provincial Grand Lodge of Saint Domingue. Grand Lodge of Pennsylvania.*
38	No. 98 La Persévérance	9/5/1803 – 1/1/1804	Abricots	*Provincial Grand Lodge of Saint Domingue. Grand Lodge of Pennsylvania.*
	No. 98 La Persévérance	5/31/1807 – 10/6/1810	St. Yago, Cuba	*Provincial Grand Lodge of Saint Domingue. Grand Lodge of Pennsylvania.*
	No. 118 La Persévérance	10/7/1810 – 8/14/1812	New Orleans, Louisiana	*Provincial Grand Lodge of Saint Domingue. Grand Lodge of Pennsylvania.*
39	No. 99 La Temple du Bonheur	12/5/1803 – 1/1/1804	Archahaye [**Archihaie**]	*Provincial Grand Lodge of Saint Domingue. Grand Lodge of Pennsylvania.*
20	No. 112 La Réunion Désirée	9/15/1808 – 3/23/1812	New Orleans, Louisiana	*Grand Lodge of Pennsylvania.*

Appendix A

RIT ECOSSAIS MASONIC LODGES
1788-1804

No.	Lodge Name	Date Founded / Changed, Demised, or Last Record	City	Mother Lodge(s)
10	Le Choix des Hommes	11/21/1787 – 1/1/1804	Jacmel	*Rit Ecossais.*
	Le Choix des Hommes	11/29/1787 – 1/1/1804	Jacmel	*Rit Ecossais.*
	Le Choix des Hommes	1/23/1805 – 1809	Santo Domingo, DR	*Rit Ecossais.*
	Le Choix des Hommes	4/28/1818 – 4/18/1818	Jacmel	*Rit Ecossais.*
	Le Choix des Hommes	4/19/1818 – 9/6/1819	Jacmel	*Grand Orient de France - R☩ Chapter.*
15	Les Frères Choisis	1789 – 1/1/1804	Fonds-des-Nègres	*Rit Ecossais.*
16	L'Unanimité	1789 – 1/1/1804	Petit-Goave	*Rit Ecossais.*

APPENDIX B

Appendix B.

No. 603 M. - La Parfaite Union to Chaillon de Joinville, Port-au-Prince, February 26, 1763.

Duplicate.

At the Orient of the Respectable Lodge *La Parfaite Union* of Port-au-Prince, Island of S[ain]t Domingue, Latitude 18° 44' North Latitude, in a place where silence, concord and peace reign. 26th February 5763.

To the Most Respectable Brother Chaillon de Joinville, Substitute-General of the Royal Order.[1]

The purpose of this letter is to express, however unsatisfactorily, the joy which we felt on hearing the happy news which Respectable Brother Morin gave us on his arrival, though we cannot hope to give you much of a description of that joy. Your appointment to the eminent grade of Substitute-General of the Order, while offering faithful Masons spread over the two hemispheres a true idea of your great efforts, also secures for the various Lodges of the French Domination a new source of light which we hasten to unanimously applaud.

The Most Illustrious Grandmaster who has chosen you to represent him and to support him in his functions has thereby convinced us of his love for the Royal Art and his fraternal charity towards all its members.

The great hopes that your appointment promises for the restoration of Masonry could not have come at a happier moment than in these times when this respectable body seems in some ways to be falling into degradation and scorn.

If the abuses which have become only too clearly apparent to the Most Illustrious Grand Master and your Most Respectable Grand Lodge located at the heart of the French capital have required him to plan a reform which he is now entrusting to you then, Most Respectable Brother, should that not tell you just how much that reform is desired by the true sectaries scattered throughout the rest of the universe? The vivacious spirit of the French nation, its capriciousness, its penchant [1r] for novelty and fashion, its international links, and the vague pretensions on the part of those who find themselves promoted to certain Degrees have undoubtedly damaged Masonic legislation inasmuch as they have distanced it from its principal sanctuaries and have reduced correspondence with the Sovereign Lodge of France.

For a long time now the various major crises, which are always preceded by less noticeable ones, have introduced into even the best Lodges a spirit of anxiety and separatism: we see trouble-making, self-interest, factionalism and a dreadful self-indulgence driving out all honest pleasure, good order, freedom of suffrage and peaceful unity.

The reckless foundation and establishment of Lodges on the basis of powers conferred by foolhardy and greedy hands have finally brought our problems to a head: there is no uniformity in our practices, customs and laws; altar is set against altar and sanctuary against sanctuary; ruination declares itself to be the sole depositary of the Masonic truths; and our own fate is dependent solely on the resistance we are able to put up against it.

---

1   Augustin-Jean-François Chaillon de Jonville (September 7, 1733 - December 8, 1807). Author, royal counselor and Worshipful Master of the Lodge *l'Exactitude* founded May 1761. General Substitute of the Grand Master, effectively making him Deputy Grand Master of the Grand Lodge of France from 1761-1771.

Once the propagation of the Royal Art ceased to be a matter of developing qualities of obedience as well as virtue, a shameful traffic arose which laid the field wide open to the indiscreet and the perjured.

So far had Masonry ceased to be a source of those virtues whose practice had made Masons more recommendable than other men that every profane who had even a slight awareness of what was going on in its internal disputes saw our gatherings as nothing more than awful conspiracies; things to run a mile from; things which people, in all conscience, felt under an obligation to severely criticise. [1v] Can I really say this without shuddering! Some virtuous Masons, motivated by a delicacy that owed more to moral scruple than to wisdom, found the best course of action was to disguise their status and simply debar themselves from entering the Lodges, such was the degree of mutual suspicion which had grown up between them.

However, certain more zealous and courageous Brethren, after taking the time and trouble to examine, understand and criticise these disorders, decided to make their best efforts to combat such great misfortunes. Profoundly aware of their commitments and duties, some reported matters to the French lodges of which they were members while others addressed their petitions to the Most Illustrious Grandmaster. If these Members have not enjoyed the protection from these personages that they were expecting to receive then we must conclude that their requests have been derailed as a result of passing through hands that have little loyalty to the task of complying with them. Finally however, all of them – through virtue, persistence and hard work – were able to gather together the errant Members, persuade others to abjure their schisms and errors, and progressively destroy and scatter the false Lodges, thus restoring confidence in those which were legitima[tely] constituted.

Such were, Most Respectable Brother, the causes of the Order's decline. To lighten your affliction we join to it the happy successes of the fundamental truths which were being carved in the hearts of faithful Masons at the same time you were considering a general reform.

It is in these circumstances and with these motives that twelve or fifteen Masters, both Scottish and Symbolic, who are members of various Lodges in France and England and resident in this town[2], conceived the plan of reconciling themselves to their exile and the privation which they had long endured of being unable to celebrate our mysteries and show the other Masons, especially by example, that they recognized a hierarchical authority. [2r]

As the Respectable Lodge of the town of S[ain]t Marc, some 16 leagues from Port-au-Prince, was conspicuous for its labors, zeal and achievements, it was to that Lodge that we addressed our petition, obtaining from them some Symbolic Constitutions under the title of *La Parfaite Union*. Its deputies presided over our establishment, as we informed the Scottish Lodges of Les Cayes du Fond and Le Cap, which have also given unchallengeable evidence of their loyalty and had preserved the Symbolic Lodges of these two towns in their original purity.

We hope, Most Respectable, that the fraternal charity of the Most Respectable Sublime Lodge which the Respectable Brother Morin has justly praised will be extended to the members of the Lodge of *La Parfaite Union* of Port-au-Prince, and that it will crown with its respectable seal of approval the work of the Scottish Lodge of S[ain]t Marc by granting us Letters Patent to confirm our establishment. This is a favor to which we aspire with the keenest ardour.

We entreat you, Most Respectable, to present our respects to the Illustrious Grandmaster and to the Sublime Grand Lodge, to assure the latter that we only recognize Masons and Masonic labors under the

---

2   Port-au-Prince.

French Domination which that Lodge will itself recognize, and that we shall remain inviolably attached to the regulations that we are petitioning the Lodge to give us, expressly promising not to admit or receive any new member above the quota of thirty-five fixed by an article of our Constitutions, nor to allow entry to any profane who might have been excluded from Lodges recognized as legitimate.

The Respectable Brother Morin, having sent us the Letters Patent with which the Most Respectable Grand Lodge has favored him, has proved by the seals and signatures of the principal [2v] dignitaries of the Lodges of France and England which he has visited that they had the same intentions.[3]

May the Great Architect of the Universe consummate the great work which He has assigned to you! May He scatter His blessings upon you, Most Respectable, upon the Most Illustrious Grandmaster, upon the Most Respectable Grand Lodge of France, and upon all the Lodges of the Universe! May every Mason recognize that he will be indebted to you for the sacred union which you are seeking to re-establish! May your name be remembered in Masonry forever! May it be eternally celebrated! May it finally be regaled with all the honours due to your Respectable Degree, your works and your virtues! We are, by the sacred and mysterious numbers which are known to you,

    Most Respectable,

        Your very humble and very obedient servants and brothers,

    Texier, D[epu]ty W[orship]ful, G[ran]d S[cot]s, Kn[igh]t of the E[as]t & W[es]t

        Br[other] Romes, Or[ator]

    Rouziers, G[ran]d Sc[ots], Kn[ight] Mas[on], Past M[aster]

        C. Gautier, P[rince of] J[erusalem]

    Le Délié, J[unior]∴ W[arden]∴ P[rince of]∴ J[erusalem]∴

        Bende, G[rand] S[cots], Kn[ight] of the E[ast]

    Delangrené, M[aster] of C[eremonies], P[rince of] J[erusalem]

        J[osep]h Raoult, Secret[a]ry Pro Temp[or]e

Morin, G[rand] P[erfec]t Elect, Sc[ots] M[aste]r, Kn[igh]t M[as]on and Master of the Lodge of *La P[arfai]te Harmonie* and Inspector.[3r]

List of Brethren of the Respectable Lodge of the Orient of *La Parfaite Union* at Port-au-Prince, Island of S[ain]t Domingue, constituted by that of *La Concorde* of S[ain]t Marc on the same island on O[cto]ber 31st.

    Brethren.

Berthomieux,[4] member of the Respectable Lodge *Française* of Bordeaux, and Deputy of that of S[ain]t Marc for the installation of the Brethren of the Lodge of *La Parfaite Union* at Port au Prince.

---

3   Further evidence that Morin's deputy patent was signed by the Grand Master of England.

4   Bertrand Berthomieux was the founder of the Élus Parfaits lodge *La Concorde* of St. Marc, and succeeded their Deputy Lamolère de Feuillas on September 18, 1753. Morin first arrived in St. Marc in January 1763 after becoming the deputy of the Grand Lodge of France.

Texier, Grand Perfect Elect, Scots Master, Knight Mason, member of the Respectable Lodge of Les Cayes du Fond of the Isle à Vache, and Worshipful Master of the said Lodge *La Parfaite Union*.

Rouzier, Scots Master, Knight Mason, Member of the Respectable Lodge *Française* of Bordeaux and Past Master of *La Parfaite Union*.

Gautier, Member of the Boston Lodge, Senior Warden.

Gabriel Rasteau, Member of the Lodge *La Fidélité*, Paris, J[unior] Warden.

De S[ain]t Romes, Member of the Lodge of Nantes, Orator.

Paul Fooks, of the Lodge of Jamaica, Scots Master, Kn[igh]t Mason.

Pellerin, idem.

William Fay[5] of the *Devil Tavern* Lodge[6] of London.

Chevalier Peyrat of the same of Rochefort.

Delangrené of the Lodge of Le Cap.

Truchasion of the Lodge of S[ain]te Foy, Secretary, absent.

Vence, Member of the Respectable Scottish Lodge of Marseilles.

Balanqué, of the same of Les Cayes du Fond.

Lescot, Member of the same of Dijon, affiliate.

Lagneau de Larisse[7], of the same of Léogane.

Parc, of the same of Jamaica.

Gastumeau, received.

Raoult, received.

De Bercy, received.

Le Delier, of the same of Rouen, affiliate.

Baron, of the same of Jamaica, affiliate.[3v]

Since the first letter

Le Chevalier de Raymond[8], of the same of Angers, affiliate.

La Forcade, Past Worshipful of the Lodge *Francaise* of Bordeaux, Grand Scots, affiliate.

---

5   See Journals of the House of Commons, Vol. 22, 1732.

6   See https://dr-david-harrison.com/freemasonry/seven-pubs-associated-with-masonic-lodges/

7   "Lagneau de Larisse, sous-ingénieur à Saint-Domingue (1er janvier 1747), nouveau brevet d'ingénieur (14 mai 1767), colonel (12 juin 1778), retiré avec la commission de lieutenant-colonel (12 novembre 1772), chevalier de Saint-Louis le 24 mars 1771" (http://anom.archivesnationales.culture.gouv.fr/ark:/61561/tu245qslla.num=20.form=complexe.start=81)

8   Presumably the author referred to here: https://www.amazon.com/Eve-Conquest-Chevalier-Raymonds-Critique/dp/0870134337

Lartigue, of the same of Guadeloupe, affiliate.

Baret, of the same of Bordeaux, affiliate.

Gerlain, of the same of Bordeaux, affiliate. [4r] [4v/blank]

No. 991 M. - Morin to Chaillon de Jonville, Port-au-Prince, June 21, 1763

Dear Sir and Most Respectable Brother,[9]

The kindness with which you honoured me during my stay in Paris and the express permission you have given me to write to you upon my arrival in the American Islands allow me to take this liberty.

I have experienced many problems, untoward incidents and setbacks but these would take too long to explain, so I shall content myself with a summary of my Masonic activities and with brief details of all the operations I have undertaken under this heading for the benefit and continued success of the Order in general.

I would therefore make so bold Sir to inform you with the great satisfaction and joy that only a truly Masonic heart can feel that the Royal Art, which has appeared to be in the doldrums for so long and which was even heading towards ruination, is today on the rise again with a new splendour and vigour.

The trips I made to different French towns, my stay in England after being captured, and what I did in Jamaica with the same intentions detained me for fourteen months before I went to Saint-Domingue, where I landed in Saint-Marc on January 20th, 1763.

During these trips I had the advantage of visiting all the regular and constituted lodges in the places where I stayed. Their respectful submissions and the ardent desire they showed me to be duly recognized by our Grand and Most Respectable and Sovereign Lodge of Paris convinced me that they will spare no efforts in earning the right to this favor by strictly observing any laws, regulations and Statutes that the Grand Lodge will deign to prescribe to them. I had the consolation of seeing that they share the same prevailing spirit, that their steps are guided by friendship, concord and peace, and that their hopes have been raised by the splendid choice which our Very Dear, Most Respectable, Most Sublime and Most Serene Grand Master the Prince de Clermont has made in appointing you his Substitute-General in the Order.

All these lodges, Sir, hope that, guided by your wise instruction, they will reach the sanctuary of virtue, the centre of the edifice that we are raising to the Eternal, where (like so many rays) our feelings and wishes find their fulfilment, with every Mason forming a point on its circumference in a circular chain composed of innumerable parts, the harmony and unity of which enable them to become one, and of which one sees neither the beginning nor the end.

---

9   Augustin-Jean-François Chaillon de Jonville was born in Brussels on September 7, 1733 and died December 8, 1807 in Paris. He was the Worshipful Master of the Parisian Lodge *Saint Antoine*. He was made Substitute General for the Grand Master of France Louis de Bourbon-Condé, Comte de Clermont who abdicated his Masonic duties in 1762, effectively making him Grand Master of the Grand Lodge of France. He was appointed to replace La Corne, Worshipful Master of the Lodge *la Sainte Trinité*, who died in office before June 1762. Both were signatories to Morin's patent dated August 27, 1761, Making him Grand Inspector of the Grand Lodge of France for Saint Domingue, and granting him the right to establish a symbolic lodge *La Parfaitie Harmonie*.

They hope, Sir, that you will be kind enough to entertain their humble pleas to be excluded from the reform and to see them numbered amongst your precious daughters, so as to finally enjoy the rights and privileges of all good Masons and to rightfully taste the sweetness of fraternity.

That, Sir and Most Respectable Brother, is the work which the Respectable Scottish Lodges and Symbolic Lodges of Bordeaux have undertaken. In response to the news (which I have given them of your appointment to the supreme post of Substitute-General of the Order) they will take immediate steps to make you part of their efforts and will address to you their most humble petitions that they might be deserving of your support whilst assuring you of their profound obedience.

At the beginning of 1762 I was captured at sea and conducted by the enemy of the French State to London, where I received all the consolations and enjoyed all the pleasures and benefits that a Freemason can expect in such circumstances, especially as I had been so highly recommended by your good self.[10]

I often had the pleasure of working with the Most Respectable Brother Earl Ferrest, Viscount Tamworth, the Grand Master and Protector of all the Lodges under English jurisdiction.[11]

I told him in open lodge about the patents you were kind enough to grant me, to which he added his approval, congratulating me and bestowing on me the title of life member of all the lodges of England and Jamaica, in which places I received in this capacity all the services which I needed until my departure for Saint-Domingue.

What a lovely surprise for me, Sir, to find upon my arrival at Saint-Marc that this town had a Respectable Scottish Lodge constituted by that of Bordeaux which I created in 1745. I found it so well organised as was also the Symbolic Lodge that I thought I should give them the same instructions in order to earn from you and our Most Respectable Mother Lodge of Paris the right to be ranked among its beloved daughters, which they received with all possible loyalty and gratitude, as also did their daughter Lodge *La Parfaite Union* in Port-au-Prince, where I am currently residing.

I have responded to their respectful demands that I take the liberty of addressing you and asking you to pass by way of Bordeaux. Regarding the Respectable Scottish and Symbolic Lodges of Les Cayes du Fond on the Ile à Vache known as *La Concorde* the praises of which I have already sung to you, I hope they will take the first opportunity to render themselves worthy of the same favor.

As for the Respectable Scottish Lodge of Le Cap Français which I founded in 1748 and its daughter the Symbolic Lodge at Fort Dauphin founded under the title of *La Double Alliance* I hope to visit this part of the island to fulfil my mission to the ultimate, and will let you have a detailed description of their work and their Masonic conduct.

I have behaved edifyingly, Sir and Most Respectable Brother, by ensuring that all the articles of the regulations included in the Constitutions sent to the Symbolic Lodges by their mother lodges the Respectable Scottish Lodges are truly Masonic and that they seek to establish order, peace and concord. However, these articles are not methodically organised, which is harmful to good morals as well as making excessive demands on the memory and causing confusion when quoting this or that article, the numbering of which almost always differs from one lodge to another.

---

10 After departing Bordeaux abord *Le Succès* for Cap-Français, Morin's ship is captured at sea and brought into Plymouth on April 9, 1762. After spending a number of months in England and Scotland Morin arrives in Jamaica, and lands in St. Marc in January 1763. HCA 32 245, National Archives, Kew, England, 115.

11 Vice Admiral Washington Shirley, 5th Earl Ferrers (5/26/1722 - 10/1/1778). Fellow of the Royal Society and Grand Master of the Premier Grand Lodge 1762-1764.

Appendix B

In some Lodges I saw articles in their Constitutions which place extreme restrictions on the members: these articles are difficult to impose and are, I think, probably innovations.

Such Lodges, led and guided by the spirit of obedience and submission and committed by the obligation into which they have blindly entered to all the articles in general of their particular Constitution dare not violate any of these articles to which they are, as it were, enslaved, but in order to avoid the abuses that could result from such innovations and especially the disgust which is experienced even by certain zealous Masons I dare, Sir, to reveal to you that I think it would be for the good of the Order if you would kindly entrust to me, for the sake of Masonic liberty, an obligation to observe one and the same regulation of the Sovereign and Grand Lodge of Paris and thus, by your authority, fully discharge the Lodges of the obligation they have sworn to all other specific regulations and articles, whatever they might be, so that they might see their fearful consciences relieved of certain obligations which they have undertaken and given, often out of the sheer necessity of having a formal constitution at any price, and so commit themselves formally, with all due solemnity and in advance to all the articles of your general regulations.[12]

That, my dear Sir and Most Respectable Brother, is the fruit of my modest endeavours, and I shall be so happy if I can earn (by my zeal and application) both your approval and the friendship of all my Brethren, but I can honestly say that all our American Lodges behave with every possible decency and regularity, especially the one at Port-au-Prince which I have had the pleasure of seeing directed, under my supervision, by our Worshipful Brother Texier, Grand Scots, Knight Mason,[13] or by our past M[aste]r Brother Rouzier, Grand Scots Knight Mason, both strict observers of our laws and men of outstanding merit, who have ordered Brother Lartigue,[14] one of our most cherished members and the bearer of the present duplicate document, to place it directly into your hands, out of fear that the first despatch may not have reached you. Since Brother Lartigue must, after completing his business in Paris, return promptly to the islands, I beseech you Sir to kindly indicate to him how happy you are that he has had an opportunity to take your orders, and to assure you that anything that you might send to us here or anything else that it might suit you to command us to do will be counted amongst the great favors with which you have honoured us up to the present day.

Some of the journeys I am obliged to make in several areas of the island will cause me to be absent from Port-au-Prince for some time: if you would do me the honour of writing to me and responding favorably to the Masonic desires that guide my steps and which direct my actions, I would therefore beg you, Sir, to address your letter to Mr. Texier, merchant, of Port-au-Prince, one of the most zealous Masons and someone in whom I have total confidence.

I will need a further two or three years to conclude my business in this colony and then return to France. I await that blessed moment with impatience Sir, but I could not long for it with any greater ardour than that with which enables me to prove to you that I am, with the most profound respect by all

---

12 This is the genesis of the Constitutions of 1762. They were first proposed by Morin to Chaillon de Jonville, to make new regulations governing the existing Scottish Lodges, as they had been constituted under the *Élus Parfaits* almost two decades earlier by Morin, and were still operating under their administration, thought the *Élus Parfaits* of Bordeaux had ceased to be an entity.

13 Jean-Jacques Texier was made a Deputy Inspector General by Morin in 1765, and installed the Les Cayes Lodge, *La Concorde*, as *Les Frères Réunis*, according to their new constitution sent to Morin in his absence in Port-au-Prince, from the Grand Lodge of France. These degrees are Grand Elect, Perfect and Sublime Mason (today the 14°) and Knights of the East (today the 15°).

14 Jean Lartigue, captain of the ships *le Saint-Jean* and *l'Orphée* of Bordeaux in 1766. Morin was detained in 1745 abord the merchant ship *La Pallas*, displacing some 250 tons, led by 1st Captain Pierre Colisson. Colisson appears in the Sharp documents, and is a central figure in the disputed legitimacy between the Scottish Lodges of Fort Royal and Saint-Pierre in Martinique. The other officers on board were 2nd Captain Jean Lartigue, and Lieutenant Eutrope Porlodee. Morin's professional and masonic networks appear to be one and the same. HCA 32 245, National Archives, Kew, England.

the S[acred] and My[sterious] N[umbers]¹⁵ which are known to us,

My dear Sir and Most Respectable Brother,

Your very humble, very loyal and very respectful Brother,

Morin

Port-au-Prince,

June 21ˢᵗ, 1763.

No. 607 M. - La Concorde to Chaillon de Joinville, Les Cayes, June 24, 1763.

I

From an enlightened place where, in a sweet and tender harmony, there ceaselessly reign silence, concord and peace, at the O[rient]∴ of Les Cayes du Fond, Île à Vache, on the Island and Coast of Saint-Domingue, on the 24ᵗʰ day of the first month of the Year of the G[reat]∴ L[ight]∴ 5763, and according to the Vulgar Calculation 24ᵗʰ June 1763.

On behalf of the B[rethren]∴ of the R[espectable]∴ L[odge]∴ of S[ain]t∴ J[ohn]∴ of J[erusalem]∴¹⁶ established at Les Cayes under the gracious title of *La Concorde* we send greetings, joy, good health and prosperity,

To the M[ost]∴ R[espectable]∴ and M[ost]∴ Exc[ellent]∴ B[rother]∴ Chaillon de Joinville, G[rand]∴ S[ublime]∴, P[erfect]∴ Sc[ots]∴ M[aster]∴, Kn[igh]t∴ of the E[ast]∴, P[rince]∴ of J[erusalem]∴, Kn[igh]t∴ of the E[agle]∴, of the S[un]∴, and of the C[ados]∴,¹⁷ G[rand Master]∴ of the Premier and Sovereign Lodge of France under the title of *Saint-Antoine* in Paris, and Substitute-General of the M[ost]∴ I[llustrious]∴ and M[ost]∴ R[espectable]∴ G[rand]∴ M[aster]∴ His Most Serene Highness the Comte de Clermont, Prince of the Blood, Protector of all the L[odges]∴ fortunate enough to be under the French Domination.

M[ost]∴ R[espectable]∴ & M[ost]∴ Exc[ellent]∴ B[rother]∴,

We cannot move quickly enough to offer you our congratulations on the decision, as glorious for yourself as it is advantageous for M[asonry]∴, that Our Most Illustrious and Most Respectable Grandmaster H[is]∴ S[erene]∴M[ajesty]∴¹⁸ the Prince de Clermont has been kind enough to make in placing you at the head of the Premier and Sovereign L[odge]∴ of France by appointing you as his Substitute-General. Kindly deign, M[ost]∴ R[espectable]∴ B[rother]∴, to receive our <u>congratulations</u>¹⁹, for we address them to you with all the sincerity you could possibly demand and with all the joy that true and zealous M[asons]∴ inevitably feel when they see this a[ugust]∴ and s[ublime]∴ art that they cherish being sustained under

---

15 Originally this abbreviation was 'Secret and Mystic' numbers, appearing in plain text in Sharp 1 and 4. The phrase first appears in the 1744 Grand Lodge constitution and is also used once by Lamolere de Feuillas. It appears abbreviated in the majority of the correspondence as 'Sacred and Mysterious' in Sharp 10, 27, 52, 56,57, 69, and 108. It appears in plain text in Sharp 129. Moreover in the 1749, 1750 and 1763 forms of the ritual that would become the 14°, the word sacred is used in plain text.

16 Cf. Georges Odo, La franc-maçonnerie dans les colonies: 1738-1960, Editions Maçonniques de France, 2001, p. 28.

17 Cadosh or Kadosh.

18 His Most Serene Highness.

19 Underlining in the original: the word is changed in the second version to 'compliments'.

the protection of its Most Illustrious and Most Respectable chief, and see his duties being performed by a R[espectable]∴ B[rother]∴ such as yourself, who has obviously impressed him as being truly worthy of his closest confidence and his most distinguished favors.

This token of the esteem, M[ost]∴ Exc[ellent]∴ B[rother]∴, that Our Most Illustrious and Most Respectable G[rand]∴ M[aste]r∴ has bestowed upon you [1r] serves us as convincing evidence of the excellence of your merits, to which he obviously believed he could only do full justice by elevating you to the sublime position to which he has appointed you. For what reward could possibly be more flattering for you? What more tangible satisfaction could there be for a M[ason]∴ who understands, as you do, the advantages and delights of his status than for you to represent, in the eyes of all the Brethren, a Prince whose virtues make him, in our eyes, as recommendable as he is respectable thanks to the noble blood from which he has sprung, for he is a Prince to whose support all the L[odges]∴ under French dominion owe their happy existence, their favorable sustenance, their gracious increase, and their most solid and unshakeable support.

Our dear B[rother]∴ Morin has informed us, M[ost]∴ R[espectable]∴ B[rother]∴, of the commission entrusted to him by virtue of the power granted to him by your M[ost]∴ R[espectable]∴ and Sovereign L[odge]∴ He has been kind enough to communicate to us everything that H[is]∴ S[erene]∴ M[ajesty]∴ Our Most Respectable and Most Illustrious Grandmaster deemed it appropriate to prescribe in order to further the interests and glory of M[asonry]∴ to all the L[odges]∴ that recognize him as their sovereign and legitimate protector. We are therefore proud to make known to you the pleasure that we feel, and we shall not hesitate to offer you proof of the zeal that has always motivated us and which motivates us ceaselessly for the prosperity of our A[ugust]∴ and S[ublime]∴ Order. We accept with the most blind obedience those judicious and even essential regulations which, through their usefulness to the R[oyal]∴ Art, prove the sagacity and wisdom of the Prince who has laid them down, and which can only contribute further to the triumph of M[asonry]∴ and make the happiness of M[asons]∴ even sweeter and more perfect.

We are therefore engaging, M[ost]∴ R[espectable]∴ B[rother]∴, in what is both a very pleasurable experience and an indispensable duty in informing you of all the operations we have performed and all the labors we have celebrated since the establishment of our R[espectable]∴ L[odge]∴ in order that, now that we have introduced ourselves to you, you will deign to interest yourself on our behalf and procure for us, through the generosity of our Most Illustrious [1v] and Most Respectable Grandmaster, some tokens of his benevolence and protection. We dare to hope that we shall receive this if the zeal and spirit of M[asonry]∴, to which we have always been loyally devoted, can earn for us these precious favors which are the object of all our wishes and of our unanimous satisfaction.

We believed and shall always do, M[ost]∴ Exc[ellent]∴ B[rother]∴, that we would still be languishing in darkness if the salutary and benevolent rays of the Great Light which shine at your O[rient]∴ had not made us aware of and at the same time kindled within us a fire whose light we conserve in all its purity and with all the fervour of which true and faithful M[asons]∴ are capable.

M[ost]∴ R[espectable]∴ B[rother]∴, we owe the happiness we enjoy to R[espectable]∴ B[rother]∴ Estienne Morin, who is today the Deputy of your M[ost]∴ R[espectable]∴ and Sovereign L[odge]∴ under the powers granted him by the M[ost]∴ R[espectable]∴ Sc[ottish]∴ L[odge]∴ of London, further certified by the M[ost]∴ R[espectable]∴ Sc[ottish]∴ L[odge]∴ of Bordeaux. He was kind enough to yield to our entreaties and now, fully convinced of our zeal and the knowledge we have acquired in the R[oyal]∴ Art, he feels he might be able to acquire for us the reward we have long solicited from the R[espectable]∴ L[odge]∴ *Française* of Bordeaux. It was he who raised our August and S[ublime]∴ edifice, which still exists today under the gracious title of *La Concorde*, and which shall last for as long as we shall feel within us a burning zeal which, ending only with ourselves, will pass to those of our B[rethren]∴ who shall succeed us, who will transmit from age to age to those who follow with us this noble and praiseworthy emulation and this inviolable devotion to the interests of M[asonry]∴ whose reign must surely extend until the end of time. All that we lack is your seal of approval. This is what we desire, and we flatter ourselves that we shall obtain it through those sentiments with which we are all intensely infused.

We have written, M[ost]∴ Exc[ellent]∴ B[rother]∴, to the M[ost]∴ R[espectable]∴ L[odge]∴ *Française* of Bordeaux, and have informed it of the [2r] operations that the R[espectable]∴ B[rother]∴ Morin has performed on our behalf. In the final instance we also passed on to them a letter via the R[espectable]∴ B[rother]∴ Gabriel Du Feu, a member of the M[ost]∴ R[espectable]∴ Sc[ottish]∴ L[odge]∴ of Bordeaux. We have reason to believe that the problems caused by the war[20] may have prevented our earlier letters from reaching their destination.

Since the moment, M[ost]∴ R[espectable]∴ B[rother]∴, that R[espectable]∴ B[rother]∴ Morin laid the foundations of our edifice we have conformed scrupulously to the laws which have been made for us and have pursued our labors with a uniformity which has never been denied. We have only admitted to our company those who have seemed to be truly worthy of our favors by virtue of the public regard they enjoy and the correctness of their morals as they are known to us. We are providing you with a precise summary of all these operations such as you will need to imagine for yourselves, as we felt we should not try your patience with monotonous details which, without providing you with any further information, would be no less tedious and tiring for you to work through.

M[ost]∴ Exc[ellent]∴ B[rother], all good M[asons]∴ must take some pride in their status: it is the only occasion when this praiseworthy and virtuous emulation in which each of us must take some pride is allowed to give way within us to feelings of conceit. Do not however judge us only by the loyalty and utter devotion we swear to you, for they are the first and the most necessary virtues that a M[ason]∴ must practise. Our dear and R[espectable]∴ B[rother]∴ Morin told us that he had kindly made us known to your M[ost]∴ R[espectable]∴ and Sovereign L[odge]∴ We now dare to present ourselves before you with confidence. We are sending you a list of all the Brethren composing our R[espectable]∴ L[odge]∴

We pray that the G[reat]∴ A[rchitect]∴ of the U[niverse]∴ may abundantly shower his favors and blessings upon your [2v] Most Illustrious and Most Respectable Grandmaster. Our prayers for his safety could not be more fervent and more far-reaching, for the prayers we are formulating for him are for the glory and prosperity of M[asonry]∴ We have sought to capture the true spirit of our A[ugust]∴ and S[ublime]∴ Order whereby, showing love to all in a spirit of cordiality and sincerity, we have displayed a unanimous interest in each other's happiness which, we flatter ourselves, may become perfect and fully accomplished through the protection of a Prince whose benevolent kindness and ready approachability form the entire joy and happiness of those who are subject to him, a Prince who is willing, when among the B[rethren]∴ he cherishes and respects, to forget the high rank that Heaven has bestowed upon him and who yet seems to be even more worthy of it thanks to all the virtues of which he is the perfect exemplar, virtues that become so beneficial to humanity through the rules they prescribe, the duties they commend and the respect they instil.

M[ost]∴ R[espectable]∴ and M[ost]∴ Exc[ellent]∴ B[rother]∴, may Heaven answer the prayers which we are addressing to it in all the fullness of our hearts, and may it shower joy and prosperity upon you! May its most favorable influences be poured out with the most abundant profusion upon all the B[rethren]∴ who compose your M[ost]∴ R[espectable]∴ and Sovereign L[odge]∴! May M[asonry]∴,

---

20 The Seven Years' War.

under the auspices of its Most Illustrious and Most Respectable Protector, be sustained in all the brilliance and splendour that should shine forth across the surface of the Universe! May it enjoy all the growth to which it is so graciously susceptible for the glory and happiness of humanity! May the equitable laws which are today being given to us, the wise regulations which are being laid down for us, and the sublime Constitutions which are generally and uniformly prescribed to us be engraved in our hearts, and in the hearts of all M[asons]∴ who, enjoying [3r] the inconceivable advantage of being subjects of the Best of Kings, also savour the delights of serving beneath the banners of an august Prince whose fatherly and benevolent attentions create the sweetest and yet at the same time the most assured happiness of which they could ever expect to be a part. May we, forever intensely suffused with the zeal that is our motivation, redouble our work and our efforts, and through a constantly and steadily sustained emulation merit the blessings we are seeking from you. Only such blessings can and must make our satisfaction and our happiness complete. This is the sole benefit to which we aspire. It forms the object of our most tender solicitudes, of our liveliest enthusiasms and of our most ardent desires. Our powers of expression are too weak to do full justice to our feelings when we dare to entertain the pleasant and flattering hope that you will deign to look kindly upon the favors we are expecting from you given your loyalty to the interests of M[asonry]∴ as well as your zeal and affection for those who, like us, have penetrated into the most secret mysteries.

M[ost]∴ Ex[cellent]∴ B[rother]∴, may those who have shown themselves to be unworthy of the blessings of a mother as tender and as affectionate as M[asonry]∴ has always shown herself to be towards her children carry ceaselessly within themselves the sufferings of their ingratitude! May they see eternally within their mind's eye the inestimable happiness we enjoy in all its sweetness and gentleness! May they endlessly pine for the singular favors which have been showered upon them, despairing of ever enjoying any further favors and remaining wholly convinced of the scorn and vilification they have merited by being wholly immersed in their shameful misconduct! May they bear within them forever a vengeful remorse [3v] which, through internal and external reproaches of their conscience, forms the subject of their torture and that of our own triumph, just like those prideful and foolish spirits which, forgetful of the benefits they had received from the infinite goodness of the Sovereign Being who created them for His glory and to form the object of His most tender kindnesses, dared to raise against Him the banner of revolt! For God was as severe in His vengeance as He was generous in His gifts and chased them from the happy abode where they shared delights and pleasures within His presence and then confounded them in floods of gall and bitterness. Their mouths which, while they showed themselves to be worthy of their happiness, were open only to the most sublime harmonies no longer uttered anything other than the most awful blasphemies. From the heights of the Heavens they have been flung headlong into the deepest abyss, from the summit of glory they have fallen to the pinnacle of humiliation, and from the bosom of supreme happiness they have passed into the keenest and most painful torments, carrying ceaselessly within them the image of the blessings they have foregone. Finally, unable to rid themselves of this memory, this image serves to even further intensify the violence of the evils they endure. They know that those who remained faithful and grateful towards their divine benefactor possess a blessedness whose endlessly renewed delights will suffer neither change nor alteration. This pure and inexpressible joy which forms the reward of the blessed spirits who have remained loyal then excites even greater anger, fury and despair within these rebellious and seditious spirits, yet their struggles are criminally useless, for they can do nothing [4r] to undermine a happiness of which God Himself did not wish to limit the duration or delight.

We salute you by 9 times 9, We are, with the feelings which are due and known to you,

Most Respectable and Most Excellent Brother,

Your very humble and very obedient servants,

F[ranço]is∴ Lamarque²¹, W[orship]ful∴, Knight M[aso]n∴

D[aniel] Suire²², Past W[orshipful], [Senior] W[arde]n∴, Kn[ight]∴ M[ason]∴

G[uillaume] Molinié²³, J[unior]∴ W[arden]∴, Kn[igh]t M[aso]n∴

Jean Charles Simon, O[rator]∴, G[rand]∴ Sc[ots]∴

George, Tyler, Grand Scots

Gellée senior, Elect Kn[igh]t, M[aster] of C[eremonies]∴

By Order of the W[orshipful] L[odge]∴

A[lexandre] Laville, S[ecretar]y∴, K[night]∴ M[ason]∴ [4v]

No. 608 M. - La Concorde to Chaillon de Joinville, Les Cayes, June 24, 1763.

II

From an enlightened place where, in a sweet and tender harmony, there ceaselessly reign silence, concord and peace, at the O[rient]∴ of Les Cayes du Fond, Île à Vache, on the Island and Coast of Saint-Domingue, on the 24ᵗʰ day of the first month of the Year of the G[reat]∴ L[ight]∴ 5763, and according to the Vulgar Calculation 24ᵗʰ June 1763.

To the Most R[espectable]∴ and M[ost]∴ Ex[cellent]∴ B[rother]∴ Chaillon de Joinville, G[rand]∴ S[ublime]∴, P[effect]∴ Sc[ots]∴ M[aster]∴, Kn[igh]t∴ of the E[ast]∴, P[rince]∴ of J[erusalem]∴, Kn[igh]t∴ of the E[ast]∴, the S[un]∴, and of the C[ados]∴²⁴, W[orshipful]∴ of the Premier and Sovereign L[odge]∴ of France under the title of *Saint-Antoine* in Paris, and Substitute-General of the Most I[llustrious]∴ and R[espectable]∴ G[rand]∴ M[aster]∴, H[is]∴ S[erene]∴M[ajesty]∴ the Comte de Clermont, Prince of the Blood, Protector of all the Lodges under the French Domination.

Most R[espectable]∴ & M[ost]∴ Ex[cellent]∴ B[rother]∴,

We cannot move quickly enough to offer you our congratulations on the decision – as glorious for yourself as it is advantageous for M[asonry]∴, that Our M[ost]∴ I[llustrious]∴ and M[ost]∴ R[espectable]∴ G[rand]∴ M[aster]∴, H[is]∴ S[erene]∴M[ajesty]∴ the Prince de Clermont has been kind enough to make in placing you at the head of the Premier and Sovereign L[odge]∴ of France by appointing you as his Substitute-General. Kindly deign, M[ost]∴ R[espectable]∴ B[rother]∴, to receive our compliments, for we address them to you with all the sincerity you could possibly demand and with all the joy that true

---

21 More usually written La Marque. This was François La Marque, 'The American', a merchant in Santo Domingo, former Master of the Loge des Frères Réunis des Cayes, member of the Lodges La Parfaite Union (Port-au-Prince), La Concorde (Saint-Marc), and L'Amitié Indissoluble (Léogâne), and Deputy of these lodges to the Grand-Orient de France. Cf. Achille Godefroy Jouaust, Histoire du Grand-Orient de France, Brisard 1865, p. 203.

22 Daniel Suire who was skippering the Benjamin in 1745. Cf. https://tinyurl.com/ybthbh5t

23 This name is spelt several different ways in the manuscripts.

24 Cadosh or Kadosh.

and zealous M[asons]∴ inevitably feel when they see this august and sublime art that they cherish being sustained under the protection of its Most I[llustrious]∴ and Most R[espectable]∴ chief, and see his duties being performed by a R[espectable]∴ B[rother]∴ such as yourself, who has obviously impressed him as being truly worthy of his closest confidence and his most distinguished favors.

This token of the esteem, Most Ex[cellent]∴ B[rother]∴, that Our Most I[llustrious]∴ and M[ost]∴ R[espectable]∴ G[rand]∴ M[aster]∴ has bestowed upon you serves us as convincing evidence of the excellence of your merits, to which he obviously believed he could only do full justice by elevating you to the sublime position to which he has appointed you. For what reward could possibly be more flattering for you? What more tangible satisfaction could there be for a M[ason]∴ who understands, as you do, the advantages and delights of his status than for you to represent, in the eyes of all the B[rethren]∴, a Prince whose virtues make him, in our eyes, as recommendable as he is respectable thanks to the noble blood from which he has sprung, for he is a Prince to whose support all the L[odges]∴ under French Domination owe their happy existence, their favorable sustenance, their gracious increase, and their most solid and unshakeable support.

Our dear and R[espectable]∴ B[rother]∴ Morin has informed us, M[ost]∴ R[espectable]∴ B[rother]∴, of the commission entrusted to him by virtue of the power granted to him by your Most R[espectable]∴ and Sovereign L[odge]∴ He has been kind enough to [5r] communicate to us everything that H[is]∴ S[erene]∴ M[ajesty]∴ Our Most R[espectable]∴ and M[ost]∴ I[llustrious]∴ G[rand]∴ M[aster]∴ deemed it appropriate to prescribe in order to further the interests and glory of M[asonry]∴ to all the L[odges]∴ that recognize him as their sovereign and legitimate protector. We are therefore proud to make known to you the pleasure that we feel, and we shall not hesitate to offer you proof of the zeal that has always motivated us and which motivates us ceaselessly for the prosperity of our august and sublime Order. We accept with the blindest obedience those judicious and even essential regulations which, through their usefulness to the Royal Art, prove the sagacity and wisdom of the Prince who has laid them down, and which can only contribute further to the triumph of M[asonry]∴ and make the happiness of M[asons]∴ even sweeter and more perfect.

We are therefore engaging, M[ost]∴ R[espectable]∴ B[rother]∴, in what is both a very pleasurable experience and an indispensable duty in informing you of all the operations we have performed and all the labors we have celebrated since the establishment of our R[espectable]∴ L[odge]∴ in order that, now that we have introduced ourselves to you, you will deign to interest yourself on our behalf and procure for us, through the generosity of Our Most R[espectable]∴ and Most I[llustrious]∴ G[rand]∴ M[aster]∴, some tokens of his benevolence and protection. We dare to hope that we shall receive this if the zeal and spirit of M[asonry]∴, to which we have always been loyally devoted, can earn for us these precious favors which are the object of all our wishes and of our unanimous satisfaction.

We believed and shall always do, Most Ex[cellent]∴ B[rother]∴, that we would still be languishing in darkness if the salutary and benevolent rays of the Great Light which shine at your O[rient]∴ had not made us aware of and at the same time kindled within us a fire whose light we conserve in all its purity and with all the fervour of which true and faithful M[asons]∴ are capable.

Most R[espectable]∴ B[rother]∴, we owe the happiness we enjoy to R[espectable]∴ B[rother]∴ Estienne Morin, who is today the Deputy of your R[espectable]∴ and Sovereign L[odge]∴ under the powers granted him by the M[ost]∴ R[espectable]∴ Sc[ottish]∴ L[odge]∴ of London, further certified by the Most R[espectable]∴ Sc[ottish]∴ L[odge]∴ of Bordeaux. He was kind enough to yield to our entreaties and now, fully convinced of our zeal and the knowledge we have acquired in the Royal Art, he feels he might be able to acquire for us the reward we have long solicited from the R[espectable]∴ L[odge]∴

Française of Bordeaux. The late R[espectable]∴ B[rother]∴ Lagère, G[rand]∴ S[ublime]∴, P[erfect]∴ Sc[ots]∴ M[aster]∴, of the Most R[espectable]∴ Sc[ottish]∴ L[odge]∴ Lodge of Bordeaux, who was in this colony at that time, joined forces with him, and together they raised our august and sublime edifice, which still exists today, and which shall last for as long as we shall feel within us a burning zeal which, ending only with ourselves, will pass to those of our B[rethren]∴ who shall succeed us, who will transmit from age to age to those who follow us this noble and praiseworthy emulation and this inviolable devotion to the interests of M[asonry]∴ whose reign must surely extend [5v] until the end of time. All that we lack is your seal of approval. This is what we desire, and we flatter ourselves that we shall obtain it through those sentiments with which we are all intensely infused.

We are committed to following whatever we might be ordered to do by the R[espectable]∴ L[odge]∴ *Française* of Bordeaux. R[espectable]∴ B[rother]∴ Morin has lodged his constitutions with our R[espectable]∴ L[odge]∴ and a copy annotated with all the formalities practised among us has been delivered to him.

On the 24th of the first month of the Year of the G[reat]∴ L[ight]∴ 5757, Most R[espectable]∴ B[rother]∴ Morin, our founder, and Joseph Lagère wrote to the Most R[espectable]∴ Sc[ottish]∴ L[odge]∴ of Bordeaux informing them of the operations which they had performed on our behalf. On several occasions we have passed on this letter in what appeared to be the most secure circumstances, but we have every reason to believe that the problems caused by the war[25] have prevented it from reaching its destination. The letter we ourselves sent on behalf of our B[rethren]∴ to this Most R[espectable]∴ L[odge]∴ at the same time met with the same fate.

We also sent a letter to R[espectable]∴ B[rother]∴ Gabriel Du Feu, a member of the Most R[espectable]∴ Sc[ottish]∴ L[odge]∴, which he had kindly offered to deliver himself. In this document we told our dear and R[espectable]∴ B[rother]∴ of this L[odge]∴ how disappointed we were that the news we had sent them about our establishment had not reached them, at the same time expressing dismay at their silence. Our letter was dated the 10th day of the 3rd month, but the mishaps that the R[espectable]∴ B[rother]∴ Du Feu suffered at the hands of the enemies[26] and the sea, which forced him to put into several different ports in this colony, meant that our latest advices to the Most R[espectable]∴ Sc[ottish]∴ L[odge]∴ of Bordeaux arrived very late.

Since the moment, M[ost]∴ R[espectable]∴ B[rother]∴, that R[espectable]∴ B[rother]∴ Morin laid the foundations of our edifice we have conformed scrupulously to the laws which have been made for us and have pursued our labors with a uniformity which has never been denied. We have only admitted to our company those who have seemed to be truly worthy of our favors. We are providing you with a precise summary of all these operations such as have taken place and which you will need to imagine for yourselves, as we felt we should not try your patience with monotonous details which, without providing you with any further information, would be no less tedious and tiring for you to work through. [6r] M[ost]∴ Exc[ellent]∴ B[rother]∴, all good M[asons]∴ must take some pride in their status: it is the only occasion when this praiseworthy and virtuous emulation in which each of us must take some pride is allowed to give way within us to feelings of conceit. We shall not however speak to you only about our loyalty and utter devotion which are the first and the most necessary virtues that a M[ason]∴ must practise. Our dear R[espectable]∴ B[rother]∴ Morin told us that he had kindly made us known to your Most R[espectable]∴ and Sovereign L[odge]∴ We now dare to present ourselves before you with confidence. We are sending you a list of all the B[rethren]∴ composing our R[espectable]∴ L[odge]∴

---

25 The Seven Years' War.
26 The English, France's enemies in the Seven Years' War.

We pray that the G[reat]∴ A[rchitect]∴ of the U[niverse]∴ may abundantly shower his favors and blessings upon your Most I[llustrious]∴ and R[espectable]∴ G[rand]∴ M[aster]∴ Our prayers for his safety could not be more fervent and more far-reaching, for the prayers we are formulating for him are for the glory and prosperity of M[asonry]∴ We have sought to capture the true spirit of our august and sublime Order whereby, showing love to all in a spirit of cordiality and sincerity, we have displayed a unanimous interest in each other's happiness which, we flatter ourselves, may become perfect and fully accomplished through the protection of a Prince whose benevolent kindness and ready approachability form the entire joy and happiness of those who are subject to him – a Prince who is willing, when among the Brethren he cherishes and respects, to forget the high rank that Heaven has bestowed upon him and who yet seems to be even more worthy of it thanks to all the virtues of which he is the perfect exemplar, virtues that become so beneficial to humanity through the rules they prescribe, the duties they commend and the respect they instil.

Most R[espectable]∴ and Most Ex[cellent]∴ B[rother]∴, may Heaven answer the prayers which we are addressing to it in all the fullness of our hearts, and may it shower joy and prosperity upon you! May its most favorable influences be poured out with the most abundant profusion upon all the R[espectable]∴ B[rethren]∴ who compose your M[ost]∴ R[espectable]∴ and Sovereign L[odge]∴! May M[asonry]∴, under the auspices of its Most I[llustrious]∴ and Most R[espectable]∴ Protector, be sustained in all the brilliance and splendour that should shine forth across the surface of the Universe! May it enjoy all the growth to which it is so graciously susceptible for the glory and happiness of humanity! May the equitable laws which are today being given to us, the wise regulations which are being laid down for us, and the sublime Constitutions which are generally and [6v] uniformly prescribed to us be engraved in our hearts, and in the hearts of all M[asons]∴ who, enjoying the inconceivable advantage of being subjects of the Best of Kings, also savour the delights of serving beneath the banners of an august Prince whose fatherly and benevolent attentions create the sweetest and yet at the same time the most assured happiness of which they could ever expect to be a part. May we, forever intensely suffused with the zeal that is our motivation, redouble our work and our efforts, and through a constantly and steadily sustained emulation merit the blessings we are seeking from you. Only such blessings can and must make our satisfaction and our happiness complete. This is the sole benefit to which we aspire. It forms the object of our most tender solicitudes, of our liveliest enthusiasms and of our most ardent desires. Our powers of expression are too weak to do full justice to our feelings when we dare to entertain the pleasant and flattering hope that you will deign to look kindly upon the favors we are expecting from you given your loyalty to the interests of M[asonry]∴ as well as your zeal and affection for those who, like us, have been admitted to the celebration of these delightful and secret mysteries.

Most Ex[cellent]∴ B[rother]∴, may those who have shown themselves to be unworthy of the blessings of a mother as tender and as affectionate as M[asonry]∴ has always shown herself to be towards her children carry ceaselessly within themselves the sufferings of their ingratitude! May they see eternally within their mind's eye the inestimable happiness we enjoy in all its sweetness and gentleness! May they endlessly pine for the singular favors which have been showered upon them, despairing of ever enjoying any further favors and remaining wholly convinced of the scorn and vilification they have merited by being wholly immersed in their shameful misconduct! May they bear within them forever a vengeful remorse which, through the constant internal prickings of their conscience, forms the subject of their torture and that of our own triumph, just like those prideful and foolish spirits which, forgetful of the benefits they had received from the infinite goodness of the Sovereign Being who created them for His glory and to form the object of His most tender kindnesses, [7r] dared to raise against Him the banner of revolt! For God was as severe in His vengeance as He was generous in His gifts and chased them from the happy abode where they shared delights and pleasures within His presence and then confounded them in floods of gall and bitterness. Their mouths which, while they showed themselves to be worthy of their happiness, were open only to the most sublime harmonies no longer uttered anything other than the most awful blasphemies. From the heights of the Heavens they have been flung headlong into the deepest abyss, from the summit of glory they have fallen to the pinnacle of humiliation, and from the bosom of supreme happiness they have passed into the keenest and most painful torments, carrying ceaselessly within them the image of the blessings they have foregone. Finally, unable to rid themselves of this memory, this image serves to even further intensify the violence of the evils they endure. They know that those who remained faithful and grateful towards their divine benefactor possess a blessedness whose endlessly renewed delights will suffer neither change nor alteration. This pure and inexpressible joy which forms the reward of the blessed spirits who have remained loyal then excites even greater anger, fury and despair within these rebellious and seditious spirits, yet their struggles are criminally useless, for they can do nothing to undermine a happiness of which God Himself did not wish to limit the duration or delight.

Seal of the Symbolic L[odge]∴

L.S.

We are by the mysterious and cherished numbers known to you,

Most R[espectable]∴ and Most Ex[cellent]∴ B[rother]∴,

Your very humble and very obedient servants and B[rethren]∴

F[rançoi]s∴ Lamarque G[ran]d Sc[ots], Kn[ight]∴ of the Sun, W[orship]ful∴

G[uillaume] Molinié, S[enior]∴ W[arden]∴

Bérindoague, J[unior] W[arde]n P[ro] T[em]P[ore]

Jean Charles Simon, O[rator]∴

George, T[reasur]er∴

Gellée senior, M[ast]er O[f] C[eremonies], Elect Kn[igh]t

By Order of the R[espectable]∴ L[odge]∴ established at Les Cayes du Fond under the title of *La Concorde*.

A[lexandre] Laville, S[ecreta]ry∴

Seal of the C[hapter] of Kn[ights] of the E[ast]∴

L.S. [7v] [1 blank leaf]

No. 912 M. - Morin to Chaillon de Jonville, Port-au-Prince, July 25, 1763

My dear Sir and Most Respectable Brother,

Suffused with your kindness and always animated as I am by Masonic zeal, the aim of all my actions is to give you proof of my sincere gratitude towards you, and to give you an account both of my own conduct and that of the Brethren with whom I am most closely associated.

I had the honour of giving you my sincere testimony regarding the Most R[espectable] Lodge of Les Cayes du Fond on the Ile à Vache and its members by means of a letter[27] sent in June which was brought to you by Brother Lartigue, who left this port a few days afterwards. I have been impressed by the Brethren's conduct from that time onwards: by way of confirmation of my first letter they have given me the enclosed letter and list of their members with a request that I send them to you. Their modesty, submissiveness and yearning for the truth will be obvious to you when you read the said letter, and I am taking the liberty of encouraging them in their sweet hope that you will support them and grant them their very humble request. The R[espectable] B[rother] Villiers Deschamps[28], a King's Purser, was happy to be the bearer of this missive. He seemed to ardently desire that the commitments associated with his official position would enable him to place the letter in your hands in person. I am also anxious for you to have the opportunity of judging the personal merits and talents and worthy sentiments of this dear Brother. If he is obliged to use the post to send the letter to you, then he will lose much by not having the pleasure of making your acquaintance, which however is compensated for by the universal testimony of those who have the advantage of knowing him. My own seal of approval in this respect would carry too little weight for me to be so prideful as to recommend him to you. After all, virtue, wisdom and probity recommend themselves, and these are the feelings which I have had about him during the time he has resided here. All this merit, which may well have eluded my own dull vision, will infallibly make itself known to your own incomparable insight if he has the honour of paying you his respects.

I beg you, Sir, to continue in your kindness towards me, of which I seek to make myself worthy by the great punctiliousness and the profound respect with which I am, according to the S[acred] and My[sterious] N[umbers] and which are known to us,

My dear Sir and Most Respectable Brother,

Your very humble, very loyal and very respectful Brother,

Port-au-Prince, Morin.

July 25th, 1763.

No. 628 M. - De Villers Deschamps to Brest de la Chaussée, Brest, October 6, 1763.

Scottish L[odge]∴ *La Véritable Union*

O[rient]∴ of Brest

Brest, 6th O[cto]ber 1763

To B[rother]∴ Brest de la Chaussée

Dear Sir and Very Dear Brother,

B[rother]∴ Morin, whom I had the pleasure of seeing in Port-au-Prince and with whom I have often worked, has sent me a parcel to send to you to pass on to M[onsieur] de Joinville, your W[orshipful] He has also delivered to me a charter empowering me to establish a Lodge of G[rand] Scots in this town, but only after it has been approved by your own R[espectable]∴ L[odge]∴, our Mother Lodge. As this charter

---

27 See No. 991 M.

28 See No. 628 M.

is pasted onto canvas I dare not risk sending it by post. I hope, my dear B[rother]∴, that you will kindly obtain for me an official permission approving what B[rother]∴ Morin has done [1r] and will attach to it the title of Lodge Inspector so that I can shut down an irregular lodge which has been established in this town. Our Lodge has been established here for some 20 years and is the daughter of *L'Anglaise* of Bordeaux. I am the only Brother who holds [the degree of] Grand Scots, and all the other degrees above it. A part of our B[rethren]∴ hold high degrees, but I shall be committing myself to abolish the Scots Masonry and the Trinitarian[29] in communication with W[orshipful]∴ Le Grand and we shall then have the pleasure of writing to you and bringing ourselves under the obedience of our R[espectable]∴ M[other]∴ Lodge.

Would you kindly let me know how much it would cost to have a collar like Brother Morin's; red with the jewel of the G[rand]∴ S[cots]∴ at the bottom and the chain with the golden cordon and the pendent Sun, all in silver-gilt, and the cordon of the Knight of the East with the little sword? [1v]

I flatter myself, my dear B[rother]∴, that you will be able to perform these services for me. I would like in turn to be of some assistance to you in this country, and shall act with the enthusiasm with which I am, with the number that is known to you,

Sir and V[ery]∴ D[ear]∴ B[rother]∴,

Your very humble and very obedient servant,

De Villiers Deschamps ∴

Scottish L[odge]∴ *La Veritable Union*

O[rient]∴ of Brest [2r]

[2v/blank]

No. 629 M. - De Villers Deschamps to Pingré, Brest, December 7, 1763.

To B[rother]∴ Pingré[30]

Dear Sir and V[ery]∴ D[ear]∴ B[rother]∴,

Having informed W[orshipful]∴ B[rother]∴, Brest de la Chaussée of my plans to enable our Lodge to establish a correspondence with your own, he informed me that he was no longer in charge but that I had only to write to you, which is why, V[ery]∴ D[ear]∴ B[rother]∴, Pingré, I have chosen this route even though I have not had the pleasure of making your acquaintance. However, every Mason and all Masons enjoy this benefit, and I am taking advantage of it with all the pleasure in the world.

B[rother]∴ Brest should have spoken to you about the Constitutions that B[rother]∴ Morin gave me in Port-au-Prince on the island of Saint-Domingue which make it possible to establish in this town [3r] a L[odge]∴ of Grand M[aster]∴ and P[erfect]∴ Scots∴ It was never my intention to separate myself from our Lodge, but rather to obtain for them the Degree <which> I have long held. The Grand Sc[ots]∴ which we have in our Lodge is not the same, and furthermore perhaps in the course of time his Constitutions may allow me to establish one. I would like, my V[ery]∴ D[ear]∴ B[rother]∴, these Constitutions to be approved by your own R[espectable]∴ L[odge]∴ and for you to procure for me the powers of Inspector

---

29 *Ecossais Trinitaire*, a variant of *Ecossais de Paris*.
30 https://fr.wikipedia.org/wiki/Alexandre_Guy_Pingr%C3%A9

for all the places where I might find myself within the French Domination. It is the zeal which I have and which I have always had for M[asonry]∴ which makes me ask you to have these favors granted to me if it is possible. Kindly inform me if I must arrange for the Con[stitutio]ns of B[rother]∴ Morin to be sent to you or if you wish me to send you a summary of them. As they are pasted onto canvas I dare not risk sending them by post because [3v] the volume is too large. Perhaps you would give me your advice on this subject.

My D[ear]∴ B[rother]∴, I can only retain for the whole of my life the most perfect gratitude towards B[rother]∴ Brest who has secured for me the pleasure of corresponding with you. Even though I am not the L[odge]∴ Secretary, please allow me to occasionally take advantage of this opportunity on my own behalf, and to assure you that I shall always be, with the most perfect friendship,

Sir and V[ery]∴ D[ear]∴ B[rother]∴,

Your very humble and very obedient servant,

De Villiers Deschamps∴

Brest, 7th D[ecem]ber 1763

If there is anything in this country which you would like then please do let me know. [4r]

No. 913 M. - Morin to Brest de la Chaussée, Port-au-Prince, May 3, 1764

My V[ery] D[ear] B[rother],

It was with genuine satisfaction that I received the letter you were kind enough to send me dated December 25th last. I am pleased to learn that you now know a little more. I congratulate you with all my heart. I would ask you to embrace him on my behalf and to ensure him of my sincere friendship which I owe to him in all respects.

B[rother] de Berey, who is the bearer of the present letter, is one of my best friends. He is our Crown Prosecutor here and is going to Paris to see his native country again, but he intends to return here. He will tell you about his plans. I warmly commend him to you. He has got as far as Grand Scots and Knight Mason. He remembered your name as soon as he saw it on your letter. He was First Secretary to the Intendant when you were at Saint-Domingue in San Miguel de la Atalaya.

I am sending you three lists which, as you will see, are continuations of those I have already sent, along with the letters in duplicate for three Lodges, namely those of Saint-Marc, Les Cayes du Fond in the Ile à Vache and Port-au-Prince. I shall send these either to you or to B[rother] Devaux Dumorier to present them to the Substitute-General. As I wanted to take advantage of the opportunity presented by B[rother] de Berey's visit, I am sending you a list of each lodge since I do not have the time to ask Saint-Marc and Les Cayes to send me their letters in triplicate. I certify those lists as true, and inform you that we have expelled from our Society a Monsieur Saint Rome, an engineer, and a Monsieur Laforeade, a merchant of this town, who have failed in the most essential obligations of our Secret Constitutions, being leaders of a conspiracy and disrupters of the basic harmony of Freemasonry.

The first of these, Saint Rome, is a Knight of Saint-Louis. He belonged to the lodge in Nantes which rebelled, and which refused to recognize the Prince de Clermont as our Grandmaster.

There is also a lodge in Le Cap called *Édouard Stuard* [31] which is similarly composed and which we certainly do not want to recognize.

B[rother] de Berey will reimburse you the relevant amount for each of the lodges on the enclosed list. I beg you not to forget about this.

B[rother] de Berey promised me that he would obtain for you a grey parrot, since I myself was still unable to find one as I would have liked. You will receive the parrot at the first opportunity along with two chitterlings from Macouba and Saint-Domingue.

Write to me often, my dear, with your news: then all your friends will be my friends also.

Send me, I beg of you, one or two jewels of the Prince of Jerusalem, which is a set of scales, along with the Small Formulary of the Order.[32]

B[rother] de Berey will reimburse you for everything. My warmest greetings to all our brothers and sisters. I will write to you at greater length in a fortnight. I remain, my dear friend and B[rother], sincerely yours,

Morin, merchant at Port-au-Prince

At Port-au-Prince, May 3rd, 1764.

I would kindly ask you to introduce B[rother] de Berey to B[rother] de Joinville [sic].

As I pointed out to you in my previous letter, when I embarked at Bordeaux to travel to America I was captured by the enemy of the French State and taken to England. I spent two months in London, where Earl Ferrest, Grand Master of all the Lodges under English jurisdiction, has appointed me Inspector of its jurisdiction for the part of the New World and has bestowed on me the sublime degrees by giving me a certificate stating that I alone am able to establish lodges of Scottish Grand Elect, Knight and Prince Mason.[33] I will share with you some of these rarities, which I admire and of which I am overcome with joy at being the depositary.

No. 604 M. - La Parfaite Union and Morin to The Grand Lodge of France, Port-au-Prince, May 3, 1764.

Port-au-Prince

Island of S[ain]t Domingue

May 3rd, 1764

List or Table

of the BB[rethr]en composing the Regular Lodge of Port-au-Prince under the title of *La Parfaite Union*, constituted by the R[especta]ble Lodge of Grand Perfect Elect Sublime Scots & Knight

---

31 Morin would loose his deputy powers to Brother Martin of the Grand Lodge on July 17, 1766. Martin arrives shortly after and finds all three lodges in Cap Français to be irregular. He regularizes the clandestine lodge *Édouard Stuard* to the horror of the existing lodges, renaming it *Le Vérité* in 1767, and establishing it as the beachhead for the Grand Lodge.

32 Morin requests a copy of the ritual of Prince of Jerusalem and its regalia, meaning he did not yet have it in August of 1764.

33 This is a reference to Morin's creation of Sublime Prince of the Royal Secret as he requests a copy of the ritual for Prince of Jerusalem and its regalia just a few lines above.

Appendix B

Masons of the Orient of S[ain]t Marc, to serve as a duplicate to their Letters of the 2ᵈ and 22ᵈ of June 1763 requesting the Grand and Sovereign Lodge of France to approve their previous labors and ratify their constitution.

Berthomieux, Sea-Capt[ai]n and Merchant, Deputy of the R[espectable] L[odge] of S[ain]t Marc for their installation, G[ran]d Perf[ec]t El[ect] M[aste]r & S[ubli]me Scots...[34] Kn[igh]t P[rin]ce Mason.

Texier, Captain of Hussars, Merchant, G[ran]d Perf[ec]t El[ect] M[aste]r & S[ubli]me Sc[ot]s, Kn[igh]t P[rin]ce Mason.

Sauveur Balanqué, Sea-Capt[ai]n, G[ran]d Perf[ec]t El[ect] M[aste]r & S[ubli]me Sc[ot]s, Kn[igh]t P[rin]ce Mason.

Rouzier, King's Receiver of confiscations, escheats, fines etc., G[ran]d Perf[ec]t El[ect] M[aste]r & S[ubli]me Sc[ot]s, Kn[igh]t P[rin]ce Mason.

Pascal Le Comte, Merchant, G[ran]d Perf[ec]t El[ect] M[aste]r & S[ubli]me Sc[ot]s, Kn[igh]t P[rin]ce M[as]on.

Delangrené, Crown Architect, Inspector of the Royal Highways, First Syndic of this town, G[ran]d Perf[ec]t El[ect] M[aste]r & S[ubli]me Sc[ot]s, Kn[igh]t P[rin]ce M[as]on.

De Berey, Crown Prosecutor, G[ran]d Perf[ec]t El[ect] M[aste]r & S[ubli]me Sc[ot]s, Kn[igh]t P[rin]ce M[as]on.

Vence, Merchant, G[ran]d Perf[ec]t El[ect] M[aste]r and Subl[i]me Scots.

Gabriel Rasteau Maison, Merch[an]t, G[ran]d Perf[ec]t El[ect] M[aste]r & S[ubli]me Sc[ot]s.

Aimé Gautier, Merch[an]t, G[ran]d Perf[ec]t El[ect] M[aste]r & Subl[i]me Sc[ot]s.

Lériés, Merchant, G[ran]d Perf[ec]t El[ect] M[aste]r & Sub[li]me Sc[ot]s.

Dubault, Merchant, G[ran]d Perf[ec]t El[ect] M[aste]r & Sub[li]me Sc[ot]s.

<*Osson de Verrières*[35], S[y]m[bolic] M[aste]r and Perfect M[aste]r>

Lagneau de Larisse, Crown Engineer, M[aste]r M[as]on

Geslin, Merchant, M[aste]r Mason.

Lartigue, Sea-captain, M[aste]r Mason.

Barret, Sea-captain, M[aste]r Mason.

Baron, Sea-captain, Fell[o]w M[as]on.

Gastumeau, Merch[an]t, App[renti]ce Mason.

L.S.

---

34 Ellipsis in original.
35 See Sachse, *Old Masonic lodges of Pennsylvania*, p. 254, https://archive.org/details/cu31924021433309

| Delangrené, Kn[igh]t Ma[s]on, Or[ator] | Rouzier | F Dubault, Secretary. |

Certified: that the present list is in conformity with that which has already been sent to the Grand Lodge of France as a duplicate as well as with the Request of May 3ᵈ, 5764.

Morin, G[ran]d Perf[ec]t El[ect] M[aste]r and S[ubli]me Sc[ot]s, Kn[igh]t P[rin]ce Mason, of the Lodge of *P[arfai]te Harmonie*.

Approved: the interlinear addition for B[rother] Osson de Verrières who was omitted. M[orin]∴[5r] [5v/blank]

No. 609 M. - La Concorde to Brest de la Chaussée, Les Cayes, May 3, 1764.

III

From an enlightened place where, in a sweet and tender harmony, there ceaselessly reign silence, concord and peace, at the O[rient]∴ of Les Cayes du Fond, Île à Vache, on the Island and Coast of Saint-Domingue, on the 3ᵈ day of the eleventh month of the Year of the G[reat]∴ L[ight]∴ 5764, and according to the Vulgar Calculation 3ᵈ May 1764.

To the Most R[espectable]∴ and Most Ex[cellent]∴ B[rother]∴ Brest de la Chaussée, Grand Guardian of the Seals and Archivist of the Premier and Sovereign Lodge of France under the title of *Saint-Antoine* in Paris,

Most R[espectable]∴ and Most Ex[cellent]∴ B[rother]∴,

We are taking the liberty of addressing to you the letter which we are presenting to your R[espectable]∴ and Sovereign L[odge]∴, for into whose hands can we better entrust it than into your own which Our Most R[espectable]∴ and M[ost]∴ I[llustrious]∴ G[rand]∴ M[aster]∴ has judged worthy of looking after the august and sacred deposit of our most sublime M[aster]∴, The R[espectable]∴ B[rother]∴ Morin to whom we are indebted for the knowledge we have acquired in the R[oyal]∴ A[rt]∴ as he laid the foundations of our R[espectable]∴ L[odge]∴, kindly wanted us to have a new Lodge, informing us to whom we could pass on the advice of which we are making you the depositary and thus proving to ourselves the pleasure of entering into correspondence with you. We hope that, on the basis of the testimony he has already submitted to Your R[espectable]∴ and Sovereign L[odge]∴ and the further testimony regarding us which he is promising to render today that we shall receive the reward for our zeal, [8r] devotion and labors. We dare to expect these blessings from our Most I[llustrious]∴ and R[espectable]∴ G[rand]∴ M[aster]∴, whose protection and benevolence extends over all those who, like ourselves, derive genuine satisfaction from serving under his banner, and who are loyal not just to the prescriptions relating to the duties which we have to fulfil but also to any future ones. We beg you, Most R[espectable]∴ B[rother]∴, to grant us your intercession in this matter, for it can only be of the greatest usefulness to us. We are requesting this only because we believe ourselves to be worthy of it thanks to the feelings within us which shall remain eternally engraved there for the glory and prosperity of Masonry, which forms the sincerest object of our labors and the sweetest delight of our leisure.

May the G[reat]∴ A[rchitect]∴ of the U[niverse]∴ shower upon you, M[ost]∴ Ex[cellent]∴ B[rother]∴, His most precious favors and most abundant blessings. These are our sincere and ardent wishes for your

Appendix B

happiness which would be lacking in nothing if they were to be wholly fulfilled.

We are, with the feelings that are due and known to you, and by all the sublime, secret and mysterious numbers,

Most R[espectable]∴ and Most Ex[cellent]∴ B[rother]∴,

Your very humble and very obedient servants,

F[rançois] Lamarque, W[orship]ful

Bérindoague

Jean Charles Simon, O[rator]∴

J[acques] Skerret

George, T[reasur]er

A[lexandre] Laville

Gellée senior, M[ast]er O[f]∴ T[he]∴, Kn[igh]ts Elect

French, S[ecreta]ry P[ro]∴ T[empore]∴ [8v] [1 blank leaf]

No. 611M. - La Concorde to Brest de la Chaussée, Les Cayes, May 3, 1764.

V

<u>Symbolic Lodge</u>[36]

Catalogue of Brethren composing the W[orshipful]∴ Symbolic L[odge]∴ of Les Cayes du Fond, l'Île à Vache, southern part of S[ain]t Domingue, under the gracious title of *La Concorde*.

Estienne Morin, Deputy Inspector of the Sovereign Lodges of France and England and Founder of the Lodge

Officers Dignitaries

J[ea]n Charles Simon, inhabitant of Le Fond, Worshipful Master

François Lamarque, merch[an]t at Les Cayes, Past Worshipful Master

Guillaume Mollinier, merchant at Les Cayes, Senior Warden

Jean George, merchant at Les Cayes, Junior Warden

Laurent Cholet, inhabitant at Le Fond, Orator

---

36 Cf. Dr. André Kervella, The First Masonic Lodges in Saint-Domingue (trans. by Murray Alford) in Harashim 75, July 2017, available online at https://issuu.com/harashimed/docs/harashim_75_july__2017

Nicolas Gellée de Boiron, inhabitant at Le Fond, Secretary

Claude Gellée senior, inhabitant at Le Fond, Treasurer

Delmas, merchant at Les Cayes, M[aste]r of Ceremonies.

Brethren

Martin Bérindoague, representing the Founder by the Letters Patent granted to him[37]

Daniel Suire, merchant at Les Cayes

Jacques Skerret, ditto[38]

Alexandre Laville, ditto

J[ean] Jacques Texier ditto

Paschal Comte, merchant at Port-au-Prince

Marraud Hue[39], inhabitant of Marchaterre

Castaing, merch[an]t at Les Cayes

Alexandre Proa, ditto

Thomas Gazan, ditto

Georges La Frézelière[40], inhabitant at Le Fond [9r]

Rolain, inhabitant at L'Islet

Pargon, merch[an]t at Les Cayes

Glié, inhabitant at Jean Deshayes

Souler, inhabitant at Lacul

Joseph Le Délié, inhabitant at Les Anses

Arthur French, merchant at Les Cayes

Joly, ditto

Le Febure des Hayes, inhabitant at L'Islet

Daniel Charpentier, ditto

Verguiol de S[ain]t Hillaire, inhabitant at Les Savanettes

Trigant de Beaumont, inhabitant at Le Fond

Meynieu, merchant at Les Cayes

---

37 Martin Bérindoague was made a Deputy Inspector General by Morin in 1764, for the southern part of Saint Domingue.
38 James Skerret was an Irish merchant naturalized in Saint Domingue in 1767.
39 Actually Hugues.
40 This would seem to be the correct spelling.

Tournér the younger, ditto

Gizot, sea-captain

Tournade de S[ain]te Colombe, inhabitant at Aquin

Germain Mercent, Notary Royal at Le Fond

Ambroise Gouin, inhabitant at L'Islet

Blactot de la Piardiere, merchant at Les Cayes

Le Noir, merchant at the said place[41]

Absent Brethren

Sauveur Balanqué[42] corsair captain} in France

Mouson[43,] ditto}

Pierre Lambert, inhabitant of Cavaillon[44]   }

Plunket, inhabitant de Tiburon   }

Tison de Langlade, Captain   } in the *Régiment*

Gellée de Prémion, Lieutenant   } *de Boulonnais*

Lefebure du Plessis, Lieutenant   } in France

L.S.

By Order of

the W[orshipful]∴ Lodge

Gellée de Boirond

Secretary. [9v]

No. 613 M. - La Concorde to Brest de la Chaussée, Les Cayes, May 3, 1764.

III

<u>Chapter of Elects</u>

Catalogue of the Knight Brothers who compose the Chapter of Elects of Les Cayes du Fond, L'Île à Vache, southern part of S[ain]t Domingue

---

41   Presumably an estate called Le Noir.

42   Captain of La Parfaite in 1748. Cf. https://tinyurl.com/y7osw3cd

43   Probably the Moulson [sic] who was skippering La Sophie in 1783, cf. Nouveau Code des Prises, vol. III, 1800, p. 207-8. https://tinyurl.com/y8nycopq

44   Pierre Lambert de Lintot, would later go to England and establish his own lodge and integrate the French high degrees into the milieu of the English high degrees in 1780.

Estienne Morin, Deputy Inspector of Sovereign Lodges of France and England, and Founder of the Chapter

Alexandre Laville, Most Illustrious Grandmaster

Jean George, Warden

Jean Charles Simon, Orator

Nicolas Gellée de Boiron, Secretary

Claude Gellée senior, Treasurer

Delmas, Master of Ceremonies

Illustrious Brethren

Martin Bérindoague, representing the Founder by Letters Patent granted to him

François Lamarque

Delmas

Jean J[acqu]es Texier

Gazan

Paschal Comte, at Port-au-Prince

Gellée

Jacques Skerret

Nicolas Gellée de Boiron

Guillaume Mollinier

George La Fresseliere

Daniel Suire

Rollain

Laurent

Cholet

Ferrier

Hugues Marraud

Glier

Sauveur Ballanqué in France

Castaing

Le Delié

Alexandre Proa

Joly

<u>Absent Illustrious B^{ren}</u>

Lambert   }

Plunket   } In France

L.S.

By Order of the Most Illustrious Chapter

Gellée de Boîrond

Sec[retary]

[12v] [12r/blank]

No. 612 M. - La Concorde to Brest de la Chaussée, Les Cayes, May 3, 1764.

VI

<u>Scots Lodge</u>

Catalogue of the Worshipful and I[llustri]ous∴ B[reth]ren∴ composing the R[espectable]∴ L[odge]∴ of Perfect Elect, Grand and Sublime Scots of Les Cayes du Fond, Île à Vache, southern part of Saint-Domingue.

Estienne Morin, Deputy Inspector of the Sovereign Lodges of France and England, and Founder of the R[espectable]∴ L[odge]∴

François Lamarque, Respectable Grandmaster

Alexandre Laville, Senior Grand Warden

Jean Charles Simon, Junior Grand Warden

Laurent Cholet, Grand Orator

Guillaume Mollinier, Grand Master of Ceremonies

Jacques Skerret, Grand Secretary

Jean George, Grand Treasurer

Worshipful Brethren

Martin Bérindoague, representing the Founder by the Letters Patent granted to him

Jean Jacques Texier

Daniel Suire

Hugues Marraud

Paschal Comte at Port-au-Prince

Sauveur Balanqué in France

Castaing

Alexandre Proa

Delmas

Gazan

Gellée senior

Gellée de Boiron

George La Frésséliere

Rolin

L.S.

By Order of the R[espectable]∴ Scottish L[odge]∴

J[acques] Skerret
Sec[retary] G[enera]l
[14r] [14v/blank]

No. 614 M. - La Concorde to Brest de la Chaussée, Les Cayes, May 3, 1764.

IIII

Council of the Knights of the East

Catalogue of the Excellent Knight Princes of the East of Les Cayes du Fond, Île à Vache, in the southern part of Saint-Domingue

Estienne Morin, Deputy Inspector of the Sovereign Lodges of France and England, and Founder of the Council

J[ea]n Charles Simon, Sovereign Prince

G[uillau]me Molinier, Army General acting as S[enio]r W[arde]n

J[ea]n George, Grand Treasurer acting as J[unio]r W[arde]n

Alexandre Laville, Minister[45], acting as Orator

Jacques Skerret[46], Grand Guardian of the Seals a[ctin]g as S[ecreta]ry∴

---

45   In the religious sense I assume.

46   Garrigus, in Before Haiti: Race and Citizenship in French Saint-Domingue (Palgrave) refers to Skerret as an Irishman who was

Appendix B

Martin Bérindoague, representing the Founder by Letters Patent granted to him

F[rançoi]s Lamarque

J[ea]n Jacques Texier

Laurent Cholet

Daniel Suire

Hugues Marraud

Paschal Comte, at Port-au-Prince

Sauveur Ballanqué, in France

Castaing

L.S.

By Order of the Excellent Knight Princes

J[acques] Skerret, Grand Guardian [of the Seals]

[10r] [10v/blank]

No. 615 M. - La Concorde to Brest de la Chaussée, Les Cayes, May 3, 1764.

G[rand] C[ouncil] of the Kn[igh]ts

of the E[ast]∴ &

of the W[orshipful]∴, P[rin]ces

of J[erusalem]∴

Catalogue of the M[ost]∴ W[orshipful]∴ P[rin]ces composing the G[rand]∴ C[ouncil]∴ of the Kn[igh]ts of the E[ast]∴ and of the W[orshipful]∴, P[rin]ces∴ of J[erusalem]∴, established at the O[rient]∴ of Les Cayes du Fond, L'Île à Vache, southern part of the island of Saint-Domingue in America, by 18 Degrees North Latitude.

Estienne Morin, Founder, Deputy Inspector of the Sovereign L[odge]∴ of France and England in the New World.

Martin Bérindoague, inhabitant at La Plaine du Fond, L'Île à Vache, representing the Founder by the Letters Patent granted to him.

François Lamarque, merch[ant] at Les Cayes, Vice-Deputy by the Letters Patent granted to him by the Founder, G[rand]∴ S[enior]∴ W[arden]∴

---

naturalised. Cf. https://www.palgrave.com/us/book/9781403971401

Guillaume Molinié, merch[an]t at Les Cayes, G[rand]∴ J[unior]∴ W[arden]∴

Jacques Skerret, merchant at Les Cayes, G[rand]∴ O[rator]∴

Jean Charles Simon, inhabitant at La Plaine du Fond, G[rand]∴ Secr[etar]y∴ G[ene]ral

Jean George, merchant at Les Cayes, G[rand]∴ T[reasurer]∴

Laurent Cholet, inhabitant at La Plaine du Fond, G[rand]∴ M[aste]r∴ of C[eremonies]∴

Daniel Suire, merch[an]t at Les Cayes, G[rand]∴ Almoner. [11r]

Alexandre Laville, merchant at Les Cayes

at the O[rient]∴ of Les Cayes du Fond, Île à Vache in the year of the G[reat]∴ L[ight]∴ 5765 and according to the Vulgar Calculation the 9th June 1765.

L.S.

By Order of the G[rand]∴ C[ouncil]∴ of Kn[igh]ts of the E[ast]∴ and of the W[orshipful]∴, P[rin]ces∴ of J[erusalem]∴

J[ea]n Charles Simon

Secr[eta]ry∴ G[ene]ral

[11v]

No. 914 M. - Morin to Deveaux du Mourier, Port-au-Prince, August 28, 1764

To Monsieur Devaux, Paris

Port-au-Prince, August 28th, 1764

My Most R[espectable] B[rother],

It was with real satisfaction that I received, via Chevalier de Villeneuve, your letter of S[eptem]ber 10th, 1763 and that of O[cto]ber 14th of the same year. I would never have forgiven you my dear Brother if you had not sent this gentleman to m[e]. He seemed to have all the qualities required for our R[espectable] Society. I did however receive him as a Brother without mystery. I am so grateful to you for enabling me to make his acquaintance. He left here during the past few days in search of Monsieur Lefranc, his uncle, who lives at Fond-des-Blancs. I obtained a carriage for him and he has already returned.

During my stay in England I received the sad news of the death of Brother Lacorne. I shall genuinely miss him.

It was with great pleasure that I learned of all the changes which have been made since my departure and the installation of the R[espectable] B[rother] Chaillon de Jonville as our Substitute-General.

I have notified our Lodges of all these changes. They are getting ready to address their petitions to the Grand Lodge. Over a period of some two years now we have written several letters to Brother De La Chaussée, but always without receiving any confirmation that the Grand Lodge has received and recorded them. I am speaking on behalf of the three Lodges of this colony, namely La Concorde in Saint-Marc, La

Concorde in Les Cayes and La Parfaite Union in Port-au-Prince. The last of these is the daughter lodge of the lodge in Saint-Marc. All these three lodges have sent their petitions several times (as well as mine) giving an account of their work. They have also sent a list of their members, degrees and civil status, just as your new regulations specify.

We have celebrated the health and prosperity of your new Lodge called S[ain]t Pierre. I wish you every success, as I am assured that its members will be amongst the best instructed. No one has a better grasp of M[asonry] than yourself and I regret all those moments that I am unable to spend with you.

During my trip to England I made a side-visit to Scotland where I met a capable man in Edinburgh. In fact, I spent 3 months with the most zealous Mason I have ever known. I can assure you that I am keeping our Grand Order in line and that I have made some discoveries which I will send you when I have an opportune moment which I received from a Brother who will be able to make sense of them. The dear Brother Brunet whom I embrace with all my heart is never forgotten amongst us. We have just welcomed Brother Pradines, a member of the same Order. He is our curé and is a very worthwhile acquisition.

I beg you, my dear Brother, to send me the Constitutions for this part of the world in my capacity as an Inspector which my various titles have acquired for me along with those that the Grand Lodge of England has granted me on the back of the patent which the R[espectable] B[rother] Chaillon de Jonville also granted me, signed by all the Masters of the Grand Lodge which are to be found in the said assembly.

M[onsieu]r Jean Cottin *fils aîné* c/o M[onsieur] Cottin, director of the Compagnie des Indes, place Vendôme,[47] should receive an order from Monsieur Pierre Isaac Rastau of La Rochelle to set aside the necessary sums which have to be paid under the new regulations of the [Grand] Lodge of France: if he has not been informed about this I beg you, my Dear Brother, to do so and to mention us to Brother Lartigue in Bordeaux or Monsieur Isaac Rastau, merchant, of La Rochelle, who will reimburse you.

I am, with most sincere feelings of friendship my Dear and R[espectable] B[rother], your very humble and very obedient servant and brother,

Morin

We have here M[onsieur]Comte d'Estin, a new General, and M[onsieur]de Magon, as Surveyor. Would it be possible for me to make use of your services to get hold of the letters of recommendation from Le Bouton? I would be infinitely obliged.

Please note that my address is "M[onsieur]Estienne Morin, merchant, Port-au-Prince". There is another Morin here, so please put Estienne Morin to distinguish me".

Please send my very best wishes to Madame, our dear sister, and to all our brothers and sisters.

Monsieur Duchaine, who will hand you this letter, has been granted a licence to set up a printing-press in this town. He is a very honourable man, and I beg you to give him all the assistance you can. He will deal with your dispatches for me and with all the orders which may wish to send to me relating to all those matters where you think I can be of assistance. Please send the mail for the Lodge and myself to "Monsieur Gabriel Rateau, merchant, at Port-au-Prince, Saint-Domingue".

---

47 Jean Cottin de Fieulaine married Marie-Anne du Rocher de Langadie in 1756 and was enobled by King Louis in 1764.

No. 915 M. - Morin to Lantoine and Daubertin, Port-au-Prince, March 7, 1765

From the Lodge *La Parfaite Harmonie* at the Orient of Port-au-Prince,

Island and Coast of Saint-Domingue, this 11th day of the 9th month of the Masonic Year 5765 or March 7th, 1765 AD.

M[ost]∴ RR[espectable]∴BB[rethren]∴ (Lantoine and Dauburtin for Daruty.)

By virtue of the powers that your Grand and Sovereign Lodge granted me in the second month of the Masonic year 5760, or in the ordinary style August 28th, 1761, signed by the M[ost] R[espectable] B[rother] Chaillon de Jonville, Substitute-General, De la Corne, Brest De La Chaussée, Maximilien de Saint Simon, Savalete de Buchelay, Saunier, Topin, Comte de Choisel, Boucher de Lenoncourt and Herbin, which powers duly appoint me Inspector of all LL[odges]∴ of America under French jurisdiction and Worshipful Master in perpetuity of a Symbolic Lodge *La Parfaite Harmonie* with the right to open this lodge wherever I can establish my residence.

The unfortunate events that befell me between my departure from France and my arrival in Saint-Domingue have deprived me for a long time now of the delicate satisfaction that all good Masons should feel when working on the further expansion of the Royal Art.

However, as soon as I arrived in Saint-Domingue, I started to use my authority by visiting and inspecting the LL[odges] which had already been established. I sent details of my work to the M[ost] R[espectable] B[rother] Chaillon de Jonville, our Substitute-General, in specific letters dated 21st July 1763. In reply this R[espectable] B[rother] sent me the new statutes and regulations adopted by the 14 Commissioners on November 25th, 1762.

The LL[odges] which I had the pleasure of visiting and inspecting in accordance with my powers were very happy to agree to having you ratify their constitutions, approve their work and offer them your protection. They addressed duplicates of their petitions, one dated February 26th, 1763, the other dated June 28th of the same year, to the M[ost] RR[espectable] BB[rethren] De La Chaussée and Devaux du Mourier, who were more than willing to assume the task of presenting them to your R[espectable] G[rand] and S[ublime] L[odge] in the same way as the Catalogue of the BB[rethren] who are members of their own Lodges.

The petitioning Lodges are:

1. *La Concorde* of Les Cayes du Fond, Ile à Vache.

2. *La Concorde* of Saint-Marc.

3. *La Parfaite Union* of Port-au-Prince.

So that you do not find me in default upon the arrival of the new Statutes and Regulations I have already chosen several BB[rethren] members of different regularly constituted LL[odges], either within the colony, or in France to form my L[odge]. *La Parfaite Harmonie*. I open it once or twice a month and have good reason to be satisfied with the eagerness to learn that all our dear BB[rethren] display. This is our sole activity, with the exception of the admission of two proselytes whose virtues certainly make them worthy to know the true light.

I enclose the catalogue of the BB[rethren] who compose the Lodge *La Parfaite Harmonie*. I hope that you will extend your friendship to them and to me also. We for our part shall not cease to wish you every success in your own work.

Brother Gourdon, a half-pay captain following the Boulonnais Regiment, who is the bearer of this letter, is a zealous Mason, a son of the Lodge *La Parfaite Union* in Port-au-Prince, and an associate member of the Lodge *La Parfaite Harmonie*. We cannot express how upset our BB[rethren] were at his departure. For my part I cannot give better testimony of my own feelings and of the case that I would make on his behalf than by recommending him to you and informing you that he is well deserving of your favors. It is however my official duty to inform you that he has already visited LL[odges] which are unknown to us. I think we should have a copy of the table of regular LL[odges] in France and her overseas dependencies, and in particular those of Paris. This would be a very good way of avoiding abuses.

As my stay in Port-au-Prince is open-ended and my business often calls me elsewhere, please ask the M[ost] R[espectable] BB[rethren] to send whatever I have had the opportunity of asking you for to B[rother] Pradines, curé of Port-au-Prince.

May the G[reat] A[rchitect] of T[he] U[niverse] shower his benign influence upon you.

I am, with the most fraternal friendship by the M[ysteriou]s N[um]bers that unite us, MM[ost] RR[espectable] B[rethren],

Your very affectionate

servant and B[rother] Morin, W[orshipful] of *La Parfaite Harmonie*.

No. 605 M. - The Grand Lodge of France to Morin, Paris, March 10, 1765.

B[rother] Morin at S[ain]t Domingue

March 10th, 1765

The Grand Lodge is ordering me to send to you the enclosed package containing the three Constitutions for Port-au-Prince, S[ain]t Marc and Les Cayes S[ain]t Louis. We beg you to convene these Lodges as soon as the package is received. By the present letter we authorize you to perform this convocation and to preside at the meeting of each of these Lodges, and at the s[ai]d meeting and not on any other occasion to open the package to install each Master after you have received from them their Oath of Submission to the G[rand] L[odge], to their Mother Lodge, to the G[rand] M[aster], and to his Substitute, and of their loyalty to the Regulations, a copy of which we are ~~enclosing~~ sending to each of these Lodges along with a table of all the regular Lodges. You will also draw up a report of all these proceedings which you will send at the first opportunity to the G[rand] L[odge] You will also attach a separate table of the s[ai]d Lodges with the ~~status~~ degrees and Masonic dates and the civil status of each Brother.

We have received from our D[ear] B[rother] Rasteau of La Rochelle the sum of 153^{ff} to cover the cost of the said 3 constitutions as ~~stated~~ as fixed by the regulations, and of a further 9^{ff} in reimbursement of the postage costs for a package addressed to our D[ear] B[rother] Devaux du Morier.

We are sure that the acquisition of the Members which compose the three Lodges in which you are interested will contribute to the honour enjoyed by the Order. We flatter ourselves and give you our word upon it that we shall contribute to it by illuminating them with your Light.

We wish you happiness, greetings and prosperity and ~~we~~ ask the G[reat] A[rchitect] of T[he] U[niverse] to keep you, V[ery] D[ear] B[rother], in His holy and worthy protection.[6r] [6v/blank]

No. 606 M. - La Parfaite Union to The Grand Lodge of France, Port-au-Prince, June 23, 1765.

From the Orient of Port au Prince on the island of S[ain]t Domingue from a very enlightened and secret place where silence, peace and perfect union constantly reign, in the Year of Light 5765 and on the 23ᵈ day of the 6ᵗʰ month.

To the Most Respectable Grand Sovereign Lodge of France.

Most Respectable and Worshipful Brethren,

We have received with the very greatest delight the Constitutions which your Most Respectable Grand and Sovereign Lodge has kindly granted us.

As the R[espectable] B[rother] Morin has been absent from this colony for some time he is not here to be able to fulfil the intentions which you have laid down for him in a letter which was sent to his address. During his departure for Jamaica, where he is currently to be found, he entrusted our Lodge *La Parfaite Union* with the task of opening indiscriminately any packages that might be addressed to him, and as for those which concerned the establishment of our Lodge he instructed us to comply with everything that he might be ordered to do. This is the course of action which we have followed with exactitude, as you will see from the report on our installation which we are sending you today, and [7r] which has been put in hand by the W[orshipful] B[rother] Lamarque as representative of and in conformity with the wishes of the R[espectable] B[rother] Morin our Inspector-General. We also enclose the list of the Officers and Members who currently make up our Lodge.

We beg you, Most Respectable Brother, to believe us when we say that nothing can equal our zeal and ardour in our efforts to propagate the Royal Order. Be assured that we shall never depart from this noble desire, and that we shall try to offer you proofs of that through the exactitude and the submissiveness with which we shall follow everything that emanates and shall ever emanate from the sublime lights of your R[espectable] Lodge and the wisdom that prevails there. It has already provided us with the most appropriate means of perfecting the condition of our illustrious society through the uniformity which you have established in all the Lodges. May labors that are so glorious and so worthy of your operations be showered upon you and upon all those who are subject to them! May the blessings of the Great Architect of the Universe reproduce eternally before your eyes the living image of this wise King who laid the foundations our Respectable Society by raising the superb edifice which the hands of our Brethren constructed to be consecrated to the temple of the true God! Finally, may your wise direction re-establish it forever in our hearts and [7v] bring us one day the reward which the Great Architect of the Universe reserves for us in the Celestial Lodge!

We are, with the most fraternal feelings, and through all the honours due to you,

Most Respectable & Worshipful Brethren,

Your very humble and affectionate Brothers,

Appendix B

C. Gautier, W[orship]ful M[aste]r P[rin]ce of Jer[usale]m

F[rançoi]s∴ Lamarque, Vice-Deputy of the L[odge]∴ *Les Frères Reunis* of Les Cayes, P[rin]ce M[aso]n &c

A. Castaing, S[enior] W[arden]

Boyer, J[unior] W[arde]n

By order of the Lodge *La Parfaite Union*

De Gradine, S[ecretary] P[ro] T[empore]

No. 181 M. - Poncet to François Lamarque, Léogane, July 19, 1765.

From Léogane, July 19th, 1765.

My dear uncle, I have a favor to ask of you, which I believe it will be easy for you to grant me, namely to obtain for me the Letters of Constitution of a Symbolic and Scottish Lodge on behalf of the town of Léogane under the title of *L'Amitié indissoluble*. These Letters must come directly from the Grandmaster our Wor[shipful] B[rother] the Comte de Clermont, but it must be done promptly. This Order is very much respected in five places in our New World, where there are five different Lodges in correspondence with each other. Our Wor[shipful] died three months ago: he alone, through his Letters Patent, had the right to constitute a Lodge, but he did not do this while he was alive, with the result that our labors would become useless if we continued without the approval of the other Lodges. This is what we have tried to anticipate this by writing to various Wor[shipfuls] who have agreed to recognize us for a period of one year, once that year has expired we have to either be constituted or cease all our labors. As we at Léogane have always been known for our punctiliousness I would be dismayed, having been elected to replace the deceased, to see the most united and best-composed Lodge in the Colony fail under my leadership.

<I beg you, my very D[ea]r B[rother]∴, to kindly take into consideration everything I have described above. In this matter I am acting solely for the benefit of Masonry, and I agree to submit to and fulfil everything that might be deemed appropriate[48], I shall oblige you, Your servant and B[rother],

Meeting of November 26th, 1765.

Poncet>

<W[orship]ful Jean Ba[ptis]te Bernard Esquire, Quartermaster Royal and Director of Mails ~~at Leganne~~ at Léogane.>[1r] [1v/blank] [2r/blank] [2v/blank]

No. 610 M. – Martin Bérindoague to Bassett, Les Cayes, July 30, 1765.

IV

---

48 This paragraph appears to be in a different hand to the rest of the letter.

Article 32

Meeting of August 12th, 1765

Sir, M[ost]∴ R[espectable]∴ P[rin]ce∴ and B[rother]∴,

Written to the W[orship]ful B[other] Basset at La Rochelle

July 30th, 1765

By Letters Patent sent to me by the R[espectable]∴ B[rother]∴ Morin dated the fifth day of the first month of the M[asoni]c∴ Year 5764 and by virtue of the powers that your S[overeign]∴ L[odge]∴, Our Mother, has granted him by bestowing upon him the title of Deputy Inspector of the G[rand]∴ and S[overeign]∴ L[odge]∴ of France and England for the New World, by the said Letters Patent he has appointed me in his stead Deputy for the southern part of Saint-Domingue. I would be sincerely flattered, my Respectable Brother, if your Grand and S[overeign]∴ L[odge]∴, Our Mother Lodge, would confirm the choice of our R[espectable]∴ and much-loved B[rother]∴ Morin who departed a short while ago for Jamaica.

He has enjoined me, my R[espectable]∴ B[rother]∴, to send you once a year the catalogues of all the L[odges]∴ of my Orient. I am sending you these under this cover, and I beg you to present them to each L[odge]∴ on my behalf and upon that of all our B[rethren]∴ As we are unable in this country to have everything we might need, in the absence of the seal for each L[odge]∴ I would like to make it clear to you that I have used for all the catalogues the seal of the Sc[ottish]∴ L[odge]∴, not having any other. [14r]

I am entrusting this parcel to our dear and R[espectable]∴ B[rother]∴ Jean-Jacques Texier who is leaving to complete his Residency in Bordeaux. I beg you to have delivered to him at his address all the parcels you would like to send us.

<u>Some time ago we sent you the sum of fifty or so livres via B[rother]∴ Rasteau, the S[enio]r∴ W[arden]∴ of the L[odge]∴ of La Rochelle, to meet the costs of our affiliation.</u>

Last year the R[espectable]∴ B[rother]∴ Morin sent me the statutes and regulations which you addressed to him. I have kept a copy of them, but as these statutes and regulations relate only to the Symbolic L[odge]∴, we would be delighted if you would do us the favor of informing us of the manner in which we have to work in the other superior L[odges]∴. I do however think that our operations do not differ from yours because [14v] we were founded by the R[espectable]∴ B[rother]∴ Estienne Morin in 1757, and if there had been any changes, then we are sure that he would have told us about them.

May the G[reat]∴ A[rchitect]∴ of the Un[iverse]∴ cast His blessings upon you and all our R[espectable]∴ B[rother]∴ and heap upon you the prosperity which we wish for with the greatest and most heartfelt sincerity.

I am by the cherished numbers and [sic] Masonry, with sincere esteem and perfect loyalty,

Sir, and M[ost]∴ R[espectable]∴ P[rin]ce∴ and B[rother]∴,

at the Orient of Les Cayes du Fond, Île à Vache, June 9th, 1765

Your very humble and very obedient servant and B[rother]∴,

Bérindoague

Due to the lack of opportunity to send these catalogues securely they will reach you a little late.[15r] [15v/blank]

No. 182 M. - François Lamarque and Jean Baptiste Perrot to M. Puisieux, Paris, November 22, 1765.

Paris, N[ovem]ber 22, 1765.

At the Hotel de la Paix, rue Richelieu

I had the honour, My Very Dear Sir, of calling upon you two days ago without having sufficient good fortune to find you at home. It was my intention to speak to you on that occasion about the matter whose success you were good enough to promise me that you would try to expedite. I have just received yet another letter on this subject begging me with the utmost earnestness to do everything possible to ensure the promptest possible execution of the matter: the qualities of the Brother aspiring to the post of Wor[shipful] are as [3r] I am [sic][49].

Jean Baptiste Bernard Perrot, Esquire, Quartermaster-Royal and Director of Mails at Léogane.

I am therefore, my very dear friend, renewing my entreaties to you on this matter, ~~and~~ for I would consider myself very lucky to have been able to further the happiness of a Brother, even though I have not been active for many years now, as well as to prevent the closure of a Lodge in the New World. Farewell. I embrace you by the required number,

L[50][3v]

No. 183 M. - M. Puisieux to Brest de la Chaussée, Paris, November 23, 1765.

Dear W[orshipful] and I[llustrious] B[rother] G[rand] M[aster],

I am enclosing two letters regarding their demands. It's B[rother] Poncet who's especially concerned that this matter succeeds. I beg you to despatch some letters[51] if it suits the Lodge. I would be obliged if you would do so. B[rother] Poncet will pay whatever is necessary. He adds his blessings to mine to assure you that he as well as I are, in a spirit of brotherly friendship,

Sir the Wor[shipful] D[eputy] B[rother] G[rand] M[aster]

Your very humble and very obedient servants,

M[onsieur]Puisieux

23rd N[ovem]ber

1765[4r] [4v/blank] [5r/blank]

To Monsieur

---

49 This sentence does not make much sense. Previous page missing?
50 Presumably François Lamarque.
51 Presumably Letters Patent.

Monsieur De la Chaussée

At the office of the Navy

cul de sacq de l'oratoire[52]

At Paris [5v]

No. 184 M. - L'Amitié Indissoluble to The Grand Lodge of France, Léogane, May 7, 1766.

L'Amitié Indissoluble, at the Orient of Léogane.

To the Most Respectable Mother Lodge, the Sovereign Grand Lodge of France.

Respectable Brothers,

It is only by placing beneath your gaze your love for Ma[sonry]∴ and your zeal for its propagation and for the idea that you have of its excellence that we can make you aware of the enormous satisfaction given to us by the reception of the splendid Letters Patent which you have kindly bestowed upon us. Ordinary terminology, although sufficiently eloquent to express appreciation for the blessings enjoyed by the Profane, would nonetheless express only imperfectly even a one-hundredth part of the delight that we feel. Unfortunately M[asonry]∴ does not have its own separate language but, even if we are unable to adequately communicate it to you, the M[asonic]∴ spirit that illuminates you is more than sufficient to enable you to appreciate it. To form an accurate idea of it, R[espectable]∴ BB[rethren]∴, you have only to consider the deplorable state from which you have just rescued us. You have only to look at us, working without a guide and, as it were, in the darkness, in the middle of a hastily-constructed temple, unknown to enlightened men, with no other consolation than our attachment to the Royal Art and our high regard for the august place of sanctuary which you know how to make worthy of respect, while on the other hand occupying yourself with ceaselessly penetrating us with the vivid light with which you have just illuminated that into which we had formed ourselves in these climes where virtue has so little illumination of its own. It is only by presenting you with this vivid picture that we can enable you to judge [6r] the importance we attach to the benefit which we derive from your kindness, so rare and precious as it is, which allows us to dedicate ourselves to the practice of wisdom under the protection of and with the assistance of its most faithful sectaries. How can we ever show our gratitude towards you! May you be content Respectable Brothers, who seek only to extend the empire of virtue, with our submission to the laws that virtue herself has laid down for us and with the ardent and perpetual vows that we are making for your happiness. Respectable Brothers, may the G[reat]∴ A[rchitect]∴ O[f]∴ T[he]∴ U[niverse]∴ look favorably upon such vows and convince you of the feelings with which we shall always be, through all the honours which you have merited,

Respectable Brothers.

Your very humble and very affectionate B[rethren]∴

Perrot, W[orshipfu]l

Sauzé, M[aste]r∴

Belloc de Monléon, S[enio]r W[arden]∴

---
52   i.e. cul-de-sac de l'Oratoire. Cf. https://fr.wikipedia.org/wiki/Rue_de_l%27Oratoire_(Paris)

Appendix B

Aurat, J[unio]r W[arde]n

Jouanel, Treasurer

Merger, M[aste]r

D'Aigalliers, Orator

Deziblais[53]∴, M[aste]r

Menand, M[aste]r

M. Le Prestre, M[aste]r

In the Year of Light five thousand seven hundred and sixty-six, on the seventh day of May.

By Order

of the R[espectable]∴ L[odge]∴ *L'Amitié Indissoluble*

Gaston Prou

Secretary[6v]

[7r/blank] [7v/blank]

No. 185 M. - L'Amitié Indissoluble to The Grand Lodge of France, Léogane, July 3, 1766.

Extract from the Register of the Secretariat of the R[espectable]∴ L[odge]∴ called *L'Amitié Indissoluble* at the Orient of Léogane, Island and Coast of Saint-Domingue./.

In the Year of Light five thousand seven hundred and sixty-six and the third day of the month of July we the Worshipful Master and the Officers of the M[ost]∴ R[espectable]∴ L[odge]∴called *L'Amitié Indissoluble* at the Orient of Léogane being regularly assembled, and after all the usual formalities, the Worshipful, assisted by his Wardens and by us the undersigned, opened the Lodge of Apprentice by its usual signs to then proceed to the appointment of new Officers as required, as is customary during the Feast of S[ain]t John. After drawing lots with the most scrupulous care, B[rother]∴ Merger, Knight of the Royal and Military Order of S[aint] Louis, was elected Worshipful Master, BB[rethren]∴ Deziblais and D'Aigalliers as Senior and Junior Wardens, B[rother]∴ Menand as Orator, B[rother]∴ Gaston Prou as Secretary, B[rother]∴ Jouanel as Treasurer, B[rother]∴ <Turgné> as M[aste]r of Ceremonies and Terrible B[rother]∴, and B[rother]∴ Le Preste as Almoner. Once this election had been completed we applauded them in the customary manner. We had a Visitor in the form of R[espectable]∴ B[rother]∴ Jean Charles Simon,[54] the current Worshipful Master of the R[espectable]∴ L[odge]∴ of *Les Frères Reunis* of the Orient of Les Cayes du Fond, Isle à Vache, [8r] whom we congratulated with all the honours of Masonry. Once midnight had come the Worshipful, accompanied as described above, and having repeated the customary Oath, closed the Lodge of Apprentice by its customary signs. The Brethren agreed that the Lodge would meet on the first Saturday in each month and signed the Register of Brethren as below, while for greater

---

53 A Pierre Leveque Deziblais, residing in Saint-Domingue, is mentioned in this document: https://www.siv.archives-nationales.culture.gouv.fr/siv/rechercheconsultation/consultation/ir/pdfIR.action?irId=FRAN_IR_042979

54 Lamarque's assistance as well as Simon's installation of the lodge demonstrates that prior to the loss of Morin's powers, *L'Amitié Indissoluble* operated in harmony with Morin's local system.

security the various signatures were also added to these presents. We then ordered our Great Seal to be applied by the depositary of the Seal, the B[rother]∴ S[ecretary]∴   Merger, W[orshipfu]l∴

Turgné Déziblais, S[enio]r W[arde]n Menand, O[rator]∴ D'Aigalliers J[unio]r∴ W[arden]∴

Jouanel, Treasurer∴

L.S.

By Order of the M[ost]∴ R[espectable]∴ L[odge]∴

L'Amitié Indissoluble

Gaston Prou

S[ecretary]∴ [8v]

[9r] [9v/blank]

No. 186 M. - L'Amitié Indissoluble to The Grand Lodge of France, Léogane, July 18, 1766.

Orient de Léogane

Amité Indissoluble

From an enlightened place where constantly reigns unity, silence,

and peace, the year of light 5766 and the 24th day of the 1st month of the

Masonic year or July 18, 1766∴

\#   -   \#

\#

To the Most Respectable Grand and Sovereign Lodge of France,

our mother, located at the Orient of Paris

Catalogue of all the bb[rethren] both absent from the colony

dead and present composing the Lodge called

l'Amitié Indissoluble

<u>Dignitary Officers</u>

\# –

<u>Brethren</u>		<u>Degree</u>
Merger	Inhabitant, kn[igh]t of the Royal and military order	
	of S[ain]t Louis Worshipful	

Deziblais	Inhabitant		S[r] Warden
D'Aigalliers	Officier in the Regiment de Forest		J[r] ditto
Mênard	Merchant		Orator
Gaston Prou	Same		Secretary
Jouanel	Same		Treasurer
Turgné	Watchmaker		M[aste]r of Ceremonies & Brother Terrible
Le Preste	Merchant		Hospitaller

Members

#.

Perrot	Guard of the King's Magazine		Past Master
Antoine	Royal Cartographer	at Versailles	Same.
Belloc de Monléon	Merchant	dead	Maitre
Antoine	Naval Commissioner	dead	Id[em].
Lebrun	Carpenter	dead	Id[em].
Sauzé	Inhabitant		Id[em].
Cézaire Sauvat	Clergy of the Order of S[ain]t John of God, in Paris		Id[em].
Sidoine Clement	Clergy of the Order of S[ain]t John of God, in Paris		Id[em].
Pruillo	Naval Captain	at Bayonne	M[aste]r & Associate
François Auras	Major Surgeon at Léogane… departed for le Mans.		M[aste]r
Filgerald	Abbot, expelled from the lodge in perpetuity		
		left for France	oooooooo
Massip de Cantaranne	Inhabitant		M[aitr]e
Lamure	Inhabitant		M[aitr]e

Saintand De Béquigur Inhabitant of Miragoane			Fellow Craft
Chiquan	Surgeon		Id[em].
Fargier	N[aval] Cap[tain] of Provence	dead	Apprentice
Coffy	N/L. inhabitant of the hills or mountains		Serving Brother

L.S.

Merger W[orshipfu]l∴

Perrot past W[orshipfu]l∴   Deziblais S^r∴ W[arde]n

Mênard O[rator]∴   Turgné   D'Aigalliers J^r∴ W[arden]∴

Jouanel Treas[urer]

By mandate of the R[espectable]∴ L[odge]∴ called
L'Amitié Indissoluble
Gaston Prou
S[ecretary]∴

[10r] [10v/blank]

No. 187 M. - L'Amitié Indissoluble to The Grand Lodge of France, Léogane, July 19, 1766.

To the Grand Sovereign Lodge of France,

Our Mother Lodge at the Orient of Paris.

Our Most Respectable and Most Illustrious Brethren,

We have pleasure in enclosing a report of our labors at the Feast of S[ain]t John l[as]t. Here are the results, which include the extract from the act of nomination of the new officers of our Orient and the List of all the Brothers composing it. We have also included those who are absent and those [11r] who have died during the course of last year. We decided that we should also include one individual who has been expelled due to his own self-deficiency.

We all live together in a close union. All that is lacking to our complete satisfaction is your powerful protection.

We greet you by all the honours due to you and are, by the most sacred of bonds,

our Respectable and Most Illustrious Brethren./.

Your affectionate Brethren./.

Merger, W[orshipfu]l∴

Perrot, Past W[orshipfu]l∴

D'Aigalliers, J[unio]r W[arden]∴

Deziblais, S[enio]r W[arde]n∴

Menand, O[rator]∴

Turgné

Jouanel, Treasurer∴

By Order of the R[espectable]∴ L[odge]∴ called *L'Amitié Indissoluble* at the Orient of Léogane, July 19th, 1766.

Gaston Prou S[ecretary]∴

I also include the annual subscription of 3ff∴ GP [11v] [12r/blank] [12v/blank]

FM2 544. - THE SOVEREIGN COUNCIL OF THE PRINCES OF JERUSALEM OF SAINT MARC RECONSTITUTES L'ÉTROITE UNION, JUNE 1, 1767.[55]

Copy of the Provisional Constitutions of the R[espectable]∴ L[odge]∴ L'Étroite Union at the O[rient]∴ of Gros-Morne, Isle of Saint-Domingue, dated the f[irst] day of the f[irst] month of the M[asoni]c Year 5767.

M[ay] t[he] G[rand] A[rchitect] o[f]

t[he Universe] m[aintain]

t[he edifice] o[n which] we are w[orking]

On behalf of the Grand Council

of the most valorous Princes of Jerusalem, Knights of the East, of all the Masonic Orders, Grand Perfect Elect, or Ancient Masters called Scots, founders of the Ancient Mastery in France, holding their meetings under the celestial vault, at the zenith, established in the Town of St Marc, Isle and Coast of S[ain]t-Domingue at 19 degrees, 8 minutes, 43 seconds, Latitude North.

We, the most valorous Princes of Jerusalem, Knights of the East, of the West and of all the Masonic Orders composing the Sovereign Council aforementioned, regularly assembled, in a respectable place where decency, silence, peace and perfect harmony constantly reign, sheltered from profane eyes, and chosen by the wisest of Kings to, in his stead and name, direct and lead all the Craftsmen employed in the re-building of the Temple of Jerusalem, trustees and guardians of the precious treasures known only to ourselves.

To all duly constituted Lodges and to all enlightened men, present and future, of whatsoever Degree or dignity they might be, who shall see these present documents, *Greetings* by the sacred and mysterious numbers.

---

55 BnF FM2 544.

Brethren Florentin Costeau, Curé of the Parish of Gros-Morne in the Jurisdiction of Port-de-Paix; Boisblau[56], former Officer of the Militia; de Morinville[57], former Captain of the Militia; Buscaille, former Commander of the Militia; Imbault, Regnier and Duluc, all former Officers of the Militia; Captain Grepain; Laplasse; de la Chaussée senior, inhabitants of Le Quartier[58]; François de la Chaussée [6r] ~~senior inhabitants~~ junior, merchant in Port-de-Paix; Levassor, de la Chaussée junior, Hatrel, Descotières[59], Grepain, Daulède and La Tourraudaye, also all inhabitants and sons of inhabitants in the locality of Gros-Morne, having respectfully represented to us that, having gathered in the town of Gros-Morne, far from the sacred sanctuaries where the mysteries are celebrated that drew them from the darkness, their zeal and sense of duty would not allow them any longer to leave in a state of uselessness and inactivity the talents and knowledge that they have acquired, as well as the virtues that are inseparable from these and which are so useful to humanity in general and so necessary to the Order in particular, and that they are dedicating themselves to the formation in the town of Gros Morne under the immediate protection of the Most Respectable Grand Lodge of France established in Paris a particular and Symbolic Lodge in order to cultivate the Royal Art in a legitimate manner and according to the Laws; that being unable to achieve this advantage according to the General Statutes of the Order and the obligations they have contracted before the G[reat] A[rchitect] of T[he Universe] without particular powers and constitutions from a Sovereign Grand Council of the Princes of Jerusalem, and clothed with the authority necessary to grant them, notwithstanding they have been given that authority by the so-called English Scots Lodge of Edouard Stuart established at Cap-Français, which is not recognized by all Lodges, Councils and Chapters except for the Symbolic Lodge La Parfaite [6v] Harmonie; and that recognising in our Sovereign Council of Princes [of] Jerusalem the supreme character and power which is an emanation of that of the Great King whom we represent; it pleased us to allow them to assemble regularly by granting to them provisional powers, pending the dispatch to them by the Grand and Sovereign Lodge of France of the Constitutions in due form and legality, which they have begged and requested from us for them and in their names, and by creating thereafter in the locality of Gros Morne a Lodge under such title and denomination as we may deem fit to give it, as well as with such Constitutions, Laws, Regulations, Obligations and generally all that we deem it appropriate and necessary to impose relating solely to Symbolic Masonry, either of General or Particular Institutions.

And as our most indispensable Obligations are not limited to maintaining Order, Discipline and Strict Observance of the Laws of pure and healthy Masonry in all Symbolic Lodges, and since our most essential functions extend to protecting the Royal Art, especially by contributing to everything that might tend to its perfection and propagation in all the places of the Earth by rewarding constancy, zeal, [7r] and fervour by new Enlightened Spirits or by the establishment of Workshops which are such striking testimonies to our fraternal tenderness and marks of the most intimate confidence, *We have believed*, in the light of our knowledge of the legitimacy of the character of the Petitioners as well as of their virtue, their personal qualities, ability, zeal, wisdom and experience necessary to enlighten, govern and lead a team of Craftsmen, that we must give favorable consideration to their request and give them provisional authorisation that their talents may bear fruit.

For these reasons and because of other careful deliberations persuading us upon his point, and with the certain knowledge, full power and authority of *King Solomon* whom, when legitimately assembled, we represent, and having regard to Article twenty-eight[60] of the Statutes and General Regulations of the

---

56 Boisbelleau?

57 Or Morenville

58 Presumably Le Quartier Colonial.

59 Gold: de la Costière

60 Art. 28 Reconstitution. – Letters of constitutions ratifying the work of the said LL[odges] since their first Constitution will be shipped

Grand and Sovereign Lodge of France enacted in consequence of the deliberations of the twenty-fifth day of November one thousand seven hundred and sixty-two, the first illegal and irregular Constitutions granted to the English so-called English Scots Lodge of Edouard Stuart, which all regularly constituted Lodges in the Colony only recognize as the Symbolic Lodge established under the name of La Parfaite Harmonie by the M[ost] Respectable Scottish Lodge of Cap Français, dated the twenty-seventh day of May one thousand seven hundred [7v] and sixty-four, ratified by this same Lodge which calls itself Edouard-Stuard on the twenty-ninth day of July following the petition addressed to Our Sovereign Council by the bb[rethren] aforementioned, dated the 1st day of December of last year to be presented to it by its deputies bb[rethren] Boisblau, Senior Warden, and Buscaille, Orator of their Lodge, on the 28th day of the same month, and having sought the advice of all the regular and legitimately constituted Lodges in this Colony with whom we correspond, *we hereby make it known* to all regular and duly constituted Lodges and to all legitimate Masons of w[hat]ever grade they might be that are spread over the surface of the land and sea *that we have permitted and hereby* provisionally *allow* the brethren as aforementioned to form a just and perfect Lodge of Symbolic Masons in the town of Gros Morne, where no legitimate one is presently to be found. And in order to give the Petitioners a singular mark of our esteem and confidence *we have hereby created and established it and do create and establish it* under the title of L'Étroite Union until it pleases the Sovereign and Grand Lodge of France to ratify the present document to be dated the twenty-seventh day of May one thousand seven hundred and sixty-four, [8r] the anniversary of its first illegitimate Constitution, promising them our sovereign protection and recommendation for the obtaining of the said Letters of Ratification for the purpose of and practising in this name all the mysteries of healthy and pure Symbolic Masonry only, *and do wish that* this Lodge La Étroite Union exercise, enjoy and make use of the rights and authorities attributed to legitimate Symbolic Lodges, as well as the prerogatives, functions and rights that pertain thereto, all as enjoyed by other Lodges, to be scrupulously conformed to at all times, without ever derogating or innovating in any way whatsoever with respect to the General Statutes of the Order or the Regulations adopted by the Grand and Sovereign Lodge of France in consequence of the deliberations of the twenty-fifth day of November one thousand seven hundred and sixty-two, of which they have a copy, and others enacted since then, and those particular ones that we reserve to ourselves and will give them thereafter, if the case requires it. We also permit them to make and compose particular regulations for the good order and internal maintenance of their Lodge, and to amend, increase or decrease them if the case demands, once only annually, at the time of the holding of the Grand Lodge of St. John the Baptist [8v] as well as expressly charging them to render and bestow all the suitable honours both due and customary to all the brethren whom they shall in future recognize as legitimate Masons who shall visit them when they shall have proved to them their quality of Mason, both by representation and by their certificates, powers and distinctive titles–by the questions customary in such cases, the whole according to the particular form which we shall give them, sent to them separately from these present documents, to which they shall have recourse when the case shall require it.

Thus are the provisional Constitutions under which the Symbolic Lodge L'Étroite Union which we are creating in the town of Gros Morne shall be regulated and governed in the future, and in order to give it its initial form and existence we have committed and deputed and do herewith commit and depute to the brethren of whom it is now composed the Most Valorous Princes of Jerusalem and Knights of the East and Very Dear brothers Princes, Knights and Members of our Sovereign Council Fleuret de Turville, Trembley[61], Lamard and Lartigault du Guerron, the first Knight of all Orders of Masons, *which* [9r] Valorous Princes and Knights we empower on our behalf and in our name to *convoke* and assemble

---

by the G[rand] L[odge] of France to LL[odges] constituted irregularly, but in good faith, by regular LL[odges], and for the said Letters of ratification the sum of 12 LL[ivres] will be paid to the Treasurer and will serve as the date, of their first constitutions.

61 Jean. See https://tinyurl.com/yckvym6d

all the aforementioned brethren and with the assistance of such other Scottish or Symbolic brethren and Masons as we permit and authorize them to appoint and choose to lay the foundation of the Symbolic Lodge L'Étroite Union and to make it provisionally just and perfect by appointing and establishing of their free choice the seven Dignitaries who shall enlighten and govern it until the General Lodge of Saint John the Baptist next, the day on which they shall either confirm their appointments or appoint others, and they should similarly give consideration, in accordance with ordinary usage, to sending *a copy* of the Minutes of Establishment to our Sovereign Council to be homologated[62] by us and deposited in our Treasury, for so have willed, decided and deliberated all the Valorous Princes of Jerusalem and Kn[igh]ts of the East regularly assembled. And for the authenticity of the present Provisional Constitutions and Powers we have caused to be affixed thereto the mysterious seal of our Sovereign Council. Given in our Sovereign Council on the first day of the first month of the Year of Light 5767, of the return from Babylon 2304, and according to the Vulgar Calculation on the twenty-fourth day of June one thousand seven hundred and sixty-seven, signed, on register [9v] by D. Duval Chef representing Darius; Trembley representing Zorobabbel; Lamand, Senior Grand Warden, Simpé[63] Junior Grand Warden, Fleuret de Turville, Grand Secretary and a Grand Orator, Touchemoulin, Durocher and Peire.

By Order of the Sovereign Council of the Princes of Jerusalem, Kn[igh]ts of the East and West &c &c. &c.

Established at the Orient of St Marc. Signed, Fleuret de Turville, G[ran]d Secretary and Grand Keeper of the Seals, Knight of all the Masonic Orders.

Sealed, in the margin, in red wax.

F[or] compared copy

By Order.

Daulède Ass[istan]t Secret[ary]

Certified in accordance with the Reg[isters] of Deliberat[ions] of the C[ounc]il of the Kn[igh]ts of Jerusalem

With its seat at the Orient of St Marc [10r] [10v/blank]

Copy of the homologation[64] of the Installation of the R[espectable]∴ L[odge]∴ of L'Étroite Union at the O[rient]∴ of Gros Morne, Isle of Saint-Domingue.

Extract from the Register of Proceedings of the Sovereign Council of the Princes of Jerusalem established at the Orient of the town of St Marc.

On behalf of the Grand Council of the Most Valorous Princes of Jerusalem, Knights of the East, of all the Orders of Masons, Perfect Grand Elect, or Ancient Masters known as Scots, founders of the Ancient Mastery in France, meeting under the Celestial Vault at the Zenith in the town of St Marc, Isle and Coast of Saint-Domingue, at 19 degrees, eight minutes, 43 seconds, Latitude North.

On the sixth day of the twelfth month of the Year of Light 5767, of the return from Babylon 2304,

---

62 Homologation is approval by a higher authority.
63 Sempé?
64 Approval by a higher authority.

and according to the Vulgar Style the 29th of May 1678 *We* the most Illustrious and Valorous Princes of Jerusalem, composing the Sovereign Council established at the Orient of St Marc, are assembled to hold council. And after the meeting had been opened with the usual formalities the V[ery] D[ear] B[rother] Fleuret De Turville said that he had been sent a letter p[ri]vately by the Worshipful Brother Florentin Costeau, Worshipful of the R[espectable]∴ Symbolic L[odge]∴ provisionally created and constituted by us under the glorious name of L'Étroite Union at the Orient of Gros-Morne in accordance with our deliberation of the first [day] of the first month of the present year through the ministrations both of V[ery] D[ear] B[rethren] Trembley and Lamard as well as of B[rother]∴ Costeau and the W[orshipful] Knight of the East, Lartigault[65] Duquairou, appointed by us, as well as the Deputies appointed for the same purpose in accordance with the same deliberation, who, assisted [11r] by the Respectable Brethren Duluc and Guyot, members of the M[ost] R[espectable]∴ Scottish L[oge]∴ established at the Orient of this town, as the Sovereign Council had permitted and chosen them to do, went on the 23d day of the sixth month of this present year to the town of Gros Morne, where they fulfilled their mission. The letter aforementioned was handed back to them by Brethren Michel Regnier, Treasurer, Daulède, Acting Secretary, and Duluc, M[aste]r of Ceremonies of this R[espectable]∴ L[odge]∴, whom it had chosen and appointed as its Deputies to our Sovereign Council for the purpose of thanking it on its behalf for and the favor we have granted to it, and who also handed over a sealed packet addressed to us by this R[espectable]∴ L[odge]∴ On being opened, the packet was found to contain two Formal Letters dated the second of this month, the first containing what has just been said, with a request to ratify and homologate the contents of the aforementioned Report of Installation following the enacting part of our deliberation as aforementioned, to which was attached a copy in certified form of that same Report of Installation.

The second Formal Letter related to the fact that we had been pleased to grant them the right to hold a Scottish Lodge in the locality for the Instruction of those brethren of this R[espectable]∴ L[odge]∴ whom our V[ery] D[ear] Prince Deputies legitimated during their stay in the locality by virtue of the Powers we have given them to grant to the same brethren thus legitimated the Power to confer this Degree upon those Brothers of this Symbolic Lodge [11v] who hold Degrees inferior to this Degree &c.

In response to which the V[ery] D[ear] P[rince] Fleuret de Turville observed that, as this request on the part of the Brethren thus legitimated by them was of importance to the Royal Art, it was vital that the Sovereign Councils of the Princes of Jerusalem established at the Orients of Cayes, St. Louis and Port-au-Prince (with whom we correspond) be informed, so that we can have their opinion of this and then decide afterwards according to circumstances.

Whereupon, the whole matter having been put to deliberation, after careful consideration, and after the Report of Installation aforementioned had been read out, our Sovereign Council said, decided and ruled that it ratifies the Report of Installation as aforementioned insofar as is necessary, and homologates it in its entirety so that it might enjoy full effect and be executed in accordance with its form and content; furthermore, to ensure the authenticity of the above, there would be delivered by the M[ost] W[orshipful]∴ P[rince]∴ Grand Secretary and Keeper of the Seals to the three brother Deputies of the R[espectable]∴ Symbolic L[odge]∴ of Gros Morne a Dispatch in the form of the present documents, bearing his signature, in the form of a certified true document, to which would be attached the seal or stamp of our Sovereign Council, to be deposited in the Archives of this R[espectable]∴ L[odge]∴ to serve as proof of its legitimacy.

Also, before judging the contents of the second Formal Letter, in order to have nothing to reproach itself with, the V[ery] D[ear] P[rince] Grand Secretary would write immediately to the [12r] Sovereign

---

65 Lartigau?

Councils of the Orients of Cayes, St Louis and Port-au-Prince, to ask for their opinions on this, and to act subsequently according to the circumstances, regarding which the brethren who had signed the Petition in question should be informed through the dispatch of these present documents so as not to cause them impatience. Thus did the V[ery] D[ear] P[rinces] composing the Sovereign Council of the Princes of Jerusalem established at the Orient of St Marc, who have signed the Register, formally desire, and decide ./.

For Dispatch, compared with the Original, on a motion of the Sovereign Council. Signed, Fleuret de Turville, Grand Secretary and Grand Keeper of the Seals, Kn[igh]t Prince of all Masonic Orders.

And, next to it: Sealed in red wax.

For compared copy.

By Order.

Daulède, Ass[istan]t Secret[ary]

Certified in accordance with the Reg[ister] of Deliberat[ion] of the C[ounc]il of the P[rin]ces of Jerusalem with their seat at the Orient of France.

Rouyer

G[ran]d Keeper of the Seals and Archives

Sealed by us, Keeper of the Seals and Archives

Thomas Duluc [12v]

No. 188 M. - L'Amitié Indissoluble to The Grand Lodge of France, Léogane, June, 1767.

At the Orient of Léogane in the Year of Light 5767 and the fourth day of the 1st month of the Masonic Year./.

To the Most Respectable Lodge of the *Grand Orient de France*,

Our Sovereign Mother

f∴ f∴ p∴[66]

Most Respectable Brethren,

We are grievously alarmed by the letter from M[ost]∴ Ill[ustrious]∴ B[rother]∴ De la Chaussée, Keeper of the Seals and Archivist of Y[our]∴ M[ost]∴ R[espectable]∴ and S[overeign]∴ L[odge]∴, Our Mother Lodge, informing us that on February 21st, 1767, on Government orders, they were suspending their labors and correspondence until happier times. As good and loyal Masons we obviously have our anxieties. We shall confine ourselves for the time being to imploring the Supreme Architect to support

---

66 Non typical abbreviation, possibly fidelité, fraternité, paix [loyalty, brotherhood, peace].

our labors and to strengthen them until the precious orders of our Most Respectable Mother Lodge should formally forbid them. As our Mother she is connected with us by an umbilical cord and [13r] and knows what we have to say to her better than we ourselves can express it to her.

Here are the appointments we have made of the BB[rethren]∴ of our Orient. The Catalogue will show you the various Members who make up O[ur]∴ L[odge]∴

We also send you the three books for the last annual use∴

We beg you to accept the compliments of the Brotherhood which we are taking the liberty of presenting to you,

Most Respectable Brothers,

Your affectionate servants and Brothers

Perrot, W[orshipfu]l∴

Jouanel, S[enio]r∴ W[arde]n∴

Massip de Cantaranne, J[unior]∴ W[arde]n∴

By Order of the R[espectable]∴ L[odge]∴ *L'Amitié Indissoluble* of the Orient of Léogane, Island and Coast of Saint-Domingue.

B[rother]∴ Gaston Prou

Secretary

P. S. We would kindly ask you to send us the General List of all the Lodges of France which we have never received. G. P. [13v] [14r/blank] [14v/blank]

No. 189 M. - L'Amitié Indissoluble to The Grand Lodge of France, Léogane, June, 1767.

Amitié Indissoluble∴

Orient of Léogane∴

5767∴

1st Masonic Month

Catalogue of the Brethren of this Respectable Lodge, regularly constituted under the immemorial title of *L'Amitié Indissoluble*.

Officer Dignitaries

BBre[thre]n

Perrot, Esquire, Quartermaster Royal and Director of Mails, Worshipful

Jouanel, Merchant, S[enio]r W[arde]n∴

Massip de Cantaranne, Esquire, J[unio]r W[arden]∴

Menand, Merch[an]t Orator

Gaston Prou, ditto, Secretary

Saremejane, ditto, Treasurer

Eauper, Hospitaller of the Order of S[ain]t John of God, M[aste]r of Ceremonies

Fauré, inhabitant Expert Tyler and S[enip]r Alm[on]er for the plain.

Miailles, Merc[han]t, Terrible and Alm[oner]∴ for the town

Lamure, Almoner for the plain.

Masters present

Merger, Knight of the Royal and Military Order of S[ain]t Louis, Past Wor[shipful]∴

Deziblais, inhabitant

Caron, merchant, affiliated to the R[espectable] L[odge] of the Orient of P[ort] au P[rin]ce

Donaud, surgeon

Demaugeis, Captain of Troops[67], Commandant at Léogane

Saintard de Bequigni, inhab[itan]t of P[eti]t Goave

Fellows present

Martin, watchmaker

Guyon, inhabitant [15r]

Apprentices present

Br[ethre]n.

G[uilla]me Samson, master builder

Réné Serault, merchant

Serving Br[ethren]:

Coffy, inhab[itan]t of the hill-country

Absentees

D'Aigalliers, officer in the *Regiment de Forest*, M[aste]r

Turgné, watchmaker, ditto

Lepretre, trader, ditto

Antoine, Royal Cartographer, ditto

J[ea]n B[aptis]te Bardet senior, ditto

---

67   Capitaine des Troupes: normally indicates a Captain of Marines.

Cezaire Sauvat   } Hospitallers of the

Sidoine Clement   } Order of S[ain]t John of God

Aurat, surgeon, ditto

Pruillo, sea-captain, ditto

J[ean] B[aptis]te Fargier of Marseille, ditto, Apprentice

Filgerald, abbé, expelled in perpetuity and without possibility of return

Deceased

Plastrier, Notary and Deputy Attorney-General

Le Brun

Antoine *Commissaire aux classes*[68]

Belloc de Monléon, merch[an]t

Du Rousset, officer in the *Regiment d'Angoumois*. [15v]

BBr[ethre]n

Leon de Traysat Chiquan, former surgeon

Perrot, W[orshipfu]l∴ Jouanel S[enio]r∴ W[arde]n∴ Massip de Canterane, J[unior] W[arde]n∴

    By Order of the M[ost]∴ R[espectable]∴ L[odge]∴ *L'Amitié Indissoluble* of the Orient of Léogane.

        B[rother]∴ Gaston Prou, S[ecretary]∴[16r]

        [16v/blank]

No. 190 M. - Jean Baptiste Bernard Perrot to Brest de la Chaussée, Léogane, June 29, 1767.

Léogane, June 29th, 1767

Received October 13th, 1767

Rep[lied] Sat[urday]. 15th.

My Most Respectable Brother,

---

68 A port official. "…le commissaire aux classes…ils sont présents dans les ports et chargés de mettre en application la législation mise en place par Colbert, l'Inscription maritime. A ce titre, ils paient des avances de solde aux épouses et aux mères quand le mari ou le fils est en mer et qu'il a « délégué ». Ils sont chargés également du recrutement des équipages au profit de l'État, les fameuses « classes » qui font que chaque inscrit maritime doit un temps de service à l'État." ["The commissaires aux classes are present in the ports and entrusted with implementation of the Colbert legislation – the Inscription Maritime, which involved paying advances on the salaries to wives and mothers when their husbands or sons were at sea which the latter had 'delegated'. They were also responsible for recruiting crews for the benefit of the State – the famous classes which required every eligible merchant seaman to spend some time in the navy in service of the State."] Cf. http://www.smlh29n.fr/memorial/livre/commissaire_de_la_marine

I received and read at our Lodge in Léogane the letter which you kindly sent me dated February 21st last. The Lodge will certainly reply to you and will never cease to follow the principles and conform to the regulations which have been sent to it by the Grand and Sovereign Lodge of France.

I am taking advantage of the opportunity you have given me to ask you for some information about the past.

It is a question of whether you would be so kind as to inform me as to whether there are several different kinds of Masonry in France. We at the Lodges in Port-au-Prince, Saint-Marc and Le Fond de l'Ile à Vache, known under the gracious titles of *La Parfaite Union, La Concorde* and *Les Frères Réunis*, dispute the right of what they call Scots Masonry, whose adherents do not wish to correspond with us in this quality to which they lay claim. In particular they all acknowledge that our Scots Masonry is, so to speak, the same as theirs, and that one cannot have a better one, but that they can recognize us only as Symbolic Masons, an Order which they claim consists of the first three degrees of the new Masonry as we do not have any constitutions for Scots Masonry.

My response to this objection is that there is just one unique Masonry, and that the first three Degrees are the beginning of Masonry from which all the other Degrees follow suit.

I then show them the vignette which runs around the parchment on which their constitutions are duly written and signed and ask them if they would kindly offer it for scrutiny to an Apprentice, Fellow or Master, whom they refer to as Symbolic Masons, so that they can explain the different emblems which this vignette represents.[17r] None of these young Masons understand anything to be found there, but in spite of that they still persist in their desire <not> to correspond with me even though they all recognize me as being a good and instructed Mason.

I would ask where they got their constitutions of what they call Scots Masonry from? They tell me from Jamaica. I think that, as Frenchmen, we should all follow uniquely all the constitutions emanating from the M[ost] R[espectable] G[rand] L[odge] of France, that same France from which, for some 28 years now, I have drawn the 1st principles of the Royal Art, in which I have been deeply immersed as far as the degree of Sublime Elect Grand M[aste]r. I have met and frequented some excellent French and English Masons who have never hesitated to receive me in all their Lodges. It is unfortunate, my Most Respectable Brother, that the three Lodges of the New World, where I have lived for some 18 years, flatly refuse to recognize in their Lodges the Masons I initiated with the agreement of our Mother Lodge, the G[rand] and M[ost] R[espectable] L[odge].

I therefore beg you to be so good as to immediately enlighten me on this subject and, if there is a need for some Constitutions to enable the continuation of the Royal Art other than those which it has pleased the G[rand] L[odge] to send us, then to obtain these for me from our M[ost] R[espectable] B[rethr]en at the Orient of Paris. Any costs will be immediately reimbursed to you by Mr. Sigoigne, a merchant in Nantes, who always holds some of my funds, and to whom I would be obliged if you would address any replies with which you might honour me so that he can forward them to me, all of them in a double envelope. Do not worry about what it will cost in the way of postage.

If, in return, I could have the pleasure of being of some service to you in my part of the world or [16v] in the Colony then please feel free to ask, and I will do my best to oblige. This part of the world provides an abundance of things which might be of interest to you as well as to our Brethren from your Orient. You only have to ask and you shall receive.

I am, with all possible fraternal esteem and friendship,

Appendix B

My Most Respectable Brother

The most humble and submissive of your Brethren,

Perrot

Quartermaster Royal and Director of Mails at Léogane. [18r]

[18v/blank]

No. 191 M. - Jean Baptiste Bernard Perrot to Brest de la Chaussée, Léogane, February 28, 1768.

Léogane, February 28th, 1768

Received in May 1768

My Very Dear Brother,

We have not taken any breaks from our labors even though we are aware of and if I dare to say so very disturbed by the reason that may have motivated the Grand Mother Lodge to cease its own sublime labors. You give me hope that these unfortunate times are coming to an end and may they never return!

I acknowledge receipt of the Catalogue of Regular Lodges which you have been kind enough to send us and which I have forwarded, as you requested, to our R[espectable] L[odge].

I can only thank you for all the useful information which you have kindly given me about the Art which we so much enjoy practising. These are the same principles that I had tried to inculcate in the minds of our Brethren, but a certain hesitancy on their part regarding the more specialised knowledge of the Lodge at Port-au-Prince which persuaded them of the contrary meant that I could not convince them < myself>. Finally the weight of evidence caused them to yield, and it is to you, dear Brother, to whom they are obliged, just as I am. I had kept telling them that the Council of Princes of Jerusalem of Port-au-Prince was not a suffragan of the Grand and S[ublime] L[odge] of France and was therefore unable to make any decisions within our Regular Symbolic Lodges. They could not believe it, any more than they could believe that, being quorate, they could be given the Degrees of Scots Masonry which are familiar to the regularly constituted Brethren of our R[espectable] L[odge].

This is no longer an issue at present, as not only would it cost us a lot of time and money to have ourselves elevated to a suffragan council of the G[rand] and S[ublime] L[odge] but it is only, I would say, a question of having from the Grand and S[ublime] L[odge] of France [19r] the same information authentically signed by several of the Master and Officers, and sealed and stamped with the seal and stamp of the said G[rand] and S[ublime] L[odge], so that having notified the other lodges of the New World they could be locked up in our Archives as an instruction from which it will not be possible to deviate. This is the favor which I dare to ask of you for the sake of our tranquillity and that of all the Brethren spread out across the territory of S[ain]t Domingue.

From time to time in this colony we see B[rothe]r Morin, whom we certainly acknowledge as Master of the Lodge of *L'Harmonie* as listed in the table of Regular Lodges, but who wishes, under titles that he has undoubtedly obtained surreptitiously from the G[rand] L[odge], to pass himself off as Inspector of Lodges of S[ain]t Domingue. We refused point-blank to recognize him as such, as he does not appear in the General Table, where we find only a B[rothe]r Martin who lives in Le Cap, and not Brother Morin who wanders backwards and forwards to Jamaica, for it should be said in passing that there is no Lodge called *L'Harmonie* in all the French territory of S[ain]t Domingue, and therefore could this not be a B[rothe]r who is making Masonry into a livelihood and living off the proceeds? He is certainly very enlightened and has all the answers at his fingertips as the saying goes, but he is definitely not my sort of man. I would be obliged if you could provide me with some clues about this Brother after you have enquired about him at the G[rand] L[odge] from which he must have originally come. He [19v] is turning upside down all the Lodges in Port-au-Prince, Les Cayes and S[ain]t Marc with titles to which he lays claim from both Jamaica and France. All the B[rethr]en of these three Orients look up to him as a tutelary deity, but as for me, speaking as someone who is not so credulous, I would be delighted to know who he really is before bestowing upon him the slightest honours other than those due to the Master of the Lodge *L'Harmonie*, and that is why I am taking this opportunity to repeat my request,

I am, with all the honours due to you dear Brother,

Your very humble and very obedient servant,

Perrot

Léogane, 28th February 1768

You will see that I am taking advantage of the permission which you gave me to ask you some favors, and I can assure you that I would like with all my heart to be of some usefulness to you in the part of the world where I live./. [20r]

To be franked in Nantes and then sent on to Paris

To Monsieur...

M[onsieur]De la Chaussée

Marine Accounts Department

Cul de Sac de l'Oratoire

Paris [20v]

FM2 543. - LA VÉRITÉ REPORT ON PARFAITIE HARMONIE, FEBRUARY 1, 1770.[69]

To the Most Sublime Grand

Lodge of France, with its seat at the Orient

of Paris

Most Respectable and Worshipful Masters∴

By virtue of the Powers and Letters of Credence entrusted to me by the Most Respectable Lodge de la Vérité, regularly established under your Constitutions at the Orient of Cap Français on the Island of

---

69 BnF FM2 543.

Saint-Domingue by the Respectable Brother Martin[70], your Inspector at the aforementioned Orient, I am laying before you for your consideration several points regarding which this Respectable Lodge begs you, by an immutable law, to resolve its doubts and perplexity, and to root out the error that has beset the majority of Lodges of the Orient of Saint-Domingue, and notably that of Cap Français[71], the enemy of the aforementioned Lodge∴ de la Vérité, thereby to re-establish the harmony of outlook that is the hallmark of true Knight Masons.

In order to fulfil a mission with all the exactitude of which my feeble knowledge of the matter renders me capable, I will start with the moment at which you entrusted the powers [33r] of Inspector to Brother Martin, in which duties he certainly wished me to participate.

Article I.

In ~~March~~ July 1766 the Sublime Grand Lodge bestowed the powers of Inspector upon Respectable Brother Martin. In consequence of the said powers he visited[72] the Lodges at the Orient of Cap Français and verified their labors and the Constitutions under which they practised the Royal Art. He did not find any of them to have a legal basis. He was firm enough to point out to them the errors of which they were guilty. You must have seen, Respectable Masters, from the report submitted to you by R[espectable]∴ B[rother]∴ Martin just how strongly attached these Lodges were to the aforementioned error. And since his departure for the Orient of France they have gone one better (or rather worse) by making remarks about him – both personal remarks and comments on the powers he wields – which are as inappropriate as they are un-Masonic, and which they have not ceased to make, right up to the present time.

No Lodge had been constituted in Le Cap, something of which it was easy to convince oneself 1) by the inspection made of the Constitutions[73] that had been granted under the auspices of Edward Stuart by a so-called B[rother]∴ de Langeron, whose name is not be found anywhere on the General Roll, and 2) by the fact that the Sublime Grand Lodge [33v] had up to that time issued only a small number of Constitutions for this region, which were known to the aforementioned Inspector and recorded on the General Roll.

One of the aforementioned Lodges, called[74] L'Harmonie, was aware of the irregular nature of its procedure and decided to remedy it by merging with another Lodge, called Ecossaise. Once it had conceived this plan it set about executing it. This merger was achieved in 1768 and please note, Respectable Masters, this Lodge Ecossaise (without any Constitutions) was not unaware of the pretty unbusinesslike behaviour of Lodge L'Harmonie, regarding which it (Lodge Ecossaise) had given Brother Martin a parcel of papers to

---

70 In 1766, Brother Martin moved to Saint-Domingue, and the R[espectable]∴ G[rand]∴ Lodge bestowed upon him these powers of Inspector. In March of that year he constituted R[espectable]∴ L[odge]∴ de la Verité.

71 The so-called Lodge Ecossaise, *Saint Jean de Jérusalem Ecossaise*.

72 There were therefore 3 Lodges: L'Harmonie, La Verité, and another called Ecossaise, all of them illegal.
  The R∴ Lodge de la Vérité was regularised by Brother Martin in March 1767.

73 The Lodge known as L'Harmonie. The Lodge known as Ecossaise did not even want to recognize it nor the Regular Lodges. I have the documents to support this statement.

74 It was when it was persuaded of the regularity of the work of B[rother]∴ Martin that it sought to join the Ecossaise, which it did in 1768, but its members' inappropriate and even insulting remarks did not cease.

take to the Sublime Grand Lodge – to what purpose I do not know.⁷⁵

Despite all this, Lodge L'Harmonie was duly received at Lodge Ecossaise, a meeting that was conducted with some pomp, all the better to taunt the Sublime Grand Lodge, its Inspector, and the R[espectable]∴ L[odge]∴ de la Verité, which had just been regularised by B[rother]∴ <u>Martin</u>, upon whom you had bestowed your powers.

The Respectable Regular [34r] Lodges of the Isle of Saint-Domingue are, due to an unpardonable irregularity, so intimately bound up with the irregular ones that they actually support their error, their paradoxical nature, and their disobedience to the laws of the Sublime Grand Lodge. They even regard them as their 'compass', a disgrace that the Respectable Lodge de la Vérité, constituted by the R[espectable]∴ B[rother]∴ <u>Martin</u> and whose Constitutions you have confirmed⁷⁶, is suffering from. The refusal of the R[espectable]∴ Regu[la]r Lodges | to recognize the R[espectable]∴ Lodge de la Vérité as regular is based on two grounds: 1) The fact that the Sublime Grand Lodge did not give them notice of the powers it had bestowed upon B[rother]∴ <u>Martin</u>, and 2) the fact that they have a <u>Council of the Prince of the Secret</u>, compared with which the Sovereign Council of the Orient is very little.

Article 2.

However, this so-called Lodge Ecossaise constitutes lodges⁷⁷* and is the Lodge most opposed to the work of R[espectable]∴ Brother <u>Martin</u>. Why does it act so un-Masonically? And all this without any title authorising it to act in this way. Why are the Respectable <Lodges> of the Orient at Saint-Domingue, constituted by the Sublime Grand Lodge of France, so intimately bound up with this Scottish Lodge (without Constitutions)? It is an irregularity from which all the schisms originated that set this Orient on fire, which has caused the work of B[rother]∴ <u>Martin</u> and the Sublime Grand Lodge to be rejected, and which prevents the recognition of the R[espectable]∴ Lodge de la Vérité.

Article 3.

Since the Respectable Lodge de la Vérité was constituted as much for the Symbolic as for the other Superior Grades [34v] forming the Masonic Hierarchy, giving sanctuary to the Sovereign Council of the Orient, and forming a section of that of the Orient of France with its seat in Paris;

---

75 It was their constitutions.

76 By the letters in the form of an Ordinance sent to it by B[rother]∴ Fauconet at the end of 1769 by which you enjoin the Lodge de la Vérité to send copies to all the Regular Lodges, which it has done, but without success, as you will see from the letters written in this regard. I shall deposit them with the Secretary.

77 * It has just constituted one at Fort-Dauphin. It has a mania for making people swear an obligation not to recognize us (i.e. the Lodge de la Vérité).

We therefore beg the Sublime Grand Lodge of France to note that if, against all expectations, this so-called Lodge Ecossaise should be regularised, then it[78] will flatter itself that it has the ~~Sublime~~ Sovereign Council of the Orient, and the Sublime Grand Lodge should also note that it is against the rules of the Masonic Order that there should be two councils at one and the same Orient. It is for this reason that the R[espectable]∴ Lodge de la Vérité begs you, Respectable Master, to ensure that the law that you will lay down in this respect is all the more precise and clear, noting that if the law is susceptible to varying interpretations it might result in schisms and disturbances that will by slow degrees destroy the regularity provided by good order, as well as the glory of the Royal Art and your own reputation.

The degradation into which the Royal Art is falling in the eyes of the Profane has its origin in these dissensions. These are disgraces that we see only too often tarnishing the lustre of many an Orient, and which the Respectable Lodge de la Vérité sincerely wishes to avoid seeing arise at its own Orient, which is why it is protesting in advance to the Sublime Grand Lodge that the latter avoid with great care everything that might render it guilty of, or an accomplice to, such misdeeds.

P.T.O. [35r]

Article 4.

The R[espectable]∴ Lodge de la Vérité is also making it a duty to point out to the Sublime Grand Lodge that the Regular Lodges at the Orient of Saint-Domingue, through a vivacity whose origin and cause cannot be guessed at, make it an equally essential duty to be subject to the Sublime Grand Lodge as well as to approve nothing that emanates either from it or from the Sovereign Council of the East with its seat in Paris. What a contrast!

Evidence in support.

How do we prevent these Lodges suffering such intellectual paroxysms? They claim that, compared with this Degree of the Princes of the Secret (which I referred to above), all the other Degrees amount to nothing. The R[espectable]∴ L[odge]∴ de la Vérité is unaware of the law they are using as a basis for such a claim. She therefore begs you, Respectable Master, to lay down the law with regard to the Degrees that must be recognized as having constitutive force in respect of Lodges and those that might be accepted as tending to perfection.

Article 5.

---

78   i.e. the Lodge de la Vérité, which is authorized in that regard by the Ordinances of Ratification that you addressed to it and which their Council of the Orient found to be in conformity with that of B[rother]∴ Martin according to the examination it made of it.

Similarly, the R[espectable]∴ L[odge]∴ de la Vérité begs you to investigate whether it would not be proper (and even essential) to avoid all sorts of schisms [35v] arising from doubts and refusals, to ensure that every time the Sublime Grand Lodge issues Constitutions it gives due notice of them to all the Regular Lodges by means of a circular[79], and to ask whether this would not be of great advantage to the cause of harmony and unanimity through the knowledge that one would have of the Degrees possessed by each Lodge, something that would excite emulation among the Brethren and avoid the abuses that ignorance breeds in the majority of the said Lodges with regard to the Higher Degrees that compose the Masonic Hierarchy.

Article 6.

It also begs the Sublime Grand Lodge to consider ways of making its correspondence more prompt and punctual, as it very often it finds itself waiting for essential replies that might stop the evil at its source and bring great benefit but finds that such replies are often received too late, especially in this hemisphere, which should be a primary object of its concern.

In this connection the R[espectable]∴ Lodge de la Vérité offers to contribute through the Annual Subscriptions to the expense of maintaining secretarial support, postage costs etc. It will fail in nothing that might contribute to the splendour of the Royal Art and to the relief of its illustrious Common Mother, being willing to send the Annual Subscriptions in advance if necessary.

P.T.O. [36r]

Article 7.

The R[espectable]∴ Lodge de la Vérité also begs the Sublime Grand Lodge to support it in the wishes it addresses to the Great Architect that by His shining light He might hasten the Great Work that it has begun towards reviving its existence by choosing Respectable Members who are as commendable for their birth as they are for their talents and their zeal for the glory of the Order, and whose example and fame, warming in the hearts of all the Brethren this essential feeling of virtue and Masonic zeal, will bring about a regeneration in every candidate which will restore to the Masonic Order the lustre and splendour over which a black cloud has cast its shadow.

---

79 This may be the only way to avoid the many schisms in which pride is always the driving-force.
    Each lodge in particular was pleased with the resolution that the S[ublime]∴ G[rand]∴ Lodge had adopted to fix the quality and number of the Degrees that each Lodge should work. This is the sort of thing that would help create a genuine Brotherhood.

These are the filial sentiments the Lodge presents to its beloved and respectable Mother,

Most Respectable Masters, I am,

Your most affectionate and zealous Brother

Vallette∴ Member of

The Lodge St. Frederic, Member of the R[espectable]∴ Lodge de la Vérité,

Knight of the East, of St Andrew of Scotland

&c. &c. and Deputy of the above-mentioned Lodge of the Grand Orient.

To the G[rand]∴ Orient de France

1 February 1771 ∴

If the wishes of the Lodge de la Vérité for the resumption of the Sublime G[rand]∴ Lodge are fulfilled then it cordially invites it to double (and even triple if necessary) the Annual Subscription in order to meet the expenses of the same. [36v]

FM2 543. - La Vérité correspondence with La Concorde, June 6, 1769 – June 1, 1770. [80]

10 July 1770

Extract from the documents lodged in the archives of the R[espectable] L[odge] La Vérité at the Orient of Le Cap Français, Isle of Saint-Domingue, evidencing the inviolable submission of the s[aid] L[odge] to the M[ost] R[espectable] and S[overeign] G[rand] L[odge] of France, as well as the gross errors, dangerous to the Order, posed by the other L[odges] of the Colony, among which is the L[odge] La Concorde in Saint-Marc, which is declaring itself as having representative powers in contravention of the perfectly consistent legality of the s[aid] L[odge] La Vérité∴ [7r] [7v/blank]

1°

Copy of the Letter from the L[odge] La Vérité to the L[odge] of Saint-Marc.

From the L[odge] La Vérité at the Orient of Le Cap Français, in the Year of Light 5769, the 6th day of the 11th M[asoni]c month, to the R[espectable] L[odge] La Concorde at the Orient of Saint-Marc.

The Most R[espectable] and Su[blime] Grand L[odge] of France and the Sub-Council of the Kn[ight]s of the East with its seat in Paris, in supporting our most ardent desires, have enjoined us to inform you, Dearest Brothers, of the diplomas that they have been kind enough to send us. The promptest diligence on the part of our R[espectable] L[odge] will serve as a token both of our obedience and of the joy that we feel that they should favor us, by corresponding with Brothers who are as dear to us as they are assiduous in legally professing the purity of the true Masonic work.

We have pleasure in sending you herewith a compared copy of the documents evidencing the legality of the mission of our R[espectable] Kn[ight] Monsieur Martin, who constituted us on 1st March 1767. We beg you to kindly assist us with any light you might be able to shed during the continuation of this correspondence, in which we are happy to engage, relating to all the Degrees of Masonry.

---

80 BnF FM2 543.

Similarly, we have received the Tableau Général in due form, listing all the constituted L[odges] [8r] of France and her dependencies, copies of which we can make available to you if necessary.

Our dearest Brothers, we are, by the mysterious numbers known only to enlightened mortals, your most affectionate and zealous Brethren. By order of the R[espectable] L[odge],

Signed, Mathéus, Secretary and Notary Royal at Le Cap Français.

The M[ost] W[orshipful] B[rother] Després, a member of the R[espectable Symb[olic] L[odge] of Le Havre du Grace, known as the St. John's Lodge, called La Vérité, who had favored us with his presence at our labors throughout his stay in Le Cap, brought us a package containing the copy of our diplomas and the above letter. This will be apparent from his own letter, a copy of which is shown below, and from the certificate of the Secretary of the R[espectable] L[odge] of La Concorde, which was delivered to him, a copy of which is also shown below. [8v]

2°

Reply from the Secretary of the R[espectable] L[odge] La Concorde

Saint-Marc, 6th April 1770

Sir,

I am beginning this letter by asking you not to be surprised that the Lodge is not addressing you as B[rother]∴, but until legal recognition has been granted it is neither permitted nor possible for us to do so.

The package you sent to the naval captain B[rother] Després at the address of the R[espectable] Symbolic L[odge] of this town, of which I am the Secretary in Charge, was opened at the L[oge] de Collège. As Bro[ther] Després was present last Saturday, he was given a receipt for this delivery, both for his own discharge and to pass on to you if he deemed it appropriate. He has personally witnesed the innumerable obstacles that the B[rothers] who compose our L[odge] have sought to overcome in order to be able to grant you legal recognition. I have been instructed to report to you about these obstacles. After I have done so, I do not think you will find it difficult to agree with our conduct as well as the precautions we are taking to avoid any unpleasant surprises. These procedures have been recommended to us in many circumstances by the G[rand] and S[overeign] L[odge] of France, which, by letters patent of 27th August 1761, appointed the M[ost] R[espectable] B[rother] Étienne Morin as its Deputy and Grand Inspector in this Colony, with the power to admit and constitute to the sublime degree of the highest perfection those B[rethren] whom he might find there to be worthy of such Degrees. This patent [9r] was recorded in our Register of Deliberations at Brother Morin's request. He travelled here for this express purpose and attended our labors. Since that time we have duly recognized him.

To the prejudice of such powers, we see from the documents enclosed in your letter that an attempt has been made to substitute the so-called B[rother] Martin who, during his stay with you, did not deign to make the slightest approach to any Regular L[odge] in this Colony, to have himself recognized in that capacity (if such existed), or to request the registration of any powers he might possess. Indeed, on the contrary, we see that he was in a hurry to constitute you provisionally without – in defiance of the *ius gentium* (law of nations) – at the very least asking the Lodges of the Colony for their advice and agreement, and without even taking the trouble to consult them about the Ancient L[odge] regularly established at the Orient of Le Cap Français. If, like us, you are imbued with the genuine principles of pure and true Masonry, you will agree with us that such conduct is extremely reprehensible, that you are in fact illegally constituted, and that ultimately we cannot and should not recognize you as legitimate.

You must know that we can only recognize the M[ost] R[espectable] B[rother] Delachaussée as Grand Keeper of the Seals and Archives of the G[rand] and S[overeign] L[odge] of France, and similarly of the Council of the Kn[ight]s of the East at the Orient of Paris, and we note with astonishment not [9v] only that the so-called constitutions that were granted to you at the request of the so-called B[rother] Martin on 8th February 1769 on the conditions mentioned therein were sealed by the so-called B[rother] Buoussay, who claims to be the Grand Keeper of the Seals of the Council of the Kn[ight]s of the East, but also that all those who appear to have affixed their signature are not those who signed the various diplomas that we have received at sundry times from this Sovereign Council of the East. This, is, at the very least, mysterious and serves to increase our already well-established doubts. As a result, we are obliged, in spite of ourselves, to decline the request you are making of us. If you can remove these obstacles, then our L[odge] will then act according to what the situation requires.

But allow me to ask you why you do not, by way of preference, have yourself recognized by the Ancient L[odge] of Le Cap Français, our Sister Lodge;[81] send it the originals of the documents that you passed on to us; and then solicit from it recognition of your legal existence, should that not fall within our Compass, since it would be a genuine pleasure for us to follow its example. We are therefore referring you back to that Lodge. Kindly ask it to write to us again, this time in your favor. We shall follow its example, but until this is done according to the observations [10r] detailed in this letter, of which you must inform them by sending this letter to them, so that they can clear up our doubts, there is no point in making any further attempts.

I have the honour to be, Sir, most sincerely

Your most humble and obedient servant,

Signed, Constant de Castelin

Notary at Saint-Marc.

On the back of the above letter is written the address: Monsieur Mathéus, Notary Royal, rue de Vaudreuil, Le Cap Français.

N° 3

Copy of the letter written by B[rother] Després concerning the packages with which he was entrusted by the R[espectable] L[odge] La Vérité, with its seat in Le Cap, to be delivered to the R[espectable] L[odge] La Concorde, with its seat in Saint-Marc.

Saint-Marc, 6th April 1770.

---

81 The Lodge *St. Jean de Jérusalem Ecossaises* initially is not included in Morin's new system, the *Sublime Princes of the Order of the Royal Secret*, when he goes to visit them on March 29, 1764 with the Foix Regiment, and are missing entirely from correspondence until this letter confirming their acceptance. Martin's regularization of *Edouard Stuart* as *Le Vérite* makes them re-align with Morin sometime after 1767. Morin founded *St. Jean de Jérusalem Ecossaises* on March 1st, 1749 and is a member of the lodge until his resignation on March 13th, 1752, for apparently serious reasons, and speaks ill of the lodge to the Élus Parfaits in Bordeaux on his immediate return. Morin loses his powers in 1753 and consequently, the lodge which had yet to have its constitutions ratified by Morin's replacement as Inspector of the *Élus Parfaits*, Lamolère de Feuillas did not even consider their founder a brother by August 7th, 1759. This accounts for their reluctance to unite with Morin until later.

Dear Sir and D[earest] B[rother],

Last Saturday I attended the L[odge] [La Concorde], where I received every possible form of welcome, but what a surprise it was for me when, on opening the packages you had entrusted to me, they were unwilling to recognize your L[odge] as being properly constituted. No matter how much I tried to explain my own point of view they did not wish to believe anything I had to say. B[rother]. Fleuret de Turville, the Worshipful Master here, told me that he would write to you about it. [10v]

You will nevertheless find enclosed the receipt for the package you entrusted to me. I shall not be able to receive any of your always welcome news, as I am leaving for France on Monday. I should be obliged if you would assure the L[odge] [La Vérité] of my good wishes and inform them about the manner in which I pleaded my case. I urge you very strongly to write to the Lodge [La Concorde] to take up with them this matter of their unwillingness to recognize your L[odge] in any way.

Meanwhile, Sir, in anticipation of the pleasure of seeing you again, I have the advantage of being, D[ear] B[rother]∴, your humble, obedient, and zealous Brother.

Signed, P. Desprès.

and addressed to Monsieur Mathéus, Notary Royal, rue de Vaudreuil, Le Cap Français.

N° 4.

Certificate from the Secretary of the L[odge] La Concorde to B[rother] Desprès in the form of a Deliberation of the said L[odge].

We, the Secretary in Charge of the R[espectable] Symbolic L[odge] legitimately established and constituted at the Orient of St. Marc, Isle and [11r] Coast of Saint-Domingue, under the title of La Concorde, hereby certify that, during the L[oge] de C[ollège][82] held on this day [31st March 1770], B[rother] René Desprès, a member of the R[espectable] Symbolic L[odge] of Le Havre du Grace, with its seat at the Orient of the said town, under the distinctive title of the St. John's Lodge called La Vérité, attended our labors, during which he presented to us a package addressed to O[ur] R[espectable] L[odge], which package was duly opened and found to be from the so-called L[odge] La Vérité of Cap Francois, submitted for the purpose of it being recognized as such, whereupon it was deliberated and decided that I would write in my official capacity to M[onsieur] Mathéus, who calls himself its Secretary, without addressing him as 'Brother', to explain to him O[ur] R[espectable] L[odge]'s reasons and well-founded considerations for being unable to recognize this alleged L[odge], in witness whereof I delivered to him at his request the present document. Done, at the Orient of Saint-Marc, the 8th day of the 10th month of the Masonic year 5769, and in the Vulgar Style the 31st of March 1770

Signed, Constant de Castelin [11v]

N° 5.

Reply by B[rother] Mathéus, Secretary of the R[espectable] L[odge] La Vérité to the previous letter of M[onsieur] Contant de Castelin, secretary of the R[espectable] L[odge] La Concorde at Saint-Marc.

Le Cap Français, 11th April 1770

---

82 College Lodge.

Appendix B

Dear S[ir] and Colleague,

If your L[odge] has authorized you to suppress the title of B[rother] then I do not require the authorisation of my own Lodge to address you as one, as this word is so much in conformity with my feelings that I will only suppress it after you have expressly forbidden me to use it, for my Masonic heart is too flattered to find in a colleague a quality that is as dear to me as the Masonic cause is precious and sublime. The only thing lacking in my happiness is my need to prove to you at this time that the reasoning used by your L[odge] against the Lodge La Vérité, of which I have the honour to be Secretary, is not only very ill-founded, but also that your Lodge is affected by an error that is very pernicious to its legality.

This latter characteristic is too close to my heart for me to defer proving it and forces me to reply to your letter by addressing myself to the item that concluded it.

Is it possible, S[ir], that it was your lawfully-assembled Lodge that dictated to you the comment that it is useless to make any further attempts to engage in correspondence with it until we have solicited letters of recommendation from the allegedly Ancient [12r] L[odge] of Le Cap, your sister Lodge! Good grief, what an illusion to be under, to use this highly illegal body as your compass, and to state that you would take genuine pleasure in following its example! We have no intention of making such a serious error! We will take great care not to fall into this precipice, and we know our duties and our status well enough to be able to avoid it. The Sub[lime] G[rand] L[odge] of France explicitly enjoins us to share its favors with all the Regular L[odges] of the Colony, and this in the form that we followed when communicating with your own Lodge first, because we found it on the Tableau Général which was sent to us by the said G[rand] L[odge] of France. If you have this Tableau (which must have been sent to you in accordance with art[icle] 30 of the General Regulations of the G[rand] L[odge]) then your conduct is unforgivable: you will find nothing there that vaguely resembles, let alone specifically refers to, this so-called L[odge] of Le Cap. I think I can even argue that its constitutions are as far from the purity of Masonic work as its alleged members are. Nothing, S[ir], escapes the knowledge and vision of the great Argus.

We note with pleasure that a so-called L[odge] under the title of St John of Jerusalem, established at Fort Dauphin [12v] using the fake constitutions of the Lodge of Le Cap, <u>your Sister Lodge</u>, has been deleted from the Tableau Général, to which it had previously been added in error. I have had the pleasure of offering you a copy of the said Tableau and pointing out to you yet again on behalf of the R[espectable] L[odge] La Vérité of Le Cap that you will not find on the said Tableau, duly sealed and stamped, any L[odge] of Le Cap other than that of La Vérité, and if you will open the Special Regulations, of which every properly-constituted L[odge] also receives a copy from the G[rand] L[odge], you will see in section 2 that [you] are prohibited in engaging in any correspondence with any Lodge other than La Vérité in Le Cap.

Assuming that you have not yet received the new Tableau Général, I enclose herewith on behalf of my L[odge] an extract from it showing those Lodges throughout the Colony that are recognized therein.

I shall conclude by formally protesting to you that this so-called Ancient L[odge] of Le Cap is irregular. However much this protest pains me, it is in the present instance forced upon me.

The other point at issue is no less interesting, but given the various obstacles and alleged difficulties encountered by the Brethren of your L[odge], should this not be considered a Norman quarrel rather than a Masonic one? This question is perhaps rather cavalier, but I think I can allow myself a style that is, at least, a little cavalier when replying to a profanomasonic letter.

We will not argue about the validity [13r] of the letters patent borne by your B[rother] Étienne Martin Morin. I believe him to be your Grand Inspector, although I have as much reason to be suspicious of him as you have to be suspicious of our R[espectable] B[rother] Martin, for ultimately the mission of your fellow has never been confirmed to me with any greater authenticity than the mission of my own. The mission of the latter is not only confirmed at the L[odge] La Vérité which he constituted, but at all the Legal L[odges] of the Colony by means of the compared extracts that the G[rand] L[odge] enjoins the Lodge La Verité to pass on, just as I passed them on, in the prescribed form, to your own Lodge in my capacity as Secretary. You accepted the Stamps and Seals of O[ur] R[espectable] L[odge] which you nevertheless refer to as a 'so-called' Lodge, and you do not dispute my status as Lodge Secretary, but you challenge the Stamps and Seals of the S[overeign] G[rand] L[odge] of France and of the Sovereign Council of the [Knights of the] E[ast], and have cast suspicions on the signatures of the R[espectable] Officers and Sublime Members which confirm the authenticity of the patents of which you have a copy. Take very great care, S[ir], for you are creating a pernicious schism, for which you will have to render account to this Respectable Body.

As a good Mason, I believe that your L[odge], before committing yourself to issuing an insult of this nature, should have [13v] acquired a little more certainty, and waited until some favorable opportunity to acquire the originals, had presented itself. By all means urge your Lodge to put a deputation together. We are only too happy to open up our Archives, and we are even assured that such a step will lead to the mutual understanding that is so essential to our Order. I boldly assert here that if it is Masons that compose the L[odge] La Concorde then they will find Masons in the L[odge] La Vérité.

Your alleged grievances against the R[espectable] B[rother] Martin are completely unjust. I cannot believe that you would wish to force this worthy B[rother] to make a Grand Tour of the Colony in order to have his powers recognized and registered in all the L[odges]! This B[rother] had private business in Le Cap, and chance alone – and certainly not violence or the duties of his office – would have taken him to other places.[83] His powers extended to rectifying the L[odges] in the places he had occasion to visit. He visited the L[odges] in Le Cap and found Masons only in the Lodge La Vérité. He forbade this Lodge to have any connection with any other, and this prohibition is confirmed by the G[rand] L[odge] of France. If B[rother] Martin had moved to Saint-Marc then he would have proceeded in the same way and would have found Masons there no doubt, [14r] as well as in all the other places.

If you are in happy correspondence with the G[rand] L[odge] of France then you will find that the Tableau G[énéral] says that B[rother] Martin is Past Master of the L[odge] St. Frederic in Paris, and an Officer of the M[ost] R[espectable] and S[overeign] G[rand] L[odge] of France, and if you have any remaining suspicions left about a Mason of this stature then frankly I have nothing more to say to you. You believe that he is <u>violating the *ius gentium* (the law of nations)</u> by not having asked the opinion of all the L[odges] of the Colony before constituting the one that subsequently proved its good faith by showing him a series of Masonic labors, <u>and by not even taking the trouble to consult the Ancient L[odge] regularly established at the Orient of Le Cap</u>. I have previously fought against such – once again, pernicious – abuse, from which I pray the G[reat] A[rchitect] of t[he] U[niverse] to deliver you.[84]

To our offer of the original documents confirming our Legality we are adding the further offer of our correspondence with the L[odges] of France. We have even decided that we can let you have the original of the letter from the R[espectable] Scottish L[odge] of Bord[eaux], which is attached herewith, but we are not allowed to do the same with the diplomas of the S[overeign] G[rand] L[odge] of France! Please be so good as to return the Bordeaux document to me in due course. See Note **A**. [14v]

---

83 Martin is isolated in Le Cap and stays briefly for a few years, mainly on business.
84 See the preceding, FM2 543.

[Marginal note:] **A** These Brethren have infringed the Law of Nations by keeping back one hundred original letters which would enable the correspondence of our L[odge] to be correlated with that of the R[espectable] Scottish L[odge] of Bordeaux, an action prejudicial to the L[odge] of Saint-Marc – Mathéus.

In just the past few days we have received a letter from Our M[ost] R[espectable] and D[ear] B[rother] Delachaussée, along with another under the same cover from Our M[ost] R[espectable] B[rother] Chaillon de Jonville, the last Substitute G[enera]l of our V[ery] Dear B[rother] the Prince of Clermont, and the first Grand Keeper of the Seals and Archives of the S[overeign] G[rand] L[odge] of France.

Never was there a more appropriate recommendation, and we enclose a compared copy for you. May these documents, by evidencing our obedience in the execution of what they enjoin us to do, dispel your doubts and confirm the legality that you unjustly deny to us!

The originals of these letters, which are sealed with the privy seals of the G[rand] L[odge], are offered to you with equal pleasure by the L[oge] La Vérité, so that your deputy may be convinced of the authenticity of the signatures and of their conformity.

I do not know, S[ir], whether, after all this, we must expect a new series of insults from a L[odge] that we have always looked upon with veneration.

I summon you and the R[espectable] L[odge] La Concorde, on behalf of the R[espectable] L[oge] La Vérité and that of the M[ost] S[ublime] G[rand] L[odge] of France, as well as of the [15r] Sov[ereign] C[ouncil] of the Kn[ight]s of the East, to acknowledge receipt of the copies in due form, which we have sent to La Concorde on behalf of the aforementioned S[ublime] G[rand] L[odge] and Sovereign Council of the Knights of the East, and to make a formal note of this in the acts of the said L[odge] La Concorde by means of an entry in its archival registers, so that we may give notice of this at the prescribed time with copies of the steps taken by our R[espectable] L[odge] at my suggestion, and of the replies by the Lodge La Concorde as well as your own, with the strict stipulation being imposed upon you that not a word should be omitted.

May the G[reat] A[rchitect] of the U[niverse] enlighten your minds and bring them to a state of eternal peace and understanding, which we for our part shall always reciprocate as true Masons and Brethren. In the meantime I remain, S[ir] and Dear Brother &c.,

signed Mathéus

Notary Royal.

Addressed to M[onsieur] Constant de Castelin, Notary Royal, at Saint-Marc. [15v]

N°. 6

Copy of the letter written by the same Brother Mathéus on the same day, April 11th, to M[onsieur] Fleuret de Turville, W[orship]ful Master of the s[aid] L[odge] La Concorde.

My Dear Worshipful,

The letter of constitution – which was as lacking in decorum as it was in Masonic spirit – that was addressed to us by your W[orshipful] Secretary, B[rother] Constant de Castelin, will never cause us to deviate either from our duties or from the respect that people of honour owe to one other. The nascent opportunity provides us with the means to avenge ourselves in the least equivocal way and in the manner most worthy of a true Mason.

Three or four days after receiving your gracious missive we received a package containing a letter from D[ear] B[rother] Chaillon de Jonville and one from D[ear] B[rother] Delachaussée. We are sending you copies of these documents in view of the importance of the advice they contain, and this amid the uncertainty in which we find ourselves that you yourselves might already have been sent the same documents. If you did receive them at the same time as we did, then perhaps they will help you to decide to display towards true Masons the respect that they owe to each other. As for ourselves, M[ost] W[orshipful], we shall never deviate from this veneration and fraternal friendship &c.

Signed, Mathéus

and addressed to M[onsieur] Fl[e]uret de Turville, Attorney to the Courts of Saint-Marc. [16r]

N° 7.

Reply from M[onsieur] Fleuret de Turville, Worshipful Master of the L[odge] La Concorde, to the previous letters. Dated Saint-Marc 4th May 1770.

Sir,

I have received your missive in the form of a letter of constitution which you have paid me the honour of writing to me on behalf of, and as Secretary of, a L[odge] whose legal existence is not sufficiently well established for me to be permitted to reply to it in the form usually encountered in the correspondence of Regular LL[odges].

Alert as I am, however, to the attention you are paying me, I take genuine pleasure in preferring to answer your letter on my own personal behalf rather than as Master of the L[odge], in order to make you aware of the considerable extent to which the answers given to you on behalf of the R[espectable] L[odge] La Concorde by B[rother] Contant de Castelin, its Secretary, are in conformity with the Laws from which we must not depart. I shall at the same time reply to what you have said to this d[ear] B[rother], to save him having to repeat to you my own observations.

The Law, S[ir], makes it perfectly clear in Article 11 of the General Regulations of the G[rand] L[odge] concerning relations with Particular L[odges] that one should only recognize packages as emanating from the G[rand] L[odge] if they are stamped and signed in the form prescribed by Art[icles] 12. and 13. of its Statutes, and that we were consequently forced to doubt the authenticity of one [16v] of the documents of which you sent us copies, seeing that, instead of being signed, as the other one was, by the M[ost] R[espectable] B[rother] Delachaussée in his capacity as G[rand] Keeper of the Seals, Stamps and Archives of the Grand and S[overeign] L[odge] of France, it was signed by M[onsieur] Duhoussay in the same capacity, and then again by M[onsieur] Bourgeois as Secretary-G[enera]l of the G[rand] L[odge], although we knew that the R[espectable] B[rother] Moët held this particular post. Nor did we see in this so-called letter of constitution any of the signatures of those Brethren whom we know to be members of the Council of the Kn[ight]s of the East in Paris, quite apart from the style and form of this letter, which seemed to be us to be very different from those used by the S[overeign] G[rand] L[odge] and by the same Council of Kn[ight]s of the E[ast], with which several of us are perfectly familiar.

Our feelings of mistrust occasioned by the absence of the signatures of the M[ost] R[espectable] B[rothers] Moët and de La Chaussée in their respective capacities was undoubtedly well-founded, since the letters, copies of which you were kind enough to send to us, and for which I thank you (having received similar ones from the M[ost] R[espectable] B[rothers] Chaillon de Jonville and de La Chaussée), far from serving to dispel them, only increased them, for in one of them the M[ost] R[espectable] B[rother] Chaillon de Jonville informs you that he has chosen B[rothers] Moët, Le Roy and Delachaussée as his confidents, [17r] <u>gives you to understand that he will acknowledge and regard as authentic and as truly emanating from the G[rand] L[odge] all patents, certificates, letters and other documents if you recognize that one of their three signatures has been affixed to them, and warns you to be on your guard and be suspicious of anything that is not signed by one of these three Brothers</u>, so as soon as we noted that none of their three Signatures appeared in your so-called constitutions, we could not for that reason consider them as having emanated from the S[overeign] G[rand] L[odge].

You must also have noticed that B[rother] Chaillon de Jonville tells you that B[rother] de Lachaussée has always been and still is the Keeper of the Seals, Stamps and Archives, and that this appointment makes him the only one of the public officers of the Order who has retained a procedural practice such that any document that does not bear his signature cannot be recognized as emanating from the G[rand] L[odge]. He adds that he has appointed him the legal guardian of Freemasonry and forbids him to divest himself of that role until he can pass it on to the true body of the G[rand] L[odge].

In his letter, B[rother] Delachaussée tells you as much as he tells us about how we can recognize as authentic a document where another B[rother] signs as Grand Keeper of the Seals, and we also see a B[rother] Bourgeois signing as Secretary of the G[rand] L[odge], while B[rother] de Jonville tells you that, of the B[rothers] who are Public Officers the only one left in office is B[rother] Delachaussée. [17v]

We also note that you are warned to be wary of anything that might come from a B[rother] Poupart, and yet there is someone of that name among the signatories of your so-called constitutions. So there you have it S[ir]. There are many reasons why we should question the validity of this document, and even if you had no others to present to us we would not have hesitated to consider your L[odge] as being badly constituted, but the copy you have sent us of the judgments both in your favor and in favor of B[rother] Martin of the Council of the Kn[ight]s of the East, with its seat in Paris, dated 27th November 1768, and which appear to have been signed by the M[ost] R[espectable] B[rother] Chaillon de Jonville, and sealed and stamped by the M[ost] R[espectable] B[rother] Delachaussée, give us reason to pause, because if the Seals, Stamps and Signatures on the despatches of these judgements are in conformity with those with which we are familiar, then we must have a great deal there to concern ourselves with. However, it remains for us to examine whether there is no good reason to return to the operations of B[rother] Martin, and if, in a town where there was not only an Ancient Scottish L[odge], very regularly constituted and laboring according to all the powers of the G[rand] Perfect Elect, Masters and Sublime Scots, but also a Sovereign Council of the Kn[ight]s of the East, he was able without their participation and approbation to form a L[odge], and if in doing so he did not abuse his powers. He was obviously not unaware of the existence of these L[odges], since he visited them, and attended their L[odge] meetings, Chapters and Councils. [18r]

The powers of the Inspectors and Deputies of the G[rand] and S[overeign] G[rand] L[odge] can only be effective in the founding of Regular Lodges in places where there is no regularly constituted L[odge], and still less so in towns and districts where there is a Scottish L[odge] and a Sovereign Council which have sufficient powers of their own for this purpose, and even if B[rother] Martin might also have been able to exercise his own powers, it can still be said that he failed to show the consideration and decency that he ought to have shown towards the B[rothers], who were very deserving of his services. If the matter were to be brought before the Tribunal of the G[rand] L[odge] of France then it would certainly express disapproval of the conduct of this B[rother]. He was not unaware that this L[odge] of Le Cap had a very ancient and very legitimate existence in Masonry, and if he was unaware of it then why, when he visited it, did he not ask to see its constitutions, for he would then have seen that they were in good order, and that they emanated from the M[ost] R[espectable] Scottish L[odge] of Bordeaux, which is recognized as legitimate by the G[rand] L[odge] of France, and all Lodges. He would therefore have been quite sure about the genuine existence in Masonry of this Scottish L[odge] of Le Cap, its only deficiency being that it was not listed in the Tableau Général in accordance with the new statutes of the G[rand] L[odge], which only date from 1763. But these new Statutes could not deprive it of its legitimacy, and it would even have appeared on the Tableau Général to confirm the date of its first constitutions if B[rother] Martin [18v] had kept the promise he had made to the Lodge to have it inserted into the Tableau on his return from Paris, given the difficulty there was in sending packages to that city. Moreover, as a Scottish L[odge], it was able to dispense with this formality, created as it was by the M[ost] R[espectable] Scottish L[odge] of Bordeaux, as well as by the Scottish L[odge] of this town. We have always corresponded with it in this capacity, as with our Elder Sister, and we would feel we were doing it a great injustice if we ceased to consider it as legally and fully constituted just because it had not enjoyed the opportunity of being registered on the Tableau G[énéra]l as a Symbolic Lodge or otherwise. And I repeat, the regulations enacted several years after its foundation could not nullify its legitimacy, or make a L[odge] that was at that time regularly constituted into an irregular one. The M[ost] R[espectable] Scottish L[odge] of Bordeaux has stated that it is recognized as legitimate by the G[rand] L[odge], having been formed long before the new Regulations, and I even believe that it may be assumed that it is recognized as legitimate by the G[rand] L[odge], and that in writing to you the B[rothers] Chaillon de Jonville and de La Chaussée thought they were writing to this old L[odge], since they say that they informed you in March 1767, as they did all the Regular L[odges], that the work of the G[rand] L[odge] had been suspended, so at that time you could not have been considered by these illustrious officers as forming a Regular L[odge], since the documents upon which you are relying only date from 9th November 1768 and February 1769. Hence I presume that they thought [19r] they were writing to the Ancient L[odge] of le Cap when they issued this notification in 1767, as at that time you did not exist, and consequently I presume also that they believed that it was to it that the letters that you received, just as we did, would be delivered.[85]

Please try therefore, S[ir], to go back to having more positive feelings towards this R[espectable] L[odge], and to show it the deserved respect – I might even say the deference and homage – that you owe to it as a Lodge composed of Masons, the majority of whom have been raised to the Higher Degrees, and at the Orient of which there presides a Council of Knights of the East, <u>which has no less authority than that of Paris</u>, regarding which I must say again that, during the suspension of the work of the G[rand] L[odge], the Council of the Kn[ight]s of the East, with its seat in Paris, <u>certainly has no more right to issue constitutions for a place where another Council of Knights of the East has its seat than it would have had to issue constitutions for Paris</u>, for a Parliament does not give orders within the jurisdiction of another Parliament. If the G[rand] L[odge] of France, which can be seen as the Council of the Most Serene G[rand] Master, is no longer in session, then the authority necessary to maintain subordination and legal guardianship of the laws of Masonry is devolved to the Councils of the Kn[ight]s of the East, the Princes of Jerusalem, the Sublime Knights of the Royal Secret etc., according to the district in which the towns in which they are established are to be found, then if in Le Cap there was a Council of Knights of the East who, in this capacity, enjoyed the right of inspection of the work of the Symbolic L[odges], then <u>it was up to this Council rather than the one in</u> [19v] <u>Paris to issue you with provisional constitutions</u>, and it is to it that you must turn to impart to your work the regularity that it lacks. Although we also have here a Sovereign Council, not only of Kn[ight]s of the East but also of the Princes of Jerusalem etc. with all the authority necessary to make a sovereign decision in such cases, we would be interfering with the rights of the Council of Le Cap if we did not leave it to its discretion to decide on your own concerns,

---

85 See No. 188M. Léogane received this notice in June 1767.

which is why we believe we can do no better than to settle upon whatever they decide on this subject. Moreover, it would be only to them that we could turn for verification of the stamps, seals, and signatures of your patents, because they must have in their archives documents that are suitable for this verification, and because nothing would be easier for us than to pass them some of the relevant material.

That, S[ir], is the arrangement to which we shall strictly adhere in order not to deviate from the fundamental laws and rules of Masonry. Will you still be calling this a 'Norman dispute' [arguing for the sake of it] rather than a Masonic one? Will you still be referring to this response as <u>Profane-masonic</u>? I do not see in the Secretary's letter anything that approaches the bitterness that persists in your reply, for neither his intention nor that of the L[odge] was to say anything to you that might cause you offence.

What you can see, S[ir], when you look at the R[espectable] L[odge] of St John of Jerusalem established at Fort Dauphin [20r] is a continuation of the error in which you find yourself, and from which I hope you will find your way back. Regarding the legitimacy of the M[ost] R[espectable] Scottish L[odge] of Le Cap, even if they are not listed in the Tableau Général recognized by the G[rand] L[odge] of France because of the remoteness of their locations and the suspension of the works of the G[rand] L[odge], they still have a very strong case for appearing in it, but until now they have not been able to secure the same facilities as yourself. With time that will come. It may even be the case that that time is not far off. What is more, since the legitimacy of the M[ost] R[espectable] Scottish L[odge] of Bordeaux speaks most decidedly in favor of the L[odge] of Le Cap, its beloved Daughter, which it created, the L[odge] of Le Cap is in the same relationship with the L[odge] of Fort Dauphin, which is *its* Daughter. Besides, the Council of Knights of the East and the [Scottish] L[odge] of Le Cap have no less authority to award provisional constitutions to this L[odge] of Fort Dauphin <u>than the Council of Knights of the East, with its seat in Paris, can have had to bestow those of which you sent us copies</u>. It is the same situation with the R[espectable] Symbolic L[odge] L'Étroite Union of Gros Morne, provisionally constituted by the Sovereign Council of the Princes of Jerusalem, Knights of the East etc., with its seat at Saint-Marc. The suspension of the work of the G[rand] L[odge] prevented this new L[odge] from receiving ratification of its provisional constitution and a listing in the Tableau Général, but that does not prevent [20v] it from being recognized as regular in all LL[odges] of the Colony, and from fraternising and maintaining a correspondence with them. Not only is this the case with the Lodges of Le Cap and Fort Dauphin, whose regularity is not contested by any of the LL[odges] in the Colony, but none of them will recognize the regularity of your own Lodge without the approval and consent of the M[ost] R[espectable] Scottish L[odge] of Le Cap. This is what you must expect to happen, and I therefore recommend you make the appropriate representations to that L[odge].

Far from 'criticising' the Seals and Stamps of the G[rand] L[odge] of France, as you reproach us for doing, we have infinite respect for them, and we shall criticise only over those documents that are devoid of them, such as one of those of which you have sent us a copy, a fact that will undoubtedly be confirmed by comparison. And let us suppose for a moment that they *are* the same, it is still true to say that they were affixed by someone other than the M[ost] R[espectable] B[rother] Delachaussée, who is the sole Keeper of the Seals, who has always been enjoined not to divest himself of them, and who has not even signed your patents. Reflect on this and you will find that my observation is justified.

There are still a few points in your letter to be dealt with, but my present letter is already too long. Unfortunately the subjects are too important to be dealt with more concisely. However, if you would be so kind as to pay some attention to the reasons for the circumspection with which we believe [21r] we must act then I trust that you will no longer find anything profanly-masonic in it. I must add that I am not writing any of this on my own initiative and authority without having conferred with the Past Masters and those holding the highest Degrees of L[odges] both Scottish and Symbolic and of the Sovereign

Councils of this Orient. You can therefore consider this reply as our unanimous view. I urge you to believe that as soon as the legitimacy of your L[odge] has been recognized by the Most Legitimate and M[ost] R[espectable] Scottish L[odge] of Le Cap, we shall take a genuine pleasure in corresponding with you, as we do with all the regular L[odges] of the Colony, and with many of those of the various Orients of France.

I have the honour to be, most sincerely Sir, your most h[umbl]e and o[bedien]t B[rother],

signed, Fleuret de Turville

and addressed to M[onsieur] Mathéus, Notary Royal, Le Cap Français. [21v]

N° 8

Reply to this previous letter by B[rother] Mathéus, Secretary of the R[espectable] L[odge] La Vérité, to the above-mentioned Worshipful of the R[espectable] L[odge] of St Marc.

Le Cap, 16th May 1770.

Sir,

I read your letter with a mixture of pleasure and surprise. I accept that it was concerned with Masonry but, for me, it does not express that delicate sense of brotherhood to the degree of purity that I would like. It is, however, far from being the case that your letter is too long-winded, for the matter we are dealing with is much too important to be briefly summarised.

I warn you, S[ir], that you are dealing here with a Mason who was initiated before the legal age, as a Lewis, and who is now in his fortieth year or so. That information should be sufficient to persuade you that I will not be content with playing word-games, and that I am capable of fearlessly delving into a subject that has fascinated me since I first knew how to fathom the most sacred mysteries. If you are a Mason, then you will not be able to deny that you know few other Masons, and that, indeed, there are not that many to know. I do believe you to be a Mason, so why then do we have the misfortune to see ourselves forced to bicker and take opposite sides in the pursuit of a goal that requires so much agreement and mutual understanding? However, I feel motivated to reply to your letter by the good faith it displays to me on the one hand and the blindness and error that I perceive in it on the other. [22r]

I hope you are as convinced of my sincerity as I am of yours. Both myself and my R[espectable] L[odge] are thoroughly familiar with the General Regulations of the G[rand] L[odge], and with all its Articles. Your observation on one of the diplomas addressed to us is fair and pleasing to me. Let us assume for a moment that this document is a forgery, although personally I am sure that it is genuine, since I am now familiar with the cause of this kind of misunderstanding. If you acknowledge the diploma of the Sovereign Council of the Knights of the East, which enjoins you to recognize my L[odge] as well-constituted, what more do you want? Are you any safer than we are ourselves from attempts to impose it upon you? Our R[espectable] B[rothers] Chaillon and de Lachaussée warn us all to be on our guard. Although we are assured of the truth of both our diplomas, we have not allowed ourselves to raise the same objections to the diploma that you have doubts about, which was sent to us subsequently. I could prove to you that this diploma at least could be genuine, and that indeed it is, but as I have no need to do so, and as that would lead me too far out of my way, I am happy for you to assume that it is a forgery for as long as you please, it being enough for me that you accept the other diploma, which should have earned for me that status that is so precious to me, namely that of a B[rother], a status that you have refused me. I shall be content simply to observe that B[rother] Bourgeois, whose signature as Secretary you reject, is the Secretary of the [22v] Provinces, and that this Colony is, in this sense, a Province. You must therefore agree that the other diploma prevents you from regarding our L[odge] as badly constituted, but that it still causes your judgement to be suspended until you are assured of the truth through comparison with the originals.

You still want to investigate whether there is any justification for resuming opposition to B[rother] Martin's operations.

Why in God's name are you so jealous that Masons exist? Why would you want to thwart the mission of a B[rother] who is an officer of the G[rand] L[odge] and who enjoys its confidence? And that is a mission that calls for a learned Brother too! Why, I say, do you harbour this enmity towards a L[odge] that professes Masonic purity, and towards B[rothers] whom you despise before you have even met them? This, S[ir], is the heart of the matter, and it is here that I can clearly see the error into which you are falling. <u>If, in a town where there is not only a very well constituted Scottish L[odge] (you are referring to the so-called L[odge] of Le Cap)</u> etc., <u>but also a Sovereign Council of Knights of the East, could B[rother] Martin have formed a L[odge] without their approval? And could he really have been unaware of the existence of such L[odges], having visited them?</u> To this I must reply that B[rother] Martin *did* visit them, and I will even confess that he was more or less satisfied with the so-called Scottish L[odge], but that then and thereafter he suffered infinite annoyance through the so-called L[odge] La Parfaite Harmonie, which is, unfortunately, [23r] united with the other Lodge. Since these two so-called L[odges] now form one body, since Bro. Martin was fully aware of the all too irregular labors of the Lodge La Parfaite Harmonie, and since the Scottish Lodge was composed mostly of Craftsmen from that Lodge, it was impossible, I say, for B[rother] Martin to grant his approval under the auspices of the Grand Orient to a body composed of several bad Craftsmen.

This, S[ir], if I am not mistaken, is the cause of the formal illegality of the so-called Scottish L[odge], although you talk about this as if it is something to be proud of. I will not dispute that, as you state, this L[odge] fundamentally deserves its constitutions, and should be listed on the Tableau Général for France, but it does *not* have these constitutions and is not listed there.

Since you have a relationship with the G[rand] Globe de France and are familiar with its operations, can you, Sir, therefore depart from the sacred statutes that you have sworn to follow and respect? Read Articles 24, 28, and 29 of the General Regulations of the G[rand] L[odge], and see if you can find there this so-called L[odge] of Le Cap. See whether Article 30 is executed in its favor. I would gladly concede if they showed me a G[enera]l Tableau addressed to it in conformity with that article. See if Article 2 of the Particular Regulations tells you whether they have any relationship with this L[odge], and qualify it to be described, as you so blindly do, as [23v] <u>Your Sister Lodge and Model</u>? Are you also compliant with Art. 3. of these regulations? And Art. 4? And Art. 5̶-6̶? I must conclude from all this, my dear W[orship]ful, that you are very lax regarding consistency of form in your Masonic ritual, something that causes me great annoyance. I repeat that this so-called L[odge] may well be deserving of a different fate, but that it is not possible for me to formally recognize it as a well-constituted Sister Lodge without prevarication and without, ultimately, being guilty of a crime in the first degree. Can you really suggest that <u>I go back to adopting a more positive view of this R[espectable] L[odge], and to paying it the deference and homage that I owe it?</u> O Supreme Architect, in what a state is thy Jerusalem to be found! I know, Sir, how much I value most of the members of this so-called L[odge]: with most of them I have bonds either of genuine friendship or of social status, but such a bond is a purely civil one, and I would even suggest that, out of an almost immeasurable number of so-called Masons, <u>G[ran]d Scots, Kn[ight]s of the East, Princes of Jerusalem, Princes of the Royal Secret etc.</u> there are probably not more than four really good Masons. It is less than two years since I affiliated with the L[oge] La Vérité. I joined it because I saw that it was well-constituted, and because I saw Masons hard at work there. I think I can say that it was just as easy for me to join the other L[odge], which was composed almost exclusively of my friends and colleagues, but I was a Mason and I liked the Masonic rituals. [24r]

In truth, S[ir], from this point of your letter to the end of it, every sentence I read provokes me to a Masonic anger with which I cannot burden you. You want this so-called Council of the Knights of the East of Le Cap, rather than the Sovereign Council of France, to be entitled to grant us constitutions, and argue <u>that it is the Council of the Knights of the East of Le Cap which must impart to our work the regularity that is lacking.</u> Such a belief is the height of fanaticism. But my dear W[orship]ful Kn[ight], as long as you persist in the error of firmly believing that this L[odge] is <u>regular, and indeed most regular, eminent, and infinitely respectable, and the Model and compass for all the regular L[odges] of the Colony</u>, then frankly that says it all, and if I am not fortunate enough to dissuade you from such a dangerous error, despite such an impressive armoury of arguments, then I really have nothing more to hope for.

I would like, with all my heart, to hear you say, as I do, that this L[odge] is simply unlucky. It wants to be composed exclusively of true Masons, and it aims for purity in its ritual. Even so, it is persistently rejected. That is a shame. It will always be irregular, in that it should neither claim nor expect in this condition to enjoy any communication with the regular L[odges]. Instilled by a similar (entirely Masonic) reasoning, I would gladly share your tears if, on our journey through life, I encountered good Brethren with whom I could not have any connection. [24v]

I swear, upon the faith of a Mason, that not the slightest trace of whimsy will be found in my approach, but that if the L[odge] of La Vérité were capable of sufficient absurdity to lower itself to the level that you so unreasonably require, then my request for its withdrawal would immediately follow upon its decision, and I would reserve the right to lodge in due course a formal complaint with the Grand G[lobe] of France.

It is not to this so-called L[odge] that you must take your commissioners to verify our original documents. The door of the Temple would undoubtedly be closed to them, and for all sorts of good reasons, if, that is, my voice could prevail.

The display you have shown me of the various Degrees of this L[odge] does not impress me. We know as well as they do how to form Councils of the Knights of the East, and unquestionably more legitimate ones too, as well as Lodges working all the other Degrees with which you adorn them. But I know of no other Masonry beyond the Symbolic, and if you have a good relationship with the G[rand] L[odge] you must be familiar only with the Degrees of English M[aste]r, Knight Rose-croix, Knight of the Sword or of the East, and the fourfold respectable Knight of St. Andrew of Scotland. It is to this last College that all Masonry is subordinate today, and it is this College of St. Andrew of Scotland that is the sovereign judge. These are the only Degrees that we work in the Respectable L[oge] La Vérité, and [25r] the only ones that we are allowed to work, to the exclusion of all others, with which we are nevertheless familiar, along with the so-called <u>Sublime Kn[ight]s of the Royal Secret of your 'Model and Elder Sister', the Lodge of Le Cap.</u>

If you obtained your information from the Grand Orient of France then you would know that, to this day, all the L[odges] in the Colony have been subordinate to our Sovereign College, which will not be (and cannot be) attached to any L[odges] in Le Cap other than that of La Vérité, and which must judge in the last resort.

But I am afraid I am unable to give you a taste of a truth of which, I presume, you have never yet had any notion. You are a Mason, and that is enough for me as far as the present matter is concerned. If you want to verify what I am saying, my dear Worshipful, then both the door of the Temple and our archives are open to you. We are more learned and more enlightened than you think, and we do not deserve the contempt of any of our Brothers. Do not pretend any longer that this so-called L[odge] (which, I state once again, is illegal) <u>makes any pronouncements upon this subject that we have in common with you</u>. They are unable, as you yourself say, to show you any <u>proper documents to verify our original ones</u>. You are offering to let them have such – well, all the worse for you. It is quite obvious that they do not have any signatures of the Members of the G[rand] L[odge] or, at least, any of its officers. [25v]

I am sorry that you detected a certain bitterness in the style of my letter in reply to M[onsieur] Constant, but how else am I to deal with such ~~a little expected~~ an unexpected obstacle? I will always be happy to submit anything I write to any competent court, with all the more confidence as I am guided in this matter by the compass of the fundamental and sacred Laws of the Order.

You may encounter in my style of writing something that comes close to bitterness, but I swear to you, my dear W[orship]ful, that I would be in despair if you saw in it anything other than an ardent zeal and a sincere desire to see people united under the same Law – people who, moreover, differ, in a cause so sublime, only on certain formal points. Do not deceive yourself that the geographical remoteness of the places involved is the reason why the so-called Scottish L[odge] of Le Cap does not appear on the Tableau G[énéra]l. Your flexibility of mind in this regard is excessive and misplaced.

I swear to you that various gentlemen, famous in both civilian life and in the Royal Art, have failed even in their most strenuous attempts to obtain constitutions for this L[odge], and have grown weary of the task.

Why then does our Lodge enjoy better fortune? *Ex tenebris fulget Veritas* ['The truth will shine forth from the darkness'] is our motto. Is it possible that in the other Lodge some well-known firmly-rooted vice is to be found? Now, if that Lodge is illegal, then all the more so is that of [26r] Fort Dauphin, which you defend. You still claim equality of rights between the Scottish L[odge] of Le Cap and the G[rand] Council of the Orient of France in order to prove that this Scottish L[odge] had the power to constitute others. This argument is untenable in every respect: Masonry is one, and as soon as it adopts a chief, nothing emanates except from him. That Lodge's power to constitute others may certainly have existed in other times, but this situation has changed, as the latest regulations will confirm to you. Your constitutions bestowed upon the L[odge] of Gros Morne have met with the same fate, and I therefore still make a clear distinction between your L[odge], which is recognized as well-constituted, and that of Le Cap, which has only ever been recognized by those people in the Colony who are blind to the facts, and by its Mother Lodge in Bordeaux, which left it in a state of error, as we proved to the present Worshipful of this French L[odge] of Bordeaux when he did us the favor of visiting us recently, on which occasion we even provided him with proof of the poor relations of his L[odge] with the G[rand] Orient of France, whose most important and fundamental work he seemed not to know anything about. This is the way we do business, and it should be the way of all good Masons.

You therefore agree on the authenticity of the diploma of the Sovereign Council of the Knights of the East addressed to Our R[espectable] L[odge] – we are therefore properly constituted. By all means send a deputy or similar, [26v] however many you please, from your own Lodge to verify our originals, but please make sure they are not members of your so-called Sister Lodge of Le Cap. Since I am writing this letter without having consulted my L[odge], I do not know what sort of reception such deputies would receive, although I have said something about this above.

I do not wish to end this letter without confessing to you that I derived a certain secret pleasure from some of your objections, and if you knew me you would find that I myself am scarcely less severe when dealing with fundamental issues. No one is more keenly aware than I am of <u>the respect that we owe to each other</u>, but beware, my dear W[orship]ful, that although you are speaking here as a Mason, I can hardly detect any of the true Masonic zeal either in your Secretary's letter or even in yours. I am not, however, used to being so initially surprised by something that I have read. I find your style of writing to be less shocking than that of your Secretary, or perhaps I find it less shocking because of the respect I have for your level of accomplishment, which causes me to assume that there is some merit in you. You will know, moreover, that a Knight of the East is characterised by firmness, and that it does not suit him to creep and crawl to people, especially when he is well-armed. I will say the same about my R[espectable] L[odge], whose sublime character is well-known to me, and where also they are familiar with all [27r] these High Degrees with which you embellish the others, and even of the most sublime Degree of all, which stands above all those known to this day in the Colony, as I had the pleasure to point out above.

Reflect carefully, S[ir], upon my replies, and reflect also upon the advantages of our Respectable Art. Open your eyes to those errors that are all the more dangerous because they have such deep roots. Let us leave aside the Diploma that bears the signature of B[rother] Delachaussée. We will clear up this question in due course.

Look again to see whether you can accept or must reject the Diploma of the Sovereign Council <of the Knights> of the East. Force us if you can to change our style of labor – my fear is that I will receive all too many complaints from you about my own way of going about things. But what else can I do if I face rejection by my tribe and <finally> become your Brother and a recognized and legitimate Mason!

I shall pass very cursorily over most of the points in your letter, because of the sheer length of mine. You are wrong, for example, to believe that a Deputy of the G[rand] L[odge] cannot constitute a L[odge] without the consent of the others L[odges] of the place where he wants to constitute it. When, for example, your General awarded you your commission, did he bother to consult anyone about it, after recognising that you deserved it by virtue of your ability, and after seeing how you lived and what your moral standards were? [27v]

I sense intuitively that B[rother] Martin was compelled to give the G[rand] Orient the most negative account of various Members of this L[odge]. Abuses are to be found everywhere, but my dear W[orship]ful, I believe that many are to be found in this so-called L[odge], and it is undesirable that all Masons use the tools of those who have made such a poor job of raising their edifice. By this I am referring only to the *majority* of the Craftsmen, and not to the whole Workshop in general. This submission to which you wish to subject this Deputy or Inspector might be acceptable as a last resort in a town where there are L[odges] of those Degrees you mention, but B[rother] Martin found that there were no constituted L[odges] in Le Cap at all, and even showed his authority to the so-called Scottish Lodge. But B[rother] Martin, armed with the most unchallengeable Diplomas, was just a vagabond in the eyes of the Lodge La Parfaite Harmonie. He did not cut a figure commensurate with his Degree, and he was therefore despised before anyone took the trouble to find out whether he was a Mason. You, Most W[orship]ful, who are a Mason, will agree at least that one would hardly recognize Masons from behaviour of this kind. Disabuse yourself, therefore, of the idea that, if the matter were to be brought before the Grand Tribunal, B[rother] Martin's conduct [28r] would be disapproved of, since this issue has already been debated there, as can easily be seen from the copies of the deliberations of the Sovereign Council which I sent you on behalf of the M[ost] R[espectable] L[odge] La Vérité. Disabuse yourself also of the belief that this L[odge] is and must be <u>the Model for those of the Colony</u>. I warn you that I am too good a Mason to allow this error, which is so dangerous to the Order, to persist, and I am unable to dispense with informing the Grand Orient of it in due course, along with the membership-list, which is so eloquent and so revealing of the poison-seed that this error contains. This so-called L[odge] appears too dominant for us not to fear that poorly-enlightened Masons will allow themselves to be seduced by its deceptive appearance.

One of the most cutting remarks that you aim at our respectable L[odge] is that the R[espectable] B[rothers] Chaillon de Jonville and Delachaussée sent the L[odge] La Vérité, by mistake, the package they thought they were sending to the Scottish L[odge] of Le Cap. This is frankly below the belt, and may I tell you that you have behaved reprehensibly in making this observation, which indicates the presence of a formal hatred without a cause, as well as a [28v] criminal hostility that injures good Masons who are undeserving of it. But it is very easy for me to disabuse you of this notion in just a few words. Here is my evidence to the contrary.

Our Worshipful B[rother] Pescay received at his address a package containing two Letters from the R[espectable] B[rothers] Chaillon de Jonville and Delachaussée, copies of which we have sent you. In this same package there was another letter, addressed to the so-called L[odge] Le Cap mentioned above. Based on the fact that these R[espectable] B[rothers] or their secretaries had certainly been mistaken in the addresses, ~~which told us to send them according to~~ and because we wished to act in the spirit of the letters addressed to us, which told us to inform the other L[odges] at our discretion, I confess that I myself was most firm in maintaining that it was unnecessary to hand over this package, but that it should be sent back to Paris, stating the reasons for our acting thus. However, in spite of my firmness, and that of other B[rothers], the said package was handed over to two of the Members of the aforementioned so-called Scottish L[odge], who certainly received it, and not in a very Masonic spirit either. Here then, Sir, is the very substantial proof that the package addressed to our L[odge] was put together expressly for it, and not for the other L[odge], and that your judgement has been proved false in this ~~respect~~ respect. [29r] What is more, both this package and the other one were addressed specifically to B[rother] Pescay, W[orship]ful Master of the L[odge] La Vérité, which is even stronger proof of your error. Cease this hatred, dear W[orship]ful, which is as unjust as it is disruptive of the harmony and development of this cherished seminary of the Sons of the Widow. ~~It is time to finish, and I do so by making it clear to you that I shall never depart from the respect due to true Brethren when they conduct themselves as such.~~ May everyone in the universe see themselves placed beneath its sacred veil. You yourself were born to experience the full benefit of this vow, so give it your full attention in order to ensure that it is fulfilled. It is time to finish now, and I do so by making it clear to you that I shall never depart from the respect due to true Brethren when they conduct themselves as such, but that I shall also never overlook any errors that I identify as manifest and dangerous to the Order, even if it be on the part of the M[ost] S[ublime] and M[ost] R[espectable] G[rand] Master of the Masters <u>ad vitam</u> (for life), for we know that <u>aliquando dormitat homerus</u> ['Sometimes even Homer nodded']. I am most definitely, Sir, your most humble and most obedient servant

Signed, Mathéus

addressed to M[onsieur] Fleuret de Turville, Attorney to the Courts of Saint-Marc. [29v]

N° 9

Copy of the reply by M[onsieur] Fleuret de Turville, Worshipful Master of the L[odge] La Concorde, to the previous letter.

Saint-Marc, 1st June 1770.

Sir,

I acknowledge receipt of the l[as]t letter you paid me the honour of writing to me on 16th May l[as]t. If you reflect upon all its contents with a lesser degree of prejudice, then you will agree with me that you display a great deal of obstinacy and that, despite everything, you are forced to admit this shortcoming in reality and in fact. The G[rand] and S[overeign] L[odge] of France has recognized the R[espectable] L[odge] of Le Cap, our dear Sister L[odge], as legitimate, since, by your own admission, a letter of constitution for it was sent to M[onsieur] Pescay, one of your good selves, without you specifying the time, but which we know for a fact was dated October 30th, 1769. You acknowledge that you held back this document for a long period, which is against the *ius gentium* [Law of Nations]. The letter of constitution was actually handed over, as you say, to this R[espectable] L[odge] against your own personal advice, which suggests a stubbornness on your part that you agree was misplaced. But, finally, this letter of constitution, despite everything you might have to say about it, establishes to an even greater extent the [30r] recognition of this R[espectable] L[odge] by the Sovereign Grand Lodge of France, in that the latter addresses it by the distinctive title of the L[odge] of St John of Jerusalem at Le Cap. All this, together with the contents of my last letter, should make you open your eyes to the error into which you have fallen, but it seems that you do not want to do anything about it, and that you are 'very much the Master'. I shall only observe that, for all that you are so little imbued with the true principles of a R[egular] L[odge], you will recognize that, in all this, you are falling into some very extreme deviations. But this is no longer an issue between us. Let things stand as they are, please. Whereas the responsibilities of my legal practice do not allow me to indulge in as much detail as you yourself have provided, I would urge you not to write to me again on the same subject for as long as you persist in refusing to follow my advice, which you reject with an unparalleled indifference. But that is your business. Nor will I complain about all the bitterness aimed at the R[espectable] L[odge] of Le Cap, our dear Sister, to be found in your [30v] last letter. We can therefore terminate all correspondence on the subject at hand. Your style of writing is too sour, and you put so much bile into it that it is simply impossible to endure,

I have the honour to be, &c.

Sir, &c.

Signed, Fleuret de Turville,

addressed to Monsieur Mathéus, Notary Royal at Le Cap.

Compared with the original documents and copies deposited by us in the archives of the R[espectable] L[oge] La Vérité, with its seat at the Orient of Le Cap Français, from which the whole has been copied word for word by us, Secretary of the said L[oge] La Vérité, for the present copy, which will be sent to the M[ost] S[ublime] and M[ost] Il[lustrious] G[rand] L[odge] of France in order to correct the observations made by the s[aid] L[odge] La Vérité to the s[aid] G[rand] L[odge] of France, and then presented to it by Our R[espectable] Kn[ight] B[rother] Vallette, our deputy.

At the Orient of Le Cap Français, isle and coast of Saint-Domingue, this 10th day of the 5th Masonic month, 5770. And we have affixed in the margin the privy seal of the R[espectable] L[odge],

By order of the same,

Mathéus, Secretary, Keeper of the Seals and Stamps. [31r]

Arturo de Hoyos, *The Knight of Disks*, by Ivan D. Ivanov (Bulgaria)

Arturo de Hoyos, 33°, Grand Cross, KYCH,
is Grand Archivist and Grand Historian of the Supreme Council, 33°, Southern Jurisdiction,
Washington, DC, and a member of the executive staff at the House of the Temple.

HIS PREVIOUS BOOKS INCLUDE:

The Cloud of Prejudice: A Study in Anti-Masonry (1992)

Rituals of the Masonic Grand Lodge of the Sun, Bayreuth, Germany (1992)

Liturgy of Germania Lodge No. 46 F&AM (1993)

The Book of the Words—Sephir H'Debarim: With an Introduction by Art de Hoyos (1999)
[Serbian edition, 2017]

Albert Pike's Esoterika: The Symbolism of the Blue Degrees of Freemasonry (2005)
[Serbian ed., 2015; Spanish ed., 2016; Bulgarian ed.,2021]

The Scottish Rite Ritual Monitor and Guide (2007)

Light on Masonry: The History and Rituals of America's Most Important Masonic Expose (2008)

Masonic Formulas and Rituals Transcribed by Albert Pike (2010)

Albert Pike's Morals and Dogma: Annotated Edition (2011)
[Bulgarian edition, 2022]

Freemasonry's Royal Secret (2014)
[Serbian ed., 2017]

Reprints of Rituals of Old Degrees (2015)

A Lecture on the Masonic Tracing Boards (2017)

Albert Pike's Magnum Opus (2017)
[Bulgarian ed., 2019]

Daniel Parker's Masonic Tablet (2019)

Curiosities and Treasures (2019)

The Freemason's Punchbowl (2020)

Insignia of Office and Honor (2021)

A House Adorned for Beauty (2022)

Supreme Council Souvenir Medallions, 1969–2021 (2023)

Albert Pike's The Porch and the Middle Chamber, The Book of the Lodge (2023)
[Bulgarian ed., 2019]

IN COLLABORATION WITH S. BRENT MORRIS:

Is It True What They Say About Freemasonry? The Methods of Anti-Masons (1994)

Freemasonry in Context: History, Ritual, Controversy (2004)

Committed to the Flames: The History and Rituals of a Secret Masonic Rite (2008)

The Most Secret Mysteries of the High Degrees of Masonry Unveiled (2011)
[Serbian ed., 2017]

Allegorical Conversations Arranged by Wisdom (2012)

Cerneauism and American Freemasonry (2019)

The Perfect Ceremonies of Craft Masonry and the Holy Royal Arch (2021)

Samuel Prichard's Masonry Dissected (2022)

IN COLLABORATION WITH JOSEF WÄGES:

Julius F. Saches's Ancient Documents Relating to the A. & A. Scottish Rite (2024)

AS EDITOR AND/OR AUTHOR OF INTRODUCTION/PREFACE/FOREWORD:

(ed.) *Collectanea* (Grand College of Rites, 1994–2024)

(ed.) *Miscellanea* (Grand Council, Allied Masonic Degrees, 2001)

(ed.) C.F. Kleinknecht, *Forms and Traditions of the Scottish Rite* (2001)

(ed.) L.P. Watkins, *Albert Pike's String of Pearls* (2008)

(ed.) L.P. Watkins, *International Masonic Collection, 1723–2011* (2012)

(intro.) S. Dafoe, *Morgan: The Scandal the Shook Freemasonry* (2009)

(intro.) A. Bernheim, *Un certaine idee de la franc-maconnerie* (2009)

(ed./intro.) R. L. Hutchens, *A Bridge to Light: A Study in Masonic Ritual & Philosophy* (2010)

(preface) A. de Keghel, *Le defi Maconnique Americain* (2015)

(preface) A. de Keghel, *American Freemasonry* (2017)

(preface) D. L. Harrison, *The Lost Rites of Freemasonry* (2017)

(foreword) Mark Stavish, *The Path of Freemasonry: The Craft as a Spiritual Practice* (2021)

Josef Wäges, *The Knight of Cups*, by Ivan D. Ivanov (Bulgaria)

Josef Wäges, 32°, is a Board Member of the Scottish Rite Research Society, and a Member of the Blue Friars (Masonic Authors)

His Previous Books Include, as Editor:

(with Reinhard Marner, and Jeva Singh-Anand as translator), *The Secret School of Wisdom: The Authentic Rituals and Doctrines of the Illuminati* (2015)

(with Reinhard Marner, and Lionel Duvoy as translator), *L'école secrète de sagesse : rituels et doctrines authentiques des Illuminés* (2017) (with Jeva Singh-Anand and Paul Ferguson as translator), *The Collected Works of Adam Weishaupt Volume One: The Illuminati Writings, Number One: On Materialism and Idealism.* (2018)

(with Stewart Clelland and Paul Ferguson as translator), *The Green Book of Élus Coëns* (2021)

(with Stewart Clelland and Paul Ferguson as translator), *The Masters Voice the Rituals & Letters of Martinés de Pasqually* - Deluxe Edition (2022)

as Translator:

(with Jean Pierre Gonet, Pierre Mollier, and Alain Bernheim), *Les Élus Parfaits une aventure transatlantique, Les Documents Sharp* (2021)

Book design by Arturo de Hoyos and Josef Wäges

This edition is based on the original layout by Elizabeth A.W. McCarthy

Related Titles from Westphalia Press

Ancient Mysteries and Modern Masonry: The Collected Writings of Jewel P. Lightfoot, Edited by Billy J. Hamilton Jr.

Jewel P. Lightfoot. Former Attorney General of the State of Texas. Past Grand Master of the Masonic Grand Lodge of Texas. From humble beginnings in rural Arkansas, he worked to become an educated man who excelled in law and Freemasonry. He was a gentleman of his time, well-known as a scholar, public speaker, and Masonic philosopher.

Essay on The Mysteries and the True Object of The Brotherhood of Freemasons
by Jason Williams

This isn't a reprint of a classic. It's a new rendition with new life breathed into it, to be enjoyed both by the layperson trying to understand the Craft and Masonic scholars taking a deeper dive into the fraternity's golden years—when the concepts of liberty and equality were still fresh.

Female Emancipation and Masonic Membership:
An Essential Collection
By Guillermo De Los Reyes Heredia

Female Emancipation and Masonic Membership: An Essential Combination is a collection of essays on Freemasonry and gender that promotes a transatlantic discussion of the study of the history of women and Freemasonry and their contribution in different countries.

Freemasonry, Heir to the Enlightenment
by Cécile Révauger

Modern Freemasonry may have mythical roots in Solomon's time but is really the heir to the Enlightenment. Ever since the early eighteenth century freemasons have endeavored to convey the values of the Enlightenment in the cultural, political and religious fields, in Europe, the American colonies and the emerging United States.

Freemasonry: A French View
by Roger Dachez and Alain Bauer

Perhaps one should speak not of Freemasonry but of Freemasonries in the plural. In each country Masonic historiography has developed uniqueness. Two of the best known French Masonic scholars present their own view of the worldwide evolution and challenging mysteries of the fraternity over the centuries.

Worlds of Print: The Moral Imagination of an Informed Citizenry, 1734 to 1839
by John Slifko

John Slifko argues that freemasonry was representative and played an important role in a larger cultural transformation of literacy and helped articulate the moral imagination of an informed democratic citizenry via fast emerging worlds of print.

Why Thirty-Three?: Searching for Masonic Origins
by S. Brent Morris, PhD

What "high degrees" were in the United States before 1830? What were the activities of the Order of the Royal Secret, the precursor of the Scottish Rite? A complex organization with a lengthy pedigree like Freemasonry has many basic foundational questions waiting to be answered, and that's what this book does: answers questions.

The Great Transformation: Scottish Freemasonry 1725-1810
by Dr. Mark C. Wallace

This book examines Scottish Freemasonry in its wider British and European contexts between the years 1725 and 1810. The Enlightenment effectively crafted the modern mason and propelled Freemasonry into a new era marked by growing membership and the creation of the Grand Lodge of Scotland.

Getting the Third Degree: Fraternalism, Freemasonry and History
Edited by Guillermo De Los Reyes and Paul Rich

As this engaging collection demonstrates, the doors being opened on the subject range from art history to political science to anthropology, as well as gender studies, sociology and more. The organizations discussed may insist on secrecy, but the research into them belies that.

The Great Transformation: Scottish Freemasonry 1725-1810
by Dr. Mark C. Wallace

This book examines Scottish Freemasonry in its wider British and European contexts between the years 1725 and 1810. The Enlightenment effectively crafted the modern mason and propelled Freemasonry into a new era marked by growing membership and the creation of the Grand Lodge of Scotland.

Getting the Third Degree: Fraternalism, Freemasonry and History
Edited by Guillermo De Los Reyes and Paul Rich

As this engaging collection demonstrates, the doors being opened on the subject range from art history to political science to anthropology, as well as gender studies, sociology and more. The organizations discussed may insist on secrecy, but the research into them belies that.

Freemasonry: A French View
by Roger Dachez and Alain Bauer

Perhaps one should speak not of Freemasonry but of Freemasonries in the plural. In each country Masonic historiography has developed uniqueness. Two of the best known French Masonic scholars present their own view of the worldwide evolution and challenging mysteries of the fraternity over the centuries.

Worlds of Print: The Moral Imagination of an Informed Citizenry, 1734 to 1839
by John Slifko

John Slifko argues that freemasonry was representative and played an important role in a larger cultural transformation of literacy and helped articulate the moral imagination of an informed democratic citizenry via fast emerging worlds of print.

Why Thirty-Three?: Searching for Masonic Origins
by S. Brent Morris, PhD

What "high degrees" were in the United States before 1830? What were the activities of the Order of the Royal Secret, the precursor of the Scottish Rite? A complex organization with a lengthy pedigree like Freemasonry has many basic foundational questions waiting to be answered, and that's what this book does: answers questions.

A Place in the Lodge: Dr. Rob Morris, Freemasonry and the Order of the Eastern Star
by Nancy Stearns Theiss, PhD

Ridiculed as "petticoat masonry," critics of the Order of the Eastern Star did not deter Rob Morris' goal to establish a Masonic organization that included women as members. Morris carried the ideals of Freemasonry through a despairing time of American history.

Brought to Light: The Mysterious George Washington Masonic Cave
by Jason Williams MD

The George Washington Masonic Cave near Charles Town, West Virginia, contains a signature carving of George Washington dated 1748. This book painstakingly pieces together the chronicled events and real estate archives related to the cavern in order to sort out fact from fiction.

Dudley Wright: Writer, Truthseeker & Freemason
by John Belton

Dudley Wright (1868-1950) was an Englishman and professional journalist who took a universalist approach to the various great Truths of Life. He travelled though many religions in his life and wrote about them all, but was probably most at home with Islam.

History of the Grand Orient of Italy
Emanuela Locci, Editor

No book in Masonic literature upon the history of Italian Freemasonry has been edited in English up to now. This work consists of eight studies, covering a span from the Eighteenth Century to the end of the WWII, tracing through the story, the events and pursuits related to the Grand Orient of Italy.

westphaliapress.org

Policy Studies Organization

The Policy Studies Organization (PSO) is a publisher of academic journals and book series, sponsor of conferences, and producer of programs.

Policy Studies Organization publishes dozens of journals on a range of topics, such as European Policy Analysis, Journal of Elder Studies, Indian Politics & Polity, Journal of Critical Infrastructure Policy, and Popular Culture Review.

Additionally, Policy Studies Organization hosts numerous conferences. These conferences include the Middle East Dialogue, Space Education and Strategic Applications Conference, International Criminology Conference, Dupont Summit on Science, Technology and Environmental Policy, World Conference on Fraternalism, Freemasonry and History, and the Internet Policy & Politics Conference.

For more information on these projects, access videos of past events, and upcoming events, please visit us at:

www.ipsonet.org

www.ingramcontent.com/pod-product-compliance
Lightning Source LLC
Chambersburg PA
CBHW081023240426
43671CB00029B/2884